THEATRE
PAST AND PRESENT

AN INTRODUCTION

MILLY S. BARRANGER

The University of North Carolina
at Chapel Hill

Wadsworth Publishing Company
A Division of Wadsworth, Inc.
Belmont, California

Editor: Kevin Howat
Production Editor: Patricia Brewer
Designer: MaryEllen Podgorski
Copy Editor: Elaine Linden
Technical Illustrator: Mary Burkhardt
Photo Researchers: Lindsay Kefauver and Jean O'Korn
Cover Photo: Max Waldman
Compositor: Dharma Press
Printer and Binder: R.R. Donnelley & Sons

Printed in the United States of America

1 2 3 4 5 6 7 8 9 10—88 87 86 85 84

ISBN 0-534-02842-X

Library of Congress Cataloging in Publication Data

Barranger, Milly S.
    Theatre past and present.

    Bibliography: p.
    Includes index.
    1. Theater—History.   2. Drama—History and criticism.
I. Title.
PN2075.B37   1984   792   83-17087

ISBN 0-534-02842-X

BRIEF CONTENTS

Preface   xvii

PART I / MODERN PERSPECTIVES   1

1 / The Theatre Event   2

2 / The Script into Performance   22

PART II / HISTORICAL PERSPECTIVES   51

3 / Greek Theatre   52

4 / Medieval Theatre   84

5 / Elizabethan Theatre   110

6 / *Commedia dell'arte* and Renaissance Italy   142

7 / Seventeenth-Century French Theatre   168

8 / The Restoration and Eighteenth-Century Theatre   194

9 / Nineteenth-Century European Theatre   226

10 / Modern Theatre: Beginnings in Realism   262

11 / Post-War Trends: Epic Theatre   292

12 / Post-War Trends: Theatricalism and the Absurd   316

13 / Contemporary Theatre:
    "New" Realism on the British Stage   354

PART III / AMERICAN THEATRE
PAST AND PRESENT   389

14 / American Theatre: 1900–1970   390

15 / American Theatre: The Present   446

Suggested Readings   482

Illustration Credits   490

Index   492

REPRESENTATIVE PLAYS

The Trojan Women   75
The Crucifixion Play   103
Macbeth   132
The Three Cuckolds   161
Tartuffe   186
The Beaux' Stratagem   215
Ghosts   254
The Three Sisters   283
The Caucasian Chalk Circle   307
The Bald Soprano   344
Look Back in Anger   377
A Streetcar Named Desire   434
Buried Child   471

DETAILED CONTENTS

Preface xvii

PART I

MODERN
PERSPECTIVES

1 / THE THEATRE EVENT 2

Theatre as Immediate Art 2

Theatre as Life's Double The Theatrical Space Actor and
Audience Theatre's Grand Illusion

Photo Essay: Types of Contemporary Theatres 6

Theatre Contrasts 8

Theatre and Film Theatre and Other Entertainment

Theatre as Collaborative Art 11

The Playwright The Director The Actor The Designers

Theatre as Discovery 13

What We Bring to the Theatre 16

The Theatrical in Everyday Life The Audience's Expectations

Summary Sources Notes

2 / THE SCRIPT INTO PERFORMANCE   22

Drama's Forms   22

Drama, Play, and Imitation   The Elements of Drama
Tragedy   Comedy   Tragicomedy   Melodrama   Farce
Adaptations

Drama's Structures   32

Climactic Play Structure   Episodic Play Structure   Situational
Play Structure   The Theatre of Images   Talking Pieces

Drama's Conventions   41

Exposition   Point of Attack   Complication   Crisis
Resolution   Simultaneous or Double Plots
The Play-within-the-Play

**Photo Essay: Styles of
Developing Scripts into Performance   44**

Summary   Sources   Notes

PART II

HISTORICAL
PERSPECTIVES

3 / GREEK THEATRE   52

A Modern Perspective   52

Representative Theatre: Theatre of Dionysus, Athens   53

Conditions of Performance   54

Background   The City Dionysia   The Performers   Visual
Elements   The Audience   Roman Theatre

Photo Essay: Greek Theatres Past and Present   64

Photo Essay: Roman Theatres Past and Present   66

Dramatic Conventions   63

Tragedy   Satyr Play   Comedy   Roman Drama

Representative Play: *The Trojan Women*   75

Background   The Tragic Action   The Scene   Character
Language   Euripides' Modernism

Essay: Greek Tragedy in Modern Performance   79

Summary   Plays to Read   Sources   Notes

4 / MEDIEVAL THEATRE   84

A Modern Perspective   84

Representative Theatre: The York Cycle   85

Conditions of Performance   86

Background   Religious and Civic Purposes   Management:
Festival Theatre   Playwriting   Acting and Rehearsals
Visual Elements   Processional Staging in Spain   Popular
Entertainments   The Audience

Photo Essay: Medieval Fixed and Processional Stages   96

Dramatic Conventions   98

Playwriting   Cycle Plays   Saint or Miracle Plays   Farces
Morality Plays

Representative Play: *The Crucifixion Play*   103

Background   The Scene   Action and Characterization
The Cycle Play's Modernism

Essay: Medieval Theatre in Modern Performance   106

Summary   Plays to Read   Sources   Notes

5 / ELIZABETHAN THEATRE   110

A Modern Perspective   110

Representative Theatre: The Globe, London   111

Conditions of Performance   111

Background   The Public Playhouse   Management and
Repertory System   Playwriting   The Acting Company   Visual
Elements   The Audience   The Private Playhouse: Blackfriars
Court Masques

Photo Essay: Elizabethan Theatre Past and Present   126

Dramatic Conventions   128
The Episodic Plot   Exposition   Scenes   Double Plots
The Ending   Language

Representative Play: *Macbeth*   132
Background   Tragic Action   The Scene   Character
Language   Shakespeare's Modernism

Essay: Shakespeare in Modern Performance   136
Trevor Nunn's *Macbeth*

Summary   Plays to Read   Sources   Notes

6 / *COMMEDIA DELL'ARTE*
AND RENAISSANCE ITALY   142

A Modern Perspective   142

Representative Theatre: The Gelosi Company   143

Conditions of Performance   144
Background   Management of the *Commedia* Companies
Visual Elements   Popular Entertainments   The Audience
Court Theatres and Festivals

Photo Essay: Theatres of Renaissance Italy   158

Dramatic Conventions   157
Scenarios   Character Types

Representative Play: *The Three Cuckolds*   161

Essay: *Commedia* **in Modern Performance**   164

Summary   Plays to Read   Sources   Notes

7 / SEVENTEENTH-CENTURY
FRENCH THEATRE   168

A Modern Perspective   168

Representative Theatre: Hôtel de Bourgogne   **169**

Conditions of Performance   **171**

Background   Management and Repertory   The Acting
Company   Visual Elements   Playwriting   Rehearsing
the Play   The Audience

Photo Essay: The Comédie Française   **182**

Dramatic Conventions   **181**

Genre   The Unities   Language   Decorum
The Messenger's Report   Poetic Justice

Representative Play: *Tartuffe*   **186**

Background   Comic Action   The Scene   Character
Language   Molière's Modernism

Essay: Molière in Modern Performance   **189**

Summary   Plays to Read   Sources   Notes

**8 / THE RESTORATION AND
EIGHTEENTH-CENTURY THEATRE**   **194**

A Modern Perspective   **194**

Representative Theatre: Drury Lane   **195**

Conditions of Performance   **196**

Background   Management and Financing   The Repertory
System   The Acting Companies   Playwriting   Casting and
Rehearsals   Visual Elements   The Audience

Photo Essay: Drury Lane Theatre Past and Present   **210**

Dramatic Conventions   **212**

Prologues and Epilogues   Afterpiece   Comedies of Manners
Ballad Opera   Sentimental Comedy   The Language of Wit

Representative Play: *The Beaux' Stratagem*   **215**

Background   The Comic Action   The Scene
Characterization   Language   Farquhar's Modernism

**Essay: Eighteenth-Century
Comedy in Modern Performance**   **220**
The Director at Work   The Production

Summary   Plays to Read   Sources   Notes

9 / NINETEENTH-CENTURY EUROPEAN THEATRE   226

A Modern Perspective   **226**

Representative Theatre: Théâtre Libre, Paris   **227**

Conditions of Performance   **229**
Background   Management: Toward National Theatres
Playwriting   Visual Elements   The Emerging Director: Goethe,
Meiningen, Antoine   The Audience   Wagner's Music-Drama
at Bayreuth

Photo Essay: Ibsen and Strindberg in Performance   **248**

Dramatic Conventions   **250**
Shakespeare as Model in Germany   The Romantic Vision
Melodrama   Realism   Naturalism

Representative Play: *Ghosts*   **254**
Background   The Scene   The Tragic Action   Character
Language and Symbolism   Ibsen's Modernism

Essay: *Ghosts* in Modern Performance   **257**

Summary   Plays to Read   Sources   Notes

10 / MODERN THEATRE: BEGINNINGS IN REALISM   262

A Modern Perspective   **262**

Representative Theatre: The Moscow Art Theatre   **263**

Conditions of Performance   265

Background   Management: The Star System   Playwriting
Acting: Stanislavsky's System   Visual Elements
The First-Night Audience   The Directors: Stanislavsky
and Meyerhold   Symbolism   Offshoots in America

Photo Essay: Moscow Art Theatre in Performance   276

Dramatic Conventions   278

The Well-Made Play   Chekhov's "New" Dramaturgy

Representative Play: *The Three Sisters*   283

Background   The Scene   The Tragicomic Action
Character   Language   Chekhov's Modernism

Essay: Chekhov in Performance   286

Summary   **Plays to Read**   **Sources**   **Notes**

11 / POST-WAR TRENDS: EPIC THEATRE   292

A Modern Perspective   292

Representative Theatre:
Theater am Schiffbauerdamm, East Berlin   293

Conditions of Performance   294

Background   Epic Theory and Practice   Epic Acting
The Alienation Effect   Visual Elements   The Berliner Ensemble

Photo Essay: Epic Theatre in Performance   304

Dramatic Conventions   303

Episodic Structure   Historical Background   The Narrator
Characterization   Gestic Attitudes   The Dialectic in Action

Representative Play: *The Caucasian Chalk Circle*   307

Background   Prologue and Frame   The Play-Within-the-Play
Linking Devices   Azdak's Story   The Chalk Circle Test
Brecht's Dialectical Meaning

Essay: Epic Theatre in Contemporary Performance **311**

Stein's Schaubühne *Peer Gynt* Epic Technique

Summary **Plays to Read** **Sources** **Notes**

**12 / POST-WAR TRENDS:
THEATRICALISM AND THE ABSURD** **316**

A Modern Perspective **316**

Representative Theatre: Théâtre des Noctambules **317**

Conditions of Performance **317**

Background Management and Stage Theatricalism
Max Reinhardt's Experiments French Directors Between
the Wars Playwriting in France Between the Wars
Post-War Directors in France Playwriting after the Second
World War Avant-garde Directors in France Visual
Elements: From Futurism to Surrealism

**Photo Essay: "Theatrical" Styles
in Scenery, Costumes, and Lighting** **336**

Dramatic Conventions **334**

Pirandello's Metatheatre Existentialist Playwright:
Jean-Paul Sartre The Absurdists: Ionesco and Beckett
Jean Genêt's Open Theatricality

Representative Play: *The Bald Soprano* **344**

Background The Scene The Action The Characters
Language Ionesco's Modernism

**Essay: Theatricalism and
the Absurd in Modern Performance** **350**

Summary **Plays to Read** **Sources** **Notes**

**13 / CONTEMPORARY THEATRE:
"NEW" REALISM ON THE BRITISH STAGE** **354**

A Modern Perspective **354**

Representative Theatre: The Royal Court Theatre   **355**

Conditions of Performance   **357**

Background   Management: The Companies   Playwriting
Acting   The Directors   Festivals and Fringes

Photo Essay: The "New" Stage Realism   **366**

Dramatic Conventions   **368**

Working-Class Realism   Pinter's Ambiguous Realism
The Open Theatricality of Stoppard and Shaffer

Representative Play: *Look Back in Anger*   **377**

Background   The Scene   The Action   Character   Language
Osborne's Modernism

Essay: *The Life and Adventures of Nicholas Nickleby*
in Modern Performance   **381**

Beginnings   Scripting and Rehearsals   Performance Style
The Audience

Summary   **Plays to Read**   **Sources**   **Notes**

PART III

AMERICAN
THEATRE
PAST AND PRESENT

14 / AMERICAN THEATRE: 1900–1970   **390**

A Modern Perspective   **390**

Representative Theatre: The Ethel Barrymore Theatre   **391**

Conditions of Performance   **392**

Background   Management: The Companies
The Commercial Theatre   Acting as Profession   Training
Programs   Visual Elements   The "Groups"   The Directors
The Playwrights   The Collectives

Photo Essay: American Musical Theatre   **414**

Dramatic Conventions   **418**

O'Neill's Eclecticism   Hellman's Melodrama   Odets' and
Miller's Social Realism   Lorraine Hansberry's Multicultural
Realism   Williams' and Albee's "New" Realism

Representative Play: *A Streetcar Named Desire*   434

Background   The Scene   The Tragic Action   Character
Language   *Streetcar's* Modernism

Essay: From Stage to Film   440

Summary   Plays to Read   Sources   Notes

15 / AMERICAN THEATRE: THE PRESENT   446

A Modern Perspective   446

Representative Theatre: The Public Theatre   447

Conditions of Performance   449

Background   The Troika: Broadway, Off Broadway,
and Off-Off Broadway   Resident Theatres   Subsidizing
the Arts   Alternative Theatres   Current Playwriting
The Changing Avant-garde

Photo Essay: American Design and Stage Technology   460

Dramatic Conventions   463

The Comic Realism of Neil Simon   The Bizarre Realism of
Shepard and Mamet   The Interior Monologue   Feminist
Plays: María Irene Fornés

Representative Play: *Buried Child*   471

Background   The Scene   The Action   Character   Language
Shepard's Postmodernism

Essay: The Mabou Mines in Performance   475

Summary   Plays to Read   Sources   Notes

Suggested Readings   482

Illustration Credits   490

Index   492

PREFACE

Written for use in the basic course, *Theatre Past and Present* discusses theatre's historical development in relation to modern performance theory and practice. The book has three goals: (1) to inform students about theatre—its historical development, conventions, styles, and vocabulary; (2) to enhance their ability to experience the theatre event; and (3) to increase their liking for live theatre. With these goals in mind, I have divided the book into three parts—the first *topical*, the second and third *historical*.

Part I (Chapters One and Two) reviews material essential to an understanding of the theatre event and prepares for the historical discussions. Here I discuss the theatrical event, aesthetics, and the types and elements of drama.

Part II (Chapters Three to Thirteen) discusses the major periods in European theatrical history.

Part III (Chapters Fourteen and Fifteen) takes up the American scene—our playwrights, resident theatres, Broadway, collectives, and people's theatres. I examine seven decades of American theatre and the social milieu in which it has developed. It ends with a discussion of new American plays and the current avant-garde.

Throughout the book I have emphasized theatre's *tradition*, *continuity*, and *change*, rather than the theatre historian's methods. I am concerned with how past and present conventions, theories, and practices evolve and synthesize, making today's theatre a vibrant and meaningful art. To present these ideas, each historical chapter contains these elements:

A Modern Perspective introduces the period from our twentieth-century viewpoint.

Representative Theatre puts the reader in the audience of a theatre typical of the period.

Conditions of Performance explores the physical and performance conditions of the period.

Photo Essay illustrates important historical theatres and productions.

Dramatic Conventions describes the development of playwriting practices.

Representative Play analyzes a significant work from the period.

Essay relates the historical material to today's theatre. These essays show modern artists—Peter Brook, Andrei Serban, Trevor Nunn, Lee Strasberg, and many others—building upon the theatre's past to capture the essence of its meaning for today's audiences.

I have provided other tools throughout the book to help students with problems of history, biography, definition, and example. There are timelines, maps, short biographies of major artists, plot summaries, sections of plays, comments and observations by artists and critics, and suggested readings. In an effort to place the book's contents within the students' cultural ambience, I have emphasized English-language theatre. However, like the theatre's history, the book is international in scope.

This book is not a comprehensive study of theatre history or of modern performance theory. I have concentrated on theatre's elements, on individual artists, and on special historical periods that continue to challenge the modern artist. If I have omitted an instructor's favorite period, topic, or playwright, I have done so out of concern for the introductory level and the length of the course. In addition, I have tried to limit the examples of plays, theatres, com-panies, and productions to avoid overwhelming the beginning student with information. However, I hope that the book's material and its presentation will excite and encourage students to look further into theatre's development—*past and present*.

My thanks are due to colleagues and students for their encouragement and assistance in the preparation of this book. Those who advised on the manuscript at various stages of its development were Ralph G. Allen (Queens College), Gregory Boyd (The University of North Carolina at Chapel Hill), David Cook (The University of Tulsa), Gresdna A. Doty (Louisiana State University), Donald Drapeau (Virginia Polytechnic Institute and State University), Tanda Dykes (Indiana University), William Elwood (University of Wisconsin at Madison), Bill J. Harbin (Louisiana State University), Clive Hardy (University of New Orleans), Kenneth Harris (Slippery Rock State College), Wandalie Henshaw (The University of Tennessee at Knoxville), Arthur Housman (The University of North Carolina at Chapel Hill), Linda Walsh Jenkins (Northwestern University), Bruce D. Podewell (Tulane University), James M. Symons (Trinity University), Randolph Umberger (North Carolina Central University), and Richard A. Weaver (Texas Tech University). My special appreciation goes to Jeffrey Grove, Nancy Lee, Deanna Ruddock, Elizabeth Snyder, and Jewell Dobbins. Also, Kevin J. Howat of Wadsworth Publishing Company deserves special mention for his efforts as editor.

Milly S. Barranger
The University of North Carolina
Chapel Hill

MODERN PERSPECTIVES

THE THEATRE EVENT

Theatre—like dance, music, opera, or film—is an art form that places imagined human experiences before a group of people—an audience. In this first chapter, we ask what makes theatre different from other arts, what makes it unique? In short, what is the theatre event?

THEATRE AS IMMEDIATE ART

Unlike a painting or a novel, *theatre* takes place as we watch it. For theatre to happen, two groups of people—actors and audience—must come together at a certain time and in a certain place. There the actors go onstage (or into a special space) and present themselves to the audience in a story. The audience shares in the story and the occasion. This is called the theatrical event.

Theatre is alive because it centers on the immediate, face-to-face relationship between these two groups of people—performers and audiences. Painting and sculpture, which are not "performed" before an audience, do not share this quality. Dance, music, and opera share with the theatre the human being as performer, but they do not share theatre's *unique* way of imitating reality: Theatre presents actual human beings playing fictional characters who move, speak, and "live" before us in recognizable places and events. For a short time we, as audiences, share in an experience with them that is immediate, entertaining, provocative, imitative, and sometimes magical.

THEATRE AS LIFE'S DOUBLE

Theatre shows men and women in action—what they do and sometimes why. Because human beings are both theatre's subject and its means of expression, theatre is one of the most immediate ways of experiencing another's idea of life—of what it means to be human.

Shakespeare and others speak of the doubleness of the theatrical experience that shows us life reflected in a special mirror—the stage. For instance, the audience experiences the actor both as actor—the living presence of another human being—and as fictional character. Likewise, the performing space is both a stage and at the same time an imaginary world created by playwright, designers, director, and actors. Sometimes this world is familiar to us—the stage might resemble a modern living room or a hotel room. Sometimes it is unfamiliar, like Othello's island of Cyprus in Shakespeare's play (c. 1604), Oedipus' plague-ridden Thebes in Sophocles' *Oedipus the King* (427 BC), or the deserted landscape in Samuel Beckett's *Waiting for Godot* (1953).

The Elizabethans thought the theatre mirrored life. Shakespeare had Hamlet describe the purpose of acting, or "playing," in this way:

> . . . the purpose of playing . . . was and is, to hold . . . the mirror up to nature, to show virtue her own feature, scorn her own image, and the very age and body of the time his form and pressure. (III, 2)

The Elizabethan idea of the stage as a mirror can help us understand the dynamics of theatre. Going to the theatre is like looking into a mirror. When we look into a mirror we see our double—an image of ourselves—and possibly a background. The image can be made to move; we make certain judgments about it; it communicates to us certain attitudes and concerns. Our humanity as reflected in the mirror has shape, color, texture, form, attitude, and emotion; it is even capable of limited movement within the mirror's frame. On stage the actor's living presence as a fictional character—as Othello or Desdemona, as Stanley Kowalski or Blanche DuBois in Tennessee Williams' *A Streetcar Named Desire* (1947)—creates the doubleness that is theatre's special quality. It is both a stage world and an illusion of a real world.

Theatre is life's double, but it is also something more. It is a form of art—*a selected and shaped reflection*. It is life's reflection *organized meaningfully*. The basic way theatre is organized is through the positioning of actors and audience in space.

> **"** I can take any empty space and call it a bare stage. A man walks across this empty space whilst someone else is watching him, and this is all that is needed for an act of theatre to be engaged. **"**
>
> Peter Brook, *The Empty Space* (1968)[1]

3

THE THEATRICAL SPACE

At the heart of the theatre experience is the act of seeing and being seen. We are told that the word *theatre* comes from the Greek word *theatron*, meaning "seeing place." At one time or another during the history of Western culture, this place for seeing has been a primitive dancing circle, a Greek amphitheatre, a church, an Elizabethan stage, an arena, a garage, a street, and a proscenium theatre (Figure 1-1). But neither the stage's shape nor the building's architecture makes it a theatre. The use of space to imitate human experience, with an audience watching and participating, makes that space theatrically special—a seeing place.

Since its beginnings in primitive ritual and in the amphitheatres of classical Greece, theatre has been a place for seeing and being seen—for viewing, presenting, perceiving, and understanding what it means to be a human being.

Places for theatre to happen are found in all societies, ancient and modern. Actors always performed in a special or privileged place. The priest, the guru, the dancer, or the actor was found in a threshing circle, a hut, a building, or an enclosure that was shared with onlookers or spectators. In some ritual spaces a circular area was surrounded by spectators. In others, special buildings were constructed for the occasion and destroyed at the end of the rite. Some primitive groups moved from place to place until the entire event was experienced.

ACTOR AND AUDIENCE

The two living components of theatre are the actor and the audience. The history of the theatre has been, in one sense, the record of the changing physical relationships of actors and audiences. The audience has moved from a

---

The Origins of Theatre

Since the publication of Sir James Frazer's *The Golden Bough* in 1890, theatre historians have connected the origins of theatre with agrarian and fertility rites and with special places for enactment of these rites. Primitive people staged mock battles between death and life in which the king of the old year, representing death, perished in a duel with the champion of the new year. In these rituals we can see the beginnings of theatrical modes of today: *enactment, imitation,* and *seasonal performances.*

There were also dramatic overtones to ceremonies designed to win favor from supernatural powers. The rain dance ceremonies of the American Southwest Indians were ways to ensure that the tribal gods would send rain to make crops grow. Early societies acted out seasonal changes—patterns of life, death, and rebirth—until their ceremonies became

formalized dramatic rituals. Harvest rituals, for example, celebrated abundant food supplies. Imitation, costume, make-up, masks, gesture, and pantomime were theatrical elements in these early rituals.

Another kind of ritual performance in early societies was the ceremony conducted by the shaman, or master of spirits, to cure illness. The shaman often performed in a trance; while he or she was curing the patient, a supernatural presence manifested itself to the patient and presumably to the onlookers surrounding the healing ceremony.

Finally, anthropologists and historians conjecture that theatre as we know it today owes a debt to the thousands of unknown magicians who carved their enemies' faces on tree trunks, performed voodoo spells, and threatened or wooed bad and good spirits.

---

ceremonial circle to the hillside of the Greek amphitheatre, to a place before the Christian altar, to standing room around the Elizabethan theatre's platform stage, to seats in a darkened hall before a curtained proscenium stage, to the floor and scaffolding of a modern environmental production. In the same historical sequence, the actor has moved from the dancing circle of the Greek theatre to the altar of the Christian church, to the open stage of the Elizabethan theatre, to the recessed stage of the proscenium theatre, to the environmental space of some contemporary productions.

The common denominators of theatre, unchanged since the legendary Greek actor Thespis stepped apart from the Greek chorus and created dialogue for the listener, are *actor, space,* and *audience.* However, whether the physical space becomes more elaborate or less so, whether the performance occurs indoors or out, the actor–audience relationship is theatre's vital ingredient. The formula for theatre is simple: *A man or woman stands in front of an audience and performs an action, usually interacting with another performer.*

Figure 1-1 Modern stages. (a) The proscenium or picture-frame stage is most familiar to us. The word *proscenium* comes from the wall with a large center opening that separates the audience from the raised stage. In the past the opening was called an "arch" (the proscenium arch), but it is actually a rectangle. The audience faces in one direction before this opening, appearing to look through a picture frame into the locale on the other side. The idea that a stage is a room with its fourth wall removed comes from this type of stage; the proscenium opening is thought of as an "invisible wall." (b) The arena stage (also called theatre-in-the-round) is at the center of a square or circle with seats for the spectators around the circle or on the four sides. This stage offers more intimacy between actor and audience because the playing space usually has no barriers separating them. (c) The thrust or open stage combines features of the proscenium theatre and the arena stage. The basic arrangement has the audience sitting on three sides or in a semicircle around a low platform stage. At the back of the stage is some form of proscenium opening for entrances, exits, and scene changes.

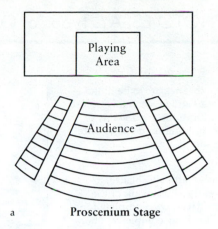

a   **Proscenium Stage**

b   **Arena Stage**

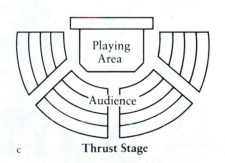

c   **Thrust Stage**

Today's theatres are to be found in large cities and in small towns. Just as their locations are diverse, so theatre buildings and stages differ in size and shape.

London's National Theatre, located on the south bank of the Thames River, was completed in 1976. This huge complex contains three theatres, rehearsal rooms, workshops, offices, restaurants, and foyers. The Olivier (named for English actor Sir Laurence Olivier) has an open stage and 1150 seats. The audience encircles the stage and has its attention focused on the playing area. The Lyttelton Theatre, seating 890, has a conventional proscenium stage; the proscenium opening can be altered by changing its width and height. The Cottesloe Theatre, a workshop theatre, is a rectangular box holding up to 400 people.

The Guthrie Theater, Minneapolis, built in 1963, has a large auditorium (1441 seats) encircling a unique seven-sided thrust stage. No seat is more than 52 feet from the center of the stage. The photo shows the audience's relationship to the actors and stage.

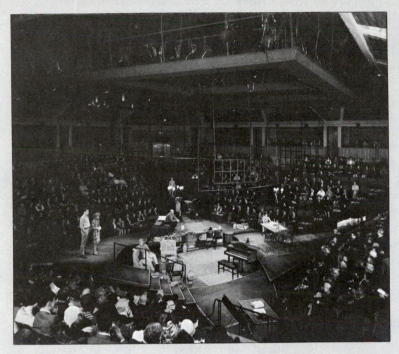

In the Arena Stage, built in 1960 in Washington, D.C., the audience completely surrounds the stage action. Lighting instruments are visible above the stage, and scenery and furniture are minimal. Actors enter and exit through alleyways visible in the photo.

The Oregon Shakespearean Festival Theatre in Ashland (founded in 1935) is an open-air theatre. The audience sits in front of a platform stage. A multilevel building serves as a permanent background for plays by Shakespeare and other playwrights. Compare this photo with the picture of Shapespeare's Globe on page 127.

THEATRE'S GRAND ILLUSION

Related to the immediacy of the art form is theatre's grand illusion, or pretense. In the theatre event, performers create the illusion that everyone (actors and audiences) is sharing an experience for the *very first time*. As members of the audience we tacitly agree with the actors that, for the time of the performance, the play is a living reality. If we think about it objectively, we know that theatre is not life, but we ordinarily suspend this knowledge for the few hours we watch a play. We share with the actors the illusion that life is being lived on stage. This is a quintessential part of the theatre event. The actors contribute to the illusion, for they are both actors and characters. For the moments they are onstage, they share a dual existence—a doubleness. We know, for instance, that Oedipus, the central character in Sophocles' *Oedipus the King*, is a character and that he is played by an actor, but when we watch a performance of the play we become caught up in the character's actions as if he—and his actions—were real. In the theatre we suspend our *disbelief* and give way to theatre's illusion and storytelling qualities.

THEATRE CONTRASTS

We can get a better sense of what theatre is by looking at the differences between theatre and film, and theatre and other forms of entertainment.

THEATRE AND FILM

The actor–audience relationship distinguishes theatre from that extraordinarily popular medium of our culture: *film*. When we go to a movie, we sit in a darkened room looking at a large screen filled with light images. We respond to the large *image* of the actor and background details of environment but not to the actor's

> *" There are, for example, privileged places, qualitatively different from all others—a man's birthplace, or the scenes of his first love, or certain places in the first foreign city he visited in youth. . . . as if it were in such spots that he had received the revelation of reality other than that in which he participates through his ordinary daily life. "*
>
> Mircea Eliade, *The Sacred and the Profane: The Nature of Religion* (1959)[2]

physical presence. The living presence of the actor is one of the key differences between the two art forms. For this reason, *film is a nonimmediate art*. For movies, as for its more recent technological relative, television, once a performance is filmed or taped, the film is placed in canisters to be released and shown whenever there is a market for it, the electronic equipment for showing it, and the screen for viewing it. In the theatre, in contrast, the interval between an actor's performance and the audience's response is minimal, and the living, breathing actor stands before us sometimes in a space where we can almost reach out and touch flesh with flesh.

In film the actors' images and activities are placed electronically on celluloid and revealed to us on a large screen; film audiences are in the presence of images from the past, not of living human beings in the present. Therefore, just as the film audience does not experience the actor's flesh-and-blood presence, the film actor does not experience the audience's instant responses to his or her performance.

Although film makes use of actors, they are subordinate to the photographic images that the film editor has arranged. Both film and theatre use people as subjects, but film as a medium is a twentieth-century technological invention, a means of recording and preserving images of reality. Theatre is immediately alive. Film captures aliveness on celluloid for all time, but by do-

ing so it takes away the living quality of the performance that is essential to the theatre event.

For example, the great performances of Marlon Brando and Vivien Leigh as Stanley Kowalski and Blanche DuBois in *A Streetcar Named Desire* are captured in the 1951 film (Figure 1-2). But the wonderful theatre performances of Laurette Taylor, Jessica Tandy (Figure 1-3), and Elizabeth Ashley in plays by Tennessee Williams are lost to us as the performance ends. Theatre is an evanescent art, lasting only those two or three hours it takes to see the play. The experience can be repeated night

Figure 1-2 This still from the 1951 movie version of Tennessee Williams' play *A Streetcar Named Desire* captures for all time this moment between Vivien Leigh as Blanche DuBois and Marlon Brando as Stanley Kowalski. Each time we see the movie (and it may be 10 times), we can experience again this moment between these two particular actors. A similar moment in the theatre is lost to us even as it takes place before us on the stage.

Figure 1-3 *Streetcar* in performance: Actors Jessica Tandy as Blanche DuBois and Karl Malden as Mitch in the original New York production (1947). The experience of this stage moment is now lost to audiences.

after night as long as the show is running, but once the play is closed and the cast dispersed, the performance is lost and the theatre dark.

This very frustrating but intriguing quality of theatre, which American critic Brooks Atkinson called the "bright enigma," is the source of its vitality and liveliness.

THEATRE AND OTHER ENTERTAINMENT

We can also distinguish between theatre as an art form that is also entertaining and activities that are designed as pure entertainment. There are many kinds of entertainment. Watching a basketball game, for example, is entertaining. What is it about the theatre that makes its entertainment value different from, let us say, that of an athletic event?

In both theatre and basketball activities we take pleasure in observing the skill of the performance. But part of the pleasure in watching a basketball game is finding out who is going to win, and it is this unpredictable or random quality of the sporting event that distinguishes it from the ritual quality of theatre. Each time a team plays another team the outcome is different, but once the theatrical performance is set, it varies little from night to night.

In a basketball game not only the audience but the players are unsure how the game will turn out. In the theatre, the playwright, actors, director, and designers have planned their event with great care from beginning to end. We say that the performance is "set" in rehearsals. Each night actors recreate the same characters and reenact the same story; at predetermined times they do certain things, move, handle props, make gestures; the stage lights change and the scenery shifts upon cue. Although we take pleasure in observing the skill, talent, and intelligence of the performers in both basketball and theatre, our special pleasure in watching actors comes from their carefully crafted, ritualized performance.

If any random quality exists in theatrical performance, it arises from the particular *feedback* the performers obtain from each separate audience, which may vary from attentive rapport to an impatient shifting about in seats. Certain kinds of feedback, like laughter and applause, are obvious. But there is another, less tangible kind of communication between actor and audience. Like the Zen archer who becomes one with the arrow in flight, a good actor establishes an emotional kinship with the audience. The audience's attention, breathing, energy, and tensions send out signals to the actor and vice versa. For a brief spell an emotional oneness is achieved between them. At the end of such a performance, the audience's applause is like the breaking of a spell, releasing energy and tension. These are the great moments we remember in the theatre, when the actors' emotional life melds with the lives of the audience.

THEATRE AS COLLABORATIVE ART

Theatre is a team effort. It is made to happen, not by one individual, but by many artists, workers, and spectators. Unlike sculpture, painting, or poetry, theatre is a collaborative art. Playwrights, directors, designers, and actors come together as artists to create the total theatre event; they transform an empty stage into an environment where actors live out special moments of their make-believe lives in their make-believe worlds. The audience, as we have seen, becomes part of this collaboration, responding at each performance to the success or failure of their collective efforts.

THE PLAYWRIGHT

Playwrights write plays to express an aspect of reality, a measure of experience, a vision or conviction about the world. Playwrights such as Henrik Ibsen write plays to expose truths about social injustice. Other playwrights, like Bertolt Brecht, have political or economic statements to make about men and governments. For others, like Adrienne Kennedy, writing is an expression of an inner, psychological state and childhood experiences.

Like every artist, the playwright shapes a personal vision of many experiences into an organized, meaningful whole. Thus a script is more than words on a page—it is the playwright's *architecture* of a special kind of experience created to appeal as much to the eye as to the ear. All in all, playwriting is the search for the truth of human experience as the playwright perceives it.

Playwrights may start with an idea, theme, or notes and work out an action; or begin with an unusual character or a real person and develop an action around that character; or start with a situation based on personal experience, their reading, or an anecdote. Other writers working with groups evolve scenarios, or play outlines, with actors and arrange a final script from the group's improvisations, situations, dialogue, and movement. Some write from scenarios or plot summaries; others write from an imagined crisis scene, images, dreams, myths, or imagined environments. The playwright's script is of major importance in the theatre because it is the usual starting point for the theatrical production.

THE DIRECTOR

The *director* collaborates with playwright, actors, and designers to create on stage a carefully selected imitation of life—a special mirror. Responsible for what is seen and heard, the director works in rehearsals and production meetings with actors and designers to interpret the playwright's world, characters, and events.

The performance reflects the director's idea of the way the play looks and sounds. This means that the director functions as an interpreter or creator. As an *interpretive artist* the director serves the playwright by translating the script as faithfully as possible into theatrical form. Director Elia Kazan has worked in this way with Arthur Miller's and Tennessee Williams' major plays on Broadway.

More recently, some directors have become *creative artists* who fashion scripts into an original work of art. In this role the director alters the play—changes the period represented, cuts the text, rearranges the scenes—and practically takes over the role of author. In his recreation of Shakespeare's *A Midsummer Night's Dream* for the Royal Shakespeare Company (1970), director Peter Brook changed the period of the play and the entire concept of how the play was to be performed.

THE ACTOR

One of the theatre's most essential collaborators is the actor, who works with script, director, and other actors to tell the character's situation in the play as effectively as possible. Learning in rehearsals to behave as a person would in the situation existing among the play's characters, the actor comes to believe in what he or she is doing on stage. The actor concentrates on the character's behavior in this special context; the performance follows.

To understand better the actor's reality (and stage reality), we can compare again the situation in a play with an event on the sports field. Like baseball, for example, a play has its own rules and regulations, the set dimensions of the playing area, and a set number of persons on the field. The interactions of the players are real, vital, and intense. For the playing time, the field is the players' whole universe. The game, like a play, has its own reality that is frequently more vivid than everyday reality.

The actor's early work occurs in scene study and rehearsals where she or he carries out the task of creating an emotional impact through carefully reconstructing personal life experiences and then relating those emotions to the character and the situation. The work of rehearsals is to condition the actor's responses, so that during performances the actor's emotions flow from his or her concentration upon the material—the character's situation and objectives. Then, on each night of the play's run, the actor recreates the character's situation for the audience. The actor's creativity continues within the boundaries set in rehearsal; this is the actor's art. Each performance requires the actor to give fresh life onstage to the character's situation—to concentrate anew on the character's speech, behavior, and theatrical effectiveness.

THE DESIGNERS

Other vital collaborators in the modern theatre are the *designers*. Designers of scenery, lighting, and costumes (and sometimes makeup, masks, sound, properties, and furniture) shape and fill the stage space. They create the actor's environment and make the play's world *visible*. Beginning with the script, designers translate the playwright's words, ideas, and imagined environments into a total evocation that can be seen, touched, and heard.

Designers collaborate with the director to focus the audience's attention on the actor in a special environment—the stage or playing space. Sometimes one person (the *scenographer*) designs all the elements, including scenery, lighting, and costumes. But whether designed by one person or many, all these elements must serve the play's dramatic action—visualizing and enriching it—without distracting the audience.

THEATRE AS DISCOVERY

Theatre people often call the beginning of a performance "magic time" because performances usually start with a certain magical effect. The house lights dim, the front curtain goes up (if there is one), and the audience *discovers* a hidden world.

In one sense, then, theatre is *discovery*. Let us briefly examine two plays to see how this discovery process works. Starting with two actors on a bare platform, the complex world of *Hamlet* (c. 1601) gradually reveals itself. As the ghost appears to Hamlet demanding that he avenge his father's murder by his uncle Claudius, Shakespeare shows us a fallen and disordered world. Appearances are deceptive. The innocent appear to be guilty, and the devious seem honest. We find out about Claudius' villainy, Hamlet's "madness," and the murderous plots that end in the fatal duel. Hamlet's delayed revenge results in the destruction of two families and a kingdom. Witnessing that destruction, we discover that Shakespeare's revenge play is, in truth, a complex tragedy about the power of evil and political disorder to paralyze the human will and corrupt the imagination (Figure 1-4).

A more recent play is Samuel Beckett's *Waiting for Godot* (1953). A curtain rises to reveal two tramps waiting under a wasted tree for someone named Godot. During the next two hours we discover that their situation is in many ways like our own. Samuel Beckett's tramps in *Waiting for Godot* eat, sleep, joke, suffer, quarrel, despair, and hope while waiting out their lives. As we watch the play we discover that, like Beckett's Vladimir and Estragon, we are also waiting for things to happen and time to pass.

The writer, too, is engaged in a process of discovery. It is not unreasonable, then, that many plays begin and end with questions. When theatre emerged from the Dark Ages after the decline of the Greek and Roman cultures, one of the earliest recorded pieces was the *Quem*

Hamlet

Hamlet (c. 1601) is Shakespeare's greatest tragedy. The play is about a man who confronts a task that seems beyond his powers.

Although the Danish court is celebrating King Claudius' wedding to Queen Gertrude (Hamlet's mother), Prince Hamlet still mourns the death of his father. The ghost of his father appears and tells Hamlet that he has been secretly murdered by Claudius. Hamlet swears to take vengeance, but he must first prove to himself that Claudius is guilty. He has a group of strolling players put on a play in which a similar murder is depicted. Claudius' reaction to the play betrays him and Hamlet plots revenge.

By accident he kills Polonius, the Lord Chamberlain and father to Ophelia, who loves Hamlet. Hamlet is exiled for killing Polonius, and Ophelia is driven mad.

Laertes, Polonius' son, vows revenge and challenges Hamlet to a duel. To ensure that Hamlet is killed, Claudius poisons Laertes' sword and prepares a cup of poison for Hamlet to drink during the duel. In the closing scene, Gertrude accidentally drinks from the poisoned cup and dies, Hamlet kills Claudius, Laertes kills Hamlet and is killed in turn by his own poisoned sword, which Hamlet picked up in the confusion. Hamlet's cousin, Fortinbras, is made king of Denmark.

Figure 1-4 A 1975 New York Shakespeare Festival production at the Delacorte Theatre in Central Park. Actor Sam Waterston as Hamlet kneels before Claudius, Gertrude, and Polonius.

Quaeritis trope, which begins with the question "Whom seek ye?" The first words of *Hamlet*, spoken by the guard on the fog-shrouded battlements, are "Who's there?" The next-to-last lines of the two acts of *Waiting for Godot* are also questions—the same questions, in fact:

> *Estragon* Well, shall we go?
>
> *Vladimir* Yes, let's go.
>
> [*They do not move.*] *Curtain* (Act I)

> *Vladimir* Well, shall we go?
>
> *Estragon* Yes, let's go.
>
> [*They do not move.*] *Curtain* (Act II)[3]

Theatre is a searching for answers about human nature and society. It is also a way of disclosing what it means to be a human being in certain situations and under certain conditions. In Sophocles' *Oedipus the King*, Oedipus searches for the cause of the plague and discovers his own identity. Shakespeare's Othello, persuaded of Desdemona's unfaithfulness, seeks revenge and finds out, too late, that he has killed an innocent wife and has been destroyed himself by Iago's malevolence. In Beckett's *Waiting for Godot* (Figure 1-5), Vladimir and Estragon keep their appointment with the absent Godot and perhaps discover in their waiting something essential about themselves and others. Vladimir says: "We have kept our appointment and that's an end to that. We are not saints, but we have kept our appointment. How many people can boast as much?" Estragon answers: "Billions."[4]

Figure 1-5 The first American production of Beckett's *Waiting for Godot* was directed by Alan Schneider. Tom Ewell played Vladimir (center) and Bert Lahr was Estragon. The play was presented in 1956 at the Cocoanut Grove Playhouse in Miami.

Waiting for Godot

Waiting for Godot, by the Irish playwright Samuel Beckett, was first produced at the Théâtre de Babylone, Paris, in 1953. On a country road in a deserted landscape marked by a single leafless tree, Estragon and Vladimir are waiting for someone named Godot. To pass the time, they play games, quarrel, make up, fall asleep. In comes Pozzo, leading Lucky by a rope tied around his neck. Pozzo demonstrates that Lucky is his obedient servant, and Lucky entertains them with a monologue that is a jumble of politics and theology. They disappear into the darkness, and Godot's messenger (a boy) announces that Mr. Godot will not come today.

In Act II, a leaf has sprouted on the tree, suggesting that time has passed, but the two tramps are occupied in the same way. They play master-and-slave games, trade hats, argue about everything. Pozzo and Lucky return; one is blind and the other dumb. Godot again sends word that he will not come today, but perhaps tomorrow. As the play ends, Vladimir and Estragon, alone, continue waiting. In this play Beckett shows us how each of us waits for a Godot—for whatever it is that we hope for—and how, so occupied, we wait out a lifetime.

WHAT WE BRING TO THE THEATRE

We the audience, as collaborators in the theatrical event, bring a wealth of informal theatrical experience to our viewing and also a set of largely unconscious expectations about what we are going to see.

THE THEATRICAL IN EVERYDAY LIFE

In recent years sociologists, psychologists, critics, and artists have become greatly interested in the theatrical in our daily lives. Sociologist Erving Goffman in *The Presentation of Self in Everyday Life* (1956) considers human beings as actors who give performances, wear costumes, even makeup and masks.

It is no accident that the word *person* means mask. It is a recognition of the fact that everyone is always, more or less consciously, role playing. In these roles we get to know each other and ourselves. Sociologists tell us that our *masks* represent the conception we have formed of ourselves—the role we are striving to live up to.

The theatrical permeates all corners of our day-to-day-lives, including our bedrooms, living rooms, coffee lounges, classrooms, and neighborhood bars. We give "performances" when we are in social situations. We "stage" events and even talk about "getting our act together." Sometimes we "act out" in public to influence friends and to shape events to our liking. The living room is frequently our most convenient stage. It is set, or arranged, with familiar furniture and properties. We use this space to convince our parents about matters important to us. We invite our friends and acquaintances into this space to share conversation and cultivate relationships.

In short, as we go about our daily affairs, we are both spectators and actors observing and experiencing our lives. Formally, we are spectators at football games, at graduation ceremonies, and at religious services. Informally, we watch television and become spectators to world events, to congressional hearings, and to political speeches. In certain situations we are outsiders observing unfamiliar customs and behavior in much the same way that we observe a play in the theatre. Sometimes circumstances make it impossible for us to remain spectators, and we become participants, insiders, actors. At other times we simultaneously act and also observe ourselves as actors.

There are certain situations, usually public ones, where we costume ourselves and think through the behavior expected of us. Our clothing and public behavior give us a way of mastering an unfamiliar world and of fitting in. These kinds of activities vary widely. What we wear to a football game, a disco, or a classroom differs from what we wear to religious services, weddings, and job interviews. The "preppy look" so popular in the 1980s requires a costume that is taken for granted and familiar: madras slacks and skirts, button-down Oxford shirts, Izod and polo shirts, wool sweaters, topsider loafers without socks, and so on. Clothing gives us a *persona*, or identity, in our daily lives just as Hamlet's "inky black" costume gives him a persona on stage.

Television increasingly has made observers of us all, distancing us from events and denying us an active involvement in them. As a result, we have a greater need, sociologists tell us, to master situations in which we find ourselves—in which we are cast as "actors." This probably accounts for the increasing theatricality of our everyday

> *I have been using the term 'performance' to refer to all the activity of an individual which occurs during a period marked by his continuous presence before a particular set of observers and which has some influence on the observers.*
>
> Erving Goffman , *The Presentation of Self in Everyday Life* (1956)

lives. Our clothes have become costumes; men and women wear makeup and frequent hair salons; our conversations are little dialogues; our homes and other environs are frequently stage settings arranged by interior decorators; and our public behavior is often a well-calculated performance.

THE AUDIENCE'S EXPECTATIONS

A modern audience enters a theatre lobby with an air of excitement and a sense of anticipation. There is usually a last-minute crush at the box office to pick up tickets, to find programs and seats. An audience is not an unruly crowd but a very special group assembling for a special occasion; it is the final, essential participant in the theatre event.

Let us think about the audience's expectations as we wait for the house lights to dim and the curtain to rise. These expectations are the same whether the audience is at the Shubert Theatre on Broadway or the Guthrie Theatre in Minneapolis.

Most audiences expect plays to be related in some way to life's experiences; they expect to be presented with the familiar, not with the strange or bizarre; and they expect to join with a group in an emotional experience of some sort.

First, let us consider that audiences expect plays to be related to life experiences. (It goes without saying that audiences expect plays and performances to hold their attention and to be entertaining.) This does not mean that audiences actually expect to have experienced the events taking place on stage. None of us would willingly exchange places with Oedipus, Othello, or Blanche DuBois. Instead, we expect the play's events (and also the actor's performances) to be *authentic* in terms of feelings and experiences. We are moved by Tennessee Williams' *A Streetcar Named Desire* because it rings true in terms of what we know about ourselves and others. It confirms what we have studied, read, or heard about human behavior. Williams' characters and situation may not be literally a part of our lives; yet we all recognize the need

for fantasies, self-delusion, and refuge from life's harsh realities. In short, we go to the theatre expecting the performance to be an authentic representation of some aspect of life as we know it or can imagine it.

Second, most people go to the theatre expecting the familiar. These expectations are based largely on plays we have already seen or on our experiences with movies and television. Audiences enjoy the familiar in plots, characters, or situations. For this reason, audiences frequently have difficulty understanding and enjoying plays from the older classical repertory or from the contemporary avant-garde. New plays often fall into the category of the unfamiliar because we do not know what to expect.

All audiences come to the theatre with certain expectations that have been shaped by their previous theatregoing experiences. If those experiences have been limited to musicals, summer stock, or local community theatre, then they may find the first experience of a play by Anton Chekhov or Samuel Beckett a jarring, puzzling, or even boring experience. But masterpieces somehow ring true! In them we find authentic life experiences, even if the language is difficult, the situations strange, and the production techniques unfamiliar.

The response to *Waiting for Godot* in the 1950s is a good example of audiences confronted with the unfamiliar and having their expectations disappointed on their first experience with the play. Audiences in Miami and New York were baffled by it. But in 1957 Jules Irving and Herbert Blau's San Francisco Actor's Workshop presented *Waiting for Godot* to the inmates of San Quentin Prison. The director and actors were apprehensive as no live play had been performed at San Quentin since Sarah Bernhardt appeared there in 1913.

Of the 1400 convicts assembled to see the play, possibly not one had ever been to the theatre. Moreover, they were gathered in the prison dining room to see a highly experimental play that had bewildered sophisticated audiences in Paris, Miami, and New York. What would be the response? It was simply over-

Figure 1-6 A radical adaptation of Shakespeare's *A Midsummer Night's Dream*, directed by Peter Brook. Oberon (Alan Howard) and Puck (John Kane) speak Shakespeare's lines while seated upon trapezes like acrobats.

whelming. The prisoners understood the hopelessness and frustration of waiting for something or for someone that never arrives. They recognized the meaninglessness of waiting and were aware that if Godot finally came, he would probably be a disappointment.[5]

By now *Waiting for Godot* is no longer experimental, and most audiences are no longer baffled by it. It has become a classic of the modern theatre. But it remains a good example of how initial audience expectations can change over a period of years in response to an unusual, profound play.

Even though audiences desire to see the familiar—this is probably the reason why there are so many revivals of *Arsenic and Old Lace* and *Charley's Aunt*—they also appreciate and look forward to joyful and exhilarating experiences in the theatre. Imagine the surprise of audiences in 1970 when director Peter Brook reinterpreted Shakespeare's *A Midsummer Night's Dream*, exploring the complications of young love in a white boxlike setting with actors on trapezes and in mod clothing and circus costumes (Figure 1-6 and the color insert). Most audiences around the world were delighted with the new concept for staging a very old play, although a few were dissatisfied by not having their expectations fulfilled.

Like all great art forms, the theatre gives us a heightened sense of life and self-awareness. Great theatre also provides a sense of *new* possibilities. We go to plays (whether we are consciously aware of our reasons) to realize a fuller and deeper understanding of our lives, our society, and our universe. Great plays and performances give us this. Satisfied, we no longer cling to our need for the familiar or the desire to have before us what we are used to.

Another facet of audience expectations is more difficult to pin down. We experience a performance as a group—as a *collective presence.* We have already remarked how theatre is a collective art. Psychologists tell us that being in an audience satisfies a deeply felt human need; that is, a need to participate in a collective response whether with laughter, tears, apprecia-

tive silence, or thundering applause. As part of an audience we become very much aware of audience dynamics at the conclusion of a powerful and moving play. Sometimes when audiences are deeply moved there are moments of silence before the beginning of applause. At other times applause is instantaneous with audiences leaping to their feet clapping and shouting "bravo." The curtain calls for *Nicholas Nickleby,* produced in 1980 by England's Royal Shakespeare Company, were of this kind. The response was immediate and unrestrained.

While applause is a theatregoing convention, it is also a genuine expression of our appreciation and approval of a performance. One major element of our experience of live theatre is this sharing of an experience with others around us. Sometimes this even happens in movie houses, but rarely does it happen when we sit before the television set at home—because we are usually alone.[6]

SUMMARY

Theatre, like life, happens within the present moment. Theatre has an immediacy that most other art forms do not have or require. For theatre to happen, two groups of people—actors and audience—must come together in a certain space. There the actors present themselves to the audience. The space, the actor, and the audience are the three essential ingredients of the theatre event. Most effectively of all the arts, theatre captures the experience of what it means to be human because human beings are both its medium and its subject.

Comparing theatre with film and other forms of entertainment helps clarify the special qualities of the theatre. Theatre's *immediacy*—the living actor *presenting* himself before a live audience—is one of the most notable differences between theatre and film. While both theatre and, say, sporting events entertain us, there is a random and unpredictable quality in sports that

Figure 1-7 Audiences responded enthusiastically to *The Life and Adventures of Nicholas Nickleby,* produced by the Royal Shakespeare Company. In this scene, Nicholas (Roger Rees) and Smike (David Threlfall) discuss their bleak future after their escape from the dreaded Dotheboys Hall.

is not found in the carefully rehearsed and performed play.

Theatre requires the participation of people with varied skills. Playwrights, directors, actors, and designers work together to bring some aspect of life experience before an audience. While theatre, unlike painting and sculpture, is a collaborative art, the collaboration is not complete until the audience is also engaged in the event.

Theatre is an act of discovery. When the curtain goes up we discover a world that is both familiar and unfamiliar to us. We discover new ways of learning about ourselves, our society, and our universe. Great plays always raise questions about what it means to be a human being in certain situations and under certain conditions. Great performances communicate this knowledge to us in fresh, entertaining, and challenging ways.

What do we, the audience, bring to the theatre? First, we bring our own experiences of the theatrical. Sociologists tell us that the theatre has permeated our everyday lives in our dress codes, our "acting out" of planned behavior, and our staging of personal events.

Second, we bring our expectations of what theatre should be. Audiences expect plays to relate in some way to life experiences. They prefer the familiar and are frequently uncomfortable with the difficult and strange, although these responses change as the familiar is glimpsed in the unfamiliar. Finally, audiences expect and have a need to participate with others in an emotional experience, an expression of collective feelings through laughter, tears, and applause.

SOURCES

Atkinson, Brooks. *Broadway,* rev. ed. New York: Macmillan, 1974. Long-time drama critic of the *New York Times,* Brooks Atkinson traces the development of Broadway from its beginnings to the early seventies by focusing on the principal plays and people of American theatre history. This is a fact-filled and amiable history of the New York commercial theatre.

Brook, Peter. *The Empty Space.* New York: Avon Books, 1969. Paperback. Peter Brook is one of today's most influential and experimental directors. Here he reexamines the essential elements of every theatrical event, along with contemporary theatre practice.

Esslin, Martin. *An Anatomy of Drama.* New York: Hill and Wang, 1977. Hardcover and paperback. Esslin writes a brief, informal discussion of the nature of theatre, concentrating on the differences among theatre, film, radio, and television.

Lahr, John, and Jonathan Price. *Life-Show.* New York: Viking, 1973. Hardcover and paperback. A richly illustrated book on "how to see theatre in life and life in theatre." Lahr and Price discuss the elements of the theatre event and show how we recreate them in our everyday lives.

NOTES

1. Peter Brook, *The Empty Space,* p. 3. Copyright © 1968 by Peter Brook. Reprinted with permission of Atheneum Publishers, New York, N.Y., and Granada Publishing Ltd., England.

2. Mircea Eliade, *The Sacred and the Profane: The Nature of Religion,* Harcourt Brace Jovanovich, Inc., 1959. Reprinted with permission.

3. Samuel Beckett, *Waiting for Godot* (New York: Grove, 1954), pp. 36, 61. Copyright © 1954 by Grove Press, Inc. Renewed © 1982 by Samuel Beckett. Reprinted by permission of Grove Press, Inc.

4. Beckett, *Waiting for Godot,* p. 52. Reprinted by permission.

5. Martin Esslin, *The Theatre of the Absurd,* rev. ed. (Garden City, N.Y.: Doubleday, 1969), pp. 1–3.

6. For a highly readable and thorough discussion of the theatre audience, see Robert W. Corrigan, *The World of the Theatre* (Chicago: Scott, Foresman, 1979), pp. 304–310.

TWO

THE SCRIPT
INTO PERFORMANCE

DRAMA'S FORMS

Over centuries of theatrical activities, drama evolved out of child's play and society's formal rituals into different forms or types: tragedy, comedy, tragicomedy, and many more. Conventions developed that allow for rapid communication between stage and audience during performances. We will examine drama's ways and means in this chapter.

DRAMA, PLAY, AND IMITATION

Drama, the playwright's art, takes its name from the Greek verb *dran,* meaning "to do" or "to act." Drama is a pattern of words and actions having the potential for "doing" or becoming living words and actions. It is the source of what we see and hear in the theatre.

On the printed page drama is mainly *dialogue*—words arranged in sequence to be spoken by actors. Often stage dialogue is similar to the dialogue we speak in conversation with friends. Often, as with Shakespeare's blank verse or the complex verse forms of the Greek plays, dialogue is more formal. But stage dialogue differs from ordinary conversation in one important way: The playwright creates it and the actor speaks it. *Performability* is the link between the playwright's words and the actor's speech.

We can begin to think about drama by discussing *play,* with which it shares similar features.

Play as Imitation Children, too, are playwrights as they imitate reality through play like cops and robbers, cowboys and Indians, "school," "store," or "hospital." Children play to entertain themselves, to imitate adult behavior, and to help fit themselves into an unfamiliar world. In play children try out and learn roles they will play in their adult lives. In their imitations they develop what the American psychiatrist Eric Berne calls *life-scripts.*

What do we mean by *imitation,* especially imitation at the psychological level? In *Play, Dreams and Imitation in Childhood* (1962), French psychologist Jean Piaget shows that we tend to imitate through play those things that arouse ambivalent emotions within us. We do this to handle the fears those things evoke because of their strangeness. We imitate the unknown as a way of mastering and gaining dominance over it. Children, adults of primitive societies, and artists all use imitation and for many of the same reasons.

So imitation is a process by which we confront and transform our fears of the strange and unknown by becoming one of them. Every drama-as-play is an imitation that confronts the mystery of human behavior. It does so concretely through *the living presence* of the actor, who is both a real person and a fictional character. The great British actor Sir Laurence Olivier has remarked that "Acting is an almost childish wish. . . . Pretend to be somebody else. . . . Let's pretend—I suppose that's the original impulse of acting. . . ."[2]

Drama as Imitation As we have seen, play and drama have much in common. The child playing firefighter or the actor playing *Hamlet* must start with a scenario or script, or imagined situation, dialogue, and locale. Both play and drama entertain. They contribute to a sense of well-being and to an understanding of ourselves and others. They have their own fixed rules. Most important, they *imitate human events.*

In the fourth century BC, the Greek philosopher Aristotle (384–322) described drama as *mimesis*—the imitation of human beings in action. In his *Poetics* (c. 335–323), he showed that the playwright used certain devices to turn written material into human action: plot, character, language, meaning, music, and visual elements. From our modern perspective we could add time and space to Aristotle's list of dramatic elements (Figure 2-1).

THE ELEMENTS OF DRAMA

Plot is an arranged sequence of events or incidents usually having a beginning, middle, and end. These incidents spring from an action or motive.

Words

Signals   Symbols

Signs   Character

Gesture —— Pattern —— Action
            for
            Doing

Space   Meaning

Plot   Time

Figure 2-1 The elements of drama are words, symbols, sounds, spectacle, plot, action, character, gesture, space, time, and meaning. Together they make up a pattern for doing. In the theatre, drama's elements become living words and actions.

Character includes the physiological and psychological makeup of the persons in the play. *Language* is the spoken word, including symbols and signs. The play's *meaning* is its underlying idea—its general and particular truths about human experience. Today we frequently use the word *theme* when we talk about a play's meaning. A play may have more than one basic theme. *Othello,* for example, is a play about false appearances, errors of judgment, social differences, passion without reason, and the nature of evil.

Aristotle used the word *spectacle* to take in all visual and aural elements: costumes, settings, music, and sound. In the modern theatre we add stage lighting to this list.

The modern idea of a play's *time* refers not to *actual time*—the length of the performance—but to *symbolic time,* which is integral to the play's structure and may be spread out over hours, days, or years. *Hamlet* frequently takes four hours to perform, although the story covers many months. In Henrik Ibsen's *Ghosts* we are asked to believe that the incidents take place in a little more than 24 hours.

The "happenings" of the 1960s introduced *event time* into American theatre. Allan Kaprow's happening called *Self-Service* (1967) was created to be done over a summer, during which the participants could do specified tasks on any weekend. Kaprow roughly combined actual time (the summer months) with event time (the task).

Action is a crucial element of drama. Aristotle did not use *action* to refer to those external deeds, incidents, situations, and events we tend to associate with a play's plot. He likened the relationship of action and drama to that of the soul and the body. He saw action as the source of the play's inner meaning. As such, it is an inward process that cannot be perceived directly through the hero's deeds. It is a spirit that moves through the play and holds all its elements together in a meaningful way as the play works its way to a conclusion.

American scholar Francis Fergusson defines action as "the focus or aim of psychic life from which the events, in that situation, result."[3] It embodies all the physical, psychological, and spiritual gestures and motivations that result in the visible behavior of the characters. It is the source of the play's outward deeds. The action of Oedipus in Sophocles' play occurs on two levels. On one level, Oedipus' action is to find the killer of Laius, the former Theban king, and to purify the city of plague by punishing the guilty person. During his investigation of the plague's cause, Oedipus discovers that he is the guilty man, that he unwittingly killed his father and married his mother. On another, deeper level, the action of *Oedipus the King* is really a man's attempt *to know himself.* In short, action is the play's all-encompassing purpose, that which is to be fulfilled in performance.

Over the centuries playwrights have developed different ways of imitating human behavior in what we call dramatic forms and styles to mirror the changing intellectual and emotional life of their cultures. (Playwright Bertolt Brecht has said: "If art reflects life it does so with special mirrors" [*The Short Organon for the Theatre*].) These dramatic mirrors fall under many categories. The main ones are tragedy, comedy, tragicomedy, melodrama, and farce. (Two highly significant forms of twentieth-century theatre, epic and absurdist theatre, are discussed at length in later chapters.)

Drama's essential forms are ways of seeing human experience. The words *tragedy, comedy,* and *tragicomedy* are not so much ways of classifying plays by their endings as ways of talking about the playwright's vision of experience—of the way he or she perceives life. They furnish clues about the play's style and how the play is to be taken or understood by the audience. Is the play a serious statement about, say, the relationship between men and women? Does it despair at the possibilities of mutual understanding? Or does it hold such attempts up to ridicule?

TRAGEDY

It is not altogether simple-minded to say that a tragedy is a play with an unhappy ending. Tragedy, the first of the great dramatic forms in Western drama, makes a special statement about human fallibility.

The Tragic Vision The writer's tragic vision of human experience conceives of people as both vulnerable and invincible, as capable of abject defeat and transcendent greatness. In tragedies like *Oedipus the King, Hamlet, Othello, Ghosts,* and *A Streetcar Named Desire,* the playwright shows the world's injustice, evil, and pain. Tragic heroes, in an exercise of free will, pit themselves against forces represented by other characters or by their physical environment. We witness their suffering, their inevitable defeat, and, sometimes, their personal triumph in the face of defeat. The trials of the hero give meaning to the pain and paradox of our humanity.

Some tragedies are concerned with seeking meaning and justice in an ordered world, others with humanity's helpless protest against an irrational universe. In both kinds the hero, alone and willful, asserts his or her intellect and energy against the ultimate mysteries of an imperfect world.

Tragic Realization The realization that follows the hero's efforts usually takes one of two directions. We may learn that, despite human suffering and calamity, a world order and eternal laws exist and people can learn from suffering, or we may learn of the futility of human acts and suffering in an indifferent, capricious, or mechanical universe, but at the same time celebrate the hero's protest against this futility. In *Oedipus the King* and *A Streetcar Named Desire* we find examples of these two kinds of tragic realization.

Aristotle on Tragedy Aristotle spoke of tragedy as "an imitation of an action . . . concerning the fall of man whose character is good (though not preeminently just or virtuous) . . . whose misfortune is brought about not by vice or depravity but by some error or frailty . . . with incidents arousing pity and fear, wherewith to accomplish the catharsis of these emotions."[4]

Aristotle and the Greek playwrights depicted tragedy's action as an imitation of a noble hero who suffers a downfall and tragedy's subjects as dealing with suffering and death. The heroes of ancient tragedies were often aristocratic to show that even the great among us suffer the fate of the human condition. In modern plays the hero's averageness speaks to us of human kinship in adversity. Whether the hero is aristocratic or ordinary, his or her action is influenced by the writer's tragic view of life, which centers on the human need to give meaning to our fate despite the fact that we are doomed to failure and defeat.

COMEDY

In the eighteenth century Horace Walpole said, "The world is a comedy to those that think, a tragedy to those that feel." In comedy the playwright examines the social world, social

Oppositions Between Tragedy and Comedy	
Tragedy	**Comedy**
Individual	Society
Metaphysical	Social
Death	Endurance
Error	Folly
Suffering	Joy
Pain	Pleasure
Life-denying	Procreative
Separation	Union/Reunion
Terror	Euphoria
Unhappiness	Happiness
Irremediable	Remediable
Decay	Growth
Destruction	Continuation
Defeat	Survival
Extreme	Moderation
Inflexible	Flexible

values, and people as social beings. Frequently, comic action shows the social disorder created by an eccentric character who deviates from reasonable values like sensibility, good nature, flexibility, moderation, tolerance, and social intelligence. Deviation is sharply ridiculed in comedy because it threatens to destroy revered social structures like marriage and the family.

The writer of comedy calls for sanity, reason, and moderation in human behavior so that society can function for the well-being and happiness of its members. In comedy, society survives the threat posed by inflexible or unnatural behavior. In Molière's *Tartuffe* (1664) (Figure 2–2) that character's greed is revealed and Orgon's family is returned to a normal, domestic existence at the play's end. For the seventeenth-century French playwright, as for some of his contemporary American counterparts, the well-being of the family unit is a measure of the well-being of the society as a whole.

At the end of almost any comedy, the life flow is ordinarily symbolized in a wedding, a dance, or a banquet celebrating the harmony and reconciliation of opposing forces. These social ceremonies allow us to see that good sense wins the day and that humanity endures in the vital, the flexible, and the reasonable.

TRAGICOMEDY

Tragicomedy, as its name implies, is a mixed dramatic form. Up to the end of the seventeenth century in Europe, the definition of *tragicomedy* was a mixture of tragedy, which went from good fortune to bad, and comedy, which reversed the order from bad fortune to good. Tragicomedy mixed serious and comic incidents as well as the styles, subject matter, and language proper to tragedy and to comedy, and it also mixed characters from all stations of life. The *ending* (up until the nineteenth century) was its principal feature: Tragicomedies were serious and potentially tragic plays with happy endings, or at least with averted catastrophes.

The term *modern tragicomedy* is used to designate plays with mixed moods in which the endings are neither exclusively tragic nor comic, happy nor unhappy. Samuel Beckett calls *Waiting for Godot* a "tragicomedy" in the play's subtitle. In this play two tramps entertain themselves with comic routines while they wait in a sparse landscape adorned by a single tree for someone named Godot to arrive. But Godot never comes. As they react to this situation, humor and energy are mixed with anguish and despair. In the modern form of tragicomedy, playwrights show people laughing at their anxieties and life's contradictions with little effect on their situations. Beckett's Vladimir summarizes the form when he says, "The essential doesn't change."

MELODRAMA

Another mixed form, *melodrama*, derives its name from the Greek word for music, *melos*. It is a combination of music and drama in which the spoken voice is used against a musical back-

Figure 2-2 Tartuffe pretends to be a person of utmost piety to Elmire, Orgon's wife, while plotting to seduce her and take her husband's property. He disrupts the household and threatens its well-being before being found out and sent to prison for his misdeeds. John Wood is Tartuffe and Tammy Grimes is Elmire in the 1977 Circle-in-the-Square production (New York), directed by Stephen Porter.

ground. Jean Jacques Rousseau, who introduced the word's modern use in 1772, applied it to his *Pygmalion*, a *scène lyrique* in which words and music were linked together in the action.

The term became widely used in the nineteenth century to describe a play without music but having a serious action ordinarily caused by the villainy of an unsympathetic character. Melodrama's characters are clearly divided—either sympathetic or unsympathetic—and the villain's destruction brings about the happy resolution. Melodrama usually shows a main character in circumstances that threaten death or ruin from which he or she is rescued at the last possible moment. Like a film's musical score, music heightens the mood of impending disaster. The term *melodrama* is most often applied to such nineteenth-century plays as *Uncle Tom's Cabin* (1852) based on Harriet Beecher Stowe's novel and Dion Boucicault's *The Octoroon* (1859). Today we apply the term to such diverse plays as Lillian Hellman's *The Little Foxes* (1938), Lorraine Hansberry's *A Raisin in the Sun* (1959), and Joseph Walker's *The River Niger* (1972) (Figure 2-3).

The melodramatic view of life sees human beings as whole, not divided; enduring outer conflicts, not inner ones, in a generally hostile world; and sees these conflicts resulting in victory or defeat as they are pressed to extreme conclusions. Melodrama's characters win or lose in the conflict. There are no complex and ambiguous resolutions, as when Hamlet wins in losing.

Even though melodrama oversimplifies, exaggerates, and contrives experience, the fact is that we see most of the serious conflicts and crises of our daily lives in melodramatic terms. We take comfort ourselves that our failures are the fault of others; we cry that our accidents are due to fate. Melodrama is the dramatic form that expresses the human condition as we perceive it most of the time.

FARCE

Farce is best thought of as comedy of situation. In farce, pies in the face, beatings, mistaken identities, slips on the banana peel—exaggerated

physical activities growing out of situations—are substituted for comedy's traditional concern for social values. The writer of farce presents life as mechanical, aggressive, and coincidental, and entertains us with seemingly endless variations on a single situation. For instance, a typical farce situation is the bedroom crowded with concealed lovers as the cuckolded husband or deceived wife arrives on the scene (Figure 2-4).

The "psychology of farce," as Eric Bentley calls it, is that special opportunity for the fulfillment of our unmentionable wishes without taking responsibility for our actions or suffering the guilt.[5] Farce as a dramatic form recklessly abandons us in a fantasy world of violence (without harm), adultery (without consequences), brutality (without reprisal), and aggression (without risk). Today we enjoy farce in the films of Charlie Chaplin, W. C. Fields, the Marx Brothers, Peter Sellers, and Richard Pryor; in the Monty Python films and television series; and in the plays of Georges Feydeau, Neil Simon, and Alan Ayckbourn. Farce has also been part of some of the world's great comedies, including those of Shakespeare, Molière, and Chekhov.

ADAPTATIONS

With the success of *Nicholas Nickleby*, a novel by Charles Dickens adapted for performance in 1980 by the Royal Shakespeare Company of Stratford-upon-Avon (England), and performed in England and America, we encounter another play form—*the adaptation*. The current explosion of interest in adaptations in contemporary French, English, Russian, and American theatres is not related to the availability of new plays but to a desire of theatre companies to create their own texts rather than to stage classical or "written" plays.

Dickens' novels, with their wealth of dramatic incident and social detail, have been prime targets for adaptation. Many theatrical adaptations (not counting films and television) have been made of *A Christmas Carol* (Figure 2-5), *Pickwick Papers, A Tale of Two Cities, David*

Figure 2-3 Paranoia, relief, and despair are the basic emotions of melo-drama. In playwright Joseph Walker's *The River Niger*, produced by the Negro Ensemble Company (1972) in New York, we feel relief that John Williams (center), played by Douglas Turner Ward, takes control of his life at the moment of his dying.

Copperfield, and *Nicholas Nickleby.* In France novels by Jack London, Voltaire, Honoré de Balzac, Gustave Flaubert, and Marguerite Duras, as well as notable adaptations of nondramatic texts, have found their way onto the stages of both established and experimental theatres. *Pariscope,* a weekly entertainment guide, showed that adaptations accounted for one out of every five Parisian productions between 1979 and 1981.

How is a dramatic adaptation created and how does it work theatrically? An adaptation is largely the director's concept and the actors' work. As French director Antoine Vitez says: "The theatre is *someone* who takes his material wherever he finds it—even things not made for the stage—and puts them on stage. Or, rather, stages them."[6] In the process of adaptation, the director emerges as primary creator. What matters is not what the author meant the text to say but how the director reads it. French director Jean-Louis Barrault (b. 1910) reasons that because great texts, especially novels, permit him to visualize their universe, his own creativeness soars when he stages them.[7]

One method of adapting novels to the stage is to retain the novel's narrative voice (with actors as narrators), substituting storytellers for characters. The aim is to blend narrative tech-

Figure 2-4 Farce's familiar situation: The hero successfully seduces the wife only to have their affair almost discovered by her husband who, by chance, is meeting his mistress at the same hotel. Louis Jourdan is the lover and Patricia Elliott the wife in the Circle-in-the-Square's 1978 production in New York of Georges Feydeau's *13 Rue de L'Amour.*

niques (descriptions, comments, interior monologues) with dramatic ones (one character speaking directly to another). In some cases social documents relevant to the action are read aloud. In others, adaptations seem *to objectify* the act of reading. For instance, the action begins at one side of the stage and moves to the other, then recommences—like turning the pages of a novel. Descriptions are also included in what is spoken. Antoine Vitez has said: "... if one wants to stage a novel, one must also stage the novel's flesh, its narrative thickness. Yes, I mean houses and streets."[8] Sometimes actors simply give voice to both descriptions and conversations, including the phrases "he said" or "she said."

Skillfully adapted novels work as theatre pieces, but they also challenge audiences to accept a kind of theatre that mirrors the life of the mind. The transformation of the novel into play script is the creation of a new psychological

Figure 2-5 Scrooge and the Ghost of Christmas Past in the University of North Carolina at Chapel Hill's 1982 adaptation of Charles Dickens' *Christmas Carol.*

theatre piece: the act of the mind structuring the world. The adaptation becomes both a laboratory for human consciousness and a collective creation on the part of the theatre company.[9]

The 1977–1978 French production of *David Copperfield* was staged to illustrate how memory is stored up and experienced. To make a theatre piece out of Dickens' 1000-page chronicle, two French companies combined their talents: Jean-Claude Penchenat's Théâtre de Campagnol and Ariane Mnouchkine's Théâtre du Soleil. Twenty-six actors from both companies in improvisations of 36 Dickens characters created a strong and unique theatre experience. Many of Dickens' lines and metaphors were

---

David Copperfield

Charles Dickens' *David Copperfield* (1850) is the story of the adventures of young David Copperfield on his way to manhood—from birth to a second, mature marriage. Along the way he encounters a myriad of characters from Peggotty, his salt-of-the-earth nurse; the mock-heroic Micawbers; Little Emily, a fallen angel; Aunt Betsey Trotwood, David's crusty savior; Uriah Heep, the villain of all villains; and the saintlike Agnes Wickfield.

retained while dialogue and movement were invented. They condensed the novel into two parts: David's childhood, the terrors of the Salem House boarding school, the introduction to the Micawbers, and his rescue by Aunt Betsey formed one-half. The second half focused on his adolescence, his encounter with Heep, his marriage with Dora, and his confession of love to Agnes. The play ended with David, the writer, taking up the narrative from the novel's beginning: "Whether I shall turn out to be the hero of my own life, or whether that station will be held by anybody else, these pages must show."

**Ariane Mnouchkine
and the Théâtre du Soleil**

Of the French directors who have come to prominence since 1965, Ariane Mnouchkine (b. 1940) has become one of the most important. She founded the Théâtre du Soleil, a commune composed of about 40 members, in the sixties. They performed until 1968 in the Cirque d'Hiver, creating a considerable stir with productions of Shakespeare's *A Midsummer Night's Dream* and Arnold Wesker's *The Kitchen.*

In 1970 the company moved to an abandoned munitions factory just outside Paris (the Cartoucherie) where they have since produced internationally celebrated environmental productions of *1789* (in 1971) and *1793* (in 1972), treatments of the early years of the French Revolution where it was argued that the revolution was more concerned about property than with social injustice. *The Age of Gold* (1975) dealt with various aspects of materialism and Molière's *Don Juan* (1978) with sexual values. The company is one of France's finest.

The theatre piece differed from the novel in the following essential way: The actors did not tell a story but reconstructed *a series of memories*—as David experienced them and as they experienced David experiencing them. The playing space, including lighting, costumes, movement, and music, divided the stage into two halves. The front portion was used as the domain of present memory, while the rear half, cavernous and dusty, was reserved for past memories. It resembled a grandparent's attic with old clothes, bric-a-brac, and furniture suspended from the flies or propped against walls. Victorian chandeliers bathed the actors in a haze of yellow light; the costumes completed the illusion of old engravings.

Audiences entered easily into the onstage memories of David Copperfield, charmed to rediscover David's and their own childhood. By transferring David's recollections to the stage, the Campagnol–Soleil companies preserved one of the principal interests of the novel—how a mind remembers and structures its past. By giving their adaptation the ever-changing shape of memory itself, the company illustrated the functioning of the audience's own mind. Hence this new method of adapting novels for the stage has resulted in a new play form—a new kind of psychological text for the contemporary theatre.

DRAMA'S STRUCTURES

In Western drama, plot and action are based on a central *conflict* and organized usually in the following progression: confrontation—crisis—climax—resolution. This generalization is true for plays written by William Shakespeare, Henrik Ibsen, or Edward Albee. The way the playwright varies this pattern determines the play's structure. In general, there have been three basic ways in which plays have been structured or organized: *climactic, episodic,* and *situational.* More recently, entirely new structures, such as "talking pieces," have been devised.

CLIMACTIC PLAY STRUCTURE

Found in classical and modern plays, climactic structure confines the characters' activities and intensifies the pressures on the characters until they are forced into irreversible acts—the climax. As the action develops, the characters' range of choices is reduced. Frequently, they are aware their choices are being limited and they are being moved toward a crisis and turning point. Climactic structure is a *cause-to-effect* arrangement of incidents ending in a climax and quick resolution.

Mrs. Alving in Henrik Ibsen's *Ghosts* (1881) (Figure 2–6) is shown progressively that the "ghosts" of her past are the cause of the present situation. Her son "looks like" his father; like his father, he makes advances to the serving girl; he also carries his father's moral corruption within him as a physical disease; and Mrs. Alving is conditioned to do what society dictates is proper and dutiful.

As Mrs. Alving faces her terminally ill son, she must decide whether or not to kill him. She has two alternatives at the play's end. She must choose *one.*

EPISODIC PLAY STRUCTURE

We associate episodic play structure with medieval plays and with plays by Shakespeare and Bertolt Brecht. Episodic structure traces the characters through a *journey* of sorts to a final action and to an understanding of what the journey meant. It can always take a new turn. In Shakespeare's plays people are not forced immediately into unmaneuverable positions. Possibilities of action are usually open to them until the very end. Events do not accumulate to confine the characters because the play takes in large amounts of time and distance. *Hamlet* takes place over several years and countries. Also, the expanding plot takes in a variety of events and activities. Frequently, Shakespeare used main plots and subplots to contrast events. In this loose structure, characters are not caught in circumstances but pass through them, as Grusha does in Brecht's *The Caucasian Chalk Circle* (1944–1945) (Figure 2–7). Grusha undergoes a variety of experiences in her efforts to save a governor's child from mercenary soldiers. She *journeys* through the countryside with the child until she is captured and brought before Judge Azdak to be tested by the chalk-circle rite. She passes the test and the judge awards the child to her.[10]

SITUATIONAL PLAY STRUCTURE

In absurdist plays of the 1950s, *situation* shapes the play, not plot or arrangement of incidents (Figure 2–8). It takes the place of the journey or the pressurized events. For example, two tramps wait for a person named Godot who never arrives (*Waiting for Godot*); or a husband and wife talk in meaningless clichés as they go about their daily routines (in Eugene Ionesco's *The Bald Soprano*).

The situation has its own inner rhythms, which are like the basic rhythms of life: day, night, day; hunger, thirst, hunger; spring, summer, winter. Although the situation usually remains unchanged, these rhythms move in a cycle.

In *The Bald Soprano* (1949) Ionesco introduces a fire chief and the Martins into Mr. and Mrs. Smith's typical middle-class English living room. After a series of absurd events, the dialogue crescendos into nonsensical babbling. The words stop abruptly and the play begins again. This time Mr. and Mrs. Martin are seated as the Smiths were at the play's beginning and repeat the Smiths' lines from the first scene. In the repetition Ionesco demonstrates the interchangeability of middle-class lives.

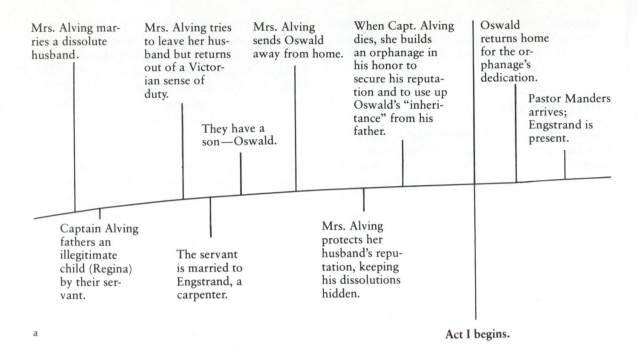

Mrs. Alving marries a dissolute husband.

Mrs. Alving tries to leave her husband but returns out of a Victorian sense of duty.

Mrs. Alving sends Oswald away from home.

When Capt. Alving dies, she builds an orphanage in his honor to secure his reputation and to use up Oswald's "inheritance" from his father.

Oswald returns home for the orphanage's dedication.

Pastor Manders arrives; Engstrand is present.

They have a son—Oswald.

Captain Alving fathers an illegitimate child (Regina) by their servant.

The servant is married to Engstrand, a carpenter.

Mrs. Alving protects her husband's reputation, keeping his dissolutions hidden.

a

Act I begins.

b

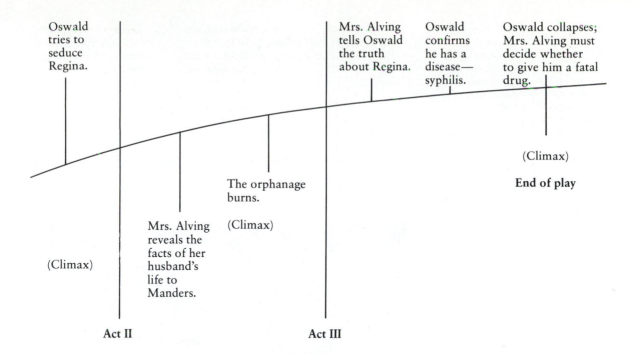

Oswald tries to seduce Regina.

Mrs. Alving tells Oswald the truth about Regina.

Oswald confirms he has a disease— syphilis.

Oswald collapses; Mrs. Alving must decide whether to give him a fatal drug.

The orphanage burns.

(Climax)

Mrs. Alving reveals the facts of her husband's life to Manders.

(Climax)

(Climax)

(Climax)

End of play

Act II

Act III

Figure 2-6 (a) Climactic play structure begins late in the story, near the crisis and climax. All the events of the story's past (to the left of the vertical line) occur before the play begins and are revealed in the exposition. Each act of Ibsen's play ends with a climax, building to the highest point of tension—Oswald's collapse. Since a climactic plot begins late in the story, the period of time covered is usually limited. The classical play usually takes place in a few hours. *Ghosts* begins in the afternoon and ends at sunrise the following day. (b) Climactic drama: Oswald and Mrs. Alving face the crisis in their lives. In climactic drama the characters are confined within time and space. There is usually a limited number of characters, and locale and events are restricted. *Ghosts* has five characters and takes place in Mrs. Alving's living room. As the pressures of the past go to work in the present, the action develops, limiting the choices the characters have open to them. An explosive confrontation becomes inevitable. In the photo Mrs. Alving (Margaret Tyzack) learns the truth from Oswald (Nicholas Pennell) about his disease in the 1977 Stratford Festival Theatre, Ontario, production of *Ghosts*.

Prologue	Narrator tells the story of Grusha, a peasant girl, saving the governor's child in the midst of a revolution.	She flees with the child Michael to the mountains, leaving her fiancé behind.	She bargains to feed the child, escapes pursuing soldiers, and marries to provide food and shelter for Michael.	The soldiers capture Grusha and Michael; they are returned to the city.
1945— people from two valleys dispute the land's ownership.				

Grusha's story

a

Figure 2-7 (a) Episodic play structure begins early in the story and involves many characters and events. The action is a journey of some kind, and place and event do not confine the characters. Instead, the plot expands to include a variety of events and activities. The Shakespearean episodic play usually has a double plot to contrast events and people. Brecht's *The Caucasian Chalk Circle* is made up of two stories, Grusha's and Azdak's. The expanding plot moves in a linear fashion, telling the two seemingly unrelated stories until Brecht combines them in the chalk circle test to make his point about decent people caught in the injustices of a corrupt political system. (b) Azdak the judge, played by Ernst Busch, in a 1954 production of *The Caucasian Chalk Circle* by The Berliner Ensemble, in East Berlin.

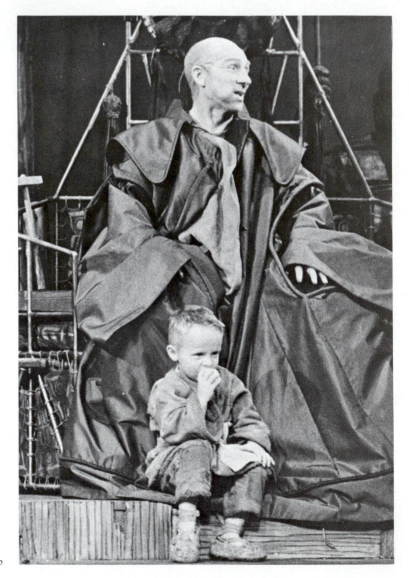

b

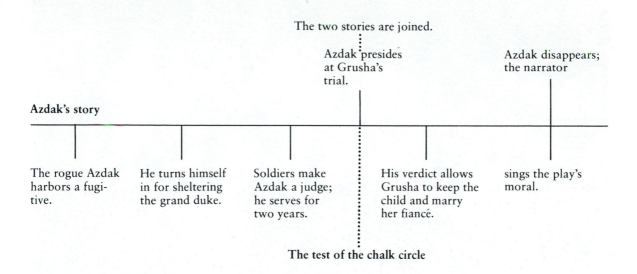

The two stories are joined.

Azdak presides at Grusha's trial.

Azdak disappears; the narrator

Azdak's story

The rogue Azdak harbors a fugitive.

He turns himself in for sheltering the grand duke.

Soldiers make Azdak a judge; he serves for two years.

His verdict allows Grusha to keep the child and marry her fiancé.

sings the play's moral.

The test of the chalk circle

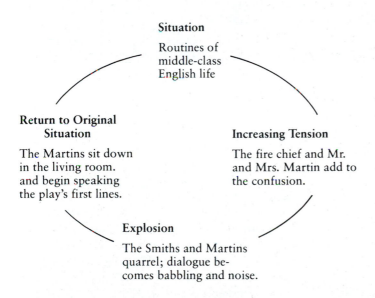

Situation

Routines of middle-class English life

Return to Original Situation

The Martins sit down in the living room. and begin speaking the play's first lines.

Increasing Tension

The fire chief and Mr. and Mrs. Martin add to the confusion.

Explosion

The Smiths and Martins quarrel; dialogue becomes babbling and noise.

Figure 2-8 Following World War II the "theatre of the absurd" emerged in Europe. Absurdist plays convey a sense of alienation, of people having lost their bearings in an illogical or ridiculous world. Situational play structure mirrors this world view.

THE THEATRE
OF IMAGES

The Theatre of Images—a label coined by New York critic and editor Bonnie Marranca in 1976—is the name given to the 1970s work of American writer-director-producers Richard Foreman (Ontological-Hysteric Theater), Robert Wilson (Byrd Hoffman School of Byrds), and Lee Breuer (Mabou Mines). Revolting against words, they create plays dominated by visual and aural images. Stage pictures, illustrations, sounds, and images replace plot, character, and theme. Wilson's *A Letter for Queen Victoria* (1974) is composed of bits and pieces of overheard conversations, clichés, newspaper blurbs, colors, radio spot announcements, television images, and film clips (Figure 2–9). Wilson creates his own *visual language* out of objects, sounds, people, and gestures. In Act II pilots talk about faraway lands against a background of gunfire sounds and bomb blasts. Instead of discussing American imperialism, the scene projects an *image* of it.

ACT IV
SECTION 4

(BREAK DROP)

(4 BECOMES 2 FROM ACT I. 3 BECOMES 1 FROM ACT I.)
(PILOTS REENTER)

PILOTS: I DON'T KNOW HOW TO THANK YOU
      (PAUSE 5 SECONDS)
    SAY
      (PAUSE 4 SECONDS)
    WHAT
      (PAUSE 3 SECONDS)
    CERTAINLY
3   MY KNOWLEDGE ABOUT YOU IS REDUCED TO A HANDFUL OF FACTS

(PILOTS EXIT)

1 AND 2 ALTERNATE   SEEM WHAT
          SEEMED WHAT
          SEEM
          SEEMS THE SAME
          SEEMED THE SAME
          SEEMS
          SIMULTANEOUSITY O'CITY O'VORST
          WHEEL WHAT WHEN NOW
          AN ALLIGATOR'S SPAN
          SEEM WHY
          SEEM WHAT
          SEEMED
          SEEMS
          SCREEN TELL A VISIONS
          SCREENED TOLDA VISIONS
          SCREEN
          SCREAM
          A MILLION DANCES

(FRAMED IN WHITE LIGHT)

A	HAP HAT HAP	AAAAAAAAAAAAO	CONFORMING	O
AO	HATH HIP HA	AAAAOAOAOA	VCONFORMIN	OK
OAOA	HAT HIT HAP	AAAOAOAOA	VECONFORMI	AOKO
XXXXX	HATH HAP HA	AAOAOAO	VERCONFORM	LAOKOK
AOAOAOA	HIP HIT HATH	AOAOA	VERYCONFOR	LLAOKOKO
XXXXXXXXX	HAP HATH HI	OAO	VERYVCONFO	ELLAOKOKOK
XXXXXXXXXXX	HAP HI HATH	AO	VERYVECONF	WELLAOKOKOK
OAOAOAOAOAOAO	HI HI HAP HA	O	VERYVERCON	AWELLAOKOKOKO

Figure 2-9 Robert Wilson's theatre of images: *A Letter for Queen Victoria* premiered at the 1974 Festival of Two Worlds in Spoleto, Italy. Wilson "assembles" actors, shapes, words, sounds, light, and shadow to make a theatrical statement. The visual image of the autistic boy, Christopher Knowles, framed in white light against the broken language projected behind him, makes a statement about communication in our computerized society. The theatrical meaning and effect are based on *visual image* rather than verbal communication. (Text reprinted with the permission of the Byrd-Hoffman Foundation, Inc.)

ROBERT WILSON

Robert Wilson founded the Byrd Hoffman School of Byrds in New York in 1970. His production of *The Life and Times of Joseph Stalin, Einstein on the Beach,* and *A Letter for Queen Victoria* "assemble" actors, sounds, music, light, and shadow to comment on American society and cultural myths. A student of architecture and painting, Wilson creates living pictures on stage—collages of sounds, sculptured forms, and visual images—requiring many hours to experience. His lengthy productions stretch the audience's attention and attempt to alter our perceptual awareness of people, places, and things. In 1981 he staged *Medea* for the Musical Theater Lab at the John F. Kennedy Center for the Performing Arts in Washington, D.C.

RICHARD FOREMAN

Richard Foreman, an American philosopher-playwright, founded the Ontological-Hysteric Theatre in 1968 to create an avant-garde theatre based on sounds, images, and illustrations. Stage pictures interrelated with words replace dialogue, characters are social types, sets are constructed before the audience. Foreman has produced, designed, and directed his own plays mostly in a New York City loft. He is author and director of numerous plays, including *Rhoda in Potatoland, Pandering to the Masses,* and *Penguin Touquet.*

TALKING PIECES

In the late 1970s the American inflationary economy and the lack of large social and political issues resulted in the disbanding of many of the theatrical collectives that had gathered momentum in the sixties over issues like the Vietnam War. Many performers, such as Spalding Gray, who had worked for a time with Richard Schechner's Performance Group in New York City, turned to creating a new kind of theatre piece for the solo performer (and also for small casts). Gray's pieces, developed for performance by himself, have been called "talking pieces." They represent a new and interesting dramatic structure, as well as theatre event.

Gray improvised his memories, free associations, and ideas of childhood, family relationships, and private emotions to create an open narrative of personal actions.[11] Using properties bought at Woolworth's, a tape recorder, old family photograph albums, slide projections, and phonograph records, he worked before small audiences that included director Elizabeth LeCompte, giving shape to his autobiographical sketches. The text as it developed was talked through with the director and audiences

> *This was the new 'play' which I found more interesting, and certainly more immediate, because it was going on all the time. I only had to stop it, and look at it, and any number of theatre situations would present themselves. It was learning how to make frames, to frame the mass of reality. I saw this act as composition. I thought of myself as performer/composer because this interplay from which these set of actions grew did not necessarily take the form of text but more often took the form of a conglomerate of images, sounds, colors, and movement.*
>
> Spalding Gray,
> "About *Three Places in Rhode Island*"[12]

in what Gray calls "an act of public memory." Once satisfied with the final product, Gray "set" the text. Because of these improvisational methods, Gray refers to the pieces as the "self-as-text" or as "talking pieces"—a series of simple actions using free associations as building blocks to create a series of images like personal, living Rorschachs.

Gray's series of monologues, or talking pieces, include *Sex and Death to the Age 14, A Personal History of the American Theatre,* and *47 Beds.* Even in the trilogy, *Three Places in Rhode Island,* the monologue remains a foundation stone. *Rumstick Road* opens with a monologue in which Gray discusses his acting career, his mother's psychiatric treatment, her Christian Science faith, her illness from cancer, and her eventual suicide.

SPALDING GRAY

Spalding Gray is a theatre creator, performer, and teacher. A graduate of Emerson College, he came to New York in 1967, where he performed in Off Broadway plays. He worked for brief periods with the Alley Theatre in Houston and with Joseph Chaikin's Open Theatre before joining Richard Schechner's Performance Group in 1969. There he played in Sam Shepard's *The Tooth of Crime* and in Bertolt Brecht's *Mother Courage.* In 1975 he and Elizabeth LeCompte, along with other former members of the Performance Group, formed The Wooster Group.

For The Wooster Group, Gray composed and/or performed in *Sakonnet Point, Rumstick Road, Nayatt School, Point Judith,* and *Route 1 & 9.* The first three are known as *The Trilogy: Three Places in Rhode Island* based on Gray's life. He also created a series of monologues, or talking pieces, with The Wooster Group.

Gray has taught in the Experimental Theatre Wing of New York University's School of Drama and has led many workshops there and in India and Europe. Like his work with The Wooster Group and his monologues, the emphasis of his workshops for both children and adults is autobiographical; participants are encouraged to develop material and theatrical metaphors from their own lives. Since 1979 he has begun a second career as a comic monologuist touring America and Europe with his autobiographical storytelling.

DRAMA'S CONVENTIONS

Over the years playwrights have worked out different dramatic structures to say different things about experience. In addition, they have worked out dramatic conventions, ground rules, to set plot and character in motion. A *convention* is an agreed-upon method of quickly getting something across to an audience. Just as we have social conventions in life to help us meet strangers or answer the telephone, so the playwright has conventions to solve problems, pass along information, develop plot and action, and create interest and suspense. Conventions make it possible for the playwright to use shortcuts to give information and to present experiences that in life would require weeks or even years, tell two stories at once, and complicate the stage action without confusing the audience. What follows is a discussion of seven dramatic conventions: exposition, point of attack, complication, crisis, resolution, double plots, and the play-within-the-play.

EXPOSITION

In a play's beginning we are given certain information about what is going on, what has happened in the past, and who is to be seen. This is *exposition*. In Aeschylus' *Agamemnon* (458 BC) a watchman tells us that it is the tenth year of the Trojan War and that Queen Clytemnestra has ordered him to keep watch from the palace roof at Argos. A succession of beacon fires set on hilltops is to announce the news from Troy when that city is captured by the Greek forces under King Agamemnon's command. We therefore anticipate the flashing beacon lights. In the watchman's hints of wrongdoing in the King's palace, we also anticipate Agamemnon's murder that is to follow.

Some plays begin with a telephone ringing; the person answering—for instance, a maid in drawing-room comedy—gives the background information by talking to an unseen party about the family, plans, and conflicts.

Other plays begin with informational exchanges of dialogue. *Othello* begins with Iago in conversation with Roderigo. Iago complains that Othello did not promote him and that he plans to serve his "peculiar end" upon Othello in the near future.

Contemporary drama makes fewer demands for information of this kind. Instead of asking who these people are and what is going to happen next, we usually, ask: "What's happening now?"

POINT OF ATTACK

The moment early in the play when the story is taken up is the *point of attack*. In *Agamemnon,* as the signal blazes forth, the watchman sends out a cry of joy and Queen Clytemnestra arrives to give thanks for Troy's fall. In *Othello* it comes when Iago and Roderigo arouse Desdemona's father to tell him that she has eloped with the Moor.

COMPLICATION

The middle of a play is made up of *complications*—the discovery of new information introduced by new characters, unexpected events, or newly disclosed facts. In *Ghosts* Mrs. Alving overhears Oswald seducing Regina in the dining room. Regina is the child of her husband and a servant with whom he had an affair and is therefore Oswald's half-sister. Mrs. Alving must deal with this complication.

CRISIS

A play's complications usually develop into a crisis, or turning point of the action. The crisis is an event that makes the resolution of the play's conflict inevitable. Othello's murder of Desdemona is the play's crisis. A play usually ends when the conflict is resolved in the climax, or highest point of intensity, and any loose strands of action are tied off. Othello's discovery that he has murdered an innocent wife and been duped by Iago is the crisis that leads to the play's climax and his suicide.

RESOLUTION

The resolution restores balance and satisfies the audience's expectations. Othello has paid for the crime, Iago is punished for his part in the affair, and Cassio becomes governor of Cyprus. In *A Streetcar Named Desire* Blanche DuBois is taken to an asylum and the Kowalski household settles back into its routines of poker, beer, and Saturday-night bowling. The absurdist play usually completes a cycle in its resolution, suggesting that the events of the play will repeat themselves over and over again. Some plays end with unanswered questions—for example, will Mrs. Alving in *Ghosts* give Oswald the fatal drug, or won't she?—to stimulate the audience to think about what kind of choice they would make in a similar situation. Whatever the case, the resolution brings about a sense of completed action, of conflicts resolved in probable ways, and of promises fulfilled.

Other dramatic conventions relate past and present events and behavior. *Simultaneous plots* and the *play-within-the-play* are two important conventions used by Renaissance and modern playwrights.

SIMULTANEOUS OR DOUBLE PLOTS

The Elizabethans used double plots to represent life's variety and complexity. Two stories are told concurrently; the lives of one group of characters affect the lives of the other group. *Hamlet* is the story of two families: Hamlet-Claudius-Gertrude, Laertes-Polonius-Ophelia. The secondary plot or subplot is always resolved before the main plot to maintain a sense of priority and importance. Laertes dies before Hamlet in the duel, resolving that family's story.

THE PLAY-WITHIN-THE-PLAY

The play-within-the-play was used by Shakespeare and is still a common plot device. In *Hamlet* the strolling players recreate a second play on stage about the murder of Hamlet's father. Claudius' reaction to it gives Hamlet proof of the king's guilt.

Modern playwrights use the play-within-the-play in a more complex way: to show that *life is like theatre* and vice versa. In his celebrated play *Marat/Sade* (*The Persecution and Assassination of Jean-Paul Marat as Performed by the Inmates of the Asylum of Charenton under the Direction of the Marquis de Sade*), written in 1964, Peter Weiss uses the play-within-the-play convention to suggest that our contemporary world is a madhouse. The inmates of Charenton Asylum in France produce a play in 1808 about the political revolutionary Jean-Paul Marat written by the Marquis de Sade, who is author, actor, director, and inmate.

Weiss uses two time frames: (1) the events of July 13, 1793—the historical setting of de Sade's play during the French Revolution—that culminates in the death of Marat and (2) the frustrations of 1808, when de Sade and other inmates are staging the events of 1793. The play's madhouse world at Charenton reflects the violence and irrationality of our modern world. The play-within-the-play forces us to see the relationships between the violence of one era and the violence of another, political ideologies of one time and another, the guillotine and the atomic bomb, and so on.

PETER WEISS

Peter Weiss (1916–1982) was born in Berlin. He took refuge from the Nazis in Sweden during the 1930s and lived there until his death. Weiss attracted the theatre world's attention with the Schiller Theater's Berlin production of *Marat/Sade* in 1964. Subsequently, the play was produced by the Royal Shakespeare Company in London and New York under the direction of Peter Brook and also filmed. Weiss is author of *The Investigation* (1965), *The Song of the Lusitanian Bogey* (1969), and *The Prozess* (Kafka's *The Trial*, 1975), and he made documentary films.

SUMMARY

Drama is a special way of imitating imagined human behavior and events. Just as children imitate adults as ways of mastering the strangeness of the world around them, so playwrights create dramatic blueprints representing physical and psychological experience to give shape and meaning to their world as they see it.

Drama comes from the Greek *dran*, meaning "to do" or "to act." From our modern perspective it defines an art form having the potential for placing *visible behavior* before us in a performance space. That behavior, which the actor brings before us, takes many forms depending upon the playwright's attitudes and interpretations of experience.

GREEK SCRIPTS
IN MODERN PERFORMANCE

For years British director for the Royal Shakespeare Company, John Barton, claimed he was fascinated by the Greek plays but disappointed and irritated by them in performance. "Translations and performances," he said, "seemed heavy, earnest, portentous, ritualistic and not *human.* I came to suspect that the heavy style of most translations does not well serve their originals in the theatre today."[13]

The RSC set about in 1979 to take 10 Greek plays by different authors, but with most of the materials based on Euripides' plays, and fashion

a new theatre work. *The Greeks*, as the production was called, was performed over three evenings as *The Wars, The Murders, and The Gods.* The production concentrated on what happened rather than on social or political meanings and aimed for a certain naiveté in the playing style, so that characters dealt with the simplest of statements: What is goodness? What is a god? What shall I do now? The representative play in Chapter 3, Euripides' *The Trojan Women,* was the final play of *Part One: The War.*

Barton and designer John Napier, in creating a basic permanent set, attempted to get away from traditional approaches to Greek tragedy. They tried to create their own world for the plays with a shifting sense of time, with a mixture of the epic and the formal, the naturalistic and domestic, the ancient and the modern. Kenneth Cavander's text (based on the Greek texts) created virtually a new work for the theatre.

Of his development of the script of *The Greeks*, Kenneth Cavander has said:

> The following pages are the ground plan for a theatrical production, not the literal or complete translation of an ancient Greek text. . . . The original plays had to be edited; mythological references explained; characters established and introduced; the story kept moving, suspense maintained. Beyond that, we had a point of view, a vision of what the entire cycle might have to say to a twentieth-century public. All these influences worked on us and led us to create what is virtually a new work for the theatre, in which some passages, perhaps more than twenty per cent of the whole, were invented for the occasion.[14]

Cavander's text from *The Tro-jan Women:*

Hecuba [*waking*] There is no Troy any more.
    I'll tell you who I was
    And then you'll pity me.
    I ruled a country once,
    My husband was a king
    And all my sons were princes.
    I have seen them lying
    With Greek spears through
    their hearts
    And have watched their father
    die.
    Now I must be a slave.
    My dress is torn and ragged
    And filthy, my whole body's
    filthy;
    It makes me ashamed.
    And this is Hecuba
    Who sat on a throne in Troy.
    What shall I do now?
    I shall sing and cry like a bird
    When her nest is destroyed
    and her children;
    I shall sing as I never did
    When the choirs sang
    And the music beat
    And I was queen of Troy.
    Wake up, wake up, my children.
    You are widows. Troy is
    burning.[15]

The Greeks, from the Royal Shakespeare Company production at the Aldwych Theatre, London, 1979. Shown here in *Part One: The War* (from *The Trojan Women*), left to right, are Deirdra Morris as Polyxena, Eliza Ward as Queen Hecuba, and Diana Berriman as a chorus member.

Opposite: John Shrapnel as Agamemnon with Celia Gregory as his captive slave, Cassandra in *Part Two: The Murders* (from *Agamemnon*).

ARTHUR MILLER'S "MODIFIED" REALISM

Arthur Miller's *Death of a Salesman* was first produced at the Morosco Theatre in New York in 1949.

Directed by Elia Kazan and designed by Jo Mielziner, the "modified realism" of the staging and setting made possible an uninterrupted flow of action and a fluid time scheme that enhanced Miller's idea of how the past and present time of Willy Loman's life (his actions and memories) come together at every moment. When Willy remembers his successful brother, Ben steps into the scene. These flashbacks are carefully signaled and offered no difficulties to audiences in following the tragic retreat of Willy Loman into suicide.

Arthur Miller on *Death of a Salesman*:

The First Image that occurred to me which was to result in *Death of a Salesman* was of an enormous face the height of the proscenium arch which would appear and then open up, and we would see the inside of a man's head. In fact, *The Inside of His Head* was the first title. . . . The *Salesman* image was from the beginning absorbed with the concept that nothing in life comes "next" but that everything exists together and at the same time within us; that there is no past to be "brought forward" in a human being, but that he is his past at every moment and that the present is merely that which his past is capable of noticing and smelling and reacting to.

I wished to create a form which, in itself as a form, would literally be the process of Willy Loman's way of mind. But to say "wished" is not accurate. Any dramatic form is an artifice, a way of transforming a subjective feeling into something that can be comprehended through public symbols. Its efficiency as a form is to be judged—at least by the writer—by how much of the original vision and feeling is lost or distorted by this transformation. I wished to speak of the salesman most precisely as I felt about him, to give no part of that feeling away for the sake of any effect or any dramatic necessity. . . . As I look at the play now [in 1957] its form seems the form of a confession, for that is how it is told, now speaking of what happened yesterday, then suddenly following some connection to a time twenty years ago, then leaping even further back and then returning to the present and even speculating about the future.[16]

Miller's text from *Death of a Salesman* (1949):

[*In this scene Willy Loman's neighbor, Charley, talks with Willy about his difficulties trying to keep up with his job as a salesman. They are playing cards.*]

Charley What're you doin' home?

Willy A little trouble with the car.

Charley Oh. [*pause*] I'd like to take a trip to California.

Willy Don't say.

Charley You want a job?

Willy I got a job, I told you that. [*after a slight pause*] What the hell are you offering me a job for?

Charley Don't get insulted.

Willy Don't insult me.

Charley I don't see no sense in it. You don't have to go on this way.

Willy I got a good job. [*slight pause*] What do you keep comin' in here for?

Charley You want me to go?[17]

Jo Mielziner (1901–1976) designed the salesman's house on several levels (kitchen, son's bedroom, porch, and forestage). The actor's movements with area lighting were the only scene-change devices. The large backdrop upstage was painted to show tenement buildings looming over Willy Loman's house in the play's present time. When lighted from the rear, the buildings washed out to show trees. Leaves were projected on the stage to indicate the pleasantness of the remembered past with its bright sunshine, surrounding leaves, and cheerful ambience.

Director Elia Kazan explains the model of Jo Mielziner's set to the actors in the original production: Mildred Dunnock, Lee J. Cobb, and Arthur Kennedy.

Six dramatic forms, from the most ancient to the most recent, are tragedy, comedy, tragicomedy, melodrama, farce, and adaptations of novels.

The structure of a play organizes the play's events in a particular pattern. Climactic or classical structure, which compresses events toward a crisis, has been a recurring dramatic pattern from Sophocles to Henrik Ibsen to Arthur Miller. Episodic play structure has been used in the theatre by such diverse writers as Shakespeare and Brecht. A more flexible structure than the classical type, it makes use of linear episodes to trace the journey of people through a variety of events, connecting one episode to another until the hero's story is concluded. More recent dramatic forms are the situational structure of absurdist plays by Samuel Beckett and Eugene Ionesco, the theatre of images, and the talking pieces of the contemporary American avant-garde.

Drama's conventions are agreed-upon methods of quickly getting something across to an audience. They are ground rules used to set plot and character in motion. These devices include exposition, complication, crisis, resolution, double plots, and the play-within-the-play.

Finally, the photo essay juxtaposes remarks by playwrights on their craft with segments of their scripts to illustrate the long, complex journey from the germ of a play in the playwright's mind to its realization in performance.

SOURCES

Bentley, Eric. *The Life of the Drama.* New York: Atheneum, 1964. Hardcover and paperback. A highly readable discussion of drama's basic elements and the forms of drama that have dominated Western theatre.

Cole, Toby, ed. *Playwrights on Playwriting.* New York: Hill and Wang, 1961. Paperback. This volume remains one of the best collections of writings by playwrights on their art. It focuses on nineteenth- and twentieth-century playwrights and contains an excellent bibliography.

Miller, Arthur. *The Theatre Essays of Arthur Miller.* Edited by Robert Martin. New York: Viking, 1978. This collection contains all of Miller's writings on the theatre up to the late seventies. It provides the student with insight into the thoughts of a major American playwright on his writings, as well as on theatre and society.

The Drama Review ("Playwrights and Playwriting Issue"), 21, No. 4 (December 1977). This special issue contains statements by contemporary American playwrights (Richard Foreman, María Irene Fornés, Adrienne Kennedy, Sam Shepard, Megan Terry, Jean-Claude van Itallie, and Robert Wilson) on their working methods. There are copious photographs.

NOTES

1. George Steiner, *The Death of Tragedy.* © 1980 by George Steiner. Reprinted by permission of the author's agent, Georges Borchardt, Inc.

2. Robert W. Corrigan, *The World of the Theatre* (Chicago: Scott, Foresman, 1979), p. 163.

3. Francis Fergusson, *The Idea of a Theatre* (Princeton: University Press, 1949), p. 36.

4. Lane Cooper, *Aristotle on the Art of Poetry* (Ithaca, N.Y.: Cornell University Press, 1947), p. 17.

5. Eric Bentley, "The Psychology of Farce," in *Let's Get a Divorce! and Other Plays* (New York: Hill and Wang, 1958), pp. vii–xx.

6. Danielle Sallenave, "Entretien avec Antoine Vitez: Faire théâtre de tout," *Digraphe* (April 1976), 117.

7. Jean-Louis Barrault, "Le Roman adapté au théâtre . . .," *Cahiers Renaud-Barrault* (October 1976), 27–58.

8. Sallenave, p. 120.

9. Judith Graves Miller, "From Novel to Theatre: Contemporary Adaptations of Narrative to the French Stage," *Theatre Journal,* 33, no. 4 (December 1981), 431–452.

10. For my understanding of climactic and episodic drama, I am indebted to material from Bernard Beckerman, *Dynamics of Drama: Theory and Method of Analysis* (New York: Knopf, 1970).

11. Spalding Gray, "About *Three Places in Rhode Island,*" *The Drama Review,* 23, no. 1 (March 1979), 31–42. Reprinted with permission of Spalding Gray.

12. Gray, "About *Three Places in Rhode Island,*" 34.

13. *The Greeks: Ten Greek Plays Given as a Trilogy,* adapted by John Barton and Kenneth Cavander (London: Heinemann, 1981), p. vii. Reprinted with permission of Heinemann Educational Books, Ltd., England.

14. *The Greeks,* p. xix. Reprinted by permission.

15. *The Greeks,* pp. 75–76. Reprinted by permission.

16. Arthur Miller, Introduction to *Arthur Miller's Collected Plays* (New York: Viking, 1957). Copyright © 1957 by Arthur Miller. Reprinted by permission of Viking Penguin Inc.

17. Arthur Miller, *Death of Salesman.* Copyright 1949 by Arthur Miller. Copyright renewed © 1977 by Arthur Miller. Reprinted by permission of Viking Penguin Inc.

PART II

HISTORICAL PERSPECTIVES

THREE

GREEK THEATRE

A MODERN PERSPECTIVE

The Greek theatre developed out of tribal rituals, religious ceremonies, and choral songs sung in honor of the god Dionysus. Today, some 2500 years later, the ancient Greek plays are still performed. The Greek National Theatre, with Alexis Minotis as director, performs yearly in the ancient theatres in Athens and Epidaurus. Other modern directors, such as Andrei Serban, Peter Brook, John Barton, and Peter Stein, engage audiences in ritual and ceremony with masks, music, flaming torches, dance, and human sounds. Greek perceptions of human travail in the world come to us in the form of plays about gods, men, women, and children.

Western theatre began with tribal rites, citywide ceremonies, choral competitions, and play contests in the great Athenian festival called the City Dionysia, begun about 534 BC, and held annually after 325 BC in the Theatre of Dionysus.

Figure 3-1 The Theatre of Dionysus with modern Athens in the background. What remains of the ancient theatre are the stone seating, the orchestra, and a stone foundation for the scene building with steps.

REPRESENTATIVE THEATRE:
Theatre of Dionysus, Athens

Crowds of Athenians and visitors carrying breakfast figs, bread, and flagons of wine converge in the early morning light upon the south slope of the Acropolis. They pay their tokens at the entrance to the Theatre of Dionysus (Figure 3-1) and find their places in the seating spaces allotted them. Each tribe is grouped together on the hillside; there are also special seats for priests, dignitaries, and city officials.

The open seats carved into the hillside fill up quickly. The crowd of 15,000 people on this day is made up of Athenian citizens as well as a mass of noncitizens: women, slaves, tradespeople, foreign visitors, and resident aliens. The state gives out two obols to paupers from a state fund so they can attend the festival. They sit with the foreigners and latecomers on the far edges of the hillside auditorium.

The second play of Euripides' trilogy about the Trojan War has just ended. The third play, *The Trojan Women,* is just starting. In the bright sunlight a masked and costumed actor appears atop a low, rectangular building set in full view of the spectators. A hush falls over the crowd, and the actor booms out the new text by Athens' controversial young playwright:

> I am Poseidon. I come from the Aegean
> depths of the sea beneath whose waters
> Nereid choirs evolve the intricate bright
> circle of their dancing feet. . . .[1]

He is Poseidon, the god of the sea. A second actor, as the goddess Athene, joins him. They plot to destroy the victorious Greek armies on their trip home by sea. Their plans agreed upon, they disappear, and the actor in the ravaged

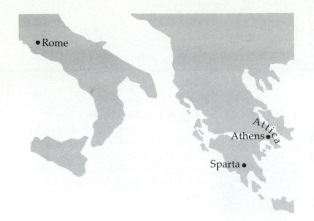

1200 BC	800 BC	600 BC

Trojan Wars
c. 1184–1174 BC

Homer's *Iliad*
and *Odyssey*
800–700

Tragic Contests
begin at
City Dionysia
534

Comedy first
produced at
City Dionysia
487–486

mask and torn garments of Hecuba, Queen of Troy, rises from the ground in front of the low building and begins to lament the destruction of Troy.

Two choruses—some 15 people in all—enter the theatre through the arched entrances. Following the flute player, they move into the flat circle of ground at the base of the hillside where the crowds are seated. This is the dancing circle, or *orchestra*, where they will sing Euripides' odes. They are dressed in simply draped garments, soft shoes, and masks. They question Hecuba about the fate of the Trojan survivors, and so begins the last part of the terrible story of the destruction of Troy and its people.

The crowds settle back to see Euripides' new version of a familiar story. This is the final play of his trilogy, lasting some three hours. It will be followed by a bawdy satyr play, *Sisyphus*, that mocks the trilogy's serious themes. It, too, is by Euripides, the young man who has challenged Athens' leading dramatists with his new methods and pacifist ideas.

When the plays are over, the citizens return as they have come through the arched entrances to the theatre. They will come back to the theatre tomorrow to see another set of plays and to learn which playwright receives the festival prize for this year (415 BC).

CONDITIONS OF PERFORMANCE

Over the centuries theatre has been performed under a myriad of conditions. Society's influence, the size and shape of the theatrical space, and the conventions of playwriting and management affect the theatre's impact. The first great period of Western theatre began in ancient Greece.

BACKGROUND

Greek civilization began with a Bronze Age (c. 2500 BC), centered on the Greek mainland, that introduced metal as an item for trade. An agrarian economy of grain, olives, and vineyards developed in the south. A seafaring economy exploited the rich trade routes of the Mediterranean from Egypt to Cyprus, Sardinia, and Crete. Homer's poems, the *Iliad* and *Odyssey*, written between 800 and 700 BC, recorded the exploits of legendary Greek heroes of the Trojan War, a war fought for control of the rich trade routes. Much of what is known about this period comes from Homer's poetry.

Over a period of 400 years, social and technological changes affected the culture; the use of

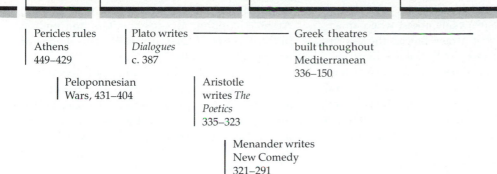

450 BC	400 BC	300 BC	200 BC	100 BC

Pericles rules
Athens
449–429

Plato writes
Dialogues
c. 387

Greek theatres
built throughout
Mediterranean
336–150

Peloponnesian
Wars, 431–404

Aristotle
writes *The
Poetics*
335–323

Menander writes
New Comedy
321–291

iron for tools and weapons became widespread; an alphabet was developed; a pantheon of gods, shrines, and religious ceremonies evolved. In the mid-seventh century the mass of people was ruled by rich and powerful citizens. In 545 BC Pisistratos (c. 600–527 BC) seized power in Athens, the largest of many city-states, increased the rights of the common people, and brought the nobility under a new rule of law. The city-state was adopted as a political, economic, and social unit. These developments led indirectly to a democratic system by which Athens governed itself for the next two centuries.

Fifth-century Athens was the birthplace of the most influential ideas in Western art, literature, philosophy, science, and politics, and the Athenian Golden Age produced a succession of gifted practitioners of these arts.

However, developing conflict between Athens and Sparta, the city-state to the south, burst into the flames of the Peloponnesian War in 431, and after nearly 30 years of war Athens capitulated to Spartan rule. A Spartan oligarchy replaced Athenian democracy for a time. Sporadic wars continued among the city-states until Philip II (382–336 BC) of Macedonia to the north conquered Greece in 338 BC and the independence of the city-states came to an end.

By the second century, the great classical age was over. But there were permanent open-air theatres and a rich heritage of plays whose traditions have influenced every age that has followed.

THE CITY DIONYSIA

Each year in honor of Dionysus, four festivals were held in Attica, the region dominated by Athens. It was at one of these festivals, the City Dionysia, that drama was first presented. The festival was held at the end of March and featured choral contests between the local tribes. Later, play contests were added to the festival, only tragic plays at first, but then satyr plays, and finally comedy.

We know few details about the line of development from ritual to choral songs to tragic drama. Aristotle tells us in the *Poetics* that tragedy developed out of improvisations by the leaders of *dithyrambs*—hymns sung and danced in honor of Dionysus.

At first the words and music of the dithyramb, sung by a chorus, were composed spontaneously, taking their inspiration from the excitement of the festivities. The dithyramb was probably also largely narrative, telling some legend relating to the god. Gradually, changes were made and poets began to compose lines for the chorus and its leader. The decisive change (attributed to Thespis) came about when an actor who was not just a member of the chorus was added to the event. With the use of masks, a single actor might impersonate several characters and exchange "dialogue" with the choral leader and the chorus. The way was then opened to develop complex themes, conflict between two or more persons, and richer characterization.[2]

Festival Events The City Dionysia, partly a civic display of Athenian wealth and culture, was supervised by the city's chief magistrate (the *archon*). The festival began with a procession that reenacted the coming of Dionysus to Athens. It included public officials, sponsors of plays, and priests carrying gifts and leading sacrificial animals. The procession wound through Athens, stopping at various altars and ending in the Theatre of Dionysus with the sacrifice of an animal on the altar.

Next came the choral contests followed by the tragedies and satyr plays. After about 487 BC, five comic writers presented a single play apiece sometime during the festivities. There were prizes offered for the best plays and later also for the best actor. The state selected the judges whose votes were kept an official secret.

Festival Management and Play Selection The city-state and its wealthy citizens subsidized the festival. Admission was at first free. Later a small sum of two obols was charged, but a public fund provided tickets for the poor. The state provided the theatre and prizes, supplied costumes, and paid actors and playwrights.

About a year before the festival, writers applied to the magistrate for permission to enter the competition. He probably listened to part of the script, then selected three tragic writers and assigned choruses to them. In Aeschylus' time (525–456 BC) the playwright acted in his plays, trained the chorus, invented music and dances, and supervised every aspect of the performance.

DIONYSUS

Dionysus, god of wine, fertility, and ecstasy, was the only Olympian god to have a mortal for a parent. The god Zeus, in love with Semele, the daughter of Cadmus, disguised himself as a mortal and visited her. A few months before the birth of their child, she begged him to appear to her as the god. He appeared in blazing majesty and Semele was burned to ashes. Zeus snatched her unborn child from her womb and sewed it up in his thigh, from whence Dionysus was born when he reached maturity.

He traveled about the earth teaching the mysteries of his worship and the cultivation of the vine, a recognizable figure dressed in a fawn skin draped about his body, a band of ivy or vine leaves in his hair, and a reed wound with ivy for his staff.

Dionysus was god of vegetation, hospitality, peace, and the arts of civilization. He was honored in Greece with festivals, the most important being the Greater or City Dionysia in Athens.

THESPIS

Thespis is the Greek actor credited with the invention of drama; he lived and worked about 534 BC. Virtually nothing is known about him, but legend has it that Thespis, a chorus leader, added to the choral narrative a prologue and lines to be spoken by an actor impersonating a character. One theory maintains that tragedy as we know it evolved from this dialogue between actor and chorus. The Greek word for actor is *hypokrites,* meaning "answerer."

THE PERFORMERS

The Tragic Actor In the earliest Greek plays the actor and dramatist were one. Early in the fifth century Aeschylus introduced the second actor, but playwrights continued to act in their own plays until the time of Sophocles (496–406 BC) who abandoned the practice and added the third actor. By using masks three actors could play any number of roles, including women's parts. "Extras" probably were used in nonspeaking roles. At first the playwright selected his actors, but once prizes were given, actors were assigned by lot to the competing dramatists.

The tragic actor was judged by the beauty, power, and timbre of his voice. Given the size of the theatre, the actor's delivery was probably declamatory in style. Gesture and movement were broad and stylized. Since the actor was masked, his facial expression was always fixed in emotions of pain, anger, or sorrow.

The Comic Actor Aristophanes' plays require three or more actors wearing masks, short buskins or boots, and phalluses. Five actors were chosen by lot and assigned to the playwrights. Since the comic actor was involved in horseplay, his gestures and movements were probably less stylized than those of the tragic actor. He engaged in a lot of physical movement, including beatings and wild twirling dances.

The Chorus In the beginning a chorus of up to 50 people dominated the tragic plays and the single actor left the stage often to change roles and masks. In Aeschylus' early plays the chorus was given as many as one-half the total number of lines. In *The Persians,* for example, the chorus is the protagonist, or main character. Later the role and the size of the chorus diminished; in Euripides' plays (written around 420 BC), the chorus is often only slightly related to the dramatic action and has been reduced to about 15 members.

As a rule the tragic chorus entered the theatre in a stately march (the *parodos*) after the

> *"The chorus serves several functions in Greek drama. First, it is an agent in the play; it gives advice, expresses opinions, asks questions, and sometimes takes an active part in the action. Second, it often establishes the ethical or social framework of the events and sets up a standard against which the action may be judged. Third, it frequently serves as an ideal spectator, reacting to the events and characters as the dramatist might hope the audience would. Fourth, the chorus helps to set the overall mood of the play and of individual scenes and to heighten dramatic effects. Fifth, it adds movement, spectacle, song and dance, and thus contributes much to theatrical effectiveness. Sixth, it serves an important rhythmical function, creating pauses or retardations during which the audience may reflect upon what has happened and what is to come."*
>
> Oscar G. Brockett, *History of The Theatre,* 4th ed. (1982)[3]

prologue and remained there until the play ended. Their last ode was called the *exodos.* Most choral passages were sung and danced in unison, although at times the chorus was divided into two groups who performed in turn. Euripides used the chorus in this way in *The Trojan Women.* Sometimes the chorus exchanged dialogue with a character. We have almost no information on their acting and dancing.

At first the playwright trained the chorus. They were usually assigned to a play some 11 months before the festival, so their training period could have been lengthy. It likely involved a special diet, exercise, and rehearsals.

Choruses for comedy and satyr plays were probably permitted more freedom of movement than the tragic ones. The chorus for Aristophanes' plays was composed of 24 members; their entrances, dances, and uses varied considerably.

Aristophanes (c. 448–c. 380 BC) was the greatest of all the ancient writers of comedy. His plays, the only surviving samples of Greek Old Comedy, mix political, social, and literary satire. He distrusted the Sophists and Socrates alike, satirized Euripides' art as degenerate, and deplored the excessive imperialism of Athens that resulted in the Peloponnesian War.

Eleven of Aristophanes' plays have survived. They are *The Acharnians, The Knights, The Clouds, The Wasps, The Peace, The Birds, Lysistrata, The Thesmophoriazusae* or *The Women at Demeter's Festival, The Frogs, The Ecclesiazusae* or *The Women in Politics,* and *Plutus.*

The typical plan of his comedy involves the protagonist undertaking some preposterous project, such as a father going to Socrates' school to learn how to outsmart his creditors or wives refusing sex with their husbands until the men stop fighting wars. The plot then is an elaboration of the main character's success or failure within the overall scheme.

VISUAL ELEMENTS

Scenery The scenic conventions of the Greek theatre differed greatly from our own. Evidence in the play texts suggests that the Greek theatre had a background with doors, a second level for actors to use for heights, and machines for special effects.

The scene building dates from about 450 BC, of later origin than the dancing circle. Initially, the building was probably a temporary, wooden structure that served as a dressing room. But playwrights quickly saw its scenic possibilities. The neutral background could easily represent many places, a palace, temple, house, cave, or whatever was needed. One or more doors opened onto the acting area and the roof served

as a second level for scenes taking place on heights, as in the opening scene of *The Trojan Women.* By the fourth century the building was made of stone, creating a permanent and elaborate architectural facade.

There is some evidence of *scene painting* in the Greek theatre, but its origin is controversial. Aristotle, writing in the fourth century BC, credits Sophocles with adding scene painting; but the Roman architect Vitruvius, writing in the first century, says that it originated in Aeschylus' time. Flat panels (called *pinakes*) were painted with architectural designs and hung on the walls of the scene building. They were changed as needed. Also, triangular prisms (called *periaktoi*) were painted, each with a different scene. Mounted on a central pivot near the building, they could be revolved to show different settings.

The Stage Was there a stage in the Greek theatre? There is no conclusive evidence for the existence of a low, raised stage in front of the scene building in the fifth century. However, some plays indicate that actors are on a higher level than the dancing circle. If not a stage, then broad steps leading up to the scene building may have been used.

Special Effects Special effects were created by the *ekkyklema* and the *mechane*. The *ekkyklema,* or "something which can be rolled out" (a wheeled platform or wagon), made it possible to present a tableau of actors posed like living statues. These tableaux usually depicted scenes of carnage and death that took place offstage; the wagon and its burden then could be pushed into sight through the building's central door. Aeschylus reveals the bodies of Agamemnon and Cassandra in this way in *Agamemnon.*

The *mechane,* or crane, was used to swing characters onto the stage in simulated flight. The crane was probably located out of sight of the audience; an actor could be attached to a kind of harness and then swung over the top of the building into the acting area. Euripides made frequent use of the crane to contrive endings to

Agamemnon, first produced at the City Dionysia festival, Athens, in 458 BC, is the first play in Aeschylus' trilogy *The Oresteia.* Plotting with her lover, Aegisthus, to kill her husband upon his return from the Trojan War, Queen Clytemnestra has ordered that a guard keep watch from the palace roof at Argos. A succession of beacon fires set on hilltops is to bring the news from Troy when that city is captured by the Greek forces under Agamemnon's command.

The play opens as the watchman waits in the dead of night. As the signal blazes forth, he sends out a cry of joy. The queen gives thanks for Troy's fall. A herald announces Agamemnon's arrival, but tells of sacrilegious acts committed by the Greeks against the gods' temples. Clytemnestra speaks of her love for Agamemnon, but the chorus hints at hypocrisy.

Agamemnon enters with the Trojan princess Cassandra, priestess of Apollo, captured in Troy and made his unwilling mistress. Clytemnestra persuades Agamemnon to walk into the palace on a rich purple carpet. He does so unwillingly, knowing that it constitutes an act of pride.

Cassandra recalls the bloody history of the house of Atreus and predicts Agamemnon's death and her own. They go into the palace and are killed. The palace doors open, revealing Clytemnestra standing over their bodies. She exults in the deed. The chorus predicts her future punishment by Zeus' law, that the doer must suffer the consequences of his deeds, and warns that Agamemnon's son Orestes will avenge his father.

The first play in the trilogy ends with the warning. The story of Clytemnestra, Aegisthus, Orestes, and Electra (his sister) is taken up in *The Libation Bearers* and *The Eumenides.*

Agamemnon, at the 1977 New York Shakespeare Festival at the Vivian Beaumont Theatre in Lincoln Center. Top: Priscilla Smith as Queen Clytemnestra. Bottom: Stylized masks and movement express the arrogant pride of the doomed characters.

his plays—so much so that the term *deus ex machina,* or god from a machine, is used today to describe any contrived ending.

Costumes Costumes and masks provided color and visual style. The tragic actor's costume, attributed to Aeschylus, was a loose-fitting, ankle-length tunic (or *chiton*) with fitted sleeves and a simple decorative border; a soft and pointed high-topped boot in common use at the time; and a mask of linen, cork, or wood. Vase shards show us members of the chorus in sleeveless chitons and soft boots. Both actors and chorus wore either short cloaks (*chlamys*) or long ones (*himation*) (Figure 3-2).

While this suggests a standardized costume, we cannot be certain that all tragic actors and choruses looked alike. Vase paintings (from which most of our evidence comes) are not wholly reliable, since most dated from a period later than the fifth century. There is some evidence that costumes showed differences of sex, age, rank, and nationality.

There were also symbolic costumes. Orientals, for example, wore a sleeveless robe with patterns of black circles with brown centers. Herakles carried a club and lionskin. Actors and chorus also carried properties: the suppliant carried his branch, the soldier his spear and shield, the king his scepter.

Although much has been written about the actor's platform shoe, or *cothurnus,* and padding beneath his costume to make him appear larger than life size, these effects were not used until the late Hellenistic period in the fourth century.

The fifth-century comic actor wore flesh-colored tights, short *chiton* (frequently with padding across the stomach), and a visible phallus. This grotesque costume was probably worn by actors playing ridiculous old men, the principal figures of Old Comedy, and by their comic slaves. Those characters who were not severely ridiculed by the playwright more than likely wore a theatrical version of clothes from everyday Greek life.

Satyrs wore goatskin loincloths with a tail and phallus over spotted tights. Silenus, usually their leader, wore shaggy tights under an animal-skin cloak. Since the actors and chorus were the same for tragedies and satyr plays, the conventions of acting, costuming, and scenery were probably similar, although the emphasis on satire was greater in the satyr plays than in the tragedies.

Masks Originally, masks were used in the worship of Dionysus to endow the wearer with the qualities of the god (Figure 3-3). Later, masks continued to be used in choruses. With the possible exception of flute players, all performers wore masks in the fifth century. Tradition has it that Phrynichus was the first to introduce female masks and that Aeschylus was the first to use painted masks. Masks, which covered the entire head, were highly detailed with color, hair style, beards, ornaments, and other features. There were special masks to signify the blind Tiresias, Actaeon wearing horns, and the Furies.

Satyr masks for the chorus usually depicted dark, uncombed hair and beards, a bald forehead, and pointed, horselike ears. Silenus was portrayed with gray hair and beard.

Masks for comedy represented a variety of people, animals, birds, and insects, such as the masks in Aristophanes' comedies depicting wasps, frogs, and birds. The masks of the main characters exaggerated "ugly" human features. There were also "portrait masks" portraying such well-known Athenians as Aeschylus and Euripides (see Aristophanes' *The Frogs*).

Music and Dance The Greeks regarded dance and music as *mimetic,* or expressing moral and artistic feelings. Dance was any expressive rhythmical movement using hand gestures, pantomime, and the body. The dramatic texts indicate that the tragic chorus moved in formal, complex patterns during the odes. The comic and satyr dances were exuberant displays of kicking, leaping, and spinning like a top. Comic dances were called the *kordax,* and the basic satyr dance, a mixture of horseplay and lewd pantomime, was called the *sikinnis.*

Music was also integral to the tragic perfor-

Figure 3-2 Greek vases as source material. (a) Black-figured Greek vases dating from around 480 BC. The large vase shows character-istic dress of the period. A flute player with mask can be seen on the smaller vase on the right. (b) This Greek-Roman vase from the fourth century BC depicts a scene with comic actors.

a

b

Figure 3-3 Greek tragic mask of a woman from the fifth century BC, Thebes.

mance. The greater part of the choral odes was sung to the accompaniment of the flute. The flute player also accompanied passages of recitative, declamatory singing with the rhythm and tempo of speech, coloring emotion and mood. The playwright from time to time composed his own music, but ordinarily this was the flute player's responsibility.

THE AUDIENCE

The Theatre of Dionysus held between 15,000 and 30,000 people. Seating in the *theatron* was divided into sections for the priests of Dionysus (the front row), archons, city officials, generals, the 10 tribes, visiting ambassadors, and women.

The audience brought wine, fruit, and other refreshments into the theatre and sometimes used these to pelt actors. As we might guess from this behavior, audiences were noisy and quick to make their feelings of approval or disapproval known. At times actors were hissed off the stage. But audiences also responded, with reverential silence and weeping, to the great tragic moments of Oedipus' suffering and to Aeschylus' political sentiments.

ROMAN THEATRE

Background Rome, founded in the eighth century BC, had extended its power over the then-known world by the beginning of the Christian era. The Romans, who assimilated the culture of the people they conquered, took to Rome the drama and types of theatre buildings they found in the Greek colonies of Sicily and southern Italy.

Other types of theatrical entertainments flourished in Rome as well. From the Etruscans the Romans had borrowed boxing, chariot racing, and gladiatorial combats. Around 364 BC, they began to hold musical and dancing events, also borrowed from Etruria, in an attempt to appease the gods during a plague that ravaged the city. In time all were presented alongside regular drama, creating a lively, circuslike atmosphere.

The first regular comedy and tragedy, by Livius Andronicus, a Greek playwright from southern Italy, were presented beginning in 240 BC. Soon other Romans were writing plays based upon the Greek models. Although many plays were written in Rome, works by only three playwrights survive: 21 comedies by Plautus, 6 comedies by Terence, and 9 tragedies by Seneca.

Management Plays were performed in Rome at the *ludi,* or festivals, that were usually official religious celebrations, although plays also were given on special occasions like the funeral of a distinguished person or the triumphal return of a victorious army. At first drama was confined to the *ludi Romani,* or Roman Games, and was probably restricted to a single day. But plays were popular, and as the number of Roman festivals increased so did the occasions for presenting plays. By AD 354, 101 of 175 public festival days were devoted to theatrical events.

The Romans mixed together religious celebrations honoring the gods with theatrical entertainment. They believed that for a festival to be effective it must be carried through according to certain rules. Hence if a mistake occurred during the scheduled events, the entire festival had to be repeated, including the plays. So, many plays were produced many times over.

Production expenses, as in Greece, were undertaken by the state or by wealthy citizens. The Roman senate made an appropriation for each festival. The officials in charge, who normally contributed additional funds to the festival, contracted for productions with managers of theatrical companies. The companies then were responsible for all details of production, including finding scripts, actors, musicians, costumes, and so on. The manager probably bought the play script outright from the author; it then became the manager's property and could be played as often as demand warranted. Festival sponsors offered prizes to the most successful troupes.

Admission to the festivals was free, seats were not reserved, refreshments were not available in the auditorium, and audiences were often unruly. The programs were long, including a variety of entertainments from plays to gladiatorial combats. Since the theatrical troupes had to compete with rival attractions, they had to provide the kind of entertainment that would satisfy a mass audience.

Plautus' Stage The state supplied a temporary theatre in the time of Plautus and Terence in the second century BC. A permanent theatre, equivalent to the Theatre of Dionysus, was not built in Rome until 55 BC. Since plays were given in connection with religious festivals honoring specific gods, it is likely that the theatre was set up near the temple of the god being honored.

The theatre of Plautus and Terence probably included a semicircular orchestra surrounded by temporary scaffolding for spectators to sit on and a long, narrow stage rising about five feet above the orchestra level. A stage house with a facade, called the *scaena frons,* bounded the back and ends of the stage. We can only guess at the design of the stage house, as no theatre remains from this period. The back wall of the stage probably contained three openings. In a comedy each might be used as the entrance of a house. The stage then became a street, and the entrances at either end of the stage were looked upon as the continuation of the street. Some comedies required windows and a second story; the background may have provided those as well. Our ideas about these early theatres are derived largely from existing stone structures dating from the first century AD or later and do not necessarily give us an accurate picture of the wooden structures used by Plautus and Terence.

Costumes and masks varied. Plautus and Terence adapted their plays from Greek New Comedy and retained Greek settings and garments. Other playwrights wrote about Roman characters and the costumes were similar to those worn everyday by Romans. Since most of the characters in Roman comedy were "types," the costumes quickly became standardized. Even certain colors were associated with particular occupations, slaves, for example, wearing red and courtesans yellow. All actors wore masks and each comic actor also wore a thin sandal or slipper, called a *soccus.*

DRAMATIC CONVENTIONS

The main conventions of Greek drama emerged early and, as late as Euripides, there was little departure from them. Three types of plays evolved—tragedies, comedies, and satyr plays— each having a chorus that remained central throughout the fifth century.

The Theatre at Delphi is typical of ancient Greek theatres. It is built on a hillside with seats on three sides surrounding the stage. The temple of Apollo is in the background. Eventually, scene buildings were built behind the playing area. Audiences could look past the stage to the mountains or the sea in the distance. The photo shows the stone benches placed on the hillside for the audience, the flat dancing circle or stage at the foot of the hill, and the remains of the stone foundation of the scene building.

The Epidaurus Festival Theatre is the best preserved of the Greek amphitheatres. In the photo we can see the relationship of the theatre to its natural environment. The scene building is of recent construction; the entranceways, or *parodoi*, are clearly marked.

Theatre of Herodes Atticus in Athens.

Theatre of Marcellus, in Rome, begun by Julius Caesar and completed in 11 or 13 BC by Augustus. It had a seating capacity of 14,000. In the twelfth century it was made into a fortress and later into a palace. The theatre's remains were restored to their original appearance in 1928.

Construction of the Colosseum, or the Flavian Amphitheatre, was begun about AD 74 and completed in AD 80. It could hold 50,000 persons. The beauty of the colossal structure contrasts sharply with the gory purpose it served. Many thousands met their deaths in the arena either in gladiatorial combat or at the jaws of wild beasts for the amusement of the masses. Much of the basic structure still stands.

An interior view of the Colosseum as it appears today. Seventy-six of the 80 arches were numbered; each spectator received a ticket with the number of the arch nearest his seat. The interior is vast, measuring one-third of a mile across. A cross section and elevation are shown below.

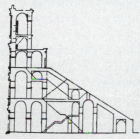 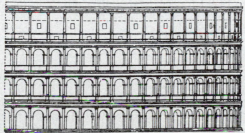

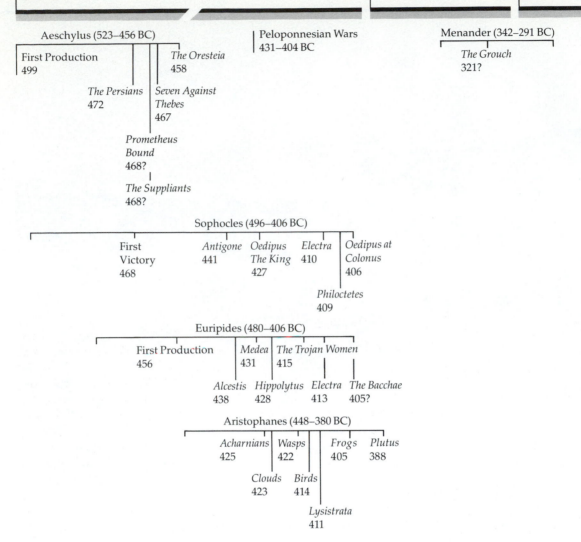

Aeschylus (523–456 BC)

First Production
499

The Persians
472

Prometheus
Bound
468?

The Suppliants
468?

Seven Against
Thebes
467

The Oresteia
458

Peloponnesian Wars
431–404 BC

Menander (342–291 BC)

The Grouch
321?

Sophocles (496–406 BC)

First
Victory
468

Antigone
441

Oedipus
The King
427

Electra
410

Philoctetes
409

Oedipus at
Colonus
406

Euripides (480–406 BC)

First Production
456

Alcestis
438

Medea
431

Hippolytus
428

The Trojan Women
415

Electra
413

The Bacchae
405?

Aristophanes (448–380 BC)

Acharnians
425

Clouds
423

Wasps
422

Birds
414

Lysistrata
411

Frogs
405

Plutus
388

TRAGEDY

Use of Mythic Material Drawing from myth, legend, saga, and recent history, playwrights developed plot, conflict, character, and theatrical effects. The stories of great houses, or tribes, appealed to their imaginations as did the myths surrounding their gods: Prometheus, Poseidon, Athene, and Aphrodite.

Greek tragedy shows humans and gods under pressure, confronting chaos and disorder and acting out of necessity, often in contradictory and immoral ways. In the *Oresteia* (458 BC) Aeschylus depicts how a civilized judicial system evolved out of a chaotic system of personal revenge (the *lex talionis*). Revenge and murder go unchecked until the goddess Athene's "new justice" takes hold, tempering the older harsh codes with pity and compassion.

Sophocles' tragedies demonstrate a divine order where humans can, through suffering, learn the meaning of their deeds. Divine order

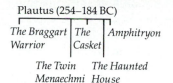

| 200 BC | 100 BC | AD 1 | AD 100 |

Plautus (254–184 BC)

The Braggart Warrior | The Casket | Amphitryon

The Twin Menaechmi | The Haunted House

Seneca (5 BC–AD 65)

The Trojan Women | Medea

Oedipus | Phaedra | Thyestes

Agamemnon

Terence (195–160 BC)

Andria 166 | Mother-in-Law 165 | Self-Tormentor 163

Eunuch 161

Phormio 161 | The Brothers 160

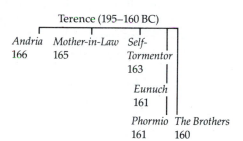

decrees and our personal choices fulfill those decrees. A man like Oedipus refuses to accept a ready-made fate. Hearing the oracle's prophecy that he will kill his father and marry his mother, he runs away from the people he presumes are his parents, but unwittingly, through anger and pride, he fulfills the oracle's prophecy. The realization of his deeds is the source of the tragedy. The Oedipus story, for Sophocles, demonstrates that we learn who we are only after paying a great price; moreover, our heroism is the anguished acceptance of who we are in a world we never made.

Euripides, who wrote during the civil war between Athens and Sparta, had a bleak vision of the universe. His plays described a morally disordered world in which gods and human beings alike were irrational, passionate, and violent.

Play Structure The way the Greeks told or revealed a story has influenced Western playwrights for 2500 years. The plays open late in the story's action or development. *Oedipus the King* begins with the city plague-stricken and Oedipus seeking remedies. *The Trojan Women* begins after the fall of Troy, just before the women are loaded onto the Greek ships. The characters then experience intense pressures until they are forced into irreversible acts. There is usually a limited number of characters, and locale and events are restricted. Also, since the plot begins late in the story, the period of time covered is usually limited to a few hours. The incidents are arranged with concern for cause and effect, building to a climax and quick resolution.

Odes and Episodes By modern standards little happens in Greek tragedy. Scenes of violence (death, battle, maiming) are reported by eyewitnesses, usually messengers. Moreover, the episodes, or scenes of action, are separated from one another by choral odes. Dramatic action as we know it is suspended while the chorus moves in stately and intricate patterns, chanting to the flute's accompaniment. The choral odes provided mythic and historical background to the main story; they expressed emotions pertinent to the action that had gone before or was to come; they reflected upon the past, warned of present transgressions; they conveyed atmosphere and mood.

Scholars date the Greek plays as early or late depending upon the length and function of the odes. Before Aeschylus the chorus was the pro-

---

Oedipus the King

Sophocles, one of several Greek playwrights whose work survives today, wrote the greatest of Greek tragedies, *Oedipus the King*, in 427 BC. He wrote three plays about the Oedipus story: *Antigone* and *Oedipus at Colonus* are the other two.

Oedipus the King is the story of a man who flees from Corinth to avoid fulfilling a prophecy that he will kill his father and marry his mother. On his journey he kills an old man (an apparent stranger but actually his real father, the king of Thebes) and his servants at a place where three roads meet. He then proceeds to Thebes and solves the riddle of the Sphinx. As a reward he is made king and married to the widowed queen, who is actually his mother, Jocasta. He rules well and has four children.

The play opens with Thebes stricken by a plague. Oedipus has sent his brother-in-law Creon to consult the Delphic oracle about the cause of the plague, declaring that he will rid the city of the infection. As Oedipus pursues the plague's source, he learns more and more about himself. Finally, Oedipus comes face to face with himself as his father's killer, as his mother's son and husband, and as his children's father and brother. He puts out his eyes when he learns the truth and Jocasta kills herself. By his own decree he is exiled from Thebes and wanders blind into the countryside.

Oedipus the King is one of the world's greatest tragedies; it is about human guilt and innocence, knowledge and ignorance, power and helplessness. Its fundamental idea is that wisdom comes to us through suffering.

---

tagonist. As the second and third actors were added, the chorus's function changed. They became the voice of a common humanity, sharing in and responding to the hero's tragic experiences very much as an interested and knowledgeable bystander shares in someone else's calamity.

Greek playwrights introduced variety and stimulated interest in several ways. They alternated odes and episodes; and they used such conventions as the *debate,* the *stichomythic confrontation* of individuals, *arias* of suffering, and the messenger's *report.*

The debate (or *agon*) between main characters was a means of putting two opposing points of view before the chorus and audience.[4] In the debates characters exchange a brisk staccato of one-liners (called *stichomythia*) for up to 100 lines at a time. The effect is like a verbal tennis match where emotions and words are volleyed back and forth between two opponents. In the *agon* the turbulence of human emotions bursts through the formal rhetoric in the hero's lonely outcries—those arias of suffering—that personalize the agony of his dilemma.

In most cases a messenger reports events of carnage and death. These descriptive reports prepare the audience for the spectacle of the hero's suffering. One such report is the account given by the messenger of how Oedipus put out his eyes when he discovered that he was cause of the plague.

Aristotle's Perspective on Classical Tragedy
Aristotle lectured on poetry and drama to students at the Lyceum in Athens around 335 BC. These lectures (called the *Poetics*) set down a critical basis for understanding classical tragedy.

Aristotle defined tragedy as an *imitation* of an action that has serious implications, is complete, and has universal implications that may be grasped in a single viewing. It is written in language that has rhythm and melody and is enacted by persons (chorus and actors) engaged in a course of events that are fearful and pathetic. Plot—the structuring of those events—is the

Messenger's Speech
from *Oedipus the King*

Second Messenger . . . our glorious queen
    Jocasta's dead . . . .
By her own hand. The worst of what was
    done
you cannot know. You did not see the
    sight.
Yet in so far as I remember it
you'll hear the end of our unlucky queen.
When she came raging into the house she
    went
straight to her marriage bed, tearing her
    hair
with both her hands, and crying upon
    Laius
long dead—Do you remember, Laius,
that night long past which bred a child for
    us
to send you to your death and leave
a mother making children with her son?
And then she groaned and cursed the bed
    in which
she brought forth husband by her hus-
    band, children
by her own child, an infamous double
    bond.
How after that she died I do not know
for Oedipus distracted us from seeing.
He burst upon us shouting and we looked
to him as he paced frantically around,
begging us always: Give me a sword, I say,
to find this wife no wife, this mother's
    womb,
this field of double sowing whence I
    sprang
and where I sowed my children! As he
    raved
some god showed him the way—none of us
    there.
Bellowing terribly and led by some
invisible guide he rushed on the two doors,
wrenching the hollow bolts out of their
    sockets,

he charged inside. There, there, we saw his
    wife
hanging, the twisted rope around her neck.
When he saw her, he cried out fearfully
and cut the dangling noose. Then, as she
    lay,
poor woman, on the ground, what hap-
    pened after,
was terrible to see. He tore the brooches—
the gold chased brooches fastening her
    robe—
away from her and lifting them up high
dashed them on his own eyeballs, shriek-
    ing out
such things as: they will never see the
    crime
I have committed or had done upon me!
Dark eyes, now in the days to come look
    on
forbidden faces, do not recognize
those whom you long for—with such
    imprecations
he struck his eyes again and yet again
with the brooches. And the bleeding eye-
    balls gushed
and stained his beard—no sluggish oozing
    drops
but a black rain and bloody hail poured
    down.

So it has broken—and not on one head
but troubles mixed for husband and for
    wife.
The fortune of the days gone by was true
good fortune—but today groans and
    destruction
and death and shame—of all ills can be
    named
not one is missing.

Oedipus the King[5]

"soul" of tragedy. It shows characters that have a defined moral character (called *ethos*) trying to prove some thesis or setting forth an opinion (called *thought* or *dianoia*).

Of the six elements that made tragedy distinctive, plot was the first, followed by character, thought, verbal expression, song composition, and visual effects. These elements made up an effective *dramatic* pattern: (a) they *imitated* by verbal expression and song composition; (b) the *manner* in which they imitated was visual adornment (with costumes, masks, scenic elements); (c) the *things* they imitated were plot, character, and thought. Aristotle said that tragedy was

> . . . an imitation not of men but of a life, an action, and they have moral quality in accordance with their characters but are happy or unhappy in accordance with their actions; hence, they are not active in order to imitate their characters, but they include the characters along with the actions for the sake of the latter. Thus the structure of events, the plot, is the goal of tragedy, and the goal is the greatest thing of all.[6]

Aristotle stressed that plot must convey a sense of wholeness by having a beginning, middle, and end. It should constitute a unified event taking place, if possible, during a single daylight period (the play's length was already determined by the festival competition). The event should also be *probable* or *necessary*.

In Aristotle's view, plots were either simple or complex. Simple plots are those where the reversal from good fortune to bad occurs without the hero's coming to a new understanding about himself or his world. In complex plots, on the other hand, the characters undergo *peripety* or recognition (a shift from ignorance to awareness). For example, in *Oedipus the King*, the peripety occurs when the man who comes to reassure Oedipus—to relieve him of his fear about his mother—by revealing who he once was, brings about a new, but unexpected, understanding.

For Aristotle a complex plot was also one in which the reversal of the hero's fortunes from good to bad took place gradually throughout the play. Aristotle admired the plot in *Oedipus the King* where the hero underwent a change of fortune, not through any real evil or wickedness, but because of some *mistake*. He thought this type of plot was the finest in tragic drama.

SATYR PLAY

The satyr play, part of the festival competition, was written by the dramatist as a comic afterpiece to the three tragedies that came before it. It was short, comic in tone, and used a chorus of satyrs, mythical goat-men, to comment on the action. Since the same actors and chorus were used for both tragedies and satyr plays, the conventions of acting, costuming, and scenery were probably similar.

One complete satyr play exists (Euripides' *Cyclops*) and part of another (Sophocles' *The Trackers*). They are divided into five sections by four choral odes and parody a serious story. In Euripides' play Odysseus encounters the Cyclops and mischief follows.

After the fifth century the writing of satyr plays declined and they eventually ceased to exist as a dramatic form.

COMEDY

Aristophanes' Old Comedy Aristotle traces the origins of comedy back to Dorian phallic rites with their dances, songs, and parades of phallic symbols and to the improvisations of those who led the singing. But the process by which phallic rites achieved comic form is unknown to us. Aristophanes' 11 comedies are our only sources of fifth-century comic writing (called Old Comedy).

Aristophanes' plays commented on contemporary issues: social, political, literary, and military. The plots were organized around a central theme embodied in a ludicrous and exaggerated idea (like the sex strike to bring an end to war in *Lysistrata*). Fantasy, farcical situations, slapstick, obscene passages, and debates over the pleasures of eating, drinking, sex, wealth, and leisure make up the fabric of his plays.

The comedies themselves are divided into two parts. The first part contains a prologue that sets forth the fantastic idea; the chorus enters, there follows a debate (or *agon*) over the merits of the idea or scheme, and a decision is made to try out the scheme.

A *parabasis* (or choral ode in which the audience is addressed directly) divides the play in half. It is the playwright's means of presenting his viewpoint on social or political issues and advocating a line of action. He may even use the *parabasis* to praise the play or to plead for the audience's indulgence.

The play's second part shows the results of such a scheme as the wives' sex strike in *Lysistrata*. The final scene (or *komos*), like the *parabasis*, is unique to Old Comedy. In the *komos* all of the characters are reconciled and they exit to a feast or celebration.

Menander's New Comedy Following the Peloponnesian War, economic prosperity returned to Athens and play festivals continued during the fourth century. Tragic writers turned to imitating earlier works; as a result, there was a falling off of public support for their plays. The same was not true for comedy. It developed a new form identified with *The Grouch,* the single surviving work of Menander (342–291 BC), and increased in popularity after the fifth century.

In the transition from Old Comedy to Menander's plays, the political satire, personal invective, and *parabasis* identified with Aristophanes' comedies dropped away in favor of events based on contemporary life and manners. New Comedy treated the domestic affairs of the Athenian middle class. It ignored social and political issues in favor of concerns for love, property, and family relationships. *The Grouch* is a series of episodes separated by choral passages having little connection with the play's events.

ROMAN DRAMA

Roman Comedy The existing comedies of Plautus and Terence were adapted from Greek New Comedy. However, these playwrights

Figure 3-4 Satyr mask. This Greek terracotta mask shows us a satyr's head.

abandoned the chorus and used the music formerly associated with it throughout the play. Plautus included a number of songs and had certain scenes recited to musical accompaniment. In Plautus' plays about two-thirds of the lines were accompanied by music; his plays are often spoken of as forerunners of modern musical comedy. Although Terence did not use songs, music accompanied at least half of his dialogue.

Roman comedy, like Greek New Comedy, deals with affairs of the well-to-do middle class. The plots turn on misunderstandings of one kind or another: mistaken identity, misunderstood motives, or deliberate deceptions. Sometimes the misunderstanding leads to farce as in Plautus' *The Twin Menaechmi* where the mistaken identity involves identical twins, or, as in Terence, it leads to sentimentality in resolving the problems of lovers or conflicts between parents and children.

Plautus typically uses a single plot and a

complicated intrigue. In an expository prologue he explains the dramatic situation and then develops the farcical possibilities of the situation in the episodes that follow. Terence, on the other hand, uses a double plot and dispenses with the expository prologue. Moreover, their characters fall into clearly defined types: the older man (usually a father) concerned about his wealth or children, the young man (usually the son) who rebels against authority, the clever slave, the parasite or hanger-on, the courtesan, the slave dealer, and the cowardly soldier. Of all the characters the Roman slave is the most famous; he helps his master devise all sorts of schemes, most of which go awry and lead to further complications. Very few respectable women appear in Roman comedy, and while love affairs may be the source of a play's misunderstandings, the women involved are most often never seen.

All action takes place in the street (and in front of the scene house) no matter how illogical, and characters must frequently explain what has happened indoors. Occasionally, the conventions of Roman comedy strain the modern reader's belief, but they were apparently accepted without question by Roman audiences.

Only the plays of two Roman comic writers have come down to us. Titus Maccius Plautus' (c. 254–184 BC) 21 surviving plays include his most famous: *Amphitryon, The Pot of Gold, The Captives, The Braggart Warrior,* and *The Twin Menaechmi.* Publius Terentius Afer (195–159 BC), known as Terence, was a native of North Africa brought to Rome as a slave and later freed. He wrote six plays, all of which survive: *The Woman of Andros, The Self-Tormentor, The Eunuch, Phormio, The Mother-in-law,* and *The Brothers.*

Roman Tragedy Tragedy, also based on Greek models, was important in the Roman theatre. Whether using Greek or Roman themes, it featured horrifying plots, characters almost totally good or depraved, and long bombastic speeches.

The only Roman tragedies to survive are by Lucius Annaeus Seneca (4 BC—AD 65), a philosopher and one of Nero's principal advisers. Of his nine surviving tragedies, five are adapted

from plays by Euripides. The most well-known are *Oedipus* and *Thyestes.*

Seneca was not a professional dramatist, and it is likely that his plays were not staged but rather read to a small group of Roman aristocrats. Much later they were read in Latin in England's schoolrooms and became a major influence on Renaissance tragedy. The characteristics of Senecan drama are important for this reason.

Seneca divided his plays into five acts by choral interludes. Although Renaissance dramatists seldom used a chorus, they did adopt Seneca's five-act structure. His plays contained elaborate speeches, *sententiae* (brief moral statements about human behavior), and sensational deeds illustrating the terrible effects of unrestrained emotion. They are filled with violence. In *Oedipus,* Jocasta kills herself on stage by ripping open her abdomen, and in *Thyestes* the flesh of children is served at a banquet. Thus moral lessons are taught through horrifying examples and moralizing statements, two practices followed by many Renaissance playwrights. Seneca also used ghosts and magical rites for effects and such technical devices as the soliloquy, aside, and *confidant* (a character whose main function is to advise the protagonist), which were to influence later playwrights.

Other Types of Entertainment After the first century BC, the Roman stage was taken over by minor dramatic entertainments, especially the *fabula Atellana,* mime, and pantomine. The *fabula Atellana,* a short farce, was one of the oldest of Roman theatrical forms, emerging from Atella, an area near Naples. It employed stock characters, improvised dialogue, music, dance, and plots involving trickery and cheating in a rural setting. Such stock characters as Maccus, a fool or stupid clown; Bucco, a glutton or braggart; Pappus, a foolish old man who is easily deceived; and Dossenus, a cunning swindler and glutton (probably a hunchback) appear again with other names in the *commedia dell'arte* during the Italian Renaissance.

The term *mime* was used loosely to refer to

almost any kind of theatrical entertainment, known especially for violent and obscene events. Mime appeared in Rome as early as 211 BC, often performed by traveling mime troupes on makeshift stages. In the beginning their plays (short, topical farces on subjects drawn from urban life) were improvised and the female roles were played by women. None of the actors wore masks.

By the first century BC, both Atellan farce and mime had been written down and became semi-literary forms. The subject of the later mime was often adultery and the language was frequently indecent. These elements set the Christian Church against the mime troupes who retaliated by ridiculing the Church's sacraments and beliefs. Thus the mime was more responsible than any other form for Christian opposition to the theatre.

Pantomime was also popular in late Rome. This silent, interpretive dance was performed by a single actor who played many roles by changing masks that had a closed mouth. A chorus narrated the story, which was usually drawn from mythology; the action was accompanied by music played by a chorus composed of flutes, pipes, cymbals, and other percussion instruments. In late Rome pantomime was especially popular with the ruling classes and largely replaced tragedy.

The theatre degenerated to such a degree in imperial Rome that plays, usually mime, pantomime, and nondramatic spectacle, were often competing with gladiatorial combats held in the orchestras and on stages of the theatres. By AD 476 Rome had twice been sacked. Although festivals were revived for a time, the last recorded performance is in AD 533.

REPRESENTATIVE PLAY

The Trojan Women
Written by Euripides and produced in 415 BC at the Theatre of Dionysus, Athens

BACKGROUND

In 415 BC the Greek playwright Euripides won second prize in the City Dionysia competition with *Alexander, Palamedes, The Trojan Women,* and *Sisyphus* (a satyr play). He presented his trilogy as three successive episodes in the story of Troy; his satyr play was a burlesque on a related theme.

The first play was the story of Paris (Alexander), how it was foretold at his birth that he must destroy his own city (Troy), how the baby was left to die in the mountains, and how he was rescued. The second play was the story of Palamedes, the wisest of the Greeks at Troy and therefore hated by Odysseus who contrived his death. The third play described the destruction of Troy, the death of its defenders and the enslavement of its women and children. Of these three plays, only *The Trojan Women* is extant.

When Euripides composed this set of tragedies, Athens was nominally at peace. Only a few years earlier, Athens had emerged from an indecisive 10 years' war with Sparta, and the city was only weeks away from launching the great Sicilian Expedition, which touched off the next and final phase of the same war that ended in 404 BC with the surrender of Athens. Incidents of genocide during the long Peloponnesian War served as background to *The Trojan Women.* Both Athenians and Spartans had systematically killed male populations surrendering to stronger forces; the fate for women and children was slavery.

In the winter of 416–415 BC, a few months before Euripides' play was presented, Athens invited the neutral island city of Melos to join the Athenian alliance. Melos refused and was besieged and captured. The Athenians put all adult males to death and enslaved the women and children.

THE TRAGIC ACTION

The Trojan Women, an antiwar play, enacted the plight of war's often forgotten victims—women and children. The action of *The Trojan Women*

EURIPIDES

Euripides (c. 480–406 BC), one of the three great tragic writers, won only four contests during his lifetime. Scholars attribute this relative unpopularity to his innovations with play structure and style and to the subjects of his dramas. The son of aristocratic parents, Euripides held political offices in Athens, where he became a member of the unpopular peace party during the Peloponnesian War and an opponent of Athenian imperialism. Toward the end of his life he sought exile at the court of Macedonia and died there.

He is credited with writing 88 plays (22 sets of 4) of which 19 plays have survived. The best known are *Alcestis* (438), *Medea* (431), *Hippolytus* (428), *Electra* (date unknown), *The Trojan Women* (415), and *The Bacchae* (produced after his death). In addition, *The Cyclops* (date unknown) is the only complete satyr play that now exists.

Aristotle, surveying Greek drama decades later, called Euripides the "most tragic of the poets," presumably because of Euripides' dark materials: sexual repression, irrational violence, human madness and savagery. Critics consider him the most modern and innovative of the three tragic poets, speaking to today's audiences of the hero's demoralization and the barbarity of men at war. His *Trojan Women* is the first great antiwar play in Western drama.

takes place shortly after the capture of Troy by the Greeks. All Trojan men have been killed; all women and children are captives, waiting to be divided as slaves among their conquerers. The play evokes in an audience, especially one on

the eve of the Sicilian Expedition, a recognition of the suffering and loss that accompany war. While the Trojan dead are absent from the acting area, their presence is felt in the emotions and lamentations of the surviving women.

The actors' restricted movements mirror the fact that they are captives *waiting* to learn of their cruel fates. Waiting in grief and fear is the play's principal activity. The women wait to be divided among their new masters: Cassandra to Agamemnon, Andromache to Achilles' son, and Queen Hecuba to Odysseus. With each announcement of a Greek general's decision, the tension of waiting is released only to be heightened again in the new horror of consignment.

In Euripides' universe gods are as vengeful and irrational as human beings. It is a universe without order; therefore, the spectacle of the human dilemma is pitiable but without moral or ethical meaning. There is a line in the play that reads: "The man who sacks cities is a fool; he makes temples and tombs, the shrines of the dead, a desert, and then perishes himself."

THE SCENE

The scene is an open space before a partly demolished city. The scene building functions as the walls of the ruined city and the "huts" that contain the Trojan captives. Two masked actors—the sea god, Poseidon, and Athene, the goddess defender of Troy—speak the prologue. We can imagine these gods appearing high up (perhaps on top of the scene building), above the level of the actors playing ordinary human beings. Poseidon points to Hecuba "lying before the doors" (of the huts) weeping for her daughter, Polyxene, killed at the tomb of Achilles, and for her husband, Priam, and children dead in the rubble of the fallen city.

As background to this scene, Poseidon describes the treachery of the Greeks' use of the Trojan horse, the collapse of the city, and fate of its defenders. Athene engages him in her revenge against the Greeks for defiling her altars in Troy. He agrees to overwhelm the Greek

Figure 3-5 *The Greeks*, first presented by the Royal Shakespeare Company at the Aldwych Theatre, London, 1979. This photo is of *Part One: The War* (from *The Trojan Women*). In the foreground is Billie Whitelaw as Andromache; in the background Eliza Ward as Hecuba holds the child Astyanax. The production was directed by John Barton and designed by John Napier.

ships during their homeward voyage to teach them to respect all gods.

These actors change masks and costumes to assume the principal human roles (with the exception of Hecuba) in the remainder of the play. Hecuba, wife of the dead King Priam and mother to Hector, the chief Trojan warrior slain in battle with Achilles, rises slowly from the ground. She describes her physical and mental suffering and calls on the chorus (the captive women) to lament Troy. They enter in two semichoruses (probably up the *parodoi*). They sing of Greece where they are to be sent.

Euripides is master of the theatrical entrance. Talthybius, the Greek messenger, arrives the first of four times to announce decisions made by the Greek generals. In four episodes the women learn about their fates and depart into captivity. These scenes are further complicated by the trial of Helen of Troy and the execution of Hector's son, the child Astyanax.

Andromache enters on a chariot with Astyanax. Hecuba counsels her to be loyal to Neoptolemos in the hope of bringing up Astyanax to reestablish Troy. The hope is immediately dashed by the arrival of Talthybius to say that the Greeks have decided to kill the child. Hecuba is left alone and the chorus sings of war.

In another startling entrance, Menelaus arrives to take his wife Helen away. He intends to kill her, but Helen defends herself as one who was prevented from returning to her homeland. In what becomes a mock trial, Menelaus accuses Helen of adultery and betrayal, and Hecuba acts as prosecutor, arguing that the "price of adultery is death." Helen pleads coercion, saying that she was Paris' "bride of force." The result of the trial is that Helen sails to Greece on another ship, Hecuba fearing that if Helen and Menelaus voyaged together Helen would seduce her husband and thereafter escape punishment.

On his third entrance Talthybius returns with the child's body carried on Hector's shield; preparations are made for his burial. Hecuba pronounces his funeral oration and the chorus sings of Helen's destruction of Paris, Hector's shield, their misery and meaningless sacrifices. The body is carried off on the shield.

Talthybius' last entrance ends the waiting period. The chorus sees flames in the huts (probably special effects with torches). Troy is being burned and the captives are ordered to the ships. Hecuba tries to run into the flames, but Talthybius stops her because she is "Odysseus' property." The play ends with Hecuba's lyric lament:

> *Hecuba* That mortal is a fool who, prospering,
> thinks his life has any strong foundation;
> since our fortune's course of action is the
> reeling way a madman takes, and no one
> person is ever happy all the time.[7]

CHARACTER

Despite the horrible and sometimes bizarre events of Euripides' plays, we can see that his main characters respond to their tragic experiences with ordinary emotions. They are recognizable people. For instance, Helen is a clever vamp, Hecuba an aging queen, and Talthybius a compassionate but loyal soldier. Euripides' gods are as mean and fickle as human beings although their powers are larger. Moreover, Euripides' characters exhibit human qualities that are to be condemned and praised: Talthybius' loyalty to his commanders is offset by his compassion for the women's plight; Helen's beauty is linked to her promiscuity; Cassandra's clairvoyance is counterbalanced by her emotional instability, and Hecuba's noble suffering is undercut by her desire for revenge against Helen.

LANGUAGE

While Euripides experimented with theatrical effects (the winged chariot in *Medea* and the burning city in *The Trojan Women*), he also varied the norms for verse in classical tragedy, mainly by blurring the contrast between spoken words and those that were sung.

Three types of language were spoken in the Greek theatre: recitatives, spoken iambics, and lyrics. The chorus technically lamented in *lyric* outpourings of emotions. Euripides interchanged these verse forms between actors and chorus to contrast sharply the beautiful mythological world of the choral odes with the misery of the captive women.

EURIPIDES' MODERNISM

Euripides' commitment to pacifism and his interest in the psychology of irrational acts make him the most modern of the Greek playwrights. The events in *The Trojan Women* show the playwright's concerns. Even though the women's fate as Greek slaves has been decided before the play begins, the episodes bring about dramatic events: the child's death and burial, the trial of Helen, and the consignment of the women to the Greek generals. Also, despite the fact that the women are trapped and their destinies determined, they do more than react passively to their fates. They rage against the cruelties of the Greeks, especially against the murder of Hector's small son. The women's characters are as complex as those in modern drama. They are not exempt from the guile and savagery shown by the men and gods. Hecuba resorts to cunning to persuade Menelaus to kill Helen, but she also displays great nobility in the presence of human waste and destruction.

Euripides, always a controversial playwright in fifth-century Athens, explored the cost of war in human lives (an entire male population is killed) and the plight of the survivors (women, children, and future generations). While the Greeks were ostensibly victors at Troy, their victory was temporary and bittersweet. King Agamemnon died on the day of his return, Odysseus wandered for 10 years, and the Greek fleet was destroyed in a storm at sea. In selecting this part of the Trojan–Greek story, Euripides was at pains to represent his nation's *hubris,* or overbearing pride. Speaking to contemporary politicians and generals, Euripides documents in Cassandra's rape and Astyanax's murder how very much the Greeks deserved their doom. The story of the Trojan women also commented indirectly on the genocide at Melos, the action of a barbaric (and degenerate) polity, and warned of disaster to come in the conduct of present and future wars.

ESSAY

The Greek plays are ageless in their concern for the relations of men, women, and their gods. To demonstrate the timeliness of these ancient plays when performed for modern audiences, we have selected *Fragments of a Trilogy.*

Greek Tragedy in Modern Performance
Fragments of a Trilogy
(Selections from Euripides' *Electra, Medea,* and *The Trojan Women*), directed by Andrei Serban, New York City, 1974

Today audiences fill the ancient theatres of Epidaurus and Herodes Atticus in Greece, and directors all over the world restage plays by Aeschylus, Sophocles, Euripides, and Aristophanes. However, there is almost worldwide disagreement over how to stage the classics. Should they be presented in something approximating their ancient form? Or should they be modernized to make them relevant to twentieth-century audiences?

Some directors believe that classical plays must be modernized if they are to be meaningful. Euripides has been staged with actors wearing tuxedos and bathrobes. Others keep their productions within the bounds of tradition, enriching them with contemporary knowledge. Still others imitate ancient productions; actors wear masks, high wooden shoes, huge gloves, and shoulder pads to give supernatural proportions to the body. Stylized gestures and exaggerated delivery are emphasized. Perhaps the most widespread concept of staging Greek tragedy is to use stark settings, actors in somber colors, and a keening chorus moving in unison.

Director Andrei Serban has moved New York audiences with starkly theatrical productions. Serban worked for three years with composer Elizabeth Swados on three plays by Euripides: *Medea, Electra,* and *The Trojan Women,* produced consecutively between 1972 and 1974. Later that year the three plays were presented as "fragments of a trilogy" in repertory at La Mama Experimental Theatre Club with two plays performed each night.

The challenge for the modern director is how to make 2500-year-old texts meaningful to a modern audience. "These texts," Serban said in an interview, "once upon a time had cosmic power, cosmic intensity, and it was lost. How can we in a way rediscover something of that energy?"[8]

Serban set about experimenting with language and the actor's voice to bring the texts to life. Different languages (Greek, Latin, Mayan, Aztec) became avenues for experiment: the way words were put together, the harsh consonants, the round vowels, the flow of lines. The greatest

Andrei Serban (b. 1943), Romanian-born director, came to the United States in 1969 at the invitation of Ellen Stewart to work at her La Mama Experimental Theatre Club on a Ford Foundation grant. After participating in Peter Brook's International Research Institute in Paris and Shiraz (Iran), he returned to New York to direct La Mama ETC productions of *Medea, Electra,* and *The Trojan Women.*

During 1975 he directed Bertolt Brecht's *The Good Woman of Setzuan* at the Berlin International Festival; and in 1976 Shakespeare's *As You Like It* for summer festivals in France. More recently, he has directed Chekhov's *The Cherry Orchard* and Aeschylus' *Agamemnon* at Lincoln Center and Chekhov's *The Seagull* at The Public Theatre (New York City). In 1983 he returned to La Mama to stage Chekhov's *Uncle Vanya.*

challenge for the actor, Serban said, was "to be able to sustain something that goes on for whole pages—a rage that just goes on, words and words and words, flowing, and coming out like bursts of flame. How do you sustain that? Still, those plays 2000 years ago were performed for the citizens of Athens by people who were just like us, so somehow we had to find a training, a technique"[9] (Figure 3-6).

Many months' work with vocal and physical exercises resulted in performances in which the material was sung, chanted, spoken, shouted, screamed, whispered, and even gasped in ancient languages. The *meaning* to the events was communicated not through words but through sounds, actions, emotions, and music.

The Trojan Women, the last part of the trilogy, began with a keening procession through the lobby of the La Mama Annex that brought both performers and audiences jointly into the vast interior playing space of the theatre, an enormous room with a proscenium stage at one end. Two tiered wooden galleries along the sides of the rectangular room were used for actors and audience. At the beginning the audience was left standing for three-quarters of an hour in the darkened space in the room's center. They became genuine participants in the action that followed—the bystanders who watched Troy's women and children being driven from their ruined towers to tumbrils on the beachhead, there to be murdered, raped, or claimed as prizes.

Then the theatre lights stabbed the darkness, picking out certain women. Andromache was illuminated in a frozen farewell to her child before plunging to her death by leaping from a balcony into the center of the crowd. On a platform above the three-person wind-and-percussion orchestra, Cassandra danced out her madness with flaming torches in her hands. Hector's wife and son were exhibited in cages at one end of the room. On a cart in the center, Helen of Troy was stripped of her clothes, her hair cut; she was dirtied, mocked, and put to death with an ax blade.

Near the end of the performance, actors guided the audience to seats in the side galleries, and the remaining action then expanded to occupy the whole space. The Trojan women destined for exile slowly boarded ships formed out of wooden frames held up by cast members. Seated in the galleries, the audience members were no longer participants in the tragedy but detached onlookers observing the human destruction that followed the fall of Troy.

Serban used a *universal language*—the sounds of music and the human voice in pain and anger—to enact Euripides' story. The meaning of the Trojan holocaust was made palpable by the intensity of the music and by the animal-like bursts of sound from the actors' throats. To

Figure 3-6 Director Andrei Serban's performance style is evident in his treatment of the Greek chorus in *Fragments of a Trilogy* (selections from Euripides' *Electra, Medea,* and *The Trojan Women*), produced at La Mama Experimental Theatre Club (New York, 1974).

bridge the gap of 2500 years, Serban experimented with and found *vocal techniques* and a *production style* to release emotions all too familiar to modern audiences. The holocaust material of Euripides' play, its victims (the dead and the living), were matters of record. Serban reenacted the ancient material in such a way that it awakened our collective memories and emotions in recognition of the pain and suffering common to all victims of war.

SUMMARY

Western theatre grew out of the ancient Greek religious rituals and tribal rites honoring gods, especially Dionysus. In the great Theatre of Dionysus in Athens, the plays of Aeschylus, Sophocles, Euripides, and Aristophanes were produced. Wearing flowing costumes and spectacular masks, actors and choruses performed plays before large audiences. Our representative play, Euripides' *The Trojan Women*, depicts the fate of the vanquished in war—refugees waiting to learn the will of their captors in an all-too-universal situation.

The Romans borrowed from Greek architecture and writings the models for their buildings and plays. They presented the first regular comedy and tragedy at religious festivals (the *ludi*) around 240 BC. The plays of Plautus and Terence were performed on temporary wooden stages by masked actors dressed in Greek or Roman clothing. In time permanent stone amphitheatres were built in Rome to contain a variety of entertainments, including plays, mime, pantomime, music, dancing, acrobatics, and, later, gladiatorial events. With the decline of Rome, theatre degenerated; the last recorded performance of a play is AD 533.

Fragments of a Trilogy (selections from Euripides' *Electra, Medea,* and *The Trojan Women*) directed by Andrei Serban in New York in 1974 demonstrates our living heritage from these ancient theatres and the variety of means used today to present classical texts to modern audiences.

PLAYS TO READ

Agamemnon from *The Oresteia* by Aeschylus

Oedipus the King by Sophocles

The Trojan Women by Euripides

The Twin Menaechmi by Plautus

SOURCES

Aeschylus I. The Oresteia. Translated with an introduction by Richmond Lattimore. From *The Complete Greek Tragedies,* edited by David Grene and Richmond Lattimore. Chicago: University of Chicago Press. Paperback, 1953. The introduction to *The Oresteia* contains notes on Aeschylus' life, early Greek drama, and the legend of the house of Atreus. There follows individual discussions of each of the three plays: *Agamemnon, The Libation Bearers,* and *The Eumenides.*

Sophocles I. From *The Complete Greek Tragedies.* Edited by David Grene and Richmond Lattimore. Chicago: University of Chicago Press. Paperback, 1954. This edition contains an introduction to "The Theban Plays" and includes texts of *Oedipus the King* (translated by David Grene), *Oedipus at Colonus* (translated by Robert Fitzgerald), and *Antigone* (translated by Elizabeth Wycoff).

The Oedipus Cycle of Sophocles. Translated by Dudley Fitts and Robert Fitzgerald. New York: Harcourt Brace Jovanovich. Paperback, 1955. The volume includes *Oedipus the King, Antigone,* and *Oedipus at Colonus.*

Euripides III. From *The Complete Greek Tragedies.* Edited by David Grene and Richmond Lattimore. Chicago: University of Chicago Press. Paperback, 1958. *The Trojan Women* in this edition is translated by Richmond Lattimore. *Hecuba, Andromache,* and *Ion* are also included.

Plautus. *Menaechmus Twins and Two Other Plays,* edited by Lionel Casson. New York: Norton, 1971.

Terence: The Comedies. Translated by Betty Radice. Baltimore: Penguin, 1976.

NOTES

1. *The Trojan Women* in *Euripides III, The Complete Greek Tragedies,* eds. David Grene and Richard Lattimore (Chicago: University of Chicago Press, 1959). Reprinted by permission of The University of Chicago Press.

2. Critic Gerald Else advances the theory that drama had its origin in oral readers, or *rhapsodes,* reciting passages from epic poems during the religious festivals sometime prior to 534 BC. See *The Origin and Early Form of Greek Tragedy* (Cambridge, Mass.: Harvard University Press, 1965.)

3. Oscar G. Brockett, *History of the Theatre,* 4th ed. (Boston: Allyn and Bacon, 1982), p. 29. Reprinted by permission of Allyn and Bacon, Inc.

4. William Arrowsmith has argued in his fine writing on Greek drama that a tradition of rhetorical speaking in the plays comes from the Athenian judicial system where language was formal but did not disguise the speaker's passionate commitment to his or her cause. ("The Criticism of Greek Tragedy," *The Tulane Drama Review, 3,* no. 3 (March 1959), 31–57.)

5. *Oedipus the King* in *Sophocles II, The Complete Greek Tragedies,* eds. David Grene and Richard Lattimore (Chicago: University of Chicago Press, 1954). Reprinted by permission of The University of Chicago Press.

6. Gerald F. Else, trans. and ed., *Aristotle: Poetics.* (Ann Arbor: University of Michigan Press, 1967), p. 27. Reprinted with permission.

7. *The Trojan Women* in *Euripides III, The Complete Greek Tragedies,* eds. David Grene and Richard Lattimore (Chicago: University of Chicago Press, 1959). Reprinted by permission of The University of Chicago Press.

8. Julius Novick, "Releasing the 'Cosmic Intensity' of the Classics," *New York Times* (January 18, 1976), p. 5. Reprinted by permission.

9. Novick, p. 5.

FOUR

MEDIEVAL THEATRE

A MODERN PERSPECTIVE

The theatre of the Middle Ages was international in scope and religious in nature. Like the Greek theatre, it began as a springtime religious observance. It was also intensely public and communal, attracting a mass audience to celebrate a common mythos—the Old and New Testaments of the Bible. Church and civil governments, clergy and laymen, collaborated to produce the outdoor festivals that often lasted from dawn to dusk over a period of days and involved 40 or more playlets and casts of hundreds.

In modern times tourists crowd the streets of Oberammergau in West Germany to witness a kind of theatre left over from medieval times. The Passion Play at Oberammergau has been performed mostly at 10-year intervals since 1634. It began months after the parish priests of a remote Bavarian valley ravaged by the plague vowed to reenact in perpetuity the story of Christ's last days if their village was spared. The Passion Play has always been performed by local people without professional training. In the 1980 version a local plumber played Judas and a dentist's son Jesus Christ, along with a cast of more than 1000. The play's 14 acts and 60 scenes, including more than a dozen living tableaux, cost $250,000 and brought a half-million visitors to the Bavarian town.

Although the Passion Play at Oberammergau occurs every 10 years, the theatre of the Middle Ages was often an annual event. The spectacles at Mons, Lucerne, and Valenciennes in France, and at Coventry, Wakefield, and York in England created a popular theatre approximated today only by the modern cinema. The *pageant* at York introduces us to medieval production methods that were handed down from generation to generation.

REPRESENTATIVE THEATRE: The York Cycle

It is early morning on Corpus Christi Day in York, a town in northeast England. The year is 1378. The actors have been up since 4:30 AM putting on their costumes and mounting the pageant wagons for a parade through the town. Already crowds are gathering in the narrow streets, before the cathedral, and in the marketplace. They watch in anticipation for the decorative wagons, which are pulled by young men and carry actors and scenery. A holiday spirit is in the air. Beggars, pickpockets, and food vendors ply their respective trades among the crowds.

Sounds of music and merriment and shouts of good cheer can be heard. A tremor of excitement passes through the crowd as the procession makes its way through the twisting streets. At the front of the procession clergymen carry the Host in a casket; craftsmen, wearing ceremo-

nial livery, carry banners displaying emblems of their craft. Wagons pulled by apprentices and journeymen appear one after the other.

On the first wagon members of the tanners' craft or trade guild stand like living statues in a colorful tableau that suggests the subject of their play, "The Creation and the Fall of Lucifer."

The narrow, double-decker wagon has two vertical levels for scenes to take place in Heaven and in Hell. Brightly painted curtains conceal the wagon's undercarriage. It is a dressing area for the actors.

The wagons—some 48 in all—stop at prearranged intervals before the houses of town dignitaries. The tanners' wagon finally comes to rest at the back of a platform stage erected in the pavement of York, a public square that serves as a place of trial, torture, and execution of criminals. In an effort to see and hear better, the crowds surge around the first wagon parked behind the platform.

The actor playing God steps forth dressed in ecclesiastical garments and announces himself to a host of angels and, by extension, to the audience gathered in the early morning light. He speaks in simple, rhyming verses that are frequently alliterative ("gracious and great," "shimmering and shining"). God "creates the world" and, when he is finished, turns to the archangel Lucifer (meaning "bearer of light") and appoints him second in command. Angels sing a hymn in praise of God's acts ("Holy, Holy, Holy, Lord God of Hosts") to the accompaniment of flute and tambour.

God then disappears into the curtained dressing area and Lucifer takes the stage. He rants, struts, and storms about while the crowd taunts and hisses this villain. With overreaching pride Lucifer announces: "I feel me so famous and fair/My power is passing my peers." Daring to set himself up in the place of God, Lucifer is

AD 900	1100
Hrosvitha writes Christian comedies c. 935–1001	Normans conquer England 1066
	Play of Adam oldest known scripture drama in vernacular 1150
	First Crusade 1095–1096

struck down and falls into "Hell," or into a lower area decorated as the gateway to Hell.

Lucifer In glorious glamour my glittering gleams!
I shall bide in bliss through my brightness of beams!
To Heaven I'll set myself, full seemly to sight,
To receive all reverence, through my right of renown.
I shall be like unto him that is highest on hight,
Oh! How I am deft—Oh!!! Deuce!!! All goes down!!
My might and my main have stopped calling!
Help, Fellows! In faith, I am FAALLLLINGGG!

The crowd cheers as the villain falls into the most admired of stage mansions, Hell's Mouth —a horrifying stage piece designed to "swallow sinners" and belch forth flames. Lucifer and his cohorts denounce one another and cry out in pain, lamenting the torment of Hell: "Hot it is here!" A general battle follows, even on the pavement among the crowd, to the general merriment of all.

The playlet ends (having taken in all about 15 to 20 minutes) with a final scene in Heaven where God, reappearing, draws the moral: "They would not worship that wrought

them./Therefore my wrath shall over go with them." Then he proceeds with Creation. He creates man, then night for the devils and daylight for mankind. He blesses the crowd, and the tanners' wagon moves on to make way for the second wagon where the plasterers' guild prepares to perform "From the Creation to the Fifth Day."

So wagon after wagon draws up to the platform stage. The festive day stretches out until each of the 48 playlets has been performed in the pavement at York. Performers and spectators have taken part once again in the great rolling spectacle of Biblical history with its moral messages. After nightfall and at the end of "Judgment Day," performed by the dealers in cloth and dry goods, the crowds disperse. Next year they will celebrate again the history of mankind at Corpus Christi time, as conceived, mimed, and enacted by the town of York and its trade guilds.

CONDITIONS OF PERFORMANCE

Performance conditions in the Middle Ages were influenced by folk mimes, pagan rites, and the Roman Catholic Church. The popular theatre in

Drama moves out of Church
Magna Carta
1215

Outdoor religious drama
1200–1600

Giotto
1266–1337,
Italian painter

Petrarch
1304–1374

Plays in Latin,
modeled on Roman drama,
written in Italy
1315–1500

Constantinople
falls to Turks
1453

Joan of Arc
burned at stake
1431

Gutenberg,
invention of
movable type
c. 1450

Introduction
of printing press
into Italy
1465

Pierre Pathelin,
one of many popular
farces in France
c. 1470

Everyman
morality play
c. 1500

Botticelli
paints *Birth of Venus*
1480

First profes–
sional acting
companies
in Spain
c. 1530

medieval Europe was a religious theatre that took its bookings, costumes, dialogue, and staging from the Church calendar, holidays, liturgy, ecclesiastical dress, and architecture. A popular theatre, the like of which had not been seen since the Dionysian festivals of Greece, was born again on the altars and naves of Christian churches.

BACKGROUND

Historians have labeled the years of European history between the fall of Rome (AD 476) and the coming of the Renaissance in the fifteenth century as the "Middle Ages." We tend to think of the Middle Ages as a transitional period when little of importance happened in the political and cultural world. We even call the first five centuries of the period the "Dark Ages" to suggest a world that had regressed from the glorious days of Greece and Rome and whose meager accomplishments are obscured if not lost to us. Yet the years that we do know well—the so-called High Middle Ages of the twelfth and thirteenth centuries—were as active and productive as any comparable period in recorded civilization. In France the great cathedrals of Chartres and Mont-Saint-Michel and the magnificent abbey of Saint-Denis were built. People of all classes of society were drawn to fight in the Crusades, and bold leaders like Richard the Lion-hearted of England divided and conquered kingdoms. Later on, Italy and the Netherlands were the birthplaces of a new economic system, founded by such families as the Medici.

The foundations of modern languages, literature, and philosophy were laid during the Middle Ages. Thomas Aquinas wrote the *Summa Theologica;* Dante, *The Divine Comedy;* and Chaucer, *The Canterbury Tales.* Indeed, the Middle Ages were more than transitional; some of the achievements of that day, like the cathedral of Chartres, have never been surpassed in magnitude and beauty.

It is difficult to trace with any certainty the fate of theatrical activities between the fall of Rome and the dominance achieved by the Roman Catholic Church by the tenth century. Although theatrical events were suppressed by the Church, many contemporary documents record the continuing presence of actors, mimes, and *jongleurs.* Moreover, pagan rites and festivities containing theatrical elements like music, dancing, and masks persisted despite the Church's opposition. Spring fertility rites were performed throughout Europe. Some historians have argued that the Church introduced its own dramatic ceremonies in order to combat the appeal of pagan rites.

Despite a variety of underground theatrical activities, Western theatre after the fall of Rome did not develop extensively until the Church began to make use of dramatic scenes in its own services. Beginning in the tenth century, these church-sponsored events were the first step in restoring the theatre to a respected place in society.

RELIGIOUS AND CIVIC PURPOSES

The Church began to use dramatized episodes in its services probably to make moral lessons more graphic and therefore more easily understood. Since most people could not understand Latin (the official language of the Church liturgy until very recently), spectacle had long been an important means of portraying Church doctrine. The theatrical interludes merely elaborated upon this tradition. Moreover, the Church calendar, organized around the principal events of the Old and New Testaments—Advent, Christmas, Lent, Easter, Pentecost, and Corpus Christi—provided occasions for the development of theatrical events.

Easter was the first event to be given dramatic treatment in Church services. The oldest existing Easter trope is the *Quem Quaeritis* trope (c. 925). It was probably sung by two groups —angels and three Marys:

Angels Whom seek ye in the tomb, O
  Christians?

The Three Marys Jesus of Nazareth, the
  crucified, O heavenly Beings.

Angels He is not here, he is risen as he foretold.
  Go and announce that he is risen from the
  tomb . . .

This trope, found in the introductory part of the Easter Mass, was the first step toward the creation of a new drama. The facts of this Easter story, as sung, are simple. Three women are

// While political power centralized during the 12th and 13th centuries, the energies of Europe were gathering in one of civilization's great bursts of development. Stimulated by commerce, a surge took place in art, technology, building, learning, exploration by land and sea, universities, cities, banking and credit, and every sphere that enriched life and widened horizons. Those 200 years were the High Middle Ages, a period that brought into use the compass and mechanical clock, the spinning wheel and treadle loom, the windmill and watermill; a period when Marco Polo traveled to China and Thomas Aquinas set himself to organize knowledge, when universities were established at Paris, Bologna, Padua, and Naples, Oxford and Cambridge, Salamanca and Valladolid, Montpellier and Toulouse; when Giotto painted human feeling, Roger Bacon delved into experimental science, Dante framed his great design of human fate and wrote it in the vernacular; a period when religion was expressed both in the gentle preaching of St. Francis and in the cruelty of the Inquisition, when the Albigensian Crusade in the name of faith drenched southern France in blood and massacre while the soaring cathedrals rose arch upon arch, triumphs of creativity, technology, and faith.//

Barbara W. Tuchman, *A Distant Mirror:
The Calamitous Fourteenth Century* (1978)[1]

looking for a tomb, intending to dress the corpse of Jesus. They meet an angel who tells them that the corpse has risen from the tomb. The emotions that accompany the situation are also simple. The women are overcome with grief as they approach the tomb. The angels' news changes their grief to joy; the choir sings the *Te Deum* and bells ring out the glad news.

This early playlet, complete with directions for its performance, is found in the *Regularis Concordia* (or *Monastic Agreement*) compiled by Ethelwold, Bishop of Winchester (in England) between 965 and 975. By the end of the tenth century, such plays were common in many parts of Europe.

For about two hundred years drama remained inside the church walls; then about 1200 religious plays began to be performed out of doors. This practice spread throughout Europe, as far east and north as Russia and Scandinavia and as far south as Italy and Spain. While the plays differed in length and complexity, they dealt largely with materials connected with Easter, Christmas, Epiphany, and Corpus Christi.

MANAGEMENT: FESTIVAL THEATRE

In the long and complicated history of medieval theatre, many reasons have been given for why performances were moved outside the Church. Some historians argue that the plays outgrew the restricted confines of church services. Others say that secular elements made the plays inappropriate for performing inside the Church. Recently, still others suggest that the series of short religious plays produced back to back (also known as cycles or pageant plays) developed quite independently of liturgical drama and that similarity between them is due to their common sources—the Bible and other religious literature.

Corpus Christi

Corpus Christi celebrated with Communion bread and wine the doctrine of transubstantiation of God as human in Christ. The Feast Day of Corpus Christi was begun in 1264 on the first Thursday following Trinity Sunday (between May 23 and June 24). It celebrated our salvation through God's decision to become human and to pay the price, through Christ's crucifixion, of redeeming us from original sin. The cycle plays centered on the Eucharist and dealt with a universal pattern: humanity's Fall, Redemption, and Judgment—in that order.

Whatever the reasons, significant changes had occurred in religious drama by 1400. Outdoor theatrical events made up of short religious plays put together to make a longer play were now staged, primarily during the spring and summer months when weather was favorable. The most usual times were at Easter and Corpus Christi. Other important changes included the substitution of everyday language for Latin, which led to spoken rather than chanted dialogue, and the use of laymen instead of clergy as actors and producers.

While the clergy participated less and less in the production process, the Church's approval was still necessary. Festival productions continued to be a cooperative effort between Church, town officials, and trade or religious guilds. The Church supplied approval and encouragement; secular groups provided money and personnel.

Under this arrangement the medieval theatre flourished. From about 1350 to 1500 it steadily grew in complexity and technical proficiency.

With the passing of drama into marketplaces and town squares, laymen took over most aspects of productions. In some areas trade guilds became the principal producers; in others municipal authorities assumed control; in still others special societies were formed to serve as charities and to present religious dramas. Of these, the Confrérie de la Passion in Paris was the most famous.

Certain common production practices can be traced in England, France, Italy, and Spain. Although records are slim, we can piece together the festival events, personnel, and costs through diaries and wills, guild and parish records, prompt books and actors' parts copied by scribes. Visual evidence of contemporary dress and tableaux survive in paintings, stained glass, frescoes, and statuary.

Throughout Europe, as clergy reduced its participation in the festivals, town halls and guilds financed and produced the festivals while the Church continued to authorize scripts. Laymen provided most of the money and materials for the stage, scaffolds, wagons, scenic devices, costumes, machinery, and special effects. Moreover, they contracted with artists and provided food and lodging for actors and spectators. Producers and stage managers (called "pageant masters" in England) were appointed to oversee financing and rehearsals. They, in turn, solicited the cooperation of choirs, artisans, nobles, and laborers. The choirs sang and played the parts of women and boys; nobles loaned costumes, donated properties and money; priests and scribes copied actors' parts and kept accounts; laborers prepared meals, built wagons, scaffolds, and bleachers. In short, entire communities were involved in producing these festivals, which could consume days. In Chester (England), for instance, the Corpus Christi festival stretched over three full days, in London a week, and in Valenciennes 25 days in 1547.[2]

PLAYWRITING

The playwright in medieval times, whether one or more persons, was anonymous. At the start the clergy wrote the four-line playlet in Latin and inserted it into the Easter services. In time, the short dialogue was expanded as they added related episodes to the simple plot along with gestures, costumes, and properties.

As the playlets grew more elaborate and were performed outdoors and in everyday language, the playwright or playwrights were recruited not only from the clergy but also from within the trade guilds. They exhibited varying degrees of talent, but the fact that individuals were assigned playwriting tasks opened the way for the professional playwright. From the anonymous "York realist" of the York pageant to William Shakespeare of the Globe Theatre is a span of little more than 200 years.

ACTING AND REHEARSALS

Rehearsals for the cycle plays took place over weeks and even months. It was usual for rehearsals to be held in the early morning between dawn and the start of the workday. The guilds paid for breakfast during the rehearsal period and gave banquets for actors, technicians,

---

The Formation and Function of Trade Guilds

"Guilds originated during the eleventh and twelfth centuries as protective organizations against local feudal lords and for merchants when traveling. By the thirteenth century, many craftsmen—bakers, brewers, goldsmiths, tailors, and so on—had formed similar organizations to regulate working conditions, wages, the quality of products, and other matters affecting their well-being. These guilds were organized hierarchically. Each was governed by a council of masters (those who owned their own shops and supervised the work of others); under each master were a number of journeymen (those skilled in the trade but who worked for wages); and below the journeymen were apprentices (young men and boys who received room and board while learning a trade, usually over a period of seven years)."

Oscar G. Brockett, *History of the Theatre,*
Third Edition (1977)[3]

---

and important guests on evenings following performances.

Rehearsals were held in large rooms and halls. The play manager levied fines for being late or absent, for not knowing one's lines, or for drunkenness. Actors frequently signed contracts stipulating fines for misconduct.

Since the cycles were divided into separate playlets, they could be rehearsed individually. With one or two dress rehearsals, the pageant master could coordinate the parts into a single performance.

Some actors in France, Germany, and England received fees for performing. At first individuals were either reimbursed for wages lost or for out-of-pocket expenses. In the late fifteenth century, some "professional" actors were recruited for major parts and paid modest fees. Records show that one actor in the town of

Figure 4-1 Isabella and her court, a detail from *The Triumph of Isabella,* Brussels, 1615. This pageant wagon has only a conjectural relationship to the English pageant wagons; the English vehicles may not have looked like this. It is one of 10 depicted in the painting by Denis Van Alsloot, now in the Victoria and Albert Museum.

Coventry was paid three shillings, four pence (about 30 cents) for playing the part of "God."

It is widely believed that women never performed in medieval plays. As a rule they did not, but there were exceptions. The wives of the town were allotted roles in the "Assumption of the Virgin" in the Chester play. In France the role of St. Catherine was played by a woman at Metz in 1468. British historian Glynne Wickham offers two reasons why women did not generally perform. First, an exclusive male hierarchy was responsible for the festivals; that is, clergy, craftsmen, and merchants. Second, choir boys, who had trained voices, could better project and speak than women and were therefore used for female roles.[4]

VISUAL ELEMENTS

Staging The outdoor festival plays were performed on fixed or movable stages (see page 96). The fixed stages were usually set against buildings on one side of a town square. Some extended down the middle of a square (and could be seen from three sides); others might be set up on an ancient Roman amphitheatre or another circular place (and could be viewed in the round). The movable stage was usually a wagon carrying background scenery (called *mansions*); they moved in procession from one location to another. The movable stage was popular in England and Spain, but both types could be found throughout Europe (Figure 4-1).

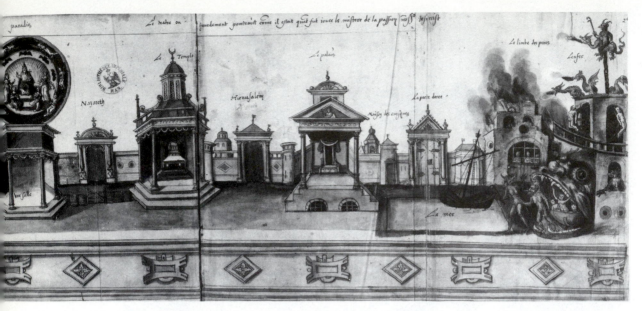

Figure 4-2 The fixed stage used for the Valenciennes (France) Passion Play in 1547. The mansions or huts represent specific locations: Paradise, Nazareth, the temple, Jerusalem, the palace, the golden door, the sea, and Hell's Mouth.

The basic approach to production was much the same everywhere. The scenic conventions were those inherited from the Church—a series of mansions or decorative huts abutting onto a generalized acting area (the *platea*). Every production involved three planes of being—Heaven, Earth, and Hell—all represented scenically. The typical platform stage set up the mansions horizontally with Heaven on the right (as one faced the audience) and Hell on the left. The earthly scenes were staged between these two points. On the wagons Heaven, Earth, and Hell were often arranged vertically, although a single wagon seldom depicted all three levels (Figure 4-2).

Scenery was both fragmentary and symbolic. No place was depicted in its entirety: a small building might represent Jerusalem, a throne under a portico might be the palace of Herod or the dais of Pontius Pilate. Since all places were presented simultaneously, there could be little illusion of a "real" place.

Special Effects Medieval producers gave great attention to special effects (called "secrets"). They welcomed the challenge posed by such episodes as the Flood or Christ's walking on water. They also took special care to depict as vividly as possible Hell and its horrors. The entrance to Hell was often represented as the mouth of a fire-breathing monster (hence the name "Hell's Mouth"), out of which issued fire, smoke, and the cries of the damned.

Stage machinery created special effects. Much of it was operated from beneath the stage, where trapdoors also aided the appearance and disappearance of people and objects. For the scenes that required "flying," pulleys and ropes were attached to adjoining buildings.

As special effects became more and more elaborate, machinists and stage managers became increasingly skilled. For a play staged at Mons (France) in 1501, 2 technicians were hired to construct secrets; 17 people were needed to operate Hell's machinery; 5 men were paid to paint scenery; and 4 actors were employed to act and help with the staging. Thus while most people connected with a production were amateurs, some workers and performers quickly achieved at least semiprofessional status as productions grew in complexity.

Costumes and Properties There were essentially two types of garments worn in medieval theatre: ecclesiastical robes and everyday clothing. God, angels, and saints wore church garments often with such added accessories as wings for angels. Emblems and properties identified certain characters. Justice was recognized by her sword and scales, Judas by his red hair, St. Peter by his keys, St. Catherine by a torture wheel, Prudence by her mirror, and Envy by her snake.

Figure 4-3 Medieval woodcut of a Devil carrying away a child under the eyes of the parents, who had made a pact with the Devil. Note the clothing worn by the parents and child and the grotesque costume of the Devil.

Dress in the Late Middle Ages

"No epoch ever witnessed such extravagance of fashion as that extending from 1350 to 1480. . . . All the forms and dimensions of dress are ridiculously exaggerated. The female headdress assumes the conical shape of the "hennin," a form evolved from the little coif, keeping the hair under the kerchief. High and bombed foreheads are in fashion, with the temples shaved. Low-necked dresses make their appearance. The male dress had features still more bizarre—the immoderate length of the points of the shoes, called "poulaines," which the knights at Nicopolis had to cut off, to enable them to flee; the laced waists; the balloon-shaped sleeves standing up at the shoulders; the too long "houppelandes" and the too short doublets; the cylindrical or pointed bonnets; the hoods draped about the head in the form of a cock's comb or a flaming fire. A state costume was ornamented by hundreds of precious stones."

Johan Huizinga, *The Waning
of the Middle Ages* (1949)[5]

Heaven's representatives were dressed to inspire awe and reverence, those of Hell were expected to arouse fear and scorn, and the common humanity that dwelt in between wore clothing appropriate to their social rank, although there was no attempt to make costumes historically accurate. Just as the greatest scenic effects went into Hell's Mouth, so the greatest imagination went into costuming the Devil, who is depicted in woodcarvings with wings, claws, beak, horns, and tail (Figure 4-3).

Music Music in medieval times was pervasive in religious ceremonies, theatre, and public entertainments of all sorts. Heavenly scenes frequently featured choruses of angels; trumpet fanfares announced God's presence and proclamations. Both vocal and instrumental music bridged the intermissions between scenes and was played for the spectators' amusement in the evenings after the performances. While songs were sung by choirboys and actors, instrumental music was played by professional musicians.

PROCESSIONAL STAGING IN SPAIN

The medieval theatre in Spain began early and finished late—by 1700. The Spanish theatre had origins similar to those of Northern Europe and England. However, religious drama in Spain maintained its close ties with the Roman Catholic Church much longer, and the Church maintained firm control over the theatre's content. During the last half of the seventeenth century, plays came to be closely associated with the festival that emphasized the power of the Church's sacraments—Corpus Christi—and with the name of one of Spain's finest playwrights, Pedro Calderón de la Barca (1600–1681).

Producing the *Autos* Medieval religious plays in Spain, similar to the cycle plays in England, were called *autos sacramentales*. They combined characteristics of both cycle and morality plays. The morality play has been said to represent the conscience, learning, and moralizing of the Middle Ages. Morality plays were developed around themes of the conflict of virtue and vice for a person's soul. Rooted in the folkways of the time, they combined elements of religious belief with farcical horseplay and moral sentiments.

Producing *autos* closely resembled practices in medieval England. Until 1550 trade guilds in Spain were responsible for staging plays. Thereafter city councils assumed control and professional companies and playwrights were employed to produce the plays, forging a close connection between public and religious theatrical events. They presented from two to four *autos*—either old or new plays—each year in various towns. Between 1647 and 1681 the *autos* in Madrid were all new plays written by Calderón. Sometimes a single company performed the plays; at other times they were performed by two companies. The companies were chosen during Lent, paid sizable fees, and authorized to give public performances and to tour the *autos* to neighboring towns. The town sponsoring the performances provided everything needed with the exception of costumes and hand properties.

The *Auto* Stage The *autos* were mounted on two wagons, called *carros*. Later, beginning in the 1640s, four wagons were used. These wagons had two stories and were made of wooden frames covered with painted canvas. The façade of the upper story was often hinged so it could be swung open and a scene played within. Many wagons also contained machinery for making actors and objects fly.

Several wagons, pulled by oxen, made up the staging unit. Before 1647 a third wagon accompanied the *carros* and functioned as an acting area. Later, staging grew more elaborate as more wagons were drawn up around the stage. By 1692 eight wagons were arranged around the platform throughout the production, a compromise combining the best features of movable staging with the conveniences of the fixed platform stage. The dimensions of the wagons were about 16 feet long by 36 feet tall, and fixed platforms for the acting area were about 45 to 50 feet long by 36 feet deep.

Performing the *Autos* The Corpus Christi festival usually extended over several days. Wagons paraded through the streets, stopping to give performances before the king in a palace courtyard, before powerful government groups and town councils, and before the general public in a town square or marketplace. In some towns the first official performance was given just outside the Church.

The processions carried the Host through the streets and paraded large carnival figures of giants and dragons; later, music, dancing, and farcical interludes added to the carnival spirit. Processional staging was abandoned in 1705; thereafter the *autos* were performed only in the public theatres, or *corrales*—so-called because they were originally adapted from existing courtyards (Figure 4-4). The *autos* became increasingly secular in spirit, and in 1765 they were finally forbidden for reasons of objectionable content and the questionable morality of the performers.

In contrast to theatrical developments in England and France, the *autos* along with pro-

Figure 4-4 A reconstruction of an eighteenth-century Spanish *corrale.*

cessional staging remained a significant part of the professional theatre in Spain for at least 200 years.

POPULAR ENTERTAINMENTS

Much of life in the Middle Ages may have been austere, but it was nonetheless colored by seasonal folk customs and entertainments, including sword dances, May games, mummings, pageants, and tournaments.

Mummings Mumming is the name given in England to masquerades connected with Shrovetide and New Year's Day. The relation of mumming to drama lay in disguise, processions, and the need for a spokesperson to explain the mummers' visitation to someone's house and to introduce the masked visitors. In time this cus-

tom was ornamented with music, song, dance, scenery, and simple texts (in the sixteenth century they were called *masques*). In rural districts mumming survived as folk dances, athletic trials of strength, and other games.

The mummers' play that comes down to us dates from the eighteenth century (there are no surviving medieval or Renaissance texts). It follows the procession of masqueraders to a predetermined house and ends with the collection of money, usually to pay for refreshments and to go to local charities. The traditions of masquing were to be fully developed on the Elizabethan stage and at the English court under James I.

Pageants and Royal Entries While the merchant class collaborated with the Church in organizing and financing cycles, saint plays, and moralities, they also supported civic pageants

A Cornish circular amphitheatre (fixed stage). A typical permanent open-air theatre in Cornwall (also called a round) was made of earth with circular turf benches surrounding a level area 130 feet in diameter. Openings on two sides of the earthen mound provided entrances and exits. This diagram (of the fourteenth-century theatre at Perranzabulo) shows the staging for a biblical cycle called *The Resurrection of Our Lord Jesus Christ.* There are eight scaffolds located in the round's center. Action requiring a specific locale took place on the scaffolds, progressing from one scaffold to another around the circle. The audience, seated on the earthen tiers of seats, could follow the scenes with ease.

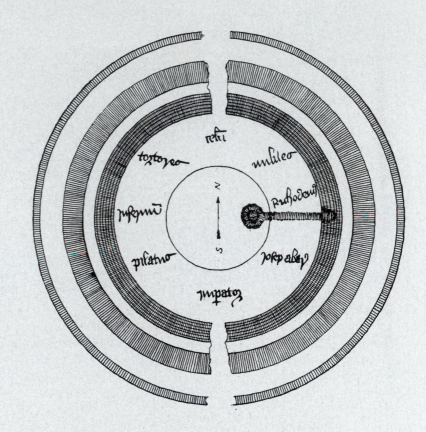

The English pageant wagon or processional stage. Glynne Wickham's drawing is a reconstruction of an English pageant wagon and ground plan of the overall playing arrangement. The drawing shows the essential features of what was to be the Elizabethan playhouse: a platform acting area, a tiring house with a recessed area (the *loca*) for interior scenes and costume changes, and an area above the cart for machinery.

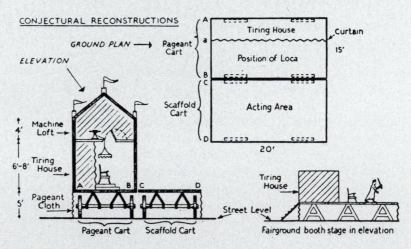

A Mardi Gras parade float (modern processional stage). This colorful float entitled "You Are My Mardi Gras Valentine," appeared around 1937 in a Mardi Gras parade in New Orleans. The platform base of the float rests on a cart drawn by horses or mules. The masked riders, called the "Krew," throw inexpensive trinkets, usually beads and doubloons, to crowds waiting along the parade route. The flambeaux carriers (bottom center) light the way for the floats.

> **"**The form of the Mummers' Play is familiar enough. A Presenter—usually Father Christmas, Headman or Fool, but occasionally a Devil or an old woman—calls out a Champion, having first cleared a space for the action. This Champion's name is frequently St. George or Prince George. He is followed by an antagonist—sometimes the Turkish Knight, sometimes the King of Morocco, sometimes Slasher. They fight and the Champion kills his boastful antagonist. A doctor is called for who effects the corpse's resurrection. Characters equipped with musical instruments and collection-boxes then appear to take money off the spectators while a dance is performed. The central combat can be extended and supplemented by subsidiary characters; and the dispute that leads up to the combat can be related to rival claims to a woman, frequently the King of Egypt's Daughter. The form is thus constant in essentials, and there is no reason to doubt that the mimetic ritual is of itself of great antiquity.**"**
>
> from Glynne Wickham,
> *The Medieval Theatre* (1974)[6]

and visits of royal dignitaries. The installation of a new mayor, for example, was an occasion for a procession through the town. Clerks and children addressed songs and speeches to the chief dignitaries riding in the procession from platform stages erected along the route, and dignitaries were expected to respond.

Street pageants provided a colorful, secular entertainment. By Queen Elizabeth's time her visits with her court to towns and manor houses were called a "progress"; these pageants were looked upon as displays of civic pride as the town and its inhabitants welcomed their ruler.

THE AUDIENCE

Spectators for medieval plays and pageants flocked in from the surrounding towns and countryside—a mix of nobility, merchants, craftsmen, women, and children. In most places

Quem Quaeritis trope—choral dialogue introduced in Church service c. 925

St. Thomas Aquinas 1266–1273 *Summa Theologica*

Dante 1265–1321 *The Divine Comedy*

plays were given every year. Performances were scheduled, posters put up on city gates, and invitations sent to neighboring towns and villages. On the day of performance heralds rode through the city sounding a trumpet and announcing the day's events. Since work was often forbidden during the hours of performance, everyone was available to take part in the festivities.

It is likely that spectators were admitted free to the English cycles, but in Europe, where scaffolding was used for seating along with a series of boxes mounted on bleachers, fees were probably charged. Also, the owners of adjacent houses may have rented space in their rooms and on rooftops for viewing. While entrance fees were not charged for many civic-sponsored productions, there are records of sponsoring organizations at Valenciennes and Rheims (in France) charging fees and dividing profits.

DRAMATIC CONVENTIONS

PLAYWRITING

What we have of medieval drama is those religious plays found in monasteries or in municipal archives of the towns that sponsored them.

1300	1400	1500	1600	1700

—————————— Medieval theatre flourishes ——————————
1200–1600

Chaucer (c. 1345–1400) writes
The Canterbury Tales

—————————— Commedia dell'arte ——————————
troupes tour Europe
1550–1750

Lope de
Vega
1562–1635

Lope de Rueda
c. 1510–1565

Valenciennes Passion Play
1547

Marlowe
1564–1593

Shakespeare
1564–1616

Ben Jonson
1572–1637

Their authors' names are forgotten, if indeed single authors were ever known. The author of the York cycle is known simply as "the York Realist" for the details of medieval life captured in the many episodes.

Although ill-preserved or, in many instances, lost, enough samples of cycles, moralities, and farces are preserved to demonstrate that the medieval theatre was international and populist. Medieval drama is not great literature, but it does offer us a varied and rich experience of theatre rooted in a living society and in a world more spiritually and culturally unified than any the West has known since. Its theatrical forms created a continuous tradition of performing and writing for a broad audience. They also prepared the way for the leap into that great period of dramatic writing—the Elizabethan Age.

CYCLE PLAYS

The religious drama of the English cycles and the continental Passion plays (especially in France and Spain) was the major achievement of the medieval theatre. The English cycles, written in Middle English, comprised a history of the world from the Creation to the Last Judgment performed as individual scenes following one after another in a chronological sequence. Taken over from the clergy but with their approval, the plays were assigned to various craft or trade guilds partly on the basis of the expertise of the guildsmen. The shipbuilders were responsible for the episode on Noah's ark, the bakers for "The Last Supper," and so on.

Written in doggerel verse, the cycles were made up of episodes based on the Old and New Testaments. They played on the religious piety of simple folk, as well as on their love for spectacle and entertainment. There was frequent interplay between stage and audience, prompted especially by the Devil who was booed and hissed vigorously. Animals needed for the performances were led or ridden through the crowds up to the wagons or fixed stages. The three wise men bearing gifts to the baby Jesus probably rode their horses through the streets

The York Cycle

The complete collection of 48 playlets, which was kept in a "register" by the York corporation, shows a great diversity of writing styles. The York plays and the guilds that presented them are as follows:

1. The Creation and the Fall of Lucifer—Barkers
2. From the Creation to the Fifth Day—Plasterers
3. God Creates Adam and Eve—Cardmakers
4. Adam and Eve in the Garden of Eden—Fullers
5. Man's Disobedience and Fall—Coopers
6. Adam and Eve Driven from Eden—Armorers
7. Sacrifice of Cain and Abel—Glovers
8. Building of the Ark—Shipwrights
9. Noah and the Flood—Fishers and Mariners
10. Abraham's Sacrifice—Parchmenters and Bookbinders
11. The Israelites in Egypt; the Ten Plagues; and Passage of the Red Sea—Hosiers
12. Annunciation and Visitation—Spicers
13. Joseph's Trouble about Mary—Pewterers and Founders
14. Journey to Bethlehem; Birth of Jesus—Tile-thatchers
15. Shepherds—Candlemakers
16. Coming of the Three Kings to Herod—Masons
17. Coming of the Three Kings; the Adoration—Goldsmiths
18. Flight into Egypt—Horse Grooms
19. Massacre of the Innocents—Girdlers and Nailers
20. Christ with the Doctors in the Temple—Spurmakers and Bitmakers
21. Baptism of Jesus—Barbers
22. Temptation of Jesus—Blacksmiths
23. The Transfiguration—Curriers
24. Woman Taken in Adultery; Raising of Lazarus—Capmakers
25. Christ's Entry into Jerusalem—Skinners
26. Conspiracy to Take Jesus—Cutlers
27. The Last Supper—Bakers
28. The Agony and Betrayal—Cordwainers
29. Peter Denies Jesus; Jesus Examined by Caiaphas—Bow and Arrow Makers
30. Dream of Pilate's Wife; Jesus before Pilate—Makers of tapestry and carpets
31. Trial before Herod—Dyers
32. Second Accusation before Pilate; Remorse of Judas; Purchase of Field of Blood—Cooks and Water Leaders
33. Second Trial before Pilate; Judgment on Jesus—Tilemakers
34. Christ Led Up to Calvary—Shearmen
35. The Crucifixion—Pinners and Painters
36. Mortification of Christ; Burial—Butchers
37. The Harrowing of Hell—Saddlers
38. The Resurrection—Carpenters
39. Christ's Appearance to Mary Magdalen—Winedrawers
40. Travelers to Emmaus—Sledmen
41. Purification of Mary; Simeon and Anna Prophesy—Hatmakers, Masons, and Laborers
42. Incredulity of Thomas—Scriveners
43. Ascension—Tailors
44. Descent of the Holy Spirit—Potters
45. The Death of Mary—Drapers
46. Appearance of Our Lady to Thomas—Weavers
47. Assumption and Coronation of the Virgin—Stablemen
48. Judgment Day—Mercers (dealers in cloth)

and right up to the wagon to present their gifts before the nativity scene. The cycles alternated high moral sentiments with low comic horse-play, the latter apparently associated with the cavorting and shouts of pain and woe emanating from Hell's Mouth.

SAINT OR MIRACLE PLAYS

Performed on days celebrating a town or guild's patron saint, these plays were devoted to repre-senting the life of a saint along with his or her martyrdom and miracles. Saint plays were common throughout Europe by the late four-teenth century. By 1402 the French king granted a monopoly to the Confrérie de la Passion in Paris for performing them, and their audiences, like those elsewhere, witnessed graphic scenes of torture, maiming, and miracle cures (see Figure 4-5).

While the Protestant Reformation in Eng-land in the mid-sixteenth century dampened enthusiasm for these plays, they continued to be highly popular in France, Italy, and Spain. Their main importance to us is that they opened the way for plays centered around the deeds, ideals, defeats, and victories of a secular hero.

FARCES

In Europe secular farces developed alongside religious plays from a variety of sources in mimes, stories, songs, and pagan rituals. The sur-viving texts of plays written after 1400 draw upon human imperfections like quarreling, cheating, and marital infidelity in their plots; the hero is usually the clever person who takes ad-vantage of the stupid and gullible. Extant farces from France and Germany are short, written in doggerel, with few characters and uncompli-cated action. In *Pierre Pathelin* (c. 1470), a pop-ular French farce, lawyer Pathelin tricks a mer-chant out of a piece of cloth; in turn, a wily peasant defended by Pathelin for stealing sheep gets away without paying the lawyer's fee. *The Second Shepherds Play* from the Wakefield cycle also deals with a stolen sheep. A clever peasant

HROTSVITHA

Hrotsvitha (c. 935–1001), a tenth-century nun of the monastery of Gandersheim, an important cultural center in northern Saxony, wrote six didactic plays to serve the Christian cause with examples of piety, chastity, and martyrdom. This evi-dently well-educated Benedictine nun, probably a "canoness," took the Roman playwright Terence as her model and created plays with well-developed char-acters, dramatic conflict, humor, and emotional interest.

Hrotsvitha wrote at a time when the new Christian drama was starting in the Easter and Christmas tropes. Her work reflects three streams of dramatic and theatrical development: the classical in-fluence, the vogue of mimes or *jongleurs* who provided popular entertainment, and the evolving liturgical drama in Latin.[7]

A link between classical and medieval drama, Hrotsvitha developed Christian themes and sentiments along with humor and theatricality. In *Dulcitius* the comic villain mistakenly kisses kitchen pots and frying pans in his effort to seduce young women, and the heroine is killed by a soldier's arrow but not until she speaks of the rewards of Heaven and the horrors of damnation.

steals a sheep from trusting shepherds; he is found out but all is forgiven within the context of the Nativity scene peopled with angels and wise men bearing gifts to the infant Jesus.

In Germany farce grew out of folk festivals preceding the Lenten season. (They are often called Shrovetide plays.) Most of the surviv-ing texts are associated with Hans Sachs (1494–1576), a shoemaker in Nuremberg who was

Figure 4-5 The miniature by Jean Fouquet is thought to show a torture scene from a play about St. Apollonia (c. 1460). Based on this assumption, the small painting depicts at least six separate locations (*loca*) as background to the stage action. It places Heaven (or Paradise) on the actor's right and Hell on the actor's left. Devils with masks, wings, and clubs can be seen. The central *loca* appears to be a throne room. The figure in ecclesiastical robes with book in one hand and baton in the other (see stage left) is taken to be a pageant master on stage during the actual performance. Called an "Ordinary," he functioned like a prompter in modern opera who cues the singers by repeating the entire text loudly enough to be audible to them but not to the audience.

master singer in a music guild as well as a member of a trade guild. One of Sachs' best plays is *The Wandering Scholar and Exorcist* in which a student outwits a clever lawyer and an adulterous couple.

Medieval farces were probably staged like the religious plays on temporary platforms, called "booth" stages, thrown up by traveling players. The farces rarely require more than one mansion. They need few actors and no complicated special effects. In their economy of staging, simple plots, and recognizable characters, they represent the best of popular humor in Europe predating the *commedia dell'arte* of Italy.

In France two kinds of farces became popular: the *sotties* and *sermons joyeux*. Both were associated with the staging of a "festival of fools" by students and lawyers. While the Church attempted to suppress the Feast of Fools, the sa-

tirical farces survived. The *sottie* was a thinly disguised satire on religion, politics, and society. All characters wore the fool's multicolored garments, including a hood with ass's ears and a cock's comb. The *sermon joyeuse* was a less elaborate burlesque of religious sermons.

MORALITY PLAYS

In a sense, morality plays represented the conscience of the Middle Ages. Important stepping stones between the medieval cycles and Elizabethan drama, they were especially popular in England from about the middle of the fourteenth century to the middle of the sixteenth.

The morality play brought moral sentiments and religious beliefs to life by combining the allegorical tendencies of medieval painting, sculpture, and poetry with the farcical horseplay of the cycles. It usually traced a person's life from birth to death. Three themes were dominant: (1) a conflict of the Virtues and the Vices for the human being's soul—called *psychomachia;* (2) a coming of Death, or "summoning" of someone to his final hours, and the Judgment to follow; (3) a debate of Mercy and Peace against Truth and Justice for the soul of the deceased. In the allegorical tradition of Dante's *Divine Comedy,* Virtues, Vices, Death, and so on, were acted out.

The most popular personification was the Vice figure, a mischief-making devil whose pranks enlivened the plays. He remained a popular stage figure in Elizabethan times in the guise of the clown and the prankster. Christopher Marlowe (1564–1593) introduced the medieval Vice figure full blown on the Elizabethan stage in the character Mephistopheles in *Dr. Faustus* (c. 1588).

The masterpiece of the English morality plays, *Everyman* (c. 1500), consisted of the summoning of the central figure (called Everyman) by Death and Everyman's appeal to relatives, good deeds, and moral qualities to justify how he has lived his life.

Morality plays were relatively short, none of them taking more than an hour to perform; they had small casts and could easily be acted indoors in a hall or on a simple booth stage in the open air. They were convenient for small companies performing in almost any situation: in schoolrooms, banquet halls, and fairgrounds.

REPRESENTATIVE PLAY

The Crucifixion Play
Performed at Wakefield, England, beginning around 1375

BACKGROUND

There are four existing cycles, or Corpus Christi plays, named for the towns in England in which they were first performed: York, Chester, Wakefield, and Coventry. The Wakefield cycle is also known by the name of the Towneley family that possessed the manuscript.

The Crucifixion play found in all cycles is based on Biblical scenes of Christ's torture at the hands of soldiers followed by his death on the cross. In the Wakefield play the various characters are Pilate, Jesus, four torturers, Mary (Christ's mother), the blind beggar Longeus, and three followers—John, Joseph of Airmathea, and Nicodemus.

THE SCENE

Let us imagine a pageant wagon decorated with Pilate's throne drawn up to a neutral platform in the town square. The throne as scenic background reminds the spectators of Pilate's villainy and the source of Christ's suffering. Once Jesus is raised on the cross by his torturers, he dominates the playing space. He becomes the central focus of all further action, including his torture and death.

ACTION AND CHARACTERIZATION

The play begins with Pilate's prologue in which he savagely threatens anyone who gets in his way. He is the chief villain of the piece, portrayed as the personification of evil. Pilate is followed on stage by Jesus bearing the cross on his bent shoulders while his plebeian torturers look on. The nameless men then torture Jesus even as they nail him to the cross. This is a scene of immense brutality. They beat him, throwing him down on the cross, stretching his limbs with a rope to make the palms of his hands reach the holes on the cross bored for the nails. With gusto they drive the nails into his hands and feet. Then, calling for and receiving assistance from the spectators, they raise the cross and fling a crown of thorns on the head of Christ. Meanwhile they taunt him with reminders that he has claimed to be God's son.

> If thou be
> God's son, as thou tells,
> Thou canst save thyself—how shouldst thou
> else?

Figure 4-6 The Crucifixion scene from the York Cycle, performed in front of the cathedral in York, England, 1980.

In the Wakefield version the torturers speak of Jesus as a "knight" and of their task as that of serving men horsing a knight before a tournament. As he fits Jesus to the cross, one torturer says, "And get upon your palfrey soon/For you are ready now."

The figure high above on the cross now dominates the scene, and for the first time Jesus speaks. His speech is a lamentation for the ills of the world that have been visited upon the son of God. It ends with the famous words from Biblical literature: "But, Father . . ./Forgive thou them this guilt." The effectiveness of this speech depends upon the fact that Christ's audience includes the torturers and spectators as well.

At the foot of the cross, Mary, Christ's mother, takes up the lament. Her words function as an outlet for the audience's instinctive feelings. Her lamentation for the sufferings of her son is taken up by the disciple John who universalizes the meaning of Christ's Passion for all to hear. While Mary is the distracted mother

before the spectacle of her son's sufferings, John is the loyal follower and believer in his master's omnipotence. Jesus speaks again, affirming God's beneficence to mankind. He groans in thirst and the torturers are quick to give him a "sop of vinegar."

The Wakefield author created a dice-throwing scene for which there is no precise source. The men toss dice for Christ's garments while Jesus cries out to God:

Eli, Eli, lama sabachthanil!
My God, my God! Wherefor and why
Has thou forsaken me?

The Biblical source has the soldiers disposing of the garments by drawing lots for them. But the Wakefield master developed a game of dice with the garments as the prize. This scene probably had a twofold purpose. It evoked within the audience a humorous release of tension while at the same time it stressed the utter

Figure 4-7 Scene from the York Cycle production in York, England, 1980, performed in the square before the cathedral.

damnation of the torturers. The robustness with which the torturers attack their victim and toss dice for his clothing fully expresses their sinfulness and earns them a place in Hell's Mouth (a scene that comes after the Crucifixion play). Also, the scene is clearly a warning to the audience against the folly and the disastrous consequences of gambling.

Christ dies during the game. The men then push the "blind knight" Longeus toward the cross to spear Jesus' side to determine if he still lives. As Longeus does so, a miracle takes place: His blindness is cured.

Joseph of Airmathea, another of Christ's followers, and Nicodemus walk to Pilate's throne set atop the pageant wagon. While they plead for permission to take Jesus' body away, the cross is lowered, facilitating the start of the final scene where they pull the nails from his hands and feet and cradle the body in a living tableau. Before they exit to place the body in the tomb, Nicodemus addresses the audience:

Save you all that now here be
That Lord that died for ye,
    And rose on Paschal [Easter] Morn.

THE CYCLE PLAY'S MODERNISM

Each play, like the Wakefield Crucifixion, functioned as a unit, usually beginning with a prologue and ending with a homiletic address to the audience. Each play was succeeded by the next until the entire journey from Creation to the Last Judgment was shown. The homiletic quality forced the play's message upon the spectators in a tradition that has continued in modern church pageants held during Christmas and Easter. The journeying of characters through life has informed many plays of the modern period, like Ibsen's *Peer Gynt*, Strindberg's *Dream Play*, and Brecht's *Caucasian Chalk Circle*. The idea of play-as-journey continues to intrigue modern playwrights as a way to make a statement about life's twists and turns. Modern poets, such as Robert Frost in "The Road Not Taken," have written eloquently on this theme.

ESSAY

While we tend to think the medieval theatre quaint and simplistic in its sermonizing, the cycles are continuously revived by townships in Great Britain to celebrate civic pride and traditions. The York cycle in northern England is one such revival by a modern township. So impressive was the staging in 1978 that the York production was invited to be performed at London's National Theatre. The environmental production in the small Cottesloe Theatre at the National is the subject of our essay.

Medieval Theatre in Modern Performance
The Passion (a selection from the York mystery plays), performed at The National Theatre, London, 1978

In 1978 the National Theatre of Great Britain produced *The Passion* as a selection in modern dress from the fifteenth-century York cycle. The performance consisted principally of "The Last Supper" and "The Crucifixion."

The Passion was performed in the small Cottesloe Theatre, a boxlike space without fixed seats. Directors Bill Bryden and Sebastian Graham-Jones staged a kind of people's theatre, evoking feelings of a crowded festival day and a busy marketplace. Overhead lighting instruments were encased in ordinary objects like dustbins (with holes punched in them), cheese graters, and road lamps. One wall of the theatre was decorated as for a harvest festival. Common laborers' tools, such as hoes, mallets, brooms, and pitchforks, were lying around for use by actors.

Since these plays were originally devised and acted by artisans and craftsmen, the company was costumed as modern-day laborers. Some were dressed as uniformed transport workers, others as miners with tunics and helmets, and still others as firemen and housewives. Pontius Pilate (played by Dave King) appeared as the put-upon mayor of an industrial town.

Figure 4-8 A scene from *The Passion* produced in the Cottesloe Theatre, 1980. The environmental staging in the small Cottesloe theatre and the eclectic costumes allowed spectators to be part of the play's action, similar to medieval times.

The actors first entered this "marketplace" chatting idly with one another and then breaking into a jig. Gradually, they launched into the play, telling the story of Christ's last week on earth that culminated in his Crucifixion and burial. The action took place all around the performance space. Actors mingled with the audience and even brushed them aside when spectators accidentally crossed or blocked their paths. Christ (played by Mark McManus) had to clear the way before him as he walked with the crucifix through the crowds of spectators.

Actors talked to the audience individually in only slightly modernized English, and the audience was cast into the role of witnesses to and participants in the scourging and crucifying of Christ. At the end of the play and in celebration of Christ's ascension, they were invited to join hands with the company and dance to music played by the Albion Dance Band, which provided folk-based rock music throughout the performance.

SUMMARY

Popular theatre in medieval Europe was a religious theatre whose conventions were based on the Church calendar, liturgy, and ecclesiastical dress, along with innovations made by laymen over a period of many years. Medieval drama was both epic in scope and festive in character, involving whole towns and villages. All in all, the medieval theatre was the largest people's theatre known to Western culture.

Beginning in the tenth century the Church revived theatre long dormant during the so-called Dark Ages by using dramatic scenes during religious services. The *Quem Quaeritis* trope, dating from 925, is the oldest example of dialogue introduced into the Easter Mass. By 1200, religious plays were performed outdoors all over Europe. Between 1350 and 1500 the medieval theatre flourished and developed complex producing organizations (the guilds) and elaborate festivals lasting anywhere from 3 to 25 days. Play managers mounted them on fixed platforms or on movable wagons and used mansions for scenic background and a generalized acting area (the *platea*) for the performers. In England the cycle plays were performed on pageant wagons; in Spain the similar *autos sacramentales* were given on wagons called *carros*. Religious drama dominated the Spanish theatre long after the public theatres in England were producing nonreligious plays for secular audiences.

Medieval drama offered a rich variety of cycle plays, saint or miracle plays, moralities, farces, and interludes. These theatrical forms created a continuous tradition of performing and writing for a broad audience. The Devil, or Vice figure, was always the most popular villain with audiences and Hell's Mouth their favorite piece of scenery.

The Crucifixion Play from the Wakefield Cycle represents the character and form of the English cycle or Corpus Christi plays, as they were also called, and a representative modern performance is the York version of Christ's Passion on the cross as performed at London's National Theatre in 1978.

PLAYS TO READ

Abraham and Isaac

The Second Shepherds Play

Everyman

SOURCES

Allen, John, ed. *Three Medieval Plays*. New York: Theatre Arts Books, 1968. Paperback. This edition, adapted into modern English, contains *The Coventry Nativity Play*, *Everyman*, and *Master Pierre Pathelin*.

Hussey, Maurice, ed. *The Chester Mystery Plays*. London: Heinemann, 1975. Paperback. This edition adapted into modern English contains 16 pageant plays from the Chester craft cycle. The appendix includes hints on production, including suggestions for acting, costumes, and music.

NOTES

1. Barbara W. Tuchman, *A Distant Mirror: The Calamitous Fourteenth Century* (New York: Alfred A. Knopf, 1978), p. 9. Reprinted with permission.

2. For my understanding of medieval production practices, I am indebted to Glynne Wickham, *Early English Stages*, 1300–1600, 2 vols. (New York: Columbia University Press, 1959–1972), and *The Medieval Theatre* (London: George Weidenfeld and Nicholson, 1974).

3. Oscar G. Brockett, *History of the Theatre*, third edition (Boston: Allyn and Bacon, 1977), p. 101. Reprinted by permission.

4. Wickham, *The Medieval Theatre*, pp. 92–93.

5. Johan Huizinga, *The Waning of the Middle Ages* (New York: St. Martin's Press, 1949), pp. 228–229. Reprinted by permission.

6. Wickham, *The Medieval Theatre*, p. 146. Reprinted by permission.

7. John Gassner, *Medieval and Tudor Drama* (New York: Bantam Books, 1963), p. 2.

FIVE

ELIZABETHAN THEATRE

A MODERN PERSPECTIVE

This chapter deals with the traditions of the Elizabethan stage and the individual talent of its greatest playwright, William Shakespeare. A look at Shakespeare's Globe Theatre, his acting company, and his dramaturgy helps us understand certain conventions and problems in the 350-year-old texts. To bridge the gap between Elizabethan practices and today's theatre, we end this chapter with a discussion of the Royal Shakespeare Company's 1976 production of *Macbeth* in England. One critic called it the RSC's finest achievement since their production of *A Midsummer Night's Dream,* directed by Peter Brook in 1970.

In evaluating modern productions of the Bard's plays we need to be sensitive to Elizabethan staging conditions, as well as to the demands these texts make upon directors, actors, and designers. We also need to understand the stage eclecticism that has emerged in the modern theatre with such directors as Tyrone Guthrie, Orson Welles, Peter Brook, and Jonathan Miller. Their productions bombard us visually with unfamiliar analogues to the time, place, dress, and situations of the texts. Shakespeare's plays are thus put into new social contexts.

Peter Brook's *A Midsummer Night's Dream*

After directing critically acclaimed productions in England of Shakespeare's *The Tempest* and *King Lear*, and Peter Weiss's *Marat/Sade*, Peter Brook decided to direct Shakespeare's *A Midsummer Night's Dream* using a concept of the actor as acrobat, circus clown, and trapeze artist speaking Shakespeare's verse. The bare, white setting has the three levels of the Elizabethan stage. First there is the audience level, which the cast contacts at the play's close when the audience responds to Puck's request for personal contact and applause: "Give me your hands, if we be friends/And Robin shall restore amends."

The stage itself is an enclosed white space—a room with doors in the rear wall through which Alan Howard as Theseus and Sara Kestleman as Hippolyta enter; later they reappear as Oberon and Titania, king and queen of the fairies.

For the working out of the premarital dream a third level—equivalent to the Elizabethan stage's balcony—is a catwalk around the top of the white room that is the principal acting area of designer Sally Jacobs's set (Photos © Max Waldman 1970.)

The actors as circus artists cavort on trapezes and stilts about the area that serves as Shakespeare's magic forest.

Above: In Brook's production there are no woodland fairies and fat, jolly Bottom wearing an ass's head. The directorial influences are circus tricks, puppet theatre, and English music hall. Bottom wears a clown's red nose when under the influence of Puck's magic spell. Bright party streamers simulate the magic forest as Titania, also under Puck's spell, makes love to Bottom.

Left: Oberon (Alan Howard) and Puck (John Kane) speak Shakespeare's lines while seated upon trapezes like acrobats.

Above: Sara Kestleman as Titania alone in her ostrich-feather bower.

Right: The quartet of lovers is caught in the steel coils dangled by the fairies from the catwalk around the top of the room. They manipulate the lovers like marionettes.

Above: The "mechanicals" or menial laborers rehearse their parts in the play that they are to perform for the court's entertainment in celebration of the multiple weddings at the play's close. *Below:* The mechanicals performing their amateurish play about Pyramus and Thisbe with Lion "roaring his angry roar" at the audience.

For instance, productions of *Coriolanus* or *Julius Caesar* set in Germany in the late 1930s remind us of recent tyrannies, and a *Measure for Measure* set in the Vienna of Sigmund Freud takes on modern theories of sexual behavior.

Our starting point is *the Globe Theatre*, the most famous public playhouse in Elizabethan London.

cries. Through another door sounds the counter demand: "Nay, answer me: Stand and unfold yourself." Another guard enters carrying a lighted lantern in one hand and a weapon in the other. The bright afternoon turns to darkness in the imaginations of 2000 people as the action begins in Elsinore Castle in faraway Denmark. On stage it is "midnight" and "bitter cold" and a "ghost" lurks in the shadows. The tragedy of *Hamlet* has begun.

REPRESENTATIVE THEATRE: The Globe, London

It is noon in Queen Elizabeth's London in the year 1601. Flags fly atop three of the taller buildings in Bankside across the Thames from the city proper. It is a performance day at the Globe, the Rose, and the Swan. Boats ferry theatregoers across the broad river. Other people are headed, on foot and by carriage, to the Fortune and Curtain theatres of Shoreditch and Golding Lane, located north of London's city limits.

In their Bankside theatre, the Globe players prepare to present a new tragedy by their popular playwright and actor, William Shakespeare. The play is called *Hamlet,* supposedly based on a play by Thomas Kyd. The noisy crowds pay a penny as the price of admission into the theatre; those who pay extra can go upstairs and take a seat on one of the benches in the gallery—the best place to see the play.

A trumpet sounds and some 2000 spectators around the stage and in the galleries turn their attention to the bare, trestled stage backed by the high façade of the tiring house. A guard enters through a side stage door. "Who's there?" he

CONDITIONS OF PERFORMANCE

Performance conditions in London in Shakespeare's time were influenced by producers like the Burbages and Philip Henslowe. They set about creating public theatres that would combine the best features of platform stages and their scenic backgrounds used for religious cycles with the temporary boothlike stages thrown up in halls and inn yards for the secular entertainment that appealed to earls, citizens, students, and apprentices alike. These stages, erected on one side of a courtyard, took advantage of the inn's overhanging galleries to provide seating on a raised level, while many spectators could stand in the yard itself. Many companies played indoors, but the arrangement of stage, players, and spectators was often the same.

BACKGROUND

Under the Tudor kings in the sixteenth century (Henry VIII was Queen Elizabeth's father), the spirit of Renaissance humanism began to be felt in England. Scholars turned to the study of an-

111

1550

Elizabeth I of England rules, 1558–1603

Globe Theatre built, 1599

The Theatre and Blackfriars, first permanent theatres in England, 1576

Curtain Theatre built, 1577

Teatro Olimpico, first permanent theatre in Italy, c. 1587

Spanish Armada defeated by English fleet 1588

cient literature and philosophy, and it was not long before these new interests affected dramatic writing. Schools and universities began to encourage the writing of plays on the Roman model and their performance in both Latin and English. Other types of plays—mostly farce plays called *interludes*—were written in English and performed by schoolboys. *Ralph Roister Doister* (c. 1534–1541) and *Gammer Gurton's Needle* (c. 1552–1563) are the best known surviving farce plays from this period.

Many plays were written and performed at the inns of Court—law schools that admitted young men who were recent graduates of Oxford and Cambridge. These wealthy and aristocratic students, who were abreast of the latest fashions in drama both at home and abroad, wrote plays to be performed on holidays and special occasions. The first English tragedy, *Gorboduc*, was written by two students, Thomas Sackville and Thomas Norton, presented in 1561 at the Inner Temple—one of the Inns of Court—and attended by Queen Elizabeth. *Gor-*

boduc shows a shift away from classical drama to plays based on English history and recent Italian works. Both were to be important sources for professional playwrights in the 1590s and 1600s.

The late 1500s in England were eventful years. Political and religious controversies had raged from the time Henry VIII broke with the Catholic Church in 1534. Following Henry's death his daughter and successor Mary tried to reinstitute Catholicism. The result was civil disruption and suffering. During her reign (1553–1558), more than 300 people were burned at the stake for heresy or sedition. Not for nothing did the people call her "Bloody Mary." After Mary's death, the Protestant Elizabeth began her long successful rule, keeping the country at peace for 30 years. In 1588 the Catholic King Phillip II of Spain sent his fleet against England, but the English defeated the Spanish Armada and established England as a major maritime power.

The 1580s also saw the end of the conflict between Mary Stuart, Queen of Scots (1542–

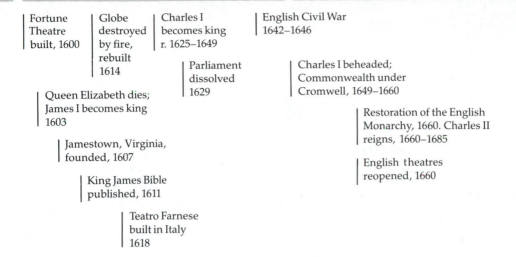

| 1600 | 1650 | 1700 |

Fortune Theatre built, 1600

Globe destroyed by fire, rebuilt 1614

Charles I becomes king r. 1625–1649

English Civil War 1642–1646

Queen Elizabeth dies; James I becomes king 1603

Parliament dissolved 1629

Charles I beheaded; Commonwealth under Cromwell, 1649–1660

Jamestown, Virginia, founded, 1607

Restoration of the English Monarchy, 1660. Charles II reigns, 1660–1685

King James Bible published, 1611

English theatres reopened, 1660

Teatro Farnese built in Italy 1618

1587), and her cousin Elizabeth I. Mary Stuart's exile in England had been the focal point of Catholic intrigue against the English queen. In 1587 Elizabeth agreed to Mary's execution. The twin events of the defeat of the Spanish Armada and the execution of Mary made English Protestantism and the throne secure from outside threats.

These religious and political controversies

The Producers

James Burbage (1530–1597) headed the first important theatre company, the Earl of Leicester's Men, in Elizabethan London around 1574 and was instrumental in building the first permanent theatre ("the Theatre") in London in 1576. Finally losing their lease, the Burbage family built the Globe in 1599 on Bankside where one son, Richard Burbage (c. 1567–1619), became the leading actor of his day. Most of Shakespeare's plays were produced here along with plays by Jonson, Beaumont, and Fletcher. The Burbages also purchased Blackfriars Theatre. Their company was renamed the Lord Chamberlain's Men in 1593, and when James I came to the throne in 1603 was renamed the King's Men, a title they retained until 1642.

Philip Henslowe (d. 1616) and actor Edward Alleyn (1566–1626) were managers of a rival company, the Lord Admiral's Men. Henslowe built the Rose, Fortune, and Hope playhouses in London, and he kept a famous diary—a record of loans made for costumes and scripts—that throws much light on Elizabethan theatre organization. He employed such writers as Thomas Dekker, John Marston, and even Ben Jonson upon occasion.

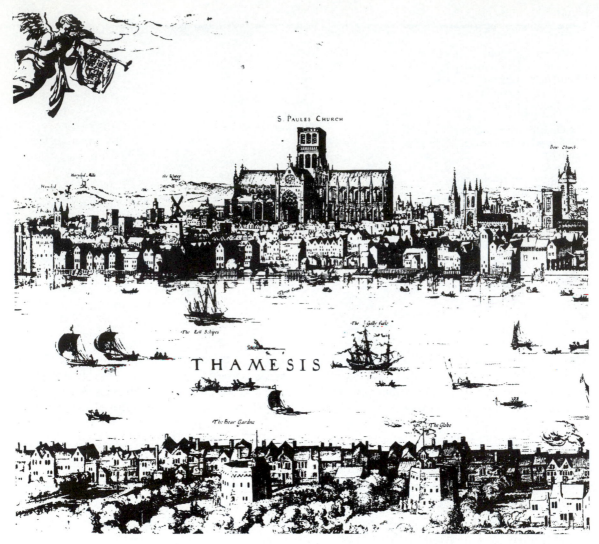

Figure 5-1 A panoramic view of London from the engraving by J. C. Visscher, c. 1616.

and the surge of nationalism that followed affected drama in several ways. Most obviously, they inspired plays conveying a strong sense of a moral force at work in the universe and human affairs. Elizabeth's ban on productions of the religious cycles (generally accepted by 1575) gave impetus to a secular and professional theatre. Producers like the Burbages and Henslowe were waiting in the wings, so to speak, to form professional companies and to build permanent theatres. But only as the school-educated writers—Marlowe, Lyly, Greene, Kyd, Jonson—began to work for professional companies did English drama enter an era of true greatness.

THE PUBLIC PLAYHOUSE

In 1599 Richard and Cuthbert Burbage, sons of James Burbage who built the first playhouse in London, put together a holding company, including Shakespeare and four other actors, and built the Globe, one of the finest theatres of its time. Like most theatres in that day, the Globe was located outside the city limits on the south bank of the Thames River. This location avoided the jurisdiction of the London city council, which sometimes banned performances. Although the Globe is the most famous of all the Elizabethan theatres, there is considerable controversy about its characteristic features. What we know about it comes from theatrical records, contemporary drawings, and from the plays produced there. The Globe was an open-air building with a platform stage in the middle surrounded by an open standing room. This space was surrounded in turn by a large enclosed balcony topped by one or two smaller roofed galleries. The audience stood around the stage or sat in the galleries or private boxes. They paid one price to get in and another price to sit in the galleries or boxes. Like the medieval audience, they were never far removed from the performers.

As an open-air theatre, the Globe was a "public" theatre as opposed to an indoor hall or "private" theatre. An example of a private theatre was Blackfriars, later used by Shakespeare's company as a winter theatre.

The Globe was only one of several theatres in London and the surrounding area. The theatres differed in shape and size. Some were round, some polygonal, and some square. The

---

ELIZABETH I OF ENGLAND

Elizabeth (1533–1603), the daughter of Henry VIII and Anne Boleyn, is generally accounted one of the most successful rulers in history. Her long and productive reign we now call the Elizabethan Age. During the years of her rule, England asserted herself as a major European power in politics, commerce, and the arts.

Elizabeth's childhood was marked by danger and insecurity from the political and religious intrigues that were a legacy of her father, Henry VIII. During the reign of her Roman Catholic sister, Queen Mary, Elizabeth was imprisoned in the Tower of London. Upon Mary's death Elizabeth, a Protestant, ruled for 45 years (1558–1603). Her wide interests—statecraft, finances, religion, scholarship, languages, the arts, exploration—were reflected in her support of these activities. She saw an average of about five professional productions a year at court, for which she paid the companies ten pounds as a standard fee. Royal patronage was to increase greatly under the Stuart kings who succeeded Elizabeth.

Despite the urgings of her advisers and various marriage plans, she never married. Outliving her trusted friends and advisers, Elizabeth was surrounded in her late years by personally ambitious men, including Robert Devereux, Earl of Essex, who was executed for high treason in 1601. On her deathbed she formally named King James VI of Scotland, Protestant son of the executed Mary, Queen of Scots, as her successor.

Globe was eight-sided (Figure 5-2). It featured a large, central unroofed space, called the *pit* or *yard*, surrounded, as already noted, by two or three tiers of roofed galleries forming the building's outside wall. A raised stage (about head high) jutted out into the center of the yard. This was the main acting area. At the back of the stage stood the *tiring house*, which looked like a two- or three- story house front; it had a multileveled façade with at least two doors at stage level. These doors accommodated not only the players but also the necessary stage properties and set pieces. Workrooms and storage areas were located within the stage wall.

While the platform stage was the main acting area, the second level of the façade was also an acting area. Scholars disagree about this second area, as well as about the *discovery space* or enclosed area on the main stage. Some believe a recessed area on the second level, which they call "the inner above," was used to represent high places such as balconies, battlements, and upper-story windows. And down below at the rear of the forestage was an "inner below," or a recessed area in the back wall with a curtain across the front. This discovery space was used for "discovering" people and things, for entrances and exits, for concealment, and for the introduction of large properties onto the stage. Others argue that the discovery space was not recessed at all but was a *pavilion* or "mansion" that jutted onto the stage and had curtains on three sides. (See C. Walter Hodges' reconstruction of the Globe in the Photo Essay.) Some also suggest there was a third level in the façade used as a "musicians' gallery," which could also have been used by actors. A thatched roof was supported by posts at the front of the stage.

In addition to the levels above the stage, the Globe and other theatres of its day had a subterranean level, entered by trapdoors in the stage floor. From here arose the ghosts and witches; here were set the graveyard scenes; and from here issued other special effects.

For playwrights, this multilevel stage allowed scenes to flow from one to the next without interruption. The Elizabethan playhouse was a theatre built by actors for actors.

MANAGEMENT AND REPERTORY SYSTEM

The Elizabethan theatre was one of the first examples of theatre as a commercial enterprise. Theatrical companies such as Shakespeare's Lord Chamberlain's Men (later called the King's Men) and its main rival, the Lord Admiral's Men, intended to make a profit. To receive a performing license from the court-appointed Master of Revels to perform, a troupe had to be under the patronage of a nobleman who would allow it to use his name. The noble patron's money came in handy as well. Although this system limited the number of companies, it nevertheless gave actors a legal status as working citizens; earlier they had been considered vagrants.

Philip Henslowe is the best-known theatrical manager of Elizabethan London, largely because his records have survived. Henslowe's diary, a detailed account of how a theatrical company was run includes records of plays performed, number of performances, and lists of expenses for costumes, properties and actors' wages.

With the appearance of the first permanent playhouses, a repertory system emerged. The

---

London Theatres

At least nine public playhouses were built in London between 1576 and 1642:
The Theatre (1576)
The Curtain (1577)
Newington Butts (c. 1579)
The Rose (1587)
The Swan (c. 1595)
The Globe (1599, rebuilt 1614)
The Fortune (1600, rebuilt 1621)
The Red Bull (1605)
The Hope (1613)

repertory system of rotating plays was complex. In two weeks playgoers could see 11 performances of 10 different plays at one playhouse. This system mandated certain customs: a large number of plays ready for performance at one time, new plays continously added to the repertory, and frequent revivals.

The demands on playwrights for new plays —and on actors' memories—were staggering. Elizabethan actors had to retain the lines of old plays that they might not perform for weeks or months and learn new plays at the same time. Leading actors, like Edward Alleyn and Richard Burbage had to learn about 52 new plays and

retain command of 71 different roles over a three-year period.

Philip Henslowe and James Burbage (and later his actor-son) managed the two most successful companies, the Lord Admiral's Men at the Rose and the Fortune and the Lord Chamberlain's Men at The Theatre and the Globe. Like other public companies they were organized into a partnership of sharers (or stockholders) who managed the company. The sharers purchased plays, bought costumes, hired actors and bookkeepers, paid licensing fees, and attended to the many duties of the company. They also shared profits and expenses. A small core of shareholders usually owned the theatre building and the company rented it from them. Shakespeare was one of seven shareholders who owned the Globe.

PLAYWRITING

The companies acquired new plays in two ways: from free-lancers and from their own actor-playwrights. Upon approval of the outline from the free-lance playwright, they paid the writer advances until the script was completed. Full payment was usually six pounds. Ben Jonson, for example, wrote for several different companies, including Shakespeare's.[1] Shakespeare, however, wrote exclusively for his company.

Among Shakespeare's contemporaries were three professional playwrights whose plays rivaled his: Christopher Marlowe, Ben Jonson, and John Webster. Christopher Marlowe (c. 1564–1593) wrote in a powerful blank verse creating theatrical events that were both exciting and bizarre. Among his plays are *Tamburlaine, Parts 1 and 2* (1587–1588), *Dr. Faustus* (c. 1588), and *Edward II* (c. 1592). Ben Jonson (1572–1637) imposed his prodigious learning upon a comic sensibility. His comedies, based upon classical play structure, included clever servants, gullible tradespeople and country squires, and benign merchants. He is best known for *Every Man in His Humour* (1598), *Volpone* (1606), and *The Alchemist* (1610). John Webster's (c. 1580–c. 1630) reputation as the second finest writer of tragedy of the period rests on two plays: *The White Devil* (1609–1612) and *The Duchess of Malfi* (1613–1614). These plays depict a world of moral and political corruption through characters who act out their unrepressed sexuality and violent impulses.

CHRISTOPHER MARLOWE

Christopher Marlowe (c. 1564–1593) was the son of a Canterbury shoemaker. His early education was at the finest grammar school of his day, the King's School, Canterbury. In 1584 he earned a B.A. degree from Corpus Christi College, Cambridge. While at Cambridge he apparently served the government in some capacity (perhaps as a spy on the queen's Roman Catholic enemies). These activities are thought to be related to his early death.

His splendid career as a playwright spanned 6 years and seven plays. Before leaving the University he wrote *Tamburlaine the Great* (2 parts by 1588). No other of his plays or poems were printed in his lifetime. *Hero and Leander,* a splendid poem, appeared in 1598.

During his brief life (he was murdered at 29), he wrote the greatest morality play of his time (*Doctor Faustus*), a psychologically penetrating history play (*Edward II*), and the most dramatically effective stage language before Shakespeare's mature plays ("Was this the face that launched a thousand ships/And burnt the topless towers of Ilium?").

Marlowe was an avowed atheist, a man of violence, and probably a member of Elizabeth's secret service. He died in a tavern quarrel in Deptford, a London suburb. Many viewed his death as evidence of God's vengeance on atheists. In modern times he is seen as one of the great dramatists of the Elizabethan age.

While there were many other professional writers—including Thomas Heywood, Thomas Kyd, Cyril Tourneur, Philip Massinger, John Marston, Thomas Middleton, Francis Beaumont, John Fletcher, and John Ford—Shakespeare, whose plays range across all dramatic forms, stands above them all as the greatest writer of his age, if not of all time.

THE ACTING COMPANY

Elizabethan acting took its style from the theory and practice of Elizabethan rhetoric, from theatrical traditions handed down from early troupes, and from the playing conditions within the public theatres.

Since rhetoric played a vital role in the Elizabethan's education, the art and techniques of oral and written communication likely found their way onto the English stage. Actors stressed meaningful delivery of lines, convincing gestures, and eloquence of expression.

An Elizabethan acting company was made up of from 5 to 14 men and boys. Each actor was required to play several roles, and the boys, for the most part, played the women's roles. The actors had little opportunity to specialize in certain roles, although a comic lead (Robert Armin in the Globe company) was an exception to this general rule. The actor's attention—since he had to memorize and retain an extraordinary number of parts—was on telling the story, not on developing character. Character was largely derived from generic or broad social types—kings, rustics, tyrants, and the like.

The stage of the public theatres also contributed to a style of acting. The actor played upon a platform some 25 feet in length projecting into the audience. Since the sightlines were poor, he was required to play at the end of the platform (where the two actors are placed in the DeWitt drawing of the Swan Theatre, page 126). These physical conditions called for "scope in delivery, grace in manner, and audacity in playing."[2]

Scenes were set in generalized locales—for instance, Macbeth's castle or Othello's island of

WILLIAM SHAKESPEARE

William Shakespeare (1564–1616) was an Elizabethan playwright of unsurpassed achievement. Born in Stratford-on-Avon, he received a grammar-school education and married a twenty-six-year-old woman when he was eighteen. He became the father of three children, Susanna and twins Judith and Hamnet.

Few other facts about Shakespeare's life have been established. By 1587–1588 he had moved to London, where he remained until 1611, except for occasional visits to his Stratford home. He appears to have found work almost at once in the London theatre as an actor and a writer. By 1592 he was regarded as a promising playwright; by 1594 he had won the patronage of the Earl of Southampton for two poems, *Venus and Adonis* and *The Rape of Lucrece*.

In 1594–1595 he joined James Burbage's theatrical company, The Lord Chamberlain's Men, as an actor and a playwright; later he became a company shareholder and part owner of the Globe and Blackfriars theatres. He wrote some thirty-seven plays for this company, suiting them to the talents of the great tragic actor Richard Burbage and other members of the troupe. Near the end of his life he retired to Stratford as a well-to-do country gentleman. Shakespeare wrote sonnets, tragedies, comedies, history plays, and tragicomedies, including some of the greatest plays written in English: *Hamlet, King Lear, The Tempest, Macbeth,* and *Othello.*

Cyprus—and played against the unchanging background of the tiring house wall. Actors were therefore not concerned with illusions of place as they are in the modern proscenium theatre, concentrating rather on the action and emotions of the scene. Moreover, the actor had a sense only of his part, for he learned his role from parts or "sides" inscribed on narrow sheets of paper, containing only the actor's lines together with brief cues for each speech and some stage directions. Altogether, it seems the Elizabethan acting style emphasized "solo" parts, the delivery of speeches, and a physical and vocal ability to dominate the stage.

Hamlet's Advice to the Players

Shakespeare talks about the purpose and style of acting:

[Enter Hamlet and Players]

Hamlet Speak the speech, I pray you, as I pronounced it to you, trippingly on the tongue: but if you mouth it, as many of your players do, I had as lief the town-crier spoke my lines. Nor do not saw the air too much with your hand, thus, but use all gently; for in the very torrent, tempest, and, as I may say, the whirlwind of passion, you must acquire and beget a temperance that may give it smoothness. O, it offends me to the soul to hear a robustious periwig-pated fellow tear a passion to tatters, to very rags, to split the ears of the groundlings, who for the most part are capable of nothing but inexplicable dumb-shows and noise: I would have such a fellow whipped for o'er-doing Termagant; it out-herods Herod: pray you, avoid it.

First player I warrant your honour.

Hamlet Be not too tame neither, but let your own discretion be your tutor: suit the action to the word, the word to the action; with this special observance, that you o'er-step not the modesty of nature: for any thing so over done is from the purpose of playing, whose end, both at the first and now, was and is, to hold, as 't were, the mirror up to nature; to show virtue her own feature, scorn her own image, and the very age and body of the time his form and pressure. Now this overdone, or come tardy off, though it make the unskillful laugh, cannot but make the judicious grieve; the censure of the which one must in your allowance o'erweigh a whole theatre of others. O, there be players that I have seen play, and heard others praise, and that highly, not to speak it profanely, that, neither having the accent of Christians nor the gait of Christian, pagan, nor man, have so strutted and bellowed that I have thought some of nature's journeymen had made men and not made them well, they imitated humanity so abominably.

First player I hope we have reformed that indifferently with us, sir.

Hamlet O, reform it altogether. And let those that play your clowns speak no more than is set down for them; for there be of them that will themselves laugh, to set on some quantity of barren spectators to laugh too; though, in the mean time, some necessary question of the play be then to be considered: that's villainous, and shows a most pitiful ambition in the fool that uses it. Go, make you ready.

[Exeunt players]

(III, 2)

VISUAL ELEMENTS

Architectural Façade as Background or Emblem Scholars tell us that the Elizabethan public theatres took over from earlier art and street pageants the principle of *architectural symbolism.* Contemporary records of writers, actors, and foreign visitors point out that the public theatres were colorful buildings with painted façades and columns, decorative flags, curtains, and canopies. We have already remarked how the Globe's architect-producers erected a permanent façade rising several stories above the platform stage. In play after play this elaborate façade with its ornamented doorways, balconies, and openings became a visual symbol of reality, an *emblem.* It symbolized at various times castles, city gates, gardens, woods, backings for thrones and tombs, or a dozen or so combinations. Actors then played as if in front, within, or anywhere about the imagined place.[3]

In *Macbeth,* the façade served as the castle; the walls surrounding the throne room, bed chambers, and banquet hall; the castle gate; the walls threatened by approaching armies; and the battlements where Macbeth fought to his death. Act V, scene 5, of *Macbeth*—the scene of the famous "Tomorrow and tomorrow" soliloquy—begins with the entrance of Macbeth and soldiers "with drums and colors." Macbeth says, "Hang out our banners on the outward walls." We can suppose that these symbolic decorations were hung on and about the façade.

Costumes and Properties We cannot overestimate the importance of the elaborate and colorful costumes as a visual element on the Elizabethan stage. Costumes, whether purchased by the company or donated by its patron, were two basic types: *contemporary* and *symbolic.* Actors wore the ordinary garments of the day in most plays for roles as kings, princes, soldiers, servants, and noblewomen. Symbolic costumes were worn by characters to set them apart from ordinary people.

By modern standards Elizabethan actors used very few properties. Sometimes they carried small hand properties (books, papers, swords, drinking cups) to lend realism to a scene. Large properties, or set pieces, were used sparingly and were frequently "discovered" within the curtained enclosure or carried on stage by actors. For example, the bed in *Othello* (V, 2) was most likely discovered, while the banquet table in *Macbeth* (III, 4) was probably carried on stage.

In the public playhouses lighting (by candlelight) was unnecessary since performances were held during the day, but actors might carry hand properties like torches, candles, and lanterns to indicate night.

The Festive Elizabethan Stage

"Most of all, the Elizabethan stage had the atmosphere of a festival. The hangings, the painted architectural structure, the processions with banners and music, the special effects of soldiers assaulting castles, of kings holding court, of gods and Virtues descending, of princes being welcomed at city gates—all created the spirit of a festival day when for the inauguration of the lord mayor or the progress of the queen or the return of a triumphant army the streets were decorated and street-shows were erected. The façade had on some occasions the appearance of a triumphal arch; on others, with black curtains hung for tragedies, it suggested a public ceremonial of mourning. It but carried a little further the principle already established in the street-shows that it keep the aspects of several different scenic devices at the same time. On some occasions it was imagined as an actual room or the front of a house or other particular place, but its principal function was to provide the atmosphere and the symbols of a show."

George R. Kernodle, *From Art to Theatre* (1944)[4]

Figure 5-3 (a) The "Peachum Print" (probably a nineteenth-century forgery) shows a mixture of contemporary Elizabethan garments worn in court or private life with Turkish trousers on one actor and an attempt at a Roman cloak on another. (b) Woodcut of elaborately costumed Dr. Faustus from the 1631 edition of Marlowe's play.

Music and Dance Music and dancing flourished in Elizabethan England and were an integral part of theatrical performances. Plays called for songs, instrumental music, military and ceremonial music, and music to accompany dances and other festivities. Shakespeare's tragedies and histories note "alarums and excursions" requiring trumpets, cymbals, and drums; fanfares and flourishes accompany King Claudius' drinking bout in *Hamlet* (I, 4); and Romeo and Juliet meet at the Capulets' grand ball (I, 5) with its lively music and dancing.

In Shakespeare's last play, *Henry VIII,* stage directions call for "drum and trumpet; chambers discharged" just before the king appeared at Cardinal Wolsey's supper dance. At the premiere performance the firing of the cannon set fire to the theatre. The audience was so engrossed with the pageantry and sound effects that it was some time before the fire was detected, and the Globe burned down.

Comedies often ended with dancing to signify the union of couples and the goodwill of the community at large. The plays included country dances as well as such popular court dances as the galliard, the lavolta, and the pavan.

The Dumb Show On the Elizabethan public stage, symbolic pageantry, or the dumb show, mimed the historical or allegorical meaning of events related to the play's main action. In most Elizabethan dumb shows, actors dressed as allegorical figures moved onto the main stage in a procession with musical accompaniment, usually military, regal, or funereal. In *Macbeth* (IV, 1), the spectacle of "Eight Kings, the last with a glass in his hand; Banquo's Ghost following" accompanied by oboes foreshadowed Banquo's royal succession.

At times a "presenter" commented on the pantomime, explaining its significance. Sometimes the dumb show was more like an arranged *tableau* concealed behind the curtain of the inner stage until it was revealed, but the most common English practice was the pantomimic procession with music on the main playing area. Shakespeare's famous dumb shows in *Hamlet, Macbeth,* and *The Tempest* were presented in this manner.

THE AUDIENCE

Elizabethan audiences, as heterogeneous as movie audiences today, were made up of a cross section of the London population: gentry, professional men, merchants, artisans, students, apprentices, women, and children. About 10 percent of the London population were gentry and professionals, 52 percent were artisans and shopkeepers, and the rest were retailers, laborers, and servants. Admission prices reflected this stratification: a penny for general admission representing one-third of the audience that stood in the yard; additional pennies for the two-thirds who sat in the galleries or private boxes.

An Elizabethan public theatre could accommodate more than 2000 people, but only about 450 or 500 attended any one theatre on an ordinary day. However, on holidays and on days when new plays were being presented, the playhouses would be jammed. In an average week of 1595, some 15,000 people probably attended the two London theatres then operating. By 1603, with five companies performing, the number rose to more than 20,000.[5]

Although the "groundlings" (those standing around the stage) were noisy and often ill mannered, audiences generally appreciated good plays and revered the famous actors (Richard Burbage, Edward Alleyn, Will Kempe); like audiences in other times and places, they responded with laughter, applause, or tears when they were emotionally moved and with hisses or boos when they were displeased.

THE PRIVATE PLAYHOUSE: BLACKFRIARS

In 1608 the Globe company took possession of a second theatre—Blackfriars, in a residential area in London originally belonging to monastic groups. The first Blackfriars was leased in 1576 to a boys' company. In 1596 James Burbage acquired the buildings in the Blackfriars area, built a "second" Blackfriars, and leased the theatre to another boys' company (The Children of the Chapel Royal) for a number of years. In 1608 Richard Burbage assumed the Blackfriars lease.

Beginning in 1610, and for the next 34 years, Shakespeare's company operated two theatres, using Blackfriars during the winter months and the Globe during the summer. As the first adult acting company to run a private theatre, they started a trend quickly followed by other companies. Within a short time Blackfriars became the company's main theatre and Shakespeare, Ben Jonson, Francis Beaumont, and John Fletcher its principal playwrights.

Like other private playhouses of its day, Blackfriars was a long, rectangular hall with a platform stage at one end; the hall was lighted by

---

The Burning of the Globe

On June 29, 1613, the roof of the Globe caught fire during the first act of Shakespeare's *Henry VIII.* Within an hour the building burned to the ground. An eyewitness described the event in the following portion of a letter:

"I will entertain you at the present with what happened this week at the Bankside. The King's Players had a new play, called All is True, *representing some principal pieces of the reign of Henry the Eighth, which was set forth with many extraordinary circumstances of pomp and majesty, even to the matting of the stage; the Knights of the Order with their Georges and Garter, the guards with their embroidered coats, and the like—sufficient in truth within awhile to make greatness very familiar, if not ridiculous. Now King Henry, making a masque at the Cardinal Wolsey's house, and certain cannons being shot off at his entry, some of the paper or other stuff wherewith one of them was stopped, did light on the thatch, where being thought at first but an idle smoke, and their eyes more attentive to the show, it kindled inwardly, and ran round like a train, consuming within less than an hour the whole house to the very ground. This was the fatal period of that virtuous fabrick; wherein yet nothing did perish but wood and straw, and a few forsaken cloaks; only one man had his breeches set on fire, that would perhaps have broiled him, if he had not, by the benefit of a provident wit, put it out with bottle ale."*

---

candles and had galleries and benches for the spectators.

The private theatres were always exclusive. They had a limited number of seats and charged six times the price of admission to the public theatres. There were subtle changes in the writing and acting for an audience of gentry and sophisticates in enclosed, quieter surroundings: Acting became less bombastic, and subjects

Figure 5-4 A reconstruction of the second Blackfriars Theatre, 1597. Notice the curtained inner stages on two levels, the candelabras, and the audience in the galleries and center area.

dealt more with faraway places and bizarre situations, like Prospero's enchanted island in *The Tempest.* Shakespeare's late plays—*Cymbeline, The Winter's Tale,* and *The Tempest*—were probably written for this theatre.

COURT MASQUES

Spectacle and pageantry had always been a part of English court life. In this tradition Henry VIII had made masques popular as a type of court entertainment. Elizabeth was interested more in elaborate spectacles given in her honor. The two Stuart kings who came after her revived and perfected the masque.

Most court masques, called "prince's toys" by one Elizabethan writer, were given at royal palaces to celebrate betrothals, marriages, and visits of foreign princes and dignitaries. Devel-

oped from scenarios provided by playwrights, they featured mythological or allegorical figures like Diana, Neptune, Reason, Splendor, and Love. Under James I, masques became expensive spectacles using the services of professional writers, scenic designers, dancers and singers, as well as courtiers and royalty. James I "walked on" in the silent title role of *The Masque of Oberon* (1610), which cost 1500 pounds—three times as much as the cost of building the Fortune Theatre the year before.

The court recruited Inigo Jones, the English architect who studied in Italy, to collaborate with playwright Ben Jonson in the creation of these spectacles. Jones's designs introduced Italianate scenery and stage machines to England, as well as the proscenium façade and front curtain. His elaborate movable scenery was to find its way onto the public stage after 1660.

Figure 5-5 (a) Inigo Jones's design for Scene 1 of the *Oberon* masque (1610). Ben Jonson described "a dark rocke, with trees beyond it." This first scene changed to a palace by means of drawing or "opening" the wings or two-sided flats on both sides. (b) This sketch of a knight's costume shows the elaborate costumes designed for the court entertainments. This semi-Roman costume was designed by Inigo Jones.

a

b

INIGO JONES

Inigo Jones (1573–1652), appointed to the English court as architect in 1604, took over the design and production of court masques. He gradually introduced the style and techniques of Italian decor and theatrical practices: three-sided revolving prisms showing different scenes on each side; two-sided painted houses with back shutters that opened to reveal cutout scenes; flat wings in grooves that introduced perspective painting; and elaborate costume designs of fantasy and myth.

With *The Masque of Blackness* in 1605, Inigo Jones and Ben Jonson began a long collaboration. Eventually, the two men quarreled over who was more important, the scenic artist or the poet. Their collaboration ended in 1631 when Jones succeeded in having Ben Jonson dismissed from his royal post as author of court masques.

Jones was Surveyor of His Majesty's Works from 1615 to 1643 when he, in turn, was dismissed from office by the Puritans. However, his contributions to the English theatre were secure; the features of the Italianate stage that he introduced were to characterize the Restoration theatre after 1660.

The De Witt drawing of the Swan Theatre (right) in London dates from about 1596; it is the first picture we have of the interior of an Elizabethan theatre.

In *The Globe Restored* (1968) C. Walter Hodges describes the Elizabethan theatre as self-contained, adjustable, and independent of any surroundings other than its audience.

Below left: The tiring house (the area around and within the house wall at the back of the stage) was divided from the stage by hangings of some sort, usually curtains opening in the middle.

Below right: The inner stage is thought to be a small, recessed area with curtains in the tiring house wall. Hodges shows a discovery area surrounded by curtains. The permanent upper level or upper stage is a characteristic feature of the Elizabethan stage; it was used for scenes like Juliet's balcony scene in *Romeo and Juliet.* Hodges's reconstruction of the inner and upper stages brings them forward into the main acting area.

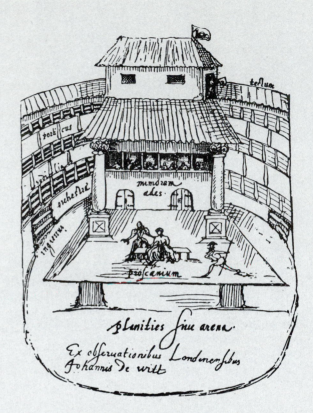

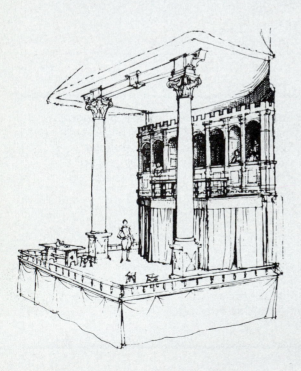

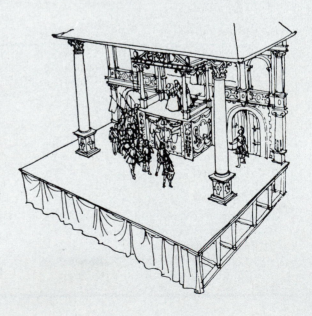

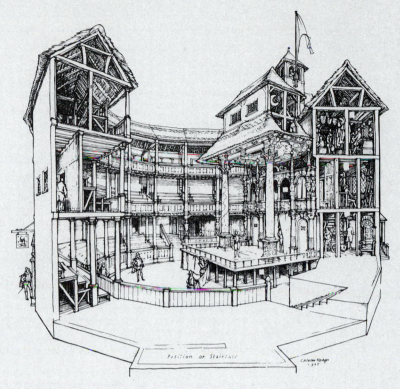

Hodge's detailed reconstruction of the Globe Playhouse (1599–1613) shows the building's superstructure, with galleries, yard, and railed stage. Notice the trapdoor in the stage, stage doors, curtained inner and upper stages, tiring house (as backstage area with workrooms and storage areas), hut with machines, the "heavens," and playhouse flag.

The Oregon Shakespearean Festival Theatre is a modern reconstruction similar to The Fortune Theatre of Shakespeare's London, which was built in 1599. Although the seating and lighting facilities are modern, the stage and tiring house are patterned after the earlier theatre.

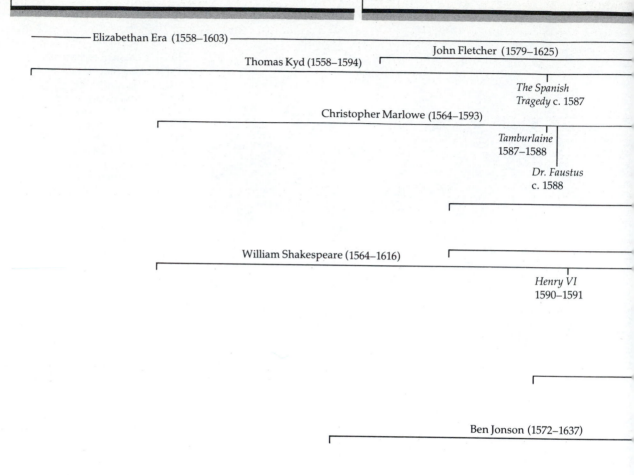

1550 | 1575

Elizabethan Era (1558–1603)

John Fletcher (1579–1625)

Thomas Kyd (1558–1594)

The Spanish Tragedy c. 1587

Christopher Marlowe (1564–1593)

Tamburlaine 1587–1588

Dr. Faustus c. 1588

William Shakespeare (1564–1616)

Henry VI 1590–1591

Ben Jonson (1572–1637)

DRAMATIC CONVENTIONS

THE EPISODIC PLOT

Several traditions influenced the form of Elizabethan plays: romantic narratives about historical events covering much time and many places and the popular idea that art reflected human behavior. The play (and the stage) was thought of as a "mirror held up to nature," as Shakespeare said, to reflect the behavior and social conventions of the time. Equally important were the plots that mirrored human events.

Most playwrights, including Shakespeare, turned to popular romances and histories for their plots. This narrative material, however, did not lend itself to tight plotting of incidents. Taking large portions of a given story, playwrights arranged the material and often *added* characters and events. For instance, Shakespeare integrated the story of Gloucester and his son with the King Lear story taken from Holinshed's *Chronicles* and an anonymous play called the *True Chronicle History of King Leir* first performed about 1594.

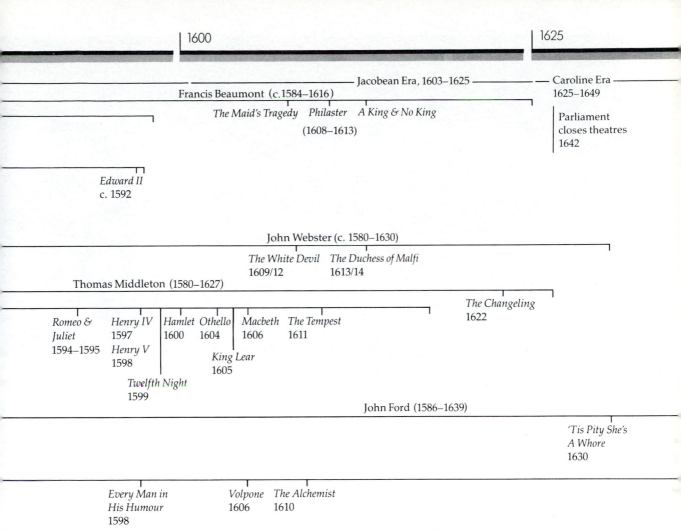

| 1600 | 1625 |

Jacobean Era, 1603–1625 ——————— Caroline Era
1625–1649

Francis Beaumont (c.1584–1616)

Parliament
closes theatres
1642

The Maid's Tragedy   Philaster   A King & No King
(1608–1613)

Edward II
c. 1592

John Webster (c. 1580–1630)

The White Devil   The Duchess of Malfi
1609/12   1613/14

Thomas Middleton (1580–1627)

The Changeling
1622

Romeo &	*Henry IV*	*Hamlet*	*Othello*	*Macbeth*	*The Tempest*
Juliet	1597	1600	1604	1606	1611
1594–1595	*Henry V*				
	1598		*King Lear*		
			1605		

Twelfth Night
1599

John Ford (1586–1639)

*'Tis Pity She's
A Whore*
1630

Every Man in   Volpone   The Alchemist
His Humour   1606   1610
1598

English playwrights, unlike classical writers, concentrated on the rapid progression of a story from high point to high point, opting chiefly for *effects* rather than causes. Shakespeare emphasized the effects of Iago's plotting, the effects of Duncan's murder on Macbeth and the kingdom, and the effects of Hamlet's procrastination. The causes of action (so important in our modern theatre of psychological realism) were often taken for granted. Therefore, plots were made up of events (or episodes) loosely strung together to tell a story from beginning to end about actions—killing kings, driving persons mad, fighting over kingdoms, avenging wrongs, and so on—which take place over months and years and in many different places.

EXPOSITION

Episodic plotting required little exposition, as not a great deal had happened before the play began. Shakespeare's minor characters address one another and we learn who and where they are and the time of day or night. Frequently, characters are waiting for something to happen. *Hamlet* begins with a changing of the guard before the castle at Elsinore:

Figure 5-6   Desdemona's death in *Othello*. James Earl Jones was Othello in this 1964 New York Shakespeare Festival Theatre production at the Delacorte Theatre.

[*Francisco at his post. Enter to him Bernardo.*]

Bernardo Who's there?

Francisco Nay, answer me: stand and unfold yourself.

Bernardo Long live the king!

Francisco Bernardo?

Bernardo He.

Francisco You come most carefully upon your hour.

Bernardo 'Tis now struck twelve; get thee to bed, Francisco.

Francisco For this relief much thanks; 'tis bitter cold, and I am sick at heart.

Bernardo Have you had quiet guard?

Francisco Not a mouse stirring.

Bernardo Well, good night. If you do meet Horatio and Marcellus, the rivals of my watch, bid them make haste.

Francisco I think I hear them. Stand, ho! Who's there?

(I,1)

In this dialogue between the guards, we learn the speakers' names, what they are doing, that it is midnight and cold, that the evening has been quiet, and also the names of the two characters entering next. In the next scene we learn about the ghost of Hamlet's father walking the battlements and why the undisturbed watch of Francisco was significant.

It is typical of the episodic play that some force occurs early in the opening scenes, or just before them, to impel the characters to act. The ghost in *Hamlet* has appeared to the guards before the play begins. In *Othello* the Moor and Desdemona have eloped; Iago has been passed over for promotion.

SCENES

Shakespeare arranged a series of events, each of which was completed before another was begun. Usually, exits and entrances marked the end of scenes together with couplets or soliloquies. Each scene had one of three functions: (1) to propel the play toward its crises and resolution; (2) to develop traits of character; or (3) to compare and contrast situations among the characters.

Elizabethans used a five-part form that they probably adopted from their classical studies of Seneca and Terence, the Roman playwrights. However, within the five parts the Elizabethans departed from the classical format, shaping the dramatic action to develop the highest tension during the middle of the play.

The fourth part of the play included events that lessened tensions, and the final part concluded with other climactic moments and a resolution of the dramatic conflict and the story's complications. The first climax in *Macbeth* occurs with Banquo's appearance at the banquet; the second with Macbeth's suicidal combat with Macduff.

DOUBLE PLOTS

Shakespeare's double plots tell two stories with similar themes, characters, and events. *Hamlet* is the story of two families: Hamlet–Claudius–Gertrude and Laertes–Polonius–Ophelia. Through comparisons and contrasts, one story highlighted the meaning of the other. Sometimes the two stories joined one another late in the action. The lesser story was usually resolved first to allow sharp focus on the main story at the play's conclusion.

THE ENDING

Shakespeare's plays usually ended with a public resolution of the conflict. Usually, an authority figure (a prince, judge, or king) meted out justice or brought lovers together. In comedy, love triumphed and even punishments were tempered with "a quality of mercy" or forgiveness. In tragedy justice prevailed, even though the hero might die in the process. In comedy the substance of the resolution was the working out

---

The Final Lines of *Macbeth*

[*Reenter Macduff, with Macbeth's head.*]
Macduff Hail, king! for so thou art: behold, where stands
The usurper's cursed head: the time is free:
I see thee compass'd with thy kingdom's pearl,
That speak my salutation in their minds;
Whose voices I desire aloud with mine:
Hail, King of Scotland!

All Hail, King of Scotland! [*Flourish*]

Malcolm We shall not spend a large expense of time
Before we reckon with your several loves,
And make us even with you. My thanes and kinsmen,
Henceforth be earls, the first that ever Scotland
In such an honour named. What's more to do,
Which would be planted newly with the time,
As calling home our exiled friends abroad
That fled the snares of watchful tyranny;
Producing forth the cruel ministers
Of this dead butcher and his fiend-like queen,
Who, as 'tis thought, by self and violent hands
Took off her life; this, and what needful else
That calls upon us, by the grace of Grace,
We will perform in measure, time and place:
So, thanks to all at once and to each one,
Whom we invite to see us crown'd at Scone.

[*Flourish. Exeunt*]

of complications that impeded love. In tragedy the substance was the overcoming of evil forces that destroyed a just order.

The *means* of bringing about a play's ending varied from the discovery of the identity of disguised persons to a trial, an execution, single combat, or suicide. Othello's confession and suicide resulted from his discovery that Desdemona was innocent. In *Macbeth* and *Hamlet* a single combat decided the issue against the forces of evil.

Following this type of climactic action, someone in authority usually pronounced judgment, declaring the meaning of the action and reasserting order. Usually, these final lines were little more than ceremonial, and they were followed by a stately exit of all persons to clear the stage.

LANGUAGE

Shakespeare was essentially a man of the theatre. With the exception of his long poems and sonnets, he was not a poet writing for readers but a playwright setting down words to be *spoken* by actors and *heard* by audiences.

Shakespeare's stage language alternates from the abstract to the concrete, from verbal image to physical deed, and back again. *Macbeth* begins with sound effects ("thunder and lightning") and with the appearance of three witches. Within 12 lines they give information about the time, place, occasion, weather, mood of battle, and announce Macbeth's impending entrance. The rhymes and ritualistic intoning of these supernatural creatures set the pattern of what is to come: fair/foul, victory/defeat, good/evil, order/chaos. The moral disorder in the political realm is foreshadowed by the conventional symbolism of the witches' storm. In Shakespeare the natural universe always reflects the moral condition of the political world. Corrupt kingdoms, for instance, breed images of shipwreck, blood, disease, storms, and eclipses.

It is usual to point out Shakespeare's use of both poetry and prose in his plays. *Blank verse* (unrhymed iambic pentameter) is reserved for

---

The Opening Scene of *Macbeth*

[*Thunder and lightning. Enter three witches.*]

First Witch When shall we three meet again
In thunder, lightning, or in rain?

Second Witch When the hurlyburly's done,
When the battle's lost and won.

Third Witch That will be ere the set of sun.

First Witch Where the place?

Second Witch Upon the heath.

Third Witch There to meet with Macbeth.

First Witch I come, Graymalkin!

Second Witch Paddock calls.

Third Witch Anon.

All Fair is foul, and foul is fair;
Hover through the fog and filthy air.

---

the lyrical moods, descriptive passages, and the emotional weight of the great soliloquies. By contrast, prose is used in the low comic scenes, like the drunken porter scene in *Macbeth* (II, 3), and in mad scenes, such as Othello's gravest moments of irrationality (IV, 1).

The *soliloquy* has been called the most characteristic theatrical device of the Elizabethan stage. Shakespeare's soliloquies represent a form of conscious thought brought to a point where it becomes speech. They serve several functions: to express deeply felt emotion, to reason aloud, and to invoke assistance from supernatural powers. The soliloquies of *Hamlet* and *Macbeth* are perhaps the most perfected form of this type of theatrical language.

Asides are of two types. The first allows two characters to exchange comments not intended to be heard by others present on stage. This is the "conversational" aside. Another type allows a character to comment briefly to himself while not being heard by others on stage. This is the "solo" aside. The first is usually introduced by some transitional phrase, such as "Bernardo, a word with you," and two speakers move away from the other characters to share their thoughts unheard. When King Duncan honors Banquo and Macbeth after the battle and names his elder son Malcolm as Prince of Cumberland, Macbeth's solo *aside* reveals his inner thoughts:

Macbeth [*aside*] The Prince of Cumberland!
　　that is a step
　　On which I must fall down, or else o'er-leap,
　　For in my way it lies. Stars, hide your fires;
　　Let not light see my black and deep desires:
　　The eye wink at the hand; yet let that be,
　　Which the eye fears, when it is done, to see.
　　[*exit*]

(I,4)

REPRESENTATIVE PLAY

Macbeth
Performed at court in 1606 by the King's Men (Shakespeare's Company) for King James I and the King of Denmark

BACKGROUND

Macbeth is the last of Shakespeare's four great tragedies, written when his creative powers were at their highest. As best we can tell, *Hamlet* (1601–1602) was produced several years before *Othello* (1604); *King Lear* (1605) and *Macbeth* (1606) followed.

Upon the accession of James I to the English throne following Queen Elizabeth's death in 1603, he took the Lord Chamberlain's Men under his direct patronage as the King's Men. It is likely that *Macbeth* was performed in the summer of 1606 as a court entertainment for the visiting king of Denmark. Whether it was performed earlier at the Globe, we do not know. However, by Shakespeare's standards it is a short play, suggesting that it was originally conceived as court entertainment; it also contains a court favorite—a masque (IV, 1).

Shakespeare's source for the story was Holinshed's *Chronicle,* which furnished him with accounts of the reigns of Duncan and Macbeth in Scotland. The playwright's imagination worked upon this story of a lawful king's brutal murder, adding the encounters with the prophetic witches, Lady Macbeth's complicity, and Banquo's ghost. It would not have gone unnoticed by King James and the English court that Banquo, an eleventh-century Scottish nobleman, was the king's ancestor and that the old women who had bargained their souls to the Devil in return for powers of witchcraft fulfilled the king's own belief in such demonic creatures. By invoking their aid Macbeth was guilty of trafficking with the Prince of Darkness. To the Elizabethan mind this was one of the deadliest of sins.

TRAGIC ACTION

Taken at its simplest level *Macbeth* is a story of crime and punishment. In the annals of Western crime stories, it ranks with Dostoevsky's novel *Crime and Punishment* (1866) as one of the great literary accounts of the power of evil to destroy its perpetrator. But first of all *Macbeth* is a great play. On stage we watch the disintegrating effects of evil act upon a once noble man and his wife. His crimes distort his judgment, poison his imagination, and isolate him from others, including his wife. A seemingly endless series of murders to conceal his original deed (Duncan's murder) destroys the revered soldier of the play's first act. Pessimism and despair take hold as he contemplates his certain punishment. At the end he revives a small part of his former self as he duels with Macduff to certain death.

Shakespeare's story is also about the destructive effects of power and ambition on the

Figure 5-7 The New York Shakespeare Festival production of *Macbeth* at the Delacorte Theatre, Central Park (1966) with James Earl Jones as Macbeth.

human psyche. Lady Macbeth learns (by letter) of the witches' prophecy and that the king has indeed named her husband Thane of Cawdor, thereby fulfilling part of the prophecy. Over-powering ambition charges her imagination and she conceives of the king's death before Macbeth arrives. In the early soliloquies she meditates upon her husband's conscience and his certain fears of punishment. Lady Macbeth then goads her husband into murdering the king.

The couple's moral dissolution follows swiftly upon the king's murder. Macbeth's is a reign of terror encompassing Banquo, Macduff, and the king's heirs. Profoundly affected by her own suppressed guilt, Lady Macbeth becomes a sleepwalker, nightly washing away Duncan's "blood" from her hands. In the sleepwalking scene, one of Shakespeare's greatest inventions, we see that it is not fear of punishment but *memory* of the events crowding the dreadful night of the murder that disturbs her psyche. At last she finds life unendurable and commits suicide.

The play is a strong, melodramatic story, pitting right against wrong. Macbeth's self-awareness, revealed in the great soliloquies, endows the action with its tragic dimension and makes his individual death seem to be an important moment in the march of human destiny. He feels his responsibility for the moral chaos around him, and he explores life's meaning in soliloquies that transcend his individual dilemma:

To-morrow, and to-morrow, and
to-morrow
Creeps in this petty pace from day to day
To the last syllable of recorded time,
And all our yesterdays have lighted fools
The way to dusty death. Out, out, brief
candle!
Life's but a walking shadow, a poor player
That struts and frets his hour upon the stage
And then is heard no more: it is a tale
Told by an idiot, full of sound and fury,
Signifying nothing.

(V,5)

THE SCENE

Shakespeare's platform stage encompassed the storms of the natural world and the military battles of the political one. Whereas *Othello* takes place almost entirely at night, concealing Iago's machinations, *Macbeth* conjures up the confusions and bloody carnage of battle. The witches appear, disappear, and reappear (probably through a trapdoor) accompanied by the rolling thunder of the tiremen (stagehands). Reports of battle are profuse and confusing. All of these activities mirror the confusion of Macbeth's mind once the witches confront him and Banquo with their prophecies: Macbeth will be Thane of Cawdor and King hereafter; Banquo will beget kings.

As in *Othello* the main events in *Macbeth* occur at night. Duncan is murdered at night. Banquo is attacked at dusk, and the famous banquet scene takes place at night. Lady Macbeth sleepwalks at night, while Macbeth's troubled conscience will not let him sleep and he becomes a "night creature."

Shakespeare's use of darkness mirrors the moral confusion that descends upon the characters. Only as the opposing armies march on Dunsinane for the final battle does daylight intrude on the scene. Just as day banishes night in Shakespeare's design, so, too, good banishes evil.

CHARACTER

Most of the characters in *Macbeth* take their identities from broad types: king, tyrant, avenger, assassin, loyal friend, retainer. Only the Macbeths have an interior life that gives them individuality. The other characters serve as contrasts to them. Unlike Macbeth, Banquo remains deaf to the witches' temptation. Macduff is the conventional avenger of private wrongs. Malcolm displays kingly virtues that Macbeth does not possess.

LANGUAGE

Macbeth contains some of Shakespeare's most beautiful soliloquies. They guide us in blank verse through the interior lives of the Macbeths—through Lady Macbeth's efforts to "unsex" herself of feminine ways as preparation for murdering the king and through Macbeth's meditation on life's meaning. These interior moments (as well as the sleepwalking incident) give dimension to characters who, without them, would be little more than a "bloody tyrant" and his accomplice.

The scene of the drunken porter answering the knock at the castle gate is the play's most famous *prose scene*. He pretends to be the porter at Hell's gate, and we know that a bitter hell is contained within the castle walls.

By and large Shakespeare's poetic images are confined to fair and foul, insidious night creatures, and blood—an image of violent death. These images reflect the ambiguous nature of existence where one can be simultaneously a winner and a loser. Blood is a source of life as well as a sign of death. The witches' prologue underlines the world's confusion: "When the battle's lost and won"; or "Fair is foul, and foul is fair."

SHAKESPEARE'S MODERNISM

Macbeth is highly meaningful to modern audiences familiar with Vietnam, Watergate, and twentieth-century tyrannies. The first level of meaning shows war breeding tyranny and further war; the second anticipates our Freudian heritage—the workings of the unconscious; and the third touches upon the postmodernist conclusion that life, after all, is absurd.

The First Level The five acts of *Macbeth* are given to war, murder, and tyranny. In the play offensive war breeds crime and makes tyrants of valorous men. In the play's second scene a soldier reports that Macbeth faced one of the traitors in battle and "unseam'd him from the nave to the chaps,/And fix'd his head upon our battlements." The king rewards him for slaughtering the enemy. But the "fair" Macbeth, honored in battle, becomes the "foul" criminal who murders his king and kills his rivals and their progeny.

The Second Level Shakespeare also explores the mind's dark recesses through Macbeth's superabundant imagination. Aware of his diseased imagination, Macbeth says: "O, full of scorpions is my mind, dear wife." He perceives both the character of his deeds and his inevitable punishment. In contrast, Lady Macbeth's failure of imagination makes her a victim of her unconscious. Walking in her sleep she says, "Yet who would have thought the old man to have had so much blood in him"; and again, "Here's the smell of the blood still: all the perfumes of Arabia will not sweeten this little hand." Earlier in the play she has assured Macbeth that "A little water clears us of this deed." Shakespeare's understanding of the unconscious as a latent reservoir of thoughts and experiences is best depicted in the sleepwalking scene where Lady Macbeth acts out her guilt.

In contrast to his wife, Macbeth's moral imagination works on a conscious level. He says after he kills Duncan:

Will all great Neptune's ocean wash this blood
Clean from my hand? No, this my hand will rather

The multitudinous seas incarnadine,
Making the green one red.

(II, 2)

The Third Level Critic Jan Kott reminds us in his lively book, *Shakespeare Our Contemporary*, that the true tragedy of Macbeth, the killer, is at the play's end where he acknowledges the human situation as *absurd*—without purpose, harmony, or meaning: "a tale told by an idiot, full of sound and fury, signifying nothing."

If death does not change anything and if his life is without meaning, why, then, does Macbeth fight Macduff? Why doesn't he surrender and die passively? For a final time Macbeth exposes his predicament in terms of the human condition. He describes himself as a *bear* tied to a stake in a bear-baiting arena, struggling to fend off an attacking dog until one of them dies:

They have tied me to a stake, I cannot fly,
But bear-like I must fight the course.

(V,7)

Macbeth is hardened to guilt. Unlike Othello he has nothing to protest about. But he does identify his plight with all humankind. In Macbeth's view we are all tied, like bears, to a stake and have no choice other than to stay life's course. Jan Kott says of Macbeth: "All he can do before he dies is to drag with him into nothingness as many living beings as possible. This is the last consequence of the world's absurdity."[6]

ESSAY

The Royal Shakespeare Company's acclaimed production of *Macbeth* produced in 1976 and directed by Trevor Nunn (more recently acclaimed for his direction of *Nicholas Nickleby* and *Cats*) did away with all audience expectations of how a Shakespeare play should be staged. Removing *Macbeth* from a proscenium theatre, elaborate scenery, and period costumes, Nunn staged the play in a small, empty space and demonstrated anew the raw power of Shakespeare's story.

Shakespeare in Modern Performance

Macbeth, directed by Trevor Nunn and designed by John Napier, presented by the Royal Shakespeare Company at The Other Place, Stratford-upon-Avon (England) in 1976

The modern director of Shakespeare has to re-create the meaning and events of a 350-year-old text for a modern audience. This is not an easy task.

To begin, directors make three major decisions: choosing the play, arranging the playing text, and creating the pictorial concept for the production. Some directors say that the choice of play is 80 percent of their work; others give cutting and arranging the acting text an equally high rating. Still others think that determining the visual style of setting and costumes is the most important preliminary work.

Modern productions of Shakespeare have used a variety of concepts and interpretations. In some of the most famous, directors have added contemporary viewpoints to the social context of Shakespeare's plays. Laurence Olivier made a strongly nationalistic statement in the 1944 film of *Henry V* made during the Battle of Britain. In 1937 Orson Welles directed *Julius Caesar* at the Mercury Theatre (New York City) with the characters in storm-trooper uniforms, drawing a parallel between the fascism of Caesar's Rome and Hitler's Germany. Tyrone Guthrie directed a "modern dress" *Troilus and Cressida* at the Old Vic (London) in 1956. He selected 1913 fashions from Edwardian England and the Kaiser's Germany, dressing Shakespeare's Greeks and Trojans in military uniforms modeled on those of turn-of-the-century German and Austrian armies. Guthrie's production suggested to a postwar generation of theatregoers that this was the last time when nations could treat war as a game.

By and large modern directors have used four basic modes to arrive at a production's visual metaphor and its ambience of setting and costume: *Renaissance, modern, historical,* and *eclectic.* The first (and most common practice) reflects the historical period in Elizabethan dress and staging. The second results in modern-dress productions to strengthen the relevance of texts for modern audiences. The third seeks out a historical period (other than Shakespeare's) as an analogue for the play's meaning. British director Jonathan Miller placed *Measure for Measure* in Freud's Vienna of the 1930s to point up the characters' sexual repressions.

The eclectic approach is highly popular today because it uses many stimuli to free audiences of a *single* interpretation. Peter Brook's staging of *A Midsummer Night's Dream* at Stratford-upon-Avon in 1970 in a "white box" suggested various environments—a circus, gymnasium, clinic, rehearsal room—and focused on love's placeless and timeless snares and vicissitudes.

Keeping in mind the principal strategies open to modern directors of Shakespeare, let us look closely at Trevor Nunn's 1976 production of *Macbeth* which used a small theatre and modern workshop techniques.

TREVOR NUNN'S *MACBETH*

Trevor Nunn has been artistic director of England's Royal Shakespeare Company since 1968. Today he shares that title with director Terry Hands. Nunn has pointed out that Shakespeare's plays were written for a permanent stage and also the audience went to the theatre fully aware of what the stage looked like and how the actors worked on it. Everyone, including the playwright, concentrated on the expression of events and characters through language, not through stage pictures.

In 1976 Nunn undertook to direct *Macbeth* (a play he had directed twice before) in a small theatre in Stratford called The Other Place, usually reserved by the RSC for low-budget productions. His intention was to take a permanent space (in this case a large room) and

TREVOR NUNN

Trevor Nunn (b. 1940), a cabinetmaker's son, grew up in Ipswich, Suffolk. At age 13 he got a part in the Ipswich Theatre's production of *Life with Father* and decided to become an actor. Educated at Cambridge University, he was involved there in some 32 undergraduate productions.

Upon graduation Nunn became Anthony Richardson's assistant director at the Belgrade Theatre, Coventry (1962–1964). He was then hired as assistant director to Peter Hall with the Royal Shakespeare Company, Stratford-upon-Avon, where he directed Tourneur's *Revenger's Tragedy* in 1966. With Hall's departure to the National Theatre in 1968, Trevor Nunn became the RSC's artistic director. What followed were his exemplary productions of *The Winter's Tale, Hamlet* with Alan Howard, the Roman plays (*Titus Andronicus, Julius Caesar, Antony and Cleopatra, Coriolanus*), *Macbeth,* and *Nicholas Nickleby.* He recently directed *Cats* for the commercial West End theatre and Broadway.

As RSC artistic director Nunn has worked to create an ensemble company, allowing younger actors to move up into larger roles, and to keep a continuity of directors.

concentrate on revealing through language Macbeth's world of moral collapse and violence.

Nunn's *economy* of staging, more than any other quality, put the play into relief. A circle was drawn on the bare wooden floor of the large room. This became the playing area surrounded by the audience against three walls. Boxes were placed just outside the circle for actors to sit on; rising from the boxes they assumed their characters as they stepped into the circle.

The production began with organ music and a sanctimonious hush emphasizing the legitimacy of Duncan's rule, interrupted by the witches' chanting and shrieks as Macbeth arrives among them.

The first scenes were presented with great simplicity. At Macbeth's return to court there was an outburst of cheers and embraces, abruptly cut off as soon as the point of a hero's welcome is made. For the coronation Macbeth (Ian McKellen) performed a stately walk around the perimeter of the circle dressed in Duncan's robe. As the Macbeths met (Judi Dench played Lady Macbeth), their endearments smothered the first hints of the murder plot. More like storytellers than dramatic characters, the actors coaxed the audience's interest until the action was fully launched.

The staging dispensed with the usual dumb show—the masquelike spectacle of the parade of kings with Banquo's ghost—and in its place the witches (sitting down) paraded voodoo dolls in front of Macbeth's face while they painted his half-naked body with witches' symbols. Banquo's ghostly presence at the banquet table was also eliminated. Instead, the scene (without banquet table) was played out with Macbeth staring into empty air terrorized by his own imagination. All the battle scenes with the exception of the last, where Macbeth's head is severed from his body, were deleted. The "armies"—three or four actors—appeared in the dim light like apparitions conjured up by the witches or by Macbeth's imagination. Their presence could easily have been another apparition, for they came into the light, stood there, spoke, and vanished.

Figure 5-8 The Royal Shakespeare Company production of *Macbeth*, 1976, directed by Trevor Nunn. (a) Macbeth (Ian Kellen) with the witches. The witches entice Macbeth with voodoo dolls and paint symbols on his body. (b) The three witches sit in the center of the circle drawn on the bare wooden floor of the large room.

a

b

Ian McKellen's cold, subdued performance of Macbeth took place largely under rehearsal lights. He was transformed by Duncan's murder from a victorious soldier to an efficient, corporate executive, ruling with unquestioned authority and skillful efficiency until his imagination tricked him into perceiving Banquo's ghost. Frightened, he was driven back to the witches and, once again taking up witchcraft, his reason was lost.

Nunn's decision to produce in the small Stratford theatre set up workshop conditions that led to this eclectic production. He used a permanent stage (the building's floor) without scenery, colored lights, or elaborate decor. Duncan's splendid robe and crown contrasted sharply with the bare setting and the actors' drab rehearsal clothes. The circle drawn on the floor to outline the playing area suggested a return to early ritual—to the privileged or sacred space—where the costumed performer enacted mysteries of death and rebirth.

SUMMARY

The Elizabethan public theatre emerged from its medieval and Tudor origins in the 1590s as full-blown commercial theatre. In 1576 James Burbage had built the first permanent theatre (simply called "The Theatre") and others had quickly followed. The most famous of all the London theatres was The Globe built by Burbage's company in 1599. Moreover, a number of professional playwrights, schooled in the study and performance of Latin plays, were active. By the late 1590s plays by Shakespeare, Kyd, Marlowe, Jonson, Webster, and others were dominating the London stage. The two most successful acting companies were Philip Henslowe's Lord Admiral's Men and James Burbage's Lord Chamberlain's Men (later to be renamed the King's Men). Audiences were made up of a cross section of London society. In addition to the "public" theatres, such

"private," indoor playhouses as Blackfriars (also owned by Burbage's company) were opened in the 1570s and leased to boys' companies; in the early 1600s Burbage's company took over Blackfriars to play to more sophisticated audiences in the winter months. Performances at court were frequent; the English love of spectacle and pageantry found its most elaborate expression in the court masques designed for the Stuart court by Inigo Jones.

Shakespeare's name dominates the age of Elizabethan drama. *Macbeth* is an example of Shakespeare's dramaturgy with its episodic structure, blank verse, powerful soliloquies, and fluid scenes. It is the last of Shakespeare's four great tragedies, written in 1606 when he was at the height of his creative powers. The Royal Shakespeare Company's 1976 production of *Macbeth* at their studio theatre in Stratford-upon-Avon (England) is a modern example of Shakespeare in performance.

PLAYS TO READ
(All by William Shakespeare)

Macbeth

Hamlet

A Midsummer Night's Dream

SOURCES

Barnet, Sylvan, editor. New York: Signet *Classics, 1963–1983.* Paperback. The editions contain thorough introductions, notes on the sources, and commentaries by major Shakespeare critics. There are also suggested references included at the end of each edition.

Harbage, Alfred, editor. Baltimore: Penguin Books, 1956–1983. Paperback. *The Pelican Shakespeare Series.* Each edition contains an introductory discussion of Shakespeare and his stage, notes on the text, and a general discussion of the play. Good notes are found at the bottom of each page of the text and an appendix contains lists of all departures from the folio text. *Macbeth* is edited by Alfred Harbage (1956),

Hamlet by Willard Farnham (1957), and *A Midsummer Night's Dream* by Madeleine Doran (1959).

Wright, Louis B., and Virginia Lamar, editors. *The Folger Library Shakespeare Series.* New York: Washington Square Press, 1974–1983. Paperback. The introductions contain critical notes on each play, sources of the play, its stage history, notes on the author, a description of Shakespeare's theatre, and references for further reading. The texts are printed with notes on the opposite page for easy reading.

NOTES

1. For my understanding of the activities of the Globe company, I am indebted to material from Bernard Beckerman, *Shakespeare at the Globe 1599–1609* (New York: Macmillan, 1962).

2. Beckerman, p. 128.

3. For my understanding of the pictorial symbolism of the façade in Elizabethan public theatres, I am indebted to George F. Reynolds, *The Staging of Elizabethan Plays at the Red Bull Theater, 1605–25* (New York: Modern Language Association, 1940) and George R. Kernodle, *From Art to Theatre: Form and Convention in the Renaissance* (Chicago: University of Chicago Press, 1944).

4. Kernodle, p. 151. Reprinted by permission.

5. Alfred Harbage, *Shakespeare's Audience* (New York: Columbia University Press, 1941), pp. 1–52.

6. Jan Kott, *Shakespeare Our Contemporary*, trans. Boleslaw Taborski (New York: Doubleday, 1964), p. 97.

SIX

COMMEDIA DELL'ARTE AND RENAISSANCE ITALY

A MODERN PERSPECTIVE

We think of the Renaissance (1400–1600) as the first great period of fully mature accomplishments since Periclean Athens in the fifth century BC, especially in architecture, painting, and government. The theatre, too, took on new life in this period, as we have seen in Elizabethan theatre. In the 1500s Italy's professional theatre emerged in *commedia dell'arte*. The itinerant *commedia* companies knew no geographic boundaries or language barriers. They toured Spain, France, England, and Germany, spreading their special brand of improvisational theatre wherever they went.

In modern times improvisation has been a significant technique in actor training, drama therapy, and creative dramatics. Silent films served as a bridge between a European *commedia* tradition and the collective work in the 1960s of such American groups as the Open Theatre and the San Francisco Mime Troupe. In the 1930s the brilliant pantomime of Charlie Chaplin breathed life on the embers of a waning tradition carried on sporadically by European mimes and circus clowns. The improvisations of master comedians like Chaplin, Buster Keaton, Harpo Marx, and Bert Lahr have found their way into Samuel Beckett's plays and Marcel Marceau's mimes.

There have been other influences on modern theatre as well. In Renaissance Italy the court theatres of Florence, Ferrara, Mantua, and Milan encouraged elaborate spectacle and stage illusion. Today's theatre of scenic illusion and spectacular effects dates essentially from the court entertainments of the Medici and their compatriots.

In this chapter we examine the court theatres and the improvisational theatres of the past and also of the present. Let us begin with a look at the Gelosi Company, a *commedia dell'arte* troupe, in sixteenth-century Italy.

REPRESENTATIVE THEATRE: The Gelosi Company

There is a buzz of excitement throughout the sixteenth-century town of Bergamo in northern Italy. The Gelosi *commedia* troupe is passing through on their way to perform for the Duke of Mantua. Their carts are laden with actors, servants, children, animals, birds, costumes, and properties. Various members of the company play brisk tunes on recorders and drums to attract the attention of the townspeople. They tease children and adults into calling for a performance, although the Gelosi Company is far too grand to perform often in streets and marketplaces.

Francesco Andreini, the company's manager and director, barks commands for the carts and carriages to be attended to, and his young wife, Isabella, the company's leading lady, gives orders for the care of the costumes and masks.

A lesser-known company would be hur-

Figure 6-1 In this painting on wood dating from about 1572, we see what is thought to be the Italian *commedia dell'arte* company of Alberto Ganassa giving a performance in collaboration with the French Court of Charles IX. The *commedia* character types are interspersed among the nobility. Downstage center is Pantalone in a black robe and hat; behind him is Arlecchino in black mask and motley costume. On stage right with a serving maid is Brighella with a sword hanging from his belt. Behind the pair appears the head of another masked character who may be another *zanni*. This painting is by Paul Porbus, called Porbus the Elder, or by Frans Porbus.

riedly setting up its stage with boards and trestles and announcing with trumpets and drums the afternoon's performance. However, the Gelosi usually play only in buildings, like the Duke of Mantua's great hall, the impressive Palladio theatre in Vicenza, or the Hôtel de Bourgogne in Paris. But on this day in Bergamo the crowd's enthusiasm persuades them to perform in the town square.

While their productions feature the familiar *commedia* characters—the clownish Arlecchino,

Italian High Renaissance, 1300–1500

Gutenberg, invention of movable type (~1440)	Spain united under Isabella and Ferdinand (1469)
Constantinople falls to the Turks 1453	Lorenzo de Medici controls Florence 1478–1492
	Inquisition in Spain 1480–1834
	Christopher Columbus sails to America 1492
	Vasco da Gama sails to India, 1497

the miserly Pantalone, and the swaggering Capitano played by Francesco Andreini himself—the Gelosi are so successful that they are sought after by kings and princes to play before their courts in France and Italy. Andreini plays the male lover and also the braggart captain. Isabella Andreini, the female lead, is famous throughout Italy for her beauty, learning, and cultivation. Very soon she will die of a miscarriage and be buried with pomp and ceremony by the governor of Lyons in France.

The company's scenarios suit almost any occasion, including royal marriages in Paris and carnivals in Venice, Genoa, and Milan. The Gelosi actors have played together so often and so successfully that their dialogue, jokes, and comic business appear to be wholly improvised. Dressed in the familiar masks and costumes of their character types, their celebrated skill at improvising dialogue, sight gags, and acrobatics set the standard for *commedia* companies for at least 100 years.

After the company performs for Bergamo's townspeople, they pack their costumes, masks, musical instruments, and portable stage into their carts. The Gelosi continue on their way to perform again and again before peasants, merchants, and courtiers.

CONDITIONS OF PERFORMANCE

Performance conditions in Italy during the Renaissance were influenced by the growth of trade routes and by the exchange of culture, artifacts, and artists. It was a sign of the times that Italy's popular theatre, the *commedia dell'arte*, was both secular and transient. Just as ideas and paintings were transportable over the mountains of northern Italy, so, too, was its theatre. To understand the theatrical rebirth that took place in Italy in the 1500s and produced companies like the Gelosi, we need to take a closer look

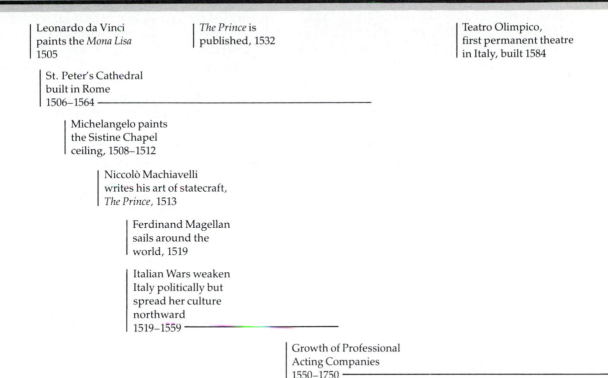

1500

Leonardo da Vinci
paints the *Mona Lisa*
1505

St. Peter's Cathedral
built in Rome
1506–1564

Michelangelo paints
the Sistine Chapel
ceiling, 1508–1512

Niccolò Machiavelli
writes his art of statecraft,
The Prince, 1513

Ferdinand Magellan
sails around the
world, 1519

Italian Wars weaken
Italy politically but
spread her culture
northward
1519–1559

The Prince is
published, 1532

Growth of Professional
Acting Companies
1550–1750

Teatro Olimpico,
first permanent theatre
in Italy, built 1584

at the new secular humanism that was sweeping northward from the Mediterranean Sea to Scotland.

BACKGROUND

The traditional picture of the Renaissance is of a gradual renewal of creative thought and learning after the "dark years" of the Middle Ages. But from today's vantage point, the years 1400–1600 in Europe were more like a cultural explosion—a cultural "big bang." The ferment of ideas was sparked by a new secular spirit and a new interest in classical civilization, which led to prodigious accomplishments in architecture, painting, sculpture, technology, exploration, and government. The famous people who crowd this historical landscape are of varied geography and

vocations. They are from Italy, France, England, Germany, and Spain; some of their names are Michelangelo, Niccolò Machiavelli, Leonardo da Vinci, Thomas More, Martin Luther, Christopher Columbus, and Ferdinand Magellan. In truth, the Renaissance was a time of unparalleled exploration and accomplishment in all areas of life.

Italy was the crossroads of the Mediterranean trade routes extending from northern Europe to Asia and Africa. Trade produced the wealth needed to support government, learning, architecture, and the arts. Two events of prime importance to the development of literature and dramatic writing were the fall of Constantinople in 1453, which brought scholars and manuscripts of Greek plays to Italy, and the introduction of the printing press into Italy in 1465, which made the wide dissemination of classical texts possible. The prosperous cities of fifteenth-century Italy (Florence, Venice, Mantua, Genoa, Milan) became centers of classical scholarship pursued under the patronage of wealthy and urbane rulers. The new learning, like the theatre that developed alongside it, was predominantly *secular*; its concerns were with the natural world, not the supernatural one. Patrons, scholars, and artists celebrated human achievement and the idea that humankind had the power to shape its own destiny. The new learning was called *humanitas* (or Humanism) and described a new concern for the value of people, their ideas, and their lives. It drew inspiration from the classical world, where it first flourished, and stimulated interest in Greece and Rome throughout Europe.

The Italian theatre during the Renaissance took its inspiration from native theatrical entertainments and from Greek and Latin plays. Italian theatre had its beginning before 240 BC in sacred festivals in Etruria (in northern Italy), which included acting, dancing, flute playing, juggling, prize fighting, horse racing, acrobatics, and competitive sports.

In southern Italy the Atellan farces were another type of popular theatre. Derived from mimes of Roman times, the farces were probably short, largely improvised, and based on domestic situations or burlesques of myths. Character types, each with its own costume and mask, were also characteristic.

Latin drama originated in Fescennine verses—named for the town of Fescennium where they were first performed—and consisted of improvised, abusive, and often obscene dialogue exchanged between masked clowns at harvest and wedding celebrations. Rome derived its name for actors (*histriones*) from these professional performers. Later, performers added improvised dialogue to music and dance to create a new form most familiar in comedies by Plautus and Terence. The Roman playwrights influenced Italy's vernacular drama written after 1500 by Ludovico Ariosto, Niccolò Machiavelli, Torquato Tasso, and Giambattista Guarini.

It was the festival theatre of improvised farces with fixed characters and masks that most influenced the growth of professional theatre in Italy. The *commedia dell'arte* was the name given to companies of professional actors performing largely improvised material. The vibrant, improvisational spirit and skill of these companies created an international theatre that lasted in Europe for almost 200 years.

MANAGEMENT OF THE *COMMEDIA* COMPANIES

The *commedia dell'arte* began in Italy in the sixteenth century. However, we are not entirely certain about its origins. It may have evolved from early Roman farces performed by wandering mimes during the Middle Ages or from improvisations based upon comedies of Plautus and Terence or even from Italian farces of the early sixteenth century. Whatever its sources, by 1580 the *commedia dell'arte* was flourishing as popular entertainment throughout Italy, France, and Spain.

The average size of a *commedia* company was 10 to 12 members, of which 3 to 4 were women. Unlike the performance conventions in England and elsewhere, in Italy female parts in *commedia* were played by women. The actors were usually divided into two sets of lovers, two old men, and several *zanni* (an array of comic servants, braggarts, buffoons, tricksters, and dupes).

The company was organized around a sharing plan. Company members shared the production costs and divided the profits. Young actors may have been salaried until they were granted full membership. The leader, or most respected actor, supervised productions. He wrote *scenarios* along with other actors and explained the plots, characters, and traditional stage business to the company. He also supervised costumes, masks, properties, and scenic pieces. Since the companies traveled constantly, everything had to be transportable. They usually hired large rooms in towns and performed on indoor court stages or on temporary booth stages set up in streets and marketplaces.

Rehearsals were held whenever schedules permitted.

Several companies became internationally famous: the Uniti, Confidenti, Accesi, and Gelosi. The Gelosi (meaning "zealous") was probably the most famous company performing between 1569 and 1604 in Italy and France. Since they were frequently invited to play at court, they were able to utilize the elaborate stage machinery of the day. Their greatest success was *La Princesse qui a perdu L'Esprit* featuring music, mechanical devices, and a naval battle. Their outstanding members were Flaminio Scala, Francesco Andreini (1548–1624), and Isabella Andreini (1562–1604), the most famous *inamorata* of her day (Figure 6-2). The company disbanded upon her death in 1604, but Scala and Andreini worked to preserve the company's history and repertory by publishing the scenarios in 1611.

VISUAL ELEMENTS

Improvisational Methods The chief characteristics of *commedia dell'arte* were improvisation and stock characters. Actors worked from a plot outline (the *scenario*), posted backstage during performances, which listed the order of the scenes and explained what each scene was about. On the basis of this outline actors improvised dialogue and action. They usually played the same characters whose attitudes, costumes, and masks never varied.

There is some question about what was improvised from one performance to the next and which bits of stage business were fixed and handed down from one actor to the next. Playing the same character throughout an actor's career must have encouraged the repetition of dialogue and sight gags that had proved popular with audiences. Many bits of comic business (called *lazzi*) were sufficiently repeated to be indicated in the plot outlines as *lazzi* of fear, *lazzi* of love, *lazzi* of jealousy, and so on. Actions like Brighella or Scapin catching a fly on the wing and chewing it with great gusto were usually show-stoppers and were eagerly anticipated by audiences.

Although some elements were fixed and others were freely improvised, *commedia* performances created a general impression of spontaneity. The companies probably followed out-lines to avoid confusing the audience, repeated popular *lazzi* as crowd pleasers, and memorized some dialogue. The actors probably also memorized rhyming couplets used to end scenes. Otherwise, in the hour-long performances, actors were free to improvise. In turn, they had to be prepared to improvise responses to unexpected dialogue and business.

Staging: Portable and Fixed As itinerant companies the *commedia dell'arte* usually carried their stage, costumes, curtains, masks, and properties with them in carts about the countryside. Their stages (boards placed on trestles) were small and high, the platform being at about eye level to the standing spectators. The platform was divided into two sections by a large painted curtain suspended between two poles, creating a forestage and backstage. Jacques Callot's etching from the seventeenth century (Figure 6-3) shows actors on a platform, others peering from behind the

---

FLAMINIO SCALA

Flaminio Scala (fl. 1600–1621) was a *commedia dell'arte* performer, stage director, and playwright who worked for a time with the Gelosi Company. During his association with the Gelosi, he preserved 50 *commedia* scenarios, which he published in 1611 as "The Theatre of the Performed Tales, or Comic, Pastoral, and Tragic Entertainments Divided into Fifty 'Days'." The collection is known briefly as "The Theatre for Fifty Days."

Scala's life, what little we know about it, was probably similar to that of other famous *commedia* actors of the time in its variety and mobility. He directed one *commedia* company in 1597 and appeared in another in 1600–1601 while it played in France at the invitation of the king. He published a comedy, performed in Mantua in 1606 at the duke's palace; he left Mantua in 1611 to take service with Giovanni de Medici in Florence and assume the direction of the Confidenti Company. In 1620 he performed in Venice. This is the last record that we have of his activities.

Gherardi, a famous seventeenth-century actor who played Harlequin, described the methods of the *commedia dell'arte*:

❝ The Italian comedians learn nothing by heart; they need but to glance at the subject of a play a moment or two before going upon the stage. It is this very ability to play at a moment's notice which makes a good Italian actor so difficult to replace. Anyone can learn a part and recite it on the stage, but something else is required for Italian comedy. For a good Italian actor is a man of infinite resources and resourcefulness, a man who plays more from imagination than from memory; he matches his words and actions so perfectly with those of his colleagues on the stage that he enters instantly into whatever acting and movements are required of him in such a manner as to give the impression that all that they do has been prearranged.❞

Gherardi, *Le Théâtre Italien* . . . (1694)

Balli di Sfessania
di Jacomo Callot

Figure 6-3 One of Jacques Callot's etchings showing *commedia* actors and staging.

curtain, and an actor standing on a ladder to the side of the stage observing the scene while waiting for an entrance. Slits in the curtain served for entrances and exits along with ladders placed on both sides of the stage. The backdrop usually had painted scenes of a public square and streets in perspective.

Most companies toured the countryside and cities, playing at fairs, on holidays, for special engagements, or at random. The more important companies (the Gelosi, for example) performed under different conditions. They were invited to play in court theatres and palaces. At Vicenza they played in the Teatro Olimpico, a permanent theatre designed by Italian architect Andrea Palladio in 1580 and completed by Vincenzo Scamozzi in 1585.

The auditorium of the Teatro Olimpico was elliptical with tiers of seats, as in the ancient amphitheatres. Its stage was divided into a main stage and proscenium platform that extended outward. The main stage was then blocked off into three sections by decorative façades that opened onto streets that, viewed from the audience, gave an effect of distance. The most complicated plots and intrigues were possible on this stage. While one group played on the proscenium, the audience could observe others along the distant street. For instance, while Isabella sat at the window serenaded by her lover from below, Brighella, a *zanni*, could overhear their love making from the shadow of the arcade. The audience was able to follow every detail of plot; Brighella was in full view of the audience and yet completely hidden from the lovers.

The fixed architectural setting was appropriate for all occasions. However, since there was no way to change scenery, actors had to recite a prologue to the audience in which the general locations of the action were described. In the event the action took place in a house, a specially constructed set (or mansion) was erected on the main stage.

Masks, Costumes, and Properties Regardless of the type of stage used, the companies depended upon masks, costumes, and properties to provide color and visual effects. Many scenarios played by the Gelosi contain lists of properties and special costumes.

Commedia masks, unlike classical masks and those of China and Japan, did not express any particular emotion like laughter or sorrow. Instead, they gave a permanent expression to a particular character, such as craftiness or greed. The mask's expressiveness varied with the angle from which it was seen. Also, the suppleness of the actor's body was required to complement the mask's effect. The masks were black, olive green, brown, and flesh colored and were supplemented with an array of hats, beards, mustaches, eyebrows, chin pieces, wrinkles, warts, hooked noses, small or large eyes, and glasses (Figure 6-4).

JACQUES CALLOT

Jacques Callot (c. 1592–1635), a French artist, spent a number of years in Italy recording in sketches, prints, and engravings the popular theatre of his day: street theatre, fairs, mountebanks, river spectacles, processions with wagons, operatic works, *intermezzi*, and the *commedia dell' arte*. His work is a rich source of details of costuming, stage business, bodily postures, properties, musical instruments, settings, physical staging, and audience behavior. While his drawings are stylized, they capture the spirit of the *commedia* performer as he practices his craft.

Callot's masterpiece on the *commedia* is a series of 23 etchings entitled *I Balli di Sfessania* (c. 1622). (We do not know what Callot meant by this title.) Almost every sketch shows a pair of actors in the foreground flanked by musicians, other actors, or a street scene. Except for the women, all the characters are masked and carry swords, slapsticks, and even syringes. (A slapstick, constructed of two pieces of wood, made a clacking noise when hit against the leg or another person.) Many wear a phallus enhanced comically with a cloth draped over it as a sight gag.

Stage Properties

Many *commedia dell'arte* scenarios include lists of stage properties, presenting as wide a range of animals, objects, and clothing as we would expect to find in a modern production. Included are rings, purse, heart, blood, dagger, Turkish clothes, turban, bow, arrows, candle, chest, washing basket with sheets, valises, hats, boots, food, books, shovel, bundles of wood, crown, gold chain, decanter of wine, flames, paper, pen, money, inkstand, ladder, flour, apples, oranges, book, sausage, two bladders, plate of macaroni, fountain, flowers, urinal, bear, lion, bull, tree, birthing chair, eagle, and a cat.

a   *Scaramucia.*   *Fricasso.*

Figure 6-4 (a) The figures called by their French names are standing back to back in a fighting pose with their capes draped over their left arms. There are various figures in the background, including musicians. (b) Brighella (called Scapino here) is playing some kind of game with a Capitano. On the ground between them is a wine bottle wrapped in raffia. In the background we see figures fighting while others look on. (c) This etching depicts a common *lazzi*: a large syringe being used to squirt at the exposed backside of another character (in this case a Capitano). In the background are dancers and spectators.

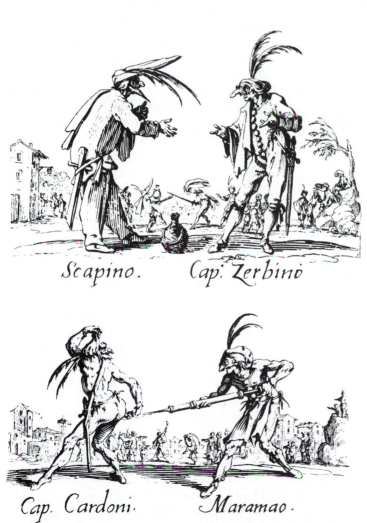

b   *Scapino.*   *Cap: Zerbino*

c   *Cap. Cardoni.*   *Maramao.*

Figure 6-5 Callot's etching of Pantalone.

Commedia costumes underwent subtle changes from company to company and from period to period. Of the *zannis*, *Arlecchino* wore a soft cap with fur or feathers; dark, multicolored patches sewn on his pants and jacket; and a bat (or phallus) and wallet hung from his belt. A black half-mask with wrinkles across his forehead, small eyes with a large wart under one eye, and an expression of craftiness and sensuality completed his character.

Brighella wore a jacket and full trousers with green braid along the seams, a short mantle, and soft hat with a green border. He carried a large leather purse and a dagger. As he became more of a servant in the plays and less of an adventurer, he was costumed in a white frock with a turn-down collar. His mask was olive green with sloe eyes, a hooked nose, sparse beard on the chin, and a twisted moustache.

The *Capitano* and other servants wore variations on the ordinary uniforms of the day. The captain, a spoof on the Spanish military of the day, wore the military dress of the period with a long sword, a flesh-colored mask with a large nose, and bristling moustaches. *Pedrolino*, a servant, was played without a mask but with a heavily powdered face in the universally familiar "clown" costume including a ruff.

Pantalone, the *Dottore*, and *Pulcinella* (or Punch) were the *commedia's* elder citizens. Whether he was married or a bachelor, Pantalone was a miserly and greedy merchant. He wore a loose black cape over a red jacket, trousers, and hose with Turkish slippers and a soft black hat and carried a large dagger and a purse at his belt. His mask was brown with a hooked nose, gray, sparse moustache, and a pointed white beard (Figure 6-5). He sometimes wore round eyeglasses. Pantalone's companion in black, the Dottore, wore garments that caricatured the ordinary dress of men of learning of the time: a knee-length black gown and a long, black robe and hat. His mask was black or flesh colored covering his forehead and nose. His cheeks were red and sometimes he had a short, pointed beard. Pulcinella was disfigured by a humpback, potbelly, spindly legs, and hooked nose. His white blouse was caught below the waist by a leather belt; a wooden sword and fat wallet hung from it. He wore wide trousers and a scarf about his neck that in time became a starched ruff. A dark mask with a large nose was adorned by a heavy moustache and beard.

The lovers wore fashionable garments of the period. The men dressed as gallants and the women wore ruffles and bodices embroidered in gold and silk. They sometimes carried a small black velvet mask, or *loup*, and used it occasionally.

Music and Dance Music and dance in Italian Renaissance theatre took varied forms. As the Callot etchings suggest, music and dance were used throughout *commedia dell'arte* performances. In contrast, "learned comedy" put music and dancing in an *intermezzi*, an entertainment with spectacle and music performed between the acts of regular drama. *Intermezzi* began as court entertainments for special occasions such as betrothals and weddings—scenic spectacles with allegory and music. In the seventeenth century they were absorbed into opera, chiefly an entertainment of the courts and academies of the time. The first great operatic composer was Claudio Monteverde (1567–1643) whose *Orfeo* (1607) first shifted theatre's emphasis from drama to music.

POPULAR ENTERTAINMENTS

Carnivals and Fairs Carnivals and fairs were highly popular in Europe as early as the twelfth century. They drew large crowds from all classes of people: nobility, fashionable women, lackeys, pages, rogues, and solid bourgeoisie. People thronged to see the marionettes, the two-headed cow, the cock fights, the games of chance, the tightrope walkers, acrobats, jugglers, magicians, and actors. The general scene was as lively as the entertainments. Vendors sold soap, bonnets, trinkets, wines, and cakes. Tooth extractors

blew horns to attract customers and entertained the onlookers with the patient's writhings.

In this setting in the seventeenth century appeared such *commedia* characters as Arlecchino, Capitano, and Brighella who performed on their small stages with skits, parades, and acrobatics. In general, the fairs displayed the spirit and comic buffoonery of Italian *commedia dell'arte*.

Marionettes Marionettes trace their origins to the early Roman (*Atellan*) farces. Some *commedia* characters were first conceived as marionettes and vice versa. Burattino, originally a *commedia* character, became a leading character of marionette theatre; his fame was such that by the end of the sixteenth century, all marionettes operated by strings and wires were called *burattini*.

THE AUDIENCE

Audiences for popular theatre in Italy, France, and Spain were as motley a group as could be found at any country fair, at carnivals during holidays, and at festivals put on by the Medicis to display their wealth and power. The *commedia* companies traveled far and wide in pursuit of employment and audiences. They performed not only for royalty but also for villagers, tradesmen, and farmers in small villages and crowded marketplaces.

COURT THEATRES AND FESTIVALS

Productions of plays at the court of Ferrara in northern Italy and at the Roman Academy began about 1486. Soon other courts and academies followed their example. By the early sixteenth century plays were considered suitable entertainment for almost all court celebrations. These festivals, symbols of princely power, were the forerunners of modern opera, ballet, and the theatre of illusion.

Figure 6-6 The Terence stage showing a scene from *Adelphi*. The name above each door identifies the house of a character. Note how the characters use the curtains as entranceways.

The Stage The long road to the modern theatre of illusion and spectacle began in Renaissance Italy with the interest in Vitruvius' treatise on Roman architecture (first century BC or AD). Printed about 1486, Vitruvius' *De Architectura* quickly became the authority on all matters relating to architecture and staging in ancient Rome. Since many of his verbal descriptions were not illustrated, producers interpreted his remarks in a variety of ways. One result was the "Terence stage" shown in late fifteenth-century illustrated editions of Terence's plays: a platform stage backed by a continuous façade, either straight or angled, and divided into a series of curtained openings, each representing the house of a different character (Figure 6-6).

Perspective Scenery The use of a stage of this type was soon modified by the addition of per-

spective painting. Perspective drawing exerted a fascination over the Renaissance mind because of its almost magical ability to manipulate illusion. Sebastiano Serlio's (1475–1554) *Architettura*, printed in 1545, best sums up the practices of early sixteenth-century painters and architects and includes a section on the theatre with illustrations of tragic, comic, and satyric scenes based on Vitruvius' descriptions (Figure 6-7).

In Serlio's day theatres were set up in already existing rooms in the great halls of palaces. The builders constructed stadiumlike seating around an orchestra (used almost exclusively to seat the ruler and his guests). The stage at one end of the room was raised to eye level and perspective scenery designed so that the ideal view of it was from the ruler's chair. The front part of the stage floor, used by the actors, was level, while the back of this floor sloped upward at a

Scena Comica.

Figure 6-7 The principles of perspective painting were introduced to theatrical scene design in the sixteenth century. Perspective scenery created the illusion of large streets or town squares, with houses, churches, roofs, doorways, arches, and balconies all designed to appear exactly as they would seem to a person standing at a single point. These painted backgrounds gave a sense of depth to the scenes. In *Architettura*, Sebastiano Serlio explained the construction and painting of scenery for comedy, including the houses, tavern, and church shown in this drawing.

sharp angle to increase the illusion of distance. All scenery (based on Vitruvius' floor plan) had the same requirements: four sets of wings and a backdrop. This scenery was not meant to be changed. However, interest in spectacle soon increased the demand for movable scenery. Of the many solutions the chief one became the use of flat wings that could be changed by sliding them in grooves set into the stage floor. Scene handlers could then withdraw the set of visible wings to reveal another set behind, as many as the number of settings needed for the play. The back scene was usually painted on two flats (or shutters) that met at the center of the stage. Sometimes painted cloths that could be rolled up were hung from the wings. In 1606 at the court of Ferrara, Giovan Battista Aleotti (1546–1636) applied new principles of perspective painting to the flat wings and

made this type of movable scenery popular for the next 40 years.

In the 1640s Giacomo Torelli (1608–1678) invented the chariot-and-pole system of scene shifting, the next revolutionary step in scenic design (Figure 6-8). Working at the Teatro Novissimo in Venice, he cut slots in the stage floor and passed upright supports (or poles) through them. Flats were mounted to the poles above the floor level; they were attached to "chariots" beneath the stage set in tracks parallel to the front of the stage. An elaborate system of ropes and pulleys attached to a winch beneath the stage could move all of the chariots simultaneously. As the chariots rolled toward the center of the stage, they carried flats into view; when they moved in the opposite direction the scenery disappeared from sight. The moving scenery was almost magical to the audiences of the day.

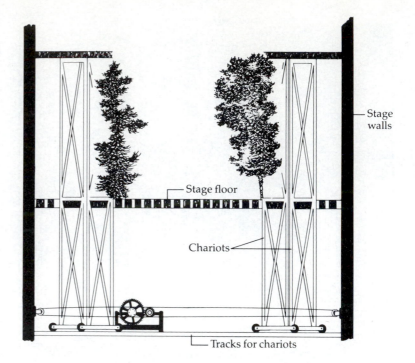

Figure 6-8 The chariot-and-pole or "continental" system shifted scenery. The chariots ride in tracks below the stage, and lines, pulleys, and levers move the chariots.

Stage walls

Stage floor

Chariots

Tracks for chariots

This system became the standard method of scene shifting in most European theatres until the late nineteenth century.

Lighting The indoor court and opera theatres required artificial lighting. Candles and oil lamps generally illuminated theatres; they could be mounted on vertical poles behind the proscenium and between the wings and borders. Chandeliers were often hung over the auditorium and the stage itself, and footlights were also used at the front of the stage. Stage directors had little control over the amount of illumination once the candles and lamps were lit, although some used stovepipe devices that could be lowered over the candles and lamps to darken the scene and then raised to bring the light back up (Figure 6-9). There were also crude effects to change the color of the light through the use of tinted glass or silk screens placed in front of the lamps. But for the most part effective control of intensity and color had to wait until the introduction of gas in the first quarter of the nineteenth century.

Court Spectacles Spectacular productions with crowds of performers and lavish movable scenery soon became associated with political prestige and power in the courts of Ferrara, Mantua, Urbino, Milan, and Rome. But the Medicis at Florence surpassed these, and court spectacle probably peaked there in the work of Bernardo Buontalenti (1536–1608), who created entertainments at the Medici court for nearly 60 years. His court spectacles with highly imaginative costumes, scenery, machinery, and special effects helped to create the visual style that was to become so elaborate in later years. In 1589 Buontalenti supervised the month-long festivities honoring the marriage of the Grand Duke Ferdinand de Medici I. Masquerades, animal hunts, a naumachia on the Arno River, *intermezzi,* comedies, and other events entertained the wedding guests. He was succeeded by his pupil Giulio Parigi (c. 1570–1635) from whom the English court designer, Inigo Jones, learned much that he was to apply in staging English masques between 1605 and 1640.

Almost immediately, the scenic splendors of

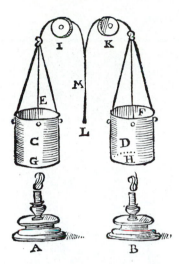

Figure 6-9 In this candle-dimming device, the light was regulated by raising or lowering the hollow cylinders. (From Sabbattini, *Manual for Constructing Theatrical Scenes and Machines*, 1638.)

Nicola Sabbattini (1574–1659) described scene-shifting practices in the seventeenth century. In 1638 he published his *Manual For Constructing Theatrical Scenes and Machines* in which he listed four methods of shifting scenery. The older method was the use of *periaktoi*—three-sided scenic pieces that could be turned toward the audience one side at a time, used by Inigo Jones in England. Two other methods were changing angled wings by maneuvering new frames around those already in place or by pulling painted canvas over the visible surfaces. These methods were clumsy and time consuming. The fourth eventually became the most popular practice: flat wings (instead of angled wings) placed across the rear of the stage in a series from front to back, each revealing a new set (or scene) as it was pulled offstage. Borders (framed pieces of cloth) were hung above each set of wings, continuing the scene overhead and also concealing from the audience whatever was above the stage. These elements— borders, wings, and back scenes—eventually became the standard parts of every set.

the court theatres influenced opera production. With the opening of the first opera houses in Venice in 1637, the spectacles of the court theatres became available to the general public. From opera they spread to the other public theatres. By the end of the seventeenth century, Italian scenic practices had been adopted by court and public theatres throughout Europe.

DRAMATIC CONVENTIONS

SCENARIOS

Commedia scenarios (*soggeto*) were divided into three acts. Like the characters, costumes, and masks, these plot outlines were passed down from one actor or company to the next. Some were even pirated from rival companies. More than 700 have been preserved.

On retiring from the stage, an actor wrote out the scenarios he or she had played. Sometimes, like Scala's, they were sold and printed. While there were serious and tragicomic scripts, the greatest number were comic, dealing with love, intrigues, disguises, and misunderstandings. The actors did not write out their dialogue but did set down directions for movement and stage business. Emotional outbursts, comic reversals, and *lazzi* moved the action along quickly with unexpected climaxes.

There were usually the following groups of characters in the comedies: old men, their wives,

Commedia dell'arte performance in the arena at Verona. Note the temporary stage and seating. The side boxes with roofs are similar to box seating in indoor theatres. Various *commedia* characters are on stage with an *inamorata* apparently center stage. (From Marco Marcola's oil painting, 1772.)

Teatro Olimpico in Vicenza was designed by architect Andrea Palladio in 1580 and completed by Vincenzo Scamozzi in 1585. Scamozzi added the perspective vistas behind the five doorways. The long, narrow stage was backed by a permanent scenic façade richly ornamented with niches, statues, and pillars. The façade had five openings or doorways that were probably closed with curtains.

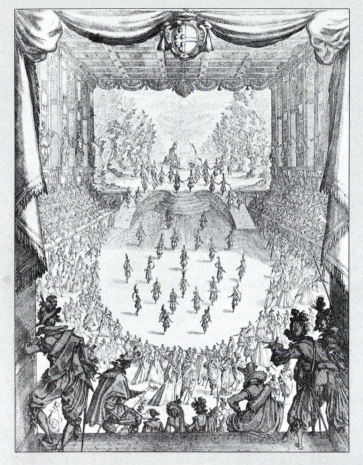

The Uffizi Teatro, sometimes called the Teatro Medici, opened in Florence in 1586 as a permanent theatre in the Uffizi building. Designed by Bernardo Buontalenti, the hall held 3000 to 4000 people. The grand duke and his guests sat on a dais in the center, ladies were seated by rank along the side walls, and men took their places on the raked floor. This etching by Jacques Callot gives us an idea of the grandeur of the auditorium and scenery as it appeared in 1617.

The Teatro Farnese, built in 1618 in Parma, was one of the early theatres with a permanent proscenium arch. An ornamental façade framed the stage and separated the audience from the actors and scenery.

lovers, clowns, and servants. Events rose out of conflicting interests; for example, fathers competing with sons for marriage with a wealthy friend's daughter. Various disguises and tricks filled out the plots. At the end love's complications were unknotted, young lovers united, husbands and wives reunited.

If we read scenarios like *The Three Cuckolds* (c. 1618) we can perceive the bare bones of characters, events, disguises, and *lazzi*. But we are left without the live antics, bright costumes, and general merriment of a *commedia* performance.

1500	1550
Lodovico Ariosto (1474–1533) *The Casket*	Serlio publishes *Architettura* 1545
Niccolò Machiavelli (1469–1527) *The Mandrake* 1513–1520	Hôtel de Bourgogne, permanent theatre built in Paris 1548
Giraldi Cinthio (1504–1573) *Orbecche,* 1541	

CHARACTER TYPES

Commedia characters were usually divided into straight and exaggerated types. The lovers were always fashionable young people of the day, and, like the serving maid (the *fantesca*), were played without masks. Exaggerated characters appeared in one form or another in all *commedia* companies: the braggart soldier, the credulous doctor, miserly tradesmen, scheming servants, and wayward clowns.

All the major *commedia* characters have had their counterparts in other countries and times. Arlecchino (also called Harlequin), one of the oldest *commedia* characters and one of several *zanni*, was a numskull with flashes of shrewdness. Sixteenth- and seventeenth-century engravings show him leaping about, somersaulting, dancing, walking on stilts, or making love to an *inamorata*. Dressed in motley with irregular patches and a black mask, he was a continual display of tricks, movement, and roguishness. His chief trait through the years has been resiliency.

Brighella (portrayed in France as Scapin and Figaro) changed over time from a swaggering and quarrelsome liar, drunkard, and even murderer to a scheming servant. His mask with slanted eyes and hooked nose gave him a sinister expression to match his schemes.

Pantalone, the Dottore, and Pulcinella were types of senior citizens. Pantalone was always the old, stingy merchant. Rich or poor, he was a dupe in love and trade. His companion, Dottore, appeared some times as a physician and others as a man of letters. In all ways he was an old windbag. The general impression of his black costume was gravity mingled with foolish self-importance. Pulcinella (Punch in England and Hanswurst in Germany) was another old bachelor type, selfish, boastful, quick witted, and cruel, his humpback, potbelly, and large nose reflecting his sensuality and gluttony. He has remained a favorite character of Punch and Judy shows. Pedrolino (later Pagliaccio and Pierrot) has become the classic clown figure dressed in loose-fitting tunic and white-powdered face. The Capitano (later Scaramouche and Cyrano in France) was a swaggering, arrogant coward similar to the *miles gloriosus* or braggart soldier in Roman comedy. As Callot's etchings suggest, the military cad was a favorite *commedia* figure.

The handsome young lovers were important to the *commedia* plots but less so to the comic business. The man (the *inamorato*) was usually named Ottavio, Orazio, or Lelio, and the woman (the *inamorata*) was called Isabella, Lavinia, or Flaminia. The women—beautiful, cultivated, charming, and accomplished singers, dancers, and musicians—mostly defined their own roles by their talents. Like the men, their chief trait

Torquato Tasso ———————— *Commedia dell'arte* companies flourish———
Aminta, 1573   1580s to 1750s

James Burbage builds   Flaminio Scala
the Theatre, London   publishes Gelosi
1576   scripts, Venice, 1611

Teatro Olimpico, designed by   Teatro Farnese
Palladio, built 1580–1584   built in 1618
                                   First proscenium
Giambattista   arch theatre
Guarini, *The*
Faithful Shepherd
1590

was being in love. Their amorous intrigues were central to the comic plots, but the horseplay was carried out by the exaggerated characters.

REPRESENTATIVE PLAY

The Three Cuckolds (Li Tre Becchi)
From the Corsini manuscript dated around 1622 and located in the Palazzo Corsini, Rome. The acting date by a *commedia* company was probably much earlier.

The Three Cuckolds, first performed in the first quarter of the seventeenth century, is a representative scenario. It was devised for a seven-member company of four men and three women. Its character types, or "masks" as they were called, are familiar: two old men, three young women, a nameless *zanni* who doubles as a husband, and a handsome young man. The chief comics are the old men—Pantalone and Coviello—married to young wives.

The main action is the pursuit of love: Pan-

talone pursues Franceschina who is married to the *zanni,* Coviello pursues Flaminia married to Pantalone, Leandro pursues Cintia married to Coviello. The *zanni* is in a constant flurry of activity to avoid being cuckolded. But all his efforts are doomed. Just as he comes to his doorway to check on his wife, he hears "caresses going on," and knocks in a fury. He threatens to burn down the house, but Franceschina persuades him to carry out a basket of newly washed sheets first. Pantalone, undiscovered, is carried out in the basket by the deceived husband. With this reprieve the comedy ends. Arm in arm, the characters gather before the *zanni's* house. Leandro explains love's confusions and reunites husbands and wives.

While the scenario describes the lovers' frantic knocking at the doorways of love, we have only the dry bones of a performance script in *The Three Cuckolds.* By exercising our imaginations we can flesh out the characters, including the foolish old men and the unscrupulous young women who are rarely models of virtue. The *lazzi* of jealousy and of cuckoldry are carefully noted in the script along with the use of stage properties, such as a chest of lemons and the basket of sheets.

A *commedia* script was a rogue's gallery of types strongly individualized by the talents of the actors. What we have in the following script of *The Three Cuckolds* is the mere outline that was posted backstage to cue the actors on the sequence of scenes and particular stage business.

The Three Cuckolds[1]

Dramatis Personae
Pantalone.
Flaminia, his wife.   Lucinda.

Coviello.   Ubaldo.
Cintia, his wife.   Ardelia.

Zanni.   Cola.
Franceschina, his wife.   Columbina.

Leandro, a young man.   Ottavio.
                             Valerio.
                             Stoppino,
                             servant.

Properties.
A washing basket with sheets; chest for lemons; cask; tow; fire; candle; broth; dress for a rogue.

ACT I

Coviello, Cintia have their scene of reciprocal jealousy. Cintia goes in and leaves Coviello to disclose his passion for Flaminia, the wife of Pantalone; he knocks at her door:

Flaminia appears. They have their love scene and in the end she tells him about the chest of lemons. Coviello goes in, Flaminia stays; at this:

Pantalone is asked to provide her with lemons; he promises to send them in a chest. Flaminia goes in. Pantalone is left to disclose his love for Franceschina, Zanni's wife; he knocks at her door:

Franceschina hears everything and declares that she favours Pantalone; he departs, she remains; at this:

Zanni tells his wife to go to work; they have many antics. Franceschina goes in and he stays saying what a nuisance she is; at this:

Coviello asks Zanni to carry him in a chest and explains everything. They go off down the street.

Leandro declares his love for Cintia and knocks at her door:

Cintia hears everything and instructs him to come dressed as a rogue, dumb and disguised. She goes in and he departs to dress up.

Pantalone can wait no longer and says that at last it is time; he knocks for Franceschina.

Franceschina leads him into the house and they have their antics over the entrance.

Zanni, Coviello with the chest, exhorts Coviello not to speak or move; he puts him inside; at this:

Leandro as a dumb beggar is forced to shoulder the chest by Zanni who does not recognize him; at this:

Flaminia receives the chest. Zanni enters. Leandro is left and knocks for Cintia.

Cintia receives him into the house, they have their scene and the act ends.

ACT II

Zanni blames Flaminia for the trick played on her husband and congratulates himself on the honesty of his wife Franceschina; meanwhile she is heard within singing and slapping up and down with the washing; then she comes out.

Franceschina appears with the cask which she puts over her husband's head, playing the trick of the tart; at this:

Pantalone comes out of Franceschina's house grinning, he goes to knock at his own home. Zanni and Franceschina go in. Pantalone is left calling his wife.

Flaminia with much circumstance recounts the dream of the eye and makes him hide his eyes from Flaminia; at this:

Coviello comes out of Flaminia's house laughing at the trick. He goes to knock at his own. Pantalone and Flaminia go in; Coviello knocks.

Cintia makes much of Coviello and caresses

Fracischina.

Figure 6-10 Fracischina (Franceschina?), another of the *commedia* etchings by Callot.

and Zanni in the end tells about the lemon-chest and goes in. Pantalone is left; at this:

Coviello is told of the hoax of the rogue; they have their scene together shouting "Cuckold" at each other.

ACT III

Franceschina to borrow a buck-basket knocks for

Cintia who promises to give it to her with the washing and takes her into the house.

Pantalone wishes to return to Franceschina who had pleased him; at this:

Franceschina comes with the basket and the clothes. Pantalone explains his intentions and she makes him get into the basket and covers him with clothes; at this:

Zanni aware of all that is going on and knowing there is someone in the basket has many antics about throwing the clothes into the copper and boiling them. He carries in the basket and coming out again tells Franceschina that he is going into the country. She is delighted and goes into the house. Zanni goes down the street.

Coviello after his former success wishes to try again, he knocks for

Flaminia who hears his wish and receives him once more and leads him into the house.

Leandro, Cintia do the same; Cintia embraces him and takes him into the house again.

Zanni comes to make sure about his wife; he draws near to the door and hears caresses going on; he knocks in a fury.

Franceschina hearing that Zanni wants to burn down the house makes him carry out the basket of clothes, before he sets fire to the place. With an uproar

Pantalone comes out among the clothes in the basket; at this

All the couples arm in arm rush to the alarm of fire in the room. Leandro explains what each has done to the other and delivers over to each his proper wife with whom he is at last content. They go in and the comedy ends.

him, and then tells him of the poor beggar she has in the house; at this:

Leandro disguised comes in with some soup. Coviello scolds and goes into the house with Cintia. Leandro laughs at the hoax and seeing Zanni approaching pretends to be dumb again.

Zanni after several jokes recognizes Leandro and tells him what has been going on in Pantalone's house. Leandro tells him what has happened at Coviello's and goes in laughing. Zanni stays; at this:

Pantalone learns from Zanni the jest of the rogue. Pantalone tells him the jest of the cask

ESSAY

The improvisations of *commedia* performances are as old as child's play. The addition of character types, standard costumes and masks, and bits of stage business have been picked up by some of our greatest comedians of this century: Charlie Chaplin, the Marx Brothers, and Marcel Marceau. In the 1960s *commedia* traditions were reintroduced by the San Francisco Mime Troupe to American audiences. While their subjects have changed over the last 20 years, the vitality of the Mime Troupe carries on ancient and modern, European and American theatrical traditions.

Commedia in Modern Performance

L'Amant Militaire, performed by the San Francisco Mime Troupe, adapted by Joan Holden from the play by Carlo Goldoni, and directed by Ronnie G. Davis, San Francisco, 1967

In the 1960s America was polarized by the Vietnam War, protest marches, riots on campuses and in ghettos, and by the deaths of the two Kennedy brothers and Martin Luther King, Jr. Just as different groups of citizens developed alternatives to the policies and politics of Presidents Lyndon B. Johnson and Richard M. Nixon, so, too, different groups of theatre people developed alternatives to the commercial Broadway and regional theatre.

Called "alternative," "radical," or "guerrilla" theatre, these new groups were made up of young, often amateur, theatre people. Their productions, dealing with sensitive social and political issues, examined the dark side of American society and culture often in controversial ways. Their theatres were garages, lofts, churches, parks, and streets. Among the best known of these companies were The Living Theatre, the Open Theatre, the Bread and Puppet Theatre, El Teatro Campesino, and the San Francisco Mime Troupe.

Ronnie Davis, founder of the San Francisco Mime Troupe, used the term "guerrilla warfare" to describe the militant assault by radical theatre groups upon America's consciousness. The new theatre's targets were the American middle class, consumer-oriented politics, American military intervention in Vietnam, the industrial—military complex, racial discrimination, and police brutality. Their methods were frequently sixteenth-century *commedia dell'arte*.

Davis, returning from Paris where he studied mime techniques with Etienne Decroux, went to San Francisco in 1959 with the idea of developing a company devoted to mime and improvisational theatre. Over a 10-year period (1960–1970) he developed a company (of some 10 to 50 people) that applied *commedia* techniques to contemporary social and political issues.

The Mime Troupe was a blend of New Left politics and outdoor popular theatre. They used *commedia* gags, characters, costumes, masks, movement, and portable stages in scripts that confronted America's "imperialism" in Southeast Asia and its racial discrimination at home. Pantalone, Brighella, and Arlecchino paraded across temporary stages thrown up in parks and public squares from San Francisco to Seattle, from Chicago to New York.

THE COMMEDIA

The troupe's productions often melded *commedia* performance style with scripts adapted from plays by Molière, Goldoni, Brecht, and Beckett. By 1967, when *L'Amant Militaire* (loosely translated as *The War Lover*) was produced, the company's production format and style had been set. The production was designed with a kind of preamble to help performers warm up in front of audiences and to let audiences in on the backstage secrets. Their portable stage was set up in a park; actors got into costume and makeup or masks before the audience. The actors played music and did warm-up exercises while singing songs (to tambourine, recorder, drum, and castanets) with audiences joining in. After the singing and physical warm-ups,

Figure 6-11 The San Francisco Mime Troupe performing *L'Amant Militaire,* c. 1967, in one of the free outdoor performances in the park. Note the *commedia*-like masks, cloaks, sword, drum, and portable stage.

the group began a Renaissance melody and paraded toward the stage. Once behind the curtain they stepped onto the platform, then leaped into view in front of the curtain, bowed to the audience, circled once around the platform, and, as the cast exited, one person spun out from the group and began the introductions:

Signor, Signora, Signorina!
Madame, Monsieur, et Mademoiselle!
Ladies and Gentlemen!
Il troupo di Mimo di San Francisco
presents for your appreciation this

afternoon . . . Joan Holden's adaptation of a play by Carlo Goldoni entitled . . . *L'Amant Militaire.*[2]

Carlo Goldoni's (1707–1793) play was about two lovers caught in the web of warfare. Davis' group shifted the emphasis from the lovers' personal problems to the social situation and reworked the plot to parallel and satirize America's involvement in Southeast Asia. The play's Spanish army had been occupying Italy to protect the Italians from their own rebellion. The first scene takes place between Pantalone, mayor

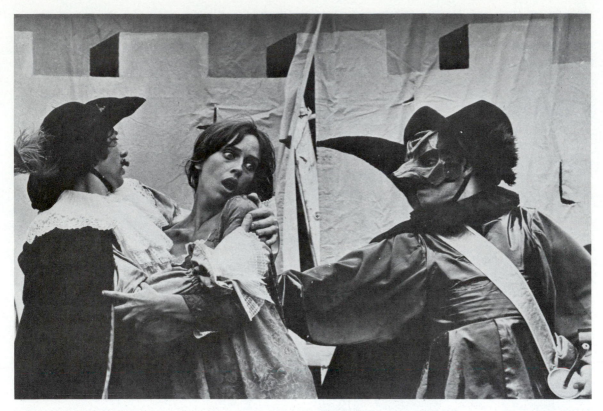

Figure 6-12 The San Francisco Mime Troupe performs *L'Amant Militaire*, c. 1967. The *inamorata* sets off a *lazzi* of distress with two would-be lovers.

of Spinacholla and father to Rosalinda, and General Garcia, Spanish commander in chief. Garcia announces that the war is drawing to a conclusion but the mayor suggests slowing down its end; he is making large profits from the war. Garcia warns that if the Spaniards stay too long it will look like imperialism. Pantalone proposes to sell his goods to the rebels if the army pulls out. They quarrel.

In the following scenes confusion reigns. Rosalinda's lover is ordered to war; she collapses, setting off a *lazzi* of resuscitation. Army recruiters are at work while everyone tries to avoid being recruited. There is much scheming and confusion until a serving maid in a conical hat interrupts the play by announcing, "I'ma de pope." Everybody freezes. "But, first, I'ma sing a

little song"; "When the moon hits your eye like a big pizza pie, dat's amore." The pope saves the day by stopping the war (she even reads a papal bull). The general runs off the stage, exiting through the audience, shouting that he will reappear another day. The lovers are married. All exit to music and dancing. For a finale the cast returns to sing a song from Peter Weiss's play *Marat/Sade* to bows and applause—"Marat we're poor. . ."—and the hat is passed among the audience for donations.

The image of the female servant as pope (a shock device) was as intrinsic to this performance as the *commedia* happy ending. The pope as *deus ex machina* brings about the ending. General Garcia exits from the stage through the audience to satirical effect; the play ends but the war continues. *"L'Amant Militaire,"* according to Ronnie Davis, "was intended to expose a pacifist's impotence, it did not intend or pretend to stop the war."[3]

SUMMARY

For nearly 200 years the *commedia dell'arte*, a theatrical form of mixed origins, was the most popular form of theatrical performance in Europe. By 1580 the *commedia dell'arte* was flourishing in Italy, France, and Spain. Such companies as the Gelosi, Uniti, and Confidenti became internationally famous for their techniques of improvisational performance.

A *commedia* performance is characterized by use of scenario, *lazzi*, stock characters, costumes, and masks. The companies performed almost anywhere: outdoors on improvised booth stages and in the great halls of their aristocratic admirers. Artist Jacques Callot's seventeenth-century etchings capture the spirit and look of a *commedia* performance. *Commedia* stage conventions have survived in modern musical comedy, comic opera, silent films, and street theatre.

The other main form of theatrical entertainment in Renaissance Italy is found first in the courts and academies around 1486. By the early sixteenth century regular plays were part of all court celebrations, which became more elaborate as architects and designers perfected movable scenery, perspective painting, lighting, and stage machinery. Soon permanent theatres were built at Vicenza, Parma, and elsewhere to house the great scenic effects of such court designers as Bernardo Buontalenti, Giacomo Torelli, and Giulo Parigi. Behind all the thinking about theatre architecture of the period lay the first-century studies of Roman buildings by Vitruvius and the Renaissance researches of Serlio into stage illusionism.

PLAYS TO READ

The Three Cuckolds (an authentic *commedia* scenario)

The Servant of Two Masters by Carlo Goldoni

SOURCES

Goldoni, Carlo. *The Servant of Two Masters.* Translated by Frederick H. Davies. New York: Theatre Arts Books, 1961. Paperback. Goldoni (1707–1793), Italy's greatest comic playwright, began his career by writing scenarios for *commedia* companies. Later he set out to refine *commedia* conventions. He abandoned masks for more subtle facial expression; he softened and humanized the stock characters, abolished improvisation, and substituted subjects based on real life for the stock situations. Among his *commedia* plays, *The Servant of Two Masters* is perhaps his finest.

Lea, Kathleen M. *Italian Popular Comedy*, 2 vols. New York: Russell & Russell, 1962. Authentic *commedia* scenarios are not readily available for classroom use. For this reason we have included the entire scenario for *The Three Cuckolds* in this chapter. Lea's book is the standard source.

NOTES

1. *Commedia* script from Kathleen M. Lea, *Italian Popular Comedy*, II (New York: Russell & Russell, 1962), pp. 582–584. Reprinted by permission of Oxford University Press, London.

2. R. G. Davis, *The San Francisco Mime Troupe: The First Ten Years* (Palo Alto: Ramparts Press, 1975), p. 173. Reprinted by permission.

3. Davis, p. 86. Reprinted by permission.

SEVEN

SEVENTEENTH-CENTURY FRENCH THEATRE

A MODERN PERSPECTIVE

The professional French theatre evolved in the early seventeenth century from medieval religious dramas and touring *commedia dell'arte* companies like the Gelosi. Unlike the situation James Burbage found in London, there was a permanent playhouse in Paris as early as 1548. This was the Hôtel de Bourgogne, built almost 30 years before Burbage built The Theatre. The Hôtel de Bourgogne dominated the Paris cultural scene for 130 years, being at one time or another home to plays by Corneille, Racine, and Molière.

If we took a poll of plays produced by major repertory theatres in Europe, Canada, and the United States, we would find that of all seventeenth-century French playwrights, Molière is the one most frequently produced today. In 1973 France celebrated the tri-centennial of Molière's death with productions of his 33 plays throughout the country. Other productions of his plays by modern directors have been highly controversial. One was a sexually charged version of *Tartuffe* directed by Roger Planchon in 1962–1963 at the Théâtre de la Cité in Villeurbane. Another took place at the 1978 Avignon Festival where director Antoine Vitez produced the

Figure 7-1 A drawing of the inside of a seventeenth-century public theatre that looks very much like the Hôtel de Bourgogne. The pit is crowded with standing spectators, and the raised platform stage is framed by galleries on either side of a rectangular hall.

Molière Cycle—four plays by Molière treated as one play in 20 acts.

This chapter opens with a look at France's preeminent theatre as it prepared for a performance in a March afternoon in 1630.

✎ REPRESENTATIVE THEATRE: Hôtel de Bourgogne

On foot and in carriages people converge on the Hôtel de Bourgogne from four directions to see a new tragedy followed by a popular farce. The theatre is located in the center of Paris between two main streets: the rue Mauconseil and the rue de Bourgogne. Shops catering to theatregoers take up one wing of the L-shaped building. At the entrance to the theatre a porter collects money from nobles and courtiers, shopkeepers and merchants, soldiers and citizens. The theatre holds about 1600 spectators.

There is a rush through the narrow foyers by the many who seek standing space in the pit, or *parterre*. Since it is a chill March afternoon, spectators gather around bonfires built on the floor of the pit for warmth. Shafts of afternoon sunlight stream in from windows near the roof, which also serve for ventilation. Smoke drifts upward past the candelabras hanging above the pit. The hall is gloomy and noisy. Spectators chat to-

Paris
Versailles • •Fontainebleau

• Nantes

Villeurbane •

Avignon •

1525   1550   1575

—————— Religious wars flourish ——————

Hôtel de Bourgogne
built in Paris, 1548

Confrérie de la Passion
holds monopoly on public
performance, 1548–1575

Etienne
Jodelle writes
first neoclassical
play, 1552

*Commedia
dell'arte*
troupes tour
Paris
1572–1588

Renovation

The Hôtel de Bourgogne was remodeled in 1647 as a proscenium theatre probably to compete with the more lavish Théâtre du Marais built in 1634 and remodeled after it burned in 1644. The Théâtre du Marais was a converted tennis court (or *jeu de paume*) with a proscenium opening and Italian scenery.

In the remodeling of the Hôtel de Bourgogne, the stage floor was raked upward toward the back so spectators in the pit could see the actors better and so Italian scenery with perspective could be used. A second acting area, called the *théâtre supérieure*, was raised on pillars at the rear of the stage to accommodate scenes on heights, balconies, and so on. A proscenium arch was built and a curtain installed. In the auditorium the galleries were curved into a U-shape to eliminate sharp angles. The result was a proscenium stage with perspective scenery and extra acting areas. In this renovation the modern proscenium theatre was being born.

gether, vendors hawk cakes and wine, pickpockets ply their trade.

Taking seats in boxes or loges on a second level, the fashionable seek refuge from the milling crowd below. Two or more galleries surround the hall on three sides. There is plenty of seating here but it costs extra. A few years later there would be limited seating for spectators on stage.

The noise increases as the theatre fills up. The raised stage at one end of the hall is framed by the side galleries. It is about 25 feet wide and about the same number of feet deep. There is as yet no curtain or proscenium arch.

The stage is set with three painted mansions. Two on either side are painted to resemble two different houses. The third, at the rear, is probably no more than a painted cloth.

The noise subsides as an actor appears to speak a prologue, a traditional means of quieting a noisy audience. Then three actors come into the center of the stage and speak their opening lines. After performing the tragedy the actors will return as Turlupin, Gaultier-Garguille, and Gros-Guillaume—favorite characters of French farce. The afternoon of two plays begins without further ado.

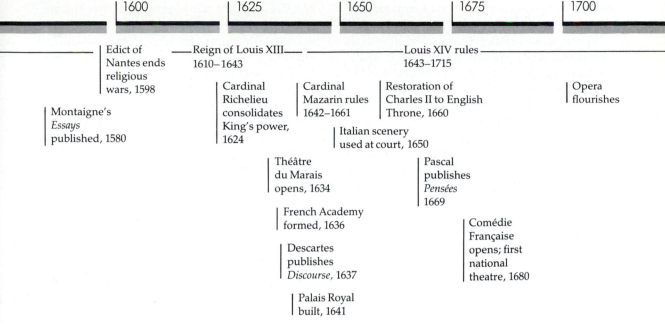

1600	1625	1650	1675	1700

—Edict of Nantes ends religious wars, 1598 ——Reign of Louis XIII 1610–1643 ——————————Louis XIV rules 1643–1715 ————————

Montaigne's *Essays* published, 1580

Cardinal Richelieu consolidates King's power, 1624

Cardinal Mazarin rules 1642–1661

Restoration of Charles II to English Throne, 1660

Opera flourishes

Italian scenery used at court, 1650

Théâtre du Marais opens, 1634

Pascal publishes *Pensées* 1669

French Academy formed, 1636

Descartes publishes *Discourse*, 1637

Comédie Française opens; first national theatre, 1680

Palais Royal built, 1641

CONDITIONS OF PERFORMANCE

BACKGROUND

The blossoming of French culture around 1500 occurred at the time of wars with Italy to the south and Flanders to the north, which resulted in the importation of new ideas and artistic styles. Italy's poets, musicians, and artists particularly (among them Leonardo da Vinci) were much admired. Also, as the French monarchy was strengthened under the Bourbon kings in the late 1500s, French art became increasingly secular. As in Italy, new modes of architecture, painting, and sculpture reflected the new modern spirit.

The years 1500 to 1700 in France were a time of expanding trade to finance wars and exploration. During this time the center of commercial activity, and therefore power, shifted from the Mediterranean to the Atlantic, from Italy and Spain to England, France, and the Netherlands. Farming and cottage industries dominated the society of early modern Europe; 90 percent of the population lived off the land. The growing middle class consolidated their wealth and improved their social status. In a time of rising prices, landowners exploited the land while those less fortunate were condemned to lives as wandering beggars. As a result labor was cheap. The combination of cheap labor and available capital encouraged improvements in agricultural and manufacturing processes.

Science gained new impetus from the invention of the telescope and microscope. Nicolaus Copernicus advanced the theory that the sun, not the earth, was the center of the universe. Galileo Galilei was the first to use the telescope to study the heavens. But his belief in a universe governed by mathematically regular laws ran afoul of Church teachings and he later recanted his ideas. In England William Harvey announced his discovery of the blood's circulation in 1628, and Isaac Newton published his three laws of motion and the law of universal gravitation in 1687.

Seventeenth-century French art, like most aspects of French life and thought, was dominated by one special quality: a profound belief in order and reason. Academies were founded with the object of setting standards and rules. (The Royal Academy of Painting and Sculpture began in 1648.) The French regarded ancient Greek and Roman forms in architecture, sculpture, and writing as models of harmonious organization; harmony was the essence of the new classicism. One of the greatest architectural monuments to the passion for order is Louis XIV's palace at Versailles, where the buildings, gardens, and fountains follow strict rules of symmetry.

When Louis XIV (1638–1715) began to exercise power after the death of Cardinal Mazarin in 1661, he set about restoring order to the nation after the turbulence of civil war—the Fronde. Order demanded restoring the crown to absolute authority and the eradication of heresy. With the revocation of the Edict of Nantes in 1685, French Protestants (the *Huguenots*) were forced to conform or go into exile. The king also set about restoring to France all territories to which it had once laid claim, and at the end of a series of wars fought continuously from 1667 onward against the Netherlands, Spain, and Germany, France emerged as a great military, naval, and mercantile power. But the cost was great. Peasants bore the brunt of taxation to finance the wars, while poor harvests and high taxes led to unrest. But the king retreated to Versailles where he lived in isolation from the rest of the nation. The great palace became the symbol of the strength and limitations of autocratic rule.

MANAGEMENT AND REPERTORY

Management Theatrical companies were usually made up of 8 to 12 actors, the most experienced member acting as manager. There was an apprentice system for young actors; Molière began as an apprentice to the Illustre Théâtre run by the Béjart family. In the early seventeenth century an actor, using two different names, would play in tragedy and also in the farce at the end of the program.

A company rented a theatre and scheduled performances that usually began at two o'clock, but on Sundays and festival days they were required to begin at three in the afternoon. The official policy was to have public amusements like the theatre end before nightfall when Paris streets became dangerous.

Profits were divided into shares and actors were paid at the end of each performance after expenses were deducted. The manager probably got at least two shares to the actor's one and apprentices no more than half a share or only bed and board. The manager received a larger share because of his many responsibilities. He purchased things for the company, including masks, beards, candles, crowns, and unusual costumes. He frequently hired musicians and scene painters and supplied transportation for the company's tours. The four most famous actor-managers during this period were Valleran Lecomte, Charles Lenoir, Montdory, and Molière.

We know a great deal about these theatrical companies and their managers and members from their contracts to build, lease, or buy theatres. Contracts were also drawn up between actors and the company. Under such contracts apprentices were to be fed, clothed, and cared for when sick. Actors received a share of the profits even when ill; they were required to attend rehearsals and performances on time and to furnish their basic costumes.

Repertory In public theatres between 1600 and 1630 in France, serious and farcical works appeared on the same program. The farces were performed last but frequently were the most popular part of the performance.

The production opened with a prologue (by the *orateur de troupe*) to quiet spectators in the pit. It was followed by one of three kinds of plays—a tragedy, tragicomedy, or pastoral—and concluded with a farce. Musicians entertained between the acts and between the two plays. After 1630 audience taste changed and there was pressure to drop the vulgar farces. By the second half of the century, serious new plays were performed by themselves and opened routinely in the winter months.

In 1658 when Molière's company (*Troupe de Monsieur*) first appeared at court before Louis XIV, they performed Corneille's tragedy *Nicomède*. However, sensing that the audience was unmoved by the tragedy, they quickly added a farce to the program. When the polite applause for Corneille's tragedy ended, Molière stepped forward and announced they would present a "small diversion" that he had written himself. This was *Le Docteur amoureux* (*The Doctor in Love*). Pleased with this farce, the king installed Molière's company in the royal theatre next to the Louvre, the Petit Bourbon, which they shared with an Italian troupe until they moved to the Palais Royal in 1660. The company performed here until Molière's death in 1673.

THE ACTING COMPANY

Acting companies were often composed of eight men and four women. (By 1607 women were accepted members of the companies.) The members (called *sociétaires*) elected new members, employed extras, scene painters, musicians, and other personnel. They voted on new plays to be produced, paid authors, and cast parts. Each company had an actor-manager. Molière was unusual as he was not only an actor-manager but also a playwright.

Actors were drawn from all classes of people. While their status in society was not demeaning, the Catholic Church nevertheless denied them funeral rites. This led to many deathbed renunciations of the profession.

The most famous farce actors of their day performed at the Hôtel de Bourgogne in the first native company headed by Valleran Lecomte. Their stage names were Gros-Guillaume, Gaultier-Garguille, and Turlupin (see Figure 7-2).

About 1625 the Players of the Prince of Orange, a new company, appeared at the Hôtel de Bourgogne with France's first famous tragic actor, Montdory (1594–1654), whose real name was Guillaume des Gilleberts. Later Montdory and his fellow actors moved to the Théâtre de Marais, becoming the second important company in Paris. Montdory played heroic figures with great physical and vocal strength, achieving particular distinction in plays by Corneille,

---

French Farceurs

Three famous farce players at the Hôtel de Bourgogne continued a strong *commedia* tradition.

Gros-Guillaume, whose real name was Robert Guérin, was known in tragedies as LaFleur. Originally a baker, he was enormously fat, and in farces he accented his belly by wearing two belts, above and below his stomach. Engravings show him wearing a flat cap, striped trousers, a loose tunic, and the two belts. As a comedian he used a white, flourlike makeup on his face, which he blew in the faces of other actors. He was a member of Les Comédiens du Roi under Valleran Lecomte and became its head before his death in 1622.

Gaultier-Garguille, acted by Hugues Guéru, was known in tragedies as Flechelles and was as thin as Guillaume was fat. In farce he wore a black cap with a plume, a mask with gray hair and pointed beard, large glasses without lenses, and black garments. In one illustration he is holding a book in one hand and a stick in the other.

Turlupin, named Henri Le Grand and called Belleville in tragedy, was the third member of the Lecomte company. Well-built and handsome with red hair, he wore a mask in farce that made him look like the Italian Brighella, the clever and roguish valet.

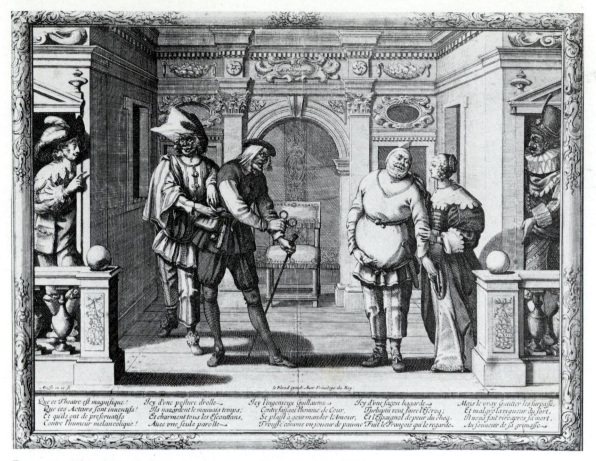

Figure 7-2 This 1630 engraving of actors performing farce at the Hôtel de Bourgogne shows a stage with two mansions or compartments with doors on either side. Either a third compartment or a painted cloth is at the back. The actors played in the open area down front. On stage (left to right) are the clowns Turlupin, Gaultier-Garguille, and Gros-Guillaume.

which he introduced. In 1636, while playing the role of Herod, his tongue became paralyzed, forcing his retirement from the stage.

At Montdory's retirement the best actors of the Marais company, Bellerose and Montfleury, returned to the Hôtel de Bourgogne, where they introduced an affected and bombastic style that became the prevailing acting style. Meanwhile, Molière, who was to become the greatest comic actor of his age, was touring the provinces with the Illustre Théâtre. After his triumph before Louis XIV in 1658 and the king's subsequent patronage, described earlier, his company became the finest company of its day, noted for its ensemble acting.

The great French tragic actors and actresses were praised for their expressive faces and striking voices. What we know about the acting style of the period we learn from engravings, paintings, and writers like Molière who objected to the extravagant style of their rivals. Acting grew more refined as audience tastes changed. One contemporary described the qualities of an actor as a fine facial expression, an impressive bearing capable of free and unconstrained movement, a clear and strong voice free of regional accent, a good mind for understanding verses, a good memory to learn lines quickly and retain them, and a good education in history and fable for correct interpretations.[1]

The actresses (first Mlle. DuParc and later Mlle. Champmeslé), famous as Racine's tragic heroines, established vocal nuances and gestures appropriate to tragic heroines of the day. Champmeslé's speech, it was said, verged on singing, and she conveyed emotion through gestures that reflected rituals of courtly etiquette.

VISUAL ELEMENTS

Scenery Mansions and simultaneous settings were routinely used by early acting companies like the Confrérie de la Passion, which began as a company producing religious plays and later produced secular plays at the Hôtel de Bourgogne. Our study of the French theatre is enriched by a book by scenic designer Mahelot containing 47 designs for plays produced at the Hôtel de Bourgogne in the 1630s: *Le Mémoire de Mahelot, Laurent et d'autres décorateurs de l'Hôtel de Bourgogne*. In it Mahelot documents how he and others (possibly George Buffequin, the major scenic designer of the period) modified medieval scenic practices with Italian principles of painted perspective and movable scenery.

Mahelot placed mansions, representing palaces, temples, and so on, in a semicircle (some with second levels) on three sides of the stage. Usually, the most important locale was placed in the rear. Sometimes merely a scenic curtain with painted landscape formed the background. Two or more compartments with doors, curtains, and

---

MARIE DESMARES CHAMPMESLÉ

The celebrated French actress known as La Champmeslé (1642–1698), joined the Théâtre du Marais in 1669, and a year later went to the Hôtel de Bourgogne where she created the part of Bérénice in Racine's play. In 1679 she joined the Théâtre Guénégaud, which, after Molière's death, was formed by the combined Marais company and the Palais Royal troupe. A year later the Marais company and the Hôtel de Bourgogne founded the Comédie Française, which has retained its name to the present day.

Champmeslé became the Comédie Française's leading actress, creating the role of Racine's Phaedra in 1680. Possessing a melodious and expressive voice, she established the chanting, declamatory style for classical tragedies that was passed on to the next generation of French actresses. She was also greatly admired (especially by Racine) for her charm and wit.

---

small inner areas for furniture were lined up on either side of the stage. At times curtains were used to hide other mansions until they were needed.

Although trapdoors do not appear to be in use in the 1630s, theatres had machines to fly clouds or goddesses above the mansions. As the elaborate Italian scenic conventions became more popular, other machines and movable scenery came into evidence. The most famous Italian designer of the day, Giacomo Torelli, was summoned to the French court in 1645 to design for the Italian company at the Petit Bourbon. Here he designed the first Paris opera and set the fashion for Italian scenic practices in theatre, opera, and ballet for the remainder of the century.

Figure 7-3 Jean Berain's costume design for *The Triumph of Love*, 1681. Berain's designs emphasize heavy lines and ornamentation. (a) An Indian maiden. (b) Notice the bell-shaped skirt, heavy ornamentation, and plumed helmet of the hero. Berain established a distinctly French style of design.

Lighting Lighting was provided by candelabras over the stage and auditorium. There is no evidence that any kind of footlights existed. However, there were crude arrangements for snuffing out candles for nighttime scenes. As in the Elizabethan theatre, actors often represented night scenes with candles, torches, lanterns, and even fireworks.

Costumes and Properties Also like the Elizabethans, costumes for the French stage were both *contemporary* and *symbolic*. Most costumes in comedy resembled ordinary dress of the period. Actors, who usually provided their own costumes, dressed in brightly colored satin in the fashions of the day. Others wore symbolic costumes, like the black robes of magicians and pedants. Tragedies required more symbolic costumes than other play types: the semi-Roman toga, turbans for Orientals, a lion skin for Hercules, and so on. However, the costume *à la Romaine* was the standard garment for the tragic actor.

By the 1630s when Mahelot wrote the notices later compiled in his *Mémoire,* costumes reflected the splendor of court fashions. Actor Charles Lenoir's wardrobe was appraised in 1637 at a value equivalent to $10,000 in today's currency.

In the latter part of the century, designer Jean Berain (1637–1711) was appointed court designer, and, in the manner of Inigo Jones, realized a visual style in scenery and costumes

> **❝** *The standard European costume for all kinds of courtly theater—opera, ballet, tragedy—was brought to a high level of formal finish by those Italian and French designers working directly for Louis XIV. . . . Many gorgeous costumes were done at court for Louis' theatricals in the mid-seventeenth century, but only at the end of it was perfect stylization finally achieved, by Jean G. Bérain. . . . Operatic and dance costume . . . took its form from the dress of noble life, but only basically, and quickly developed . . . into an independent stage style. . . . For both sexes, all opera and ballet costumes, no matter what the character, encased the torso closely and had a stiff, bell-shaped skirt—shoe length for women, thigh length for men . . . . The stiff, overwrought skirt, plumes, and train of Bérain's heroines, however, became the suitable trappings for all European operatic stars and for the heroines of tragedy, too. . . . Jason and Coriolanus wore the male version, usually with the classical musculated torso above the stiff knee-length bell skirt, all topped with a flowing curled peruke and plumed helmet . . .* **❞**
>
> Anne Hollander, *Seeing Through Clothes* (1980)[2]

Figure 7-4 Louis XIV costumed as the Sun King in an engraving for *The Ballet of the Night* in 1653.

associated with the reign of Louis XIV. This distinctively French style influenced costuming for European theatre, opera, and ballet for the next century (Figure 7-3).

Special effects consisted of clouds, fire, smoke, and sound effects. Such properties as lances, flambeaux, writing paper, masks, trumpets, shields, human heads, and sponges filled with blood are listed in Mahelot's *Mémoire*. Furniture was restricted to an occasional throne, stool, chair, or writing desk.

Music and Dance Acting companies hired two or three musicians to play before and during performances. Usually, there were two violinists and a third musician with flute and drum. Placed in the wings or on stage, the musicians were later moved into the loges and then between the stage and *parterre* at the Hôtel de Bourgogne. Today musicians are traditionally placed in what is called the "orchestra pit."

Dances followed the fashion of the day both in the public theatres and at court. As the Italian production ideal gained favor, ballet became fashionable first at court and then in opera. Called *ballets d'entrées,* these entertainments—more like English masques than modern ballet—were allegorical stories explained by a spoken libretto and pantomimed by performers in movements based upon ballroom dances of the time. One of the most famous, *The Ballet of the Night* (1653) performed at the Petit Bourbon, featured hunters, bandits, gypsies, astrologers, Venus, and Aurora. At the ballet's climax the Sun, danced by Louis XIV, appeared to disperse the darkness (Figure 7-4). This production helped to create the flattering image of Louis XIV as the Sun King.

PLAYWRITING

The work of France's first professional playwright, Alexandre Hardy (c. 1572–1632), first appeared in 1597. He is said to have written about 500 plays (only 34 have survived) during his 35 years of writing for the public theatre. He wrote "potboilers" that appealed to a broad popular taste, mixing neoclassical devices that attracted aristocratic audiences with the suspenseful story lines and violent scenes beloved by lower-class audiences. Writing at a time when farce reigned on the public stage, he made tragedies, pastorals, and comedies equally popular. His success encouraged others to write for the theatre, including the three greatest writers of the period—Corneille, Racine, and Molière.

Corneille stands out in the 1630s for writing the best tragicomedy of the period—*The Cid*. He is also credited with establishing the neoclassical mode in French theatre. Unfortunately, his greatest play turned out to be his most controversial and the furor over it resulted in Corneille's early retirement as a professional playwright. Corneille took the plot of *The Cid* from an older Spanish play (Guillén de Castro's *Las Mocedades del Cid*); he compressed the events into 5 acts, 24 hours, and 4 locations in a single town. His theme, a popular one, revolved around love versus honor. The hero, Rodrigue, and the heroine, Chimène, are forced by the turn of events to choose between their love for each other and their duty to family and state.

The Cid was an enormous popular success, but it was attacked by purist critics on the grounds that it violated the neoclassical rules. It was neither a tragedy nor a comedy; it resembled tragicomedy in the variety of incidents and in the happy ending. Moreover, Chimène's agreement to marry Rodrigue, who has killed her father less than 24 hours earlier, violated the rules of decorum. Corneille was censored by the French Academy. When he next wrote for the stage, he restricted himself to tragedies that ad-

---

PIERRE CORNEILLE

Pierre Corneille (1606–1684), educated as a lawyer, began his career in theatre with *Mélite, or The False Letter*, a comedy performed in Paris by the famous actor Montdory. Following its success Corneille wrote seven plays between 1630 and 1636, the last being his most famous play, *The Cid*. The academic outcry over its performance resulted in Corneille's temporary retirement from the stage.

Thereafter Corneille wrote tragedies that adhered strictly to the unities of time and place and took their subjects from ancient Roman history. He became a member of the foremost literary salon of his day, the Hôtel de Rambouillet, and in 1647 was admitted to the French Academy. He retired after his success in the theatre began to wane in the late 1640s; then in 1659 he was persuaded by France's finance minister and arts patron, Nicholas Fouquet, to come out of retirement. His *Oedipus* was produced at the Hôtel de Bourgogne. But his success was soon overshadowed by a rival playwright, Jean Racine. The two clashed openly in 1670 when they both produced plays based on the Titus and Berenice love story. Racine's *Bérénice* was clearly the audience favorite. In 1674 Corneille retired permanently from the theatre and spent his last years in poverty. He died in Paris in 1684.

hered closely to the rules. In *Horace* (1640), *Cinna* (1640), *Polyeucte* (1642–1643), and *The Death of Pompey* (1643), heroes of indomitable will choose death rather than dishonor.

It is fortunate for world drama that the sensibilities of Racine and Molière were more in tune with the dramatic conventions of the time. Racine, the greatest writer of tragedy of his age, over a 10 year period wrote *Andromaque* (1667), *Britannicus* (1669), *Bérénice* (1670), *Bajazet* (1672), *Mithridate* (1673), *Iphigénie* (1674), and *Phaedra* (1677). His acknowledged masterpiece is *Phaedra*, which centers on the inner struggles of characters torn between their sense of duty and their uncontrollable desires. Whereas Corneille placed simple characters in complex plots, Racine placed complex characters in relatively simple plots. Fully aware of their dilemma (spoken aloud to their confidants), Racine's heroes and heroines wrestle with their inner conflict, which has no resolution, and they are destroyed.

Racine retired from the stage after the disappointing reception of *Phaedra*. He was appointed historiographer to Louis XIV and abandoned his literary life. Some years later he wrote *Esther* (1689) and *Athalie* (1691). Neither play was performed professionally during his lifetime.

Molière, like Shakespeare before him, was a man of the theatre. Beginning as an actor in a provincial company, he became an actor-manager-playwright with his own company. While Molière wrote farces in the manner of the *commedia dell'arte* and entertainments for the court, his greatest achievements were his comedies of character and manners: *The School for Husbands* (1661), *The School for Wives* (1662), *Tartuffe* (1664, 1667, 1669), *The Misanthrope* (1666), *The Miser* (1668), *The Learned Ladies* (1672), and *The Imaginary Invalid* (1673). These comedies set in drawing rooms observe the neoclassical ideal of five acts, the unities, and verse; but they triumph over the rules in their good-natured exposure of contemporary life and manners.

JEAN RACINE

Jean Racine (1639–1699) was educated at the Jansenist seminary at Port Royal, where he encountered rigid and puritanical views that greatly influenced his life and artistic vision. He also acquired a knowledge of Greek literature, whose characters became the subjects of his finest plays.

In Paris at age 25, he sprang into prominence with the play *La Thébaïde* (1664), written with Molière's encouragement. It was followed by five masterpieces: *Andromaque, Britannicus, Bérénice, Iphigénie en Aulide,* and *Phaedra.* The last was to be his greatest play of all. However, the opening night performance of *Phaedra* ran afoul of Racine's enemies, and a rival play on the same theme by a minor playwright was announced a greater success. Responding to his disappointment over the critical failure of his play, Racine retired from playwriting at age 38 to become historian and biographer to the king.

Racine did not write another play until 1689 and then not for a professional production. Then, at the request of the king's longtime mistress and second wife, Madame de Maintenon, he wrote the Biblical play *Esther* (1689) for performance by young girls at her school at St. Cyr. Madame de Maintenon was so pleased with the play that she prevailed upon Racine to write another for the school. The result was *Athalie* (1691), his last play.

Racine died in 1699 never having returned as a professional playwright to the French stage, but he has proved, along with Molière, to be one of the seventeenth century's greatest playwrights.

MOLIÈRE

Molière (Jean Baptiste Poquelin, 1622–1673), French playwright-actor-manager, was the son of Louis XIV's upholsterer. Poquelin spent his early years close to the court and received a gentleman's education. He joined a theatrical troupe in 1643 and became a professional actor with the stage name Molière.

Molière helped to found the Illustre Théâtre Company in Paris, which soon failed, and spent twelve years touring the French provinces as an itinerant actor and company playwright. He returned to Paris to become the foremost comedian of his time. Within thirteen years (1659–1673) he wrote and acted in *Tartuffe, The Misanthrope, The Doctor In Spite of Himself, The Miser,* and *The Imaginary Invalid.* Writing during France's golden age, Molière's comedies balance follies of eccentric humanity against society's reasonable good sense.

" The business of comedy is to represent the flaws common to all men, and especially the men of our time. It would be impossible for Molière to dream up people who resembled nobody you've ever met. If he is going to be challenged with pillorying every living person who has the same faults as his characters, he will indeed have to stop writing plays."

Molière, *The Rehearsal at Versailles* (1663)

REHEARSING THE PLAY

In *The Rehearsal at Versailles* (1663) Molière constructed a play-within-a-play in which his acting company rehearsed a script by "Molière" for performance before the king. The one-act play not only represented a rehearsal but it also stated Molière's ideas on theatre. As director-playwright in the *Rehearsal*, Molière casts roles and advises actors on characterization, line readings, stage business, makeup, and movement. In addition, he satirizes the actors of the rival company at the Hôtel de Bourgogne for their affectations—their declamatory speech and exaggerated gestures—while stressing the more natural acting style of his company (Figure 7-5).

Similar to Shakespeare's rehearsal in *A Midsummer Night's Dream*, Molière's play was one of the few contemporary accounts of seventeenth-century actors and their director-playwright at work. Molière went a step beyond Shakespeare's play-within-a-play, for his company played at being *themselves*; Molière, Madeleine Béjart, and so on. In this respect he is the ancestor of modern dramatists, such as Luigi Pirandello and Jean Giraudoux, who use the play-within-a-play to comment on stage practices as well as on the nature of existence.

THE AUDIENCE

By 1630 a cross section of Paris society was attending performances at the public theatres, an amalgam of pages, valets, pickpockets, soldiers, merchants, gentlemen, and nobility. Noisy and ill-mannered, they crowded into the pit and loges, and a few sat on benches placed along two sides of the stage. Seating for spectators on stage became popular, some scholars believe, with the success of Corneille's *The Cid* in 1636.

It is estimated that about 1000 spectators could be crowded at half price into the pit at the Hôtel de Bourgogne; another 1000 could be seated at full price in the loges, galleries, and amphitheatre. Respectable women probably did not attend the theatre early in the century; those who did likely wore masks and sat in the loges.

Figure 7-5 Molière in the costume of the character Sganarelle. (From the original engraving by Simonin in the Bibliothèque Nationale.)

DRAMATIC CONVENTIONS

The French theatre during the reign of Louis XIV evolved a kind of dramaturgy associated today almost exclusively with Molière's comedies and Racine's tragedies. Several dramatic conventions used by these writers, particularly the three unities and the *commedia dell'arte* characters, came from the Italian theatre and the reconstruction of classical dramatic theory by such Italian critics as Lodovico Castelvetro (1501–1571). Others grew out of Cardinal Richelieu's efforts to elevate French literature through the French Academy, a kind of standards commission legislating style and conventions. The academy imposed rules about genre, the unities, decorum, verisimilitude, poetic justice, and verse forms. The result was a writing and theatrical style very different from those found in the Elizabethan theatre.

GENRE

The French classical theatre reduced drama to two basic types—tragedy and comedy. All others, including tragicomedy, were considered inferior because they were "mixed forms." According to accepted theories of the time, tragedy drew its characters from rulers or nobility; its stories dealt with affairs of state and the downfall of rulers; its endings were always unhappy; and its style was lofty and poetic. Comedy, on the other hand, drew its characters from the middle or lower classes; its stories dealt with domestic affairs; there was no danger of death; its endings were always happy; and its style was characterized by the use of ordinary speech appropriate to the people represented.

Interior of the Comédie Française in the eighteenth century. Note the boxes, galleries, and elaborate proscenium arch.

Opposite: The present-day Comédie Française, the state theatre of France.

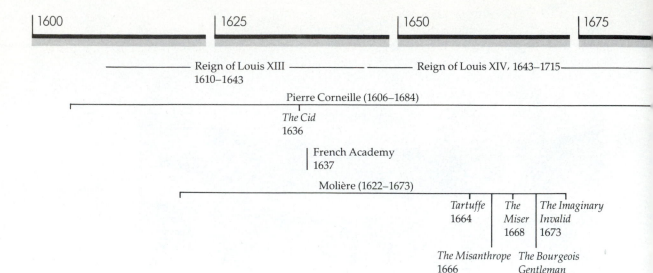

| 1600 | 1625 | 1650 | 1675 |

Reign of Louis XIII ———— ———— Reign of Louis XIV, 1643–1715———
1610–1643

Pierre Corneille (1606–1684)

The Cid
1636

French Academy
1637

Molière (1622–1673)

| *Tartuffe* 1664 | *The Miser* 1668 | *The Imaginary Invalid* 1673 |

The Misanthrope   *The Bourgeois*
1666   *Gentleman*
                                 1671

Racine (1639–1699)

La Thebaide   *Andromaque*   *Phaedra*
produced by   1667   1677
Molière
1664

THE UNITIES

In an effort to achieve *verisimilitude*—the appearance of truth or credibility on stage—unities of *action*, *time*, and *place* were established based on precedents found in the classical and Italian theatres. A play, it was argued, should have a single action (there should be no subplots). The play's events should coincide with the 2 or more hours of the performance or at least should not exceed 24 hours. Its events should occur within a single locale or setting.

LANGUAGE

French classical tragedy depicted an artificial, constricted world, populated by kings and queens speaking a kind of language never heard in real life. Tragedies were written in a carefully constructed verse form—the *alexandrine* (a 12-syllable line). They focused on the austere presentation of moments of truth. Things came to light—secrets were revealed—only as language (the character's spoken thoughts) brought these inner realities into the external world. No act or thought existed on the French classical stage until it was expressed in dialogue. *Language* was the means of organizing reality and displaying it for all to see and hear.

Racine's verse, for example, *exposes* the ambition, passion, despair, and terror of his characters. It is Phaedra's spoken dialogue that clarifies the blind forces of passion at work within her.

DECORUM

Decorum was a principle of character portrayal. It dealt with the *appropriateness* of characters to their situation and to the language they spoke. Characters were ranked according to their age group, social class, profession, and sex. Characters in tragedy were restricted to kings, princes, and their associates. *Phaedra* has eight characters (plus several guards). Of these eight, two are *confidants* (Theramenes and Oenone), the characters to whom the protagonist spoke his or her inner thoughts, secrets, and plans. In the French theatre the confidant replaced the soliloquy as a more realistic stage convention.

Comic characters were restricted to the middle and lower classes and included merchants, their wives, children, friends, and servants. They had their source in the popular Italian and French farces seen at the Hôtel de Bourgogne and elsewhere. In *Tartuffe*, for instance, we recognize the stock Italian prototypes remolded into types from the French middle class: the foolish and tyrannical father (Orgon), the bland lovers (Valere and Mariane), the clever servant (Dorine), and the domineering mother-in-law (Madame Pernelle).

THE MESSENGER'S REPORT

In tragedy and comedy a messenger was used to report offstage events that bring about the play's resolution. In *Phaedra* Theramenes returns from the scene of Hippolytus' death and describes the violent event resulting from the father's curse.

Molière resolves *Tartuffe* with a variation on two conventions of classical drama: the messenger's report and the *deus ex machina*—a person (or fact) who has not entered the action before and who steps in to resolve a deadlocked situation. The latter is Louis XIV's representative who arrests Tartuffe. Nothing earlier in the play has led us to expect the officer's appearance. Molière not only resorts to praising his royal patron as an earthly representative of divine providence but he also makes the point that sometimes an all-powerful hand is needed to rectify the consequences of human error and evil (see the box). Orgon's discovery of his error and his sincere remorse are simply not enough to correct the situation. Orgon *needs* kingly assistance.

Phaedra

Phaedra, Racine's last play, was written for the public theatre and produced at the Hôtel de Bourgogne in 1677. It was based on *Hippolytus*, the classical tragedy by Euripides.

In her husband's absence Phaedra falls in love with her stepson, Hippolytus. She realizes that her love is wrong, but she is powerless to resist it and contemplates suicide. News arrives that her husband, King Theseus, has died. Oenone, her confidante, convinces Phaedra that she can now declare her love to Hippolytus. But he fails to respond to her declaration; just then, news comes that Theseus is alive and entering the city. Phaedra finds it difficult to greet her husband and his suspicions are aroused. To save her mistress, Oenone accuses Hippolytus of making advances to the queen, and Theseus calls down a terrible curse upon his son and banishes him.

As Phaedra starts to tell Theseus the truth, he reveals that Hippolytus is in love with someone else. She becomes jealous and conceals the truth that could save Hippolytus' life. As Hippolytus leaves, his horses, frightened by a sea creature, bolt and drag him to his death. Oenone commits suicide and Phaedra, driven by remorse, takes poison. Before she dies she confesses her guilt to Theseus and he realizes he has cursed an innocent son.

Racine adhered to the neoclassical unities of *time* (a few hours elapse during the play), and *place* (in and around Theseus' palace). Unity of *action* is observed in the concentration on Phaedra's psychological conflict. Like all Racine's characters, she wants to act rationally but is swayed by irrational forces. It is Phaedra's departure from decorous behavior that brings doom to all. Racine's plays, especially *Phaedra*, mark the peak of French classical tragedy.

POETIC JUSTICE

From early Roman times drama was expected not only to *entertain* but also to *teach* moral lessons. Playwrights were expected to show ideal moral patterns in which wickedness was punished and goodness rewarded. It would have been unthinkable for Racine's Phaedra to escape punishment or for Molière's villain to escape the law.

REPRESENTATIVE PLAY

Molière's *Tartuffe*
First produced before King Louis XIV at Versailles in 1664, with Molière as Orgon, his wife Armande Béjart as Elmire, and DuCroisy as Tartuffe

BACKGROUND

Tartuffe has been the most controversial of Molière's plays. When first performed, religious bigots at Louis' court found the play offensive and convinced the king to ban it. Molière revised the play and it was performed again in 1667. He changed the play's title to *The Imposter* to make clear that he was attacking false piety (hypocrisy) and not the clergy and even dressed Tartuffe as a fop rather than a priest. But the play still offended religious authorities. It was not until 1669 that the king permitted the play with its original title and present form to be produced.

Molière wrote and directed *Tartuffe* for his own company, and he and his wife took two of the principal roles—Orgon and Elmire. The role of Tartuffe was written for DuCroisy, a large man with a ruddy complexion, whose physical appearance was used as a source of humor. The actor's obvious corpulence easily contradicted Tartuffe's talk about fasting and scourges.

COMIC ACTION

In general, comic action shows the social disorder created by one or more eccentric characters who deviate from reasonable values, such as sensibility, good nature, flexibility, moderation, tolerance, and social intelligence. Comic action generally affirms the well-being of society against the havoc wrought by social misfits.

Molière's play is named for his chief deviant character. Tartuffe's deceptions *threaten* family harmony, true love, property rights, a wife's fidelity, and a daughter's chastity. Tartuffe persuades the foolish Orgon at every turn that he, Tartuffe, is the soul of Christian humility. Orgon's gullibility and obstinance are a kind of lunacy. His affection for Tartuffe blinds him to reason. He decides to give his daughter in marriage to a man who is hateful to her; he disinherits his son in favor of that person; and he turns over his gravest secret (the strongbox) to this outsider. Once Tartuffe is arrested instead of Orgon, property is returned to the legitimate owner and lovers are reconciled; but only because a king intervenes to keep evil from winning out against good.

This ending (in which, thanks to the king, Tartuffe is discovered to be a notorious criminal and arrested) satisfies our sense of justice. However, it is obviously contrived; the sudden and unexpected appearance of the king's officer brings into question the playwright's skills and intentions. Why did the playwright employ such an artificial ending? He did it partly to underscore his essentially serious intent. Orgon is not completely reformed. He has learned that Tartuffe *deceived* him, but he has failed to learn the difference between hypocrisy and piety, for he says to Cleante: "I'm through with pious men:/Henceforth I'll hate the whole false brotherhood,/And persecute them worse than Satan could."[4]

Molière's artificial resolution instructs us in the nature of human deception and gullibility. Sometimes human situations become so complicated that a larger force *must* come to the rescue. Whereas in art a rescue can be forced by

Deus ex Machina
(the King's Officer)
in *Tartuffe*

Officer I owe an explanation, but not to you.
[*To Orgon.*] Sir, all is well; rest easy, and be grateful
We serve a Prince to whom all sham is hateful,
A Prince who sees into our inmost hearts,
And can't be fooled by any trickster's arts.
His royal soul, though generous and human,
Views all things with discernment and acumen;
His sovereign reason is not lightly swayed,
And all his judgments are discreetly weighed.
He honors righteous men of every kind,
And yet his zeal for virtue is not blind,
Nor does his love of piety numb his wits
And make him tolerant of hypocrites.
'Twas hardly likely that this man could cozen
A King who's foiled such liars by the dozen.
With one keen glance, the King perceived the whole
Perverseness and corruption of his soul,
And thus high Heaven's justice was displayed:
Betraying you, the rogue stood self-betrayed.
The King soon recognized Tartuffe as one
Notorious by another name, who'd done
So many vicious crimes that one could fill
Ten volumes with them, and be writing still.
But to be brief: our sovereign was appalled
By this man's treachery toward you, which he called
The last, worst villainy of a vile career,
And bade me follow the impostor here
To see how gross his impudence could be,
And force him to restore your property.
Your private papers, by the King's command,
I hereby seize and give into your hand.
The King, by royal order, invalidates
The deed which gave this rascal your estates,
And pardons, furthermore, your grave offense
In harboring an exile's documents.
By these decrees, our Prince rewards you for
Your loyal deeds in the late civil war,
And shows how heartfelt is his satisfaction
In recompensing any worthy action,
How much he prizes merit, and how he makes
More of men's virtues than of their mistakes.

(V,7)[5]

a benevolent playwright flattering his king, in life a reprieve from the fruits of human error does not always take place. As Oscar Wilde wrote in *The Importance of Being Earnest*:

The good ended happily, and the bad unhappily. That is what Fiction means.

THE SCENE

The place is Orgon's drawing room, probably depicted at the Palais Royal by painted wings and a cloth background. The play requires a few basic pieces of furniture: a table with cloth for

Figure 7-6 Title pages from Molière's *Works* (1666). Volume I shows Molière in the costumes of Mascarille and Sganarelle. Volume II shows Molière in the costume of Arnolphe and Mlle. de Brie as Agnes in *The School for Wives.*

Orgon to hide under and a wardrobe in which Damis, his son, can hide.

The drawing room is the social world of Orgon's family into which Orgon has introduced Tartuffe. The family quickly finds its values under attack, especially its women, property, and money. Tartuffe tries to seduce Elmire; he betrays secrets entrusted to him; he tricks Orgon out of his house and estate; and he connives Orgon's imprisonment for treason against the king.

Molière carefully observes unities of place, time, and action. There is no change of scene and all characters, including the king's officer, are introduced *into* Orgon's drawing room. This is the play's microcosm: a middle-class family whose values and well-being come under attack from without.

CHARACTER

Molière's characters are created out of broad stereotypes: the foolish and tyrannical father, the hypocritical villain, the level-headed wife, the clever servant, the rash son, the devoted lovers, the wise friend, and the garrulous mother-in-law. Cleante stands out as the voice of moderation and reason, and is thought to be the spokesman for Molière's personal viewpoint, although even in Cleante there are no complexities or ambiguities.

LANGUAGE

Molière writes a rapid-fire, deliberately formal dialogue with artificial rhymes and stilted speeches. In the play's first scene Madame Pernelle is leaving her son's house and chastising the members of the household at the same time. Everyone tries to interrupt her harangue but only succeeds in drawing her attention and verbal abuse. While her speech is "unnatural," it sets up a certain rhythm that, when unbroken, becomes a torrent of words:

Elmire . . . But, Mother, why this hurry? Must
you go?
Mme. Pernelle I must. This house appalls me.
No one in it
Will pay attention for a single minute.
Children, I take my leave much vexed in spirit.
I offer good advice, but you won't hear it.
You all break in and chatter on and on.
It's like a madhouse with the keeper gone.
Dorine If . . .
Mme. Pernelle Girl, you talk too much, and I'm afraid
You're far too saucy for a lady's-maid.
You push in everywhere and have your say.
Damis But . . .
Mme. Pernelle You, boy, grow more foolish every day. . . .

(I,1)[6]

In another famous scene (I, 4), Orgon has just returned from a trip to the country and asks Dorine how everyone has been during his absence. She tells him that his wife has been ill, to which he replies, "Ah! And Tartuffe?" She says he is comfortable and in excellent health, and Orgon exclaims, "Poor fellow!" This sequence of four speeches is repeated three times to establish a pattern (p. 190). From this repetition we gather an impression of Orgon's distorted values, Tartuffe's grip on the household for personal gain, and the wildly funny clash between sense and foolishness.

MOLIÈRE'S MODERNISM

For 300 years Molière's plays have entertained audiences. Many of his themes seem especially modern: women's oppression, human gullibility, and middle-class consumerism. His broad character types are familiar reflections of human behavior at its most ludicrous. The miser, the fool, and the hypocrite appear again and again in modern comedies by Woody Allen, Jules Feiffer, and Mel Brooks. Moreover, Molière's message appeals to our present-day cynicism. If our movies and television shows are a gauge of our attitudes, we apparently believe that stupidity and evil are far more characteristic of human behavior than reason and goodness.

ESSAY

Molière's plays continue to be performed today all over the world. After looking at the traditions of the seventeenth-century French theatre and their reading of *Tartuffe*, it is fascinating to see how directors have reinterpreted the text for modern audiences, sometimes in surprising and shocking ways. Roger Planchon, one of France's most well-known directors currently working in the theatre, gave the theatre world a new look at *Tartuffe* in 1962. That production is the subject of our performance essay.

Molière in Modern Performance
Molière's *Tartuffe*, directed by Roger Planchon at the Théâtre de la Cité in Villeurbane, France, 1962–1963

Few productions of Molière in this century have received either the critical acclaim or the condemnation accorded the Théâtre de la Cité's 1962–1963 production of *Tartuffe*, directed by Roger Planchon and designed by René Allio for the 1200-seat theatre located 300 miles from Paris in the industrial town of Lyons.

Planchon's *Tartuffe* explored the play's psychology, particularly Orgon's attitudes and feelings toward Tartuffe. In an interview about the production, Planchon explained:

From *Tartuffe*

Orgon [*To Dorine*] Dorine . . .
[*To Cleante*] To put my mind at rest, I al-
    ways learn
The household news the moment I return.
[*To Dorine*] Has all been well, these two
    days I've been gone?
How are the family? What's been going
    on?

Dorine Your wife, two days ago, had a bad
    fever,
And a fierce headache which refused to
    leave her.

Orgon Ah. And Tartuffe?

Dorine Tartuffe? Why, he's round and
    red,
Bursting with health, and excellently fed.

Orgon Poor fellow!

Dorine That night, the mistress was
    unable
To take a single bite at the dinner-table.
Her headache-pains, she said, were
    simply hellish.

Orgon Ah. And Tartuffe?

Dorine He ate his meal with relish,
And zealously devoured in her presence
A leg of mutton and a brace of pheasants.

Orgon Poor fellow!

Dorine Well, the pains continued strong,

And so she tossed and tossed the whole
    night long,
Now icy-cold, now burning like a flame.
We sat beside her bed till morning came.

Orgon Ah. And Tartuffe?

Dorine Why, having eaten, he rose
And sought his room, already in a doze,
Got into his warm bed, and snored away
In perfect peace until the break of day.

Orgon Poor fellow!

Dorine After much ado, we talked her
Into dispatching someone for the doctor.
He bled her, and the fever quickly fell.

Orgon Ah. And Tartuffe?

Dorine He bore it very well.
To keep his cheerfulness at any cost,
And make up for the blood *Madame* had
    lost,
He drank, at lunch, four beakers full of
    port.

Orgon Poor fellow!

Dorine Both are doing well, in short.
I'll go and tell *Madame* that you've ex-
    pressed
Keen sympathy and anxious interest.

(I,4)[7]

I found Orgon's attitude to Tartuffe very strange. Actually, Tartuffe is not the aggressive one. Orgon gives everything to Tartuffe who, of course, accepts it all. It was not Tartuffe's idea to marry Marianne—it was Orgon who proposed the marriage. Orgon also wants to disinherit his own children and make Tartuffe his heir. It is Orgon who gives Tartuffe the strongbox (Tartuffe has no idea it even exists). Perhaps one could argue that Tartuffe leads Orgon on; but from the point of strict morality—and I am a moralist—the one who acts is the guilty man. Orgon is an important man, a friend of the king. He met Tartuffe in church, brought him home, fed him, clothed him, etc. For the past three hundred years these actions have not been understood. Critics have called Orgon stupid—but a man's actions cannot be explained away that easily. Orgon is not stupid, but profoundly homosexual. It's obvious that he doesn't know it—the play would fall apart if he were conscious of it, if

he simply tried to sleep with Tartuffe. Our production focused on this relationship between the two men. . . . The play doesn't change over the centuries, but our understanding of it does.[8]

Planchon presented the beguiling Tartuffe (Michael Auclair) as an attractive young man, and Orgon (Jacques Debary) as a plump burgher whose chief fault is not his flaming temper but his infatuation for Tartuffe. Dorine warns Orgon (in the same scene as the dialogue opposite) that he has too much "affection" for the young man. When Orgon comes to see Tartuffe's lust and fraudulence, he is not so much enraged as heartbroken. By the play's end Planchon has transformed *Tartuffe* from a comedy into a tragedy with some comic relief—a play about a forthright soul (Orgon) deceived by the man (Tartuffe) to whom he gave all.

Planchon strengthened his psychological interpretation of Molière's text by using props, furniture, and costumes to show the confusion of sex and religion in the play. As Orgon's family is introduced, we see them getting out of bed, dressing, and eating breakfast. The scene is highly naturalistic, for this is what families do every morning. But the domestic activity works in tandem with Planchon's religious symbolism. The breakfast table becomes the table beneath which Orgon hides to witness his wife's seduction. The table is very large, and, as Tartuffe and Elmire lie on top of it (with Orgon hidden beneath), the action suggests that their sexual relationship will be consummated here just as the family's breakfast meal has been consumed here. Within these contexts the white tablecloth takes on various meanings: a *bedsheet* where Tartuffe will "know" the woman sexually; a *tablecloth* where he will "consume" her as a meal; an *altar cloth* where the cleric will ceremoniously offer Elmire as a "host" to God.

In addition to napkins and tablecloths, *clothes* (the actors' costumes) take on special meanings. When we first see Orgon, he has just returned from a trip. He undresses, removing his garments, shoes, and wig. He puts on a robe and

ROGER PLANCHON

French director, actor, and playwright Roger Planchon (b. 1931) created a theatre for factory workers—the Théâtre de la Cité in Villeurbane, a suburb of Lyons. Planchon opened his first company (the Théâtre de la Comédie de Lyons) in 1952, where he directed and acted in plays by Marlowe, Jonson, Brecht, Ionesco, and Adamov. In 1957 he moved the company to the Théâtre de la Cité. There he became internationally known for his new interpretations of classics, including his adaptation of Dumas's *The Three Musketeers* (1957–1958) in which he played D'Artagnan, Marlowe's *Edward II* (1960–1961), and Molière's *Tartuffe* (1962–1963).

In 1972 France's minister for culture offered Planchon the codirectorship of the Théâtre National Populaire (known as the TNP) in Paris. Planchon refused the post but later, in a reorganization of the National theatres, Planchon's company in Villeurbanne was renamed the Théâtre National Populaire and placed under the direction of Planchon and Patrice Chereau.

house slippers. While changing clothes he discusses his wife's health with Dorine, but mostly he inquires about Tartuffe. As he removes his clothes he also *exposes* his feelings for Tartuffe and his lack of interest in his wife.

Only two people undress in this play: Orgon and Tartuffe. In the same way that Orgon exposes his emotions, Tartuffe *reveals* his lust for Elmire (and to the hidden Orgon) as he takes off his clothes to seduce Elmire on the table. No other characters are either ignorant of their feelings or attempt to hide them, and their clothes are not used symbolically.

Planchon uses the stage to make statements about the social, political, and psychological realities of Western culture. The text is his starting point, but he also uses a number of bold scenographic effects: disappearing walls, large marionnettes, projected scenery, and the "calendar"—a strip of material on which comments to the audience are written.

Planchon has a reputation for flamboyance, parody, and adventure. In some productions he concentrates on the social and political conduct of his characters. In others he concentrates on the psychological motivation of the characters' outward behavior. His production of Moliere's *Tartuffe* was a psychological study in human passion—of one man's passion for another at the expense of family, property, and reputation.[9]

which kings and courtiers took part, its creation of a "national" theatre in the Comédie Française in 1680, and its neoclassical dramaturgy represented in plays by Corneille, Racine, and Molière.

Molière's *Tartuffe*, our representative play, while showing the playwright's adherence to neoclassical conventions like the unities, decorum, verisimilitude, and poetic justice, also shows how a great playwright triumphed over those rules in his depiction of human fraud and gullibility. *Tartuffe*, directed by the well-known and often controversial French director, Roger Planchon, emphasizes the play's psychology more than its farce. Planchon's interest in Orgon's feelings toward Tartuffe brought a new dimension to a play that has been popular for more than 300 years.

SUMMARY

The professional French theatre evolved in the early sixteenth century from medieval religious drama and touring *commedia dell'arte* performances. The Confrérie de la Passion, a society of religious brothers, built the Hôtel de Bourgogne in Paris in 1548, the first permanent theatre in France. Its original features and later renovation trace the history of the public theatre in seventeenth-century France. The court theatres (the Palais Royal, the Petit Bourbon, and the Theatre at Versailles) of cardinals and kings introduced Italian scenic practices onto the French stage. Perspective and movable scenery, backstage machines, the front curtain, and the proscenium arch came to dominate theatrical practice by the mid-1600s. Still, the focus was on the actor and scenic effects served as mere background for Montdory, Bellerose, Montfleury, Molière, Du Parc, and Champmeslé.

The French theatre under Louis XIV, the Sun King, is best remembered for its permanent theatres converted out of halls and tennis courts, its pseudo-Roman costumes created by designer Jean Berain, its fashionable *ballets d'entrées* in

PLAYS TO READ

The Cid by Corneille

Tartuffe by Molière

Phaedra by Racine

SOURCES

Corneille, Pierre. *The Cid*. Edited and translated by John C. Lapp. Crofts Classics Series. Arlington Heights, Ill.: Harlan Davidson, 1955. Also translated by John Cairncross. Penguin Classics Series. Baltimore: Penguin, 1980. Paperback. These are two excellent student editions with solid introductions and notes.

Guicharnaud, Jacques, ed. *Seventeenth-Century French Drama*. Translated by Morris Bishop and Kenneth Muir. New York: Modern Library, 1976. The six plays included are Molière's *Tartuffe*, *The Would-Be Gentleman*, and *The Precious Damsels*; Racine's *Phaedra* and *Athaliah*; and Corneille's *Cid*. Guicharnaud has written an excellent introduction to this anthology.

Molière. *Tartuffe*. Translated by Richard Wilbur. New York: Harcourt Brace Jovanovich, 1968.

Also edited by Haskell M. Block. Crofts Classics Series. Arlington Heights, Ill.: Harlan Davidson, 1958. Paperback. The Wilbur translation is outstanding.

Racine, Jean Baptiste. *Phaedra*. Edited and translated by Oreste F. Pucciani. Crofts Classics Series. Arlington Heights, Ill.: Harlan Davidson, 1950. Also *Phaedra and Other Plays*. Translated by John Cairncross, Penguin Classics Series. Baltimore: Penguin, 1964. Paperback. The Penguin edition also includes Racine's *Iphigenia* and *Athaliah*.

NOTES

1. W. L. Wiley, *The Early Public Theatre in France* (Cambridge, Mass.: Harvard University Press, 1960), pp. 96–97.

2. Anne L. Hollander, *Seeing Through Clothes* (New York: Avon, 1980). Copyright © 1975, 1976, 1978 by Anne L. Hollander. Reprinted by permission of Viking Penguin Inc.

3. Jacques Guicharnaud, *Seventeenth-Century French Drama* (New York: Random House, 1967), pp. vii–viii. Reprinted by permission.

4. Molière, *Tartuffe,* translated and © 1961, 1962, 1963 by Richard Wilbur (New York: Harcourt, 1963), pp. 104–105. All excerpts reprinted by permission of Harcourt Brace Jovanovich, Inc.

5. Molière, *Tartuffe*, p. 90. Reprinted by permission.

6. Molière, *Tartuffe*, p. 3. Reprinted by permission.

7. Molière, *Tartuffe,* pp. 104–105. Reprinted by permission.

8. Bettina L. Knapp, "Interview with Roger Planchon," *Tulane Drama Review*, 9, No. 3 (Spring 1965), 190–193. Reprinted by permission.

9. For a detailed description of Planchon's *Tartuffe* see Andre Merle, "*Tartuffe*: Mise en Scène par Roger Planchon," *Travail Théâtral*, No. 17 (October–December 1974), 40–45.

EIGHT

THE RESTORATION AND EIGHTEENTH-CENTURY THEATRE

A MODERN PERSPECTIVE

English stage history was interrupted for a period of 18 years when the public theatre was closed and acting prohibited between 1642 and 1660 on orders of Oliver Cromwell, who had emerged victorious from the Civil War. Although plays and theatrical entertainments did not wholly disappear, these 18 years represent an unusual hiatus in stage history. The reopening of the English theatres in 1660 with the restoration of Charles II to the English throne marked the beginning of the modern proscenium playhouse in England and the emergence of an especially "English" brand of comedy, the *comedies of manners.*

Today, comedies of manners continue to dominate the stages of the fashionable London West End theatres. And the plays of the late seventeenth-century playwrights—Etherege, Wycherley, and Congreve—are retained in the repertories of the major companies. Goldsmith and Sheridan are even well-known names in college and university theatres on this side of the Atlantic. The interest of audiences in the behavior of fashionable society has not dwindled with the passage of time.

In bringing the English theatre to life again in 1660, managers, playwrights, actors, and audiences developed practices that set the pattern for the London professional theatre for the next 150 years. These practices are closely associated with the history of the *playhouse in Drury Lane* —one of two theatres in London today that traces its beginnings to the Restoration.

REPRESENTATIVE THEATRE: Drury Lane

On this cold January afternoon in 1675 people hurry along on foot and in hackney coaches through the mud and dirt of London's narrow streets in the quarter between Bridges Street and Drury Lane. Lines have already formed outside the doorway to the new Theatre Royal in Drury Lane. Footmen crowd into the narrow entranceway to hold seats for their masters. Fops, beaux, wits, and would-be wits struggle through the narrow foyers and stairs to gain access to the boxes and pit. As soon as the footmen are released from their duties, they retire to the third gallery to sit on benches with other servants, country cousins, and apprentices. Only the boldest gallants gain the few coveted seats on stage where they can be seen and heard along with the actors. Smoking chandeliers above the stage and auditorium drip wax on the spectators, but the artificial light is needed on this dark January day.

The play today is by a new playwright, William Wycherley, and is called *The Country Wife.* It is reputed to be wicked in its portrayal of sexual dalliance between a man who claims to be sexually impotent and the ladies who discover to their delight his "hidden" charms. Mr. Hart and

Figure 8-1 A drawing of the frontispiece to the play *Ariane* (published in 1674) shows the stage of the Drury Lane Theatre. The stage opening separates the proscenium and the scenic stage flanked by Corinthian pilasters with a curved stage front.

Mrs. Boutell are acting today; they have drawn a particularly large crowd.

The theatre has just been rebuilt on the same site as a smaller theatre that burned three years ago. The famous court architect, Christopher Wren, designed the building. The pit has been raked (slanted) to give audiences a better view of the stage. The backless benches are covered with green cloth that lends vibrant color to the motley crowd in the pit. There are three galleries, the lower partitioned into boxes, the middle one partially devoted to boxes near the proscenium and the remainder to benches, and the top gallery having rows of benches.

Musicians have been playing in the small orchestra gallery under the stage. The chatter of

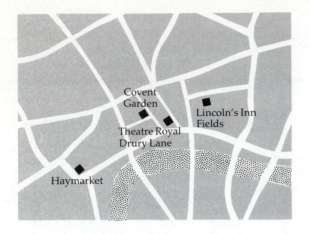

King Charles II
(r. 1660–1685)
restored to
English throne

King Charles
dies (1685),
succeeded by
his brother
James II
(r. 1685–1688)

Theatre Managers,
Davenant and Killigrew,
receive patents to open
theatres, 1660

Theatre Royal,
Drury Lane, built, 1663

Great Fire of
London, 1666

Paradise Lost by John Milton,
published, 1667

Dorset Garden Theatre
opens, 1671

the audience is partially silenced by the appearance before the curtain of the veteran actor Charles Hart to speak the prologue. He finishes to applause and the curtain opens to reveal the new fashion in movable scenery from Paris. The painted wings and shutters behind the proscenium delight the eyes of the spectators. Wycherley's first scene is an interior. The scenery is part of the spectacle and provides background only for the actors playing Horner and Dr. Quack, who enter from one of two doors on either side of the forestage.

The stage is deep (about 34 feet) and raked from front to back. It is divided roughly into equal parts by the proscenium. Standing in front of the proscenium arch on an open, semicircular platform, Mr. Hart, as Horner, speaks Wycherley's opening lines:

> [*aside*] A quack is as fit for a pimp as a midwife for a bawd; they are still but in their way both helpers of nature.—Well, my dear doctor, hast thou done what I desired?

And so the play begins.

CONDITIONS OF PERFORMANCE

BACKGROUND

Life was unsettled during the 1640s in England. The Royalists and Puritans were fighting a civil war. King Charles I was captured, tried, and beheaded by the Puritans. Parliament appointed their leader, Oliver Cromwell, as head of a committee, called the Protectorate, to govern England, and Cromwell ruled as a virtual dictator until his death in 1658. Then, tired of civil and religious strife, Parliament restored the monarchy, and in 1660 Charles II returned from his long exile in Europe.

While England's "merry monarch," as Charles was called, settled down to align the various political and religious factions, he also restored the theatre as a major form of entertainment. Still, politics and religion divided the nation at every turn. Whigs and Tories clashed;

Parliament establishes
constitutional monarchy, 1689;
William of Orange and Mary
(James II's daughter) become
co-rulers (1689–1702)

Covent Garden
Theatre opens
with John Rich
as manager, 1731

William Hallam opens
theatre company in
America, 1752

America declares
Independence from
Great Britain, 1776

Queen Anne
comes to throne
(r. 1702–1714)

David Garrick
manages Drury Lane
1747–1776

Queen's theatre in
Haymarket opens
1704

King George I
(r. 1714–1727)
rules. Robert Walpole,
first prime minister

CHARLES II AND HIS SUCCESSORS

Charles II (1630–1685), King of England, Scotland, and Ireland, spent his early years in exile in Paris with his mother, Queen Henrietta Maria of France, and his brothers and sisters during the civil war that pitted royalists against the rising merchant class. After Cromwell's death in 1658, disenchantment with the Commonwealth rapidly spread and the monarch was welcomed back. Charles arrived in London on May 29, 1660. His rule was characterized by conciliation of the various English factions and religious toleration at a time of strong anti-Catholic bias.

Charles was married in 1662 to a Portuguese princess, Catherine of Braganza. They had no children, but Charles had at least 14 illegitimate children by various mistresses, including the actress Nell Gwyn. He died at age 54 to be suc-

ceeded by his unpopular brother James II, who ruled only three years until 1688. Having abused his prerogative powers and facing an invading army led by Protestant Dutchman William of Orange (James's son-in-law married to his Protestant daughter Mary), James fled England and spent his last years in exile in France.

William and Mary came to the English throne during the "Glorious Revolution" of 1688. They assured the supremacy of Protestantism and Parliament, for they ruled under a constitutional monarchy.

Queen Anne, the last Stuart monarch, who reigned from 1702 to 1714, was the second daughter of James II. She became queen on William's death in 1702. Her children died in infancy, and she named as her successors the Hanoverian descendants of King James I of England.

Protestants and Catholics quarreled. It was an age of plot and counterplot to secure the throne, the wealth of great families, and the influence of power.

The great event of the early years of the Restoration, recorded by diarist Samuel Pepys, was the fire that ravaged London in 1666. Another grander city was rebuilt on the ruins of the old. In the early eighteenth century the new London ranked with Paris as a cultural center and with Amsterdam as one of the world's two greatest trading centers. It was the seat of government, the home of royalty, and the heart of England's business district. There fashion was set, favorites made, fools and those out-of-fashion scorned. London was the final judge for the rest of the country of what was written, act-ed, sung, and worn. Westminster was the seat of Parliament, Buckingham Palace the place of royalty, and the theatres, along with the coffee-houses, St. Paul's, the Mall, and Hyde Park, the places where all society met. The river carried people down to Hampton Court and up to Greenwich. They rode horseback in the parks and sedan chairs carried fashionable ladies abroad shopping. But there were parts of London that were less picturesque, where the fashionable did not go and to which the playwrights gave no thought. These were the foul, miserable parts of the city—the "Gin Lanes"—preserved in engravings by artists like William Hogarth (Figure 8-2).

Too little liberty under Cromwell led to too much license under Charles. The carefree court and fashionable drawing rooms were filled with gallants and profligate young rakes. The Restoration, moreover, was as cynical as it was pleasure loving. The theatre was a microcosm of this society, expressing its mores in comedies about fops, seducers, adulterers, and cuckolds. Marriage for fortune, like infidelity, was taken for granted; the interest lay merely in the twists and ruses by which it was carried out; and the laugh lay in insolently deceiving some dullpate of a husband or suitor.

This attitude could not last. It was not a matter of people becoming more virtuous but wishing to appear better than they were. Decorum and correctness were bound to reappear among the fashionable and middle class, and a premium was soon placed on a person's public deportment rather than on his or her private morals. The celebrated Augustan Age of Queen Anne's reign enjoyed a perhaps undeserved reputation for reformed morals. However, its arts succeeded in realizing its ideals. On the whole, society under Queen Anne was simply hypocritical rather than truly virtuous. Gross flattery, back stabbing, and political squabbling defined the age. By the early eighteenth century, Louis Kronenberger wrote, society was only a bad compromise between the indulgence of natural instincts and the practice of empty forms.

The eighteenth century also had its share of

SAMUEL PEPYS

Samuel Pepys (1633–1703) is known to us primarily as the writer of the celebrated *Diary* that gives a valuable and entertaining picture of the social and theatrical life of the Restoration.

From a humble background Pepys rose to become England's earliest secretary of the Admiralty, a member of Parliament, and president of the Royal Society. Although he never intended it to be read by others, Pepys began his *Diary* on January 1, 1660, but failing eyesight made him discontinue it in 1669. The *Diary* was written in cipher (a system of shorthand) and was not deciphered until 1825 by a Rev. John Smith.

The *Diary* is far more than an ordinary record of its writer's thoughts and social life during the Restoration. It is most valuable to us as a spontaneous account of the Restoration and coronation, the horrors of the plague, the great London fire, and the theatre of the day (see page 208).

Figure 8-2 *Gin Lane* by William Hogarth.

fops, venal politicians, wits, bullies, and boors. People ate and drank far too much; gout was overwhelmingly an upper-class malady. The coffeehouse was possibly the most important institution of Augustan society where scholars at the Grecian, wits and writers at Button's or Will's, and businessmen at Lloyd's transacted serious business and indulged in gossip. With the coffeehouse, the English club for drinking, gambling, and socializing was established at the Whig, the Kit-Kat Club, and White's.

All in all, the English theatre over a period of about 150 years reflected changing mores, sentiments, and fashions; and throughout the comings and goings of the great and the near great, two theatres—Drury Lane and Covent Garden—were home to the best of Restoration and eighteenth-century plays.

MANAGEMENT AND FINANCING

When King Charles II licensed William Davenant and Thomas Killigrew to open the first new theatres in 1660, he created the theatrical manager who leased and built theatres, ran the companies, and assumed the financial risks. Davenant, unlike Killigrew, was a theatre artist, having produced plays and operas for private performance at his home, Rutland House, and this experience was valuable to him as a manager. Killigrew's company soon fell on hard times and a change of managers began.

While actors like Thomas Betterton became successful managers, the financial risks were so great that few managers survived long. Many failed because they knew little about theatre or because they tried to exploit it.

Between 1660 and 1700 there were three theatres of importance: Drury Lane, Lincoln's Inn Fields, and Dorset Garden. Between 1700 and 1800, there were five: Drury Lane, Lincoln's Inn Fields, the King's Theatre, the Haymarket, and Covent Garden.

As the theatres grew larger so did the companies. Whereas the typical acting company of the Restoration had included 35 to 40 persons, a company by 1800 had about 80. In addition to actors, each company employed a treasurer, ticket takers, barber, bookkeeper, prompters, singers, dancers, musicians, bill distributors, scene painters, candle snuffers, stagehands, wardrobe keepers, dressers, laundresses, and maintenance personnel. By the 1800s the major companies were employing more than 200 people.

To support the companies, *shares* were sold in buildings used as theatres. In return for their investment, shareholders were paid a fixed sum for each day the building was used for performances. Shares were also sold in a company and its productions. For a time after 1660 actors shared in the company's risks and profits, but as expenses increased and the financial risks grew larger, actors came to prefer a fixed salary. Today the situation is somewhat similar: actors are paid fixed salaries and "backers" buy into productions.

In the early 1700s the average daily expenses of a company were about 40 pounds; by 1790 they had increased to 105 pounds. Managers were dependent upon ticket sales for income; to increase income they either raised ticket prices or increased attendance by having special events, such as "benefits" for popular actors. Basic ticket prices (*boxes,* four shillings; *pit*, two shillings six pence; *upper gallery*, one shilling) changed little during the period. However, ticket prices were raised for premieres, for plays with *new* costumes or scenery, or for added attractions, such as a new pantomime performed as an afterpiece.

THE REPERTORY SYSTEM

The repertory system was a holdover from Elizabethan times. A company performed 35 to 40 plays divided about equally between old, pre-Commonwealth plays and new plays (or highly popular plays from recent seasons).

The system required actors to play several types of characters, perhaps to sing and dance, to speak prologues and epilogues, and to remember a large number of roles. Thomas Betterton during his 40 years on stage (1660–1700) played 132 major roles (Figure 8-3).

By the early 1800s the repertory had increased to 75 plays and by the late 1800s was up to about 90. However, only about one-third of this number represented new plays. The others were drawn from Shakespeare (with revisions to bring the texts in line with contemporary tastes) and Restoration plays by John Dryden, William Congreve, and others.

During the Restoration period performances usually began at about three o'clock in the afternoon; by 1800 six o'clock was the fixed hour for beginning a performance. A performance was a lengthy affair, about three hours. It included music, prologue, play, between-act entertainment, epilogue, and afterpiece. The season was usually October to June, the theatres being dark on Sundays and holidays. An initial run for a new play was two or three consecutive performances. The author's benefit performance occurred on the third day and sometimes on the sixth and ninth. A new play that ran for 14 consecutive days was an unqualified success.

THE ACTING COMPANIES

The Restoration opened with two official theatrical companies: the King's Company made up of experienced actors of the day and managed by Thomas Killigrew and the Duke's Company made up of young actors and managed by William Davenant. The companies included women, reflecting the King's tastes for foreign fashions in theatre as well as in other arts. Other nonpatent companies were formed with varying degrees of success, and some companies ran "nurseries" where young actors could train and perform.

Contracts signed by actors restricted them to a single company, stated their salary, and set forth penalties for missing rehearsals or for removing costumes and properties from the theatre. The *benefit* performance was an additional source of income for an individual actor or

---

The Licensing Act of 1737

By 1730 the legal status of the patents issued by Charles II to Davenant and Killigrew was being debated. Many theatre managers were illegally defying the monopoly, whereas others, such as Thomas Betterton, had received a license from King William III in 1695 and were therefore still operating legally. Confusion reigned. The 1737 Licensing Act, passed during the reign of George II, restricted plays and theatres to those licensed by the lord chamberlain. It was as much an effort to bring about government control over the theatres as it was Prime Minister Robert Walpole's revenge against political satires being performed at unlicensed theatres.

The Licensing Act was rushed through Parliament in 1737. It restricted authorized theatres to the City of Westminster (the government seat), making Drury Lane and Covent Garden (opened in 1732) the only legitimate theatres in England. It also prohibited the acting of any play not previously licensed by the lord chamberlain.

The law was obeyed for a while but then managers sought ways to circumvent it. They charged admission for concerts or for food; the plays themselves were free. Towns outside London petitioned for theatres; finally, other theatres like the Haymarket were licensed in London. Another Licensing Act in 1788 tried once again to settle some of the confusion by licensing theatres outside London proper and plays performed throughout Britain. This new law was not fully challenged until the nineteenth century when managers again tried to avoid its restrictions.

Figure 8-3 In the closet scene of *Hamlet* (II, 1), at the moment when the Ghost appears, all early illustrations show Hamlet standing aghast with one stocking loose, the chair from which he has leaped lying overturned behind him. This tradition of playing the scene remained unbroken from the time of Thomas Betterton until the last quarter of the eighteenth century. David Garrick contrived an effective crash by use of a trick chair, but he did not do away with the stage business. (From an engraving of 1709.)

for the playwright. Presumably, the first benefit for an individual performer was for Elizabeth Barry in 1694–1695. It quickly became a part of nearly every contract between actor and management. So important was the benefit that Anne Bracegirdle came out of retirement to play a benefit for her adopted father, Thomas Betterton (Figure 8-4).

During this entire period theatre in England was an actor's theatre, as distinct from a playwright's or a director's theatre. During the Restoration, theatre in London was looked upon as a

The Indian Queen

J. Smith ex. *W. Vincent fe.*

Figure 8-4 Anne Bracegirdle in the title role of *The Indian Queen.*

ANNE BRACEGIRDLE

Anne Bracegirdle (c. 1663–1748) was both actress and singer. The daughter of a Northampton coachman, or perhaps coachmaker, who fell on hard times, she was placed as an infant with the childless couple Thomas and Mary Betterton. Through them, she became associated with the theatre. Her name first appears as a member of the United Company in 1688 where she was an ingenue playing breeches parts, or parts requiring men's clothing. Exceptionally talented, she was apparently best suited to tragic roles and to sophisticated heroines of comedy. Her private life was often as dramatic as her stage life. She was associated with a well-known duel between her lovers, actor William Mountfort and Lord Mohun, in which the actor was killed, and was also linked romantically with playwright William Congreve.

The finest role ever written for her was Millamant in Congreve's *The Way of the World* (1700). Six years later, at age 44, she retired from the stage, giving little explanation. She died at 80 and was buried in Westminster Abbey.

DAVID GARRICK

Manager, patentee, playwright, and poet, David Garrick (1717–1779) was also the greatest actor of his day. He was responsible for the radical change to a new naturalism in the style of English acting.

During his long management of Drury Lane, he instituted many reforms, the most important being the introduction of stage lighting that was concealed from the audience and the banishment of the audience from the stage. He has also been credited with the revivals of Shakespeare's texts, freeing them from the changes of seventeenth-century hack writers; even so, he continued to make alterations, omitting, for instance, the gravedigger's scene in *Hamlet* and the fool from *King Lear*.

Of Huguenot descent, Garrick grew up in Lichfield, the son of an army officer, and early showed an inclination for the stage. He studied under Dr. Samuel Johnson and accompanied his teacher to London. Rejected by the managers of both Drury Lane and Covent Garden, he made his formal London debut at Goodman's Fields Theatre in 1741 as Richard III. Playgoers crowded to see him. Garrick was now embarked on a triumphant career of acting, managing, and writing that would last until his retirement in 1776. He was unsurpassed in such parts as Hamlet, Macbeth, and King Lear. His greatest comic roles were Falstaff in Shakespeare's plays and Abel Drugger in Ben Jonson's *The Alchemist*. [2]

court toy and actors and actresses as fashionable playthings. The actor's personal glamour and talent got attention, not the quality of the repertory or the plays. Actors displayed their polish in comedy and their abilities for high passion in tragedy. They also became associated with certain parts and stage business.

The leading actor of the Restoration stage was Thomas Betterton (c. 1635–1710), who appeared with Elizabeth Barry in tragedy and with Anne Bracegirdle in comedy (Figure 8-4). The playwright William Congreve wrote his greatest comedies for Betterton and Bracegirdle. Colley Cibber (1671–1757) was known for his "fops" (Figure 8-5), and Charles Macklin (1699–1797) is best remembered for discarding the tradition of portraying Shylock in Shakespeare's *The Merchant of Venice* as a low comic type or as a villain and playing him rather as a tragic, dignified figure.

The greatest actor of the eighteenth century was David Garrick (1717–1779). Equally effective in tragedy and in comedy, he radically changed the style of English acting, substituting natural delivery and movement for the stiffness and pomposity of older actors. All contemporary accounts of his performances take note of his expressive eyes and exceptionally mobile features. His career ran triumphantly from his debut as Shakespeare's Richard III in 1741 to his retirement in 1776. Most of his time was spent as actor and manager at Drury Lane.

Another actor, destined to play a large part in English stage history, was John Philip Kemble. With his sister Sarah Siddons, they dominated the next generation of English actors.

PLAYWRITING

With the reopening of the playhouses in 1660, the companies presented old plays until new ones could be written. Beaumont and Fletcher, Shakespeare's contemporaries, were immediate favorites with court audiences. John Dryden emerged as a new playwright whose specialties were rhymed heroic dramas and comedies of

Figure 8-5 Colley Cibber as Lord Foppington in Vanbrugh's *The Relapse; or Virtue in Danger*, 1696.

manners. In 1676 London audiences saw premieres of three comedies of manners: Sir George Etherege's *The Man of Mode,* Thomas Shadwell's *The Virtuoso,* and William Wycherley's *The Plain Dealer.* Comedies by William Congreve, Sir John Vanbrugh, and George Farquhar continued the tradition as late as 1707.

Many different types of plays were written—satire, burlesque, neoclassical plays, heroic drama, ballad opera, manners, intrigues, adaptations, comedies, and tragedies. By 1700 audiences were becoming more varied and less sophisticated, and a new style of play called sentimental comedy emerged. Almost in defi-

ance of the witty comedies of the Restoration, the later bourgeois tragedy and domestic drama joined with sentimental comedy in elaborating the problems of middle-class heroes and heroines.

A long period of mediocre playwriting set in. In the 1770s playwrights Oliver Goldsmith and Richard Brinsley Sheridan reacted against the fashionable excesses of sentiment in current plays. Sheridan's *The Rivals* (1775) and *The School for Scandal* (1777) were written in the tradition of Restoration comedy with wit but with much less license. Sheridan's two plays, along with Goldsmith's *She Stoops to Conquer* (1773), have survived in the repertory of English and American theatres.

As we noted earlier, the playwright's main source of revenue was the benefit where he or she derived income from the third performance of a new play's run and sometimes from the sixth and ninth performances. While Aphra Behn (1640–1689), the first woman of the period to earn her living as a playwright, declared in the preface to *The Lucky Chance* (1686), "I am not content to write for a third day only," this was usually the case nevertheless. The playwright's other sources of income were gifts from patrons or profits from the sale of printed copies of the play. Neither source was very lucrative or dependable. Some playwrights, like John Dryden, bought shares in a company; others, like Richard Brinsley Sheridan, derived their main income from managing the theatre where they, in turn, produced their own plays.

CASTING AND REHEARSALS

It was informally agreed that popular actors were given the good roles. Betterton, for instance, played Shakespeare's heroes; Colley Cibber excelled as fops; and Nell Gwyn (1650–1687) was given, according to Pepys, parts beyond her talents. Occasionally, the playwright had a hand in casting his plays. Charles II also sometimes intervened in casting decisions.

The repertory system demanded almost continuous rehearsing. The companies prepared new plays at the same time they were recasting and refreshing "stage business" and lines for revivals. It appears likely that formal rehearsals were held in the mornings and at midday, while work on scenes, songs, and dances continued after the audience had left the theatre. A new play was normally rehearsed about two weeks in advance of opening.

VISUAL ELEMENTS

Scenes and Machines William Davenant, one of the first Restoration producers, had a profound interest in movable and changeable scenery. He used machines for creating illusions and startling events, such as the rise and descent of chariots, angels, tables, and other objects. Davenant developed the principle of drawing back the curtain after the prologue, revealing a scene followed by others. The curtain stayed open until after the speaking of the epilogue. All scene changes took place in full view of the audience and were part of the visual entertainment. Richard Southern tells us that a scene represented a grouping of side scenes (wings), shutters, and "relieve" scenes.[3]

When a text read, "the scene opens," it meant that the scenery actually moved, and "the scene closes" indicated the drawing together of the two halves of the back scene. A bare stage ordinarily indicated the end of an act; the interval was used for song, dance, musical interludes, and even specialty acts while scenery was set up again.

Out of necessity each theatre accumulated a stock of scenery that was used over and over again. It was possible to reuse scenery in this way because staging emphasized the *general* features of a place, rather than the particular. Scenes were designated as a drawing room, chocolate house, St. James' Park, palace exterior, palace interior, a prison, a garden, and so forth. The audience's delight in spectacle led to the practice of raising ticket prices if new settings or costumes were to be seen. Also, the talents of the scene painter were rewarded with fees far in excess of the actor's wages or the playwright's fees. In 1669 Killigrew was sued by Isaac Fuller, who claimed he had not been paid for one setting, which he testified had taken him six weeks to paint; the court awarded him 335 pounds for his work (at a time when a leading actor was paid about two and one-half pounds a week).

In the late eighteenth century the most important scenic designer working on the English stage was the French artist Philip James de Loutherbourg (1740–1812), whose reproductions of "real" places on stage became extremely popular. The designer introduced several new techniques to increase the illusion of reality. He broke up the stage picture with "cutouts" to gain

Figure 8-6 Stage of the Dorset Garden Theatre showing a scene from Settle's *The Empress of Morocco*, produced in 1673. Note the elaborate perspective scenery and proscenium arch.

a greater sense of depth and reality. He painted backgrounds emphasizing the detail and color of particular places; he coordinated sound effects, such as waves, rain, hail, and distant guns. He also made lighting more elaborate by using silk screens to simulate weather conditions and times of day.

Costumes and Properties Our chief sources of information about costumes of the period are diaries, letters, engravings, paintings, and records kept by John Downes, a prompter for the Duke's Company. Costumes were elaborate and expensive. Charles II and his courtiers some-

times loaned their clothes to enhance a scene. When Davenant staged *Love and Honour* (1661), Charles II allowed Betterton to wear the coronation robes. Like the practice in Elizabethan England and in France, actors wore contemporary clothing as costumes. Little regard was given to historical accuracy although there were specialty costumes, such as the Roman *habit* and the Oriental turban. For an exotic character like the Indian Queen in a lavish work of the same name, Anne Bracegirdle wore a costume bedecked with feathers and plumes.

Information about properties is relatively scarce. Only essential pieces of furniture (like the two chairs on stage for *Hamlet* or the screen and chair in *The School for Scandal*) were used. Other furniture was painted on scenery. Smaller objects for stage use were more abundant. Pepys describes a visit to the property room in Drury Lane where he saw "a wooden-leg, a ruff, a hobbyhorse, and a crown." Many plays called for the eating of food, and contemporary property lists included claret, beer, and bread in addition to chinaware.

All the theatres employed property masters, wardrobe persons, and dressers.

Lighting Between 1660 and 1800 remarkable innovations occurred not only in movable scenery but also in stage lighting. Wax or tallow candles provided the principal light sources over the stage in hanging chandeliers and in wall sconces in the auditorium. In Garrick's day Drury Lane had a large chandelier suspended over the center of the auditorium and six others above the stage. Earlier, Pepys complained of candle wax dripping on the spectators and of the candlelight hurting his eyes. While candles (supplemented by oil lamps) may have been snuffed out to darken the stage for night scenes, the general practice was to light the candles before the curtain was opened and to snuff them out when the play was over. By the 1740s candles apparently were being mounted on vertical stands behind each wing and dimmed by the use of "scene blinds" lowered between the light source and the stage. During the 1770s De Loutherbourg added transparent silk screens to add and control color. Footlights were probably in use by 1672.

Lighting improved again in 1785 when the Argand, or "patent," oil lamp was added. It produced a much brighter and steadier light than candles, and the glass chimney could be painted, increasing color effects. However, the auditorium continued to be lighted during performances.

Music and Dance After 1660 the growth of between-act entertainments meant a greater de-

---

February 4, 1667:

". . . the house being very full, and great company; among others, Mrs. Stewart, very fine, with her locks done up with puffs . . . and several other great ladies, had their hair so. . . . Here I saw my Lord Rochester and his lady, Mrs. Mallet, who hath after all this ado married him; and, as I hear some say in the pit, it is a great act of charity; for he hath no estate. But it was pleasant to see how everybody rose up when my Lord John Butler, the Duke of Ormond's son, came into the pit towards the end of the play, who was a servant to Mrs. Mallet, and now smiled upon her, and she on him. I had sitting next to me a woman, the likest my Lady Castlemayne that ever I saw anybody like another; but she is a whore, I believe, for she is acquainted with every fine fellow, and called them by their name, Jacke, and Tom, and before the end of the play frisked to another place.*"*

Samuel Pepys, *Diary* (1661–1669)

---

mand for dancers, instrumental and vocal musicians, and performers with skills in both acting and specialties. Ordinarily, actors were not expected to sing; professional singers were employed when needed. But Nell Gwyn, for example, did act, sing, and dance, and Anne Bracegirdle was the first known professional actress to train her singing voice.

Dances during the play and between acts, plus rope dancing (a combination of dancing, rope skipping, and twirling) were very popular. There was also a growing vogue for music at court, in theatres, and in concert halls. The eighteenth century brought Italian opera into fashion and the creation of the Royal Academy of Music by a company of wealthy nobles.

In the theatres an orchestra played an overture before the prologue, concerts and solos with the acts, accompanied vocalists, and played

background music. Many plays, both tragic and comic, had at least one song, and new songs were composed for revivals of old plays. Henry Purcell (c. 1659–1695) was the most famous composer of the time, composing music for songs, overtures, and operas.

THE AUDIENCE

Restoration and eighteenth-century audiences were composed of a diversity of classes, education, and tastes (Figure 8-7). The divisions of the auditorium into boxes, pit, and galleries reflected this diversity. In the pit were writers, critics, professional men, and the like. The boxes held persons of rank and fashion. Merchants and tradesmen sat in the first gallery, and in the upper galleries were citizens, clerks, servants, apprentices, and soldiers. By 1700 the range of social classes and professions was as great as the taste and motives of the spectators. Some, like Samuel Pepys, were fascinated by the stage. Others, like John Dryden, attended as arbiters of taste. Still others went to be seen and to make assignations.

In 1672 a fire gutted the Theatre Royal in Bridges Street built in 1663, and plans were laid for the construction of a new playhouse, with Christopher Wren as the architect. Except for an architectural section, drawn by Wren, the only contemporary view of the interior is a view of the stage shown in Figure 8-1.

Engraving of the interior of Drury Lane after it was remodeled by the Adams brothers in 1775. David Garrick made frequent attempts to increase the capacity of Drury Lane. In 1775 the interior was remodeled. The galleries were pushed back to the exterior wall, doubling the number of rows. Wren's great pilasters were replaced with narrow pillars, enabling patrons in the side boxes to see more of the stage. The ceiling was raised and a third tier was added to the sides. It is this Adams version of Drury Lane that is most frequently reproduced. Unfortunately, the scale of the engraving was changed to make the house seem monumental.

Interior of the Drury Lane before the theatre was destroyed by fire in 1809. Private boxes on each side enclosed the pit. The dress circle and galleries circled the auditorium.

The modern Drury Lane, designed in 1921–1922. The modern Drury Lane is a traditional picture-frame theatre; the auditorium is divided into orchestra stalls, a dress circle, and three cantilevered tiers of balconies facing a large proscenium opening. Two groups of seven boxes are on each side of the opening. It has an orchestra pit, fire curtain and sprinkler system (required by British law), fly galleries and grid, counterweight system, hydraulic lifts, and electrical system. It has a large area of stage floor with a side dock for the storage of scenery required in a current production. This type of orthodox picture-frame stage is most common in modern British, American, and European theatres.

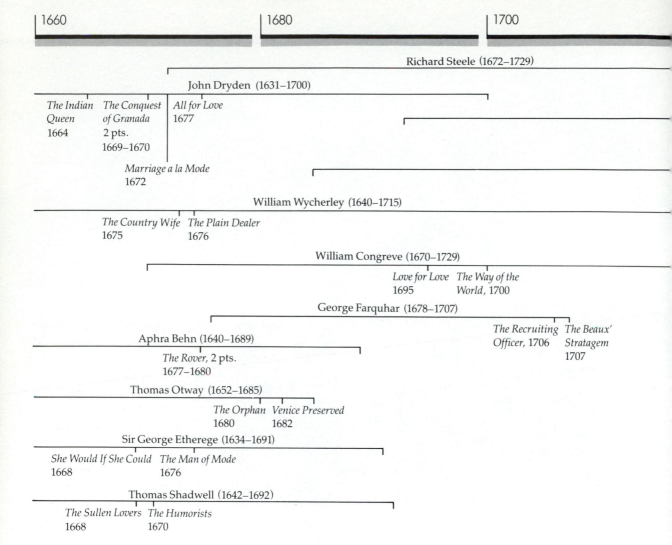

1660   1680   1700

Richard Steele (1672–1729)

John Dryden (1631–1700)

| The Indian Queen 1664 | The Conquest of Granada 2 pts. 1669–1670 | All for Love 1677 |

Marriage a la Mode 1672

William Wycherley (1640–1715)

The Country Wife 1675   The Plain Dealer 1676

William Congreve (1670–1729)

Love for Love 1695   The Way of the World, 1700

George Farquhar (1678–1707)

The Recruiting Officer, 1706   The Beaux' Stratagem 1707

Aphra Behn (1640–1689)

The Rover, 2 pts. 1677–1680

Thomas Otway (1652–1685)

The Orphan 1680   Venice Preserved 1682

Sir George Etherege (1634–1691)

She Would If She Could 1668   The Man of Mode 1676

Thomas Shadwell (1642–1692)

The Sullen Lovers 1668   The Humorists 1670

DRAMATIC CONVENTIONS

When London theatres opened in 1660, it was quickly apparent that the most devastating effect of the 18-year hiatus was the absence of new plays. Davenant and Killigrew turned to pre-Commonwealth plays and quickly cultivated courtiers and others with playwriting pretensions. Soon the names of Dryden, Etherege, Wycherley, Congreve, Otway, and Shadwell

appeared on playbills. Their works, like the playhouses they were writing for, revealed a blending of native traditions with foreign influences.

PROLOGUES AND EPILOGUES

Almost all new and revived plays had a prologue and epilogue spoken by popular actors like Nell Gwyn, Thomas Betterton, and Anne Bracegirdle.

The prologue's chief purpose was to gain the

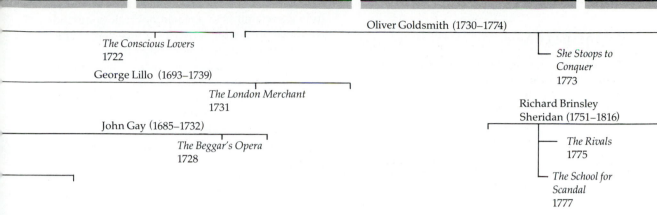

1720   1740   1760

Oliver Goldsmith (1730–1774)

The Conscious Lovers
1722

*She Stoops to
Conquer*
1773

George Lillo (1693–1739)

The London Merchant
1731

Richard Brinsley
Sheridan (1751–1816)

John Gay (1685–1732)

The Rivals
1775

The Beggar's Opera
1728

*The School for
Scandal*
1777

---

audience's attention. It was spoken after the overture with the curtain opening at the end of it. The epilogue set about to win applause for the play and its actors. It also signaled the end of the performance.

AFTERPIECE

The afterpiece was a short play performed after the main event. There was usually no connection between the two; the afterpiece might be a farce, burlesque, pantomime, animal act, or musical entertainment. The afterpiece did not gain full acceptance until the early part of the eighteenth century, but, by the time of Garrick, it was an established part of the program.

COMEDIES OF MANNERS

The term *comedy of manners* denotes a large and varied body of Restoration prose plays whose plots, expressed in witty dialogue, consisted mainly of sexual intrigue among Londoners of high fashion. The greatest of these plays were written by George Etherege, William Wycherley, and William Congreve. They have been categorized by Joseph Wood Krutch as plays about "politeness" and "pretenders to the polite."

Samuel Johnson described the purpose of drama in his prologue for the opening of Drury Lane in 1747:

*The Stage but echoes back the publick Voice
The Drama's Laws the Drama's Patron's give,
For we that live to please, must please to live.*

In the 1680s there was a shift away from the harsh sex comedies of Etherege and Wycherley. A new group of playwrights (Congreve, Vanbrugh, and Farquhar were among the best) contributed a body of comedies that united the older sexual intrigues with the newer taste for feelings, sentiments, and moral maxims. Many consider Congreve's *The Way of the World* (1700) the finest comic achievement of the period.

After 1700 a type of "genteel comedy," characterized by four acts of intrigue and flippant dialogue followed by a fifth act of repentance and reformation, found general acceptance. John Vanbrugh's *The Relapse* (1696), Colley Cibber's *The Careless Husband* (1704), and George Farquhar's *The Beaux' Stratagem* (1707) are the best examples. At the close of the eighteenth century, Oliver Goldsmith and Richard Brinsley Sheridan revived the witty dialogue of fashionable society but tempered it with a generosity of spirit.

BALLAD OPERA

The first quarter of the eighteenth century in England saw the introduction of the works of George Frederick Handel, Italian opera, and ballad opera, the most popular of which was John Gay's sensational *Beggar's Opera* (1728). Gay set the scene of his ballad opera around Newgate Prison and in it satirized musical traditions of the time along with aristocratic and middle-class ideals. His 69 ballads, or popular songs, were spread throughout three acts as was the custom in opera. His method was to take a tune associated with a ribald or erotic song and compose for it a tender lyric, or vice versa. This discrepancy between the familiar tunes and the lyrics delighted audiences. So did the satirical portraits of famous Whig leaders of the day in the guise of thieves and prostitutes. The portrait of Prime Minister Robert Walpole, in the figure of Peachum the underworld fence, was so clear that Walpole banned Gay's sequel to *The Beggar's Opera*, *Polly*.

The remarkable success of *The Beggar's Opera* (it ran for 32 consecutive performances)

❝ The Restoration Comedies belong almost exclusively to one type—what we call 'society comedy' or the 'comedy of manners.' The scene is usually London, and the chief persons, with few exceptions, members of high society. If the country or any city besides London is introduced, it is only for the purpose of ridicule. . . . The scene moves usually in a restricted circle: the drawing room, the park, the bed chamber, the tavern, then the drawing room again, through which scenes move a set of ever-recurring types—the graceful young rake, the faithless wife, the deceived husband, and, perhaps, a charming young heroine who is to be bestowed in the end on the rake. . . .

They are, briefly, comedies depicting realistically and in a sinister spirit the life of the most dissolute portion of the fashionable society of the city. The hero is ordinarily a man pursuing the pleasures of drink, play, and love, with a complete disregard for the well being of others; and the heroine is a woman whose scruples, if she has any, are based on prudence rather than virtue. Great emphasis is laid on repartee for its own sake, and upon epigrams propounding an elaborate and systematic code of immorality.❞

Joseph Wood Krutch, *Comedy and Conscience After the Restoration* (1949)[4]

WILLIAM CONGREVE

William Congreve (1670–1729) was considered by many to be the greatest writer of Restoration comedy.

Born in Ireland, he was educated at Trinity College, Dublin. In 1689 he appeared in London as the author of *The Old Bachelor*, produced at Drury Lane in 1693. It was followed the next year by *The Double Dealer*. But *Love for Love* (1695) was Congreve's most successful play, pleasing audience taste for sexual intrigue and moral sentiments. His last play, *The Way of the World* (1700), which today is regarded as his best, was coldly received. Congreve's masterpiece made plain in witty dialogue the difficulties of sustaining an authentic marriage within fashionable society (see opposite). Disappointment and possibly ill-health drove Congreve from the stage.

Congreve's comedies are prized for their pictures of fashionable society, along with their stylistically elegant and superlative wit.

launched a vogue for ballad opera for the next 20 years. Two hundred years later Bertolt Brecht's adaptation of Gay's play with music by Kurt Weill, *The Threepenny Opera* (1928), proved as sensational as the original.

SENTIMENTAL COMEDY

Sentimental comedy was a product of the tastes of the rising middle class. These comedies exhibited the virtues and sufferings of middle-class characters, replacing the sex intrigues of the earlier comedies by the admirable conduct of people in unfortunate circumstances. Sentimental characters experienced anguish and sorrow, but their conduct under stress was exemplary. This "genteel comedy" was best exemplified in Colley Cibber's *The Careless Husband* and Richard Steele's *The Conscious Lovers* (1722). In these plays women are cruelly mistreated by husbands and lovers only to have their steadfastness rewarded in the end with the reform of the miscreant.

THE LANGUAGE OF WIT

Comedies of manners were written in the polished, sophisticated language of fashionable London society. Dialogue was characterized by "wit combats" (lovers railing against each other) and by lengthy similes (called *similitudes*). For centuries *wit* had been considered the perception of similarities in things dissimilar. Thus the simile becomes the measure of a character's perception of the world around him or her. Congreve writes for his hero and heroine in *The Way of the World* some of the most extravagant and brilliant dialogue in all of Restoration comedy:

Mirabell I say that a man may as soon make a friend by his wit, or a fortune by his honesty, as win a woman with plain dealing and sincerity.

Millamant Sententious Mirabell! Prithee, don't look with that violent and inflexible wise

---

> **The Beggar's Opera**
>
> At the opening of John Gay's *Beggar's Opera*, Peachum sits at a table with a large book of accounts before him and sings the first song of the ballad opera after the tune "An old woman clothed in gray":
>
> Through all the employments of life,
>   Each neighbor abuses his brother;
> Whore and rogue they call husband and wife:
>   All professions be-rogue one another.
> The priest calls the lawyer a cheat,
>   The lawyer be-knaves the divine;
> And the statesman, because he's so great,
>   Thinks his trade as honest as mine.
>
> (I,1)

face, like Solomon at the dividing of the child in an old tapestry hanging.

(II, 6)

REPRESENTATIVE PLAY

The Beaux' Stratagem
Written by George Farquhar, produced at the Queen's Theatre in the Haymarket, March 1707, with Robert Wilks as Archer and Anne Oldfield as Mrs. Sullen

BACKGROUND

George Farquhar is one of a line of distinguished Irish playwrights—namely, William Congreve, Richard Brinsley Sheridan, Oscar Wilde, and George Bernard Shaw—who have furthered the traditions of English comedy. Farquhar made his debut with *Love and a Bottle* at Drury Lane in 1698, and wrote eight plays before his early death in

1707. His last plays, *The Recruiting Officer* and *The Beaux' Stratagem,* are comic masterpieces.

Farquhar straddles two periods of English dramatic writing. He carried on the comic tradition of such Restoration playwrights as Etherege, Wycherley, and Congreve, while embracing the spirit of a changing age. His plays are filled with fortune hunters, highwaymen, predatory innkeepers, sullen husbands, flirtatious women, scheming servants, virtuous heroines, good-hearted beaux, and loyal domestics. While society may be corrupt, his plays suggest, a person can be virtuous and a rake can reform.

The Beaux' Stratagem deals with the marriage game, its vicissitudes, triumphs, and failures. It takes place in Lichfield, a village in central England. The setting is an inn and Lady Bountiful's house. The plot turns on the strategies of two penniless rakes from London (one disguised as master, the other as valet) who must, between them, marry an heiress or join the army. Farquhar treats the social problems caused by *inheritance laws* favoring the firstborn son to the exclusion of other siblings (Aimwell and Archer) and the *divorce laws* that ignore problems of marital maladjustment (Squire and Mrs. Sullen).

From the conduct of the two male leads, we can observe Farquhar's comic world pointing in two directions: Archer toward the older sex comedies of the Restoration and Aimwell toward the new drama of sensibility, in which a display of emotions was paramount.

THE COMIC ACTION

Farquhar's comic energies are focused on the schemes and ploys of two gallants, traveling under false pretenses, pursuing marriage with wealthy heiresses. Aimwell and Archer tell us that if they do not prove lucky in Lichfield, then they will travel on to Nottingham, Lincoln, and Norwich. Dorinda and Aimwell are an example of an idealized, romantic relationship between the virtuous young woman and the beau reformed by her good example. (It is only a minor point that Aimwell literally turns wealthy over-night and gives Dorinda's dowry of 10,000 pounds to his friend Archer.)

These intrigues for fortune, sex, and marriage are sustained by three plot strands dealing with thieves, Count Bellair, and Cherry, the innkeeper's daughter. Highwaymen (Gibbet, Hounslow, Bagshot) led by Boniface, the innkeeper, set about to rob the inn's guests and Lady Bountiful's house. The sex intrigues of Aimwell and Archer are compounded by Cherry, who dotes upon the disguised Archer, and by Count Bellair, a French officer held prisoner in Lichfield and would-be lover to Mrs. Sullen.

Farquhar was also interested in the ethical problem of women, like Mrs. Sullen, who lose out when the marriage game ends. Mrs. Sullen says of her plight:

> Were I born an humble Turk, where women have no soul nor property, there I must sit contented. But in England, a country whose women are its glory, must women be abused? where women rule, must women be enslaved? nay, cheated into slavery, mocked by a promise of comfortable society into a wilderness of solitude? I dare not keep the thought about me. . . .
>
> (IV,1)

The playwright's thoughtful speeches on divorce are influenced by John Milton's *Doctrine and Discipline of Divorce* (1643), a series of pamphlets written nearly half a century before. These pamphlets criticized England's stringent divorce laws, in which separation could only be granted by ecclesiastical courts, and only in rare cases, and incompatibility of temperament was not an admitted ground. Under English law women upon marriage turned over all of their "moveable goods" to their husbands; they were then completely dependent upon their husbands' support. Farquhar set about creating the moral justification for more lenient divorce laws by showing the plight of the Sullens.

The play's comic intrigues are resolved with Aimwell and Dorinda promised to each other in

GEORGE FARQUHAR

Usually classed among writers of Restoration comedy, George Farquhar (1678–1707) nevertheless stands apart from them. He shows more variety in plotting, location of scenes, and depth of feeling than his playwright contemporaries. In his last and best plays he makes a conscious effort to adapt the licentiousness of the early comedies of manners to the changing taste of the time for sentiment and moral maxims.

Born in Ireland and educated at Trinity College, Dublin, Farquhar was for a short time an actor, but left the stage after accidentally wounding a fellow actor by attacking him with a real sword instead of a property sword. With the assistance of actor and lifelong friend Robert Wilks, he went to London where his first play, *Love and a Bottle* (1698), was produced at Drury Lane. With *The Constant Couple; or, a Trip to the Jubilee* (1699), Farquhar established his reputation as one of the outstanding dramatists of the day.

Farquhar left London for some time after a sudden marriage with a penniless lady whom he believed to be an heiress. During the remainder of his life, he was harassed by financial debts.

He returned to the theatre in 1706 with *The Recruiting Officer,* based on his experiences in Shropshire, where he was sent to recruit a company for the War of the Spanish Succession. It was followed by what many critics regard as his finest play, *The Beaux' Stratagem.* This was Farquhar's last work, written in six weeks while he was lying terminally ill in poor lodgings. His early death was a great loss to the English stage, since *The Beaux' Stratagem* shows clearly the way in which he might have developed.

---

marriage; the Sullens freed of each other by Sir Charles Freeman's intervention; and Archer, with money in hand, in pursuit of his next gratification. In Farquhar's balanced view of human nature, one beau is reformed, the other unscathed.

THE SCENE

Farquhar took his setting out of fashionable London (the scene of earlier comedies of manners) and placed it in the country where there was opportunity for introducing a greater variety of characters and events. He created the milieu of a country inn with its collection of tradespeople, robbers, country squires, foreign soldiers, and pretenders. Lady Bountiful's house becomes a second setting where various intrigues are played out to almost everyone's satisfaction with the exception of the would-be robbers. Here natural goodness triumphs over the ways of the fashionable and legal world. Here, as the social matriarch, Lady Bountiful administers to her neighbors' diseases with expertness, while her fondness for her foolish son Sullen prevents her from seeing him for what he is. Here Mrs. Sullen, the daughter-in-law, chafes in a miserable marriage to a boorish husband and longs for a return to London or for an intrigue or two. Archer and Aimwell introduce the manners of the town into Lady Bountiful's house where their schemes of fortune hunting and sexual dalliance are modified by intrinsic virtue and innate good sense.

Figure 8-8 Engraving from 1711 edition of *The Beaux' Stratagem* by Farquhar.

CHARACTERIZATION

Farquhar transforms the comic stereotypes of self-indulgent beaux, neglected wives, country bumpkins, and scheming servants into amazingly naturalistic characters. Archer and Aimwell represent London; Lady Bountiful and her household, the Lichfield gentry; Bellair and Foigard, the army; Gibbet and his friends, lawless gentlemen of the road; Boniface and Cherry, the small tradespeople.

Lady Bountiful, as her name implies, is a benevolent person. Squire Sullen is a drunken sot who married only to get an heir to his estate, and, being disappointed, treats his wife abominably. Mrs. Sullen is a fine lady removed from her London milieu and pining to get back to it. Her would-be lover, Count Bellair, is characterized chiefly by gallantry and an accent. The priest Foigard, posing as a Frenchman, is really an Irishman in disguise. The predatory innkeeper and his cronies are thieves who know their legal rights on the scaffold. These low-life characters prefigure John Gay's famous underworld types in *The Beggar's Opera*.

Farquhar's gallants and ingenues are typical of the period: handsome, charming, self-centered. Although they do not display the keen wit of Wycherley's and Congreve's earlier characters, their characters are enhanced by other, very human, qualities. The virtuous and reasonable Dorinda yearns for fashionable London life; Mrs. Sullen, aware that flesh is weak, is realistic about her powers to resist temptation; Sullen's head "aches consumedly" from too much drinking; and Aimwell is too much the man of sentiment to take advantage (even for marriage) of Dorinda's distress. Archer says of him:

> Ay, you're such an amorous puppy, that I'm afraid you'll spoil our sport; you can't counterfeit passion without feeling it.
>
> (I,1)

Since the English church did not countenance divorce, Farquhar introduces Sir Charles Freeman, Mrs. Sullen's brother, as a *deus ex machina* to extract her from the dilemma of mismarriage, by persuading the Sullens to admit their incompatibility and to part. He performs the same role in rescuing Aimwell from poverty when he announces that Aimwell's older brother is dead, making Aimwell in name and deed "Lord Aimwell," as he had pretended. The play concludes with *couples joined* and *couples parted*: "the one rejoicing in hopes of untasted happiness, and the others in their deliverance from an experienced misery."

LANGUAGE

Farquhar had a keen ear for the dialogue of low comic characters (innkeepers, thieves, and servants). He likewise was sensitive to the comic aspects of foreign accents on stage. By changing the scene from London to the country, Farquhar embraced a cross section of provincial society whose speech ranges from the gallant's sophis-

---

Mrs. Sullen's Character Portrait of Her Husband

O sister, sister! if ever you marry, beware of a sullen, silent sot, one that's always musing, but never thinks. There's some diversion in a talking blockhead; and since a woman must wear chains, I would have the pleasure of hearing 'em rattle a little. Now you shall see, but take this by the way. He came home this morning at his usual hour of four, wakened me out of a sweet dream of something else, by tumbling over the tea-table, which he broke all to pieces; after his man and he had rolled about the room, like sick passengers in a storm, he comes flounce into bed, dead as a salmon into a fishmonger's basket; his feet cold as ice, his breath hot as a furnace, and his hands and his face as greasy as his flannel night-cap. O matrimony! He tosses up the clothes with a barbarous swing over his shoulders, disorders the whole economy of my bed, leaves me half naked, and my whole night's comfort is the tuneable serenade of that wakeful nightingale, his nose! Oh, the pleasure of counting the melancholy clock by a snoring husband!—But now, sister, you shall see how handsomely, being a well-bred man, he will beg my pardon.

The Beaux' Stratagem (II,1)

ticated *similitudes* to the cockneyed dialects of Scrub and Cherry. Also, the moral maxims addressing poverty, marriage, and ladies in distress are in keeping with new stage fashions. Archer expresses a typical one: "for 'tis still my maxim, that there is no scandal like rags, nor any crime so shameful as poverty."

FARQUHAR'S MODERNISM

We perceive comedies of manners today as the playwright's measure of the customs and mores of polite society. *The Beaux' Stratagem* held the dramatic mirror up to these mores in its depiction of the problems of marriage and divorce.

Farquhar's modernism lies in his broad social perspective: The divorce laws of the time did not recognize the problems of maladjusted couples, nor did the inheritance laws take into account the welfare of second sons. Farquhar clearly sets forth a serious social message within the dramatic framework popularized by Etherege, Wycherley, and Congreve.

ESSAY

Restoration and eighteenth-century plays still have their appeal to modern audiences who delight in the rapid-fire conversations between lovers and would-be lovers, the period costumes, and the attention to "manners." If we judge by the sales of etiquette books, as well as by the plenitude of gossip columnists, our attention to manners has diminished very little in modern times. We can see the popularity of plays from this period of British theatre by the warm reception, both in England and the United States, of William Gaskill's production of *The Beaux' Stratagem* at London's National Theatre and on tour.

Eighteenth-Century Comedy in Modern Performance

The Beaux' Stratagem by George Farquhar, directed by William Gaskill at the National Theatre, London, 1970

In one of Farquhar's best similitudes, Mrs. Sullen compares the value of women in the eyes of their foolish husbands to the value of paintings at an auction:

"I think one way to rouse my lethargic, sottish husband is to give him a rival. Security begets negligence in all people, and men must be alarmed to make 'em alert in their duty: women are like pictures, of no value in the hands of a fool, till he hears men of sense bid high for the purchase."

(II,1)

William Gaskill is well known for producing the work of new British playwrights with the English Stage Company at London's Royal Court Theatre. He is also credited with revolutionizing attitudes toward staging Restoration comedies of manners, beginning with *The Recruiting Officer* (1963), *The Double Dealer* (1969), and *The Beaux' Stratagem* (1970). Gaskill's methods and interpretation tell us a great deal about the durability of these comedies.

Gaskill's decision to direct Farquhar's two best comedies—first *The Recruiting Officer* followed by *The Beaux' Stratagem*—was the outcome of his search for a mature Restoration playwright, one who kept various social types moving through his plays and one who had something meaningful to say about *society*. Two other factors were also involved. The first was the availability of a new kind of actor who was being brought into British repertory companies in the sixties—actors who were skilled at playing working-class characters so important to plays by Harold Pinter, John Osborne, and Ann Jellicoe. The second factor was Gaskill's desire to create the type of ambience that the Berliner Ensemble had displayed in their London tour of 1956, through, for example, their use of "broken down" or "distressed" costumes to make them look worn and lived in. In 1956 mud on the clothes of officers and gallants in Restoration comedies was *revolutionary*.

THE DIRECTOR AT WORK

As he started work on *The Beaux' Stratagem*, Gaskill was largely concerned with the play's social context, text interpretation, and economy of staging. He began by writing to the cast telling them not to think of their roles in terms of accents, because he knew that the first thing they would do was to put on funny peasant voices. Next, he loosely blocked the play to give the actors something to do with their bodies while they worked on their voices. Gaskill is rather strong in his beliefs about actors using "mannerisms" of the period:

> I don't think anyone cares . . . about whether they bow in the right manner or any of those "quaint" period things. But here are two problems to solve. One is class attitudes, which have changed, and which actors often find difficult to identify. . . .
> The other problem is that there are certain things which women do now which they couldn't do then.[5]

Gaskill cut the Count Bellair subplot in order to strengthen the Mrs. Sullen–Archer relationship. Squire Sullen (David Ryall) was not played as the usual clown or country rustic but as an intelligent person; his best scene is almost at the end where his long dialogue with Sir Charles Freeman is very much like a set piece to prepare for the "divorce" in the final scene. Gaskill argues that there is no basis in the text for the usual interpretation of Sullen as a buffoon.

Gaskill's concern for creating social relationships among characters is related to his refusal to sentimentalize or romanticize Restoration comedy. For him, Restoration comedy is *about people's social behavior.*

THE PRODUCTION

The Beaux' Stratagem began with bright sunlight on an empty stage with a Hessian back wall.

WILLIAM GASKILL

William Gaskill (b. 1930) was born in Yorkshire and educated at Oxford where he directed for the University Dramatic Society and Experimental Theatre Club. After a period as actor and stage manager, he directed his first London production (N. F. Simpson's *A Resounding Tinkle*) in 1957 for the English Stage Company at the Royal Court Theatre, then under the artistic direction of George Devine. Since then he has directed for the Royal Shakespeare Company and has been associate director of the National Theatre (1963–1965) and artistic director of the English Stage Company (1965–1975).

As associate director at the Royal Court from 1958 to 1960, he ran a writer's workshop that included John Arden, Arnold Wesker, Ann Jellicoe, and Edward Bond. As George Devine's successor, he quickly became known as the leading British director of Bertolt Brecht's plays. Also, his productions of Restoration comedies at the National Theatre revoluionized attitudes toward their staging. Under Gaskill's direction plays by Congreve and Farquhar became detailed portraits of society, instead of the "camp" versions of preening gallants and twittering coquettes so often presented to modern audiences.

Then, like rapid brush strokes, René Allio's beautiful and economical sets descended from the flies to create a charming panorama of Lichfield, circa 1707. Down from the flies came a distant bridge, streets, and houses, creating an advancing perspective toward the audience. The first scene took place in the timbered interior of the George Inn with a coachman pulling up outside and Boniface and Cherry bustling about to receive the visitors. The air was already thick with expectation.

Figure 8-9 *The Beaux' Stratagem* at the National Theatre, London, 1970. Left to right: Sheila Reid as Dorinda and Maggie Smith as Mrs. Sullen deplore their plight in the country.

In the foreground, Robert Stephens as Archer woos Maggie Smith as Mrs. Sullen.

Gaskill stripped away the usual period bric-a-brac of most modern productions of Restoration comedy. Gone were the familiar walking sticks, wigs, spotless clothes, superfluous flourishes with hats and the routine displays of eighteenth-century style with handkerchiefs, fans, and smelling salts.

The settings and production alike were designed to project the play's unimpeded action. Allio's foreground set pieces—half-walls and galleries and a single house façade—follow through the style of the panorama typical of the flat background of eighteenth-century staging —a two-dimensional environment that projects the living, three-dimensional actor forward in the audience's direction.

Instead of the usual playing of Restoration comedy at a nonstop speed, Gaskill's production purred along, as London *Times* critic Irving Wardle said, "like the most expensive car on the road with a sense of inexhaustible horse-power held in reserve."[6]

At a glum tête à tête over the tea table with Dorinda (Sheila Reid), Mrs. Sullen (played by Maggie Smith) remarked: "How a little love and good company improves a woman." At this point they have neither. Mrs. Sullen seems incurably stiff and listless until Archer's arrival. As she thaws out under the assaults of Archer (Robert Stephens), she undergoes a marvelous development into a woman of great life, wit, and sensuality.

From the moment Aimwell (Ronald Pickup) and Archer gain entrance into Lady Bountiful's house, the performance is pitched in two keys. There is a shell of elegant artifice, which repeatedly masks the hungry, sensual people within. This swooping descent from decorum to appetite comes out in many small touches—a sidelong look or an abrupt, predatory gesture. When Archer refuses Mrs. Sullen's money with a bow, she stands, purse still in outstretched hand, her eyes running up and down his extended leg.

While Gaskill focused on the serious matter of Farquhar's plea for divorce *by mutual consent,* the genuine merriment of the play came out in

Maggie Smith's cadences and comic effects. When Archer grabs her hand, clearly intent on seduction in the nearby bed, her "What, sir! Do you intend to be rude?" is a masterpiece of comic timing and farcical euphemism. In his staging Gaskill's intention came across clearly as a contrast between male freedom in sexual and matrimonial matters and feminine servitude in almost all matters.

Gaskill's production at the National Theatre (which later toured the United States) established Farquhar for modern audiences as a playwright of simplicity, warmth, and wit, who had the ability to take a social grievance and set it elegantly at the core of the comedy.

SUMMARY

In 1660 the English theatres reopened after a hiatus of 18 years and immediately became a beehive of activity. New theatres were built, old ones renovated; new playwrights encouraged, old ones revived. The Theatre Royal in Drury Lane and the Duke's Theatre in Dorset Garden were the first of the new theatres. Others quickly followed, including Covent Garden and the Queen's Theatre in Haymarket. The European vogue for proscenium arches, female actresses, movable scenery, and scenic spectacle was introduced by those courtiers who had spent their exile with King Charles II in Paris.

The English theatre between 1660 and 1800 was predominantly an actor's theatre run by two principal companies, the King's Company, first managed by Thomas Killigrew, and the Duke's Company managed by William Davenant. As long as they could they maintained a monopoly on theatrical activity in London.

The names of the famous actors and actresses of the period were legion, among them Thomas Betterton, Nell Gwyn, Anne Bracegirdle, Elizabeth Barry, Colley Cibber, Charles Macklin, and David Garrick. Between 1660 and 1709 Thomas Betterton was the most important actor on the English stage. Upon his retirement Betterton was soon replaced by David Garrick, an actor without peer who developed a natural acting style that won the acclaim of his contemporaries.

While such playwrights as Dryden, Etherege, Wycherley, Otway, Congreve, Vanbrugh, Farquhar, Goldsmith, and Sheridan were synonymous with the theatre of the period, the actor-managers were equally well known, notably Betterton, Rich, Macklin, and Garrick. During his long management of Drury Lane, Garrick developed a repertory of stage plays, especially revivals of Shakespeare, that treated his audience to first-class dramatic writing. Also, under his management significant innovations in scenic design and stage lighting were made by the talented designer Philip James de Loutherbourg.

By 1700 there is no question that the large middle-class audiences were dictating theatrical taste. Witty sex comedies went out of vogue and sentimental plays featuring middle-class characters in distress came into fashion. Later, playwrights like Goldsmith and Sheridan tried to combine the wit of Restoration comedies with the sentiment of those of the Augustan Age. Through it all Drury Lane remained a weathervane of the changing times, featuring, over a period of 100 years, plays as diverse as their writers and audiences.

In our representative play, George Farquhar's *The Beaux' Stratagem* (1707), Farquhar straddles the period's two chief phases of dramatic writing, carrying on the witty, comic tradition of the early Restoration playwrights while at the same time embracing the sentimental spirit of the changing age. In William Gaskill's landmark production of *The Beaux' Stratagem* at London's National Theatre in 1970, Gaskill dispensed with the traditional British playing of these comedies as pretty, effete romps and brought to bear his own social consciousness on Farquhar's scene. Gaskill stripped away the usual period bric-a-brac—the wigs, handkerchiefs, fans, and spotless clothes—to get at the slightly distasteful hygiene, dress, social mores, and grievances that he believes are at the core of Farquhar's comedy.

PLAYS TO READ

The Country Wife by William Wycherley

The Beaux' Stratagem by George Farquhar

The School for Scandal by Richard Brinsley Sheridan

SOURCES

Farquhar, George. *The Beaux' Stratagem*. Edited by Charles N. Fifer. The Regents Restoration Drama Series. Lincoln: University of Nebraska Press, 1977. Paperback. The introductory materials, accompanying notes, and chronology are first rate. Also edited by Michael Cordner. The New Mermaid Series. New York: W. W. Norton, 1977.

Salgado, Gamini. *Three Restoration Comedies*. Penguin English Library Series. Baltimore: Penguin, 1968. Paperback. This volume consists of George Etherege's *The Man of Mode*, William Wycherley's *The Country Wife*, and William Congreve's *Love for Love*. The introduction contains discussions of the period and major plays. The texts of the plays are printed with facsimiles of the title pages of the first editions; prologues and epilogues are included. Good notes are printed with the texts.

Sheridan, Richard Brinsley. *The School for Scandal*. Edited by C. J. Prince. New York: Oxford University Press, 1971. The introduction and notes in this expensive paperback are excellent. Also, edited by John Loftis. Crofts Classics Series. Arlington Heights, Ill.: Harlan Davidson, 1966. Paperback. Another excellent edition.

Wycherley, William. *The Country Wife*. Edited by Thomas H. Fujimura. The Regents Restoration Drama Series. Lincoln: University of Nebraska Press, 1965. Paperback. This edition has perhaps the most thorough introductions with accompanying notes and chronology of the playwright and period. Also edited by John D. Hunt. The New Mermaid Series. New York:

Norton, 1976. Paperback. Also in *The Complete Plays*. Edited by Gerald Weales. New York: Norton, 1972. Paperback.

NOTES

1. Louis Kronenberger, *Kings and Desperate Men: Life in Eighteenth-Century England* (New York: Alfred A. Knopf, 1942), p. 63. Reprinted by permission.

2. There have been many biographies and specialized studies of Garrick's life and career. The earliest biography is Thomas Davies' *Memoirs of the Life of David Garrick* (1790). The best modern biographies are Carola Oman's *David Garrick* (1958) and George W. Stone and George M. Kahrl's *David Garrick: A Critical Biography* (1979).

3. Richard Southern, *Changeable Scenery: Its Origin and Development in the British Theatre* (London: Faber and Faber, 1952).

4. Joseph Wood Krutch, *Comedy and Conscience After the Restoration* (New York: Russell and Russell, 1949), pp. 2–7. Reprinted by permission of The Trustees of Columbia University in the City of New York. All rights reserved.

5. William Gaskill, "Finding a Style for Farquhar," *Theatre Quarterly*, 1, No. 1 (1971), 15–20. Reprinted by permission.

6. Irving Wardle, "Farquhar Restored," *The London Times* (April 9, 1970), 18. Reprinted by permission of Times Newspapers Ltd (London).

NINE

NINETEENTH-CENTURY EUROPEAN THEATRE

A MODERN PERSPECTIVE

In less than 100 years, theatre in Northern Europe (Scandinavia and Germany) evolved from secular farces presented by local and foreign touring companies performing on improvised stages to a theatre of the stature of Shakespeare's or Molière's.

Unlike other countries Germany did not have a geographical center for its cultural life—an equivalent of Paris, Rome, London, Stockholm, Oslo, or Copenhagen. Instead, by 1800 there were a number of German principalities, each with its own court theatre. Out of a hodge-podge of small cultural centers, each competing with the other, emerged the famous theatre at Weimar. Goethe and Schiller, the two greatest playwrights of their day, converged at Weimar in the early 1800s. For the time they were there, the Weimar theatre achieved an ideal of playwriting and performance equal to Shakespeare's at the Globe or Molière's at the Palais Royal.

For a period of about 150 years, the European arts scene was a changing panorama. Farce gave way to historical drama and to romanticism in the early 1800s, to the Meiningen realists in the 1870s, and to Wagner's music-drama in the late 1870s.

From the north Henrik Ibsen and August Strindberg crossed national boundaries and shook the foundations of the establishment theatres from Stockholm to Berlin and Paris. In the 1890s a group of little-known producer-directors made Ibsen's and Strindberg's plays the hallmark of the independent theatre movement. These small, avant-garde theatres introduced the "new" plays and a production style of *stage realism* (and for a short time naturalism). Stage realism remains the dominant style of our theatre today. Moreover, our resident theatre movement, which has resulted in hundreds of professional theatres located all over the United States, is somewhat similar to the many competing theatres in nineteenth-century Europe.

It is astonishing that the trends and tastes in theatre, opera, and music that characterize modern Europe up until World War II were set in such a brief period of time. The small court theatres and the offbeat independent theatres throughout Europe were *seminal* to the unfolding of this larger picture. Let us begin with an unexpectedly daring theatrical enterprise run by a clerk for the Paris Gas Company—the *Théâtre Libre*.

REPRESENTATIVE THEATRE: Théâtre Libre, Paris

At 8:30 on an evening in 1887, we tread our way among the booths in Montmartre, the Bohemian section of Paris, carefully avoiding the water puddles on the pavements of the Place Pigalle. There are no bright lights ahead in the narrow, winding street to suggest that a theatre lies ahead. We follow a line of horse-drawn cabs

Figure 9-1 Invitation to opening night of Théâtre Libre, March 30, 1887.

slowly climbing the hill of a dimly lit alleyway. Lining the narrow streets on either side are shadowy buildings in ruins; at the far end of the narrow passageway is an obscure flight of steps leading into an old wooden building. Our search has at last ended in the Passage de l'Elysée des Beaux Arts.

The Théâtre Libre (meaning "free" or "independent theatre") is run by André Antoine, a clerk from the Paris Gas Company, who opened his experimental theatre on March 30, 1887 (Figure 9–1). To keep himself outside the world of the commercial theatre and the authority of city censors and tax collectors, Antoine organized the evening as a subscription performance (as a club, so to speak). He distributed announcements in the form of invitations to a private event, a practice he continued for later productions.

On this evening the one-act *Jacques Damour*, written by the great naturalistic writer Emile Zola, is being presented. Largely for this reason we are crowding our way into this rickety build-

Figure 9-2 Théâtre Libre, circa 1887.

ing—to see what has interested Zola in the small theatre and in the man Antoine.

Zola's play turns out to be a great success, drawing a favorable review on the front page of the leading Paris newspaper, *Le Figaro*. He is offered a production of his play at the Odéon Théâtre where the play had been rejected once before.

The original Théâtre Libre, which we had so much trouble finding on the evening of Zola's one-act, was an intimate theatre seating 242 spectators. The audience was like one large family. The building had been rented to Antoine only for the evening's performance, forcing the producer-director and his actors to rehearse elsewhere. The hall itself resembled a town concert hall. The stage and actors (all amateurs, including Antoine himself) were so close to the audience that you could easily stretch out your hand to the actors across the footlights and put your legs up on the prompter's box. The stage was so narrow that only the most elementary scenery could be used. Not until Antoine moved into a larger building could he carry out his basic principles of naturalistic production for which the Théâtre Libre became internationally famous. On the night of Zola's play, we were so near the stage in this cramped space that scenic illusion was impossible, although Antoine had borrowed his mother's dining room furniture to make the setting absolutely convincing.

Antoine began his theatre with slice-of-life original plays. Most were one-acts. As soon as he moved the Théâtre Libre into new quarters, the Théâtre Montparnasse in the Boulevard Strasbourg, a space that seated 800, he ventured more ambitious productions by Ibsen, Strindberg, and Tolstoy—the pioneers of stage naturalism. Antoine's theatre became forever after associated with naturalistic staging, emulated by others in Berlin, London, and Stockholm.

It was in the third season of 1889–1890 that Antoine, over the objections of friends and advisers, commissioned a new translation from the Norwegian of Ibsen's *Ghosts*, written in 1881, and presented Ibsen's play to Paris audiences for the first time in 1900. *Ghosts*, a thoroughly shocking play for its time, had already been used as the opening shot fired in the dramatic battles to bring new, although unpleasant, subjects to the stage.

In this famous production Antoine himself played the afflicted son Oswald and found the role one of the most rewarding of his long career. Shortly after the performance he wrote of his experience onstage:

I experienced a sensation hitherto unknown to me, the almost complete loss of my own personality. From the beginning of the second act, I remembered nothing, neither the public, nor the effect of the performance, and when the curtain fell, I found

ANDRÉ ANTOINE

Starting as a part-time actor, André Antoine (1858–1943) founded in 1887 a theatre and a naturalistic production style that became world famous. The Théâtre Libre became a showcase for new plays (Ibsen's *Ghosts* was one) and new production techniques. Seeking authentic detail, producer-director Antoine tried to reproduce exact environments on stage, in one play hanging real beef carcasses from the set. In his effort to stage "real" life, Antoine developed three important principles: realistic environments, ensemble acting, and the director's authority.

myself shuddering, enervated, incapable of pulling myself together for moments.[1]

In the seven years that Antoine produced the Théâtre Libre, he introduced new French and foreign plays to Paris audiences, revolutionized production styles, and influenced the spread of stage naturalism throughout Europe. The modern theatre owes a great debt to this "free theatre" on an obscure street in Paris.

CONDITIONS OF PERFORMANCE

BACKGROUND

Modern Germany and Scandinavia share a common heritage of languages, politics, and culture. The Scandinavian countries, including Denmark, Norway, and Sweden, developed along the lines of constitutional monarchies which, like Britain's, have remained stable in modern times. Their literature can be traced back to the age of the Vikings (800–1050). By the eighteenth century each had developed national theatres as either municipal or court theatres. The first legitimate theatre in Oslo, the capital of Norway, opened in 1827, and their National Theatre opened in Bergen in 1850. Today Oslo has six repertory theatres together with government-subsidized traveling companies. Sweden's leading theatre is the Royal Dramatic Theatre in Stockholm, founded in 1788 by King Gustav III. The Drottningholm Court Theatre, the famous eighteenth-century court theatre located just outside Stockholm, is mainly used today in the summer but retains its original scenery, costumes, and stage machinery.

Out of these North European countries came writers, philosophers, critics, playwrights, and actors, who changed the character of modern European thought and art, including Immanuel Kant and Sören Kierkegaard (philosophers), Georg Brandes (writer and critic), Henrik Ibsen and August Strindberg (playwrights), G. W. F. Hegel (social philosopher), and Karl Marx (political theorist).

Germany's effect on the mainstream of the modern theatre and the fine arts has been no less significant. Modern Germany grew out of a loose federation of states created by the Congress of Vienna in 1815 and intended to replace the Holy Roman Empire (dissolved in 1806), which had loosely bound together various ethnic groups, political states, and mercantile and agrarian interests. However, the confederation was weakened at its inception by the antagonism of the two large European powers, Austria and Prussia, and by the insistence of the many small German states on their sovereignty. The confederation broke up after the Austro-Prussian War of 1866, when Prussia's victory forced Austria to retire from German affairs.

German art, architecture, and literature do not have a clearly defined and continuous tradition. The political and religious fragmentation of the German-speaking people accounts in part for this. Nevertheless, the arts grew vigorously within the mix of German cultures. In the eleventh century great Romanesque cathedrals rose

1600

English and Italian
companies tour
Germany, 1600–1650

The Thirty Years
War, 1618–1648

1650

Jesuit schools and
court theatres
flourish

in Mainz and Worms as symbols of the Holy Roman Empire. The German Renaissance (1500–1600), like its counterparts elsewhere in Europe, burst into a visual culture of remarkable richness. In painting Albrecht Dürer, Hans Holbein the Younger, and Matthias Grünewald were Germany's Michelangelos. Salzburg's Cathedral was begun in 1614; Vienna's splendid palaces were built in an Italian style. In the eighteenth century the music of Bach, Haydn, and Mozart floated beyond the borders of any single state. And Meissen porcelain emerged as a new medium for artistic expression. Among the 300-odd independent German states, a system of state-supported theatres developed that nourished a rich repertory system still characterizing the German theatre today.

MANAGEMENT: TOWARD NATIONAL THEATRES

While theatres in England, France, Russia, and Scandinavia flourished in the mid-eighteenth century, a native German theatre developed slowly. Several factors impeded its development. Constant warfare among the ducal states resulted in the country's political decentralization. Religious wars also divided people and

states. As a result, actors and playwrights were deprived of close contact with one another and of a tightly knit society to encourage their efforts and set standards of taste.

English and Italian touring companies brought the first professional theatre to Germany in the early 1600s. There they competed with the amateur theatrics of guildsmen and schoolboys performing farces on temporary platform stages. The Fool in cap and bells (called *Narr*) became the most popular character in early German farce and was quickly adopted by the professional companies. He shared affinities with the comic Devil of religiously based theatre and the sly *zanni* of the *commedia dell'arte*.

Secular farces were soon taken over by guilds of Mastersingers and given more lavish staging. Hans Sachs (1494–1576)—known to later operagoers through his appearance in Richard Wagner's *The Mastersinger of Nuremberg* —was one of Germany's early playwrights. He wrote moral folk comedies in doggerel verse, which were performed on an improvised stage in one of Nuremberg's abandoned Catholic churches. Hans Sachs is perhaps best remembered for opening Germany's first playhouse in 1550. Here audiences sat like churchgoers in pews facing a raised stage with visible steps from floor level to stage, curtains were hung at the back and sides of the stage, and actors en-

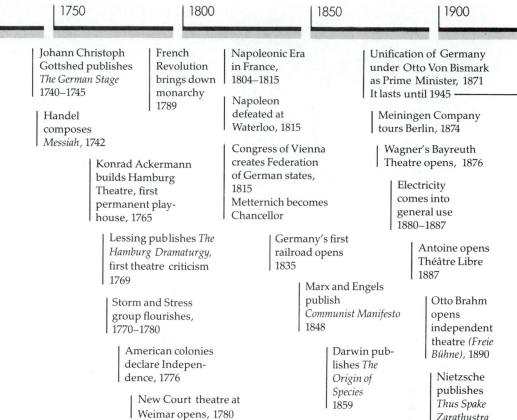

tered through the gaps in the curtains carrying properties and furniture with them.

Foreign touring companies played in noblemen's halls and in large towns on temporary stages. These were projecting platform stages (in the Elizabethan manner) with a curtained room at the back for interior scenes and perhaps a gallery above for musicians and balcony or window scenes. Their repertory consisted mainly of severely cut Elizabethan plays spoken in English along with music, dancing, and mime. Between acts a low-comic fool entertained. *Hanswurst,* or John Sausage, a local fool acted by Joseph Anton Stranitzky (1676–1726), became the most popular clown of all (Figure 9-3).

In general, seventeenth-century German theatre was made up of students, guildsmen, and professional actors (including women) whose improvisations took the place of the playwright's work. Before long, however, translations of Shakespeare's plays opened up a new dramatic world for German audiences, along with domestic dramas and sentimental comedies imported from France. The way was prepared for the local acting companies and Germany's first significant playwrights.

A number of acting companies—several dominated by women—were important in the formation of Germany's national theatre. In the early eighteenth century their chief aim was to establish permanent playhouses and to develop

Figure 9-3 One rendering of the German clown Hanswurst. He was a mixture of Harlequin, the medieval fool, and various English clowns. He developed in the eighteenth century as a beer-drinking clown with a Bavarian accent. He usually dressed in a white neck ruff, green pointed hat, and yellow trousers. Actor Joseph Anton Stranitzky (1676–1726) became the most famous Hanswurst of the German public theatre.

native playwrights. Caroline Neuber's Company (active 1727–1760) set the pace. She set up in Leipzig, a major cultural center, and teamed up with playwright and literary adviser, Johann Christoph Gottshed (1700–1766). Their company became a model for others to follow. They put together professional actors with a playwright and literary adviser; they performed regular drama (translations and new plays); and their production techniques were arrived at after careful rehearsals. Others followed Neuber's lead in Hamburg, Mannheim, and Weimar, in particular.

PLAYWRITING

The Germans At the outset German playwrights were part of a patronage system. With few exceptions, as companies and theatres emerged within the ducal states, playwrights were subsidized just as were actors, managers, and other personnel. Because of this system we associate certain playwrights with certain theatres: Johann Wolfgang von Goethe and Friedrich Schiller with Weimar, Gotthold Ephraim Lessing with Hamburg, and August Friedrich von Kotzebue with Berlin. As Berlin became the cultural center of the new nation, it also became the center of theatrical life. But this was not until 1870.

These playwrights and the later Heinrich von Kleist, Georg Buchner, Friedrich Hebbel, Franz Grillparzer, Gerhart Hauptmann, and Frank Wedekind represent about 130 years of dramatic writing. Their plays have certain characteristics in common that even today mark German playwriting. In general, their plays were discursive, filled with ideas about politics, society, metaphysics, love, and death. Goethe and Schiller both were noted for their powerful blank verse and Buchner for his images of corrupting flesh. Play structure tended toward the episodic (this was Shakespeare's influence) and ranged from the cinematic episodes of Goethe's *Götz von Berlichingen* and Buchner's *Woyzeck* to the formal classicism of Schiller's *Mary Stuart*.

In the early 1770s Lessing fused a popular middle-class interest in domestic tragedies (both in novels and plays) with sharp criticism of contemporary social conditions. *Emilia Galotti* (1772) incisively portrays the social differences between commoners and nobility. In his treatment of theme and character Lessing set the pattern for domestic tragedy with stern fathers, virtuous daughters, highborn seducers, and discarded mistresses.

About 20 years later Goethe abandoned the episodic form for plays written on Greek models and in blank verse. Schiller in *Don Carlos* (1787) shifted his thematic emphasis from personal suffering to political and humanitarian issues. This became the direction of playwriting for the next 20 years.

While Goethe and Schiller were fashioning a "classical" tradition at Weimar, August Kotzebue (1761–1819) was carving out another theatrical tradition—melodrama. A prolific writer and master of stage effects, he wrote some 200 melodramas. Even the high-minded Goethe produced Kotzebue's plays at Weimar because of their box office appeal.

The romantic school of writing that developed about 1800 was literary, political, and dramatic. The themes of the plays stressed the emotions and attempts to define reality through feelings and intuition. The recurring features of romantic literature are well known to us: use of the supernatural, the mythical, the mysterious, accents on abnormality, and indefiniteness of form.

Goethe's and Schiller's rebellious heroes highly influenced the romantic writers. August Wilhelm Schlegel (1767–1845) and Ludwig Tieck (1773–1853) called themselves romantics. They wrote plays and essays celebrating feelings and instincts as guides to moral behavior. They argued against political despotism and contributed to shaping a new view of human nature, political theory, and literary forms. Shakespeare was the mainstay of the early nineteenth-century German theatre.

Heinrich von Kleist (1777–1811), who should have had a meteoric career among the romantics, failed almost entirely to establish himself with the stage during his lifetime. He committed suicide without having seen any of his plays produced. His plays combined a classical concept of fate with the psychological and sexual dimensions of such Shakespeare characters as Lady Macbeth. In *Penthesilea* (1808) the savagery of his Amazon's passion has no parallel in classical tragedy. There was also no precedent for Kleist's treatment of mind and emotions in his masterpiece, *The Prince of Homburg* (1810).

Tenets of Romanticism

Truth There is a higher truth than that observed in everyday social forms and natural phenomena. All things (including nature and human beings) are part of a whole created by an absolute being, called God, Spirit, Idea, or Ego.

Subjects All creation has common origins and through observation of any part, the whole can be seen. The more innocent or unspoiled a thing or person is, the more likely it is to embody some fundamental truth about the world. Hence, romantics preferred subjects about unspoiled nature or human beings in rebellion against restraints imposed by a despotic society.

Doubleness of Human Nature Humanity has dual qualities: body and soul, physical and spiritual, temporal and eternal. Human beings live in a physical world while spiritually they try to transcend the demands of the flesh. Art is one means of confronting what it means to be human and of glimpsing a full awareness of humanity's artistic, social, and political potential.

Vision Only the exceptional imagination of philosopher and artist can fully perceive the unity within the diversity of existence. Thus, art and philosophy are superior forms of knowledge.

Playwriting Romantic writers rejected the notion of the unities and strict forms of drama like tragedy or comedy. They adopted Shakespeare (rather than Racine or Molière) as models because of Shakespeare's apparent freedom from rules and because he wrote about many varieties of experience.

With Kleist's suicide, Schiller dead of tuberculosis, and Goethe's disenchantment with his work at Weimar, German drama in the second decade of the nineteenth century seemed to have lost its momentum. Nor was the political scene conducive to the arts. The disruptions of the Napoleonic Wars forced artists to move from place to place for reasons of safety and sustenance. After the Battle of Waterloo, the reactionary Metternich regime excluded social, political, and religious subjects from public discussion. That left very little for the theatre to deal with and it became solely a place of entertainment. Once more Kotzebue's melodramas were popular.

During this period of internal dissension, the German playwright most admired today was writing his two masterpieces. Georg Buchner (1813–1837)—undiscovered in his lifetime—wrote *Danton's Death* (1835) and *Woyzeck* (1836), both extraordinary plays that have attracted attention from naturalists and existentialists.

Fortunately, Friedrich Hebbel (1813–1863) did not share the same fate as Kleist and Buchner. He was a forerunner to the realistic and naturalistic movements of the 1870s and later, dealing with contemporary social problems growing out of a rapidly changing society. His masterpiece was *Maria Magdalena* (1844). Hebbel's and Buchner's realistic treatments of feelings of rootlessness and moral decline and the destructiveness of outdated social forms called for a new production style. But there was as yet no contact between the new playwrights and the staging innovations already underway at the Duchy of Saxe-Meiningen that would lead to a new ensemble performance style.

Ironically, it was Germany's political and industrial successes that produced a new breed of playwright, a new kind of theatre, and the "discovery" of Georg Buchner. In the 1860s Germany's successful wars had unified the various states into a modern nation. They had also stimulated the growth of industry and the sudden rise in prosperity of the middle class. The mood of the country has been described as one of extravagant hope, naive national self-conceit, and rampant materialism. Serious drama once again found its reason for being in *revolt*: A young generation of playwrights, shocked by the national complacency and by the misery of the working classes under the new industrialism, wrote plays as vehicles of social criticism. But censorship kept the doors of the state theatres closed to the new wave of dramatists. The enterprising Otto Brahm (1856–1912) developed his own independent theatre. To get around the monopoly in 1889, he formed a private company, called the Freie Bühne, modeled on Antoine's Théâtre Libre in Paris. It had no fixed habitat and played at matinees only. His campaign for the "new" drama opened with Ibsen's *Ghosts*, along with plays by Tolstoy, Strindberg, and Zola. But the fame of the movement rested on the work of the young Gerhart Hauptmann (1862–1946). His most celebrated play, *The Weavers* (1892), gave a naturalistic picture of the abominable working conditions of the Silesian weavers. As in France, stage realism and the new naturalism had captured the imaginations of the younger generation of writers, actors, and producers.

Revolt was followed by counterrevolt. Frank Wedekind (1864–1918) reacted against the new naturalism and pointed the way toward another "ism"—*expressionism*—which was an effort to "express" the inner spirit rather than to imitate external objects and appearances as the realists had done. Expressionism flowered in Germany in the 1920s. Wedekind exchanged individuals for significant character types. His predilection for animal passions, however amoral, and his eye for the grotesque outraged Munich audiences. Wedekind acted his own heroes with flamboyant irony, in garish settings that suggested the cabaret (shortly to become Bertolt Brecht's milieu). *Spring's Awakening* appeared in 1891 and his "Lulu" plays in 1904.

Buchner, Hauptmann, and Wedekind seem almost not to belong to the same century as Goethe and Schiller. Still, these older writers were in their way as eclectic as the premoderns.

As a group their plays encompass all the major trends in nineteenth-century playwriting: neo-classicism, romanticism, music-drama, realism, naturalism, and even expressionism.

The Scandinavians The late nineteenth-century Scandinavian (and European avant-garde) theatres were dominated by two playwrights: Henrik Ibsen of Norway and August Strindberg of Sweden. Other Scandinavian writers, such as Ludvig Holberg, Bjorn Bjornson, and Pär Lagerkvist, failed to have the impact on the theatres of Europe that Ibsen and Strindberg did.

Both Ibsen and Strindberg began by writing romantic historical plays (verse dramas) dealing with events of Scandinavian history. Ibsen had the advantage of spending his early years as director and writer-in-residence at the National Theatre in Bergen (Norway). There in the 1850s he produced his early verse plays with colorful backgrounds of history and folklore, such as *The Feast at Solhaug*. He left Bergen to become artistic director at the National Theatre in Christiania (now Oslo), where he wrote and directed *The Vikings of Helgeland* (1858) and *The Pretenders* (1863); these marked the end of his active involvement in the practical theatre. His dramaturgy, not his production techniques, would change the European theatre for all time.

Brand (1865) and *Peer Gynt* (1867) grew out of Ibsen's first contact with European culture in Italy. Both were given highly successful productions by the pioneering Swedish director Ludvig Josephson. However, stung by adverse criticism of *Peer Gynt*, Ibsen determined to move with the times. "If I am no poet, then I shall try my luck as a photographer."[2] What followed were plays on contemporary themes dealing with stifling marriages, sexually repressed women, rigid social conventions, and corrupt town officials. His early experiences as a director possibly accounted for his sensitivity to environment and to the psychological states and spiritual conditions of his characters. His stage directions contain detailed descriptions of setting, costumes, properties, and lighting (p. 236).

HENRIK IBSEN

Henrik Ibsen (1828–1906) is frequently considered the most influential playwright since Shakespeare. He published his first play, *Catiline*, a verse tragedy, in 1850. His early plays celebrating his country's past glories were poorly received. As stage manager and playwright with the National Theatre in Bergen, and later artistic director of the Norwegian Theatre in Christiania, he developed a knowledge of stagecraft.

After years of failure and poverty, Ibsen immigrated to Italy where he wrote *Brand* (1865), which brought him immediate fame. For 27 years he remained with his family in self-imposed exile in Rome, Dresden, and Munich. During this time he wrote such plays as *A Doll's House, Ghosts, An Enemy of the People, The Wild Duck, Rosmersholm,* and *Hedda Gabler*. These plays changed the direction of the nineteenth-century theatre. In 1891 he returned to Norway, and in 1899 completed *When We Dead Awaken*, the play James Joyce considered his finest. He died there in 1906.

Called the father of modern drama, Ibsen wrote plays dealing with problems of contemporary life, particularly those of the individual caught in a repressive society. Although his social doctrines, radical and shocking in his own day, are no longer revolutionary, his portraits of humanity are timeless.

> **❝** A large garden room, with a door in the left-hand wall, and two doors in the wall to the right. In the middle of the room a round table with chairs grouped about it; on the table lie books, magazines, and newspapers. In the left foreground, a window, and next to it a small sofa with a sewing table in front of it. In the background, the room is extended into a somewhat smaller greenhouse, whose walls are great panes of glass. From the right side of the greenhouse, a door leads into the garden. Through the glass walls a somber fjord landscape can be glimpsed, half hidden by the steady rain. **❞**
>
> Ibsen, *Ghosts*, Act I stage directions (1881)[3]

Ibsen's decision to become a dramatic "photographer" brought forth his great realistic plays: *Pillars of Society, An Enemy of the People, A Doll's House, Ghosts,* and *Hedda Gabler.* As early as 1882 Ibsen insisted in a letter to the Norwegian director of *An Enemy of the People* that the staging should reflect, above all, "truthfulness to nature —the illusion that everything is real and that one is sitting and watching something that is actually taking place in real life."[4]

Ibsen's plays written between 1877 and 1890 brought the immediacy of real life into the theatre. They demanded real rooms with transparent fourth walls, actors dressed and moving in believable fashion among the furnishings, and authentic properties. He was supported in this by Strindberg, who pioneered the need for authentic environments and production styles. Strindberg's preface to *Miss Julie* inveighed against the old production styles and set forth the tenets of the "new" staging (see box).

Ibsen and Strindberg were the giants of the new dramaturgy. Their plays were sought by producers as far apart as Copenhagen, Paris, and London. But as early as 1884 Ibsen began to refine his photographer's role, setting out to explore "new symbolic territories" first in *The Wild Duck.* This exploration ended in 1899 with his last play, *When We Dead Awaken.* Strindberg, too, was changing direction. The epoch-making premiere of his *To Damascus I* (1898), opened the floodgates to the postnaturalistic modern theatre.

Strindberg was Sweden's greatest dramatist and one of the most versatile and creative innovators in the modern theatre. His 40-year career

> **❝** As regards the scenery, I have borrowed from impressionist painting its asymmetry and its economy; thus, I think, strengthening the illusion. For the fact that one does not see the whole room and all the furniture leaves scope for conjecture—that is to say imagination is roused . . . I have succeeded too in getting rid of those tiresome exits through doors, since scenery doors are made of canvas, and rock at the slightest touch. They cannot even express the wrath of an irate head of the family who, after a bad dinner, goes out slamming the door behind him, "so that the whole house shakes." On the stage it rocks. I have also kept to a single set, both in order to let the characters develop in their métier and to break away from over-decoration. When one has only one set, one may expect it to be realistic; but as a matter of fact nothing is harder than to get a stage room that looks something like a room . . . it seems about time to dispense with painted shelves and cooking utensils. We are asked to accept so many stage conventions that we might at least be spared the pain of painted pots and pans. . . .
>
> I have few illusions about getting the actors to play *to* the audience instead of *with* it, although this is what I want. That I shall see an actor's back throughout a critical scene is beyond my dreams, but I do wish crucial scenes could be played, not in front of the prompter's box, like duets expecting applause, but in the place required by the action. So, no revolutions, but just some small modifications, for to make the stage into a real room with the fourth wall missing would be too upsetting altogether. **❞**
>
> Strindberg, preface to *Miss Julie* (1888)[5]

AUGUST STRINDBERG

Born in Stockholm of a shipping agent father and a domestic servant who had been his father's mistress, August Strindberg (1849–1912) became a writer of prodigious accomplishment. His collected works take up 55 volumes, including novels, poems, essays, and plays.

In his youth he attended Uppsala University in Sweden to study medicine. Failing chemistry, he next turned to acting at the Royal Dramatic Theatre. Encouraged to pursue a writing career, he returned to the university where he wrote historical plays. Thereafter, he worked as a journalist, teacher, and librarian, and in 1877 married the first of three wives—Siri von Essen. His novel *The Red Room* (1879) won him international attention.

Moving to Copenhagen he set about creating an independent theatre, modeled after Antoine's Théâtre Libre, called the Scandinavian Experimental Theatre. This opened in 1889 with *Miss Julie* but failed after one performance. Strindberg's marriage to Siri von Essen ended in 1891. In grief and poverty he moved to Berlin where he married Frida Uhl, an Austrian journalist. They divorced in 1897.

The years 1892 to 1897 were desperate ones. His physical and mental health deteriorated. Between 1894 and 1896 in Paris, he experienced five psychotic episodes, commonly called his "inferno crises." In 1896 Strindberg managed to free himself from his state of near insanity and returned to Sweden, where he wrote 36 plays between 1898 and 1909. He married 23-year-old Swedish actress Harriet Bosse in 1901, but his jealousy and overprotectiveness soon destroyed the marriage. In 1907 Strindberg realized a lifelong dream and opened his Intimate Theatre. However, audiences were largely bewildered by his unorthodox "chamber" plays—*Storm Weather, The Burned House, The Ghost Sonata,* and *The Pelican*—and the theatre closed in 1910.

Above all Strindberg was an experimental playwright who expanded the parameters of the early modern theatre, pioneering stage naturalism, exploring the disconnected logic of dreams, and applying musical concepts to the drama. Several American playwrights have spoken of their indebtedness to Strindberg, including Eugene O'Neill, Tennessee Williams, and Edward Albee.

as a writer reveals an art characterized by the restless search for new forms capable of meeting the changing demands of the consciousness of his time. The range and energy of his genius were reflected in the sheer bulk of his writings, which include plays, fiction, poetry, autobiography, criticism, philosophy, and scientific theory. In all, he wrote 62 plays.

Strindberg first gained world recognition as a naturalistic playwright with his masterpieces *The Father* (1887), *Miss Julie* (1888), and *Creditors* (1888), all of which deal with great battles of will between men and women.

Strindberg considered *Miss Julie* the first naturalistic tragedy in Swedish drama. In his famous preface (added after the play was written), Strindberg set out to promulgate the ideas of theatrical reform championed by Zola and Antoine in Paris. In so doing he wrote one of the most succinct descriptions of the aims of naturalism in the theatre. In performance *Miss Julie* is the story of the midsummer eve seduction and suicide of an aristocratic woman under the influence of her valet-lover. Strindberg intended the play to be perceived as an unbroken (without intermission) "slice-of-living" reality. Following Antoine's lead, he called for the actors to disregard the audience beyond the fourth wall and to perform *within* the solidly three-dimensional kitchen decorated with real pots, pans, utensils, tables, and chairs.

The plays he wrote after his several mental breakdowns, of which *A Dream Play* (1902) and *The Ghost Sonata* (1907) are perhaps the most famous, revealed two new directions in Strindberg's work, one psychological, the other visual, one dealing with dream states (even nightmares) and the other with the idea of replacing conventional painted backdrops with projected pictures by using a large magic lantern or sciopticon. The projections were soon abandoned in favor of painted scenery again because the front of the stage had to be kept so dark to see the projections that it was impossible to see the actors clearly. But the new psychological direction was to have considerable influence.

In *A Dream Play* Strindberg prefigured the Freudian age. The play is written from the viewpoint of the dreamer. In his preface Strindberg wrote:

> . . . the Author has sought to reproduce the disconnected but apparently logical form of a dream. Anything can happen; everything is possible and probable. Time and space do not exist; on a slight groundwork of reality, imagination spins and weaves new patterns made up of memories, experiences, unfettered fancies, absurdities, and improvisations.[6]

In other words Strindberg imitated the dreamer's thought processes. In doing so he destroyed limitations of time, place, and logical sequence of events. One event flowed into an-

other without logical explanation, characters dissolved or were transformed into other characters, and widely separated places and times were blended to tell a story of tortured and alienated human beings searching for ways to explain or justify their sufferings.

Strindberg's contribution to world drama in *A Dream Play* and later in *The Ghost Sonata* was to introduce a new, although bizarre, realistic dimension—the *unconscious*. The role of the unconscious in determining ordinary behavior and the use of dreams as keys to unlock the door to the unconscious were to consume the interests of the scientific and the artistic worlds for the next half century.

VISUAL ELEMENTS

Trends in scenery, costumes, and lighting did not differ remarkably in Germany and Scandinavia from those already traced in England and France. Early in the eighteenth century the court theatres imported Italian designers to create lavish perspective scenery. Wings and drops, movable scenery, and later the chariot-and-pole system were used with opera, ballet, plays, and spectacles.

Scenery The necessity for touring forced early companies to use few settings, furniture, and properties. Before 1750 three settings were considered sufficient: a painted forest for exterior scenes, a hall for palaces, and a cottage room for domestic interiors. While stock settings increased in number when permanent theatres were built, the introduction of the chariot-and-pole system of scene shifting in the 1770s brought about new possibilities for detailed settings and authentic costumes to go with them.

Friedrich Schroeder's (1744–1816) production of Goethe's early romantic play, *Götz von Berlichingen* in 1774, was probably the first to use period costumes to evoke a historical milieu. By the turn of the century new plays were demanding complex set pieces. Doors and windows were set between the wings, marking the

first steps toward the box set. However, the trend toward greater realism and accuracy of detail was not to be fully exploited until the nineteenth century. The box set was in common use by 1875.

Costumes and Properties In the early days of a struggling company, actors were expected to own a pair of black breeches; the company manager supplied coats and waistcoats. Actresses supplied the most fashionable dress they could afford. These basic costumes were adapted to various roles by adding accessories. Kings carried scepters; classical heroes draped a scarf across their chests and wore helmets. With the influence of French drama appeared the *habit à la romaine* and the Oriental costume of turban and baggy trousers. We have already traced these types of costumes in France and England.

With Schroeder's production of *Götz von Berlichingen*, stage costuming took on a new, *visual* dimension. He dressed knights in armor; monks and bishops in ecclesiastical garments; and courtiers, citizens, and peasants in what was considered authentic clothing. Thereafter, plays with historical backgrounds used "historical" costumes from a single period—usually the sixteenth century. One exception was the popular

Figure 9-5 Gouache designs by Carl Grabow for the world premiere of Strindberg's *A Dream Play* in 1907. (a) The cloverleaf door. (b) Fairhaven.

" *No one knows just when wings parallel to the footlights were first replaced by continuous walls for the right and left sides of rooms. Eighteenth-century plans show wings so hinged that they could be aligned from the proscenium to the backing. At the Court Theater of Mannheim, Germany, in 1804, a stage designer joined pairs of wings with flats that contained practicable doors or windows. About that time the French stage must have had something like the walls of a box set; for in 1811 Goethe inveighed in his autobiography against the French stage for "shutting up the sides of the stage and forming rooms with real walls." There is good evidence that Mme. Vestris [in England] used a box-set in November, 1832, for a critic wrote that the stage's more perfect enclosure gives the appearance of a private chamber, infinitely better than the old contrivance of wings. In 1834, when Drury Lane produced a new play by Planche, a reviewer reported that the "stage was entirely enclosed" and even suggested that there was a ceiling instead of a row of hanging 'borders.'* **"**

Kenneth Macgowan and William Melnitz,
with Gordon Armstrong,
Golden Ages of the Theater (1979)[7]

plays with war backgrounds where managers borrowed uniforms from local garrisons and even used soldiers as extras.

Lighting Trends in stage lighting differed little from those in England and France. Tallow and wax candles were replaced by oil lamps. Gas lighting was introduced in 1830 along with footlights. Then, with the introduction of electric lighting in the 1880s, came the theories of the brilliant Swiss designer Adolphe Appia (1862–1928) on the use of stage lighting, which influenced much of the best modern work in this medium. In his pamphlets called *The Staging of Wagner's Music Dramas* (1895) and *Music and the Art of the Theatre* (1899) he prescribed lighting that, like Richard Wagner's music, gave a three-dimensional effect to the actor and setting. Light for Appia was plastic—infinitely malleable—capable of evoking mood and emotion. His ideas became the norm of twentieth-century stage production.

THE EMERGING DIRECTOR: GOETHE, MEININGEN, ANTOINE

As in other European theatres, the director emerged in the nineteenth century out of the tradition of the actor-manager—the leading actor who also managed and rehearsed the company. In both Scandinavia and Germany directors were part of the formation of national theatres subsidized by cities, states, and courts. Ibsen's apprenticeship at the National Theatre (Bergen) followed this pattern.

Goethe Of the many theatrical companies and playhouses that developed in Germany's major cultural centers in the late eighteenth century, one was an attractive court theatre at Weimar, which received a new artistic director in 1780. His name was Johann Wolfgang von Goethe. Goethe became Germany's first modern director by exercising a single, consistent artistic vision and performance style on his company, a style that came to be called "Weimar classicism."

Goethe persuaded the Duke of Weimar to rebuild the small court theatre set in a pleasant landscape against a background of open sky and tall trees and to convert the stage, hitherto used to "star" the court or to "showcase" touring companies, into a *professional resident theatre*.

To impose an ensemble style on a mediocre company with various accents and experience, Goethe devised his *Rules for Actors*, which prescribed how actors should speak, stand, move, and behave. His rehearsal procedures were as precise, if not dictatorial, as his acting rules. He began each new production with reading rehearsals, setting line readings, pronunciation, and interpretation. He blocked the play by dividing the stage into squares and specified the

JOHANN WOLFGANG GOETHE

Poet, novelist, playwright, and director, Goethe (1749–1832) has been called Germany's greatest man of letters. Goethe was born of a wealthy Frankfurt family and studied law at Strasbourg although he was interested in medicine and literature, too.

In 1773 he wrote *Götz von Berlichingen*, the first play to suggest a new, specifically German style of playwriting. Its idealized robber baron hero was shown as an honorable man in revolt against tyranny. After Goethe published his first romantic novel, *The Sorrows of Young Werther* (1774), he was invited to Weimar as a companion to the young duke. Goethe remained there taking on many official duties, such as supervisor for agriculture, mining, forestry, and the treasury, and at the same time continuing his literary output.

In 1786 he went to Italy for two years; during this period his themes and writing style changed. He wrote for a time in the classical mode, rejecting the romantics' desire to reproduce life as they saw it or to escape into emotionalism and fantasy. Goethe's new style used ancient myths to show humanity's evolution from narrow concerns about the self to broader concerns about society and universal truths. He wrote his classical plays *Iphigenie auf Tauris* in 1787 and *Torquato Tasso* in 1790. One expresses the belief that human salvation can come about only through renunciation. The other portrays the artist's temperament in conflict with the world of action.

Goethe spent 26 years as producer, director, and playwright at Weimar. His greatest work—*Faust, Part I* (published 1808) and *Part II* (1831)—depicted an individual's struggle with the satanic forces within himself and with his quest for salvation.

actor's movements in them. Tradition has it that Goethe, who was concerned with rhythm and cadence, especially in verse plays, beat time with a baton like an orchestra conductor.

Goethe's aim was not to create an illusion of reality but to achieve in his staging a harmonious and graceful picture. Despite his autocratic ways, Goethe created the most perfect ensemble yet seen anywhere in Europe. It would be almost 75 years before the Meiningen company appeared on the scene.

It was almost by accident that Goethe was appointed as the theatre's director in the first place. Since the population of the city of Weimar was only about 6000, the duke could not afford a first-rate company rivaling those springing up in Mannheim, Stuttgart, and Hamburg. Failing to attract a "name" director, he appointed his friend and playwright to the post. In turn, Goethe invited his friend, the playwright Schiller, to Weimar. Together they drew the attention of all literary Germany to this hitherto insignificant theatre to see such new plays as Schiller's *Mary Stuart* (1800), Kleist's *Broken Jug* (1806), and Goethe's *Faust, Part I* (1808).

Those crowding into this theatre for the first time found an elegant, intimate theatre seating about 500. Eight hundred could be squeezed in for a special attraction like Mozart's *Magic Flute* or for Schiller's *Mary Stuart*. Under Goethe's artistic management (which lasted for 26 years), the Weimar theatre became part of the resident theatre movement in Germany that included by midcentury about 65 state theatres. The theatre at Weimar was one of the best.

Meiningen Another small court theatre at the Duchy of Saxe-Meiningen in Germany emerged in the 1870s. It would further change the course of theatrical production in Europe and Russia.

Duke Georg II of Meiningen took over the court theatre in 1866 and established the supremacy of the *regisseur*—the director who unifies the production through his or her complete control of every moment of the actor's interpretation and movements and every detail of

---

❙❙ 35. First of all, the player must consider that he should not only imitate nature but also portray it ideally, thereby, in his presentation, uniting the true with the beautiful. . . .

37. The body should be carried in the following manner: the chest up, the upper half of the arms to the elbows somewhat close to the torso, the head slightly turned toward the person to whom one is speaking. But this should be done only slightly so that three quarters of the face is always turned to the audience.

38. For the actor must always remember that he is on the stage for the sake of the audience.

39. Nor should actors play to each other as if no third person were present. This would be a case of misunderstood naturalness. They should never act in profile nor turn their backs to the spectators. . . .

68. In rehearsal nothing should be tolerated that would not also occur in performance.

69. The actresses should lay aside their small purses. . . .

71. In rehearsal the actor should make no movement that is not appropriate to the part. ❙❙

Goethe, *Rules for Actors* (1824)[8]

Goethe's staging of *Wallenstein's Camp* (1798)

For the production of Schiller's *Wallenstein's Camp*, Goethe collected woodcuts and other pictorial material of the Thirty Years' War, even carrying off an old stoveplate with a seventeenth-century camp scene embossed on it from the public house in Jena. With the aid of Georg Melchior Kraus as costume designer and Henrich Meyer as scene painter, Goethe created a lively and picturesque composition with a richness of detail unlike anything yet seen on the German stage.

Goethe described the opening scene in a letter written on October 15, 1798: "Soldiers of all types and colors were gathered around a canteen tent. There were empty dishes that seemed to promise still more guests, there were heaps of rubbish and trash. To one side lay Croats and sharpshooters around a fire with a kettle hanging over it, and not far from them other soldiers playing dice on a drum. The canteen proprietress and her assistants wandered here and there, serving the humblest and the most important with equal care, while the rough song of the soldiers resounded continuously from the tents."[9]

---

setting, lighting, costume, and makeup. Meiningen's company became synonymous with intensive rehearsals; emphasis on the ensemble, not the star; and historically accurate settings and costumes to create realistic pictures. He designed scenery and costumes along with every movement and position on stage. He even dictated the folds of an actor's costume. The duke's methods of directorial control inspired other directors who had yet to make a name for themselves, namely André Antoine in Paris and Constantin Stanislavsky in Moscow.

The duke was assisted by Ludwig Chronegk, an actor responsible for supervising and rehearsing the company. Their innovations ranged from historically accurate scenery and costumes to techniques for staging "authentic" crowd scenes. The duke used English actor Charles Kean's method of dividing the crowd into small groups each with a highly competent actor as its leader. Thus while on tour "supers" or extras could be recruited locally and quickly integrated into the scene. The duke also insisted that star actors should occasionally play minor roles.

The Meiningen tours to Berlin, London, Brussels, and Moscow beginning in the 1870s brought them renown for their realistic crowd scenes and superb ensemble playing. Watching the company's productions of *Julius Caesar* and *Mary Stuart*, for example, made every important European director conscious that scenery must be designed to fit the movements of actors; that costumes, properties, and lighting contribute to the creation of the mood and atmosphere of the stage picture; and that no detail of interpretation or stage business is so small that it is not worth careful research, planning, and rehearsal.

Antoine At the Théâtre Libre Antoine took the actors behind the fourth wall into a recognizable environment and, along with Stanislavsky at the Moscow Art Theatre (opened in 1898), established the main style of the modern theatre—stage realism.

Rejected by Paris' principal acting school, the Conservatoire, Antoine was thrown back on his own resources. He set about creating a theatre for new plays and a production style that was "lifelike." Antoine recognized that the director's role—which he was defining for himself in the late 1880s—fell into two distinct parts. First, the director had to find the right environment for the action and the appropriate movements of characters within the scene. Second, the director had to oversee the text interpretation and conversational flow of dialogue. Every detail of environment must be original, striking, and authentic. Antoine argued that an interior setting should be first sketched on paper with

---

LUDWIG CHRONEGK

Ludwig Chronegk (1837–1891), a comic actor, was for 20 years the associate director of the Meiningen company. He was responsible for the Meiningen tours to Berlin and other cities where the company's work gained international fame.

Trained as a singing comedian, Chronegk played with companies in Berlin, Hamburg, and Leipzig before joining the Meiningen company. At age 34 he became the theatre's associate director and eventually gave up acting altogether. He earned a reputation as a thoroughgoing tyrant in the theatre. The most famous account of his methods is Stanislavsky's in *My Life in Art*, which describes him at rehearsals giving the signal for its beginning by ringing a large bell. At the end of a scene the company watched in absolute silence until Chronegk rang the bell again as a signal that he was going to make comments on the scene just played.

Despite Chronegk's despotic methods, the actors respected him. The importance of his work with the Meiningen company is frequently overlooked in favor of the Duke's bold innovations in performance style.

❧ In my opinion, modern directing must perform the same function in the theatre as descriptions in a novel. Directing should—as, in fact, is generally the case today—not only fit the action in its proper framework but also determine its true character and create its atmosphere. ❧

André Antoine, *La Revue de Paris* (1903)[10]

Figure 9-6 Sketch of Elizabeth's throne room in Meiningen's *Mary Stuart*.

four walls (and indeed the whole house) included. The fourth wall would later disappear to enable the audience to see what was going on.[11]

To these ends Antoine sought out amateur actors (untrained in the classical style of the Comédie Française, for example) who could live their parts. His actors came onto a stage prepared with a variety of properties and with real furniture placed about the room without regard to the audience (or the fourth wall).

By 1900 the director's art had been defined. No longer the actor-manager, the director had become an *artist* in his or her own right: one who clearly grasps the author's ideas, explains them patiently to the actors, watches over the play's development, and harmonizes all to achieve the play's interpretation; one who attends to scenery, costumes, furniture, properties, and to lighting. After fusing all elements, including the actors, the director steps back as an observer to take in the finished production as a whole.

THE AUDIENCE

In the state theatres in Scandinavia and Germany, the division of social classes was maintained by dividing the auditorium into pit, balconies, and galleries. But the bulk of a middle-class population had its impact (a) on the sentimental and melodramatic plays that expressed the ideals and emotions of a thoughtful and moralistic middle class, (b) on the popularity of opera, and (c) on the eventual emergence of a modern drama.

The audience for opera in all European cities was massive, and the works of Mozart, Donizetti, and Verdi (and later Wagner) filled the large opera houses in Stockholm, Vienna, Berlin, and Salzburg. In the construction of the Bayreuth theatre Wagner did away with the traditional auditorium of pit, boxes, and galleries. There were no class or economic distinctions while the audience was moved by the symphonic and spectacular illusions of Wagner's operatic world of Rhine maidens and dying warriors.

WAGNER'S MUSIC-DRAMA AT BAYREUTH

Richard Wagner (1813–1883) was a major innovator of nineteenth-century operatic composing and staging. He wrote his own librettos, set them to music, conducted his own operas, and developed a theory of music-drama.

Wagner had his first critical success in 1842 with the opera *Rienzi*, which led to his appointment as conductor at the Dresden Opera House. Banished for taking part in the 1848 revolution, Wagner spent 12 years in exile during which he set down his ideas of music-drama and staging in *The Art-Work of the Future* (1849) and *Opera and Drama* (1851). Wagner was convinced that the impact of music-drama depended upon composition as well as performance; the author-composer should then be the director that brought together in performance all elements of the *Gesamtkunstwerk,* or "master art work."

Wagner's ideal theatrical world was one of stupendous illusion based on stories and characters from myth. He rejected all contemporary trends toward stage realism. He combined drama and music, arguing that music, through melody and tempo, permitted greater control over performance than was possible with the spoken word alone. Moreover, the author-composer should supervise all aspects of production. With these ideas Wagner reinforced the need for a strong director and a unified production.

All of Wagner's creative efforts came together in the first production of *The Ring of the Niebelungs* at his new opera house in Bayreuth (Bavaria) in 1876. At a single stroke the Bayreuth theatre changed the course of theatre design and operatic staging. Almost every axiom of standard theatre architecture developed over the last century was broken. Wagner, along with two architects (Gottfried Semper and Otto Brückwald), eventually agreed upon a semicircular auditorium (almost like a classical amphitheatre). Every seat faced the proscenium and the auditorium floor was steeply raked, so that every spectator could see and hear without being blocked by heads or posts. The seating (about 1300 seats in all) was not divided by aisles—we now call this "continental seating." A single row of boxes was placed behind the seats and above that was a gallery seating 300 more people.

To place the musicians where they would not distract the audience, the orchestra pit was dropped beneath the stage. The stage itself was 80 feet deep by 93 feet wide; it was raked toward the back and opened onto the outdoors behind the theatre. Wagner darkened the house as the overture started; once the curtain was up, no latecomers were permitted to enter and break the illusion (Figure 9–7).

Since Wagner wrote about gods and human beings, a double proscenium (the opening was about 40 feet across) was designed that divided the forestage into two areas. When the singers came into the forward part of the stage, they were separated from the mortals of the "real" world behind them on stage. Since Wagner also wrote about great forests, cavernous castles, and the chasms of the Rhine River, the theatre had the highest stage house in Europe, so that scenery of enormous proportions could be flown entirely out of sight.

a

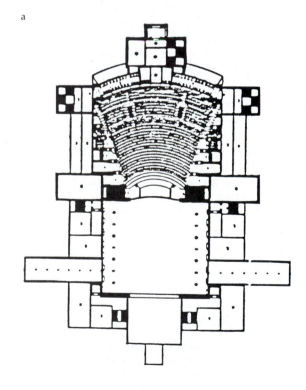

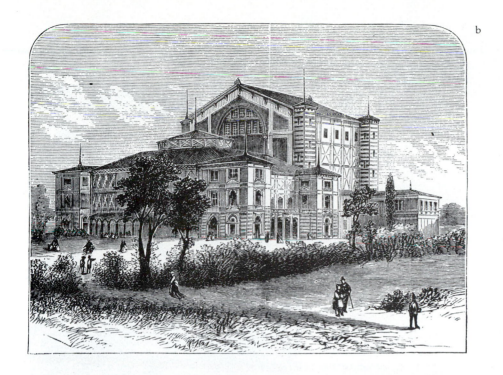

b

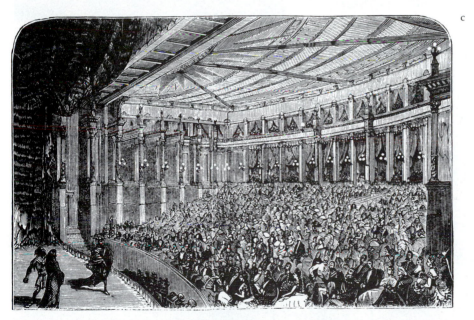

c

Figure 9-7 The Bayreuth Theatre, 1876. (a) Floor plan. (b) Exterior. (c) Interior.

PHOTO ESSAY: Ibsen and Strindberg in Performance

Alla Nazimova as Mrs. Alving in *Ghosts* at the Empire Theatre, New York, 1935. Nazimova also directed.

Swedish director Ingmar Bergman directed *A Dream Play* at Dramaten's Lilla Scene, Stockholm, in 1970. It was designed by Lennart Mork. Here are the Officer, Agnes, and the Stage-Door Keeper in the Theatre Corridor scene.

The world premiere of Ibsen's *A Doll's House* at the Danish Royal Theatre, 1879. Betty Hennings as Nora Helmer dances the Tarantella as instructed by her husband.

Ingmar Bergman originally staged *Hedda Gabler* at the Royal Dramatic Theatre in Stockholm in 1964 and restaged the play at London's National Theatre in 1970. In this photo from the London production, Maggie Smith, as Hedda Gabler, takes aim at Judge Brack with her dueling pistol.

English and
Italian com-
panies tour
Germany,
1600–1650 ————

Jesuit and
court theatres
flourish
after 1650

Gotz von   Egmont
Berlichingen 1778
1773

Gotthold Ephraim Lessing (1729–1781)

Miss Sara   Emilia Galotti
Sampson   1772
1755
          Minna   Nathan the
          von Barnhelm   Wise
          1767   1779
          The Hamburg
          Dramaturgy
          1767–1769

The Robbers
1781

*Intrigue
and Love
1784*

DRAMATIC CONVENTIONS

SHAKESPEARE AS MODEL IN GERMANY

As the court and state theatres emerged in Germany, they created demands not only for Italian scenic spectacles and operas but for plays as well. To provide them quickly, critics, translators, and playwrights turned to French and English plays.

Shakespeare's plays caught on almost immediately. Their broad spectrum of humanity, their episodic structures with main and subplots, their larger-than-life heroes and villains, exotic settings, and bizarre coincidences, and their richly imagistic verse appealed to playwrights, actors, producers, and audiences. German playwrights imitated Shakespeare's handling of plot, dramatic techniques, and language. Plays by Goethe, Schiller, Kleist, and Buchner show this influence.

THE ROMANTIC VISION

The roots of German romanticism lie more in philosophical, political, and social movements than in artistic ones. The American rebellion against the English for "life, liberty, and the pursuit of happiness" were ideals echoed on European stages. The Napoleonic Wars (1803–1815) were fought with these same ideals of patriotism and liberty. Against this background developed a literature of moods and caprices. Rules were no longer considered sacred. Young German playwrights—the "Storm and Stress" group—extolled emotions over reason, intuition over scientific facts, and Shakespeare over Racine. Goethe was celebrated by the romantics for his plays *Götz von Berlichingen* (1773) and *Egmont* (1778). *Egmont*—for which the German composer Beethoven wrote an overture—shows a national hero fighting for the independence of his country from an oppressive foreign rule.

Goethe also wrote the quintessential play of the romantic movement: *Faust*. Part I sets up the rebel as hero. Faust marches to the beat of a different drummer. He responds with instinct rather than reason, and he survives. Goethe's

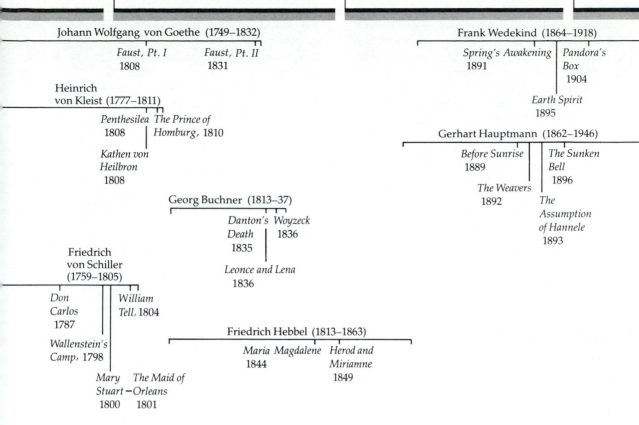

Johann Wolfgang von Goethe (1749–1832)

Faust, Pt. I
1808

Faust, Pt. II
1831

Heinrich von Kleist (1777–1811)

Penthesilea
1808

The Prince of
Homburg, 1810

Kathen von
Heilbron
1808

Georg Buchner (1813–37)

Danton's
Death
1835

Woyzeck
1836

Leonce and Lena
1836

Friedrich von Schiller (1759–1805)

Don
Carlos
1787

William
Tell, 1804

Wallenstein's
Camp, 1798

Mary
Stuart
1800

The Maid of
—Orleans
1801

Friedrich Hebbel (1813–1863)

Maria Magdalene
1844

Herod and
Miriamne
1849

Frank Wedekind (1864–1918)

Spring's Awakening
1891

Pandora's
Box
1904

Earth Spirit
1895

Gerhart Hauptmann (1862–1946)

Before Sunrise
1889

The Sunken
Bell
1896

The Weavers
1892

The
Assumption
of Hannele
1893

hero represents the indomitable human will in its search for experience.

In *The Death of Tragedy* (1963) George Steiner argues that the evasion of the tragic is central to the romantic temper. Christopher Marlowe's Faustus goes to hell, but Goethe's survives. Goethe's four acts of tragic violence and guilt are followed by a fifth act of redemption and innocence regained.

Romantic characters experience either timely *remorse* or *redemption* through love. Kleist's plays have reversals that deliver his heroes from the emotional chaos and unreality of their dream-filled lives. Faust's social conscience is awakened (Part II) and he is redeemed from damnation. Wagner's heroes experience remorse followed by a state of grace.

MELODRAMA

The popularity of melodramas by Kotzebue and others revealed a new mass audience made possible by a rising middle class and drawn together by new modes of transportation, such as railroads and steam engines. Kotzebue had mastered the formula in some 200 plays. In melodrama life was simplified; the good opposed the bad (and won out). Plots were uncomplicated and moral issues were clear. Physical action took precedence over subtlety of thought and beauty of language. A string of exciting (no matter how implausible) situations placed the hero and heroine in predicaments from which they extricated themselves at the last possible minute by strength, superior moral qualities, or sheer luck. It was taken for granted that virtue would be triumphant and vice defeated. Mass audiences thrilled to fights, escapes, and natural disasters in much the same way as modern film audiences cheer the heroics of Burt Reynolds, Jane Fonda, and Clint Eastwood.

Melodrama sustained romantic elements long after the movement gave way to the realists. As kindred spirits, both play forms championed the primacy of emotion over reason; the cultivation of the colorful, the exotic and bizarre; and the victory of the common man over forces of repression (a harsh landlord or a corrupt politician). Melodrama entertained. It provided vicarious excitement to audiences seeking escape from the monotony of lives caught up in industrial routine.

REALISM

Realism developed in the European theatre about 1860, and it influenced everyone working

in the theatre. The new realism demanded that playwrights, through direct observation of the real world around them, depict that world truthfully. They should write about the society they observed and should be as objective as possible.

The French philosopher Auguste Comte (1798–1857) and the English naturalist Charles Darwin (1809–1882) were two major influences

A classical understanding sees the world primarily as underlying form itself. A romantic understanding sees it primarily in terms of immediate appearance. If you were to show an engine or a mechanical drawing or electronic schematic to a romantic it is unlikely he would see much of interest in it. It has no appeal because the reality he sees is its surface. Dull, complex lists of names, lines and numbers. Nothing interesting. But if you were to show the same blueprint or schematic or give the same description to a classical person he might look at it and then become fascinated by it because he sees that within the lines and shapes and symbols is a tremendous richness of underlying form.

The romantic mode is primarily inspirational, imaginative, creative, intuitive. Feelings rather than facts predominate.

Robert M. Pirsig, *Zen and the Art of Motorcycle Maintenance* (1974)[12]

Romanticism and revolution are essentially related. . . . There is, both intuitively and practically, a liberation of the individual from predetermined hierarchies of social station and caste. . . . Hair is allowed to fall freely where once sat the confining majesty of the powdered wig. Carried over into politics, romanticism became the French Revolution, the chain reaction of the Napoleonic wars, and the tremors that ran through the structure of Europe in 1830–1848. . . . For at the heart of their liberating energy lay a conviction inherited from Rousseau. The misery and injustice of man's fate were not caused by a primal fall from grace. They were not the consequence of some tragic, immutable flaw in human nature. They arose from the absurdities and archaic inequalities built into the social fabric by generations of tyrants and exploiters. The chains of man, proclaimed Rousseau, were man-forged. They would be broken by human hammers. It was a doctrine of immense implications, signifying that the shape of man's future lay within his own moulding. If Rousseau was right (and most political systems are, to this day, heirs to his assertion), the quality of being could be radically altered and improved by changes in education and in the social and material circumstances of existence. Man stood no longer under the shadow of original corruption; he carried within him no germ of preordained failure. On the contrary, he could be led toward tremendous progress. He was, in the vocabulary of romanticism, perfectible.

George Steiner, *The Death of Tragedy* (1963)[13]

on the theatre of realism. Comte argued that the key to understanding the world around us was careful observation and even experimentation. These methods could reveal the cause and effect behind all events. Darwin's *The Origin of Species* (1859) carried Comte's thesis even further. Darwin argued that all forms of life had developed over millions of years from a common ancestry and that "survival of the fittest" explained the evolution of species.

Comte's and Darwin's theories had certain implications for drama. If heredity and environment—natural rather than supernatural factors—were the causes of everything that people are or do, behavior is determined by factors largely beyond our control. Thus, no individual is really responsible for his or her actions. Who or what, then, is to assume the blame? For some, the answer is *society.* Obviously, then, science and social reforms can achieve benefits for people. Also if *Homo sapiens* evolved from simple forms to their present level of complex organization, was not further evolution inevitable? Although evolutionary theory reduced human beings to the status of natural objects that could therefore be studied and controlled, both people and society would surely be better as a result.

Responding to these intellectual currents, the new playwrights emphasized details of contemporary life based on the five senses of sight, hearing, taste, smell, and touch and brought a new kind of truth to the stage by introducing subjects not previously seen. The new realism shocked audiences and created controversy with such subjects as society's responsibility for prostitution, poverty, industrial conditions, and disease. The most influential playwrights adopting the realistic mode were Henrik Ibsen, August Strindberg, George Bernard Shaw, and Gerhart Hauptmann.

NATURALISM

Realism and naturalism as theatrical movements were closely linked in their concern for a truthful depiction of life on stage. While the natural-

ists accepted that reality was discoverable only through the five senses, they also insisted that art must adopt scientific methods in its approach to human behavior. The two most important factors to observe were heredity and environment.

French author Emile Zola (1840–1902) championed the naturalist movement. He argued that the artist should emulate the scientist both in searching out subjects and in analyzing them and that like a medical doctor, the writer should remain detached, selecting subjects and examining them without prejudice. In practice, naturalistic writers emphasized the more degraded aspects of lower-class life—the social and physical maladies afflicting the poor. Some abandoned traditional dramatic structure with its complications, crises, and resolutions to present a "slice of life"—a segment of reality transferred to the stage as faithfully as possible.

Because of their belief in environment as a determinant of character and action, the naturalists wanted to reproduce this environment as accurately as possible on stage. Zola's essay on *Naturalism in the Theatre* (1881) and Strindberg's preface to *Miss Julie* (1888) were manifestos of stage naturalism.

Important naturalistic plays of this period were Emile Zola's *Thérèse Raquin* (1873; based on his earlier novel of the same title), Henri Becque's *The Vultures* (1882), Henrik Ibsen's *Ghosts* (1881), August Strindberg's *Miss Julie* (1888), Gerhart Hauptmann's *The Weavers*

> *❝ The future is with naturalism. . . . it will be proved that there is more poetry in the little apartment of a bourgeois than in all the empty, worm-eaten palaces of history; in the end we will see that everything meets in the real. ❞*
>
> Emile Zola, *Naturalism in the Theatre* (1881)

(1892), and Maxim Gorky's *The Lower Depths* (1902).

As an artistic movement naturalism had peaked by 1900 and was reabsorbed into stage realism. However, through focusing attention on the need for close observation of life, on the close relationships between environment and behavior, and on the details of stage production—the character's environment—its influence has been lasting.

REPRESENTATIVE PLAY

Ghosts
Premiered in Norwegian at the Aurora Turner Hall in Chicago, May 20, 1882

BACKGROUND

Ibsen's *Ghosts* was written in answer to critics of *A Doll's House* in which his heroine, Nora Helmer, involved in an impossible marriage, walks out on husband, children, and home in a gesture of emancipation. *Ghosts*, however, is the story of the widow who remained with a dissolute husband and who guards his reputation to gratify her own misguided selflessness and to preserve appearances. At the end, faced with the knowledge of her son's syphilitic disease and her own desperation, she realizes that the "virtues" of the past are really vicious. Oswald's congenital syphilis is only a partial symbol for the more pervasive "ghosts" in society—the moribund ideas and outworn conventions to which people cling and which stultify their lives.

Ghosts became the *cause célèbre* of the Free Theatre movement throughout the continent in the late 1880s and the landmark naturalistic play. Late nineteenth-century theatre was searching for a new kind of drama characterized by scientific accuracy, a new kind of tragedy and tragic hero, and a realistic reproduction of language and setting. *Ghosts* provided all of these elements.

Antoine at the *Théâtre Libre* fired the opening shot in the battle for a new kind of theatre experience, not only by first producing Ibsen's play in Paris, but also by establishing a new acting style—by *becoming* the character of Oswald. In Germany the *Freie Bühne* with Otto Brahm as its head began its career in 1889 with *Ghosts*, and in England J. T. Grein produced the play for the opening in 1891 of his Independent Theatre. Although the London press was hostile, calling the play "a revolting obscenity," a "dirty deed done in public," the play was not without its defenders. Moreover, the various productions of *Ghosts* that followed signified that the course of the modern theatre could not be reversed, although critical acceptance remained decidedly mixed.

Since its first production in 1882, Ibsen's play has been variously interpreted as an illustration that the sins of the fathers are visited upon the children, as a scientific discussion of the influence of heredity, and as a commentary on incestuous marriage and mercy killing. All of these interpretations are due largely to changes in the fashions of moral controversy rather than to Ibsen's intentions. For the most part Ibsen's play is about the *consequences* of human action projected through a middle-class woman's struggle to hide the corruption of her home and to shelter her child and society from the knowledge of that corruption.

THE SCENE

Ibsen's copious stage directions describe interior settings together with the gloom of the fjord landscape. This landscape, half hidden by a steady rain, can be glimpsed through large windows in the back wall of the setting. Oswald associates the dreary weather with the lack of happiness (*joie de vivre*, he calls it) in the Alving home and in the Norwegian countryside. In Oswald's mind this setting stands in sharp contrast to the sunlight of Paris and the happiness of his relationships there.

Ghosts, written by Henrik Ibsen in 1881, is the story of the Alving family. Mrs. Alving, widow of the admired and respected Captain Alving, has been living alone on her husband's estate with her maid Regina, carrying on her husband's philanthropic projects. Her son, Oswald, has returned from Paris for the dedication of an orphanage she has built.

The play opens with a conversation between the carpenter Jacob Engstrand and his supposed daughter, Regina. He tries to convince the girl to do her duty to her father and become the "hostess" of a sailors' hostel, which he plans to open with his savings. Regina refuses; she hopes for a more genteel life. Pastor Manders, a longtime friend of the family, arrives to dedicate the orphanage. He and Oswald heatedly discuss new moral codes. Oswald goes into the dining room, where sounds of his advances to Regina are heard. Mrs. Alving remarks that the "ghosts" of the past have risen to haunt her.

In Act II, Mrs. Alving explains that Regina is actually Captain Alving's daughter by a serving girl, and that his upstanding reputation has been falsely derived from her own good works. At the end of Act II the orphanage burns to the ground as a result of Engstrand's carelessness.

In Act III, it is revealed that Manders' fear of scandal has led him to bribe Engstrand. (Engstrand has convinced Manders that Manders himself started the fire.) Engstrand goes off with Regina to open the sailors' "home." Oswald confesses that he suffers from a venereal disease inherited from his father—another ghost. Mrs. Alving promises to give him a deadly drug should he become insane as the disease progresses. As the play ends, Oswald's mind disintegrates under a final seizure, and Mrs. Alving must decide whether to administer the drug as she has promised or to let her son live as a helpless invalid. The curtain falls as she tries to decide.

As we shall see in our discussion of Ibsen's language, this inclement weather is relieved only by the light from the burning orphanage (Act II) and by the truth about their lives revealed too late by Mrs. Alving. On the revelation of this truth in Act III, a brilliant morning sunlight illuminates the beauty of the glaciers and mountain peaks in the distance. However, the "sun," as a symbol of truth revealed (and ghosts exorcised), has come too late for them all.

THE TRAGIC ACTION

Joseph Wood Krutch, writing in *"Modernism" in Modern Drama*, suggested that in our age "man tends to become less a creature of reason than the victim of obsessions, fixations, delusions, and perversions."[14] More so than her son Oswald, Mrs. Alving is a tragic victim of a past that haunts the present in the shape of delusions and conflicts. The debilitating "ghosts" that Ibsen is talking about are both obvious and hidden. Specifically, Oswald "looks like" his father; like his father he uses sex and liquor to relieve his depression in the gloomy Norwegian environment; his sexual feelings toward Regina parallel his father's seduction of Regina's mother years ago. (Oswald's half-sister, Regina, the serving maid, is yet another ghost.) Oswald's secret, his syphilitic inheritance from his father's promiscuity, is a concealed ghost. Not too concealed is Pastor Manders' influence over Mrs. Alving.

She decides to insure the new orphanage, but he talks her out of it, arguing that it would appear she had no faith in Divine Providence if she "secured" her money from disaster. Mrs. Alving's secret is that she concealed her husband's degenerate behavior all these years and has built the orphanage with the last of his money to prevent her son from inheriting anything from his father.

Although Oswald's brain is being consumed by tertiary syphilis, the central tragedy is Mrs. Alving's. Oswald is little more than innocent victim. Ibsen's play centers on a woman of courage, intelligence, and business acumen who finds her ideals and enlightened views in conflict with her emotional life—which is based on an outworn system of social convention and respectability. As the play evolves it becomes apparent that Mrs. Alving is doomed because she has no control over this social inheritance.

Ibsen shows us clearly that Mrs. Alving's tragedy is not simply the realization that her son is fatally ill. It is that every significant *choice* she has made in the past, as well as in the play's present time, is finally *determined* by the ghosts of the past rather than by reason. Her socially conditioned choices begin with her marriage to Alving in conformity with her family's wishes. Unhappy in the marriage, she turns to Pastor Manders who influences her to return as a wife "should" to her husband. Oswald's birth soon results. Mrs. Alving then chooses to hide her husband's degeneracy from society. In the play's present time, she is unable to condone the Oswald–Regina relationship because of her thoughts of what is respectable. She withholds the truth about his father even from the adult Oswald. She decides not to insure the orphanage when Manders argues that the community would question her religious faith.

At the play's conclusion she is asked by her son to commit a mercy killing. Not wanting to live in a comatose state, he has a lethal dose of morphine that he asks his mother to give him at the appropriate moment. Our final view is of Mrs. Alving holding the morphine, but we do not see her act. The curtain comes down on the agony of her dilemma and a question mark.

Ibsen does not explicitly tell his audience whether Mrs. Alving administers the fatal drug to the afflicted Oswald. *Ghosts* is purposely open-ended. It is as though Ibsen wished to force his audience to identify with Mrs. Alving's dilemma and to consider whether their own lives illustrate a similar entrapment between worn-out value systems and meaningful action:

Mrs. Alving [*shaking with fear*] What is it? [*in a shriek*] Oswald! What's wrong! [*drops to her knees beside him and shakes him*] Oswald! Oswald! Look at me! Don't you know me?

Oswald [*in the same monotone*] The sun—the sun.

Mrs. Alving [*springs to her feet in anguish, tears at her hair with both hands and screams*] I can't bear this! [*whispers as if paralyzed by fright*] I can't bear it! Never! [*suddenly*] Where did he put them? [*Her hand skims across his chest.*] Here! [*She shrinks back several steps and shrieks.*] No, no, no!—Yes!—No, no! [*She stands a few steps away from him, her fingers thrust into her hair, staring at him in speechless horror.*]

Oswald [*sitting motionless, as before*] The sun—the sun.[15]

CHARACTER

Ibsen's characters are respectable middle-class types from a provincial Norwegian community, circa 1880. They dress, speak, and behave as we would expect them to if we entered the Alving home.

Mrs. Alving is the widow of Captain Alving, formerly chamberlain to the king of Norway. (Chamberlain was an honorary title conferred by the king on men of wealth and position.) Like many of Ibsen's women protagonists, she is trapped between an inherited value system (symbolized in the "ghosts" of the past and made visible in Pastor Manders' sermonizing and in Oswald's illness) and a desire for progressive social and moral action.

Oswald and Regina, the son and the serving

girl, are visible symbols of Mrs. Alving's inability to break with the old value system in which a wife was considered chattel. The children are literally ghosts from the past—one legitimate and diseased, the other illegitimate and promiscuous.

Pastor Manders, a pillar of Ibsen's provincial society, stands for the time-honored bourgeois; he is conventionally orthodox in his responses to any situation. He is also as destructive in his self-righteousness as Captain Alving was in his degeneracy. As the guardian of the community's moral and spiritual life, his foremost concern is with the appearance of respectability and the avoidance of scandal and opprobrium.

The carpenter, Jacob Engstrand, and his "daughter," Regina (Mrs. Alving arranged a marriage between Engstrand and Regina's mother when it was discovered that the maid was pregnant by the captain), are representatives of the world's opportunists (what Ibsen called "philistines") who take advantage of the conscience-ridden middle class. Regina deserts Oswald the moment she learns that he is terminally ill and cannot take her to Paris. She joins her father's enterprise, a "home for sailors" (Engstrand's euphemism for a brothel), which he finances from funds extorted from Manders after the orphanage burns. Although it is likely that a drunken Engstrand turned a candle over thereby setting the orphanage on fire, he persuades Manders that the pastor will be held responsible for the catastrophe. Manders pays him off and buys his silence.

LANGUAGE AND SYMBOLISM

With the advent of stage realism, dialogue approximates everyday conversation. In addition, nonverbal symbols, taken from the play's environment, assume as much significance as do verbal symbols in Shakespeare's verse. Within the play's symbolic design, Mrs. Alving, Oswald, and Regina are visible symbols of the ghosts that pervade the play's action—victims of

their heredity and environment—forces over which they can exercise little, if any, control.

Light is another visible symbol. The play begins on a gloomy day; Oswald complains that he can never remember anything but the dark fjord. Sunlight soon becomes a synonym for truth. The light of the burning orphanage brings some truth into the Alving home, forcing Mrs. Alving to tell the truth about Oswald's father. In the last act it is the introduction of *light*—the sunrise accompanied by Oswald's calling for "the sun" as his mind collapses—that reveals the meaning of the play's completed action. But truth (the sunrise) has come too late to the Alving home; Oswald's collapse is irreversible; Regina's promiscuity is a foregone conclusion. Mrs. Alving's awareness likewise comes too late to reverse the total collapse of her world.

IBSEN'S MODERNISM

While some argue that Ibsen was making a case for the cause of feminist liberation in *A Doll's House* and *Ghosts*, Ibsen's plays are far more universal than specific political causes or social problems could make them. The dissociation of the *ideals* people live by and the *facts* of their lives is a central theme in Ibsen's work. His modernism stems from his perception that well-meaning, intelligent people are victimized and defeated by nonrational forces over which they have no control. The nineteenth century blamed heredity or environment for this condition; the twentieth century has added the unconscious as a breeding ground for human ills. If people lack meaningful control over their lives, then existence is futile. This theme of Ibsen's plays dominates a great deal of modern drama from Georg Buchner to Samuel Beckett.

ESSAY

Ibsen's *Ghosts* continues to be a popular serious play in the modern repertoire because, first, it is a great vehicle for actresses. Eva Le Gallienne,

Margaret Tyzack, Irene Worth, and Liv Ullmann are only four among many actresses who have played the part of Mrs. Alving in recent years. Moreover, *Ghosts* continues to intrigue modern audiences because of its universal truths about human behavior. We all deceive ourselves, tell "white lies," conceal the skeletons in our mutual family closets, and struggle with conventions received from our families and society. *Ghosts* confirms these living truths.

Ghosts in Modern Performance
Directed by John Madden, with Liv Ullmann as Mrs. Alving and John Neville as Pastor Manders in The John F. Kennedy Center production, Washington, D.C., 1982

Swedish actress Liv Ullmann is known to American audiences through many films directed by Ingmar Bergman such as *Face to Face, Persona, Scenes from a Marriage,* and *Autumn Sonata.* She has also been seen on Broadway in a revival of Eugene O'Neill's *Anna Christie* and in an ill-fated musical, *I Remember Mama.*

As a result of an absurd misunderstanding, she agreed in 1982 to play Mrs. Alving in Ibsen's *Ghosts,* which was part of The John F. Kennedy Center's tenth anniversary season. While her English is fluent, it is not always perfect. When her agent asked if she would consider playing in Ibsen's *Ghosts* in America, she was under the impression that she was being offered Ibsen's last play, *When We Dead Awaken,* which she had always wanted to do. The Norwegian word for "ghosts" literally translates as "the walking-againers." Some months later when she was talking with Norwegian friends about going to America to do *When We Dead Awaken,* they asked what the play was called in America. She replied, "*Ghosts.*" They informed her that she was, in fact, doing another Ibsen play.

In a new adaptation by American playwright Arthur Kopit, especially commissioned for this production, Liv Ullmann, then 43, played Mrs. Alving encased in a Victorian gown with her honey-colored hair tightly coiled into braids and wound in a knot on top of her head. The conformity of her dress signified the conformity of her spirit.

Ullmann interpreted Mrs. Alving "like Nora Helmer of *Doll's House* who did not leave home." The Ullmann role explored the flip side of Nora Helmer—a worthwhile woman who stayed home and then spent a lifetime lying to herself and the world around her. "If somebody could touch her," Ullmann said of Mrs. Alving, "if life could touch her, she could blossom the next day."[16]

Ullmann's Mrs. Alving, as directed by John Madden, was a repressed, emotionally blighted woman who, for many years, smugly fed her sense of duty and her considerable intelligence and starved her feelings. Ullmann made Mrs. Alving plain looking and gave her a severity and a tight, purposeful dignity assumed by people who fail to feel at home with who they are and what they have become.

SUMMARY

In nineteenth-century Scandinavia and Germany, in major cities and minor principalities, a system of state-supported municipal and court theatres developed, which nourished a rich repertory system. Henrik Ibsen began his theatrical career at the National Theatre in Bergen (Norway) and Johann Wolfgang von Goethe at the Weimar Court Theatre (Germany).

It was an age of tremendous eclecticism in staging and writing. Extravagant romantic acting styles gave way to the Meiningen company's ensemble playing. Declamatory speech and prescribed gestures gave way to the naturalism of Antoine's amateurs playing the character's inner life at the Théâtre Libre. Stock scenery with wings and borders was displaced by the box setting with historical details of costumes, properties, and furnishings. Antoine's theory of "the fourth wall removed" dominated design and production styles after the 1880s. At about the same time electric lighting replaced gas

Figure 9-8 Kevin Spacey as Oswald and Liv Ullmann as Mrs. Alving in *Ghosts* at The John F. Kennedy Center for the Performing Arts, Washington, D.C., 1982.

lighting and made way for modern light design pioneered in the work of Swiss designer Adolphe Appia. The modern director (*regisseur*) emerged to coordinate all of these complemen- tary elements. Contributing to this development were Goethe, Meiningen, Chronegk, Wagner, Brahm, and Antoine.

Goethe's work at Weimar inspired the "total

work of art" envisioned by Richard Wagner where words, music, mime, scenic and vocal effects worked in harmony toward a single end—the performance. The idea of a production unified by a single artistic consciousness developed out of Goethe's rules for actors, the Duke of Saxe-Meiningen's scrupulous attention to stage detail, Wagner's amalgam of music and drama at Bayreuth, and Antoine's insistence on authenticity in all elements of play production.

The eclecticism in staging was repeated in the rapidly changing trends in playwriting. The historical verse plays that nearly all early nineteenth-century playwrights cut their teeth on were superseded by those in which the rebel heroes of romanticism took over history. Goethe's *Faust* remains the quintessential nineteenth-century romantic play. August Kotzebue wrote the popular melodramas that brought mass audiences into the theatres.

In the 1880s Henrik Ibsen and August Strindberg radically changed European playwriting with their realistic and naturalistic plays, which the great French naturalist writer Emile Zola and the Independent Theatre movement had called for in their revolt against the "falsity" of nineteenth-century drama. Realism remains the dominant production style of today's theatre, associated with precise observation of everyday details of dress, speech, behavior, and environment. The realists stressed that events must be understood in terms of cause and effect; the naturalists further stressed that causes and effects had their sources in heredity and environment.

At the close of the century Wedekind and Strindberg pointed the way toward the new expressionist movement that was to catch hold in Germany in the 1920s. Strindberg's *Dream Play* (1902) prefigured the Freudian age by introducing the dimension of the unconscious into the modern theatre.

Ibsen's *Ghosts*, our representative play, became the *cause célèbre* of the Free Theatre movement in Europe in the late 1880s. It is associated with Antoine's best work as producer, director, and actor (he played Oswald) at the influential Théâtre Libre. In *Ghosts* Ibsen shows us how well-meaning and intelligent people are victimized by nonrational forces over which they have no control. Ibsen's themes, language, symbols, setting, characters, and lighting call to mind the best practices of nineteenth-century stage realism. In the 1982 production of *Ghosts*, performed at The John F. Kennedy Center for the Performing Arts in Washington, D.C., Liv Ullmann played Mrs. Alving—the emotionally repressed woman who spent a lifetime lying to herself and the world around her.

PLAYS TO READ

Faust, Part I, by Johann Wolfgang von Goethe

Woyzeck by Georg Buchner

Ghosts by Henrik Ibsen

Miss Julie by August Strindberg

SOURCES

Georg Buchner: Complete Plays and Prose. Translated with an introduction by Carl Richard Mueller. New York: Hill and Wang, 1963. This edition includes Buchner's three plays (*Danton's Death, Leonce and Lena*, and *Woyzeck*); *Lenz*, a narrative prose work; and *The Hessian Courier*, a political tract. Mueller's introduction is one of the best critical writings on Buchner in English.

Goethe's Faust, Part I, A New American Version. Translated by C. F. MacIntyre. New York: New Directions, 1957. Paperback. This edition contains a brief biography of Goethe without introduction or notes.

Goethe's *Faust.* Translated with introduction by Walter Kaufman. New York: Doubleday Anchor, 1961. Paperback. The volume contains an excellent introduction and parts one and two of the play.

Henrik Ibsen: The Complete Major Prose Plays. Translated with introductions by Rolf Fjelde. New York: New American Library, 1978. Paperback. New translations of 12 plays from *Pillars of Society* (1877) to *When We Dead Awaken*

(1899). Fjelde has written short introductions for each play. The appendix contains a complete list of Ibsen's plays, a selected bibliography, and stage histories of these plays in the American theatre.

Ibsen, Henrik. *Four Major Plays,* Vol. 1: *Doll's House, The Wild Duck, Hedda Gabler,* and *The Master Builder. Four Major Plays,* Vol. 2: *Ghosts, Enemy of the People, The Lady from the Sea,* and *John Gabriel Borkman.* Translated by Rolf Fjelde. New York: New American Library, 1965, 1970. Paperback.

Six Plays of Strindberg. Translated with introduction by Elizabeth Sprigge. New York: Doubleday Anchor, 1955. Paperback. Long a standby of American students, this edition has a prefatory note on Strindberg by Eric Bentley. The edition contains six plays (*The Father, Miss Julie, The Stronger, Easter, A Dream Play,* and *The Ghost Sonata*), and Strindberg's prefaces to *Miss Julie* and *A Dream Play.*

NOTES

1. Samuel M. Waxman, *Antoine and The Théâtre Libre* (Cambridge: Harvard University Press, 1926), p. 115.

2. Frederick Marker and Lise-Lone Marker, *The Scandinavian Theatre: A Short History* (Totowa, N.J.: Rowman and Littlefield, 1975), p. 154. Reprinted by permission.

3. Henrik Ibsen, *Ghosts,* Act I stage direction, 1881. From *Henrik Ibsen: The Complete Major Prose Plays,* trans. Rolf Fjelde. Copyright ©1965, 1970, 1978 by Rolf Fjelde. Reprinted by arrangement with The New American Library, Inc., New York.

4. Marker and Marker, p. 167. Reprinted by permission.

5. August Strindberg, preface to *Miss Julie,* 1888. From *Six Plays of Strindberg,* trans. Elizabeth Sprigge. Copyright ©1955 by Elizabeth Sprigge. Reprinted by permission of Curtis Brown, Ltd.

6. August Strindberg, preface to *A Dream Play,* 1902. From *Six Plays of Strindberg,* trans. Eliza-beth Sprigge (New York: Doubleday, 1955). Reprinted by permission of A. P. Watt Ltd. and the Executors of the Estate of Elizabeth Sprigge.

7. Kenneth Macgowan and William Melnitz, with Gordon Armstrong, *Golden Ages of the Theater,* p. 168. © 1979 by Prentice-Hall, Inc. Reprinted by permission of Prentice-Hall, Inc., Englewood Cliffs, N.J.

8. Goethe, *Rules for Actors* (1824). See A. M. Nagler, *A Source Book In Theatrical History* (New York: Dover, 1959), pp. 428-435.

9. Goethe, from Marvin Carlson, *Goethe and the Weimar Theatre* (Ithaca, N.Y.: Cornell University Press, 1978), p. 113.

10. Toby Cole and Helen K. Chinoy, eds., *Directors on Directing: A Source Book of the Modern Theater* (Indianapolis: Bobbs-Merrill, 1976), p. 90. Reprinted by permission.

11. Cole and Chinoy, p. 95.

12. Robert M. Pirsig, *Zen and the Art of Motorcycle Maintenance: An Inquiry into Values* (New York: William Morrow, 1974), p. 73. Reprinted by permission.

13. George Steiner, *The Death of Tragedy* (New York: Oxford University Press, 1963), pp. 124–125. © 1980 by George Steiner. Reprinted by permission of Georges Borchardt, Inc.

14. Joseph Wood Krutch, "Modernism" in Modern Drama: A Definition and an Estimate (Ithaca, N.Y.: Cornell University Press, 1953), p. 22.

15. Henrik Ibsen, *Ghosts,* 1881. From *Henrik Ibsen: The Complete Major Prose Plays,* trans. Rolf Fjelde. Copyright © 1965, 1970, 1978 by Rolf Fjelde. Reprinted by arrangement with The New American Library, Inc., New York.

16. Helen Dudar, "Liv Ullmann Inspirits 'Ghosts,'" *New York Times,* 29 August 1982, II, 1, 4. © 1982 by The New York Times Company. Reprinted by permission.

MODERN THEATRE: BEGINNINGS IN REALISM

A MODERN PERSPECTIVE

Our modern theatre of psychological and social realism dates from the late nineteenth-century European and Russian theatres. The movement away from the artificiality of the theatre and its conventions toward a theatre of inner and outer truth is by and large the story of the modern theatre since its beginnings in the 1870s.

The modern theatre began as a playwright's and director's theatre. Ibsen, Strindberg, and Chekhov were the principal writers of the new stage realism that demanded a "new" director and a "new" kind of actor. Antoine in Paris, Brahm in Berlin, and Stanislavsky in Moscow created the new, realistic style for the new plays. Their impact on the American theatre has been immeasurable. Our playwrights, actors, directors, and teachers of acting—Eugene O'Neill, Tennessee Williams, Arthur Miller, Elia Kazan, Marlon Brando, Lee Strasberg, and the American "group" theatres—are synonymous with psychological realism in writing and performance. This has been the mainstream of American theatre (exclusive of musicals) for five decades. This great heritage is associated largely with the name of Constantin Stanislavsky at one of the most famous theatres of our century—the *Moscow Art Theatre*.

REPRESENTATIVE THEATRE: The Moscow Art Theatre

On a summer day in 1897 in a Moscow restaurant called the Slavic Bazaar, Constantin Stanislavsky and Vladimir Nemirovich-Danchenko met in a conference that lasted for 15 hours. Their meeting has since become a legend. These two men had much to talk about. Nemirovich-Danchenko was a stage director at the school of the Moscow Philharmonic Society and Stanislavsky was director of a semiprofessional acting company known as the Society of Art and Literature. They agreed that the time had come to start a theatre in Russia devoted to the quest for "inner truth"—a theatre that would place the truth of human feelings and experiences on stage. They pledged to form a theatre company and reform production techniques and acting methods. So the Moscow Art Theatre began over an afternoon and evening of borscht, brown bread, blintzes, vodka, and tea.

The two directors, having carefully selected a company from among members of the Moscow Philharmonic Society and the Society of Art and Literature, moved to the countryside to begin intensive rehearsals in a barn about 10 miles from the city. Returning to Moscow in the fall of 1898, the Moscow Art Theatre opened in an old beer garden (the Hermitage Theatre) with Alexei K. Tolstoy's historical drama, *Tsar Fyodor.* At the outset the company created a sensation because of its painstaking recreation of Russia, circa 1600, its ensemble acting, and its absence of "star" performers.

Four other plays made up the repertory that first season. But it was not until the production of a play by a new playwright, Anton Chekhov, that MAT (the acronym that developed for the Moscow Art Theatre) was established as a serious, innovative company. Chekhov's *Seagull*—produced unsuccessfully a year and a half earlier at a theatre in St. Petersburg—established the originality of both the author and the company. The first season ended in triumph.

By 1902 the Moscow Art theatre had made theatrical history with productions of *Hedda Gabler, The Death of Ivan the Terrible, Uncle Vanya, The Enemy of the People, The Three Sisters,* and *The Wild Duck.* The company was so popular for its new style of stage realism that they were able to build their own theatre (Figure 10-1). As the Moscow Art Theatre is today, so it was then, a proscenium theatre seating 1200 and equipped with an electrical lighting system, cyclorama, and revolving stage. There was also plentiful space in the building for offices, workshops, and rehearsal halls. The walls were gray-green, the woodwork of dark oak; there was carpeting on the floors, and the seats were upholstered. The curtain had a seagull as its emblem, taken from Chekhov's play, painted on the center. As the curtain opened the seagull parted revealing the stage behind.

In 1902 the original acting company of 39 was increased to 100 members. While MAT had no stars, a number of actors stood out. In addition to Stanislavsky, there were Olga Knipper (1870–1959), who became Chekhov's wife and the company's principal actress; Ivan Moskvin (1874–1946), a man of small stature who played self-effacing roles; and the handsome Vassily Kachalov (1875—1948), best in the roles of romantic heroes. Others, later to emigrate to the United States, were Alla Nazimova, Richard Boleslavsky, and Akim Tamiroff.

Nemirovich-Danchenko's (1858–1943) share

Figure 10-1 The Moscow Art Theatre as it appeared in the days of Stanislavsky's work there. Below: Inside the present-day Moscow Art Theatre.

in making the Moscow Art Theatre one of the finest theatres in modern Europe is frequently overshadowed by the careers of Stanislavsky and Chekhov. Nemirovich-Danchenko, who was also a playwright, asked for the original meeting with Stanislavsky, and, by the initial agreement between them, Stanislavsky had absolute control over production matters, while Nemirovich-Danchenko was in charge of financial and literary matters. It was Nemirovich-Danchenko who selected the plays and lured Chekhov back to playwriting. As literary adviser he had the right to determine how each play was to be approached to bring out its meaning. The collaboration between Nemirovich-Danchenko and Stanislavsky became one of the longest and most successful in theatrical history.

CONDITIONS OF PERFORMANCE

BACKGROUND

Russia emerged from Slavic settlements in northeastern Europe with Kiev as its center. Since the Byzantine Empire was its chief trading partner, Russia accepted the cultural heritage of Byzantine Orthodox Christianity, the Cyrillic alphabet, icon painting, and Byzantine styles of architecture. It was not until eastern Russia was overrun by Mongol tribes in the twelfth century that Moscow (Muscovy) became a major city. The Mongol rule was broken by Ivan III ("the Great," 1440–1505), and the Russian state was consolidated on the basis of a mercantile and agrarian economy. Peter the Great (1672–1725) and Catherine the Great (1729–1796) transformed Russia from a medieval kingdom into a powerful nation. They created large armies and navies, founded universities, and began a civil service system that created a new social class.

CONSTANTIN STANISLAVSKY

Constantin Stanislavsky (1863–1938) was producer-director-actor and co-founder of the Moscow Art Theatre. As a director, Stanislavsky aimed for ensemble acting and the absence of stars; he established such directorial methods as intensive study of the play before rehearsals began, the actor's careful attention to detail, and recreation of the play's milieu after visiting locales or extensive research. The Moscow Art Theatre's success was seen in Anton Chekhov's plays depicting the monotonous and frustrating life of the rural landowning class.

Stanislavsky is remembered most for his efforts to perfect a method of acting. His published writings in English—*My Life in Art* (1924), *An Actor Prepares* (1936), *Building a Character* (1949), and *Creating a Role* (1961)—provide a record of the "Stanislavsky System" as it evolved.

While in the latter part of the nineteenth century, the czars instituted social and political reforms (the serfs were emancipated in 1861), the winds of revolution were already blowing across the Russian steppes. Student disorders and peasant uprisings led to the 1905 revolution. Czar Nicholas II, the last of the Romanov rulers, made concessions, convoked an advisory national assembly (called a *Duma*), and created constitutional government. Two revolutionary parties were formed and one, the Social Democrats, soon split into the Mensheviks and the Bolsheviks, the latter led by Vladimir Illich Lenin (1870–1924). General strikes, disorder, and terrorism continued.

In 1914, at the beginning of World War I,

Russia sided with Serbia against Austria after the assassination of Archduke Ferdinand by Serbian terrorists. The Russian army was defeated at every turn. In 1917, with civil unrest at home and the army routed on the battlefield, the revolutionaries toppled the monarchy. Several months later the Bolsheviks killed the royal family. A bitter civil war followed during which the Bolsheviks (now renamed Communists) overpowered military and political opposition. By 1922 a new nation, the Union of Soviet Socialist Republics (U.S.S.R.), was formed. A succession of Soviet rulers followed, beginning with Vladimir Lenin and Joseph Stalin, and, following World War II, an expansion of Soviet satellite states (including East Berlin, Poland, Hungary, and Czechoslovakia).

Russia today is a powerful military giant whose industrial factories and space program rival our own but whose repressive measures have touched off a series of defections to the West by writers, dancers, musicians, military officers, and scientists.

MANAGEMENT: THE STAR SYSTEM

In the late nineteenth century the star system prevailed on the stages of the Russian theatres in the major cultural centers of Moscow and St. Petersburg. Likewise, theatre management differed very little from that of other nineteenth-century European theatres. Painted scenery provided background for the actor, and plays were mere vehicles to feature the talents of major actors. However, in Russia this system was shaken by the Meiningen company's tours to Moscow in 1885 and again in 1890. Their productions opened up visions of a new theatrical world to two young Russians seated in the audiences; they were Constantin Stanislavsky and Vladimir Nemirovich-Danchenko.

PLAYWRITING

Russian playwriting of the early nineteenth century was dominated by Nikolai Gogol (1809–1852), Alexander Ostrovsky (1823–1886), and Ivan Turgenev (1818–1883). Leo Tolstoy (1828–1910), Anton Chekhov (1860–1904), and Maxim Gorky (1868–1936) followed.

Chekhov, the most influential of them all, was himself influenced by the movement toward realistic writing of the earlier trio. In *The Inspector General* (1836), Gogol satirized petty corruption among provincial government officials. Ostrovsky in his greatest play, *The Thunderstorm* (1859) closely observed the everyday lives of the merchant class and lower aristocracy. Primarily a novelist, Turgenev is remembered in the theatre for *A Month in the Country* (1850), which deals with the boredom, jealousies, heartbreak, and compromises of people living on a remote country estate. Chekhov built on the realism of

Chekhov
dies, 1904

First Studio
opens, 1905

MAT tours
outside
Russia, 1906

World War I
1914–1918

Russian
Revolution, 1917
Communists
seize power

MAT comes to New York
1923–1924

Stalin comes
to power, 1928

Socialist
Realism declared
style for all
art, 1934

World War II
1939–1945

these writers who in their portrayal of nonheroic characters were concerned with inner motivations and the quiet disappointments of ordinary lives.

The team at the Moscow Art Theatre established Anton Chekhov as the house dramatist for the short span of his life and, it appears, for all time. They also introduced Russian realists like Leo Tolstoy and Maxim Gorky and the great international pioneers Henrik Ibsen and Gerhart Hauptmann to Moscow audiences.

ACTING: STANISLAVSKY'S SYSTEM

Prior to 1900 actors learned their craft in different ways. In the classical Greek theatre the playwright was responsible for training actors, singers, and dancers; in Japanese Noh and Kabuki theatres the men of whole families often made up the companies and young boys served long apprenticeships learning their craft and roles from their parents and relatives. Elizabethan and French classical theatres had highly developed programs for actor training and apprenticeships; the Restoration theatres had their "nurseries." In the eighteenth and nineteenth centuries, in addition to playing the lead roles, staging the productions, and operating the theatres, the actor-managers also trained young actors. At the beginning of this century, the theatre still trained its young actors, usually

within the context of a performing company. However, the Russian actor-director-teacher, Constantin Stanislavsky, is the person most responsible for changing this system.

Stanislavsky's approach to actor training, worked out over a period of 40 years, was essentially *psychological*. He developed a system of exercises and techniques that enabled the actor to discover from his or her own experiences the feelings and motivations of the character he or she was to play. Using such methods as concentration, relaxation, sense memory, and improvisation, Stanislavsky believed the actor would eventually come to identify with the character to such a degree that this identification would be maintained throughout the performance. In Stanislavsky's system these methods can be practiced and applied in a context separate from the rehearsal of a specific role or play; they are relevant to every acting situation. It was this recognition that led to the emergence of acting schools, studios, and training programs.

VISUAL ELEMENTS

The new plays and acting style called for a special kind of stage setting. For Stanislavsky and his designers, scenery was no longer decor but environment. The setting had to be the place of dramatic action itself, as if you walked into it off the street or as if you had grown up there.

With Antoine and Strindberg, Stanislavsky demanded a recognizable reality—stage realism.

Scenery The setting as an exact reproduction of life characterized most of the Moscow Art Theatre's productions. With great care Stanislavsky documented settings for the first play, *Tsar Fyodor*, and many that followed. He searched Moscow libraries for data on the life and times of the czar. He looked for engravings, old armor, clerical robes, and Russian headgear. He took designers and actors in a private railroad car to visit ancient towns, gathering "atmosphere" and buying genuine period costumes and properties. When he produced Maxim Gorky's *The Lower Depths* (1902), the MAT company visited the hideouts of thieves and outcasts in the Khitrov Market in the center of the city.

A study of Stanislavsky's promptbook (his *Regiebuch*) for Chekhov's *The Seagull* reveals the change in attitude toward the stage setting. It was no longer considered a mere background—an arrangement of painted side wings and backdrop—but an *environment*. His notebook contains the play's ground plan. He drew maps of the Sorin estate; the park of birch trees; the house with its veranda; the lawn, the path, the lake, and a stream with wooden bridges. Only after he understood the whole geography of the neighborhood could the stage setting be designed.

Costumes, Lighting, and Properties The romantics of the nineteenth century had introduced historically accurate costumes onto the European stage. But the Meiningen productions had the greatest impact on the new generation of actors, directors, and producers. Every detail of

> *The Stanislavsky system is really only a conscious codification of ideas about acting which have always been the property of most good actors of all countries whether they knew it or not. Its basis is the work of the actor with himself in order to master 'technical means for the creation of the creative mood, so that inspiration may appear oftener than is its wont.' That is what Stanislavsky was seeking when he began to formulate his thoughts into a system. 'This does not mean,' he wrote in his Life in Art, 'that I was going to create inspiration by artificial means. That would be impossible. What I wanted to learn was how to create a favorable condition for the appearance of inspiration by means of the will, that condition in the presence of which inspiration was most likely to descend into the actor's soul.*

Norris Houghton, *Moscow Rehearsals* (1936)[1]

> *In the other theatres of the time the problems of scenery were solved in a very simple manner: there was a backdrop and four or five wings in arched form. On these were painted a palace hall with entrances, passages, open and closed terraces, a seascape, and so on. In the middle there was the smooth, dirty theatrical floor and enough chairs to seat the dramatic* persona, *no more. . . .*
>
> *"The usual* mise en scène *and scheme of properties, established once and for all for each and every play, was as follows: on the right a sofa, on the left a table and two chairs. One scene of the play would take place near the sofa, the next near the table with the two chairs, the third in the middle of the stage near the prompter's box; then again near the sofa, the table and the prompter's box. . . . Polkas and castanets in the intermissions, the exits of actors with applause, the sudden and unexpected return of heroes who had just died on the stage, endless curtain calls in the intermissions or at the end of the performance—all these ridiculous habits of the time were the changeless accompaniments of each performance.*

Constantin Stanislavsky, *My Life in Art* (1924)[2]

setting, costumes, and properties was considered part of a total impression. Even sound effects were drawn from life to heighten emotional effects: alarm bells, weapons pounded against wooden doors, explosions, the clash of swords fading into the distance. Light was used at varying intensities as candlelight, moonlight, and bright sunshine.

At the Moscow Art Theatre Stanislavsky gave immense care to the selection of costumes, furniture, eating utensils, and rugs. Antique clothing was often collected; contemporary clothes were treated to give them a lived-in look. In one famous account Chekhov disagreed with Stanislavsky over Trigorin's costume in *The Seagull*. After seeing the production Chekhov went backstage and told Stanislavsky that instead of the elegant white suit the actor had worn, Stanislavsky should have costumed the character with "torn shoes and trousers." Years later, Stanislavsky said, he finally understood what Chekhov had meant.

Sound Effects While sound effects have always been part and parcel of theatrical performances, a change in sound conventions came about with Chekhov's writing and Stanislavsky's staging. Heretofore, the Elizabethans had had their thunder machines in the tiring house. Musicians in all theatres underscored changes in mood with pipes, flutes, trumpets, and drums. But Chekhov called for more. He enjoyed off-stage, realistic effects of fire alarms, dogs barking, birds and crickets chirping, carriages approaching and departing. Sound brought the outer world to impinge upon the inner lives of his characters, adding to the conventions of stage realism in the twentieth-century theatre.

THE FIRST-NIGHT AUDIENCE

The Seagull was the last production of MAT's first season. While their first production of *Tsar Fyodor* had been a success, the other plays had been less so. The company needed the financial and critical success of Chekhov's play to con-

> *A year or more passed. Again I played the part of Trigorin in* The Seagull—*and during one of the performances I suddenly understood what Chekhov had meant.*
>
> *"Of course, the shoes must be torn and the trousers checked, and Trigorin must not be handsome. In this lies the salt of the part: for young, inexperienced girls it is important that a man should be a writer and print touching and sentimental romances, and the Nina Zarechnayas, one after the other, will throw themselves on his neck, without noticing that he is not talented, that he is not handsome, that he wears checked trousers and torn shoes. Only afterwards, when the love affair with such 'seagulls' is over, do they begin to understand that it was girlish imagination which created the great genius in their heads, instead of a simple mediocrity. Again, the depth and the richness of Chekhov's laconic remarks struck me. It was very typical and characteristic of him.*
>
> Constantin Stanislavsky, *My Life in Art* (1924)[3]

tinue in operation. There were other complicating factors. *The Seagull* was a risky choice. It had been produced earlier at the Alexandrinsky Theatre in St. Petersburg with disastrous results, and Chekhov had very reluctantly released the script to MAT. Also, the playwright was ill of tuberculosis in Yalta, and it was feared that another failed production would make his condition worse. Chekhov's reputation, perhaps even his life, and the company's future were being placed on the line.

The first night of *The Seagull* was played before a small but chosen audience of critics, friends, and patrons. In his autobiography, *My Life in Art*, Stanislavsky described the palpable tension on stage during the first act. The curtain came down on Act I and the audience sat in gravelike silence. On stage, Olga Knipper, playing Madame Arkadina, fainted. The other actors, hearing nothing from the audience, headed in despair for their dressing rooms. Suddenly a roar of applause burst from the auditorium. The curtain then rose and fell to prolonged and enthusiastic clapping. At the end of the play there were congratulations, embraces, and ovations, especially for the actress playing Masha. Her words at the end of the first act had stunned the audience, who after what seemed an interminable silence, then began to "roar and thunder in mad ovation."[4] Afterward, a telegram was sent to Chekhov with the good news.

This story of the opening night of *The Seagull* is now a theatrical legend. The success of this one play affected the future of the Moscow Art Theatre and the direction of Western theatre for half a century.

THE DIRECTORS: STANISLAVSKY AND MEYERHOLD

Stanislavsky and Vsevelod Meyerhold represent two directions in the modern theatre—psychological realism and stage theatricality. One treats the stage not as a stage but as a living room; the other treats the stage as a stage with all of its artifices exposed to the audience.

The Stage as Reality Stanislavsky began as a director with the Meiningen company's ideals of external realism uppermost in his mind. In addition to the historical research he engaged in before starting rehearsals, he wrote out a detailed *mise en scène* (in Russian the term means all action and stage business). Gradually, Stanislavsky moved away from the external realism of his early work toward psychological realism. His staging of Gorky's *The Lower Depths* at MAT's new theatre in 1902 was the beginning of the change.

Stanislavsky's work more and more dealt with the actor as the heart of the theatre, rather than with the details of environment. As his attitude changed he gave up the elaborate historical study. "The best analysis of a play," he now said, "is to act it in the given circumstances. For in the process of action the actor gradually obtains mastery over the inner incentives of the actions of the character he is representing, evoking in himself emotions and thoughts which resulted in those actions."[5]

The Stage as Artifice Meyerhold, a former student of Nemirovich-Danchenko, played the part of Treplev, the young playwright, in *The Seagull* at the Moscow Art Theatre. He soon broke with Stanislavsky and went his own way, experimenting with theatrical style and setting out to create a modern equivalent of the openly theatrical theatres of the past, such as the *commedia dell'arte*.

Meyerhold was perhaps our first modern *creative* as opposed to *interpretive* director. He removed the front curtain, footlights, and proscenium arch; he extended the forestage into the auditorium; he kept the house lights on during performances; and he used stagehands to change properties and scenery in full view of the audience. He also cut and rearranged dramatic texts to explicate the author's purpose in a clear, theatrical way. He prepared no written notes, but his 8 to 15 assistants prepared a kind of super-promptbook—a record of Meyerhold's work on a production. Keeping everything clearly in his head, he staged scenes using improvisations.

Talking about his methods during a rehearsal of three Chekhov one-acts in 1935, Meyerhold described his use of *jeux de théâtre*, or theatre games.

> Two things are essential for a play's production. . . . First, we must find the thought of the author; then we must reveal that thought in a theatrical form. This form I call a *jeu de théâtre* and around it I shall build the performance. Molière was a master of *jeux de théâtre*: a central idea and the use of incidents, comments, mockery, jokes—anything to put it over. In this production I am going to use the technique of the traditional vaudeville as the *jeu*. Let me explain what it is to be. In these three plays of Chekhov I have found that there are thirty-eight times when characters

either faint, say they are going to faint, turn pale, clutch their hearts, or call for a glass of water, so I am going to take this idea of fainting and use it as a sort of leitmotif [a continuous theme] for the performance. Everything will contribute to this *jeu*.[6]

Meyerhold applied such terms as *constructivism* and *biomechanics* to his new methods of staging and actor training. *Constructivism*, a term taken from the visual arts, described Meyerhold's staging with platforms, scaffolds, slides, ladders, ramps, turning wheels, and trapezes. *Biomechanics* was Meyerhold's term for his new acting style. He trained actors in gymnastics, circus techniques, and ballet. He took his system from the facts of behaviorism, the observation that a particular pattern of muscular activity elicited certain emotions. "The bio-mechanical actor says, 'I make these movements because I know that, by making them, what I want to do can most easily and directly be done . . .' A tiger springs not in answer to its emotions but because it instinctively knows that its spring will bring it at once to its prey!"[7]

In short, Meyerhold replaced Stanislavsky's emphasis on inner motivation with an emphasis on response. The Meyerhold actor plummeted down slides or swung on trapezes on an open stage instead of sitting in drawing rooms, holding teacups and talking in quiet tones.

Meyerhold's most famous production was of Nikolai Gogol's *The Inspector General* presented in 1926. Meyerhold transferred Gogol's scene from a provincial town to a large city more like the capital St. Petersburg. He based costumes and properties on stylized nineteenth-century motifs, accompanied the action by period music, and used a few tables and chairs on a stage without curtain or footlights. The setting was an open space surrounded by a high wooden wall with an arc of 11 double doors. Another 2 pairs of double doors was in front of the proscenium. He also used a small platform stage, which advanced toward the audience in full light, with actors and props placed upon it (Figure 10-2).

The most striking scene was one in which 11

VSEVELOD MEYERHOLD

Vsevelod Meyerhold (1874–c.1940), who became one of the major influences in twentieth-century experimental theatre, began as an actor in the original Moscow Art Theatre company. He eventually rejected Stanislavsky's psychological techniques (working from the inside out) and developed his system of actor training known as "biomechanics," approaching a part from the *outside* through mastery of physical skills and vocal techniques.

After his break with MAT, Meyerhold was appointed, in turn, director of the Imperial Opera, the Marinsky Theatre, and the Alexandrinsky Theatre. With the 1917 revolution, he became a political activist and was placed in charge of the Theatre Section of the new Commissariat of Education. In 1922 he acquired his own theatre (the Meyerhold Theatre), and continued to experiment with biomechanics and constructivist settings.

In the 1930s when socialist realism emerged as the official style of art, Meyerhold's eclectic productions were criticized. He defended his point of view and was arrested. All traces of his name and work were removed from the Soviet theatre. He died probably in 1940. In 1956, after the Stalinist era, he was hailed posthumously as a brilliant exponent of the director's art.

government officials emerged simultaneously from each of 11 doors to offer the inspector a bribe. The effect presented bribery (political corruption) as a way of life in czarist Russia. As the 11 doors opened simultaneously with a crack and 11 hands could be seen holding out 11 white packages, the effect suggested that all czarist Russia was one large "bribe machine."

To compound the statement at the play's end after the corrupt townspeople learn that they have been duped by the false inspector, they left the stage with shrieks and wails of horror in a kind of medieval Dance of Death. A white curtain rose slowly upward out of the orchestra pit with the words spelled out: "A government inspector, appointed by imperial decree, has arrived from St. Petersburg. He is waiting at the inn and requires your presence there immediately." After the curtain disappeared, fully clothed, life-sized dummies, each a replica of a character in the play, formed a half-circle on the empty stage. They made a spectacle of grotesque effigies facing the audience, illuminated by the auditorium lights. This famous Meyerhold production strongly influenced other modern directors intent upon creating "the theatre theatrical."

Other Russian directors, such as Nikolai Evreinov (1879–1953), Alexander Tairov (1885–1950), Yevgeny Vakhtangov (1883–1922), and Nikolai Okhlopkov (1900–1966), either continued Stanislavsky's experiments or, like Meyerhold, struck out on their own with new theatrical styles. Despite the restrictions of the Soviet government on the arts, theatre has remained central to Russian society as a medium of ideas and as a showcase of its cultural achievements.

SYMBOLISM

While we tend to associate the Moscow Art Theatre almost solely with production styles and writers of stage realism and naturalism, Stanislavsky was also open to the new staging ideas of the young Meyerhold and to the reactions against realism that went under the name of *symbolism*.

Symbolism, the first important European revolt against realism, emerged in the 1880s in France and lasted less than two decades. But it has had subtle, far-reaching effects on playwrights, many of them followers of Sigmund Freud (1856–1939), who were interested in suppressed feelings, states of mind, and the unconscious. The symbolists held that truth was to be understood intuitively and not supplied by the five senses or by rational thought. Dialogue and action were relegated to positions of unimportance by the symbolist writers. They avoided social problems and precise details of physical

---

The Inspector General

The mayor of a provincial Russian town receives news that an inspector general is traveling incognito from St. Petersburg to inspect his administration. The mayor calls a meeting of his officials to decide what to do. The news terrifies them for they are petty, corrupt officials. Coincidentally, Khlestakov, a young government clerk who has spent all his money on cards, clothes, and women, arrives in town and lodges at the local inn. In their fright and paranoia, the town officials assume that Khlestakov must be the inspector in disguise. They present themselves to him.

Taking advantage of their mistake, Khlestakov moves into the mayor's house and accepts bribes from both the town council and the local merchants who come to complain about the officials. He even courts the mayor's willing wife and proposes to his daughter. Finally, tiring of the deception, Khlestakov hires the town's best coach and horses to take him on his way, promising to return the next day to claim his bride. Meanwhile, the local postmaster has opened a letter Khlestakov has written describing his adventures in the town. At a prewedding gathering the postmaster reveals the swindle. As recriminations begin to fly, a policeman enters to announce the arrival of the real inspector and to summon everyone to appear before him.

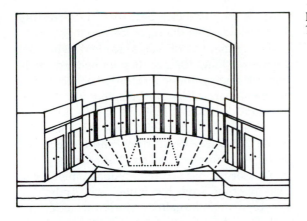

Figure 10-2 Meyerhold's drawing of the basic set for *The Inspector General.*

Figure 10-3 Gogol's *The Inspector General* staged by Meyerhold at the Meyerhold Theatre, Moscow, 1926.

environment. Instead, truth was expressed indirectly through symbols that evoked feelings and states of mind. Believing that truth lay in intuition, feelings, and the unconscious, their dramas tended to be static, mysterious, and ambiguous, and production styles had to change accordingly to encompass mood and mystery.

It is interesting that the plays most closely associated with the symbolist movement are written by many of the pioneers of stage realism. Ibsen's *The Wild Duck* and *When We Dead Awaken* fall into this category. So do Hauptmann's *The Assumption of Hannele* and Strindberg's chamber plays. But the most famous symbolist playwright was Maurice Maeterlinck (1862–1949) whose important work was written for the French theatre in the 1890s and later produced by Stanislavsky. *Pelléas and Mélisande*

(1892) is Maeterlinck's best play and probably the best symbolist drama of its time.

Few pioneers of stage realism remained purists for long. Rather, they embedded many symbols and symbolic meanings in their realistic dramas, and these symbols, like Ibsen's wild duck and the pistols in *Hedda Gabler*, keep the plays alive today. The wild duck symbolizes all of the play's fragile creatures who instinctively destroy themselves when hounded by the hunters of this world, and Hedda Gabler's pistols, inherited from her father, are symbols of her repressed sexuality. Moreover, both the realists and the antirealists (the Stanislavskys and the Meyerholds) found common ground and shared common interests with the symbolists in their quest to stage universal truths.

OFFSHOOTS IN AMERICA

Almost since its beginnings, the American theatre has had its proponents of stage realism. A production of *Ben Hur* (1899), adapted from a novel by General Lew Wallace, called for, among other things, a scene on board a Roman galley engaged in a battle. The ship is destroyed and the hero—one of the galley slaves—is thrown into the sea and saves himself by climbing onto a raft.

Like the modern film version, the play climaxed with a chariot race with eight horses galloping madly on eight treadmills so they seemed to be racing neck and neck into the audience. A moving diorama in the background added to the sensation of speed and motion.

This kind of spectacular stage realism has always been part of our theatrical tradition, ranging from *Ben Hur* to the modern musical *Sweeney Todd* (1979). However, American actors and directors have excelled in their sensitive recreations of "life" on stage. And while there are always reactions against a carefully realized stage realism, it remains the staple of our Broadway, regional, and campus theatres. Associated with the development of American stage realism are two "groups" and a "method."

Figure 10-4 Harold Clurman (right) addresses members of the Group Theatre, New York, 1937.

The Group Theatre (1931–1941) During the summer of 1931, Lee Strasberg, Harold Clurman, and Cheryl Crawford brought together a group of actors and directors to start an actor-training workshop and a producing organization. They called themselves "the Group" (Figure 10-4). Living in several houses on property near Danbury, Connecticut, and rehearsing in a big barn, the Group Theatre's first production began under conditions very much like those of the Moscow Art Theatre.

Without question, the MAT was the Group's inspiration. During the ten years of their existence, the Group produced at least four major American plays and a number of minor ones. It also arrived at a distinct production style.

The Group Theatre foundered during the war years from a lack of good plays and from the exhausting effort to remain viable in an often hostile, commercial environment. But for 10 years it worked to make theatre an art, served by a technique that made it possible to create that art on stage.

Of its members, Harold Clurman, Robert Lewis, and Elia Kazan became Broadway directors; Cheryl Crawford became an independent producer; Clifford Odets, Paul Green, and William Saroyan became major playwrights; and Lee Strasberg became a leading acting teacher whose name is almost synonymous with The Actors Studio.

The Actors Studio (1947–   ) Located today at 432 West 44th Street in New York City, the Actors Studio and its famous method of acting are part of a tradition that has its roots in the explorations of Stanislavsky. Strasberg, with whom the Actors Studio is most closely identified, was not part of its beginnings. Elia Kazan, Harold Clurman, Cheryl Crawford, and Robert Lewis (all part of the Group Theatre) set about in 1947 to start another acting workshop. At first, Strasberg declined to join them. The workshop began with 26 actors in a beginner's class and with 52 in an advanced class. A playwright's unit and a production wing were soon added. Two years

The Cherry Orchard (1904): In an effort to help the actors create the play's inner life, Stanislavsky invented all sorts of details. He wrote: ". . . the singing of birds, the barking of dogs, and in this enthusiasm for sounds on the stage I went so far that I caused a protest on the part of Chekhov, who loved sounds on the stage himself." Chekhov remarked so Stanislavsky could overhear him: "How wonderful! We hear no birds, no dogs, no cuckoos, no owls, no clocks, no sleigh bells, no crickets."[9]

The famous curtain at the Moscow Art Theatre. The seagull is a sign of the importance of Chekhov's plays in the establishment of the theatre.

Actress Olga Knipper (Chekhov's wife) as Masha in *The Three Sisters,* first staged in 1901 at the Moscow Art Theatre.

Hamlet at the Moscow Art Theatre, 1911, with scenery by Edward Gordon Craig. In designing *Hamlet* for MAT, Craig tried out his theories of using large movable screens that could be quickly arranged to transform the setting without closing the front curtain. This setting shows Craig's efforts to create a single setting with mobile parts so that scene changes would not disturb the stage space as a whole.

Lee Strasberg (1901–1982), one of the best-known acting teachers in America, transformed Stanislavsky's system of acting into an American "method." His main emphasis was on the actor's creation of true emotion by way of improvisation and exercises in emotional recall.

Born in the Galician village of Budzanow, now part of the USSR, Strasberg came to America at age seven. When he arrived in New York he spoke only Yiddish. He began as an actor in amateur Yiddish productions on Manhattan's Lower East Side and soon joined the Students of Art and Drama, a group of amateurs who gathered socially at the Chrystie Street Settlement. It was there he met his wife, Nora Z. Krecaun; they married in 1926 and had one daughter, Susan Strasberg.

Having dropped out of high school in 1918 to support his family, Strasberg spent a lifetime reading books on theatre and acting. He studied acting at the American Laboratory Theatre, founded by Russian emigré actors Richard Boleslavsky and Maria Ouspenskaya, both trained in the Stanislavsky system. Strasberg also began directing there. He worked with the Theatre Guild before cofounding the Group Theatre in 1931. In the later 1930s Strasberg directed Broadway plays and spent the 1940s in Hollywood learning the film business. He returned to New York in 1947 where for the rest of his life he devoted himself to training actors. His teaching methods have been recognized as his greatest contribution to the American theatre.

Strasberg appeared in films, *The Godfather II* and *Going in Style*. He wrote articles on acting and introductions to books, his most famous being the entry on "Acting" in *Encyclopaedia Britannica* (beginning with the 14th edition printed in 1957 and in subsequent editions) and his analysis of acting in *Strasberg at The Actors Studio* (1965).

---

later, Strasberg conducted his first class at the Studio and in 1951 assumed its leadership.

The Actors Studio has had a controversial history. It has become almost synonymous with "method acting" and with names like Marlon Brando, James Dean, Karl Malden, Geraldine Page, Al Pacino, Maureen Stapleton, Julie Harris, and Dustin Hoffman. Even though the Studio has undertaken productions from time to time, it was Strasberg's consistent policy that the Studio was a *workshop for actors*. Almost single-handedly, he became the consistent interpreter of Stanislavsky's system among American actors.

DRAMATIC CONVENTIONS

Realism as a conscious writing and production style emerged in Europe in the 1850s. It first developed in France and was perhaps most fully expressed in Russia in the masterpieces of Tolstoy, Turgenev, and Dostoevsky. Simply defined, *realism* is writing in which the natural world is candidly and objectively presented. As the writer becomes increasingly concerned with objectivity, special techniques are needed for its representation.

THE WELL-MADE PLAY

Between 1850 and 1880 French playwrights with their leader Eugène Scribe (1791–1861) devised the "well-made" play, which dealt with details of contemporary life—usually unpleasant ones. In his 400-odd plays Scribe worked out a successful play structure that was adopted by the new realistic school of writers, including Emile Zola and Henrik Ibsen.

For a play to be considered well-made, it had to have the following: clear exposition of the situation; careful preparation of events; unexpected but logical reversals; continuous and mounting suspense; an obligatory scene explaining the writer's social and moral viewpoints; and a logical resolution. While this structure is as old as Sophocles' *Oedipus the King,* Scribe added to it a highly dramatic situation in which character and meaning were sacrificed to suspense and thrilling climaxes to produce a workable formula. Nevertheless, the well-made play was easily adapted by the realists to contemporary social problems and to subjects of poverty, prostitution, venereal disease, divorce, illegitimate children, harsh working conditions, and white-collar crime.

CHEKHOV'S "NEW" DRAMATURGY

Anton Chekhov wrote plays that described the lives of "quiet desperation" of ordinary people in rural Russia around the turn of the century. Chekhov's characters—provincial gentry, writers, professors, doctors, farmers, servants, teachers, government officials, and garrisoned military—go about their daily existence eating, drinking, falling in and out of love, playing cards and billiards. Chekhov avoided the "big" moments expected in the theatre by nineteenth-century audiences and promoted by the well-made play. If there are murders or suicides, they take place offstage. The fabric of the Chekhov play is the daily humdrum of unspectacular lives, and its dramatic action is contained within inconsequential acts.

ANTON CHEKHOV

Anton Pavlovich Chekhov (1860–1904) was born in southern Russia and studied medicine at Moscow University. During his student years he wrote short stories to earn money. He began his playwriting career in the 1880s with one-act farces, *The Marriage Proposal* and *The Bear. Ivanov* (1887) was his first full-length play to be produced.

Chekhov redefined stage realism during the years of his association with the Moscow Art Theatre (1898–1904). The meaning of his plays is not in direct, purposive action, but in the truth of the representation of a certain kind of rural Russian life, which he knew first hand. Stanislavsky's style of interpreting the inner truth of Chekhov's characters and the mood of his plays resulted in one of the great theatrical collaborations.

During his last years Chekhov lived in Yalta, where he had gone for his health, and made occasional trips to Moscow to participate in the productions. He died of tuberculosis in a German spa in 1904, soon after the premiere of *The Cherry Orchard*, and was buried in Moscow.

During his short life Chekhov wrote four masterpieces of modern stage realism: *The Seagull, Uncle Vanya, The Three Sisters,* and *The Cherry Orchard.*

Chekhov's comedies deal with ordinary human survival. For example, the Chekhov discovery scene is unlike, say, Othello's discovery that he has been the dupe of Iago and murdered an innocent wife. Instead, Chekhov's characters "discover" that life has passed them by. "Where has it all gone?" is their anguished cry.

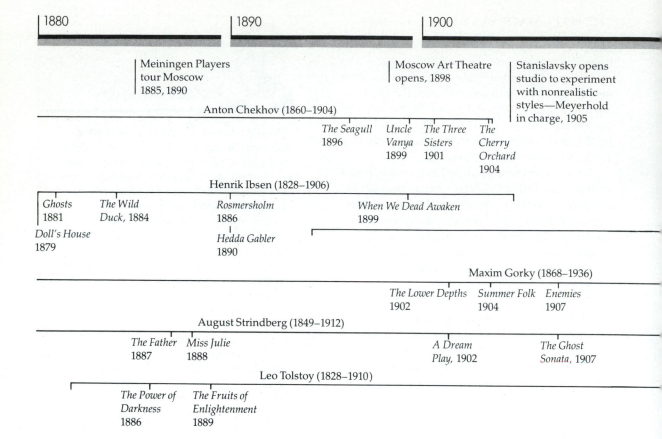

1880	1890	1900

Meiningen Players
tour Moscow
1885, 1890

Moscow Art Theatre
opens, 1898

Stanislavsky opens
studio to experiment
with nonrealistic
styles—Meyerhold
in charge, 1905

Anton Chekhov (1860–1904)

| *The Seagull* 1896 | *Uncle Vanya* 1899 | *The Three Sisters* 1901 | *The Cherry Orchard* 1904 |

Henrik Ibsen (1828–1906)

| *Ghosts* 1881 | *The Wild Duck,* 1884 | *Rosmersholm* 1886 | *When We Dead Awaken* 1899 |

Doll's House 1879

Hedda Gabler 1890

Maxim Gorky (1868–1936)

| *The Lower Depths* 1902 | *Summer Folk* 1904 | *Enemies* 1907 |

August Strindberg (1849–1912)

| *The Father* 1887 | *Miss Julie* 1888 | *A Dream Play,* 1902 | *The Ghost Sonata,* 1907 |

Leo Tolstoy (1828–1910)

| *The Power of Darkness* 1886 | *The Fruits of Enlightenment* 1889 |

Chekhov's Realism When Chekhov was asked about the meaning of life, he replied:

> You ask what is life? It is the same as asking what is a carrot. A carrot is a carrot, and that's all that's known.[10]

To show the truth of human experience, as he saw it, a different kind of dramaturgy was required and a new production style. "After all," Chekhov wrote, "in real life, people don't spend every moment in shooting one another, hanging themselves, or making declarations of love. They do not spend all their time saying clever things. They are more occupied with eating, drinking, flirting, and saying stupidities, and these are the things which ought to be shown on the stage. . . . People eat their dinner, just eat their dinner, and all the time their happiness is taking form, or their lives are being destroyed."[11]

In the 1890s Chekhov's type of dramaturgy was unexpected and even puzzling. He dispensed with cause-and-effect plotting where life's pressures build up to large climaxes with onstage murders, duels, suicides, and the like. He built his plays around the lives of a group rather than an individual and around a condition—the indolence, boredom, and social amenities of provincial Russia during his lifetime. In keeping with his sense of realism, Chekhov often suspended the action at the end of the play rather than resolving it. The three sisters watch the army march away. Firs, the old family retainer in *The Cherry Orchard*, has been forgotten and left behind by the departing family. He lies down in the parlor as in the distance are heard sounds of a breaking string and axes in the distance chopping down the orchard.

MAT produces
Hamlet with
scenery by
Gordon Craig
1912

Russian
Revolution
1917

Stanislavsky's
My Life in Art
published, 1924

World
War II
1939–
1945

World War I
1914–1918

Vladimir Mayakovsky (1894–1930)

Mystery- Bouffe
1918

The Bedbug
1929

The Bathhouse
1930

Redemption
1900

To the seemingly aimless dialogue, often spoken at cross-purposes, Chekhov added the nonverbal symbol. The seagull and the cherry orchard are not entirely abstractions; they can be seen, heard, and even felt by the characters. They are part of the characters' lives—of their external reality. The dead seagull is both itself and a symbol of nature's creatures, including human beings, who are victimized from time to time by callous, unthinking people.

Chekhov's Mood Much has been written of the mood of a Chekhov play. He achieved tragicomic effects which in the hands of a lesser playwright might have led to the tragic or the melodramatic. "Why do you always wear black?" asks Medvedenko of Masha at the very beginning of *The Seagull*. But the reference to the black dress is not, as one might think, a sym-

bolic introduction to a tragic theme, as it is in *Hamlet*, for instance. Masha's reply ("I am in mourning for my life. I am unhappy.") at once reveals to us the mood in which we are to accept the following scenes. This encounter is serious, but somehow not tragic. The two start

> **"** A play ought to be written in which the people should come and go, dine, talk of the weather, or play cards, not because the author wants it but because that is what happens in real life. Life on the stage should be as it really is and the people too should be as they are and not stilted. **"**
>
> Anton Chekhov[12]

Madame Arkadina, a successful but aging actress, visits the country estate of her brother Sorin; she is accompanied by her lover, the celebrated novelist Trigorin. Her son, Konstantin, wanting to impress his mother, stages a symbolist drama he has written to star his sweetheart Nina. His mother's careless remarks during the production cause him to stop the play.

Dazzled by Trigorin's fame and sophistication, Nina rejects Konstantin. To symbolize his feelings Konstantin kills a seagull and lays it at her feet, indicating his readiness to commit suicide. As Madame Arkadina abruptly decides to end her stay in the country, Nina declares her love for Trigorin and tells him that she is going to Moscow to become an actress. He arranges to meet her.

Two years later Madame Arkadina and Trigorin are once again at the Sorin estate. Konstantin, now a published writer, feels his life blighted by the loss of Nina who has become an actress in a provincial company. Nina slips into Konstantin's study and, almost incoherently, tells him of her hard life and of her struggle to become a great actress. She repeatedly refers to herself as a seagull. He begs her to stay but she still loves Trigorin. After she leaves, Konstantin tears up his manuscripts and leaves the stage.

In the next room, unaware of what is happening, Madame Arkadina plays cards with her friends. They hear a pistol shot. The family doctor goes to investigate; he returns and, away from Arkadina, quietly announces Konstantin's suicide.

to argue over which one is the more miserable, while each is intent wholly on his or her own thoughts. The mood evoked is ironically comic.

Medvedenko Why? [*hesitatingly*] I don't understand. . . . You're in good health; perhaps your father isn't very rich, but he's got enough. My life's very much harder than yours. I get twenty-three roubles a month in all, and from that a deduction's made for pension, and yet I don't go about in mourning.

[*They sit down.*]

Masha It isn't a question of money. Even a beggar can be happy.

Medvedenko In theory, yes, but in practice it's like this: I, and my mother and my two sisters and my little brother—with a total income of twenty-three roubles. I suppose we must eat and drink, mustn't we? I suppose we must have some tea and sugar? And tobacco? There's the rub.

Masha [*glancing at the platform*] The play will begin soon.

Medvedenko Yes, Miss Zarechni will act, and the play is by Konstantin Gavrilovich. They're in love with each other, and to-day their souls will unite in the effort to present one and the same artistic image. But my soul and yours do not have any common point of contact. I love you; I'm so miserable I can't stay at home; every day I walk six miles here and six back again, and from you I get only indifference. That, of course, is to be understood. I am without means, I've a big family on my hands. . . . What inducement is there to marry a man who hasn't enough to live on?

Masha Nonsense. [*Takes a pinch of snuff.*] Your love touches me, but I can't return it, that's all. [*Offers him her snuff-box.*] Have some?

Medvedenko I don't want any.

(I)[13]

REPRESENTATIVE PLAY

The Three Sisters

First produced at the Moscow Art Theatre on January 31, 1901, with Olga Knipper as Masha, Stanislavsky as Colonel Vershinin, and Vsevelod Meyerhold as Baron Tusenbach

BACKGROUND

The Three Sisters, the most frequently revived of Chekhov's major plays, was Chekhov's first play written specifically for the Moscow Art Theatre and with definite actors in mind.

After the success of *The Seagull*, Nemirovich-Danchenko urged Chekhov to write a new play for the still struggling theatre. Despite increasingly poor health, Chekhov finished the play by October of 1900. The first version was

---

The Three Sisters

In a garrison town in rural Russia, the cultured Prozorov sisters think longingly of the excitement of Moscow, which they left 11 years ago. Olga, the oldest, is constantly exhausted by her work as a school teacher; Masha, married at 18 to a man she considered an intellectual giant, bitterly realizes that he is merely a pedant; Irina, the youngest, dreams of a romantic future and rejects the sincere love of Lieutenant Tusenbach and the advances of Captain Solyony. Their brother, Andrey, an unambitious man, courts Natasha, the daughter of a local family. Into this circle comes Lieutenant Colonel Vershinin. He is the father of two daughters and, like Masha, is unhappily married. They are immediately attracted to one another.

The Prozorovs and their friends recognize the frustration of their lives, but hope in some vague future keeps their spirits high. For the sisters it is a dream of returning someday to Moscow. The atmosphere changes when Andrey marries Natasha. The sisters' immediate prospects of returning to Moscow are dashed. Irina tries to find relief in her job in the telegraph office. Natasha takes control of the household and as time goes on the sisters are moved about in the house to make room for her two children. Andrey takes refuge in gambling and mortgages the house that he and his sisters own jointly.

News that the garrison is to be transferred brings depressing prospects for the future. Irina decides to marry Tusenbach, an unattractive but gentle man, who resigns his army commission in the hope of finding more meaningful work. As Masha and Vershinin, who have become open lovers, bid each other goodby and the regiment prepares to leave, word comes that Tusenbach has been killed by Solyony in a duel over Irina. The sisters cling to one another for consolation. As the military band strikes up, the gaiety of the music inspires them to hope that there is a new life in store for them in another "millennium."

read to the company in Moscow, and Chekhov saw some early rehearsals. While *The Three Sisters* was coolly received on its first night, it has since become the longest-running play in Russian theatrical history.

THE SCENE

The story of *The Three Sisters* tells of the provincial lives of the Prozorov family made up of three sisters (Olga, Masha, and Irina), their brother (Andrey), and his wife (Natasha), their lovers, a brother-in-law, and military friends. All the action occurs in and around the Prozorov home. Act I takes place in their large first-floor drawing room, which is flooded with sunlight (Figure 10-5). This room with the dining room upstage suggests comfort and style, even though it is slightly shabby. By including essentially three areas in the first-act setting (the drawing room, dining room, and window to the outdoors), Chekhov symbolically expanded the frame of the proscenium arch without disturbing the realistic details within it. The divided set draws the eye into the first room and then into the dining room where we hear male voices around the table raised in laughter.

In Act III the scene is Olga's room, which she shares now with Irina at Natasha's insistence (Figure 10-6). Curtains have been hung to provide some privacy, but the limited space and cluttered beds suggest the physical and emotional discomfort to which the sisters have been reduced. As we move from the spacious drawing room to Olga's cramped quarters, we have a visual impression of the process of dispossession that is under way. Life is closing in on the sisters.

In the final act (IV) the scene, for the first time, is set outdoors. Birch trees are on one side of the house, and on the other side is a veranda. The sisters are trapped in their provincial world while a wider world mockingly beckons to them. The military band plays cheerful tunes in the distance and people pass upstage on different destinations. Constant movement, shouts of farewell, and the bustle of the midday departure animate the scene until the regiment has gone.

THE TRAGICOMIC ACTION

The play's only action in the traditional sense consists in showing the departure of a military regiment from a small provincial town after an interval of three and a half years. Each of the three sisters is a fully drawn individual with her own special longing to go home to Moscow. We know that their picture of Moscow is unreal. What holds our interest is the increasing remoteness of the wish. As the sisters fail to make an active protest about the quality of their lives, we become aware of their limitations. In this static situation we see a pattern of happiness, hope, and despair. For four acts the sisters dream of escape from their routine, but, unlike the regiment, they are unable to move on. Irina has acquiesced to a colorless life with Baron Tusenbach, but he is killed. Masha has pursued an illicit affair with Vershinin, but he moves on with his wife, children, and regiment. Olga has no officer and no hope of marriage. Thus at the play's end the regiment departs and the sisters are further isolated with their broken dreams.

While Chekhov called *The Seagull* and *The Cherry Orchard* comedies, he labeled *The Three Sisters* "a Drama in Four Acts." As we scrutinize the seriocomic quality of the play, a theme emerges: *the value of living in the face of social change.* The play is not prophetic of a new society, as Soviet authorities have tried to make it, but, rather, is critical of the old one. The three sisters are emotionally adrift in a society whose forms supply avenues of change for the military, the upstart, and the entrepreneur. Unable to take advantage of these forms, the weak and ineffectual are locked into a way of life that is neither emotionally nor intellectually rewarding. The most one can do is endure the stultifying marriage, the job routine, and the tyrannical sister-in-law.

Figure 10-5 *Three Sisters*, Act I, at the Moscow Art Theatre, 1901.

Figure 10-6 *Three Sisters*, Act III, at the Moscow Art Theatre, 1901.

CHARACTER

Of an earlier story Chekhov wrote: "The artist must not be the judge of his characters or of what they say, but only an objective observer."[14] This moral objectivity on Chekhov's part colors his portrait of the Prozorov family. The characters of the three sisters and their brother are carefully drawn with details of gesture and dress as well as speech. Andrey's lonely violin playing reminds us of his failed ambition to be a university professor. Masha's black dress underscores her sense of loss; her disillusioned love for her teacher-husband is akin to her equally unsatisfactory love for the self-centered Colonel Vershinin. Natasha's scrubbed cheeks and inappropriate pink dress with a green sash in the first act emphasize the social differences between the Prozorovs and herself.

The villain in the play is the unseen Protopopov, the wealthy merchant who steals Natasha from her husband, controls Andrey's work with the town council, and eventually buys the sisters' house, dispossessing them. Solyony, who shoots Irina's fiancé offstage, is awkward, quick-tempered, and jealous, but he is also a misfit. Natasha is single-minded in her social climbing; she is unfaithful to her husband and capable of petty cruelties to her in-laws. Her narrowness of spirit makes her the most satirically comic character in the play.

LANGUAGE

Chekhov's language exposes the vital, inner life of the group. Characters talk to each other; sometimes they listen and sometimes they do not. The dialogue is best described as *oblique*; it does not develop toward explosive moments but peels back layers of social forms to expose the characters' inner lives: their loneliness, anger, fears, disappointments, happiness, and boredom. The silences are as poignant and meaningful as the social chatter. For instance, Masha, the only married sister, is seen in Act I sitting apart, dressed in black, reading fiction. Her silence hints, more than words would, of her mood of deep-seated discontent. Feeling trapped as the wife of a provincial school teacher, she reads fiction as her only possible escape.

Much has been written about how Chekhov's characters resort to work as a panacea for the emptiness of their lives. *The Three Sisters* ends on a similar note. As they hold on to each other for strength and consolation, the sisters talk about how they propose to get through the rest of their lives. Irina will teach school and work for others; Olga talks about the future when others will live in happiness and peace; and Masha, with no prescription for the future, says only that "we've got to live."

CHEKHOV'S MODERNISM

Chekhov's modernism lies in the way in which he exposes the lives and feelings of ordinary people, not by using aristocrats, traditional plots, and stage business, but by building up the details of everyday existence. In Chekhov's view the suicides, duels, and infidelities that make up conventional plays are peripheral to the hard often dull business of day-to-day living. In Chekhov's dramaturgy, we experience the stultifying lives of teachers, postal clerks, husbands and wives as they live out their unremarkable lives. Chekhov antedates the existential and absurdist writers of the mid-twentieth century in his concern for the routine and habitual quality of the human condition.

ESSAY

Chekhov's plays offer a special challenge to the modern actor; that is, to become part of an ensemble that creates an illusion of intimate relationships. Actors and directors have responded to the Chekhov texts as creating the greatest realism of mood and spirit of any plays in the last

100 years. To play Chekhov in their own theatre with Lee Strasberg as director was the great dream of the members of the Actors Studio since its beginning in 1947. Our performance essay describes that challenge and its outcome in the Broadway theatre of the 1960s.

Chekhov in Modern Performance

Chekhov's *The Three Sisters*, produced by the Actors Studio Theatre and directed by Lee Strasberg, at the Morosco Theatre, New York City, on June 22, 1964

The Actors Studio Theatre, formed in 1962, aspired to high ideals, but the Theatre—the Studio's production wing—floundered and died after one and a half seasons. At first it seemed the fulfillment of the Studio members' dreams, which were to show in performance their ideals of ensemble acting, to be of service to the American playwright, and to develop a producing organization of artistic merit. David Garfield, in his recent history of the Actors Studio, wrote that the Studio's theatre wing was victim to poor planning, bad luck, and to several ill-conceived artistic decisions.[15]

The theatre was started on the enthusiasm of its members without a clear plan for its organization and operation. The Studio's production board with Strasberg as artistic director took a long time to select the first season of plays. In one incident the board missed out entirely on producing a new script, Edward Albee's *Who's Afraid of Virginia Woolf?*, which became the hit of the 1962 New York season. The board finally agreed to a list of five plays: Eugene O'Neill's *Strange Interlude*, June Havoc's *Marathon '33*, Arnold Weinstein and William Bolcom's musical *Dynamite Tonight*, James Costigan's *Baby Want a Kiss*, and Chekhov's *The Three Sisters*. The latter was to be directed by Lee Strasberg.

At the outset casting problems arose. Geraldine Page wanted to play Natasha, but Strasberg cast her as Olga, the eldest sister. Barbara Baxley was cast as Natasha, the sister-in-law. All along

Strasberg had intended Kim Stanley to play the part of Masha. Susan Strasberg was announced to play Irina, but she withdrew and Shirley Knight assumed the role. For Vershinin, the romantic lead, Strasberg wanted Marlon Brando, but he refused, saying that he was just too nervous to return to the stage. Instead, Kevin McCarthy played Vershinin. Strasberg also invited certain nonstudio actors to participate in the production. These included Tamara Daykarhanova (a former MAT actress), who played Anfisa and served as consultant on Russian customs and dress, and Luther Adler, a former member of the Group Theatre, who was cast as the doctor.

Following a turbulent rehearsal period, the play opened on June 22, 1964, at the Morosco Theatre on Broadway. *New York Times* critic Brooks Atkinson called it "a tender, spontaneous, truthful performance [which captured] the grace of Chekhov's compassionate spirit."[16] Taking a cue from the MAT production, the setting was heavily detailed; offstage sounds, such as a baby's cry, and window curtains moving with a gentle breeze established the play's milieu. The first act was a deliberate effort to show the good nature, the kindness, and the jollity of Chekhov's people, conventionally thought of as steeped in gloom. Some scenes were blatantly casual, so much so that relationships were passed over, concealed, or taken for granted.

All agreed on the outstanding quality of Kim Stanley's performance. As Masha she was closest to the play's center. From the opening scene, where she lay on a couch without speaking, she dominated the stage in her silences as in her speeches. Some pointed out that the sheer brilliance of her portrayal tended to disturb the balance of the play. Some of her fellow actors felt that she was a little too dramatic and a little too strong. Reportedly she agreed, saying that "her Masha *would* have gone to Moscow!"[17]

Because of the critical raves for Kim Stanley's performance, audiences were drawn to *The Three Sisters*. It ran for 119 performances and

Figure 10-7 *The Three Sisters*, with Kim Stanley (standing) as Masha, Shirley Knight (left) as Irina, and Geraldine Page as Olga in the Actors Studio Theatre production, Broadway's Morosco Theatre, 1964.

closed soon after Stanley became ill and withdrew from the cast.

The failure of the Studio's theatre after one and a half seasons points up an interesting paradox in the American theatre. American actors have excelled in portraying psychological realism associated with Stanislavsky and "the method." Three stunning examples are Marlon Brando's performance in *A Streetcar Named Desire* (1947), Kim Stanley's in *The Three Sisters* (1964), and Al Pacino's in *American Buffalo*

(1981). All three are quintessential method actors. The practice of the method, though, requires long hours of intensive rehearsals, and our commercial theatre is geared to the financial pressures of short rehearsal periods and the hit-or-miss syndrome. The two are difficult to reconcile. The success of the Actors Studio, under Lee Strasberg's directorship, was in creating workshop conditions where actors could hone their skills apart from the pressures of the commercial theatre.

SUMMARY

Social and psychological realism in the modern theatre had its beginnings in the work of late nineteenth-century theatrical companies and playwrights. The early generation of nineteenth-century Russian playwrights—Gogol, Ostrovsky, and Turgenev—laid the groundwork for the celebrated realists Chekhov, Tolstoy, and Gorky.

In 1897 the young Constantin Stanislavsky and Vladimir Nemirovich-Danchenko planned the Moscow Art Theatre as a theatre that would place the truth of human feelings and experiences on stage. In their first season of 1898 they produced plays by Tolstoy and Shakespeare, but it was a new play, *The Seagull*, by a new playwright, Anton Chekhov, that established the originality of both the author and the company. Stanislavsky's unique approach to production complemented the new dramaturgy of Ibsen, Chekhov, Maeterlinck, Hauptmann, Gorky, and others. His company also attracted some of the major acting talent of the day in Olga Knipper, Ivan Moskvin, Vassily Kachalov, Alla Nazimova, Richard Boleslavsky, and in Stanislavsky himself.

Stanislavsky also made room for experiments in open staging by Vsevelod Meyerhold. Consequently, the Moscow Art Theatre reflects two main styles in the modern theatre: one toward stage realism and the other toward open theatricality. In terms of playwriting Stanislavsky advocated the new realistic dramaturgy of Chekhov along with the symbolism of such European writers as Maurice Maeterlinck.

We have attempted to assess here the tremendous influence of the Moscow Art Theatre both as a production company and as an environment for developing new methods of actor-training and staging. The ensemble style of performing complemented Chekhov's dramaturgy that relied on group dynamics, intimate scenes, and conversations that attempted to conceal feelings rather than to expose them for all to hear.

The modern American theatre shares its roots with the Moscow Art Theatre not only in the many revivals of Chekhov's plays on campuses and in regional theatres, but also in two institutions that are an integral part of our theatrical history. The Group Theatre in the 1930s and The Actors Studio (founded in 1947) are associated with the American "method" of acting best exemplified in performances by many fine stage and film actors. Moreover, the importance of Stanislavsky and the Moscow Art Theatre is still being assessed by acting teachers, historians, and theorists the world over.

Chekhov's *The Three Sisters*, our representative play, is the one most frequently revived in European and American theatres. It exemplifies those techniques spoken of as uniquely *Chekhovian*: the avoidance of traditional plots and stage business, oblique dialogue, and the unveiling of the humdrum lives and universal feelings of ordinary people. In the Actors Studio Theatre 1964 production of *The Three Sisters*, director Lee Strasberg and his Studio actors attempted to bring their workshop methods and Stanislavsky-based techniques into the Broadway theatre. This production demonstrates how closely our theatre is tied to the work of the Moscow Art Theatre, Constantin Stanislavsky, and Anton Chekhov.

PLAYS TO READ

The Inspector General by Nikolai Gogol

The Three Sisters by Anton Chekhov

The Lower Depths by Maxim Gorky

SOURCES

There are several paperback editions of Anton Chekhov's major plays:

Plays. Translated by Elisaveta Fen. New York: Penguin, 1959. This edition, which contains an introduction by the translator, includes *Ivanov*, *The Seagull*, *Uncle Vanya*, *The Three Sisters*, *The Cherry Orchard*, *The Bear*, *The Marriage Proposal*, and *Jubilee*.

Anton Chekhov: Four Plays. Translated by David Magarshack. New York: Hill and Wang, 1969. The volume includes *The Seagull, Uncle Vanya, The Three Sisters*, and *The Cherry Orchard*. The introduction is by Magarshack, one of the principal translators and biographers in English of Chekhov.

Chekhov, The Major Plays. Translated by Ann Dunnigan. New York: New American Library, 1964. This inexpensive Signet Classics edition includes *Ivanov, The Seagull, Uncle Vanya, The Three Sisters*, and *The Cherry Orchard*.

Chekhov. Translated by Ronald Hingley. New York: Oxford University Press, 1968. Contains *Ivanov, The Seagull*, and *The Three Sisters* without introduction or notes. It is compiled from *The Oxford Chekhov*, edited by Ronald Hingley.

Gogol, Nikolai V. *The Government Inspector*. Adapted by Peter Raby. Edited by Michael Langham. Minneapolis: University of Minnesota Press, 1972. Paperback. This edition was prepared in response to a commission by director Michael Langham for the 1967 production at the Stratford National Theatre, Canada. It includes Langham's director's introduction to his 1973 staging of the script at The Guthrie Theatre where he was then artistic director. Also, *The Inspector General*. Translated by Andrew Mac-Andrew. New York: Avon Books, 1976. Paperback. The introduction is by the general editor, Henry Popkin.

Gorky, Maxim. *The Lower Depths and Other Plays*. Translated by Alexander Bakshy with Paul S. Nathan. New Haven: Yale University Press, 1959. Paperback. This edition includes *The Lower Depths, Enemies*, and *The Zykovs* plus a fine essay by Bakshy on "The Theater of Maxim Gorky." Each of the three plays is prefaced with a short essay giving the play's stage history and its social and political background.

NOTES

1. Norris Houghton, *Moscow Rehearsals: An Account of Methods of Production in the Soviet Theatre* (New York: Harcourt Brace, 1936), p. 57. Reprinted by permission of Norris Houghton.

2. Constantin Stanislavsky, *My Life in Art* (New York: Theatre Arts Books, 1952), pp. 318–319. Copyright 1924 by Little, Brown and Company. Copyright 1948 Elizabeth Reynolds Hapgood. Copyright renewed 1952. Reprinted by permission of the publisher, Theatre Arts Books.

3. Stanislavsky, pp. 358–359. Reprinted by permission.

4. Stanislavsky, p. 359.

5. *Directors on Directing: A Source Book of the Modern Theatre*, edited by Toby Cole and Helen Krich Chinoy (Indianapolis: Bobbs-Merrill, 1976), p. 36.

6. Cole and Chinoy, pp. 54–55. Reprinted by permission.

7. Houghton, p. 94.

8. Maurice Maeterlinck, "The Tragical in Daily Life," in *Playwrights on Playwriting*, ed. Toby Cole (New York: Hill and Wang, 1960), pp. 32-34.

9. Stanislavsky, p. 420. Reprinted by permission.

10. Anton Chekhov, *Letters of Anton Chekhov*, ed. Avrahm Yarmolinski (New York: Viking Press, 1973), p. 169.

11. See Maurice Valency, *The Breaking String: The Plays of Anton Chekhov* (New York: Oxford University Press, 1966), p.249. Reprinted by permission of Maurice Valency.

12. David Magarshack, *Chekhov the Dramatist* (New York: Auvergne, 1952), p. 84.

13. Anton Chekhov, *The Seagull*, 1896. From *Plays*, trans. Elisaveta Fen. Copyright © Elisaveta Fen 1951, 1954. Reprinted by permission of Penguin Books Ltd.

14. Valency, p. 66. Reprinted by permission.

15. David Garfield, *A Player's Place: The Story of The Actors Studio* (New York: Macmillan, 1980), p. 214.

16. Brooks Atkinson, "Critic at Large," *New York Times*, July 28, 1964, 26.

17. Garfield, p. 239. Reprinted by permission.

ELEVEN

POST-WAR TRENDS: EPIC THEATRE

A MODERN PERSPECTIVE

The influence of epic staging, especially Bertolt Brecht's productions, on contemporary performance theory and practice is monumental. Although other European and American theatre artists experimented with an epic production style, it is Brecht whose name is now practically synonymous with epic theatre. He is the progenitor of ensemble companies, designs, and staging techniques that use the stage as a platform for social and political criticism aimed at heightening the audience's awareness of the possibility as well as the need for change.

It is a testament to the durability of Brecht's work that in 1979 the Metropolitan Opera Company in New York City produced for the first time on its stage *The Rise and Fall of the City of Mahagonny,* written in 1927, with book and lyrics by Brecht and with music by Kurt Weill. In England Brecht has influenced the work of the Royal Court Theatre and directors Peter Brook, John Dexter, and Peter Hall; in Italy, the productions of Giorgio Strehler at the Teatro Piccoló; in France, Roger Planchon at the Théâtre de la Cité; in West Berlin, Peter Stein at the Schaubühne. Many of Brecht's plays are standards in repertory companies both in America and Europe.

Brecht began his international career in 1928 at the Theater am Schiffbauerdamm in Berlin with *The Threepenny Opera.* After World War II and at the invitation of the East Berlin government, he returned to East Germany to establish the Berliner Ensemble, today one of the most famous companies in Europe. The theatre where Brecht first began his career is now the permanent home of the company.

REPRESENTATIVE THEATRE: Theater am Schiffbauerdamm, East Berlin

The Theater am Schiffbauerdamm, a nineteenth-century German baroque theatre, is typical of elaborate proscenium theatres of the era. It featured elegant decor, tiers of boxes and galleries around the sides and back of the auditorium, orchestra seats on the main floor, a musicians' pit, and a picture-frame stage.

In 1954 Brecht supervised the theatre's remodeling and made significant changes in the theatre's decor and technology. He replaced the traditional plush velvet curtain of the proscenium stage with a white half sheet as an act curtain and exposed the workings of the theatrical production to audiences. He removed musicians from the orchestra pit and placed them on stage; he exposed overhead lighting instruments and substituted harsh white light for the usual amber, pink, and blue colors. For effects, he used a rear cyclorama, movable scenic pieces, film projections, and a turntable stage.

The purpose of these changes was to turn the

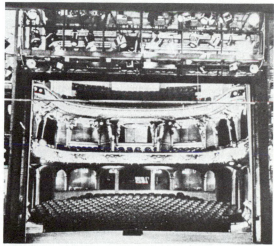

Figure 11-1 Brecht's Theater am Schiffbauerdamm after the renovation. Notice the technical innovations on stage and the auditorium with continental seating and galleries.

1914	1920	
World War I 1914–1918	Economic inflation in Germany	Stalin comes to power in Russia 1928
Brecht serves in war as a medical orderly	German Expressionist movement in art, 1919–1924	Brecht's *Threepenny Opera* produced to critical acclaim 1928
	Mussolini becomes dictator in Italy, 1922	

stage for epic theatre into a "machine" equipped to use large, mobile settings, sophisticated sound and light systems, and equipment for projecting films and slides. The renovation of the Theater am Schiffbauerdamm under Brecht's scrutiny transformed a proscenium theatre designed for stage illusion into a modern machine for epic staging and anti-illusory effects.

CONDITIONS OF PERFORMANCE

BACKGROUND

Theatre in the pre-Weimar Republic years before World War I was partly a traditional theatre of classical and romantic plays produced by permanent companies in the old, opulent baroque theatres of the preceding century. Berlin theatre was dominated by three great producer-directors—Max Reinhardt, Leopold Jessner, and Erwin Piscator—but there was also a blatantly commercial theatre of cheap farces, drawing room comedies, and musical shows.

However, the avant-garde movement, called expressionism, soon became highly influential in the arts. While short-lived (its most significant years were 1919–1923), it became the foundation of later trends in theatre, dance, and painting. The movement attempted to present emotional rather than external reality and bold psychological interpretation of people and events (Figure 11-2). Reinhard Sorge wrote the first expressionist play, *The Beggar,* in 1912. He was quickly followed by such playwrights as Walter Hasenclever, Georg Kaiser, Oscar Kokoschka, Ernst Toller, and the young Bertolt Brecht.

With their antecedents in symbolism and romanticism, the expressionists as a group were defined by revolt, distortion, and boldness of innovation. They rebelled against propriety and common sense, against authority and convention in art and in life. In theatre they rejected the conventions of the well-made play and the plausibility of stage realism. In their place we find bizarre events, disjointed plots, poetic and obscene language, stage images symbolizing mental states, and characters who merely signify their social functions. The movement was closely allied with humanitarian causes, pacifism, and progressive social reforms. Thematically, the expressionists attacked the mores and

Hitler's rise
to power, 1933

World War II
1939–1945

Brecht
returns to
Europe, 1947

Death of Stalin,
1953; Khrushchev
Era, 1958–1964

Spanish Civil
War, 1936–1939;
Franco comes to
power

Creation of
East and West
Germany, 1949

Brecht dies
1956

Brecht and
other artists
go into exile

The Berliner
Ensemble
created, 1949

Hungarian
Revolt
crushed
1956

institutions of middle-class society. Both Erwin Piscator and Bertolt Brecht owe many of their ideas about epic theatre to the expressionists.

In the 1930s political and economic forces changed the shape of German arts as well as the map of Europe. Rampant inflation in the twenties was followed by severe depression. Its effects were worldwide. Out of this economic chaos, Mussolini, then Hitler and Franco rose to power. Russia had already embraced the totalitarian model. In Germany the Weimar Republic succumbed to the Third Reich.

Caught up in the economic struggles, non-state-supported theatres in Germany tried to survive, tailoring new works to popular tastes. Others engaged in experimental works. After Hitler became chancellor in 1933 artistic experimentation disappeared. Many artists emigrated; others went underground or were arrested. Under the Third Reich, German theatre became a propaganda machine for Nazi ideology.

At the war's end the West Berlin government set about reestablishing the city as a cultural center with lively state-supported theatres. In East Berlin the Communist regime rebuilt theatre to celebrate the accomplishments of the workers. Here Brecht's views about theatre and society found a congenial home.

EPIC THEORY AND PRACTICE

The two staples of the German commercial theatre—productions of the classics and realistic dramas of everyday life—contrived to give audiences an emotional uplift, after-dinner entertainment, and an illusion of reality. In the 1920s—and throughout his career—Brecht reacted against this dramatic fare and against the production style of the well-made play and the proscenium theatre. To achieve a different production style with political and social themes, Brecht adapted methods from his contemporaries, Chinese opera, Japanese Noh drama, chronicle history plays, English music-hall routines, and modern films. Out of these he created his concept of epic theatre.

Erwin Piscator (1893–1966), a left-wing experimenter in agitprop, or propaganda theatre, perfected many of the staging techniques later associated with Brecht's epic theatre. When Piscator staged *The Good Soldier Schweik* in 1928 he used conveyor belts for bringing on scenes; a translucent drop in the rear for projections; lantern slides of photographs, cartoons, and explanatory captions; musical numbers; and loudspeakers. In *The Good Soldier Schweik*, the story of a bumbling survivor in the middle of a world at war, Piscator's aim was to create a

Figure 11-2 (a) The skeleton scene of the 1922 New York production of German playwright Georg Kaiser's *From Morn to Midnight* is a good example of expressionist design and production style, which stressed imaginative lighting (a tree has been transformed into a human skeleton), symbolic decor on an almost empty stage, and the distortion of natural appearances. The setting was designed by Lee Simonson. Notice how the actor is dwarfed by the huge projection.

(b) Erwin Piscator used drawings by George Grosz as projected scenery in his production of *The Good Soldier Schweik.*

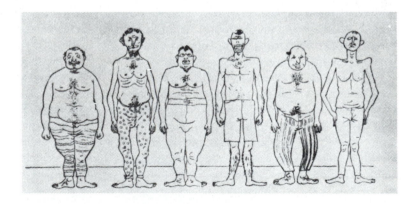

theatre that was political, technological, and epic in scope. In Piscator's terms "epic" meant loosely constructed scenes in the shape of a serious theatrical revue.

Brecht's idea of epic theatre was more complex than Piscator's. While, like Piscator, he thought that to represent historical process in the theatre the stage should be used as a *platform* on which political and social issues could be debated, he also thought of drama as *episodic* and *narrative:* a sequence of incidents or events narrated without artificial restrictions as to time, place, or formal plot. He reminded us that history is not "well-made"; it does not end but moves on from episode to episode. Why should plays do otherwise? Brecht's plays therefore were built of a series of loosely knit scenes, each complete in itself. The total effect was achieved through the juxtaposition of contrasting *episodes.* In the same way, the nonliterary elements of production—music, scenery, acting style, lighting, and moving scenery—also retained their separate identities.

For Piscator and Brecht epic theatre was a way to teach lessons about the exigencies of history and to call upon audiences to learn the processes by which the modern world lived. While Brecht's staging practices resembled Piscator's, Brecht's have been far more influential. His theoretical writings, which span 40 years, and his staging practices at the Berliner Ensemble, which he directed for 7 years, have made his name synonymous with *epic theatre.*

EPIC ACTING

Early in his career Brecht admonished actors not to regard themselves as impersonating characters so much as *narrating* the actions of people in a particular time, place, and situation. The model he used to demonstrate this approach was the behavior of an *eyewitness to a traffic accident.*

In retelling the event, eyewitnesses clearly differentiate between themselves and the victim, although they may reconstruct the victim's reactions and gestures. So, too, Brecht argued, actors clearly differentiate between themselves

BERTOLT BRECHT

Bertolt Brecht (1898–1956) was born in Augsburg, Germany, where he spent his early years. In 1918, while studying medicine at Munich University, he was called up for military service as a medical orderly. He began writing poems about the horrors of war and his first play, *Baal* (1918), dates from this period.

After World World I Brecht drifted as a student into the Bohemian world of theatre and literature, singing his poetry in Munich taverns and coffeehouses. By 1921 Brecht had seriously entered the theatre world as a reviewer and playwright. During the 1920s in Berlin, Brecht became a Marxist, wrote plays, and solidified his theories of epic theatre. *The Threepenny Opera* (1928)—produced in collaboration with the composer Kurt Weill—was an overnight success and made both Brecht and Weill famous.

With the rise of the Nazi movement, many German artists and intellectuals fled Germany. Brecht took his family and fled in 1933, first to Scandinavia and then to America, where he lived until 1947. In October of 1947 Brecht was subpoenaed to appear before the House Committee on Un-American Activities to testify on the "Communist infiltration" of the motion-picture industry. He left the United States the day following his testimony, eventually settling in East Berlin, where he founded the Berliner Ensemble.

Brecht's greatest plays date from his years of exile (1933–1948): *The Good Woman of Setzuan, Mother Courage and Her Children, Galileo,* and *The Caucasian Chalk Circle.*

as actors and the characters they play. The eyewitness never becomes the victim: "He never forgets, nor does he allow anyone to forget, that he is not the one whose action is being demonstrated, but the one who demonstrates it."[1] Just as Brecht wanted to get rid of the audience's identification with the characters, so he also rejected the *actor's* identification with the character. The actor did not "become" the character as in the Stanislavsky approach to acting. Rather, in Brecht's view, actors "demonstrated"

the characters' attitudes while retaining freedom to comment on the actions of the person whose behavior they were displaying. This device of the actor as eyewitness to the play's events was also part of Brecht's efforts to *distance* or *alienate* the audience emotionally from what was happening on stage.

THE ALIENATION EFFECT

Brecht called this jarring of the audience out of its sympathetic feelings for what was happening on stage the alienation effect (sometimes cited as A-effect or *Verfremdungseffekt*). He wanted to break down the audience's "willing suspension of disbelief," to force them to look at everything in a fresh light, and, above all, to think. Brecht's goal was that audiences should absorb his social criticism and carry their new insights out of the theatre into their lives.

Brecht was certainly aware of the entertainment value of theatre. For Brecht, pleasure in the theatre came from observing accounts of past situations, discovering new truths, and enlarging upon an understanding of the present. What he opposed was a theatre solely of catharsis where the audience lost its critical detachment by identifying emotionally with the characters. All of the epic devices—music, scenery, acting style—reminded audiences that they were in a theatre, that the stage was a stage and not someone's living room.

VISUAL ELEMENTS

Epic stage settings have been anti-illusory in style, avoiding exact reproductions of life or atmospheric stage pictures. First Piscator, later designers Caspar Neher, Georg Grosz, and Teo Otto in Germany and Howard Bay and Mordecai Gorelik in America created epic settings by supplying such fragments of environment as were needed to show the play's meaning. Let us examine the *mise en scène* at the Berliner Ensemble during Brecht's years there, including scenery, costumes, and properties for the 1949 production of *Mother Courage and Her Children*.

Piscator's 1928 production of *The Good Soldier Schweik*

"Three thin portals spanned the depth of the stage—Baroque fashion—and were closed in with a translucent drop in the rear. Between the portals, and parallel with the footlights, were two treadmills . . . whose combined widths formed the depth of the stage. That was all; and as the stage darkened it was filled with the lilt of a Czech folksong played on the hurdy-gurdy.

But now the backdrop springs to life, turning into a large motion picture screen as the projector strikes it from the back. A black dot jumps to the blank screen; it races over the white brilliance with fantastic speed, leaving behind it lines as jagged and scratchy as barbed wire. Rapidly it traces in the distinctive style of the artist Georg Grosz, a mustachioed and puffy Austrian general. The hilt of a heavy sword appears in the general's right hand; his other hand clasps that of the neighboring figure, who emerges as a German field marshal, . . .

The treadmill begins to work. From the left a little corner of a room trundles on by itself, a flea-bitten room as dog-eared as the cur in Schweik's lap. Schweik, in shirt-sleeves, puffs away at his tassled pipe while his landlady, Frau Muller, sweeps the conveyor belt energetically."

Mordecai Gorelik, *New Theatres for Old* (1952)[2]

Scene Design Brecht's favorite designers—Caspar Neher, Teo Otto, and Karl von Appen—did not create illusions of real places but provided background materials—projections on a rear cyclorama, placards, signs and emblems, and set pieces—that commented on the play's historical period and the characters' socioeconomic circumstances. Brecht used a white half curtain across the proscenium opening rather than a full-length act curtain. The half curtain revealed the preparations of stagehands and served a practical function, as titles of scenes could be projected onto it. The *setting* itself was used to make the action and individuals appear "strange," or unfamiliar, without disguising the fact that all was taking place in a theatre under lights and before an audience.

> *It is comparatively easy to set up a basic model for epic theatre. For practical experiments I usually picked as my example of completely simple, 'natural' epic theatre an incident such as can be seen at any street corner: an eyewitness demonstrating to a collection of people how a traffic accident took place. The bystanders may not have observed what happened, or they may simply not agree with him, may 'see things a different way'; the point is that the demonstrator acts the behaviour of driver or victim or both in such a way that the bystanders are able to form an opinion about the accident. . . .*
>
> *One essential element of the street scene must also be present in the theatrical scene if this is to qualify as epic, namely that the demonstration should have a socially practical significance. Whether our street demonstrator is out to show that one attitude on the part of driver or pedestrian makes an accident inevitable where another would not, or whether he is demonstrating with a view to fixing the responsibility, his demonstration has a practical purpose, intervenes socially.*

Bertolt Brecht, "Streetscene: A Basic Model for an Epic Theatre" (1938)[3]

Dramatic Theatre and Epic Theatre

Brecht's table, published in 1930, shows the difference between dramatic theatre (for example, Ibsen's *Ghosts*) and epic theatre.

Dramatic Theatre	Epic Theatre
Plot	Narrative
Implicates the spectator in a stage situation	Turns the spectator into an observer, but
Wears down his capacity for action	Arouses his capacity for action
Provides him with sensations	Forces him to take decisions
Experience	Picture of the world
The spectator is involved in something	He is made to face something
Suggestion	Argument
Instinctive feelings are preserved	Brought to the point of recognition
The spectator is in the thick of it, shares the experience	The spectator stands outside, studies
The human being is taken for granted	The human being is the object of the inquiry
He is unalterable	He is alterable and able to alter
Eyes on the finish	Eyes on the course
One scene makes another	Each scene for itself
Growth	Montage
Linear development	In curves
Evolutionary determinism	Jumps
Man as a fixed point	Man as a process
Thought determines being	Social being determines thought
Feeling	Reason

Bertolt Brecht, "The Modern Theatre Is the Epic Theatre" (1930)[4]

At the Berliner Ensemble initial preparation for a production usually took about half a year. The settings, costumes, and properties were developed on paper and from small models (Figure 11-3). Brecht thought of a setting as space where actors told a certain story to the audience. His sketches and models were designed first of all to give the actor the appropriate space and architectural structures needed to tell the story.

Brecht's working notes on the setting for *Mother Courage and Her Children* reveal his careful attention to screens, projections, scene titles, lighting, and the positioning of Mother Courage's wagon:

There was a permanent framework of hugh screens, making use of such materials as one would expect to find in the military encampments of the seventeenth century; tenting, wooden posts lashed together with ropes, etc. Three-dimensional structures, realistic both as to construction and as to material, were placed on the stage to represent such buildings as the presbytery and peasants' house, but . . . only so much being shown as was necessary for the action. Colored projections were thrown on the cyclorama, and the revolving stage was used to give the impression of travel. We . . .

Mother Courage and Her Children
(*Mutter Courage und ihre Kinder*)

Brecht's *Mother Courage* (produced in 1941) is a chronicle play of the Thirty Years' War based on Hans Jakob Grimmelshausen's picaresque novel *Simplicissimus* (1699), with music by Paul Dessau.

Anna Fierling, nicknamed Mother Courage because of her daring in saving her goods under enemy fire, is a canteen manager with three children. Eilif, Swiss Cheese, and Kathrin all have different fathers. As types, Eilif is brave, Swiss Cheese honest, and Kathrin sensitive but a mute. As the four cross many lands drawing the canteen wagon behind them, the wars begin to take Mother Courage's children and her goods one after the next. Eilif is conscripted by the Swedish Protestant Army. Swiss Cheese becomes an army paymaster and loses his life trying to hide the regimental funds from the enemy. Mother Courage forfeits the chance to buy his life by haggling too long over the ransom price of her wagon.

Although she curses war, Mother Courage continues to subsist because of it. During a short truce she fears that her business will be ruined. During peacetime, Eilif is executed for plundering, an act he was decorated for in wartime. Now only Kathrin, Mother Courage, and her companion, a Cook, are left. The Cook inherits a small inn in Holland that will support two people, and he proposes marriage. Mother Courage rejects his offer because she would have to leave her daughter behind. As they near Halle, Kathrin overhears a Catholic plan to seize the city. Realizing that children will be killed in the attack, she climbs on a cottage roof and beats a drum to warn the citizens. Soldiers shoot her down, but she has managed to waken the town. Mother Courage, having lost all her children as well as her companion, goes on pulling the wagon alone.

Mother Courage's main concern throughout is to keep her business going. As she changes sides during the wars and as she loses her children in the fighting, she expounds her materialist view of war. In the end, having failed to learn from her experiences, she is still determined to get her cut.

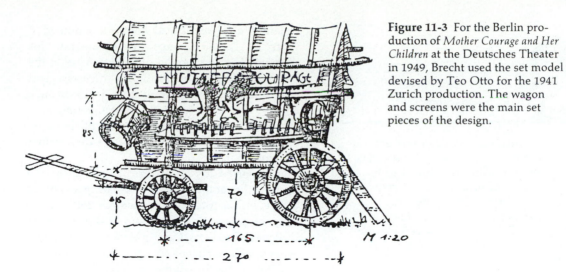

Figure 11-3 For the Berlin production of *Mother Courage and Her Children* at the Deutsches Theater in 1949, Brecht used the set model devised by Teo Otto for the 1941 Zurich production. The wagon and screens were the main set pieces of the design.

suspended the names of the various countries over the stage in large black letters. We used an even, white light, as much of it as our equipment permitted. In this way we eliminated any vestige of "atmosphere" that could easily have given the incidents a romantic tinge. We retained almost everything else [from the Zurich production] down to the smallest details (chopping block, hearth, etc.), particularly the admirable positionings of the wagon. This last was very important because it determined much of the grouping and movement from the outset.[5]

Costumes and Properties This same careful attention to detail was used also in the creation of costumes and properties. Costumes showed both the characters' individuality and social class. Properties, especially those connected with working and eating, were carefully made, including the belt buckle that Mother Courage sells while, unknown to her, her son is being recruited into the army.

Lighting In the same spirit as the white half curtain, Brecht required stage lighting to dispense with effects of atmosphere and mood. He exposed the lighting instruments and used "white" light. The effect was like spotlights over a boxing ring. It further dispensed with any "illusion" of staged reality.

Music Brecht placed musicians on stage in full view of the audience. Just as he no longer concealed the musicians' presence, so, too, he no longer introduced musical numbers by having the actor's speech burst into song when the emotional charge of a scene rose to a climax, as in musical comedy. Brecht's songs interrupted the story's flow, broke the illusion of the scene, and rendered the action strange and unfamiliar. The music itself frequently did not express the mood of the lyrics, but instead contradicted it. As in Gay's ballads for *The Beggar's Opera*, the musical score for *The Threepenny Opera* comments on and reveals the falsity of the sentiments expressed in the lyrics. Brecht's favorite composers were Kurt Weill, Paul Dessau, and Hanns Eisler.

THE BERLINER ENSEMBLE

When Brecht returned to Europe after his wartime stay in the United States, the East German authorities offered to let him direct a production of *Mother Courage and Her Children* with his wife,

HELENE WEIGEL

Born in Vienna, the great German actress Helene Weigel (1900–1971) was associated with Bertolt Brecht for almost a lifetime as creator of principal roles in his plays and as director of the Berliner Ensemble from 1949 until her death in 1971. The collaboration between Helene Weigel and Brecht began in 1927 when she appeared in *Man Equals Man.* They were married in the early 1930s and spent 15 years in exile with their children Barbara and Stefan. With the creation of the Berliner Ensemble in 1949, she appeared as Mother Courage in the play of the same name in that year and in 1952 as Natella in *The Caucasian Chalk Circle.* Her international reputation as one of the greatest actresses of her time was assured with the Berliner Ensemble's appearance in London in 1956 and 1965.

In a tribute written upon her death, American director Alan Schneider describes his memories of her: "She had the face not of an actress but of a woman, a woman who had lived with the soil, a peasant woman browned by wind and sunlight, with high cheekbones half-Spanish, half-Oriental. She was small, almost tiny, but on stage seemed a giant; lean as an animal who has had to hunt for food and who has been hunted as prey. Her eyes, alert and crinkly with crow's feet, carried the sadness and pain of the world, and her mouth cried out—and also was able to laugh."[6]

Helene Weigel, in the lead. For the first time in 15 years he had a chance to demonstrate his theories. The production opened in 1949 at the Deutsches Theater in East Berlin and was a great critical success. Following this breakthrough and an invitation from the East German government, Brecht drew together old collaborators and formed a permanent company—the Berliner Ensemble.

Supported by government subsidies, the Berliner Ensemble began as a company of 60 actors with a total complement of 250. Of the original company the most well-known were designers Teo Otto, Caspar Neher, and Karl von Appen; actors Helene Weigel, Therese Giehse, and Ernst Busch; composers Hanns Eisler and Paul Dessau; and assistants Erich Engel, Elisabeth Hauptmann, and Ruth Berlau.

Working with Actors As a director Brecht adopted a wait-and-see attitude, working with actors on positions, movements, and gestures. One of his collaborators remarked that during rehearsals Brecht sat unobtrusively in the auditorium. He rarely interrupted rehearsals, not even with suggestions for improvement. There was never the impression that he wanted to get actors to "present some of his ideas." Rather, he searched, together with actors, for the story which the play told, and helped each actor to his or her strengths. Brecht's work with actors has been compared to the efforts of a child to direct straws with a twig from a puddle into the river itself, so that they may float.[7] Much has been said by friends and collaborators about Brecht's patience with actors, his good humor, and his keen appreciation of the actor's work.

Rehearsals New productions at the Berliner Ensemble were rehearsed for three to five months; about 200 hours were spent. Brecht blocked the play in three to four months; then he worked on details of acting. Carl Weber, one of his directing assistants, has written on this part of the process:

The most meticulous attention was paid to the smallest gesture. Sometimes it took an hour to work out whether an actor should pick up a tool one way or another. Particular attention was devoted to all details of physical labor. A man's work forms his habits, his attitudes, his physical behavior down to the smallest movement, a fact usually neglected by the stage. Brecht spent hours in rehearsal exploring how Galileo would handle a telescope and an apple, how the kitchenmaid Grusha would pick up a water-bottle or a baby, how the young soldier Eilif would drink at his General's table, etc.[8]

After all the details had been examined, Brecht had the first run-through followed by more rehearsals. A week was given to technical rehearsals. Then there were five to eight previews after which, taking advantage of the audiences' reactions, rehearsals continued.

DRAMATIC CONVENTIONS

EPISODIC STRUCTURE

We chiefly associate episodic play structure with medieval cycle plays and with Shakespeare's chronicle history plays. The epic play is also episodic in form. It begins early in the story and involves many characters and events. Since the action is a journey of some kind, it focuses upon one or more central figures as they move from place to place and into different situations.

Brecht's *Caucasian Chalk Circle* is made up of two stories, Grusha's and Azdak's. The plot moves in a linear fashion, telling the two seemingly unrelated stories until they are combined in the chalk circle test to make Brecht's point about decent people caught in the injustices of a corrupt political system.

In this loose structure, characters are not trapped in circumstances but pass through

them. Grusha undergoes a variety of experiences in her efforts to save the Governor's child from mercenary soldiers. She *journeys* through the countryside until she is captured and brought before Judge Azdak to be tested by the chalk circle rite. She passes the test and Azdak awards the child to her.

Each scene in the epic play is usually developed as a unit, complete in itself. One scene follows the next, carrying the characters through their journey. As each new scene begins, *subtitles* identify the new locale and describe the basic situation.

HISTORICAL BACKGROUND

While the chronicle history play uses historical events as background to the dramatic action, Brecht enlarged the function of the historical setting. He treated the play's *story* as historical as well as unique. By emphasizing the pastness of events, Brecht felt audiences could relate the past to their present lives and times. As we noted earlier, while Brecht believed that plays should entertain audiences, he also argued that art had a larger social function: to show society's ills in such a way as to convince audiences that social change is possible and desirable. Mother Courage, according to Brecht, does not learn from her wrong choices that result in the deaths of her children. Nevertheless, the audience learns from observing her choices, her children's fates, and her diminishing circumstances.

THE NARRATOR

Brecht's use of the actor-as-narrator was influenced largely by the traditions of the Japanese Noh theatre where a chorus sings the actor's lines while he is dancing and also narrates many of the play's events. Brecht's actors narrate as well as perform, and frequently criticize the course of events. In *The Caucasian Chalk Circle* actor Ernst Busch played both the narrator and Azdak, the judge, in the 1954 Berliner Ensemble production. (See pages 36–37.)

The mounted messenger saves Macheath in Brecht's *The Threepenny Opera*, Berliner Ensemble production, 1960

The Berliner Ensemble's production of Brecht's *Mother Courage and Her Children*, 1949. In the final scene, Helene Weigel as Mother Courage, alone, pulls the wagon toward another war.

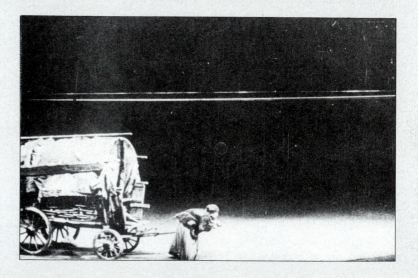

"The Living Newspaper" production of *One Third of a Nation*, New York, 1938, with setting designed by Howard Bay. "The Living Newspaper" was a form of play developed by the Federal Theatre Project in America during the 1930s. It integrated factual information with a story line about current social injustices. *One Third of a Nation*, about slum housing, used many techniques borrowed from epic theatre, like the use of loudspeakers with actors reading from *The Congressional Record*.

CHARACTERIZATION

Brecht's characters, such as Macheath in *The Threepenny Opera* and Mother Courage in *Mother Courage and Her Children,* are social types as well as recognizable individuals. This type of characterization dates back to morality plays where Everyman is both an individual and a representative of all humankind. In Brecht's plays character emerges from the individual's social function and changes with that function.

GESTIC ATTITUDES

Brecht's concept of *gest* or *gestic* language was a matter of the actor's overall attitude to what was going on around him and what he was asked to do on stage. Brecht insisted that words follow the *gest* of the person speaking. His most famous example was the Biblical line: "If thine eye offend thee, pluck it out." Here the object of concern ("the eye") was presented first; then it was followed by the advice or attitude of the speaker. Moreover, the offending eye requires an explicit gesture and attitude on the actor's part. It cannot be avoided.

The *test* of the chalk circle made visible the characters' gestic attitudes. The materialistic attitudes of the lawyers and the Governor's wife

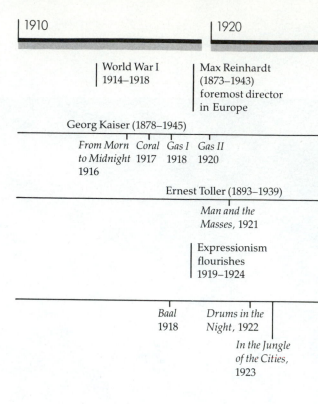

Brecht's Subtitle for the Beginning Scene of
The Caucasian Chalk Circle

Scene One

THE DISPUTE OVER THE VALLEY

Amid the ruins of a war-torn Caucasian village the members of two kolkhoz villages, for the most part women and old men, but also a few soldiers, are sitting in a circle, smoking and drinking wine. With them is an expert from the state reconstruction commission in the capital.[9]

---

toward the child were contrasted with Grusha's humanitarian feelings. Grusha refused to tug at the child while the Governor's wife pulled the child twice out of the circle. The wife's attitudes, words, and gestures betray the fact that her access to wealth and power depends upon the return of the child to her. We see that she is selfish and "grasping," while Grusha is loving and kind (Figure 11–4).

THE DIALECTIC IN ACTION

Brecht's epic plays show people as social beings caught in situations where they are forced to make decisions. One decision is related to another, just as one episode is loosely related to the next.

Throughout a lifetime of social and political theorizing, Brecht consistently emphasized the

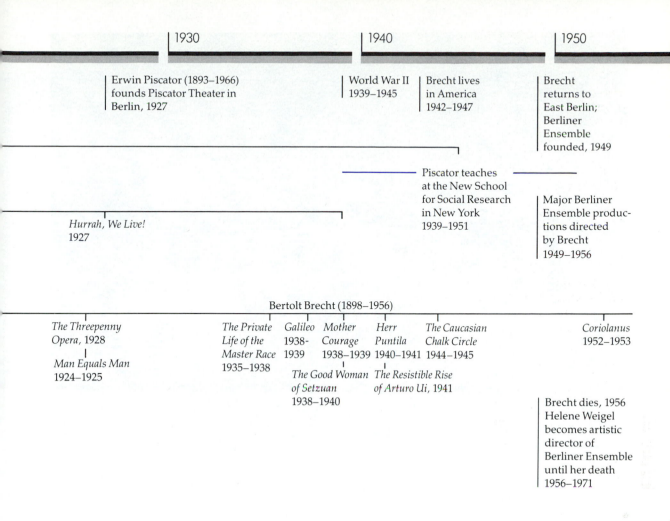

| 1930 | 1940 | 1950 |

Erwin Piscator (1893–1966) founds Piscator Theater in Berlin, 1927

World War II 1939–1945

Brecht lives in America 1942–1947

Brecht returns to East Berlin; Berliner Ensemble founded, 1949

Piscator teaches at the New School for Social Research in New York 1939–1951

Major Berliner Ensemble productions directed by Brecht 1949–1956

Hurrah, We Live! 1927

Bertolt Brecht (1898–1956)

The Threepenny Opera, 1928

Man Equals Man 1924–1925

The Private Life of the Master Race 1935–1938

Galileo 1938-1939

Mother Courage 1938–1939

The Good Woman of Setzuan 1938–1940

Herr Puntila 1940–1941

The Resistible Rise of Arturo Ui, 1941

The Caucasian Chalk Circle 1944–1945

Coriolanus 1952–1953

Brecht dies, 1956 Helene Weigel becomes artistic director of Berliner Ensemble until her death 1956–1971

contradictions (a chain of conflicts) in human affairs. His subjects mirrored his concerns about economic injustice, human exploitation, class conflicts, and power struggles. In his plays Brecht expressed a dialectical view of history as a force pulling people (individuals, families, societies) in different directions at once. Mother Courage's conflicting interests are visible in scene after scene. She is torn between bargaining for her son's life and selling a belt buckle; she must choose between caring for her disfigured daughter and a husband who offers her a roof over her head.

REPRESENTATIVE PLAY

The Caucasian Chalk Circle
Written between 1944 and 1945, produced by the Berliner Ensemble at the Theater am Schiffbauerdamm (East Berlin, June 15, 1954), with scenery by Karl von Appen, with Angelika Hurwicz as Grusha, Helene Weigel as the Governor's wife, and Ernst Busch as Azdak

Figure 11-4 The circle drawn in white chalk on the stage floor signifies a test of true motherliness and rightful ownership based upon mutual interests and well-being. The Governor's wife (left) and Grusha (right) pull at the child as Judge Azdak looks on in the 1965 production of *The Caucasian Chalk Circle* at the Guthrie Theater. Grusha (Zoe Caldwell) releases the child before harming him.

BACKGROUND

Bertolt Brecht called *The Caucasian Chalk Circle* a "parable for the theatre." The chalk circle test is a story of ancient wisdom found in a fourteenth-century Chinese play. It also has a Biblical counterpart in King Solomon's sword test. In Brecht's version the chalk circle is a test of motherhood as well as a model of practical socialist wisdom about how to settle disputes of ownership. The valley goes to the people who can make it most useful and the child goes to the mother who takes the best care of it.

PROLOGUE AND FRAME

The Caucasian Chalk Circle is made up of two plays. The prologue (scene 1) establishes the meeting of persons from two collective farms in Soviet Georgia in 1945. The meeting is to determine the ownership of a valley to which both claim rights. A government representative arrives to settle the dispute amicably and in a style satisfactory to both parties. At the conclusion of the debate, a singer-narrator comes forth to entertain the gathering. He introduces the tale of the chalk circle and links the outer play (the settling of the dispute) with the inner one (the stories of Grusha and Azdak).

Like a Greek chorus the narrator introduces and comments upon each scene and sums up the lesson that the play teaches the kolkhozes (members of the collective), as well as the audience. He also "sings" Grusha's thoughts when circumstances of her overpowering emotions force her to remain silent. The technique is similar to a voice-over narration in film and television.

As Brecht staged it, all the actors had two roles—one in the outer and one in the inner play. The play moves from one plane of reality where the actors play collective farm workers to a second plane of reality where they enact the ancient Chinese tale. This doubling of roles stresses the actor's part as observer versus character and also bridges the various parts of the play.

THE PLAY-WITHIN-THE-PLAY

The first part of the play-within-the-play (scenes 2–4) is balanced between Grusha's actions and the singer's narration and songs. These scenes tell the story of Grusha and the Governor's child before they arrive to be judged by Azdak. The singer begins the story of "the noble child" in an ancient city where a wealthy Governor, his wife (Natella), and his iron-shirted soldiers rule over beggars and peasants. A revolt against the Governor takes place and his child (Michael) is left in the care of Grusha, a servant girl and fiancée to the soldier Simon. In spite of warnings that she risks her life if she attempts to protect the child, Grusha makes her way to her brother's hut in the northern mountains.

Thus Grusha undertakes a seven-day journey. As in *Mother Courage and Her Children*,

Brecht used the revolving stage turning against her progress as the actress mimed the long journey. One after the next, Grusha's efforts to feed, shelter, and protect the child endanger her own life. Under the legal system, the rescuer of the child is a thief. Her poverty also places the child in jeopardy as she bargains for milk, blankets, and a "legitimate" father for him. She even risks losing Simon on account of Michael. Over three episodes we see her become the child's true mother through her love and sacrifice.

After Grusha's many risks and losses, the soldiers capture her, and the story of Azdak interrupts the narrative to prepare for the trial and verdict that will reward Grusha's sacrifices and make the child legally her own. Since Grusha (like the Rosa Luxemburg kolkhoz of the prologue) proves there is no difference between her interests and those of the child, Azdak gives the child to her.

LINKING DEVICES

The scenes in *The Caucasian Chalk Circle* are linked together in several ways. First, the narrator sings of events that happen but are not shown. Second, time is compressed. Grusha's decisions are translated immediately into action, such as her decision to save the child. The baby wrapped in a blanket for the journey becomes the child Michael in the hut once the blanket is removed. Third, the revolving stage visually links each day of the seven-day journey.

Fourth, the role change of narrator and judge is a strong link. At the end of scene 4, Michael is taken by the soldiers back to the city to the Governor's wife, his biological mother. Grusha follows demanding his return. The narrator provides a kind of cinematic montage by singing of Azdak who will judge the case. Then as he changes roles, the audience is transferred to Azdak's story and to the scene of judgment. Finally, the original music by Paul Dessau binds the scenes together in a unity of mood.

Figure 11-5 Grusha (Zoe Caldwell) baptizes the child (in this production, a rag doll) at the river in the 1965 production of *The Caucasian Chalk Circle* directed by Edward Payson Call, at the Guthrie Theater, Minneapolis.

AZDAK'S STORY

Azdak, a village scribe, is a rogue, thief, and coward who inadvertently shelters the villainous Grand Duke. When Azdak discovers what he has done, he demands that the soldiers punish him for sparing the villain's life. Having just hanged the local judge, the drunken soldiers dress Azdak in judicial robes and make him their judge. Azdak goes rampaging into the countryside accepting bribes from the wealthy and delivering sentences that reverse accepted standards of justice. He makes an award in favor of a poor woman who has been helped by a bandit, arguing that only a miracle could explain how a "leg of pork" came to fly into the poor woman's house. When an attractive young woman accuses a farmhand of rape, he considers her luxurious figure and finds her guilty of assault and battery with a dangerous weapon; he then goes off with her "to examine the scene of the crime."

Azdak, one of Brecht's most colorful characters, is corrupt, licentious, and contemptuous of the law that favors the wealthy. Although he has spent a life in careful adaptation to society's moral standards, he reveals an unexpected generosity and wisdom in dealing with human complaints. Two years later he is still the judge when Grusha, the child, and the Governor's wife are brought before him.

THE CHALK CIRCLE TEST

Scene 6 is the test of the chalk circle. Azdak hears the pleas of Natella's lawyers for her rights as the child's biological mother and for her desire to establish a legal heir to the Governor's estates. Grusha argues that she is the true mother because she took care of Michael when he was deserted and in need. To resolve the debate Azdak calls for the test. A circle is drawn on the floor with a piece of chalk. The child is placed in the middle and the two women are ordered to pull. Twice Natella pulls the child from the circle while Grusha protests that she cannot tear the boy to pieces. The judge awards the child to Grusha and gives her a divorce so that she can marry Simon. The Governor's estates are confiscated by the city to be named "Azdak Park." A celebration begins during which Azdak disappears into the crowd. The narrator then steps forward to sing of the wisdom of the story of the chalk circle:

> And you who have heard the story of the chalk circle
> Bear in mind the wisdom of our fathers:
> Things should belong to those who do well by them
> Children to the motherly women that they may thrive
> Wagons to the good drivers that they may be well driven
> And the valley to those who water it, that it may bear fruit.[10]

BRECHT'S DIALECTICAL MEANING

For historians, dialectics is a process in which opposing ideas are synthesized or reconciled. In the beginning Grusha is torn between her interest in the child and her interest in her own survival. On the long journey she proves her reliability, her usefulness, and her fitness to mother the child. As the two interests become one and the same, the conflict is resolved.

Brecht's play shows an alternative system of justice that takes into account necessity and usefulness rather than biology and rules of ownership. The Biblical parable identifies the biological mother and casts out the stepmother as a false claimant. In contrast, Azdak's deliberations settle upon the rights of the child to care and nurturing by those who serve it best.

While at the outset, we seem to be observing a parable instructive to the kolkhozes in settling their property dispute, the stories of Grusha, Azdak, and the test manifest a kind of *human* wisdom that can be exemplary in an actual dispute over ownership of property and the like.

The play's prologue gives a historical background (rural Russia in 1945) in which the practicality of this type of collective wisdom is demonstrated.

In the ancient Chinese tale, we are shown people's greed and humanitarianism at odds with one another. In Brecht's "parable for a modern audience," we see the contradictions and ambiguities in human behavior but also the forces of good sometimes triumphing despite human nature.

ESSAY

Brecht's theories of epic staging (what some today call "the theatre theatrical") are alive and well in various guises in American, British, and European theatres. They are most evident in staging, especially in design and directing. One of Brecht's most fervent disciples is West German director Peter Stein, whose work is the subject of this essay on the continuing influence of epic theatre on contemporary performance.

Epic Theatre in Contemporary Performance

Peter Stein directs Ibsen's *Peer Gynt* at the Schaubühne am Halleschen Ufer, West Berlin, 1971

Brecht's theatre has had a great influence on post-war directors and producers. In England Peter Brook's 1964 production of *Marat/Sade*, a play by German-language playwright Peter Weiss, displayed Brecht's influence in "announcements" about the play's action, in songs and music, in the use of actors as asylum inmates performing characters in de Sade's play, and in the staging of the great debate between the characters Jean-Paul Marat and the Marquis de Sade.

Major German-language playwrights to develop after the war were the Swiss authors Max Frisch (b. 1911) and Friedrich Duerrenmatt (b.

1921) and Swedish-based Peter Weiss (1916–1982). Frisch built his reputation on *The Chinese Wall* (1946), *Biedermann and the Firebugs* (1958), and *Andorra* (1961), all of which treated the question of German guilt for the Holocaust. Durrenmatt's fame came with *The Visit* (1956) and *The Physicists* (1962), both concerned with the moral responsibility of individuals as well as society. Weiss's reputation rests largely upon *The Persecution and Assassination of Jean-Paul Marat as Performed by the Inmates of the Asylum of Charenton Under the Direction of the Marquis De Sade* (1964) and *The Investigation* (1965). These plays explore the inhumanity of people acting on a scale of mass destruction.

A new post-war generation of German playwrights, including Rolf Hochhuth, Peter Handke, Wolfgang Bauer, and Thomas Bernhard, has explored the themes of national guilt, personal anxieties, and the dehumanizing effects of a mechanistic and sterile culture—all Brechtian themes.

PETER STEIN

Peter Stein (b. 1932), at age 28, was working as an assistant director at the Munich Kammerspiele under director Fritz Kortner, a former Brecht associate. In 1967 Stein's production of Edward Bond's *Saved* opened at the Kammerspiele's experimental workshop. He then directed Peter Weiss's *Vietnam Discourse* there, but the production was canceled because of its political viewpoint. Moving to Bremen in 1968, he became associated with designer Karl Ernst Hermann and actor Michael Konig. There Stein put together a company. In 1969–1970 Stein's company merged with the management at the Schaubühne in West Berlin, and became identified as a permanent ensemble working in a collective process. The group has since become one of the leading theatre companies in Western Europe.

STEIN'S SCHAUBÜHNE

Brecht's influence has been most visible in the work of Germany's newest leading director, Peter Stein. In 1970 Stein took over the Schaubühne, one of West Berlin's major theatres, and modeled it after the Berliner Ensemble. The Schaubühne is *political*, its staging techniques *epic*, and its working methods *collectivist*.

In combining art with politics, the main policy of Stein's company has been to stage revivals of nineteenth- and twentieth-century German middle-class plays. Since the company grew up in a postwar, middle-class society, they see these revivals as a coming to terms with their roots while, at the same time, confronting audiences with the recent past. Productions of Henrik Ibsen's *Peer Gynt* (in 1971), Peter Handke's *The Ride Across Lake Constance* (in 1971), and Friedrich von Kleist's *The Prince of Homburg* (in 1972) have been used in this way. Other plays speak directly to workers about social ills and the need for social change.

Stein advocates a democratic production process. Play selection starts with suggestions from the company. When a suggestion is accepted, the text and relevant materials are studied by a team (a director, dramaturge, designers, actors—about 12 people in all). This team, under the director's guidance, establishes a concept for the play, defines its themes, and maps out a work plan.

PEER GYNT

The company interpreted Ibsen's play, written in 1867, as an allegory and satire on the political thinking and ideological attitudes of nineteenth-century capitalist Europe. Peer, the central figure, was played as a typical *petit bourgeois*—one of a class of people made up of minor civil servants, white collar workers, and owners of small shops and businesses. The viewpoint that the petit bourgeoisie had participated wholeheartedly in capitalist Europe's expansionism and imperialism without reaping the profits was the source of the company's satire. At the Schaubühne Peer Gynt became an individual chasing after illusions of grandeur, misusing and abusing his imagination and talents in this vain pursuit so that in the end he was depleted instead of fulfilled.

EPIC TECHNIQUE

Ibsen's play follows his roguish hero through experiences of youth, middle and old age as he searches for his identity among trolls, capitalists, and madmen. Adopting an epic production style, Stein's *Peer Gynt* opened with the announcement over the sound system that we are about to see:

> Peer Gynt by Henryk Ibsen, a play from the nineteenth century. Part I: Youth in the Gudbrandstal. Four scenic chapters with different actors in the title role.[11]

The play was given in two parts (corresponding to Ibsen's Acts I–III and IV–V) on successive evenings with a total playing time of more than six hours. At the end of the first evening a trailer announced Part 2:

> Peer now leaves Norway and emigrates to America. . . . Danger is everywhere. Will Peer reach his goal in spite of them? Will he find his true self? Tomorrow at eight o'clock, *Peer Gynt,* Part 2, "In Foreign Parts and the Homecoming."[12]

To accommodate the epic style, designer Karl Ernst Hermann converted the proscenium theatre into a theatre-in-the-round. He erected a contoured sand-colored platform in the middle of the theatre with a hill at one end and a dip at the other. The audience sat on two platforms, which faced one another down the long sides of the stage. The neutral acting area was then set for each episode, either with properties that were carried on or with built-in set pieces that could be operated mechanically.

The floor plan enabled Peer to make his journey through the whole theatre while leaving certain localities—for example, Peer's hut—visible throughout the entire play. Music and sound effects—like the yacht sinking while the band plays and gurgling sounds are heard—highlighted the story's events. Also, stage machinery was exploited for fantastic and amusing effects, as in a scene in Egypt where a huge white sphinx built into the floor is cranked up on hinges.

The final result was a spectacular epic production that questioned the validity of the Victorian dream of personal success embodied in Peer Gynt, the quintessential nineteenth-century man.

SUMMARY

Epic staging—based on the theories, plays, and practices of Bertolt Brecht—has been a creative force in the theatre for four decades. In the 1920s in Berlin, Piscator and Brecht experimented with a new production style, which they called epic theatre.

For Brecht, epic theatre was, first of all, political and theatrical. It argued against the capitalist system as a mode of life that enslaved masses and made unfeeling criminals of people as they fought for survival. Epic staging used the theatre as a theatre with bare stage, exposed lighting instruments, cyclorama for projections, explanatory placards, and loudspeakers. Brecht's plays themselves were episodic with loosely constructed scenes, the one following the next until the story was fully told. Brecht also developed theories of an epic acting style, of an alienation or distancing effect, and of the use of historical backgrounds to heighten our awareness of current events.

Brecht's coterie of artists and friends included Caspar Neher, Kurt Weill, Lotte Lenya, Paul Dessau, Hanns Eisler, Elisabeth Hauptmann, Ruth Berlau, and his famous actress-wife, Helene Weigel. Throughout the war years they continued to write, experiment, and theorize about epic theatre. Their ideas encompassed acting, rehearsal, design, and the general treatment of the stage as a platform where world issues could be held up for scrutiny with an aim to changing society.

Brecht spent six years (1942–1947) in the United States with family and friends as a refugee from Nazi Germany. In 1947 he returned to Europe and in 1949 mounted the internationally famous production of *Mother Courage and Her Children* with Helene Weigel in the lead. Shortly thereafter, Brecht, with a subsidy from the East German government, formed a permanent company called The Berliner Ensemble. Here he produced for the first time plays written during his long exile, and he put into practice the theories of staging, acting, and directing that have influenced so many theatre artists in our time.

The Caucasian Chalk Circle, written in 1943–1945, demonstrates the dramatic conventions found in Brecht's major plays. Based on the old Chinese parable of the chalk circle rite, it shows Brecht's use of episodes and historical setting to emphasize the pastness of events to convince audiences that social change is both desirable and possible. The play contains Brecht's most representative themes: economic injustice, human exploitation, class conflicts, and power struggles.

The work of the young German director Peter Stein exemplifies a new post-war generation of theatre artists who continue to adapt Brecht's techniques and ideas to another time and to new audiences. A major task after 1945 was to assess the events of the preceding decade and the war years. Brecht's mode of theatre represented a kind of documentation of a significant part of mid-twentieth-century reality. This assessment continues today in the work of post-war playwrights, especially the German-language writers who have such close ties to the war and to the Holocaust period. Director Peter Stein, putting epic techniques to the service of his strong political views, has made the Schaubühne, one of West Berlin's major theatres, part of this assessment.

PLAYS TO READ

All by Bertolt Brecht

The Threepenny Opera

Mother Courage and Her Children

The Caucasian Chalk Circle

SOURCES

For a number of years several Brecht plays were available in English translation by Eric Bentley and published by Grove Press. Beginning in 1971 American and British translators Ralph Manheim and John Willett began a series of new translations of the entire Brecht canon with introductions, editorial notes, text variations (Brecht rewrote scenes many, many times), and Brecht's production notes and writings pertinent to the staging of his plays. The introductions are excellent analyses of Brecht's work during the particular historical period of the plays found in each volume.

The three plays recommended above can be found in the following volumes published as Vintage paperbacks by Random House:

The Threepenny Opera in *Bertolt Brecht Collected Plays,* Vol. 2, 1977, along with *A Man's A Man* and *Rise and Fall of the City of Mahagonny.* The appendix contains Brecht's and Weill's notes to *The Threepenny Opera* and a unique conversation between Brecht and Giorgio Strehler, the Italian director of the Teatro Piccoló, on Strehler's forthcoming production of *The Threepenny Opera* in 1955 in Milan.

Mother Courage and Her Children in *Bertolt Brecht Collected Plays,* Vol. 5, 1972, along with *Life of Galileo,* and the radio play *The Trial of Lucullus.*

Also included are Charles Laughton's rehearsal notes on creating the role of Galileo and Brecht's *Model Book* for *Mother Courage and Her Children.*

The Caucasian Chalk Circle in *Bertolt Brecht Collected Plays*, Vol. 7, 1975, along with *The Visions of Simone Machard, Schweyk in the Second World War,* and Brecht's adaptation of *The Duchess of Malfi.* The appendix contains Brecht's notes to *The Caucasian Chalk Circle,* including comments on staging, setting, and incidental music.

NOTES

1. *Brecht on Theatre: The Development of an Aesthetic,* ed. John Willett (New York: Hill and Wang, 1964), p. 125. Copyright © 1957, 1963, 1964 by Suhrkamp Verlag, Frankfurt am Main. Translation and notes copyright © 1964 by John Willett. Reprinted by permission of Farrar, Straus & Giroux, Inc., and Joan Daves.

2. Mordecai Gorelik, *New Theatres for Old* (New York: Samuel French, 1952), pp. 382–383. Reprinted by permission of the author.

3. *Brecht on Theatre,* pp. 121–122. Reprinted by permission.

4. *Brecht on Theatre,* p. 37. Reprinted by permission.

5. Bertolt Brecht, *Collected Plays,* translated by Ralph Manheim and edited by Ralph Manheim and John Willett (Vintage, 1972), vol. 5, pp. 336–337. Reprinted by permission of Vintage Books, Division of Random House, Inc.

6. Alan Schneider, "Helene Weigel 1900–1971," *New York Times,* May 23, 1971, II, 3. © 1971 by The New York Times Company. Reprinted by permission.

7. Hubert Witt, ed., *Brecht As They Knew Him* (New York: International Publishers, 1974), adapted from p. 126.

8. Carl Weber, "Brecht as Director," *The Drama Review,* 12, No. 1 (Fall 1967), 101–107. Reprinted by permission of Carl Weber.

9. Bertolt Brecht, *Collected Plays* (Vintage, 1975), vol. 7, p. 139. Reprinted by permission.

10. Brecht, *Collected Plays* (Vintage, 1975), vol. 7, p. 229. Reprinted by permission.

11. Jack Zipes, "The Irresistible Rise of the Schaubühne am Halleschen Ufer: A Retrospective of the West Berlin Theater Collective," *Theatre,* 9, No. 1 (Fall 1977), 7–47.

12. Hugh Rorrison, "Berlin's Democratic Theatre and Its *Peer Gynt,*" *Theatre Quarterly,* 4, No. 13 (February–April 1974), 15–36. Reprinted by permission of *Theatre Quarterly.*

TWELVE

POST-WAR TRENDS: THEATRICALISM AND THE ABSURD

A MODERN PERSPECTIVE

Post-war trends in European and American theatre, from the end of World War I to 1960, reflect what sociologist Christopher Lasch has called a "schizoid society." From the Moscow Art Theatre on the one hand to the experiments in circus arenas of German director Max Reinhardt on the other, we find two broad performance styles dominating the modern theatre—*realism* and *theatricalism*.

In the realistic style all stage elements—the playwright's words, actors' performances, and designers' art—simulate details of everyday life appropriate to the play's characters and environment. Realism dominates the theatre of our time. But there has been a countermovement almost since the century began. Some theatre artists, feeling constrained by the limitations of stage realism (by box settings and stage illusionism) have turned to more theatrical modes of expression. They have increasingly sought out purely theatrical devices—open stages, minimal scenic pieces and properties, spectacular lighting effects, ritual with highly stylized sounds and movement, and even actor-audience participation.

In the post-war European theatre, directors like Max Reinhardt, Jean Vilar, Jean-Louis Barrault, and Roger

Blin dominated the new stage theatricalism, while playwrights used new dramaturgical conventions to express their changing vision of the universe. In the 1950s Eugene Ionesco, Samuel Beckett, and Jean Genêt pioneered their theatrical vision of an absurd universe into a full-fledged theatre movement. One of the small art theatres of Paris where these "bizarre" plays have been staged is the Théâtre des Noctambules where, in 1950, director Nicolas Bataille staged a new play by an unknown playwright, Eugene Ionesco, and another offshoot of modern stage theatricalism was born—*absurdist theatre.*

REPRESENTATIVE THEATRE: Théâtre des Noctambules, Paris

The Théâtre des Noctambules, one of many small art theatres located in the Paris suburbs, can be reached by car or by the Paris Metro. Like others of its type, it is an "art" theatre, much like Antoine's Théâtre Libre in its early days. It is small, off the commercial theatre beat, and used by companies of young theatre people for experimental, avant-garde work. In the United States it would be an Off-Off Broadway house.

In 1950 the Théâtre des Noctambules became the scene of a landmark production. Director Nicolas Bataille's small company was handed a play by a friend, without a title, and by a wholly unknown playwright. Bataille directed and performed in the play that was eventually called *The Bald Soprano.*

On May 11, 1950, about 50 people crowded into the small auditorium of the theatre—friends of the company and author plus several influential critics. The curtain opened on a recognizable English living room. There sat the characters Mr. and Mrs. Smith in the utmost normality after their evening meal of fish and chips. Only when the large grandfather clock struck 17 times and Mrs. Smith began to speak could that first-night audience have any inkling that this new playwright, Eugene Ionesco, would transform the European theatre in the next decade. At the time, however, there were few favorable notices, and because there was little money for publicity, the actors donned "sandwich" boards and for about an hour before each performance paraded the streets advertising the play. But the theatre remained almost empty; on several occasions people were given their money back because there were so few in the audience. The company persevered for about six weeks and then closed the play. Nevertheless, the damage was done and the Theatre of the Absurd had been launched by Ionesco's *The Bald Soprano* in a small, out-of-the-way theatre in the suburbs of Paris.

CONDITIONS OF PERFORMANCE

BACKGROUND

Post-war Europe falls into two time segments: the period 1918 to 1939 (the hiatus between the two world wars) and the period following the Second World War (1945–1960) prior to the armed conflicts in Vietnam, Cambodia, and the Mideast.

Together the two world wars, which were

World War I
1914–1918

Russian
Revolution
1917

Mussolini
comes to
power
in Italy
1922

Austria's Archduke
Franz Ferdinand
assassinated
June 1914 by
Serbian nationalists,
setting off
World War I

USSR
formed
1922

Sinking of
the *Lusitania*
in 1915 provoked
U.S. to enter
War by 1917

Communist
Party formed
1918

League of
Nations
formed
1919

fought mostly on European soil, were the most destructive and costly wars of all times. The causes of World War I grew out of political and economic competition among European powers, a new spirit of rising nationalism, and shifting military alliances to ensure a balance of power. The Allies and the Central Powers assembled the largest armies in history on the battlefields of Europe, equipped with new instruments of destruction, including tanks, airplanes, bombs, submarines, and torpedoes. Before the armistice in November 1918, 8,300,000 people had died and more than $337 billion was spent. An American slogan called it "the war to end all wars."

After Germany's surrender a wave of optimism swept Europe, England, and America. The League of Nations was formed in 1919 to arbitrate national disputes and to avoid future military confrontations among the great powers. Republics replaced monarchies in several nations. But the optimism soon faded in the wake of rampant inflation in the 1920s and severe depression in the 1930s. The peace treaties that concluded the war had placed severe economic demands on the defeated, which, on top of the terrible toll in human life and materiel, exacerbated people's fears and discontent. New ideologies (fascism and communism) developed and charismatic dictators emerged to urge their

"new" politics on the people: Mussolini in Italy, Stalin in Russia, Hitler in Germany, Franco in Spain, and Hirohito's war marshals in Japan. The League of Nations soon proved ineffective to arbitrate conflicts over ideologies and territorial claims. Between 1933 and 1939 tensions grew, and in 1939, with Hitler's invasion of Poland, they erupted into a second world conflict—this time to be fought across the face of the globe.

The Second World War was fought with even deadlier weapons, with mass destruction and genocide. Nine million people, two-thirds

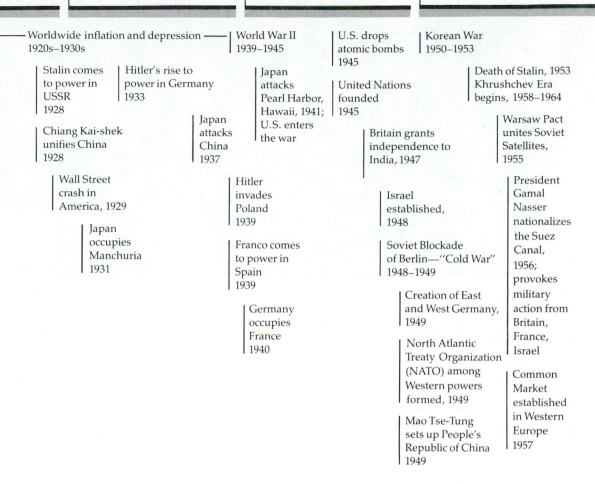

1930   **1940**   **1950**

Worldwide inflation and depression ——
1920s–1930s

| Stalin comes to power in USSR 1928

Hitler's rise to power in Germany 1933

Chiang Kai-shek unifies China 1928

Japan occupies Manchuria 1931

Wall Street crash in America, 1929

Japan occupies Manchuria 1931

World War II 1939–1945

Japan attacks Pearl Harbor, Hawaii, 1941; U.S. enters the war

Japan attacks China 1937

Hitler invades Poland 1939

Franco comes to power in Spain 1939

Germany occupies France 1940

U.S. drops atomic bombs 1945

United Nations founded 1945

Britain grants independence to India, 1947

Israel established, 1948

Soviet Blockade of Berlin—"Cold War" 1948–1949

Creation of East and West Germany, 1949

North Atlantic Treaty Organization (NATO) among Western powers formed, 1949

Mao Tse-Tung sets up People's Republic of China 1949

Korean War 1950–1953

Death of Stalin, 1953 Khrushchev Era begins, 1958–1964

Warsaw Pact unites Soviet Satellites, 1955

President Gamal Nasser nationalizes the Suez Canal, 1956; provokes military action from Britain, France, Israel

Common Market established in Western Europe 1957

of them Jews, died in extermination camps; as many as 45,000,000 (largely civilians) were killed by weapons of mass destruction, including the atomic bomb.

At the war's end the map of Europe had been redesigned, and the two superpowers that emerged—Russia and the United States—confronted each other almost immediately in a competition to extend their influence and maintain national prestige. New nations emerged in Palestine, Egypt, Africa, India, China, Taiwan, and in South America. All the anxieties of the atomic age—the buildup of nuclear arsenals, the fear of tensions among Third World nations erupting into worldwide conflict, the concern of European nations that they may be used as a nuclear battlefield—have had a profound effect on people's lives. In the immediate post-war era, the concentration camps and the mass murders that occurred, along with the development of the means for the total annihilation of the human race, raised philosophical questions among intellectuals and artists about humanity's capacity to act responsibly and to avoid a total holocaust.

The philosophy of *existentialism* addressed questions of human choice and acts; anxiety and

Figure 12-1 Pablo Picasso's *Guernica*.

guilt became major themes of novels, paintings, and plays. The arts reflected these deep concerns for humanity's survival in a wide range of forms and styles, ranging from pure entertainment to distract people from their cares to experiments dramatizing the world's horrors and absurdities.

MANAGEMENT AND STAGE THEATRICALISM

In spite of the disruptions of war on the lives of artists and theatre companies, there was a surprising stability among companies in England, France and Germany and a continuing fermentation of ideas and experiments in performance writing and styles. In England the Old Vic Company maintained a consistent style for playing Shakespeare and other classics. In Germany the Deutsches Theater under the management of Max Reinhardt (1873–1943) and in Paris the Théâtre du Vieux Colombier under the management of Jean Vilar (1912–1971) introduced a new theatricalism that was to challenge the proponents of stage realism. The experiments in theatricalism occurred largely in Germany and in France. Let us first consider the open theatricality of the new artistic directors-managers.

Theatricalism refers to plays performed in a nonrealistic mode and can apply to such diverse works as Reinhardt's mammoth productions at Salzburg Cathedral in Austria and to the absurdist plays performed in the small Paris art theatres. In its broadest sense *theatricalism* represents a revolt against realism by insisting that the stage be used in an openly theatrical way. Under the auspices of such modern directors as Max Reinhardt, Peter Brook, Tom O'Horgan, and Andrei Serban, *theatricalism* has come to be associated with large, spectacular productions; new interpretations of classics or familiar plays; emphasis on pageantry and sensory effects and often a deemphasis on the script's verbal qualities; unusual interpretations of scripts; and the stage used as a stage rather than transformed into a realistic environment.[1]

MAX REINHARDT'S EXPERIMENTS

Critic Martin Esslin has called Max Reinhardt the "high priest of theatricality." Reinhardt's early years as an actor heavily influenced his directorial methods. In his eyes the theatre was an actor's medium and the literary quality of a text was of secondary importance.

Reinhardt's spectacular career began in 1895 as an actor for Otto Brahm, the champion of naturalism, at the Deutsches Theater in Berlin. By 1905, not quite 32 years old, Reinhardt became the national theatre's artistic director, at which point he set about to define his eclecticism. To create an intimate theatre where the psychological subtleties of postnaturalistic theatre could be displayed, Reinhardt built the *Kammerspiele*, an intimate theatre seating about 400 people. Here the rigid division between ac-

> **"** For me the frame that separates the stage from the world has never been essential; my imagination has only reluctantly obeyed its despotism; I regard it merely as a necessary tool of the illusionistic stage, the peep show concept of theatre that emerged from the specific requirements of Italian opera and is not valid for all time; and everything that breaks that frame open, strengthens and widens the effect, increases contact with the audience, whether in the direction of intimacy or monumentality, will always be welcome to me. As everything is welcome to me that is apt to multiply the undreamt-of potentialities of the theatre. **"** [2]
>
> Max Reinhardt, *Works* (1901)

MAX REINHARDT

Max Reinhardt (1873–1943) was an Austrian actor, director, and producer. In Berlin he directed a classical repertoire at the prestigious Deutsches Theater, intimate psychological dramas in the small Kammerspiele theatre adjacent to the Deutsches Theater, and spectacular productions in circuslike spaces elsewhere. His company toured the United States in 1927–1928.

After Hitler's assumption of power in 1933, Reinhardt, a Jew, spent most of his time abroad. He left Europe permanently for the United States in 1938 and worked in Hollywood and New York until his death.

In the United States Reinhardt is best known for the 1935 Warner Brothers film of *A Midsummer Night's Dream* with James Cagney as Bottom the Weaver and Mickey Rooney as the mischievous Puck.

---

tor and audience was broken down by lowering the stage so that it was only a small step above the audience.

The Kammerspiele opened in 1906 with a performance of Ibsen's *Ghosts*, with sets designed by the great Scandinavian painter Edvard Munch (1863–1944) (Figure 12-2). This old masterpiece of stage naturalism heralded by André Antoine and Otto Brahm in the 1890s was transported by Reinhardt into a world of nightmare. Munch's garish colors expressed an inner world of psychological turbulence, and Reinhardt's interpretation of *Ghosts* moved beyond social realism into depth psychology.

The work that firmly established Reinhardt as the leading director in Germany and as a world figure was his treatment of the classical repertoire at the Deutsches Theater, where he mingled the supernatural, the heroic, and the coarsely comic in performance. He also abandoned flat, painted scenery for revolving stages and three-dimensional and solid scenic pieces like towers and arches, which could be moved on the revolving stage into different positions to indicate change of locale.

Figure 12-2 Painter Edvard Munch's designs for Max Reinhardt's production of *Ghosts* (1906) at the Kammerspiele in Berlin.

Figure 12-3 Max Reinhardt staged theatre events outdoors in gardens and town squares and beside lakes. He staged Shakespeare's *Merchant of Venice* in 1934 in a square in Venice, the Campo San Trovaso.

To bring all the disparate elements together, like Meiningen before him Reinhardt became a *Regisseur*—the head and coordinator of a team of artists and technicians, each of whom made a distinct and original contribution, but always under the dominant influence of the director's overall conception.[3]

Reinhardt's international reputation as a creator of spectacular stage effects (some called him a "showman") developed out of his third idea for a theatre—the *Grosses Schauspielhaus* (Great Spectacle House). Exploring the use of circus buildings and arenas for performances, Reinhardt first transformed the Zirkus Schumann in Vienna into his "theatre of five thou-

sand." Here in 1911 he staged Hugo von Hofmannsthal's adaptation of the English morality play *Everyman* (*Jedermann*). The First World War intervened before his new building could be completed, but in 1919 the Grosses Schauspielhaus opened with a performance of Aeschylus' *Oresteia*. The audience was led from narrow foyers into a vast arena that contained a central open stage allowing the action to take place in the center of the auditorium.

Although the theatre of the five thousand never quite succeeded with the critics or audiences, by 1919 Reinhardt had already turned toward new experiments in stage theatricalism. He persuaded the officials of the beautiful cathedral

Figure 12-4 By involving the entire city of Salzburg, its great cathedral and its architecture, Reinhardt enlarged the scope of theatre into total environmental staging. The scenery was minimal; a platform raised to the level of the cathedral's entrance. The play opens with the voice of God, who summons Death to bring him the rich Everyman to give an account of his life on earth. The voice of God sounded mightily from high up inside the cathedral. When the figure of Death appeared, it was as though one of the statues adorning the cathedral façade had come to life. When Everyman himself was summoned, voices called to him from all sides, echoing and reechoing from the towers of the many churches in Salzburg where actors had been posted.

When the time came for Everyman to die, dusk was falling upon the city (the time of the start of the performance varied with the hour of sunset each day) and the figures of Faith and Good Works that appeared to assist Everyman seemed again to be no more than statues of the façade miraculously come to life. When Everyman's soul was finally received into paradise, the interior of the cathedral lit up (for it was now dark). The cathedral's massive doors opened, organ music and hymns resounded from inside, and all the bells of the city's many churches began to peal. The only light in the square came from the marble-and-gold interior of the great baroque church.

city of Salzburg to create the Salzburg Festival, and in 1920 staged there an open-air production of *Everyman* on the cathedral square. A more effective setting could hardly be imagined. The square is completely enclosed; the street that passes through it enters and leaves by two archways. The facade of the cathedral fills one side; its entrance is faced by large baroque statues cf saints. The square gives the impression of being a large room.

Everyman became the classic among Reinhardt's works and was restaged regularly at Salzburg until 1937 (the last year before Hitler's takeover of Austria); it was resumed again after the war (Figure 12-4).

Unlike directors that came before him, Reinhardt believed that each play required a different style. Further, his conception of theatrical style included the actor, the physical arrangement of the theatre, and the spatial relationship of the audience to the actors. For each play he prepared a *Regiebuch* (promptbook) that recorded all details of movement, interpretation, setting, properties, sound, lighting, and costume.

Reinhardt's technical achievements in the theatre and especially his vision of theatre as "theatrical experience" inspired others. Reinhardt believed that theatre should create a lasting impression in the spectators' minds and be an emotional highpoint in their lives. This kind of theatre was his greatest achievement.

FRENCH DIRECTORS BETWEEN THE WARS

In 1913 the French director Jacques Copeau (1879–1949) assembled a company that included Louis Jouvet and Charles Dullin, and he converted a hall seating 400 into the Théâtre du Vieux Colombier. This small art theatre had a forestage forward of an inner proscenium, no machinery except for a set of curtains, and asbestos hangings that could be moved on rods to effect rapid changes of locale. Only a few pieces of essential furniture and set pieces were used.

Copeau's approach represents another type of stage theatricalism—minimal staging rather than the spectacular.

Before the war forced him to close the theatre, Copeau presented some 15 plays, including Shakespeare and Molière. Between 1917 and 1919 he toured the United States before returning to Paris to reopen the theatre. Copeau's work at the Théâtre du Vieux Colombier is impossible to overrate. With his manifesto of translating the playwright's text into a "poetry of the theatre," Copeau elevated the actor's presence on a bare platform over that of the playwright, text, or scenic elements. The actor, for Copeau, became the "living presence" of the playwright.

Although Copeau produced plays for only five years after reopening his theatre in 1919 in Paris, his ideals influenced Louis Jouvet (1887–1951), Charles Dullin (1885–1949), Georges Pitoeff (1884–1939), and Gaston Baty (1882–1951), directors who played a major role in the French theatre until the Second World War. In 1927 they formed an alliance, the *Cartel des Quatre* (the Cartel of Four), under which they agreed to counsel each other, to share publicity, and to negotiate jointly with theatrical unions.

Louis Jouvet formed a company in 1924 with many members of Copeau's disbanded troupe and developed an association with playwright Jean Giraudoux. In 1934 Jouvet opened the Théâtre de l'Athenée where he remained until 1941. He went into voluntary exile between 1941 and 1945—the years of the Nazi occupation of Paris. Like Copeau, Jouvet put primary emphasis on the text in combination with a theatrical style.

PLAYWRITING IN FRANCE BETWEEN THE WARS

Michel de Ghelderode (1898–1962), Jean Giraudoux (1882–1944), and Jean Anouilh (b. 1910) dominated French playwriting between the wars.

Ghelderode, a Belgian playwright, was influenced by the surrealists and expressionists, especially by Alfred Jarry and Antonin Artaud. He wrote more than 30 plays in which he depicted humankind as trapped by the sins of the flesh. Corruption, death, and cruelty are always part of Ghelderode's world. His often-exaggerated characters, descended from clowns of music halls, circuses, and fairs, move through scenes of degradation. He favored spectacle and downgraded language. His best-known plays today are *Escurial* (1927), *Chronicles of Hell* (1929),

---

ALFRED JARRY

Alfred Jarry (1873–1907), French poet and playwright, wrote perhaps the first absurdist play, *Ubu Roi* (*King Ubu*), performed in Paris at Lugne-Pöe's Théâtre de l'Oeuvre in 1896. This wild symbolic farce, a kind of parody of *Oedipus the King*, caused a scandal. It savagely attacked bourgeois society through its depiction of a grotesque world without human decency. Its crude, violent images of the world were reflected in the activities of the monstrous tyrant Ubu, who makes himself king of Poland and keeps himself in power by killing and torturing everyone who opposes him. Ubu is eventually driven out but promises to continue his exploits elsewhere.

Jarry wrote sequels to *Ubu Roi*, the best known being *Ubu enchaîné* (*Ubu Bound*), published in 1900 but not performed until 1937. Jarry's Ubu plays have been highly influential on absurdist writers.

---

and *Pantagleize* (1929). Discovered by the absurdists, his reputation has gradually risen since 1949.

Jean Giraudoux, probably the most important French playwright between the wars, wrote most of his important works for director Louis Jouvet, including *Amphitryon 38* (1929), *The Trojan War Shall Not Take Place* (1935), and *Ondine* (1939). Giraudoux considered language the highest expression of human reason and tried to return its literary worth to the drama. His plays turn on such antitheses as peace and war, life and death, liberty and destiny, but throughout them runs a deep faith in human goodness.

Jean Anouilh challenged Giraudoux's position of preeminence in the 1930s. As Jouvet's secretary, he was inspired by Giraudoux to write plays. He is best known for *Carnival of Thieves* (1938), *Antigone* (1943), *Waltz of the Toreadors* (1952), *The Lark* (1953), and *Becket* (1960). *Antigone*, one of his most frequently produced plays, with its confrontation between human ideals and forces of tyranny was a thinly disguised story of the occupation of France by Nazi Germany.

One of the most influential foreign playwrights on the French theatre was Luigi Pirandello (1867–1936). The Italian playwright pioneered the philosophical view that truth is necessarily personal and subjective. In a Pirandello play, like *Right You Are, If You Think You Are* (1917), issues cannot be resolved by a recourse to facts because each one of us has his or her own version of truth.

While Pirandello began by writing Sicilian folk comedies and drawing room comedies, he pioneered theatricalist scripts. His famous theatre trilogy—*Six Characters in Search of an Author* (1921), *Each in His Own Way* (1924), and *Tonight We Improvise* (1930)—uses the stage as a stage and shows how much like life the theatre actually is. *Six Characters in Search of an Author* is his most theatricalist play, opening on a rehearsal of a "Pirandello play" and evolving into a play-within-a-play where characters search for an author to complete their script.

ANTONIN ARTAUD

Antonin Artaud (1896–1948) was a French poet-actor-playwright-essayist. During the 1920s in Paris, Artaud wrote plays, essays, poems, film scripts; he acted, produced, and directed. He established one theatre company that failed, the Alfred Jarry Théâtre, and conceived of the Theatre of Cruelty. In 1938 Artaud published *The Theatre and Its Double*, a collection of lectures and articles on theatre. The most powerful essay is "The Theatre and the Plague" in which Artaud draws parallels between theatrical action and a plague as purifying events. Ill health drew him to a dependency on drugs. Confined to many institutions, the most famous being Rodez, Artaud was released five years before his death in 1948.

Though Artaud's theatrical successes were few, it is almost impossible to discuss modern theatre without mentioning his theories. He called for theatre to purge the audience's feelings of hatred, violence, and cruelty by using nonverbal sounds, lighting effects, unusual theatre spaces, violent movements. Artaud wanted to assault the audience's senses, to cleanse it morally and spiritually, for the improvement of humankind.

Figure 12-5 Jean-Louis Barrault in costume, 1952.

POST-WAR DIRECTORS IN FRANCE

The leading French directors in the years following World War II were Jean-Louis Barrault (b. 1910) and Jean Vilar (1912–1971). Barrault, one of the greatest actors of our time, studied with Charles Dullin and worked with Artaud and mime teacher Etienne Decroux. In 1940 he became a member (a *sociétaire*) of the Comédie Française, and in 1943 his production of Paul Claudel's *The Satin Slipper* made his reputation as a theatricalist director. A masked actor represented a wrecked ship floating among waves; actors recreated the motions of the sea; a man riding a horse was symbolized by a horse's head; and so on. With Barrault the "theatre theatrical" had arrived on stage at the Comédie Française.

Considered unplayable because of its length and symbolic complexity, Claudel's play was reshaped by Barrault into a theatre event. A play's text is like an iceberg, declared Barrault, since only about one-eighth is visible. For Barrault the director's task was to complete the playwright's work, revealing the hidden portions by using all the theatre's resources.

In 1946 after resigning from the Comédie Française, Barrault, with his actress-wife Madeleine Renaud, formed the Madeleine Renaud–Jean-Louis Barrault Company. They have since produced plays ranging from Aeschylus' *Oresteia* to Jean Genêt's avant-garde *The Screens*.

Jean Vilar was a fellow student with Barrault at Dullin's school. Vilar's fame came with the organization of the Avignon Festival (France) in 1947. His work there and in Paris (most notably as Henry IV in the Paris production of Pirandello's play) led in 1951 to his appointment as director of the Théâtre National Populaire (TNP). By 1954 TNP was one of the most popular companies in France. In his productions Vilar emphasized the actors and reinforced their preeminence by costumes and lighting. Scenery was usually restricted to platforms and a few set pieces. TNP soon commanded great popular support, developing branches at the Palais de Chaillot in Paris, the Avignon Festival, and most recently in Villeneuve.

PLAYWRITING AFTER THE SECOND WORLD WAR

The Existentialists Jean Paul Sartre (1905–1980) and Albert Camus (1913–1960) exerted an enormous influence on novelists and playwrights with their existentialist writings. Sartre in such plays as *The Flies* (1943), *No Exit* (1944), and *The Condemned of Altona* (1959) argued that to be a responsible, authentic being, each individual must choose his or her own values and live by them without regard to received ideas. Unthinking conformity turns people into robots. Sartre's plays, like his novels, show characters faced with choices that require them to reassess their outlooks and to forge new personal standards of behavior. Sartre, believing that conformity and the refusal to make choices had made the Nazi atrocities possible, stated that people must be politically engaged even though the choices open to them were seldom ideal.

Albert Camus, editor of a clandestine newspaper during the German occupation of France, turned from journalism to the novel and the theatre after the war. Although his dramatic output was small—*Cross-Purposes* (1944), *Caligula* (performed in 1945), *State of Seige* (1948), and *The Just Assassins* (1949)—his influence on the theatre world was considerable. This influence came in part from his famous essay "The Myth of Sisyphus" written in 1943 in which he argues that the human condition is *absurd* because of the gap between people's hopes and the irrational universe into which they are born. For Camus the only remedy lies in each person's search for a set of standards (admittedly without any objective basis) that will allow him or her to bring order out of this chaos. Suicide, he argued most eloquently, was no way out of the human dilemma.

Although Sartre and Camus often differed bitterly in their ideas about engagement, they nevertheless supplied the philosophical basis for the absurdist movement, which emerged in the early 1950s. Despite their assumption that the world is irrational, their plays retained a traditional dramatic form (almost a well-made one), as we will see later in this chapter.

The Absurdists Samuel Beckett (b. 1906), Eugene Ionesco (b. 1912), and Jean Genêt (b. 1910) assimilated the ideas of Sartre and Camus and created what Martin Esslin called the *Theatre of*

❚❚ *A world that can be explained even with bad reasons is a familiar world. But, on the other hand, in a universe suddenly divested of illusions and lights, man feels an alien, a stranger. His exile is without remedy since he is deprived of the memory of a lost home or the hope of a promised land. This divorce between man and his life, the actor and his setting, is properly the feeling of absurdity.*❚❚

Albert Camus, *The Myth of Sisyphus* (1942)[4]

the *Absurd.* In his landmark book of that name, written in 1961, Esslin defined the absurd as being out of harmony with reason and propriety; ridiculous, incongruous, and unreasonable. The so-called absurdist writers set about not to argue about life's absurdities but to show an absurd universe in concrete stage images and in language that was emptied of meaning.[5]

Ionesco called his first work, *The Bald Soprano* (written in 1948 and performed in 1950), an "antiplay" to point up his rebellion against conventional drama. The themes of his plays of the fifties parody materialistic bourgeois society, clichés of language and thought, and human irrationality. In his full-length plays of the sixties—*The Killer, Rhinoceros, A Stroll in the Air,* and *Exit the King*—his protagonists struggle against social and political conformity, although they can offer no rational basis for their actions.

Samuel Beckett's *Waiting for Godot* (1953) was the first of the early absurdist plays to win international fame. Beckett strips his characters and situations of their social, psychological, and political contexts. His characters exist in ravaged landscapes as creatures of the human condition in a metaphysical sense only. They despair and console one another, raise questions that cannot be answered, and struggle to keep going in an unhospitable environment. Probably more than any other writer of our time, Beckett has expressed the postwar writer's doubts about our capacity to understand and control our world. *Come and Go* (1966) and *Not I* (1973) take us into the stream of consciousness of the protagonist's mind where impressions are received but not sorted out in any logical way.

Jean Genêt spent most of his life in prison where he began writing novels, journals, and plays. In 12 years (1949–1961) he wrote five highly controversial plays whose characters are

---

❝ *The staging of a play is always the result of compromise. Compromise, at least, between the visual and aural imagination of the director and the living, anarchic reality of the actors. For my part, I never set anything definitely or precisely before the first rehearsals. I have no papers, no notes, no written plans. Nothing in my hands, nothing up my sleeve:* Everything in the minds and bodies of others. *Facing me, the actor.*

To compel an actor to integrate voice and body into a predetermined harmony or plastic composition smacks of animal-training. An actor is more than an intelligent animal or robot. Slowly and patiently, I believe, a sort of physical rapport *grows up between him and me, so that we understand each other without need of many words. It is essential for me to know him well, and to like him even if he isn't very likeable. It is impossible to produce successfully a work dependent on the good will of so many, to direct* a play well, *with people one doesn't like. To* love the theatre is nothing. To love those who practice it may be less 'artistic,' but it gets better results. Nevertheless, though I do not 'attempt to mold the various parts' . . . to a concept of* ensemble, *it is still true that after a (variable) number of rehearsals one sometimes has to guide some of the actors (without their being necessarily aware of it) toward* ensemble *play, to bring them into a certain harmony of tone with the rest. Not that the director arbitrarily selects this tone; it is born of the polygamous interaction of the voices, bodies, and minds of the other actors and the script.*

When this point is reached, it must be "set." It is the first, mysterious moment when the fate of the production is decided. The actor is sometimes unaware of it, and so much the better, for he would otherwise freeze what should remain spontaneous. **❞**

Jean Vilar, "Theatre Without Pretensions" (1963)[6]

social misfits, outcasts, rebels against organized society. The source of the absurd in his work is that nothing has meaning without its opposite—law and crime, judge and criminal, saint and sinner, religion and sin, love and hate, and so on—and that the way we assign values to these opposites is entirely arbitrary. In the theatre he transforms life as he sees it into a series of ceremonies and rituals that give universal meaning to otherwise nonsensical and arbitrary behavior.

While these three playwrights have led the absurdist movement, other writers have followed their lead and their work has been performed in the Paris avant-garde theatres. Arthur Adamov (1908–1971), born in Russia and educated in Switzerland, was attracted to surrealism. He turned to playwriting in the late 1940s and wrote *The Invasion* (1950), *Parody* (1952), and *All Against All* (1953). Adamov created seriocomic, nightmarelike situations in which characters exist in a cruel world of moral destructiveness and personal anxieties and people are condemned to failure by their inability to communicate. Adamov's later plays take on a more social and political orientation. His most famous one, *Paolo Paoli* (1957) uses a Brechtian form to comment on the materialism and hypocrisy that preceded the First World War. *Spring '71* (1960) idealizes the people who created the Paris Commune in 1871.

Jacques Audiberto (1899–1965), Georges Schéhadé (b. 1910), and Jean Tardieu (b. 1903), like Adamov, never achieved the international reputations of Ionesco, Beckett, and Genêt. However, Fernando Arrabal (b. 1932) achieved international recognition with *The Automobile Graveyard* (1966), *The Architect and the Emperor of Assyria* (1967), *And They Handcuffed the Flowers* (1970), *Young Barbarians Today* (1975), and *King of Sodom* (1979).

Perhaps the best-known French-language playwright since 1960, Arrabal was born in Spain, moved to Paris in 1955, and has written all of his plays in French. His early plays explore thoughtless, meaningless cruelty and are couched in a dramatic form similar to that used by the absurdists. In *Fando and Lis* (1958), for example, two childlike protagonists try to reach the town of Tar but always arrive back at the same place. Despite his love for the paralyzed Lis, Fando leaves her exposed for strangers to look at her. As a result, she becomes ill, falls, and breaks his drum. Fando beats her severely and she dies. Fando then misses her but fails to understand his part in her death.

Sometime in 1962 Arrabal devised what he called *théâtre panique* ("panic theatre"): a term that combines the usual sense of the word *panic* or *terror* with, according to Martin Esslin, the original connotation of "pertaining to the god Pan."[7] Arrabal's théâtre panique is a celebration of *all* of life: death and life, the sacred and the profane, the mystical and the erotic. *The Architect and the Emperor of Assyria* is the finest example of Arrabal's panic theatre. The play has only two characters who enact a series of ritualized human situations: master and slave, judge and criminal, mother and child, male and female, sadist and masochist. Eventually, one decides that he must be punished and asks the other to kill and eat him. As the act of cannibalism takes place, the new figure appears (as the two merge), and the whole cycle begins over again. A play like *The Architect and Emperor of Assyria* challenges all values and exposes the hidden corners of the human psyche.

AVANT-GARDE DIRECTORS IN FRANCE

Playwrights like Ionesco, Beckett, and Genêt were ignored by the commercial theatres in Paris, but, fortunately, there were adventurous directors in the small art theatres who understood the new material and were anxious to present it. Many were heavily influenced by Artaud's ideas on a "theatre of cruelty" that operated directly on the audience's senses, forcing them to confront moral and psychological truths about themselves. As Artaud put it in

Figure 12-6 Samuel Beckett's tramps, Vladimir and Estragon, entertain themselves by searching for a missing boot. Although Godot has not kept his appointment with them, the tree has grown leaves between the first and second acts. With Godot's absence and the tree's growth, Beckett juxtaposes despair with hope, loss with gain. The photo is from the 1961 Paris revival of *Waiting for Godot* directed by Jean-Marie Serreau with Lucien Raimbourg as Vladimir and Etienne Berg as Estragon. The tree was designed by sculptor Alberto Giacometti.

The Theatre and Its Double (1938), "the theatre has been created to drain abscesses collectively."[8]

In the 1950s the most influential of these directors were Nicolas Bataille (b. 1926), Roger Blin (b. 1907), and Jean-Marie Serreau (1915–1973). Most of them had worked with Charles Dullin and Jean-Louis Barrault. Bataille introduced Ionesco's plays to Paris audiences at the small Théâtre des Noctambules; Rober Blin staged Beckett's and Genêt's plays at the Théâtre du Babylone. Jean-Marie Serreau staged the first productions of Adamov's plays before opening the Théâtre de Babylone with Roger Blin in 1952. He directed the Paris revival of *Waiting for Godot* in 1961; the single tree central to the play's meaning was designed by the world-famous Italian sculptor Alberto Giacometti (Figure 12-6).

These members of the avant-garde in the fifties were later to work regularly with such established companies as the Comédie Française and the Théâtre de France.

VISUAL ELEMENTS: FROM FUTURISM TO SURREALISM

Theatricalism in stage design has been influenced by theatre artists like Adolphe Appia, Edward Gordon Craig, and Antonin Artaud, and by major European art movements—symbolism, expressionism, futurism, dadaism, constructivism, and surrealism. These "isms" or art movements of several past decades have had a great and varied influence on the theory and practice of modern theatre design. It appears that no sooner did one "ism," such as futurism, become influential (and even voguish) than another appeared to take its place. This, in part, accounts for the eclecticism of modern theatre design and performance styles.

Eclecticism is not found in the theatre of stage illusionism where the aim is to replicate the everyday environment of middle-class life, but is associated with the open theatricality in theatre design and performance styles between the years 1920 and 1960.

We have already considered expressionism, constructivism, and symbolism in earlier chapters. Let us examine here the influence of futurism, dadaism, and surrealism on designers and writers looking for ways to break out of realistic modes. While realism is the dominant mode of twentieth-century theatre, the new styles (both theatricality and the absurd) basically have been reactions against the realistic theatre. The recent work of the brilliant scenic artist Joseph Svoboda at Prague's National Theatre in Czechoslovakia shows these multiple influences.

Futurism In 1909 in Italy cries of "Burn the Museums!" burst from the throats—and pens—of the futurists upon the consciousness of an astonished public. The term *futurist* was coined in 1908 by the Italian poet, editor, and art promoter Filippo Tommaso Marinetti (1876–1944) as a label for his own explorations in poetry. His manifesto was published on the front page of the respected Paris newpaper *Le Figaro* in 1909 and the futurists were born.

The futurists, like the later absurdists, were concerned with humanity's estrangement from the world. Unlike the expressionists, they did not define this estrangement in terms of historical ills like materialism and industrialism but rather saw it as personal. They wanted art (music, poetry, theatre, and painting) to restore a

---

JOSEF SVOBODA

Josef Svoboda (b. 1920) is the chief designer at Prague's National Theatre in Czechoslovakia, where he has earned the title of "National Artist," his nation's highest award. Most of his scenic experimentation began in the 1950s when the restrictions of socialist realism in the arts were loosened. He has been highly influenced by the 1930s multimedia experimentation of designer Miroslav Kouril (b. 1911) and by the experiments at the Prague Institute of Scenography founded in 1957.

The turning point in Svoboda's career came in 1958 when he collaborated with director Alfred Radok on *Polyekran* and *Laterna Magika,* for which he used film projections on large screens, platforms, live actors, mirrors, plastics, and netting. Shown at the Brussels World's Fair in 1958, Svoboda's work elicited great excitement. His work is unique for his use of surfaces to project images around the living actor.

He has designed settings in every conceivable style to create a flexible playing space and to alter our perceptions of spatial relationships and even the size of the acting area. Svoboda is one of the best and most influential international designers working today.

sense of daring and assertiveness to living. "We want to reenter life," they wrote. To them, "life" meant *action*. They used the word *dynamism* to signify the difference between life and death—between participation in an expanding universe and withdrawal into personal isolation. "We are the primitives of a new sensibility," they boasted, and this sensibility gave emotional value to a technological world.[9]

Beginning in 1910 the futurists gave performances and produced plays, concerts, and art exhibits that aimed to change the modes of perception of the bourgeois spectator. Their model for the theatre of the future was the "variety theatre," or popular entertainments of French music halls, cabarets, and circuses. What the futurists valued was interaction between performers and spectators, as well as the overall dynamism of the performance. They wanted to compress into the shortest possible time span many situations, ideas, sensations, facts, and symbols. Many of the pieces (called *sintesi*) took only a minute or less to perform, compressing life's diversity into, say, a moment in a subway, café, or train station. These short pieces became symphonies of gesture, words, noises, and light, mingling kinetic sculptures and collages, performers with nonhuman shapes and abstract forms. Most important, the futurists rejected the cause-and-effect logic of the traditional theatre. They dismissed the notion that the public must always understand the whys and wherefores of every scenic action.

After 1930 futurism declined but it had pioneered staging innovations that extended into the 1950s, including theatricalist art, the intermingling of performers and audiences, use of modern technology for multimedia performances, antiliterary texts, and a breaking down of barriers between the arts.

Dadaism   World War I severely curtailed most serious theatrical activity in France. Popular entertainment continued to dominate the boulevard theatres of Paris during and after the war. But between the wars a series of revolts in the arts—fauvism, expressionism, cubism, futurism, constructivism, dadaism, and surrealism—helped to loosen the hold of stage realism and provided an alternative to popular entertainment. Dadaism was launched in 1916 in Switzerland where many artists had taken refuge. Its principal spokesman was Tristan Tzara (1896–1963), a Rumanian poet who published seven manifestoes between 1916 and 1920 in the magazine *Dada*.

The dadaists, responding to the horrors of the war and to the insanity of the world, sought to replace logic and reason with calculated madness in art. Working mainly at the Cabaret Voltaire in Zurich, they substituted discord and chaos for unity, balance, and harmony. Like the futurists they confronted audiences with collages and other visual art, "sound poems," dance, and playlets. Tzara favored "chance

"Essentially, each 'ism' is a single angle of vision on the totality of human experience that is either reflected by the playwright in the script or imposed as a style of production by the director. . . . This parade of 'isms' did not occur in a historical vacuum. Generally, each new 'ism' was a violent reaction—both aesthetic and philosophic—to the dominant 'ism' that preceded it. . . . Once a style of production goes out of fashion it does not disappear for good. Expressionism, for example, flourished in Germany in the first two decades of this century. But the expressionist's way of looking at life and thinking about theatre has been regularly used as a theatrical style by playwrights, directors, and designers ever since. . . . in spite of the great diversity of styles that characterizes the modern theatre, each new style has basically been a reaction against naturalism."

Robert W. Corrigan,
The World of the Theatre (1979)[10]

poems," which he created by cutting sentences from newspapers, putting them in a hat, mixing them up, and then drawing them out and reading them. By 1920 dadaism had run its course and surrealism, crystallized by André Breton (1896–1966) in his surrealist manifestoes of 1924, had captured the avant-garde imagination.

Surrealism Surrealism, which emphasized elements of spontaneity, chance, and juxtaposition in the process of creation, had from its beginnings a specific course of action based upon well-stated principles. Deeply influenced by Freud's psychoanalytic theories, Breton summarized their consequences for modern art in the first surrealist manifesto. Here he defined surrealism as "pure psychic automatism, by which is intended to express, verbally, in writing, or by any other means, the real process of thought. Thought's dictation, in the absence of all control by the reason and outside all aesthetic or moral preoccupations."[11]

Surrealism celebrated literature and art as the ultimate fulfillment of the unconscious, which was the source of the artist's most significant perceptions. Guillaume Apollinaire's (1880–1918) *The Breasts of Tiresias* (written in 1903 and produced in 1917) became one of the most seminal plays of the movement. In surrealist drama familiar human situations occurred in unusual surroundings; seemingly unrelated scenes were juxtaposed together, and an illogical progression of scenes broke the bonds of ordinary reality.

Among the most famous advocates of surrealism were Breton, Antonin Artaud, Jean Cocteau, Roger Vitrac, and such visual artists as Pablo Picasso, Henri Matisse, and Georges Braque. Surrealism as a movement dissipated in the 1920s because of political dissension among its leaders. Breton, for example, tried to make communism a fundamental tenet of the movement. However, unlike futurism and dadaism, surrealism has lived on in various guises, most successfully in French absurdist theatre.

DRAMATIC CONVENTIONS

PIRANDELLO'S METATHEATRE

The *metatheatrical* has become a central dramatic convention of certain twentieth-century playwrights, including Luigi Pirandello, Eugene Ionesco, Samuel Beckett, and Jean Genêt. The play-within-the-play convention has always been used to mirror details of a main plot, such as Hamlet's "mousetrap" in Shakespeare's play to expose King Claudius' guilt. However, the metatheatrical play uses the convention in more universal terms. In the older usage the inner play convinces us of the reality of the outer play. In contrast, the metatheatrical play says that all life is performance and that the theatre is the most appropriate art form for capturing life's plots, role playing, feelings, and conflicts. In other words, the theatre is more like life than life itself appears to be. In life we play out our small dramas, our "living" roles, and our crises with happy or unhappy endings.

Pirandello wrote within the metatheatrical convention. He said: "I think that life is a sad piece of buffoonery; because we have in ourselves, without being able to know why . . . the need to deceive ourselves constantly by creating a reality (one for each and never the same for all) which, from time to time, is discovered to be vain and illusory."[12] For Pirandello both life and art were illusory and he worked to find a dramatic form to assist him in making this statement. What he eventually came up with is what Marshall McLuhan would call "the medium is the message" type of drama.

Pirandello stated that life is a masquerade in which "without knowing it, we mask ourselves with that which we appear to be." In drawing room comedy, characters define themselves as individuals against a background of society, a clash of wills, and moral experiences. But Pirandello's concerns for our existential dividedness—our knowing about several persons within ourselves—was too complex for drawing room comedy. So in *Right You Are, If You Think You Are* he used a central mirror on stage for the *raissoneur* (the principal spokesman for the writer) to talk to himself about the problem. The character Laudisi gives essentially a "Who am I?" speech before a mirror, in which he questions his true identity. Is it the image that he sees in the mirror or is it the thinking and feeling person he knows himself to be?

Pirandello's version of metatheatre is born in Laudisi's mirror speech. In *Six Characters in Search of an Author*, Pirandello turns to the bare stage itself to weld form to his vision of life. Here Pirandello abandoned naturalistic production techniques to show us the very essence of our nature as he sees it; the duality of the masks we put on for society and the faces beneath our masks. By using a bare stage and by putting on the stage the person that we feel ourselves to be along with the actor that we inevitably become as we live among others in society, the dramatic technique complements the theme; the two roles become visible to audiences as one.

In *Six Characters* the father in the unfinished script confronts the leading man's interpretation of the father's suffering. In this confrontation between "actor" and "character," Pirandello shows how society interprets the surface of our lives while underneath we are probably suffering and bleeding to death unnoticed.

The Father . . . It will be difficult to act me as I really am. The effect will be rather—apart from the make-up—according as to how he supposes I am, as he senses me—if he does sense me—and not as I inside of myself feel myself to be. It seems to me then that account should be taken of this by everyone whose duty it may become to criticize us . . .[13]

(II)

While Pirandello has been criticized for pursuing one theme ("What is reality?")

The Mirror Speech

[Laudisi, *left alone, walks up and down the study a number of times, nodding his head and occasionally smiling. Finally he draws up in front of the big mirror that is hanging over the mantelpiece. He sees himself in the glass, stops, and addresses his image.*]

Laudisi So there you are! [*He bows to himself and salutes, touching his forehead with his fingers.*] I say, old man, who is mad, you or I? [*He levels a finger menacingly at his image in the glass; and, of course, the image in turn levels a finger at him. As he smiles, his image smiles.*] Of course, I understand! I say it's you, and you say it's me. You—you are mad! No? It's me? Very well! It's me! Have it *your* way. Between you and me, we get along very well, don't we! But the trouble is, others don't think of you just as I do; and that being the case, old man, what a fix you're in! As for me, I say that here, right in front of you, I can see myself with my eyes and touch myself with my fingers. But what are you for other people? What are you in their eyes? An image, my dear sir, just an image in the glass! They're all carrying just such a phantom around inside themselves, and here they are racking their brains about the phantoms in other people; and they think all that is quite another thing!

Pirandello,
Right You Are, If You Think You Are
(1917), Act II[14]

Josef Svoboda is perhaps the most imaginative scenic artist of the last several decades. Left: *Oedipus the King,* designed and directed by Svoboda at the Smetana Theatre, 1963. Below: Svoboda's design for Capek's *The Insect Comedy,* produced at the Prague National Theatre, 1965.

Production of Richard Wagner's *Tristan* at the Festspielhaus, Bayreuth, 1962–1969.

Alwin Nikolais' multimedia productions have been among the most innovative in American contemporary dance theatre. *Scenario* premiered at the Anta Theatre, New York, February 25, 1971.

Albert Camus (1913–1960)

Cross Purposes 1944   Caligula p. 1945   State of Siege 1948

Luigi Pirandello (1867–1936)

Henry IV 1922   Each in His Own Way 1924   Tonight We Improvise 1930

Six Characters in Search of an Author, 1921

As You Desire Me 1930

Right You Are, 1916

Jean Paul Sartre (1905–1980)

The Flies 1943   No Exit 1944   Dirty Hands 1948

Jean Anouilh (b. 1910)

Traveller Without Baggage 1937   Carnival of Thieves 1938   Antigone 1943

Michel de Ghelderode (1898–1962)

Escurial 1927   Chronicles of Hell 1929

Pantagleize 1929

The Maids p. 1947

Jean Giraudoux (1882–1944)

Amphitryon 38 1929   Judith 1931   The Trojan War Shall Not Take Place 1935   Ondine 1939

"To man is given at birth the sad privilege of feeling himself alive, with the illusions which come from it—namely to assume a reality outside himself and that interior feeling of life, change-able and various. The forms in which we try to stop and fix the continuous flow are the concepts, the ideals within which we want to keep coherent all the fictions we create, the condition and status in which we try to establish ourselves."

Luigi Pirandello, *On Humor* (1908)

throughout his 30-odd plays, his importance to the development of the modern theatre cannot be ignored. He inverted the central convention of modern dramaturgy. Instead of pretending that the stage was not a stage but a living room, he insisted that the living room was not a living room but was really a stage. In short, he popu-larized the metatheatrical play in the modern theatre.

Not only did Pirandello use the stage to comment upon life as theatre, but he also used it to examine the nature of art. He argued that a work of art can capture the truth of any given

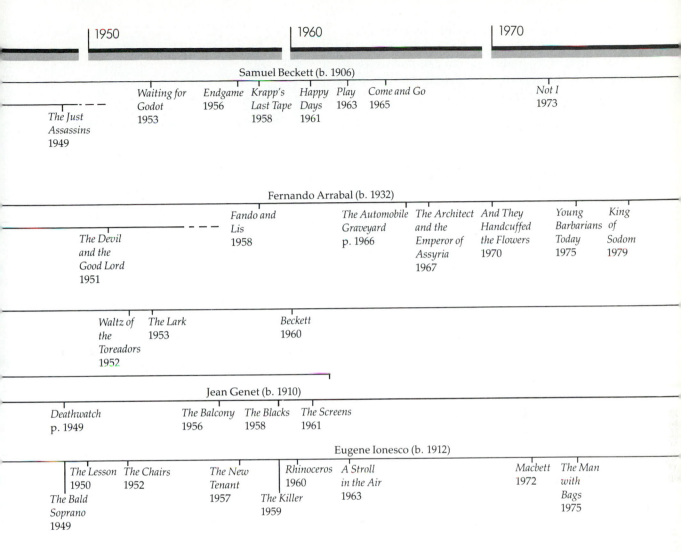

| | 1950 | | | 1960 | | | 1970 | |

Samuel Beckett (b. 1906)

The Just Assassins 1949

Waiting for Godot 1953 — *Endgame* 1956 — *Krapp's Last Tape* 1958 — *Happy Days* 1961 — *Play* 1963 — *Come and Go* 1965 — *Not I* 1973

Fernando Arrabal (b. 1932)

The Devil and the Good Lord 1951

Fando and Lis 1958 — *The Automobile Graveyard* p. 1966 — *The Architect and the Emperor of Assyria* 1967 — *And They Handcuffed the Flowers* 1970 — *Young Barbarians Today* 1975 — *King of Sodom* 1979

Waltz of the Toreadors 1952 — *The Lark* 1953 — *Beckett* 1960

Jean Genet (b. 1910)

Deathwatch p. 1949 — *The Balcony* 1956 — *The Blacks* 1958 — *The Screens* 1961

Eugene Ionesco (b. 1912)

The Lesson 1950 — *The Chairs* 1952 — *The New Tenant* 1957 — *Rhinoceros* 1960 — *A Stroll in the Air* 1963 — *Macbett* 1972 — *The Man with Bags* 1975

The Bald Soprano 1949 — *The Killer* 1959

moment and freeze it for all time. Life, in contrast, is in a continuing state of change and flux. For Pirandello it was our tragedy that we try to arrest time and to fix life in stable and permanent forms. Since we are unable to do this, we are thrown into states of confusion and unhappiness.

EXISTENTIALIST PLAYWRIGHT: JEAN-PAUL SARTRE

Jean-Paul Sartre and Albert Camus, the two leading post-war existentialist playwrights,

poured the new wine of their ideas into old bottles, into inherited dramatic forms. George Steiner has written that "like Diderot, Sartre and Camus make dramatic action a parable of philosophic or political argument."[15] They work in the convention of the play of ideas (or thesis drama) where dramatic form is taken for granted as a vehicle for ideas.

Like Camus, Sartre's dramatic output was slight. His early plays, *The Flies* (1943), *No Exit* (1944), and *Dirty Hands* (1948), are centered around a single, violent event. *The Flies*, based on the Greek myth of Orestes, shows how a man could take the responsibility of committing a crime, even though it filled him with horror. Sartre shifted the traditional insistence in Greek legend on the importance of fate to the significance of freedom of choice.

The Flies opens with the arrival of Orestes and his tutor in Argos. The only living things seem to be flies, which buzz incessantly. The flies have been sent by the gods to remind the people of their guilt in the death of King Agamemnon, which they share by not having done anything to prevent his murder.

Orestes, a homeless wanderer, longs to commit some action—even a criminal one—that would give him a right to live in Argos. Zeus warns Orestes to leave the city, but Orestes, reflecting that to do good always seems to involve acceptance and submission, suddenly realizes he is free to avenge his father's death and thus acquire the right to live among the people of Argos. As Orestes and his sister Electra set out to kill their mother, Clytemnestra, and her lover, Aegisthus, Zeus warns Aegisthus who asks why Zeus doesn't strike Orestes with a thunderbolt. Zeus replies that once liberty has exploded in a man's soul, the gods can do nothing against him. Orestes then performs the double murder.

In the last act Sartre shows us the difference between Orestes, the man who is truly free and accepting of the consequences of his deeds, and Electra who cannot bring herself to accept responsibility for the crime. Instead of the traditional scene of Orestes fleeing the wrath of the furies, Sartre's man of freedom assumes the consequences of his acts and walks out of Argos drawing the flies after him.

THE ABSURDISTS: IONESCO AND BECKETT

In *Notes and Counter Notes: Writings on the Theatre* (1962), Ionesco defined *absurd* as "anything without a goal . . . when man is cut off from his religious or metaphysical roots, he is lost; all his struggles become senseless, futile and oppressive."[16]

EUGENE IONESCO

Eugene Ionesco (b. 1912) is a Rumanian-born school teacher and refugee from Nazism who lives in France. Twenty-five years ago he puzzled and outraged audiences with plays about bald sopranos, octogenarian suicides, homicidal professors, and human rhinoceroses as metaphors for the world's absurdity. Today *The Bald Soprano, The Chairs, The Lesson,* and *Rhinoceros* are modern classics.

Since *The Bald Soprano* was first produced in Paris at the Théâtre des Noctambules in 1950, Ionesco has written more than 30 plays in addition to journals, essays, and children's stories. Ionesco says that his theatre expresses the malaise of contemporary life, language's failure to bring people closer together, the strangeness of existence, and a parodic reflection of the world. Breaking with the theatre of psychological realism, Ionesco pioneered a form of theatre closer to our dreams and nightmares.

Absurdist writers made their breakthrough in dramatic form by *presenting*, without comment or moral judgment, situations showing life's senselessness and irrationality. The common factors in the absurdist plays of Ionesco, Beckett, Adamov, and others are unrecognizable plots, mechanical characters, dreams and nightmares, and incoherent dialogue.

The meaning of Ionesco's plays is simply what happens on stage. The old man and old woman in *The Chairs* (1952) gradually fill the stage with an increasing number of empty chairs. They address absent people in the chairs.

At the play's end the two old people leave the message of their life's meaning to be delivered by an orator, and jump out of windows to their deaths. The orator then addresses the empty chairs, but he is a deaf-mute and cannot make a coherent statement. The subject of Ionesco's play is the chairs themselves—the emptiness and unreality of the world.

Ionesco subtitled his first play, *The Bald Soprano* (1949), "the tragedy of language." This farce, like many of his early plays, demonstrates the emptiness of middle-class life in a world devoid of significant problems.

In more recent plays Ionesco has given his concerns about middle-class conformity a more political cutting edge. In *Rhinoceros*, written in 1958, Ionesco's hero, Berenger, is an individual in a world of conformists. Ionesco's political concern is with people who are brutalized by dogma (in this case, fascism) and changed by it into beasts. The rhinoceros, with its thick hide, clumsy gait, and small brain is Ionesco's almost perfect analogue for dull-witted bestiality. Berenger emerges as a lonely but authentic hero, for he resists the physical and moral conformity that overwhelms his world and his loved ones. Like other Ionesco heroes, he represents a genuine assertion of personal value in a world dominated by nationalism, bureaucracy, conformity, and "groupthink."

In his more recent plays, such as *Exit the King* (1962), *Macbett* (1972), and *Man With Bags* (1975), Ionesco has written parables on human evil, the will to power, and the inevitability of death.

Virtually unknown at the age of 50, Samuel Beckett had published a few books, an essay on Marcel Proust, poetry, and short stories. In the early 1950s in Paris, he then published three novels and produced *Waiting for Godot*, one of the most influential plays of our time. Like Ionesco, Beckett freed playwriting from the bonds of such conventions as the full-length play, plot, character development, recognizable environments, and a well-defined progression of dramatic time.

As absurdist writers there are significant differences between Ionesco and Beckett. While Ionesco's dramatic world has its source in the irrationality of dreams, the banality of language, and the nightmare image, Beckett's theatre has its source in Camus' vision of the absurd: a universe that no longer made sense because there was no God to resolve the contradictions. Beckett's theatre, reflecting this absurdity, depicts human isolation and its counterpart, physical emptiness. Beckett's characters repeat endlessly that there is "nothing to be done"; yet they go on doing. Vladimir and Estragon in *Waiting for Godot* keep on waiting; Clov in *Endgame* (1958) threatens to leave his master but always stops just short of the door; Winnie in *Happy Days* (1961), although buried up to her neck in sand, keeps up her ebullient remarks about the weather (Figure 12-7).

> **"**There were a few of us who shook up the theatre in the fifties. We didn't destroy the commercial theater. In fact, we didn't want to. We believed in coexistence. For me, the revolution was in the language: to write differently is to think differently. But we initiated a new theater which, during the sixties, has followed the course we set. . . .
>
> In the past, as I think I've already mentioned, the theater followed in the wake of other forms of artistic expression. But today I have the impression that something quite remarkable is happening, and that the avant-garde is going to lead the way for other systems of expression. I think we're moving toward a kind of magical theater, which assaults the spectator, and that for the next few years we shall see little else. . . . Speaking for myself, I feel relatively removed from this wave. I go to the theater not to be assaulted, violently or primitively, I go to the theater to see what's happening and to be able to judge it freely.**"**
>
> "An Interview with Eugene Ionesco,"
> *Evergreen Review* (1970)[17]

Figure 12-7 Irene Worth as Winnie sits in sand buried to her waist in Beckett's *Happy Days* produced in 1979 by Joseph Papp at the Public Theatre, New York, and directed by Andrei Serban.

In Beckett's plays there are no beginnings and no endings. As audiences we are present in the *existential void*, for Beckett condenses life into a single stunning image that is both visual and aural. We find two tramps in a wasted landscape, two old people contained in garbage cans, time burying Winnie in sand, an old man listening without comprehension to tapes made in his youth, a woman's two large red lips emit-

ting a relentless torrent of words, and another woman reliving her life as she rocks herself into extinction. Beckett's staging captures significant aspects of our humanness surrounded by a void (the stage itself): crying, lips moving, footsteps, disconnected memories, waiting, frustration, dependency, and habituation.

Beckett's more recent works have dealt with the immobility that comes with aging, with

SAMUEL BECKETT

Samuel Beckett (b. 1906) is an expatriate Irishman living in France. Beckett grew up near Dublin and attended Trinity College, where he received two degrees in literature and began a teaching career. In the 1930s Beckett left his teaching position, traveled in Europe, published his first book (*More Pricks Than Kicks*), and wrote poetry in French. During World War II he worked with the French Resistance and barely escaped capture by the Nazis.

Since 1953 Beckett has written some 30 theatrical pieces, including radio plays, mime sketches, monologues, and four full-length plays (*Waiting for Godot, Endgame, Krapp's Last Tape, Happy Days*). *Endgame*, like *Waiting for Godot*, is a modern classic.

Recently, Beckett's plays have become minimal. *Come and Go* (1965) is a 3-minute play, *Breath* (1966) is a 30-second play, and *Not I* (1973) consists of eight pages of text. With these brief pieces Beckett constructs a theatrical image of how we come and go on this earth, briefly filling a void with our bodies and voices, and then disappear into darkness without a trace.

strokes or other incapacities. Only the characters' minds have free play, but they have turned inward to contemplate physical aches, feebleness, and partial memories of happier times. In his short prose work, *Ill Seen Ill Said* (1981), Beckett has written: "If there may not be no more questions let there at least be no more answers."[18]

JEAN GENÊT'S OPEN THEATRICALITY

While Martin Esslin included Jean Genêt among the absurdists of the 1960s, it is difficult to place his work entirely in this context. Of his five works for the theatre, written between 1946 and 1961, he has demonstrated an open theatricality and sociopolitical concerns that go beyond our definition of the absurd.

Genêt's many convictions for theft are well known. Jean-Paul Sartre, his great admirer and apologist, devoted a major work to a discussion of the significance of Genêt's life and attitudes in *Saint Genêt: Actor and Martyr* (1952). Sartre argued that Genêt had made a conscious existential choice to become a thief; he resolved to be the thief society had labeled him. In prison, where Genêt spent most of his life until age 38, he began writing novels and plays.

What is special about Genêt's theatre is his use of ceremony, dressing up, and repetition of action. Beginning with his earliest plays, *Deathwatch* (written in 1946 and produced in 1949) and *The Maids* (produced in 1947), Genêt dealt with reality as a "negation of roles." If we strip away enough veneer from the various social roles that we play as judge, servant, policeman, politician, and so on, we will eventually arrive at the reality of our true selves—at authenticity. This concept of reality is perfectly tailored for the conventions and artifices of the theatre. His most recent plays, with their explicitly social themes, such as the color question in *The Blacks* (1958) and colonialism in *The Screens* (1961), continue to make use of costume and ceremony (Figure 12-8).

In the modern French theatre, Genêt is the true successor of Pirandello. For Genêt theatre is a place of ritual and sacred mystery; all details of his theatre create a magical world where characters ceremoniously enact the relationships and dramas of life. All the while, Genêt's characters insist that they are actors in life's dramas and that their rituals belong to their special worlds.

Like Ionesco and Beckett, Genêt avoids the stage realism of traditional middle-class theatre.

JEAN GENÊT

Jean Genêt (b. 1910) was illegitimate, born in Paris to parents he never knew. His mother abandoned him and he was adopted by a peasant family in the French province of Morvan. At age 10 he was caught stealing and was sent to a reformatory. After many years in similar institutions for similar crimes, he finally escaped and joined the French Foreign Legion, but soon deserted.

Thereafter, he wandered throughout Europe as a felon, beggar, and smuggler. During this period he was imprisoned in almost every country through which he passed. In 1948, after 10 convictions for theft in France, he was to be sentenced automatically to life imprisonment. However, a group of eminent writers and artists submitted a petition to the president of France on his behalf and he was granted a pardon.

His literary career began in 1942 during a long prison term. Over a five-year period, he write several prose works (*Our Lady of the Flowers, The Miracle of the Rose, Funeral Ceremonies,* and *Querelle de Brest*); two plays, *Deathwatch* and *The Maids*; a volume of poems; and the autobiographical *Thief's Journal*. Since his release from prison, he has seen his plays produced and has written three more plays: *The Balcony* (1956), *The Blacks* (1958), and *The Screens* (1961).

Unlike his contemporaries, he stages dramas of social and psychological implication by seizing upon the central issues of life on that borderline of death or sleep where our most repressed wishes and fears come into consciousness. His theatre is artificial—openly theatrical. Charac-ters express their essence through a theatrical acting out of social roles. He blurs the sharp boundaries between fantasy and reality, art and life, sleep and waking. Through this open theatricality the audience is brought to an unsettling reversal of perspectives and to a reappraisal of social relationships.

REPRESENTATIVE PLAY

The Bald Soprano
First produced at the Théâtre des Noctambules in Paris, on May 11, 1950, directed by Nicolas Bataille, with actors Paulette Frantz, Simone Mozet, Odette Barrois, Nicolas Bataille, Claude Mansard, and Henry-Jacques Huet

BACKGROUND

In 1948 Eugene Ionesco decided to learn English and bought an *English-French Conversation Manual for Beginners*. The inspiration for *The Bald Soprano* grew out of these self-taught English grammar lessons. He copied the phrases, memorized vocabulary words, and found himself learning some surprising truths that he had never before considered seriously. For example, he learned there were seven days in the week, the floor was below us, the ceiling above, and so on. The general soon gave way to the particular as the lessons progressed. By the third lesson two characters, Mr. and Mrs. Smith, were introduced. They spoke "dialogue" to one another. Some years later Ionesco said:

> To my great surprise Mrs. Smith informed her husband that they had several children, that they lived in the outskirts of London, that their name was Smith, that Mr. Smith worked in an office, that they had a maid called Mary, who was English too, that for twenty years they had known some friends

Figure 12-8 Madeleine Renaud as Warda in the 1966 Paris production of Genêt's *The Screens*, performed at the Théâtre de France by the Madeleine Renaud–Jean-Louis Barrault Company. Sets and costumes were designed by André Acquart.

called Martin, and that their home was a castle because "An Englishman's home is his castle."[19]

By the fifth lesson, the Martins were introduced and more complex truths were developed. For instance, "The country is more peaceful than the city."

At this point Ionesco claimed that he was inspired to communicate these essential truths to a wider audience. So he wrote *The Bald Soprano*, first under the title *English Made Easy*, then *The English Hour*. He retained the Smiths, the Martins, and the maid. He also retained much of their grammar-book dialogue by stringing phrases together. But Ionesco's absurdist vision tampered with the formal logic of the grammar

book and that logical world became topsy turvy: A week suddenly had three days; the Martins no longer recognized each other as husband and wife; and identity became a problem when three-quarters of the town, including citizens and animals, were named Bobby Watson. Moreover, the placid Martins and Smiths began to speak language that was disjointed and emptied of content. At the end they quarreled and hurled syllables, consonants, and vowels at one another, not lines of conventional dialogue.

Ionesco's "tragedy of language," as he subtitled *The Bald Soprano*, showed a collapse of reality. Words, like empty shells, were devoid of meaning; characters had been emptied of psychology; and the world appeared to be governed by arbitrary laws where the fire chief could foresee (and even note in his diary) that a fire would break out three days later.

Ionesco's script was first shown by a friend to Nicolas Bataille, the director of a young company then performing at a small art theatre in Paris. At that point no suitable title had been found for the play; the use of "English" in the working title suggested that the play was to be taken as a satire on the English. When an actor's slip of the tongue substituted "bald soprano" for another phrase, "blond schoolteacher," Ionesco immediately recognized the appropriateness of the phrase because, as he later said, no prima donna, with or without hair, appears in the play. There is only a brief reference to the "bald soprano" in the play itself. At the end of scene 10, the fire chief is about to leave and asks about the bald soprano. There is general embarrassment and he is told that she still wears her hair the same way.

The play's ending also proved a problem. Ionesco had envisioned two different endings—both of an explosive variety. One ending called for the two couples to leave the stage, the audience to start a row, and the police to enter with pistols and open fire on the audience. A second ending called for the maid to arrive at the height of the Smith–Martin quarrel and announce the author in ringing tones. The author was to come on stage, be applauded by the actors, and then denounce the audience. Since neither of these endings was workable, Ionesco decided to end the play as it had begun—but with the Martins as the main characters. The idea of replacing the Smiths with the Martins emphasized the interchangeability of the characters and their lives.

THE SCENE

The scene is a parody of drawing room comedy so popular in the Paris commercial theatres of the day. The interior setting is very "English," including the armchairs, Mr. Smith, his newspaper, his wife who darns her husband's socks, their maid, and even their grandfather clock. The normality of the scene is jarred by the clock that strikes 17 times and by Mrs. Smith's announcement, "There, it's nine o'clock."

THE ACTION

The play's action is not built upon plot but is rather a presentation of mechanical living. In Ionesco's view the middle class is characterized by fixed ideas, slogans, and predictable behavior. The Smiths, the Martins, the maid, and even the bizarre fire chief are ubiquitous conformists. The couples are interchangeable because of the mechanical routines of their lives, their language, and their actions. All of them talk for the sake of talking because they have nothing personal to say to one another. Husband and wife no longer recognize each other; they are habituated in their relationship. The Smiths and Martins lose the ability to form coherent speech because they no longer know how to think or feel. They exist without identity in an impersonal world.

While *The Bald Soprano* is without an identifiable plot, it does have a definite rhythm. Ionesco has spoken in interviews of a three-part rhythm to his plays: acceleration, proliferation, and destruction.[20] In *The Bald Soprano* the action follows a similar pattern but then returns to its beginning. The vacuity of the language accelerates with the Smiths' discussion of Bobby Watson. Proliferation occurs with the Martins' presence and their efforts to recognize one another, as well as with the fire chief's recounting of his nonsense fables. Destruction takes place as the Martins and the Smiths quarrel and language disintegrates. Then there is a blackout and words abruptly cease. As the stage lights come up again, Mr. and Mrs. Martin are seated like the Smiths at the play's beginning. The play begins again before the curtain falls.

THE CHARACTERS

Ionesco's characters are stereotypical. Like puppets they are emptied of psychology and distinguishing traits. The Smiths, the Martins, the

Figure 12-9 In *The Bald Soprano* Ionesco presents the banality and purposelessness of his characters' lives in an effort to show us the world's absurdity. The maid dominates this scene with the Smiths, the Martins, and the fire chief in the original 1950 Paris production at Théâtre des Noctambules.

maid, and the fire chief are purely social characters recognizable only by their skins and clothes. Their conformity has emptied them of all individuality.

LANGUAGE

Ionesco's language more than any other quality of the play captured attention of critics. Here was a writer presenting an absurdist universe, declaring through nonsensical dialogue that words had become meaningless—overburdened with clichés, empty formulas, and slogans. Although charged at the time with stating that communication between people was impossible, Ionesco responded that the very fact of writing and presenting plays was testimony to his belief that, although difficult, one could make oneself understood.

While his approach to language in the theatre was to point up its emptiness and mechanical quality, he was also arguing for the eradication of fossilized language. *The Bald Soprano* was a call to renew language and thereby renew the conception of society and the world as meaningful, a place where we must confront sadness, the pain of living, fear of death, and the thirst for the absolute in order to realize our humanity. What Ionesco achieved was a statement of old truths in new ways.

The "Bobby Watson" Speech

The "Bobby Watson" speech in *The Bald Soprano* presents aural and visual images showing the banality of middle-class suburban life. Mr. and Mrs. Smith, seated in their middle-class English living room discussing their middle-class English dinner, engage in conversation about Bobby Watson.

[*Another moment of silence. The clock strikes seven times. Silence. The clock strikes three times. Silence. The clock doesn't strike.*]

Mr. Smith [*still reading his paper*] Tsk, it says here that Bobby Watson died.

Mrs. Smith My God, the poor man! When did he die?

Mr. Smith Why do you pretend to be astonished? You know very well that he's been dead these past two years. Surely you remember that we attended his funeral a year and a half ago.

Mrs. Smith Oh yes, of course I do remember. I remembered it right away, but I don't understand why you yourself were so surprised to see it in the paper.

Mr. Smith It wasn't in the paper. It's been three years since his death was announced. I remembered it through an association of ideas.

Mrs. Smith What a pity! He was so well preserved.

Mr. Smith He was the handsomest corpse in Great Britain. He didn't look his age. Poor Bobby, he's been dead for four years and he was still warm. A veritable living corpse. And how cheerful he was!

Mrs. Smith Poor Bobby.

Mr. Smith Which poor Bobby do you mean?

Mrs. Smith It is his wife that I mean. She is called Bobby too, Bobby Watson. Since they both had the same name, you could never tell one from the other when you saw them together. It was only after his death that you could really tell which was which. And there are still people today who confuse her with the deceased and offer their condolences to him. Do you know her?

Mr. Smith I only met her once, by chance, at Bobby's burial.

Mrs. Smith I've never seen her. Is she pretty?

Mr. Smith She has regular features and yet one cannot say that she is pretty. She is too big and stout. Her features are not regular but still one can say that she is very pretty. She is a little too small and too thin. She's a voice teacher.

[*The clock strikes five times. A long silence.*]

Mrs. Smith And when do they plan to be married, those two?

Mr. Smith Next spring, at the latest.

Mrs. Smith We shall have to go to their wedding, I suppose.

Mr. Smith We shall have to give them a wedding present. I wonder what?

Mrs. Smith Why don't we give them one of the seven silver salvers that were given us for our wedding and which have never been of any use to us? [*Silence.*]

Mrs. Smith How sad for her to be left a widow so young.

Mr. Smith Fortunately, they had no children.

Mrs. Smith That was all they needed! Children! Poor woman, how could she have managed!

Mr. Smith She's still young. She might very well remarry. She looks so well in mourning.

Mrs. Smith But who would take care of the children? You know very well that they have a boy and a girl. What are their names?

Mr. Smith Bobby and Bobby like their parents. Bobby Watson's uncle, old Bobby Watson, is a rich man and very fond of the boy. He might very well pay for Bobby's education.

Mrs. Smith That would be proper. And Bobby Watson's aunt, old Bobby Watson, might very well, in her turn, pay for the education of Bobby Watson, Bobby Watson's daughter. That way Bobby, Bobby Watson's mother, could remarry. Has she anyone in mind?

Mr. Smith Yes, a cousin of Bobby Watson's.

Mrs. Smith Who? Bobby Watson?

Mr. Smith Which Bobby Watson do you mean?

Mrs. Smith Why, Bobby Watson, the son of old Bobby Watson, the late Bobby Watson's other uncle.

Mr. Smith No, it's not that one, it's someone else. It's Bobby Watson, the son of old Bobby Watson, the late Bobby Watson's aunt.

Mrs. Smith Are you referring to Bobby Watson the commercial traveler?

Mr. Smith All the Bobby Watsons are commercial travelers.

Mrs. Smith What a difficult trade! However, they do well at it.

Mr. Smith Yes, when there's no competition.

Mrs. Smith And when is there no competition?

Mr. Smith On Tuesdays, Thursdays, and Tuesdays.

Mrs. Smith Ah! Three days a week? And what does Bobby Watson do on those days?

Mr. Smith He rests, he sleeps.

Mrs. Smith But why doesn't he work those three days if there's no competition?

Mr. Smith I don't know everything. I can't answer all your idiotic questions! . . . [21]

IONESCO'S MODERNISM

Eleven years after the first production of *The Bald Soprano* Martin Esslin was to label Ionesco's antitheatre, "the theatre of the absurd." By 1961, there was a recognizable body of avant-garde work that as a whole mirrored a new attitude to the world in our time: the *absurd*. This attitude is profoundly articulated by Ionesco in *The Bald Soprano*. Ionesco's themes and visual-aural stage images (even the nonsensical title) introduced in 1950 a new theatre for the modern world.

ESSAY

Many say in the 1980s that the Theatre of the Absurd as a theatrical movement has come and gone. However, the influence of the absurdist writers, their understanding of existence, and their unique way of stating their viewpoints in the theatre continue to be influential. Jerome Savary's Grand Magic Circus in France demonstrates the continuing influence of the absurdists on changing performance styles.

Theatricalism
and the Absurd
in Modern Performance
Zartan at Jerome Savary's Grand Magic Circus, France, 1971

We have selected Jerome Savary's Grand Magic Circus and his production of *Zartan* for our essay on modern performance because Savary's productions combine spectacle and theatricality, the surreal and the absurd.

In the late sixties, as in the early fifties, dissatisfaction with traditional theatre organizations in Paris caused some dissident theatre people to take to the suburbs to establish new theatres, while others sought out nontheatrical environments, such as streets, parks, and hospitals, to stage performances. Their purpose was to deal with large social issues in effectively theatrical ways. One of the most successful of the new theatre organizations was Savary's Grand Magic Circus.

Jerome Savary (b.1945), who began his career in 1967 and later worked with Ellen Stewart's La Mama Experimental Theatre Club in New York, conceived an innovative new company called the Grand Magic Circus. In 1970 he attracted critical attention with *Zartan*, "the story of Tarzan's deprived brother," described by Savary as the "marvelous story of colonialism from the Middle Ages to the present." *Zartan* was followed by *The Last Days of Solitude of Robinson Crusoe* (1972), *From Moses to Mao: 5000 Years of Love and Adventure* (1972, 1974), and *1001 Nights* (1978).

Savary's productions are thinly veiled commentaries on the contemporary world, but, he argues, theatrical messages are not primary in his productions. The function of the theatre is to be a "life show"—a pretext for bringing people together in a joyous celebration. He has tried to appeal to all types of audiences without being either cerebral or esoteric. His productions, which have the zest of children's theatre, circuses, and carnivals, are filled with improvisations, acrobatic feats, direct exchanges with audiences, and stunning theatrical effects. Savary clearly has been influenced by Reinhardt's outdoor spectacles, Genêt's theatricality and social concerns, and Ionesco's parodies of a mechanical society. People, according to Savary, cannot seem to talk to single individuals. The theatre is an excuse, a way to force people to communicate—to destroy the walls that isolate them from each other.

Zartan, which takes place outdoors, is a spectacle of the wars and atrocities promoted by the defenders of colonialism. Zartan, sporting his leopard skin, wages war against everyone, including the audience. The theatrical space is divided into three parts. The audience sits on a hill in the center of the playing area. They are the Silent Majority. Nearby a businessman, oblivious to what is happening around him, sells hot dogs and root beer. On one hill Zartan savages everything and everybody from a palm tree to a woman. But his efforts are futile, for each time he blows up the palm tree another blooms in its place, and each time he stabs the woman, a baby is born.

On the other hill is an idyllic corner of the earth where actors sing and dance, make love, and grow cabbages. At all times the audience is involved. As the Silent Majority they witness the massacres that occur around them, or they play "war correspondents" on the battlefield, or they help reconstruct the palm tree that Zartan destroys, or they help Zartan operate the enormous bazooka he uses to destroy the palm tree. Savary says that it is not impossible that the spectacle end in mass confrontation with a barrage of bananas.

In the sixties, the surrealism, theatricality, and social commentary of the post-war European theatre were combined by young theatre artists and small companies to deal in exciting and effectively theatrical ways with large social issues, such as Algeria, Vietnam, and Cambodia. Savary's Grand Magic Circus is a good example of one company that works in a straight line of descent from Reinhardt to Ionesco to Genêt.

SUMMARY

In the two post-war periods in the European theatre—1918–1939 and 1945–1960—stage realism remained the production style of the commercial, boulevard theatres, but it was challenged from all corners by the avant-garde experiments of expressionism, futurism, dadaism, constructivism and surrealism. *Theatricalism* is the broad term we have applied to all productions staged in a nonrealistic mode.

Perhaps the most flamboyant of the early theatricalists was German-born Max Reinhardt who staged spectacles in the Zirkus Schumann, the Grosses Schauspielhaus, and in the square of Salzburg Cathedral. *Everyman* at Salzburg was Reinhardt's classic achievement, for it represented his ultimate vision of theatre as a theatrical experience.

In contrast, the open theatricality of French directors Jacques Copeau, Jean Vilar, and Jean-Louis Barrault was characterized by minimal staging. With a bare stage and only essential furniture and set pieces, this group created a new "poetry of the theatre" in which the text was considered only the tip of the iceberg in the creation of the theatrical event. Under their leadership the major performance style of the postwar French theatre passed from naturalism to theatricalism.

Both post-war periods in France saw major changes in playwriting. Michel de Ghelderode, Luigi Pirandello, Jean Giraudoux, and Jean Anouilh dominated the French theatre between the wars, and the influences of Alfred Jarry and Antonin Artaud were felt by the younger directors and writers. The greater change in playwriting occurred in France during and shortly after the Second World War. The existentialist philosopher-writers, Jean-Paul Sartre and Albert Camus, stressed the importance of free will and responsibility, although people lived in an absurd universe in which there were no guidelines for action. During the German occupation of Paris, Sartre and Camus wrote two of their best plays, *No Exit* and *Caligula*. In his seminal essay, "The Myth of Sisyphus," Camus discussed his concept of the *absurd* and supplied the name for the theatrical movement that was to follow.

With the plays of Eugene Ionesco and Samuel Beckett in the early fifties came a startling breakthrough in playwriting. *The Bald Soprano* and *Waiting for Godot*, produced three years apart in Paris, changed the direction of avant-garde theatre. These writers and others set about not to argue about life's absurdities but to show the universe as absurd in concrete stage images and in language emptied of meaning. New dramatic conventions were introduced by the absurdists: no recognizable plots, puppetlike characters, mechanical behavior and language, illogical acts, dreams and nightmares replacing social commentary. Jean Genêt's open theatricality also included fantastic costumes, masks, and rituals, which he used to probe the idea of social role playing as central to people's lives.

In *The Bald Soprano,* our representative play, first produced at a Paris art theatre in 1950, Ionesco was the first to confront the absurdity of the universe with new dramatic techniques. This and other of his plays of the 1950s parodied conformist middle-class society, clichés of language and thought, and human irrationality. In a world where people are cut off from religious or transcendental roots, all human actions, including speech, become senseless, useless, absurd.

Jerome Savary's Grand Magic Circus represents an amalgam of Reinhardt's theatricality, Genêt's social concerns, and Ionesco's parodistic techniques. His productions are spectacular and wildly theatrical, combining the surreal and the absurd. The Grand Magic Circus has the zest of children's theatre, circuses, and carnivals. While it addresses contemporary social issues, its purpose is to force people to communicate with each other, to bring them together in celebration.

PLAYS TO READ

The Flies by Jean-Paul Sartre

The Bald Soprano by Eugene Ionesco

Waiting for Godot by Samuel Beckett

The Maids by Jean Genêt

SOURCES

Beckett, Samuel. *Waiting for Godot.* Translated by the author. New York: Grove, 1954. The paperback edition contains a short biography of Beckett and a brief note on the original Paris production.

Genêt, Jean. *The Maids.* In *The Maids and Deathwatch.* Translated by Bernard Frechtman. New York: Grove, 1962. This revision of the original 1954 publication contains a lengthy introduction by Jean-Paul Sartre, a short biography of Genêt, and a note on the 1947 Paris production.

Ionesco, Eugene. *The Bald Soprano.* In *Four Plays.* Translated by Donald M. Allen. New York: Grove, 1958. This edition also contains Ionesco's *The Lesson; Jack, or the Submission; The Chairs;* and brief notes on the original productions of these plays. Paperback.

Sartre, Jean-Paul. In *No Exit and Three Other Plays.* Translated by Stuart Gilbert and Lionel Abel. New York: Vintage Books, 1955, 1961. The volume includes *The Flies, Dirty Hands,* and *The Respectful Prostitute* plus brief notes on the original productions of these plays. Paperback.

NOTES

1. See John Gassner, *Theatre in Our Times* (New York: Crown, 1954), and "The Theatricalism Issue," *The Drama Review,* 21, No. 2 (June 1977).

2. Martin Esslin, "Max Reinhardt: High Priest of Theatricality," *The Drama Review,* 21, No. 2 (June 1977), 10. Reprinted by permission of *The Drama Review,* MIT Press Journals.

3. Esslin, "Max Reinhardt," *The Drama Review,* 11.

4. Albert Camus, *The Myth of Sisyphus and Other Essays* (New York: Vintage Books, 1955), p. 5. Reprinted by permission of Alfred A. Knopf, Inc.

5. Martin Esslin, *The Theatre of the Absurd,* rev. ed. (Garden City, N.Y.: Doubleday, 1969), pp. 5–6.

6. Jean Vilar, "Theatre Without Pretensions" in *Directors on Directing: A Source Book of the Modern Theatre,* eds. Toby Cole and Helen K. Chinoy (Indianapolis: Bobbs-Merrill, 1976), pp. 267–268. Reprinted by permission of Bobbs-Merrill Educational Publishing.

7. Martin Esslin, *The Theatre of the Absurd,* 3rd ed. (New York: Penguin, 1982), p. 291.

8. Antonin Artaud, *The Theatre and Its Double* (New York: Grove, 1958), p. 31.

9. From the program for "Fantastical Explosions: A Modernist Repertoire," ed. Julianne Singer (Pomona, Calif.: The Claremont Colleges Comparative Literature Conference on Modernism, 1982), p. 5.

10. Robert W. Corrigan, *The World of the Theatre* (Glenview, Ill.: Scott, Foresman, 1979), pp. 224–225.

11. André Breton, *First Manifesto of Surrealism* (Paris, 1924) in *What Is Surrealism?* (London: Faber and Faber, 1936), p. 122.

12. Luigi Pirandello, *One-Act Plays*, trans. William Murray (Garden City, N.Y.: Doubleday, 1964), p. viii.

13. Luigi Pirandello, *Six Characters In Search of an Author* in *Naked Masks: Five Plays*, ed. Eric Bentley (New York: E.P. Dutton, 1958), p. 245. Copyright 1922, 1952 by E. P. Dutton & Co., Inc. Renewal 1950 in the names of Stefano, Fausto & Lietta Pirandello. Renewal 1978 by Eric Bentley. Reprinted by permission of the publisher, E. P. Dutton, Inc.

14. Luigi Pirandello, *Right You Are, If You Think You Are* in *Naked Masks: Five Plays*, ed. Eric Bentley (New York: E. P. Dutton, 1958), pp. 101–102. Copyright 1922, 1952 by E. P. Dutton & Co., Inc. Renewal 1950 in the names of Stefano, Fausto & Lietta Pirandello. Renewal 1978 by Eric Bentley. Reprinted by permission of the publisher, E. P. Dutton, Inc.

15. Garry O'Connor, *French Theatre Today* (London: Pitman, 1975), p. 24. Reprinted by permission of A & C Black (Publishers) Ltd.

16. Eugene Ionesco, *Notes and Counter Notes: Writings on the Theatre*, trans. Donald Watson (New York: Grove, 1964), p. 257. Copyright ©1964 by Grove Press, Inc. Reprinted by permission.

17. Frederic de Towarnicki, "An Interview with Eugene Ionesco," *The Evergreen Review*, 85 (Dec. 1970), 73.

18. Samuel Beckett, *Ill Seen Ill Said* (New York: Grove, 1981), p. 43. Copyright © 1981 by Grove Press, Inc. Reprinted by permission.

19. Ionesco, *Notes and Counter Notes*, p. 176. Reprinted by permission.

20. Claude Bonnefoy, *Conversations with Eugene Ionesco*, trans. Jan Dawson (New York: Holt, Rinehart and Winston, 1971), p. 57.

21. Eugene Ionesco, *The Bald Soprano* in *Four Plays*, trans. Donald M. Allen (New York: Grove, 1958), pp. 11–13. Reprinted by permission of Grove Press, Inc.

THIRTEEN

CONTEMPORARY THEATRE: "NEW" REALISM ON THE BRITISH STAGE

A MODERN PERSPECTIVE

While psychological realism has dominated the American stage since World War II, in England stage realism has undergone a radical change. In the early 1950s in London's West End (Britain's equivalent of Broadway), drawing room comedies and verse plays were frequent fare. In 1956 the newly founded English Stage Company introduced a new subject matter and a new performance style to the British theatre with John Osborne's *Look Back in Anger,* a play about disaffected working-class people. What followed was an explosion of new playwrights, plays, subjects, and a new performance style.

The history of the postwar British stage has been largely the story of three theatres: The National (formerly the Old Vic), the Royal Shakespeare Company (formerly the Stratford Festival Company), and the Royal Court. Since the days of Thomas Betterton and David Garrick, the English theatre has been thought of as an "actor's theatre." This is heard today from persons reflecting upon the great talents of Laurence Olivier, John Gielgud, Peggy Ashcroft, and Ralph Richardson. Moreover, a younger generation of actors has emerged since 1950, including Alan Bates, Glenda Jackson, Vivian Merchant, Albert Finney, Ian McKellen, and Ian Richardson. These actors have "grown up" in at least one of these three companies, which have nourished playwrights as well. Playwrights Harold Pinter, Tom Stoppard, and Peter Shaffer are well known on both sides of the Atlantic.

To study the postwar British theatre, we should look closely at these theatrical institutions that have been substantially subsidized by the government. Let us examine the Royal Court Theatre, the home of George Devine's English Stage Company, where a revolution of sorts was begun in 1956.

REPRESENTATIVE THEATRE:
The Royal Court Theatre

The Royal Court Theatre, home of the English Stage Company since 1956, is located in Sloane Square away from the bustle surrounding London's densely packed group of commercial theatres in the West End. By stretching an analogy to the New York theatre, we might think of the Royal Court as an Off-Broadway theatre.

The Royal Court (sometimes just called the "Court") has a long history, dating back to 1870 when a chapel close to the present site was converted into a theatre. Over the years this theatre has had three names: the New Chelsea Theatre, the Belgravia, and finally the Royal Court Theatre. The old theatre closed in 1887, and a new theatre, the present Royal Court, was built on a nearby site in 1888.

The front of the theatre is imposing; it is built

of stone and red brick, freely treated in the Italian Renaissance style (Figure 13–1). Originally a three-tiered proscenium theatre, it had a gallery rising behind the upper circle and held 642 people. In 1934 the theatre became a cinema; in 1940 bombs fell in Sloane Square and it was finally put out of use. The Royal Court remained derelict until 1952 when it was renovated by the London Theatre Guild. Shortly thereafter, in 1955, it was leased by the English Stage Company, the interior was redecorated, a forestage added to the proscenium stage, and the lower boxes on either side of the stage turned into stage doors with balconies above. The theatre now seated about 430. The old rehearsal room was also converted into a restaurant for the club premises incorporated into the new theatre.

The English Stage Company was founded with George Devine as its artistic director and Oscar Lewenstein as general manager. Devine's philosophy was that "a theatre must have a recognizable attitude. It will have one, whether you like it or not."[1] The company's goals were to commission new plays, to produce noncommercial works including foreign plays, and to stage plays for festivals. Inspired by the work

Artistic Directors at the Royal Court	
George Devine	1956–1965
William Gaskill	1965–1972
Oscar Lewenstein	1972–1975
Robert Kidd and Nicholas Wright	1975–1976
Stuart Burge	1977–1979
Max Stafford-Clark	1979–

Figure 13-1 The Royal Court Theatre in Sloane Square, London, as it appears today.

When George Devine (1910–1966) unexpectedly died of a heart attack, *The London Times* paid eloquent tribute to his place in English theatre: "George Devine was one of the three important animating figures of the postwar theatre. He was the complement of Peter Hall and Laurence Olivier. They have made a producer's [director's] theatre and an actor's theatre. At the Royal Court, Devine made a Writer's theatre, stamping it with his own thought and independent personality . . . Devine made the English Stage Company the principal socially conscious theatre in the English speaking world."[2]

of Jacques Copeau at the Vieux-Colombier in Paris, Devine at first designed a fixed setting for the Royal Court because of the limited financial resources for scenery; he also gathered a permanent acting company to play in repertory.

Bertolt Brecht's *Threepenny Opera*, never seen before in London, was the preseason opener in 1956. The official season began with plays by Angus Wilson, a British novelist, and Arthur Miller, the American playwright. The third was a new play by a little-known actor, John Osborne. In the beginning Osborne's play received mixed reviews, but Kenneth Tynan, writing for *The Observer*, proved prophetic:

> I agree that *Look Back in Anger* is likely to remain in a minority taste. What matters,

> **"** *You should choose your theatre like you choose a religion. Make sure you don't get into the wrong temple. For me the theatre is really a religion or way of life. You must decide what you feel the world is about and what you want to say about it, so that everything in the theatre you work in is saying the same thing. This will be influenced partly by the man who is running it, and the actual physical and economic conditions under which he works . . .*
>
> *For me, the theatre is a temple of ideas and ideas so well expressed it may be called art. So always look for the quality in the writing above what is being said.*
>
> *This is how to choose a theatre to work in, and if you can't find one you like, start your own. A theatre must have a recognizable attitude. It will have one, whether you like it or not.* **"**
>
> George Devine, in *Playwright's Theatre* (1975)[3]

however, is the size of the minority. I estimate it at roughly 6,733,000, which is the number of people in this country between the ages of twenty and thirty . . . I doubt if I could love anyone who did not wish to see *Look Back in Anger*. It is the best young play of its decade.[4]

Osborne's play caught on; it was even revived within the year at the Royal Court. In his attack on British class distinctions Osborne had captured the contemporary rebellious mood of a large number of young people.

Over the years the company has developed new playwrights and new directors not yet ready for the main stage by a playwright-in-residence program and the Theatre Upstairs, an open flexible space for short runs of new plays. It brought in experimental groups, such as the Open Theatre and La Mama ETC from the United States and the Renaud-Barrault Company from Paris. Ground-breaking revivals of old plays and first productions in England of internationally significant foreign plays also gave a noncommercial character to the Royal Court.

Devine's original policy of producing plays in repertory using a permanent company of actors did not last long. What has lasted is Devine's policy of championing new playwrights, which has led to a renaissance in the British theatre. In 1981 the Royal Court celebrated its twenty-fifth year and a tradition for the new and experimental that has no end in sight.

CONDITIONS OF PERFORMANCE

BACKGROUND

While England survived two global wars in this century, the British Commonwealth of nations did not remain intact. The sun has been setting on the Commonwealth for some time—first in South Africa, then in India, Pakistan and the Caribbean, and now perhaps in Ireland as well. But Britain has survived as an industrial country in the North and Midlands and as a maritime and agricultural enterprise in the South. London remains the hub of government, religion, and the arts.

Modern England reveals a striking unity in its continuation of the monarchy, the centuries-old educational centers at Oxford and Cambridge universities, a two-party democracy, and a Parliament that has lasted 800 years. In London opera, music, ballet, and theatre flourish.

The contemporary British theatre frequently has been the envy of Americans. London, the center of theatrical activity, has more than 300 theatres in or near its West End and three national theatre companies. Outside London there are some 40 commercial theatres in large cities and about 60 theatres occupied by subsidized repertory companies in Bristol, Birmingham, Chichester, Coventry, Leicester, and Nottingham.

1930   1940

World War II
1939–1945

Hitler
invades
Poland
1939

Republic of
Ireland founded
1937

Tyrone Guthrie
heads the Old
Vic Theatre
1937–1944

United
Nations
founded
1944–1945

Atomic
bombs
dropped on
Hiroshima
and
Nagasaki
1945

As we shall see, the conditions of performance in the present British theatre differ remarkably from those in the United States, starting with a system of large government subsidies and the implicit idea that theatre artists are *national treasures.*

MANAGEMENT: THE COMPANIES

Prior to 1940 England had never provided subsidy for the arts. However, during the Second World War German bombs so damaged the theatres that at one point only one theatre remained open in London. To sustain the theatre during these dark days, the government appropriated funds to send companies on tour as a means of building morale. At the war's end subsidies to the arts became a permanent policy and financial support (both national and local) has steadily increased since that time.

The Old Vic Following the war the English theatre gained a considerable international reputation based largely on two companies—the Old Vic (to become the National Theatre) and the Stratford Festival Company (to become the Royal Shakespeare Company). In the late fifties, a third—the English Stage Company—emerged to take its place alongside the other two.

Between the wars (1918–1939) the English theatre broke no important new ground. During the 1930s John Gielgud (b. 1904) and Tyrone Guthrie (1900–1971) raised the level of production through their outstanding directing, and after the war the Old Vic was for a time the best of the English companies under the direction of Laurence Olivier, Ralph Richardson, and John Burrell. From 1946 to 1952 the Old Vic also had an excellent acting school run by Michel Saint-Denis. By the 1950s the Old Vic had become perhaps the best-known company in the English-speaking world. Then it began to decline and was dissolved in 1963 to be replaced by the National Theatre.

The National Theatre The National Theatre had been Laurence Olivier's dream for many years. It was inaugurated in 1963 and placed under Olivier's direction. Housed in the Old Vic's theatre near Waterloo Station, the new company rapidly built a reputation for excellence. In 1973 Peter Hall replaced Olivier as director and in 1976 the company moved into its new building, which includes three performance spaces: the Olivier open-stage theatre; the Lyttelton proscenium theatre, and the Cottesloe laboratory theatre (see page 6). Since the National Theatre receives more than twice the

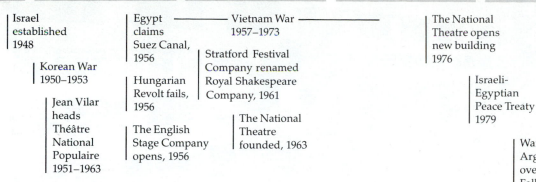

1950	1960	1970	1980

Israel established 1948

Korean War 1950–1953

Jean Vilar heads Théâtre National Populaire 1951–1963

Egypt claims Suez Canal, 1956

Hungarian Revolt fails, 1956

The English Stage Company opens, 1956

Vietnam War 1957–1973

Stratford Festival Company renamed Royal Shakespeare Company, 1961

The National Theatre founded, 1963

The National Theatre opens new building 1976

Israeli-Egyptian Peace Treaty 1979

War with Argentina over the Falkland Islands, 1982

Royal Shakespeare Company opens the Barbican Centre, London 1982

subsidy of any other theatre in Great Britain, much has been expected from it. Productions that have originated at the National and made their way recently to New York are *Equus* (1973) and *Amadeus* (1979). Playing a standard repertory that includes Shakespeare, classics, established British and foreign playwrights, certain actors have been associated with the theatre since its inception: Laurence Olivier, Michael Redgrave, Frank Finlay, Robert Stephens, Max Adrian, Maggie Smith, and Joan Plowright.

The Royal Shakespeare Company As the Old Vic declined in the sixties, the Shakespeare Memorial Theatre in Stratford-upon-Avon steadily grew in reputation, attracting major actors and adventuresome young directors.

In 1961 the Memorial Theatre at Stratford-upon-Avon (the place of Shakespeare's birth) was awarded a new charter and renamed the Royal Shakespeare Theatre, home of the Royal Shakespeare Company (RSC). The new status owed much to Peter Hall (b. 1930) who was named artistic director in 1960. At the outset Hall leased the Aldwych Theatre in London (near the West End) and transformed what had been a summer operation into a year-round one. In 1982 the RSC opened in its new London home, the Barbican Centre—a nine-story con-

crete arts and business complex (Figure 13–2). At the Barbican the company has two modern theatres: the 1162-seat, thrust-stage Barbican Theatre and the small 200-seat, arena-shaped theatre called "the Pit."

Since 1960 the company has divided its energies between Stratford-upon-Avon and London. Many of its productions have shaken the artistic world to its foundations. In the beginning Peter Hall set about rescuing Shakespeare's plays from a phony Victorian tradition of genteel heroes and rhythmical verse speaking. In 1964 he directed Shakespeare's *Henry VI* plays (*The War of the Roses*) as a horrific analysis of power politics and violence. Peter Weiss's *Marat/Sade*, directed by Peter Brook in 1965, rocked London and New York theatre with its visual images and sounds of a world gone mad (Figure 13-3). The RSC had become London's most innovative company. In 1968 Peter Hall

Figure 13-2 The Barbican Centre, London home of the Royal Shakespeare Company. The thrust stage and auditorium were designed to give the actor the sensation of speaking to every person in the audience. In this intimate atmosphere there are 1162 seats.

Figure 13-3 *Marat/Sade,* directed by Peter Brook for the Royal Shakespeare Company in 1965. Jean-Paul Marat in his bath (played by Ian Richardson), debates the importance of violent revolution while asylum inmate Simonne Evrard (Susan Williamson) attends to him. Brook used debate, mime, song, dance, and chanting to comment upon the irrationality of human events.

and Peter Brook left the company to go on to other projects, but their policies have been continued by Trevor Nunn, the present artistic co-director. Although plagued by inflation, the theatre continues its ambitious programs of revivals and new plays in its main theatres and low-budget productions in experimental spaces. *Nicholas Nickleby,* seen both in London and New York in 1980–1981, is another of the company's recent triumphs.

The English Stage Company Since 1956 the English Stage Company set about to foster new playwrights and to produce new English plays as well as foreign plays not previously seen in England. John Osborne's *Look Back in Anger* marked the beginning of a playwriting revival.

There are now a number of playwrights recognized as "Court" writers. The list is long: John Osborne, N.F. Simpson, Arnold Wesker, John Arden, Ann Jellicoe, Edward Bond, Heathcote Williams, Christopher Hampton, Howard Brenton, Joe Orton, David Storey, David Hare, and Caryl Churchill.

Not only did the Court produce a new kind of play but it also produced a "new" actor to portray largely working-class characters. Colin Blakely, Alan Bates, Peter O'Toole, Joan Plowright, and Albert Finney are perhaps the best known.

PLAYWRITING

While sex comedies, thrillers, musicals, revues, and comedies of manners are to be seen in the West End commercial theatres (along with American musicals), the major companies and resident theatres outside London have consistently encouraged the writing of new plays. It is taken for granted that Shakespeare is the house dramatist for the Royal Shakespeare Company and the National Theatre. Nevertheless, with the success of *Look Back in Anger* at the Royal Court, its tours and revivals, the idea got around that it might be profitable to produce young playwrights and new plays. Two generations of playwrights have since developed. Some are associated with repertory theatres outside London; others with certain directors and actors; others with radio and television. Many have been nurtured in low-budget productions supported by the Royal Shakespeare Company and the National Theatre.

Of the new writers emerging over the last 25 years, many have become well known in the United States. Their names are seen on Broadway theatre bills, in popular films, and in the repertories of our regional and university theatres. Foremost among them is Harold Pinter (*The Caretaker* and *The Homecoming*), followed closely by Tom Stoppard (*Rosencrantz and Guildenstern Are Dead*), John Osborne (*Look Back in Anger*), and Peter Shaffer (*Equus*).

ACTING

Since the days of David Garrick in the eighteenth century, the British actor has been considered the finest in the English-speaking world. British actors have been part of a continuous tradition since 1660, honing their skills on Shakespeare's verse and the rapid, highly mannered dialogue of Restoration comedy. Moreover, the star system dominated the theatrical scene as late as 1950.

The Old Vic, under the management of Lilian Baylis (1874–1937), was the first of the major theatres to be formed anew into the home of Shakespeare. Here Sybil Thorndike, Edith Evans, Flora Robson, John Gielgud, Laurence Olivier, Ralph Richardson, Maurice Evans, Peggy Ashcroft, Michael Redgrave, and Alec Guinness achieved their fame. In the twentieth century, English acting has been subtly changed by an elaborate network of repertory companies with training programs for young actors, the many commercial theatres, the experimental repertory companies, and by the semiprofessional and amateur groups. Actors also learned their art with Sir Barry Jackson's Birmingham Repertory Theatre, his Malvern Festival, and the Shakespeare Memorial Theatre in Stratford-upon-Avon. Acting schools also have sprung up: the Royal Academy of Dramatic Art (RADA), the London Academy of Music and Dramatic Art (LAMDA), the Central School of Speech and Drama, the Drama Centre, the Rose Bruford College, the Guildhall School of Music and Drama, and many more.

In addition to the continuous tradition of articulate verse-speaking and energetic characterization, modern British actors have added realistic playing to their special style, especially in film. New dramas with working-class characters demanded new acting styles, and English acting has become in our time an eclectic art.

As in the United States, successful British actors divide their time among the stage, films, and television. They also do commercials. Still, the National Theatre, the Royal Shakespeare Company, and the regional repertory theatres offer the only possibilities for work with a continuous management, an ensemble company, and even a known audience.

THE DIRECTORS

Contemporary British directors from Tyrone Guthrie, Laurence Olivier, Ralph Richardson, and John Burrell to Peter Brook, John Dexter, Peter Hall, and Trevor Nunn share a theatrical tradition. They have all worked in the mainstream of British drama, pioneering new approaches to performing Shakespeare and putting adventurous new words before the public.

Figure 13-4 Director Joan Littlewood rehearsing at the Theatre Workshop, Theatre Royal, Stratford East in 1961.

In 1947 Olivier reinterpreted *Hamlet* based on psychiatrist Ernest Jones' Freudian analysis of the central character. Peter Brook in 1965 shook the theatre world with a new German play, *Marat/Sade.* While actresses have certainly shared in English stage traditions, few women directors have attracted international attention. Joan Littlewood (b. 1914) is an exception.

Joan Littlewood at Stratford East In 1945 Joan Littlewood became dissatisfied with the commercial theatre and formed a workshop where she set about creating theatre for working-class audiences. Littlewood, herself working class by birth, moved the workshop in 1953 into the Theatre Royal in Stratford East, a working-class suburb.

She was greatly influenced by Stanislavsky's methods and by Brecht's alienation devices and worked collectively with writers and actors to achieve the same effects. She also drew on popular theatre techniques: improvisations and popular songs, the staging devices of circuses and music halls. Criticized for allowing actors to contribute creatively to a text, she claimed never to have altered an actor's lines without his or her consent. Until her resignation in 1971 as artistic director of the Theatre Workshop, she directed classical and modern plays, the most notable modern ones being Brendan Behan's *The Quare Fellow* (1956) and *The Hostage* (1958), Shelagh Delaney's *A Taste of Honey* (1958), and *Oh, What a Lovely War!* (1963).

Oh, What a Lovely War! perhaps best demonstrates Littlewood's methods in performance. In this biting satire on the First World War, she used actors, songs, improvisations, projections, and dialogue to express antiwar attitudes. She transformed the "war to end all wars" into a Pierrot or clown show, recreating the horrors of trench warfare alongside the patter of music hall stand-up comics and nostalgic period songs. These were performed against a background of still battle photographs and casualty figures flickering across an electrified ribbon screen (Figure 13-5).

Figure 13-5 A chorus line from Joan Littlewood's production of *Oh, What a Lovely War!* at the Theatre Workshop, 1963, designed by John Bury. In this satire on the first world war, the soldiers are costumed as clowns with army regulation hats and rifles.

Peter Brook's Experimentation In the early sixties the RSC encouraged experimental work apart from its traditional London and Stratford-upon-Avon productions. Peter Brook, along with Charles Marowitz, devised a "Theatre of Cruelty" season in 1963–1964.

Brook had long been aware that actors do most of their best work in rehearsals. He considered repetition a deadly enemy of creativity and the long run play even more so. The program to the Theatre of Cruelty season carried a note comparing the experiment to a scientific research project and warning the audience that it was watching "a public session of work-in-progress: improvisation, exploration, and a reexamination of accepted theatre forms."[5] Brook's production of Peter Weiss' *Marat/Sade* (1965) at the RSC evolved from this experiment.

Since founding the International Centre for Theatre Research in Paris (1971), Brook has spent most of his time experimenting with actor training and developing new scripts from ideas taken from myths, anthropology, and fables. His work at the Centre has focused on the actor, developing sounds and movements as substitutes for dialogue, and perfecting the actor's voice and body as performing instruments for the purpose of transcending language and cultural barriers. The Centre has performed periodically for the public, having such international successes as *The Ik, Conference of Birds, The Cherry Orchard,* and *La Tragédie de Carmen.*

John Dexter's Rituals John Dexter—current director of productions at New York's Metropolitan Opera Company—works with writers in quite different ways from either Joan Littlewood or Peter Brook. On the thrust stage at the Chichester Festival Theatre, he directed Peter Shaffer's *The Royal Hunt of the Sun* (1964), staging spectacular Inca rituals with sound effects, mime, gold costumes and masks.

In *Equus* (1973), also by Shaffer, Dexter seated a jury of spectators on stage behind and above the action. They became "tribal" witnesses to Shaffer's attack on modern civilization (specifically, on modern psychiatry). The play develops around the behavior of a stable boy who blinds six horses because they "witnessed" his abortive sexual encounter with a girl. Collaborating with the playwright, Dexter strengthened the ritualistic and unrealistic elements in the play, using actors in cagelike masks to represent the horses and having them mime and sound a chanting hum as background for the terror and mystery of the dialogue.

Peter Hall's Eclecticism Peter Hall directed the first London production of Samuel Beckett's *Waiting for Godot* in 1955. Since then he has made a remarkable career as artistic director of the Royal Shakespeare Company, stage director for the Royal Opera Company in Covent Garden, and, since 1973, successor to Laurence Olivier as head of the National Theatre.

Two results of Hall's years at the RSC were the creation of a superb ensemble company and his close association with Harold Pinter. As a director he is eclectic. He speaks of Shakespeare's plays as operatic scores whose end product is a *complex image*; he talks about getting at the "melodrama" of Pinter's plays. He has directed both Shakespeare and Pinter to critical acclaim.

Equus

In *Equus* the focus is divided between the boy, Alan Strang, and the psychiatrist, Dr. Dysart, who, in trying to cure him, fights a lack of conviction that the boy will be "better off" when cured. Dysart experiences a crisis of faith in his own healing powers and in his profession:

Dysart . . . I'll erase the welts cut into his mind by flying manes. When that's done, I'll set him on a nice mini-scooter and send him puttering off into the Normal World where animals are treated *properly*: made extinct, or put into servitude, or tethered all their lives in dim light, just to feed it! I'll give him the good Normal World where we're tethered beside them—blinking our nights away in a nonstop drench of cathoderay over our shrivelling heads! I'll take away his Field of Ha Ha, and give him Normal places for his ecstasy—multilane highways, driven through the guts of cities, extinguishing Place altogether, even the idea of Place! He'll trot on his metal pony tamely through the concrete evening—and one thing I promise you: he will never touch hide again!

Peter Shaffer, *Equus* (1973)[6]

In an interview Peter Hall spoke of his intuitive sense of directing and his rehearsals methods:

" I don't believe you can do a play unless you can say as a director what you think the spine of it is. It is about many things, of course—but you must know what its centre is to you. I'm not sure you should say what it is to your cast, and I'm pretty certain you shouldn't say it to the public or the Press, but you should know it yourself. . . . One has to read the play over and over and over again so that you actually know it in your blood. "

Peter Hall in *Directors' Theatre* (1974)[7]

Scene from Shakespeare's *Henry VI,* the first in the series of history plays produced by the Royal Shakespeare Company as *The War of the Roses.* Directed by Peter Hall. Center are Peggy Ashcroft as Queen Margaret and David Warner as King Henry VI.

Roots by Arnold Wesker, at the Royal Court Theatre, 1967. A family gathers around the dining room table complete with dishes, food, and silverware.

The Contractor by David Storey, at the Royal Court Theatre, 1969, directed by Lindsay Anderson. Actors as workmen raise the wedding tent on stage as part of the action.

The Changing Room by David Storey. In the locker room the rugby players are treated for their injuries. A Royal Court Theatre production, 1971, directed by Lindsay Anderson.

Many other fine directors are currently at work in the English theatre: Trevor Nunn, John Barton, Clifford Williams, and Terry Hands at the RSC; Jonathan Miller, John Dexter, Peter Gill, and Harold Pinter at the National; William Gaskill and Max Strafford-Clark at the Royal Court.

FESTIVALS AND FRINGES

In the 1950s festivals like those at Edinburgh, Chichester, Malvern, Glyndebourne, and Canterbury added considerably to the vitality of the English theatre. In the late sixties other groups, influenced by touring American companies like the Open Theatre and La Mama ETC, spawned a theatrical counterculture in England. Called the fringe, it is similar to the Off-Off-Broadway movement in the United States.

Fringe companies came into existence after government censorship was abolished in 1968, performing in pubs, meeting halls, playgrounds, basements, churches, and schools. Their greatest assets were their flexibility, variety, and adventurousness.

Jim Haynes, an American, launched the first fringe theatre in 1968–1969—the Arts Lab in London's Drury Lane. The Portable Theatre, Freehold, the People Show, Pip Simmons Group, Inter-Action, and the Traverse Theatre Workshop quickly followed. They performed on portable stages with improvised settings, in open, free-wheeling styles. Their subjects were mostly taken from outside their experiences—urban guerrilla warfare, criminal violence, psychopathic murder, and so forth. Sometimes performances were developed from scripts. Writers David Hare, Snoo Wilson, and Howard Brenton are associated with the Portable Theatre. Others worked as collectives, creating scripts with actors and writers during rehearsals.

While the fringe movement appears to be on the wane today, it has proved two important things: Audiences can be found almost anywhere and at any time, and solid new civic buildings and vast amounts of public monies are not always needed to create *exciting theatre*.

DRAMATIC CONVENTIONS

Let us look at three categories of British playwriting that developed after 1956 out of the ferment generated by the Royal Court: the working-class realism of Edward Bond and David Storey, the "ambiguous" realism of Harold Pinter, and the open theatricality of Tom Stoppard and Peter Shaffer.

WORKING-CLASS REALISM

Following the successes of John Osborne's *Look Back in Anger* (1956) and *The Entertainer* (1957), the language, subjects, passions, and characters of the working class gained a secure foothold on the British stage.

Bond's Urban Violence Edward Bond's *Saved* (1965) arrived at the Royal Court amid a storm of protest from the government censor. Banned in its entirety by the lord chamberlain for its language and its depiction of the stoning of a baby, the play became a *cause célèbre*. The result was litigation that ended stage censorship in England, which had lasted 125 years. Since then Bond's reputation has been firmly established as a provocative, frequently shocking, playwright.

Bond's characters are violent, inarticulate people—products of their urban environment—restless, aimless young people resentful of their ineffectual and selfish parents. Bickering, fight-

> *Like most people, I am a pessimist by experience, but an optimist by nature, and I have no doubt that I shall go on being true to my nature. Experience is depressing, and it would be a mistake to be willing to learn from it.*
>
> Edward Bond, "Author's Note," *Saved* (1965)[8]

ing, and casual sex make up their day-to-day lives. Bond uses realistic lower-class speech to deal with the theme of the corruption of natural innocence by "upbringing and environment." Neither individuals nor governments escape his harsh indictment.

Storey's "Staged" Events David Storey made his reputation at the Royal Court with plays built around some strenuous physical activity. These activities become violent metaphors for the way Storey's rough, inarticulate tradesmen play the game of life. His best-known plays are *In Celebration, The Contractor,* and *The Changing Room.*

In *The Contractor* (1969) putting up a tent for a wedding breakfast is the play's centerpiece. The setting is Yorkshire and workmen come to their boss's house to erect a tent for his daughter's wedding to an upper middle-class doctor. Extremely detailed realism is called for since everything is done on stage: frying an egg, making an apple strudel, raising the tent. The play's tensions and social messages flow from the physical labor of the main task. The workmen's desultory manner and casual back-chat reveal their strengths and weaknesses, the class barrier be-

---

EDWARD BOND

Born to working-class Jewish parents in London's East End, Edward Bond (b. 1935) has been a highly prolific and controversial writer. Along with his first play, *Saved* (1965), *Early Morning* (1968), *Lear* (1971), *The Sea* (1973), and *The Fool* (1975) were produced first at the Royal Court. More recently, *The Woman* (1978), *The Worlds* (1979), *Restoration* (1981), and *Summer* (1982) have continued Bond's concerns with the brutalization of human beings by a society that he views as economically corrupt and socially unjust.

Saved

Saved, by Edward Bond, was produced at the Royal Court in 1965 and directed by William Gaskill. The play develops the relationship between Len and Pam who meet through a casual pick-up and immediately settle down with Len as a lodger and lover in Pam's home. They quarrel constantly. Her parents, who live in the same house, have not spoken for years. Len nearly seduces Mary, Pam's mother, or she nearly seduces him, in a humorous scene where he is persuaded to darn a hole in her stocking while she is still wearing it. Pam's father, Harry, comes in and speaks to his wife, breaking the silence of years. The result is a physical attack, but at least they are now communicating. Even Harry and Len begin to talk.

Pam, however, speaks more and more savagely to Len, particularly after she has a baby by Fred (she says), one of a group of casually violent types whom she and Len know. The baby soon becomes Len's main reason for staying with Pam. At this point the notorious scene that caused the censorship fight takes place. The baby is left in its pram in a park and is tormented by a gang of teenage boys, among them Fred, the baby's alleged father. They rub the baby's face with excrement and finally stone it to death.

Bond said of the baby's death: "Clearly the stoning to death of a baby in a London park is typical English understatement; compared to the 'strategic' bombing of German towns it is a negligible atrocity, compared to the cultural and emotional deprivation of most of our children its consequences are insignificant."[9] Clearly, Bond had found a frightful stage image to bring the atrocities perpetrated by civilized society closer to home.

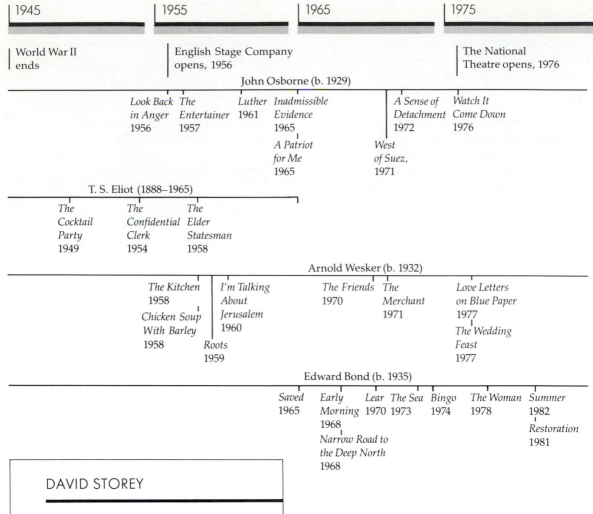

1945 — 1955 — 1965 — 1975

World War II ends | English Stage Company opens, 1956 | The National Theatre opens, 1976

John Osborne (b. 1929)

Look Back in Anger 1956 | The Entertainer 1957 | Luther 1961 | Inadmissible Evidence 1965 | A Sense of Detachment 1972 | Watch It Come Down 1976

A Patriot for Me 1965 | West of Suez, 1971

T. S. Eliot (1888–1965)

The Cocktail Party 1949 | The Confidential Clerk 1954 | The Elder Statesman 1958

Arnold Wesker (b. 1932)

The Kitchen 1958 | I'm Talking About Jerusalem 1960 | The Friends 1970 | The Merchant 1971 | Love Letters on Blue Paper 1977

Chicken Soup With Barley 1958 | Roots 1959 | The Wedding Feast 1977

Edward Bond (b. 1935)

Saved 1965 | Early Morning 1968 | Lear 1970 | The Sea 1973 | Bingo 1974 | The Woman 1978 | Summer 1982

Narrow Road to the Deep North 1968 | Restoration 1981

DAVID STOREY

Born (1933) in Yorkshire, David Storey studied at the Slade School of Art (London), attracting attention in 1959 with his novel *This Sporting Life*. He turned to playwriting in 1967 with *The Restoration of Arnold Middleton* at the Royal Court. Since then *In Celebration* (1969), *The Contractor* (1969), *Home* (1970), *The Changing Room* (1971), *Cromwell* (1973), *The Farm* (1973), and *Life Class* (1974) have been produced at the Royal Court, where he was associate artistic director in 1972–1974. He continues to write novels and plays that examine class differences, social distinctions, and the harsh rituals of work and play.

tween themselves and their boss, and their routine-filled lives. At the end of the play the tent is taken down.

The Changing Room (1971) takes place in a men's locker room during a semiprofessional rugby match in northern England. Storey reveals the thoughts and passions of the tradesmen-players while their bruised bodies and egos are on display after the intensity of the game.

PINTER'S AMBIGUOUS REALISM

From the beginning Harold Pinter's plays have defied pigeonholing. In answer to the usual

1945	1955	1965	1975

Harold Pinter (b. 1930)

The Room 1957	The Caretaker 1960	The Homecoming 1965	Old Times 1971	No Man's Land 1975	Betrayal 1978

The Birthday Party 1958

The French Lieutenant's Woman (screenplay 1981)

David Storey (b. 1933)

The Restoration of Arnold Middleton 1967	In Celebration 1969	The Changing Room 1971	Life Class 1974	Early Days 1980

The Contractor 1969 — Home 1970

The Farm 1973 — Cromwell 1973

Peter Shaffer (b. 1926)

Five Finger Exercise 1958	The Royal Hunt of the Sun 1964	Equus 1973	Amadeus 1979

Tom Stoppard (b. 1937)

Rosencrantz and Guildenstern Are Dead 1967	Jumpers 1972	Travesties 1974	Night and Day 1978	On the Razzle 1982

journalistic question at a writer's meeting ("But what would you say your plays were *about*, Mr. Pinter?"), he answered, "The weasel under the cocktail cabinet"[10]—a nonsensical reply that has since been taken seriously by Pinter's critics.

Since 1957 Pinter has written full-length plays, one-acts, television and radio plays, revue sketches, and film scripts. But his ambiguous realism and characteristic techniques are best associated with plays like *The Birthday Party, The Caretaker,* and *The Homecoming.* Usually the situation is simple, the characters' language is an almost uncannily accurate reproduction of everyday speech; yet in these ordinary surroundings (the run-down boarding houses, the

lived-in flats) lurk mysterious terrors and uncertainties.

In *The Birthday Party* sinister intruders threaten Stanley, a mild, self-effacing boarder in a seaside town. Who are these people? Who is Stanley? Why do the intruders humiliate him? What is going on? The questions are only partially answered in the play. The ambiguity creates an unnerving atmosphere of doubt and uncertainty. It also helps to generalize and universalize the fears and tensions to which Pinter's characters are subject.

In his more recent plays (from *The Caretaker* to *Betrayal*), Pinter gives closer and closer attention to realism, although ambiguity re-

Figure 13-6 The notorious final scene of Edward Bond's *Saved,* staged by the English Stage Company at the Royal Court Theatre in 1965. It was directed by William Gaskill.

mains. There are no mysterious strangers entering private worlds to terrorize and humiliate. The room in *The Caretaker* contains no outside menace but simply a clash of personalities within it that results in one of the inhabitants being displaced by another. Only Davies, an old tramp who wants to cover his tracks and to keep people guessing about him, shows the characteristic Pinter ambiguity. In *The Caretaker* the characters seem to amuse or taunt one another. Gradually the tone changes. Anxiety, pathos, or fear takes hold as the characters confront some predicament or try to defend them-

selves against some danger—real or imagined. Davies wants a place of refuge and fears that it will be denied him. In the end his worst fears are realized.

In the single-room setting of *The Homecoming,* six people explore their uncertain relationships. Teddy, a philosopher-teacher, and his wife, Ruth, arrive at his childhood home from the United States late one night to get acquainted with the family: his father, Max, an ex-butcher; his older brother, Lenny, a fast-talking pimp; his brother Joey, an unsuccessful boxer; and Uncle Sam, Max's put-upon brother.

Figure 13–7 David Storey's *The Changing Room* at the Royal Court Theatre, London, 1971, directed by Lindsay Anderson. Inside the locker room (the changing room), the captain of the rugby team takes a last look at his team before the game begins. Far right is their trainer (Barry Keegan).

In many ways it is more Ruth's homecoming than Teddy's. She is the quintessential Pinter woman who uses her body and her brains to manipulate the men in her life. In this household she knows intuitively the rules of the tribe. She manipulates Max, Lenny, and Joey, staying with them as her husband returns to the United States. But there are no clear-cut relationships here. Has Teddy really wanted Ruth to stay? Or has she manipulated him into bringing her "home"?

In creating his brand of ambiguous realism, Pinter has stripped us of our safe assumptions

about people and life. According to Pinter we cannot understand other people; we cannot even understand ourselves; and the truth of any situation is almost always beyond our grasp. If this is true in life, why should it not be true in the theatre?[11]

Pinter is capable of masterful play construction. He works up little by little to decisive climaxes: Stanley is taken away in *The Birthday Party*; Davies is ejected in *The Caretaker*; Ruth stays behind with her new family in *The Homecoming*. Pinter says of himself: "I am very concerned with the shape and consistency of mood

HAROLD PINTER

Harold Pinter (b. 1930) is an actor, playwright, director, film writer. Like Bond, Pinter grew up in a working-class Jewish family (his father was a tailor) in London's East End. He studied briefly at the Royal Academy of Dramatic Art and at the Central School of Speech and Drama in London. In 1949 he toured as a repertory actor under the name David Baron.

His first plays (*The Room* and *The Dumbwaiter*, 1957) were one-acts. His first full-length play, *The Birthday Party* (1958), received mixed reviews. But Pinter's subsequent plays have earned him the reputation as Britain's finest playwright. Six of his plays have been given stage premieres by the Royal Shakespeare Company. *The Homecoming* (1965), *Old Times* (1971), *No Man's Land* (1975), and *Betrayal* (1978) have been seen on Broadway. He has directed Robert Shaw's *The Man in the Glass Booth* (1967) and Simon Gray's *Butley* (1971) and *Otherwise Engaged* (1975) in London. Since 1971 he has been an associate director of the National Theatre.

The Homecoming

The Homecoming was first presented by the Royal Shakespeare Company in 1965 at the Aldwych Theatre, London, and directed by Peter Hall.

After teaching philosophy at an American university for six years, Teddy brings his wife home to London to meet his family: father Max, Uncle Sam, and brothers Lenny and Joey. The family has been womanless since the death of Jessie, Teddy's mother, many years before.

Teddy and Ruth arrive unexpectedly in the middle of the night and walk about the house separately. Teddy confronts Lenny but goes to bed without mentioning Ruth. When Lenny meets her, they do not know each other and Ruth obliquely offers herself to him. In the morning Teddy and Ruth see the rest of the family, and Max calls her a tart. After breakfast Teddy, sensing danger, suggests that he and Ruth leave early and return to the states, but she does not respond. Joey and Lenny make love to her while Max and Teddy stand by impassively. Teddy leaves without Ruth and the family sets her up as harlot, cook, mother, and housekeeper. She, in turn, plans to rule the roost.

in my plays. I cannot write anything which appears to me too loose and unfinished. I like a feeling of order in which I write."[12]

THE OPEN THEATRICALITY OF STOPPARD AND SHAFFER

Tom Stoppard achieved fame almost overnight when *Rosencrantz and Guildenstern Are Dead* was produced at the National Theatre in 1967. Influenced by the freewheeling fantasy of the Goon Show, the absurdist theatre of Samuel Beckett, and by his own sense of the theatrical, Stoppard in his play deals with the lives of attendant gentlemen at the beck and call of the great. Rosencrantz and Guildenstern (minor characters in Shakespeare's *Hamlet*) are summoned for brief moments into the glare of dramatic attention. Then they disappear forever.

Stoppard sees them as living suspended in existential doubt—forever on life's fringes. While waiting in the wings, so to speak, of Hamlet's court world, they play endless games of coin tossing, which defy all rules of chance by coming up heads 85 times in a row. Virtually nothing happens in their lives; they are waiting to be called to centerstage. The question is, can they decide to act instead of merely being acted upon?

In the end they go so far as to acquiesce in the choice of another, but it is only death that they choose (already arranged by Hamlet, as we remember). Their deaths at last define and give shape to their pointless lives.

In *Rosencrantz and Guildenstern* Stoppard uses the play-within-a-play and the open spaces of the Elizabethan stage. In *Jumpers* (1972) and *Travesties* (1974), he uses narrators, acrobats, and

---

Pinter's Dialogue

In Pinter's plays, words, gestures, pauses, and silences "uncover" the facts of his characters' lives. Pinter has said: "There are two silences. One when no word is spoken. The other when perhaps a torrent of language is being employed. The speech is speaking of language locked beneath it. That is its continual reference. The speech we hear is an indication of that which we don't hear. It is necessary avoidance, which keeps the other in its place."[13]

Pinter's most talked about method is the pause. The "Pinter pause" occurs when a character has said what he or she has to say and is waiting for a response. Or, the character simply cannot find words to say what he or she wants to say. Simply put, the character is caught up short and waits in silence for something to happen. But the pauses and silences are not neutral. If anything they are coercive, even defensive.

In *The Homecoming* when Lenny and Ruth meet for the first time late at night, they have a drink together. Their conversation is loaded with sexual innuendoes and threats.

Lenny And now perhaps I'll relieve you of your glass.

Ruth I haven't quite finished.

Lenny You've consumed quite enough, in my opinion.

Ruth No, I haven't.

Lenny Quite sufficient, in my own opinion.

Ruth Not in mine, Leonard.

　　　　[*Pause.*]

Lenny Don't call me that, please.

Ruth Why not?

Lenny That's the name my mother gave me.

　　　　[*Pause.*]

Ruth No.

　　　　[*Pause.*]

Lenny I'll take it, then.

Ruth If you take the glass . . . I'll take you.

　　　　[*Pause.*]

Lenny How about me taking the glass without you taking me?

Ruth Why don't I just take you?

　　　　[*Pause.*]

Lenny You're joking. . . . [14]

Figure 13-8 Tom Stoppard's *Rosencrantz and Guildenstern Are Dead* as performed on Broadway in 1967 with John Wood, Paul Hecht, and Brian Murray.

telecasts of men walking on the moon in an openly theatrical way.

Peter Shaffer's plays are meant for an open stage. After a long apprenticeship writing, and tearing up, plays during intervals of working in a New York library and for a London music publisher, his first major play, *Five Finger Exercise* (1958), was a West End success. Shaffer took the framework of a conventional English drawing room comedy and subjected his characters to a psychological scrutiny that introduced new subjects into West End drama: libido, Oedipal conflict, and homosexuality.

Shaffer is best known for his plays of spectacle, *The Royal Hunt of the Sun, Equus,* and *Amadeus*, all produced by the National Theatre. Each play is about the conflict between two protag-

onists; each requires two big performances. In *The Royal Hunt of the Sun,* the atheist Pizarro, the Spanish conqueror of Peru, and the god Inca Atahualpa, square off against each other among glittering golden sets and eye-catching Inca costumes and masks. The central question is how the idea of God is defined by these two men—each the other's prisoner, both illiterates and unscrupulous men of action.

Shaffer's large acting parts (Pizarro and Inca of *The Royal Hunt of the Sun; Dr. Dysart and Alan Strang of *Equus;* Salieri and Mozart of *Amadeus*) require spectacular staging. In *Equus* a psychiatrist and a stableboy who has put out the eyes of six horses square off in a struggle to exorcise the boy's destructive gods. We noted earlier John Dexter's use of actors in cagelike masks to

Figure 13-9 Peter Shaffer's *Amadeus,* originally staged at London's National Theatre in 1979, directed by Peter Hall and designed by John Bury. Left to right: Frank Finlay as Antonio Salieri, Morag Hood as Constanze Weber, and Richard O'Callaghan as Mozart.

represent the horses. The psychiatric treatment of the boy culminates in a physical climax. In a stylized way the boy reenacts his blinding of the horses.

Amadeus (directed by Peter Hall at the National Theatre) tells the story of the relationship between the musical genius Wolfgang Amadeus Mozart and the jealous court musician Antonio Salieri. Swelling music, costume and scene changes before the audience, and a crotchety narrator (the older, dying Salieri) make for splendid theatrical effects. *Amadeus* also has a play-within-a-play. We see characters (especially Salieri) both as participants in their lives and as aloof observers commenting on why they did what they did—interpreting, revising, moralizing.

Shaffer uses the stage to show human beings as both actors in and witnesses to their lives. Meaning, therefore, is relative—it changes with the time, place, mood, age, and memory of the actor-observers. Life is a staged event.

REPRESENTATIVE PLAY

Look Back in Anger
Written by John Osborne; produced by the English Stage Company at the Royal Court on May 8, 1956; directed by Tony Richardson with Alan Bates, Mary Ure, and Kenneth Haigh

BACKGROUND

John Russell Taylor has called John Osborne the first of the "angry young men" and *Look Back in Anger* as "the biggest shock to the system of British theatre since the advent of Shaw."[15]

What was the reason for the excitement generated at the Royal Court? Why did this play startle the London theatre establishment? There is little in the form of this well-made play, with its tensions and climaxes all in the right places and its general dependence on a solid realistic tradition, to make it unusual or distinguished.

JOHN OSBORNE

John Osborne (b. 1929) is both playwright and film writer. Born in London, Osborne was a little-known actor in repertory companies before he established himself in 1956 as a playwright with *Look Back in Anger* (a film version appeared in 1958). The play established Osborne as the most important of the "angry young men." He quickly followed this play with *The Entertainer* (with Laurence Olivier), *Luther* (with Albert Finney), and *Inadmissible Evidence* (with Nicol Williamson), consolidating his reputation.

In 1958 Osborne became codirector of the Woodfall film company for which he wrote the screenplay of *Tom Jones* (1962), also starring Albert Finney. His later plays have been produced at the Royal Court and also at the National Theatre. His more recent ones include *A Patriot for Me* (1965), *West of Suez* (1971), and *Watch It Come Down* (1976). Osborne's *A Better Class of Person: An Autobiography 1929–1956* (1981), describes his childhood and early struggles in the theatre; it ends with the optioning of *Look Back in Anger* for the English Stage Company.

What distinguishes Osborne's play is its *content*. The play deals with a post-war generation of young, disaffected working-class characters. Jimmy Porter represented a generation who became disillusioned, sullen, and full of rage when a brave new world failed to materialize. Osborne's character immediately became the cult figure of an under-forties generation of theatre-goers.

THE SCENE

The action takes place in Jimmy Porter's one-room flat in a Midland town in 1956. Osborne describes it as a large attic room at the top of a large Victorian house. It is a combination bedroom, living room, and kitchen where Jimmy lives with his wife, Alison. All of their living, loving, and quarreling take place here among the simple furnishings: a double bed, bookshelves, a chest of drawers, gas stove, cupboard, ironing board, dining table and chairs, and two shabby armchairs. The bathroom and water for washing and cooking are down the hall. The radio, newspapers, and weekly magazines provide Jimmy's main recreation, along with going to the local pub in the evening.

THE ACTION

Jimmy Porter is Osborne's rebel without a cause, or at least without an explicit cause. In the first act we learn that, although working class, he is a university graduate and a cultural snob. He reads only good books and "posh" Sunday papers, but he lives in a drab flat and makes his living by running a candy stall in the local marketplace.

Everything in life dissatisfies Jimmy: his wife, his friend Cliff, his government, his in-laws and their friends. His tone of conversation is consistent railing and complaint; his style of conversation is the monologue.

Alison Porter is the chief sufferer from Jimmy's unremitting anger. Jimmy cannot forgive her for her upper middle-class background and he constantly torments her, looking for

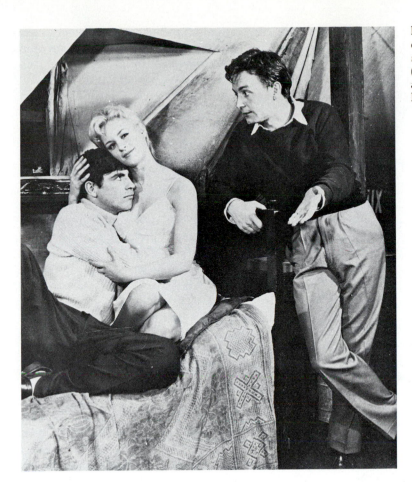

Figure 13-10 The original production of Osborne's *Look Back in Anger*, 1956. Left to right: Cliff (Alan Bates), Alison (Mary Ure), and Jimmy Porter (Kenneth Haigh).

some reaction. Alison's defense is to maintain a cool demeanor for as long as she can. But finally they "have a go at" each other under the sympathetic eye of Cliff. Into this cheerless situation arrives Alison's actress friend, Helena. She has an air of being "the gracious representative of visiting royalty" and soon makes the situation intolerable for everyone. At the end of the second act, Helena packs off Alison, who is expecting a baby and has not told Jimmy, to her family before taking Jimmy for herself.

In the third act Jimmy turns out to be settled down comfortably with Helena, as comfortably as he can be with anyone. She stands up to him more than Alison; also, their relationship is based on a rather uncomplicated lust. When

Cliff announces that he is going to leave the area, Jimmy is torn between friendship and his sexual relations with women:

Jimmy . . . It's a funny thing. You've been loyal, generous and a good friend. But I'm quite prepared to see you wander off, find a new home, and make out on your own. And all because of something I want from that girl downstairs, something I know in my heart she's incapable of giving. You're worth a half a dozen Helenas to me or to anyone. And, if you were in my place, you'd do the same thing. Right? . . .

Why, why, why, why do we let these women bleed us to death? Have you ever had a letter, and on it is franked "Please Give Your Blood Generously"? Well, the Postmaster General does that, on behalf of all the women of the world. I suppose people of our generation aren't able to die for good causes any longer. We had all that done for us, in the thirties and the forties, when we were still kids. [*in his familiar, semi-serious mood*] There aren't any good, brave causes left. If the big bang does come, and we all get killed off, it won't be in aid of the old-fashioned, grand design. It'll just be for the Brave New-nothing-very-much-thank-you. About as pointless and inglorious as stepping in front of a bus. No, there's nothing left for it, me boy, but to let yourself be butchered by the women.[16]

Alison returns after losing the baby. She admits that she is now what Jimmy has always wanted—a woman groveling, crawling, "in the mud at last." Faced with this example of his own handiwork, Jimmy reaches out to her in grief, tenderness, and fear of losing everything. At last he and Alison are reunited—perhaps never to make it in the real world around them.

CHARACTER

Osborne's characters suffer from discontent. These young adults from working-class backgrounds saw their parents demean themselves and wear themselves out just to put bread on the table; their fathers fight in wars of good causes and return without hope, maimed and dying. Their world has lost its traditional values of work, justice, and dutiful relationships. Their relationships with long-suffering friends and lovers are reduced to emotional endurance contests. As Jimmy says of Alison: "Don't think I could provoke her. Nothing I could do would provoke her. Not even if I were to drop dead." He describes her quality of imperturbability as "pusillanimous." ("It sounds like some fleshy Roman matron, doesn't it? The Lady Pusillanimous seen here with her husband Sextus, on their way to the Games.")

But Jimmy is not without elemental values. He values loyalty to people, like his dying father, who confided in him when he was a 10-year-old boy, and a friend's mother who treated him as a son and bought him the candy stall. His anger over their fates is chronic: "The injustice of it is almost perfect! The wrong people going hungry, the wrong people being loved, the wrong people dying." He does not hesitate to do the right thing by going to their deathbeds and funerals because "there was no one else to go."

Osborne's other characters are two-dimensional: the long-suffering wife, the sympathetic friend, the defensive girlfriend, the upper-class father.

LANGUAGE

Osborne's language is as much responsible for the play's impact as the action and characters. It is the "smart" language of the postwar generation, detached in its disillusionment with

---

In the opening stage direction, John Osborne describes his hero of *Look Back in Anger*:

" ** *Jimmy is a tall, thin young man about twenty-five, wearing a very worn tweed jacket and flannels. Clouds of smoke fill the room from the pipe he is smoking. He is a disconcerting mixture of sincerity and cheerful malice, of tenderness and freebooting cruelty; restless, importunate, full of pride, a combination which alienates the sensitive and insensitive alike. Blistering honesty, or apparent honesty, like his, makes few friends. To many he may seem sensitive to the point of vulgarity. To others, he is simply a loudmouth. To be as vehement as he is is to be almost noncommittal.* **"

John Osborne, *Look Back in Anger* (1957)[17]

---

politics, social movements, and the arts. Jimmy and Alison are educated; Cliff tries to adopt their tone, style of speaking, and interests. They live their lives out of the "posh" papers, disparaging the clergy, the intelligentsia, and the "American Age." Their conversation is sprinkled with clever allusions to novels, concerts, and sex. Osborne's dialogue does not so much represent shared ideas between people as Jimmy's stream-of-consciousness monologues on Alison's family and other subjects. Most of all Osborne's language is taunting, savage, and uncompromising.

OSBORNE'S MODERNISM

Twenty-five years later *Look Back in Anger* is still a remarkable play. It was the first to express the feelings of a postwar generation that rejected the experiences of the previous generation as meaningless. His characters turned their backs on the middle-class world—on the values of work, getting ahead, and life in suburbia with wife, children, and two cars. Osborne's characters are city dwellers whose life-support system is their rage at a world they did not make nor ask to be brought into and who take their anger out on each other in their defiantly shabby milieu. Ten years later the negativism of Osborne's generation would be transformed into antiwar activism and counterculture experimentation.

ESSAY

The English theatre has had a tremendous impact on the American theatre since the 1750s when the Hallams arrived with their company on American shores. Today more and more Broadway producers are depending on importing British productions for commercial success. At one point in the 1982–1983 season, four major British plays were playing in Broadway houses. At the same time *Nicholas Nickleby*, which had taken London and New York theatres by storm, was being shown on prime-time American television

for four consecutive nights. The excitement generated by the Royal Shakespeare Company's *Nicholas Nickleby* is still being felt in the American theatre; regional theatres, in particular, are commissioning many new adaptations. *Nicholas Nickleby* continues the tradition of British writing and performance styles that since the eighteenth century have challenged American audiences and theatre artists with the old remade into the new, with socially relevant statements made in openly theatrical ways.

The Life and Adventures of Nicholas Nickleby **in Modern Performance**
Produced by the Royal Shakespeare Company, adapted from Charles Dickens' novel by David Edgar, directed by Trevor Nunn and John Caird, at the Aldwych Theatre, London, 1980

Nicholas Nickleby has been the Royal Shakespeare Company's greatest success since Peter Brook's *A Midsummer Night's Dream* in 1970. Its daring concept was to stage a well-known novel with 42 actors in a production that runs more than eight and one-half hours. The play follows the story of Charles Dickens' young hero, Nicholas Nickleby, through his myriad experiences in the world of early Victorian England.

Many things about the production are a tour de force: the size of the cast, the performance's length, the scenery by John Napier, the use of a collective method to adapt Dickens' serialized novel for the stage. Despite its unusual features *Nicholas Nickleby* floats on the mainstream of stage realism that has dominated the serious British stage since George Devine established his writer's theatre in 1956. It conjures up the seaminess, filth, and violence of Victorian England with its extremes of cruelty and compassion, wealth and poverty, corruption and innocence.

BEGINNINGS

In 1979 the Royal Shakespeare Company was in financial trouble; it could afford only one major

Figure 13-11 *The Life and Adventures of Nicholas Nickleby* with the Royal Shakespeare Company, Plymouth Theatre, New York, 1981. Stage left are Roger Rees as Nicholas Nickleby and David Threlfall as his friend Smike confronting the Crummles, the theatrical family with whom they will tour in an up-beat musical version of *Romeo and Juliet.*

new production, instead of five, for its next London season. The problem was acute. How could Trevor Nunn, the artistic director, come up with one play with enough parts to engage a full company? The possibility of adapting one of Dickens' novels with its sprawling scenes, multitude of characters, and strong social messages had long been in his mind. This seemed the perfect time.

The merits of *Nicholas Nickleby* (written in 1838–1839) soon became apparent. It told of the adventures of an attractive and virtuous hero. It had a thriller plot and marvelous theatrical events like the scene in Dotheboys Hall where the schoolboys were starved, caned, blinded, and even murdered and the scene where the Crummles' theatrical troupe performed their lame, cut version of *Romeo and Juliet.* Moreover, the novel had tremendous social sweep moving from gutters to carriages, from starvelings to corpulent merchants.

The company agreed that Dickens' characteristic theme about the power of money to corrupt those who had it and to destroy those who did not was as appropriate today as yesterday.

Also, the novelist's moral concerns, his debate about human nature, were embodied in his central characters—Ralph Nickleby who thinks that human existence is nasty and brutish; his nephew, Nicholas, who believes that good always triumphs over evil.

SCRIPTING AND REHEARSALS

Like the American musical *A Chorus Line* (1975), *Nicholas Nickleby* evolved out of company improvisations, discussions, scene work, and long rehearsals. During the first days, each actor was given a chapter of the novel to narrate in a minute. Then exercises and rehearsals became more elaborate. The company was divided into four groups and asked to stage certain passages but in different styles—as mime, as naturalistic drama, as agitprop, even as opera. Some presented a slide show about the early Victorian theatre; others researched the class system, education, medicine, and hygiene—anything that might prove relevant. Then the actors were invited to choose characters that interested them

Figure 13-12 Christopher Benjamin as Vincent Crummles, Roger Rees as Nicholas, and David Threlfall as Smike. Nicholas and Smike decide to cast their fortunes with the Crummles Theatrical Company.

and, using Dickens' dialogue, to prepare three-minute extracts from the novel. Afterward the 42 actors chose parts among the 300-odd roles. Most chose the "big" parts—Nicholas, the hero; Smike, the abused boy rescued by Nicholas from Dotheboys Hall; Kate Nickleby, Nicholas' beautiful sister; Wackford Squeers, the cruel schoolmaster; and Crummles, the ham actor.

Playwright David Edgar was brought in to telescope Dickens' plot, tighten the middle, and to devise climactic endings. Edgar provided more than half the dialogue himself. To convince a modern audience, he also made the institutionalized violence at Dotheboys more brutal; Dickens had understated this for his nineteenth-century readers. The sympathetic women, Kate Nickleby and Madeleine Bray, were given firmer identities. He also created two highly effective endings to the two parts of the production.

Figure 13-13 Smike struggles to communicate his feelings to his friend Nicholas against the noises of Victorian London, as provided by the actors at left.

The first half ends with a parody of Shakespeare (staged by the Crummles family of touring actors) in which the star-crossed lovers are restored to life with song. Edgar wanted a scene of false happiness to get across the idea that the overall situation at that point was far from a happy one.

The second half ends with Nicholas cradling a starved child in his arms, reminding us that there will always be another crippled Smike and that Nicholas will always go out into the cold and bring the dying child back into the warmth.

PERFORMANCE STYLE

Early decisions influenced the final performance style. Children were not cast as the pupils at Dotheboys because they would have appeared too well fed. Instead, the cast limped and stumbled on stage telling the audience the boys' ages and afflictions. There would be no narrator-novelist in a smoking jacket to relate the action while expressing his moral outrage at poverty, disease, and child abuse. Instead, the "collective storyteller" was born. "We decided that the entire company was the narrator," said Trevor Nunn. "It was in possession of the entire story and felt very strong about it. If forty-one of the forty-two actors failed to turn up, the individual who was left would in theory be able to perform the whole show."[18]

The gravest danger for the actors was caricature. So many actors, although not all, in adaptations of Dickens' novels (*A Christmas Carol, Oliver Twist, David Copperfield, A Tale of Two Cities,* and *Great Expectations*) for television

Director Trevor Nunn talked about the emotional, even melodramatic, impact of *Nicholas Nickleby:*

" *It's like life, but more pleasant than life, because it's easier to work out whose side to be on. People found it purgative to be able to yell at Squeers, or applaud some act of heroism, and know their reaction was the right one. It was refreshing to go to something where the moral arguments didn't cancel each other out, something that wasn't contradictory and complex but said there were judgments to be made and goodness did exist. And some very fundamental English virtues were being emphasized. I mean that element of Dickens which says, why can't we behave decently, why can't we all be nicer to each other, why can't it be Christmas 365 days a year?* **"**

Trevor Nunn, *New York Times*
(October 4, 1981)[19]

and movies have opted for the easy caricature of Dickens' eccentrics. The Nicholas Nickleby company set out to be *real.*

The RSC told Dickens' story of a young innocent in the first years of Queen Victoria's reign on a bare stage surrounded by scaffolding that rose to the rafters and ringed the balcony. Each scene began almost before the previous one had ended. Where possible the cast mimed the scenery, a carriage, even Ralph Nickleby's house with its glittering lights. Actors carried their own props on and off. They created their own sound effects: a seagull, an owl, the wind. There were no elaborate disguises as all the actors played several characters (with the exception of Roger Rees as Nicholas).

THE AUDIENCE

Like *Look Back in Anger, Nicholas Nickleby* was not an immediate success. The first reviews were uneven. But a rave from Bernard Levine in *The Times* of London soon brought sold-out houses.

The play developed a cult following in London. Some sat through it 3, 5, even 10 times. At its closing (to prepare for the New York tour), the scene in the theatre was wild abandon: cheers, tears, flowers piled up to the cast's knees at the curtain call and banners unfurled in the dress circle reading, "We love you, we'll miss you!"

SUMMARY

The contemporary British theatre is an eclectic mix of subsidized and commercial theatres; national institutions and fringe groups; repertory troupes and limited-run companies. Britain's three national theatres are the National Theatre, the Royal Shakespeare Company, and the Royal Court (home of the English Stage Company). The Royal Court, under the direction of George Devine, was largely responsible for the revival of British playwriting in the sixties, chiefly characterized by working-class subjects, characters, and language. John Osborne's *Look Back in Anger* (1956) was the first of the new realistic plays.

Since the time of David Garrick in the eighteenth century, the British theatre has been looked upon as an actor's theatre in which the classically trained repertory actor set standards of versatility, articulateness, and energized performing. However, with Tyrone Guthrie, John Gielgud, Ralph Richardson, Laurence Olivier, and John Burrell, the director emerged as a force in the postwar theatre. The Old Vic (now the National Theatre) was the first significant postwar theatre. It was followed in the 1960s by the Royal Shakespeare Company (formerly the Stratford Memorial Theatre in Stratford-upon-Avon) under the direction of Peter Hall. The National Theatre opened in 1963 with Laurence Olivier as its first artistic director. Peter Hall became its second artistic director in 1973, and

Trevor Nunn replaced him as director of the Royal Shakespeare Company. When the Royal Court arrived on the scene, London had a third, major noncommercial theatre dedicated to producing serious theatre, especially the works of new playwrights.

With George Devine, Joan Littlewood, Peter Brook, William Gaskill, John Dexter, and others, the British theatre was jolted by experimentations in writing, directing, acting, and production styles. In the 1960s and 1970s the festivals and fringe groups offered alternatives to the national theatres, the commercial West End, and the provincial repertory theatres. Also, with the coming of the working-class play, modern British actors added realistic playing to their special style. Actors like Alan Bates, Colin Blakely, Joan Plowright, and Albert Finney are good examples of the eclectic art of English acting.

Over the past 25 years, the new playwrights have enormously enriched English-language drama. John Osborne, Harold Pinter, Tom Stoppard, Shelagh Delaney, and Peter Shaffer have become familiar names on both sides of the Atlantic in much the same way that Shakespeare, Sheridan, and Goldsmith had before them. Among the outstanding plays in the "new" British realistic mode are *Look Back in Anger* (Osborne), *A Taste of Honey* (Delaney), *Saved* (Bond), *The Contractor* (Storey), *The Caretaker* and *The Homecoming* (Pinter). While Shakespeare remains the house dramatist at the Royal Shakespeare Company and the National Theatre, Tom Stoppard, Harold Pinter, and Peter Shaffer consistently have their new plays produced by these theatres. Stoppard and Shaffer, in contrast to Osborne and Pinter, use the stage in an openly theatrical way.

Our representative play, Osborne's *Look Back in Anger*, expresses the disillusionment of the postwar generation with traditional, middle-class values.

Our representative modern performance of *Nicholas Nickleby*, produced by the Royal Shakespeare Company in 1980, combines the major features of contemporary performance on the British stage: open theatricality and working-class realism. Director Trevor Nunn's staging conjures up the extremes of Charles Dickens' early Victorian England: poverty and wealth, cruelty and compassion, corruption and innocence. Nicholas Nickleby's 300-odd characters played by the company's 42 actors perform on a bare stage surrounded by scaffolding, mime the scenery, create their own sound effects, and carry their own props on and off the stage. However, despite its uniqueness of form and staging, *Nicholas Nickleby* floats on the mainstream of stage realism that has dominated the serious British theatre since George Devine established his writer's theatre at the Royal Court in 1956.

PLAYS TO READ

Look Back in Anger by John Osborne

The Homecoming by Harold Pinter

Equus by Peter Shaffer

SOURCES

Osborne, John. *Look Back in Anger* (Penguin Play Series). New York: Penguin Books, 1982. Paperback.

Pinter, Harold. *The Homecoming*. New York: Grove, 1966. Paperback.

Shaffer, Peter. *Equus*. New York: Avon Books, 1977. Paperback.

These scripts are published without introductions. The only additional materials are notes on the first London productions of the plays, including producing company, theatre, date of first performance, director, and original cast.

NOTES

1. Terry W. Browne, *Playwrights' Theatre: The British Stage Company at the Royal Court Theatre* (London: Pitman, 1975), p. 10. Reprinted by permission of A & C Black (Publishers) Ltd.

2. *The London Sunday Times* (January 23, 1966).

3. Browne, p. 10. Reprinted by permission.

4. Browne, p. 10. Reprinted by permission.

5. Ronald Hayman, *British Theatre Since 1955: A Reassessment* (New York: Oxford University Press, 1979), p. 137. Reprinted by permission of Oxford University Press.

6. Peter Shaffer, *Equus* (London: André Deutsch, 1973), p. 104. Reprinted by permission of Peter Shaffer.

7. Judith Cook, *Directors' Theatre* (London: George G. Harrap, 1974), p. 71. Reprinted by permission of Harrap Ltd.

8. Edward Bond, "Author's Note," *Saved* (London: Methuen, 1965), p. 7. Reprinted by permission of Methuen, London.

9. John Russell Taylor, *The Second Wave: British Drama for the Seventies* (New York: Hill and Wang, 1971), p. 83. Reprinted by permission of A.D. Peters & Co. Ltd.

10. Taylor, *The Second Wave*, p. 323.

11. John Russell Taylor, *The Angry Theatre: New British Drama* (New York: Hill and Wang, 1962), p. 356.

12. Taylor, *The Angry Theater*, p. 260.

13. Harold Pinter, "Writing for the Theatre," *Modern British Drama*, ed. Henry Popkin (New York: Grove 1964), p. 579. Reprinted by permission of Grove Press, Inc.

14. Harold Pinter, *The Homecoming* (New York: Grove, 1966), pp. 33–34. Reprinted by permission of Grove Press, Inc.

15. Taylor, *The Angry Theatre*, p. 39. Copyright © 1962, 1969 by John Russell Taylor. Reprinted by permission of Hill and Wang, a division of Farrar, Straus and Giroux, Inc.

16. John Osborne, *Look Back in Anger* (New York: Criterion Books, 1957), pp. 104–105. Reprinted by permission of Faber and Faber Ltd.

17. Osborne, p. 2.

18. Benedict Nightingale, "How 42 Actors and 2 Directors Assembled 'Nicholas Nickleby,'" *New York Times* (October 4, 1981), pt. 2, p. 6. © 1981 by The New York Times Company. Reprinted by permission.

19. Nightingale, *New York Times*, pt. 2, p. 6. Reprinted by permission.

PART III

AMERICAN THEATRE PAST AND PRESENT

FOURTEEN

AMERICAN THEATRE: 1900–1970

A MODERN PERSPECTIVE

American theatre has its roots in the eighteenth-century British theatre—in its playwrights, actors, managers, and proscenium stages, first introduced to the American colonies by English touring companies in the 1750s. By World War I American theatre had evolved from producing plays on the English model into a truly indigenous theatre.

American theatre has been characterized by eclecticism and experimentation. One way to think of its development is as a revolving ferris wheel. Facing opposite one another in time and space, we find commercial and noncommercial theatres, regional theatres and Broadway houses, resident companies and touring groups, community theatres and ethnic theatre groups. As the wheel has gone around, playwrights, actors, designers, producers, directors, and companies have emerged, shaping and reshaping the American theatrical experience. This chapter deals with more than half a century of American theatre, perhaps its most significant years.

REPRESENTATIVE THEATRE: The Ethel Barrymore Theatre

It is December 1947 and the Ethel Barrymore Theatre is the scene of an opening-night ritual. But this will be no ordinary opening night. It is the eagerly awaited first performance of *A Streetcar Named Desire* by Tennessee Williams.

Although the evening is cold and windy, Times Square is thronged with hurrying theatregoers, street vendors selling steaming chestnuts from pushcarts, taxis vying with one another to deposit their customers in front of the many theatres. Policemen on horseback keep order in the streets. Theatregoers jostle each other hurrying across Broadway to the open doorways of the theatres.

Like most Broadway theatres—small, nineteenth-century-style proscenium houses—the Barrymore opens its doors directly onto the streets and alleyways of the teeming city. High overhead the theatre marquee spells out in brilliant lights the names of the play and playwright. Crowds hurrying from subways, taxis, and buses push through the gilt doors on 47th Street into the narrow foyer to purchase tickets and then pass by ticket takers into the red interior. Moving to the left and right, the spectators take their seats in the orchestra, or walk upstairs into the first and second balconies overhead. Refreshments, candy, and alcoholic beverages are sold from bars or narrow tables set up in the foyers.

The Barrymore—like the older Shubert, Booth, and Majestic theatres—is an elliptical auditorium with red curtain, narrow apron, and several balconies and side boxes. Racks of piping for hanging lighting equipment are located in or near the boxes. The stage itself is equipped with counterweight and lighting systems operated by union stagehands and electricians. In short, the Barrymore, operated by the Shubert Organization, is a standard Broadway house.

ETHEL BARRYMORE

Ethel Barrymore (1879–1959) was born in Philadelphia of a famous theatrical family; her grandmother was Louisa Lane Drew and her uncle John Drew, revered nineteenth-century actress and manager, and her parents were actors Maurice and Georgiana Drew Barrymore. Ethel and her two brothers John and Lionel grew up with their grandmother (Louisa Drew) because their parents were constantly on tour.

Ethel first appeared on stage at age 12 and went on to a long and successful career. She became famous for the roles of Nora in Ibsen's *A Doll's House*, Ophelia in Shakespeare's *Hamlet*, and Lady Teazle in Sheridan's *School for Scandal*. But Miss Moffat in Emlyn Williams' *The Corn Is Green* became her most famous stage role. Opening with the play in New York in 1940, she played in 477 performances. Brooks Atkinson called the role "a jewel in her crown." Ethel was admired both on stage and in films for her beauty and her extraordinary talent as an actress. The Broadway theatre on 47th Street was named for her in recognition of her lifetime achievements.

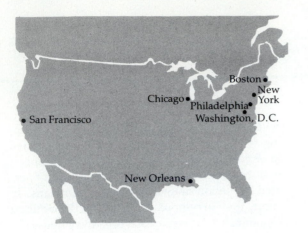

1920	1930
Woodrow Wilson, President, 1912–1920	The Great Depression 1929–1933
World War I ends, 1918	Herbert Hoover, President, 1929–1933
Voting rights extended to American women 1920	Franklin Delano Roosevelt, President, 1933–1945
Warren Harding, President, 1921–1923	

As with all opening-night audiences, there is an expectant murmur throughout the house. *The Glass Menagerie* had its successful Broadway opening in March 1945, winning the New York Critics' Circle Award for Williams. Williams' new play is being directed by Elia Kazan (former member of the Group Theatre), and features four relatively new Broadway actors: Marlon Brando, Jessica Tandy, Kim Hunter, and Karl Malden.

The house lights dim and the curtain rises on designer Jo Mielziner's setting of a two-story New Orleans tenement house located on Elysian Fields, a street that runs between the railroad tracks and the Mississippi River on the edge of the famous French Quarter.

After the applause for the splendid setting subsides, two actors walk onstage. They look up at the women sitting on the stairs leading up to the second floor. Marlon Brando, as Stanley Kowalski, begins the role that was to make him a household name. Stanley bellows to his wife (actress Kim Hunter): "Hey, there! Stella, Baby!" and the Barrymore once again becomes the scene of a history-making play. The next day's rave reviews will establish Williams' reputation as one of the nation's most distinguished dramatists and the play as an American classic.

CONDITIONS OF PERFORMANCE

BACKGROUND

During the first half of the nineteenth century, the United States grew from a small cluster of 13 states huddled against the Atlantic coast into one of the largest nations in the world. Hunters and explorers opened up the West from the Atlantic Ocean to the Pacific, from Canada in the north to Mexico in the south. The Homestead Act of 1862 brought farmers with families into the Great Plains. Beginning in 1869 the railroad brought miners, ranchers, and industrialists into the West. The American Indians, continually pressed by these forces of change, were swept aside and slaughtered; those remaining were relegated to reservations.

As the West was being "colonized," the industrial northern states and the agrarian southern states fought a bitter Civil War (1861–1865). Slavery was the focal issue. President Abraham Lincoln issued the Emancipation Proclamation on January 1, 1863, freeing the slaves. The struggle ended with about 620,000 Americans dead, a deeply divided nation, and a prostrate

Timeline

1940 | **1950** | **1960** | **1970**

Hitler invades Poland 1939

World War II, 1939–1945
America in war 1943–1945

Atomic bombs dropped on Japan, August 1945

Germany and Japan surrender, 1945

United Nations created, 1945

National television broadcasting 1946

North Atlantic Treaty Organization (NATO) formed, 1949

Harry S. Truman, President, 1945–1953

Korean War 1950–1953

Joseph R. McCarthy hunts Communists in entertainment industry 1953–1954

U.S. Supreme Court declares segregation of public education unconstitutional, 1954

American civil rights movement, 1955–

Russians launch Sputnik; Space Age begins 1957

Dwight D. Eisenhower, President, 1953–1961

John F. Kennedy, President, 1960–1963, assassinated in Dallas November 22, 1963

Cuban Missile Crisis, 1962

Lyndon B. Johnson, President 1963–1968

Medicare and Medicaid created, 1965

Vietnam War, 1957–1975 —————

Civil rights leader Martin Luther King, Jr. assassinated 1968

Robert Kennedy assassinated 1968

Richard M. Nixon elected President 1968

South. In the remaining years of the century and by the time of the country's entry into World War I in 1917, the United States developed from a predominantly rural nation into the world's largest industrial power.

Key factors responsible for these changes were a huge population increase, the discovery and exploitation of large mineral resources, and the building of railroad networks (called "hoops of iron") throughout the land. Capitalists like Andrew Carnegie, John D. Rockefeller, and John P. Morgan built powerful steel, oil, and banking industries. The labor force, steadily expanded by waves of European immigration, seemed inexhaustible. But housing was often inadequate, wages low, and poverty widespread. These conditions gave rise to the U.S. trade union movement, whose stormy history began with the Knights of Labor, founded in 1869, and continued with the American Federation of Labor (AF of L), which became a powerful indus-

trial and political force. Today the AF of L-CIO, a merger of craft and industrial unions, is the nation's largest.

Following World War I the United States, like Europe, faced severe economic problems. In 1929 the Wall Street crash brought multiplying bankruptcies, falling farm prices, and massive unemployment. The Great Depression touched everyone. In 1932, campaigning on the promise of a "New Deal" for all Americans, Franklin D. Roosevelt was elected president over incumbent Herbert Hoover. The New Deal set about to restore the economy with welfare legislation, public works, and agricultural aid. But the United States did not fully recover from the Depression until a wartime economy got under way in the 1940s. After the Second World War, American society underwent a period of unprecedented economic expansion, bringing prosperity, innovation, and some growing pains.

All of these social changes, both good and

bad, had their effect on the arts: the Depression, rapid technological change, political corruption, conservative politics, racial discrimination, and middle-class prosperity. Broadway's commercial theatre flourished in the late 1920s but steadily declined throughout the 1930s. In the thirties the Federal Theatre Project gave employment to out-of-work theatre artists; playwright Elmer Rice wrote about industry's effects on the human psyche; Eugene O'Neill wrote about the effects of possessiveness and materialism on the American family. In the forties and fifties Arthur Miller and Tennessee Williams wrote about the fragile victims of this changing society.

MANAGEMENT: THE COMPANIES

Like the country as a whole, the modern American theatre evolved both from within and from without. Conventions of theatrical performance from Blacks, Hispanics and American Indians have always been part of the multicultural richness of the American theatre, although their full significance did not surface until the 1960s. Commercial theatre evolved from touring companies during the late nineteenth century. They were led by such pioneer managers as Edwin Forrest, John McCullough, Lawrence Barrett, Laura Keene, Edwin Booth, Augustin Daly, Steele MacKaye, and Mrs. John Drew (Louisa Lane). New York, Boston, Philadelphia, Washington, D.C., and San Francisco became leading theatre centers. For managers and their companies, America was the land of opportunity.

Resident Companies Although countless touring companies played out-of-the-way mining and river towns, the "star" supported by a resident company was the standard American theatrical organization between 1850 and 1870. The United States had about 50 such companies in 1860. A successful play usually was given about 15 times and then placed in the repertory to alternate with other plays. But *Uncle Tom's Cabin*, based on Harriet Beecher Stowe's novel of 1852, changed this pattern. It played for 300 consecutive performances in one season, introducing a new trend for resident companies (Figure 14-1). These extended runs reduced the number of plays in the repertory and brought a greater emphasis on new plays. Whereas Shakespeare's plays and other standard works had once made up the repertory, by the turn of the century most long-running plays were new. All-black minstrel troupes, burlesques featuring songs and dances, melodramas, and vaudeville (essentially a collection of variety acts) also became popular.

Touring Companies The resident companies began to be undermined by the touring companies bringing new plays, stars, and scenery into the provinces. In the last decades of the nineteenth century, New York became the center of production. What we today call the "bus and truck" company was originally called the "combined company"—(one that travels with star and full company). These companies were put together in New York and sent out on the road with complete productions, including the star and supporting actors. Joseph Jefferson toured as Rip Van Winkle and Sarah Bernhardt as Camille.

As local support was withdrawn from the resident companies in favor of the touring attractions, local managers disbanded their companies and leased their theatres to the traveling troupes. Many famous theatres closed. The resident theatre movement was not to be fully revived again until the 1960s—almost 100 years later.

THE COMMERCIAL THEATRE

Theatre became a commercial venture. The long-run hit became the goal and New York the major theatrical center. Over the years various groups contributed to this development.

Managers like Augustin Daly (1839–1899) and David Belasco (c. 1854–1931) were also cre-

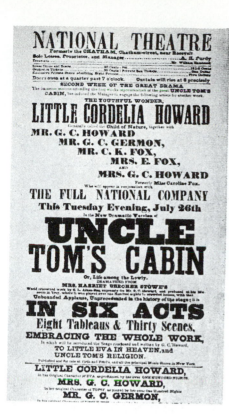

Figure 14-1 Playbill of *Uncle Tom's Cabin* at the National Theatre, New York, 1853, with the original cast.

ative artists. In the later years of the nineteenth century, managers who were exclusively business people and money makers took their place alongside them. The Frohman brothers, Daniel (1851–1940) and Charles (1854–1915), were the most successful of the new breed. In 1896 Charles Frohman with a small group of business people—producers, agents, and theatre owners —organized the Syndicate to gain control of the American theatre. By 1900 they had succeeded. The new organization offered local managers a full season of star-studded shows. Managers who refused had their theatres boycotted; actors who refused to tour in their productions found themselves unable to get work. In some cases the Syndicate built rival houses and booked the best productions at reduced prices until the competing theatre went bankrupt.

The Syndicate created a commercial mentality. It accepted only plays likely to appeal to a mass audience and favored productions that featured stars with large personal followings. However, the Syndicate provided plays that were crowd pleasers and launched many new stars, among them Otis Skinner, Maude Adams, and Ethel Barrymore.

Significant opposition soon developed among producers and stars. Actors Joseph Jefferson, Minnie Maddern Fiske, James A. Herne, and James O'Neill refused to be controlled by the Syndicate. David Belasco and the three Shubert Brothers—Sam, Lee, and Jacob J.—finally broke the Syndicate's monopoly.

Belasco is remembered as a producer and writer as well as for his opposition to the Syndicate. Like his American predecessors, managers Augustin Daly and Steele MacKaye, Belasco controlled every aspect of production. A master of stage realism that was intimate, photographic, and naturalistic, he brought the con-

Figure 14-2 *The Governor's Lady* produced by David Belasco, showing the reproduction of Childs Restaurant in New York with complete kitchen and dining area. In the last scene the building catches on fire.

tents of boardinghouse rooms, including wallpaper and kitchen odors, on stage. For the *Governor's Lady* (1912), he reproduced Childs Restaurant and the restaurant chain stocked it daily with food that was consumed during performance (Figure 14-2).

Belasco's productions were so popular that he readily defied the Syndicate; soon others followed. In 1905 the Shuberts established a rival chain of theatres. By 1915 the Syndicate's grip was broken. As producers the Shuberts favored lavish musicals and soon became as dictatorial as the Syndicate had been. However, the road show business dwindled as motion pictures caught on from coast to coast. The Great Depression of the 1930s completed the decline of the road show as a money-making enterprise.

The Shuberts continued to control what was left of "the Road" until 1956 when the government ordered them to sell many of their theatres. Today the Shubert Organization controls 17 theatres and continues as a major New York producer.

ACTING AS PROFESSION

With the triumph of the traveling company, actors had to go to New York to seek employment, and by the turn of the century actors' employment was New York based. They were hired for the run of the play, rather than for a season. Without a union to protect their rights, they were not paid for rehearsals and were often stranded when productions closed on the road.

These working conditions gradually improved with the founding of the actors' union, the Actors' Equity Association (AEA), in 1912.

The star system, which encouraged a presentational acting style to show the actor's best qualities and effects, began to be supplanted in the 1930s by the ideal of the ensemble. American actors moved increasingly toward psychological truth as found in the character's inner motivations.

The Actors Studio, which introduced the American "method," was founded in 1947 by former members of the Group Theatre: Robert Lewis, Elia Kazan, Harold Clurman, and Cheryl Crawford. Lee Strasberg soon became associated with the Studio and assumed its leadership in 1951. Until his death in 1982 Strasberg was the most influential acting teacher in America and the foremost interpreter of Stanislavsky's acting methods. Marlon Brando (b. 1924), with his characterization of the inarticulate, uneducated, and macho Stanley Kowalski of *A Streetcar Named Desire,* came to epitomize the studio's acting style.

While the Actors Studio (and American acting in general) has been criticized for the use of substandard speech, fumbling movements, and self-indulgence, the criticism is largely undeserved. Strasberg and the American method elevated the idea of inner truth as the basis of good acting. The work of many of the best American actors—Brando, the late James Dean, Karl Malden, Geraldine Page, Al Pacino, Maureen Stapleton, Julie Harris, Dustin Hoffman—reflect Strasberg's principles. But by the 1960s the influence of the Actors Studio began to decline as interest turned toward nonrealistic and period drama, for which the studio's approach seemed, to some, too limited. Also, the emergence of collective or avant-garde groups like the Living Theatre and the Open Theatre, brought new materials and working methods into the American theatre.

TRAINING PROGRAMS

Almost since the theatre's beginnings, actors and designers had been trained in the theatre by other professionals. Not until around 1900 did this system begin to change when drama programs were introduced into American colleges and universities. Although students had studied plays as literature and had produced plays in

---

Theatre Unions

During the war years even commercial theatre productions declined, falling to 80 by 1939–1940. Severe economic pressures and the emergence of powerful labor unions contributed to theatre's difficulties. The stagehands' union, the National Alliance of Theatrical Stage Employees, received full recognition in 1910–1911, and in 1918 the United Scenic Artists (the designers' union) was formed. Actors' Equity Association, founded in 1912, was recognized as the actors' official union in 1919. Equity became a closed shop in 1924 and established a minimum wage scale in 1933. The Dramatists' Guild, formed in 1912, became the bargaining agent for all playwrights in 1926. The newest union is the Society for Stage Directors and Choreographers.

As each union improved working conditions, it also demanded higher pay for its members, contributing to the theatre's economic problems. Today all professionals working in the theatre, except producers, have union status, and wage scales cover professional theatres of all types from Broadway to our resident theatres.

universities since the seventeenth century, the important change came in 1904 when George Pierce Baker (1866–1935) began to teach playwriting at Radcliffe College of Harvard University in Boston. A year later he established a similar course at Harvard, his famous English 47. By 1913 he had organized an extracurricular 47 workshop where students could learn (without credit) about acting, directing, scene design, and lighting. Many of America's most talented young writers and designers were attracted to Baker's workshop, including Eugene O'Neill, S. N. Behrman, Philip Barry, and Sidney Howard. Among the designers were Robert Edmond Jones, Kenneth Macgowan, and Lee Simonson.

In 1925 Baker moved to Yale University in New Haven, Connecticut, where he established a graduate school of drama to provide professional training for young theatre artists. He directed this program until his death in 1935. Other university pioneers followed Baker's lead. Thomas Wood Stevens established a curriculum at the Carnegie Institute of Technology (now Carnegie-Mellon University) in Pittsburgh in 1914, the first in the United States to grant degrees in theatre. Frederick Koch founded the influential Carolina Playmakers at the University of North Carolina in Chapel Hill in 1918. Many other theatre programs soon followed, including Alexander M. Drummond's at Cornell University. By 1940 theatre education was an accepted part of most American colleges and universities. The 1982 American Theatre Association *Directory* lists 1500 theatre departments all across the country.

VISUAL ELEMENTS

America's "new" stagecraft, which began to develop around 1910, is linked with the names of designers Robert Edmond Jones, Norman Bel Geddes, and Lee Simonson. They, in turn, were influenced by new European trends in open staging, spectacular lighting, and the design theories of Appia, Craig, and Reinhardt. Jones had studied in Europe between 1912 and 1915,

but it was not until the end of World War I that European practices became assimilated into the American theatre.

The new stagecraft was primarily a *visual* movement, aiming at simplified realism in production. *Theatre Arts Magazine*, launched in 1916 by Sheldon Cheney, became the principal means of disseminating the new ideas. (*Theatre Arts* ceased publication in 1963.) The new designs featured bold conceptions: towering steps, soaring platforms, mammoth abstract shapes, and imaginative lighting. In the late 1940s the new stagecraft was superseded by the selected realism of Jo Mielziner, Howard Bay, and others.

THE "GROUPS"

There was a time lag between Europe's independent theatres and those in the United States. Not until around 1915 did America develop nonprofessional groups fully aware of trends and innovations in Europe, although the Hull House Players in Chicago in 1900 was probably the first. Several "little theatres" were established in 1915 in emulation of Europe's independent theatres: the Neighborhood Playhouse, the Washington Square Players, and the Provincetown Players.

For the most part the groups depended upon unpaid volunteers for personnel and upon subscribers for financial support. Most produced a series of plays each year, using new drama and production methods widely accepted in Europe. After 1920 the little theatres became indistinguishable from modern community or civic theatres. However, they prepared the way for the Group Theatre and the Actors Studio.

The Group Theatre For ten years (1931–1941) the Group Theatre was the most distinguished, launched by Harold Clurman, Cheryl Crawford and Lee Strasberg and modeled on the Moscow Art Theatre, whose methods and ensemble acting style they emulated. The theatre was dedicated to high social and artistic ideals.

Commercial managers were not interested in

the new plays of social protest that reflected the unrest of the Depression years. New companies were needed to produce them. However, many of the companies were leftist and dedicated to political action. They enjoyed a brief flurry of activity and then vanished. The Group Theatre, whose aim was artistic instead of political, became highly influential. (See the discussion on page 275 in Chapter 10.)

The Group included actors, directors, and playwrights who were to shape the American theatre for four decades. Among them were actors Stella Adler, Morris Carnovsky, Fran-

chot Tone, and Elia Kazan; directors Harold Clurman, Lee Strasberg, and Cheryl Crawford; playwrights Paul Green, Sidney Kingsley, Irwin Shaw, William Saroyan, and Clifford Odets.

The Federal Theatre The Depression was responsible for the creation of a unique experiment, called the Federal Theatre Project. Started in 1935 under President Franklin D. Roosevelt's administration and the Works Progress Administration (WPA), and headed by Hallie Flanagan Davis (1890–1969) (Figure 14-3), then director of the Vassar College Experimental Theatre,

---

The New Groups

The triumph in the United States of the new European ideals in production and playwriting owed much to the Neighborhood Playhouse of New York, the Washington Square Players of New York, and the Provincetown Players of Provincetown and New York. They are the forerunners of the Group Theatre, among others.

The Neighborhood Playhouse grew out of the activities of the Henry Street Settlement. Its theatre on New York's lower East Side was built and endowed by Alice and Irene Lewisohn. During its first five years, the amateur company produced colorful revues, concerts, and plays for the settlement's largely immigrant clients. Later, it became professional and presented a variety of plays, some of them experimental. The producing group disbanded in 1927, but the name has survived in the influential Neighborhood Playhouse School of Theatre, directed for years by Sanford Meisner.

In 1915 a group of young amateurs and would-be professionals founded the Provincetown Players on Cape Cod, Massachusetts. A year later they moved to New York, concentrating on plays by new American playwrights, among them Eu-

gene O'Neill. By 1925 they had presented 93 plays by 47 authors and included Robert Edmond Jones, Kenneth Macgowan, and Donald Oenslager among their designers. Financial pressures forced the group to close in 1929.

Also formed in 1915, the Washington Square Players was led by Edward Goodman and made up of talented nonprofessionals who wanted to present plays of artistic worth. Designers Robert Edmond Jones and Lee Simonson, playwrights Zoe Akins and Philip Moeller, and actors Katherine Cornell and Roland Young were involved in this experimental group. The group disbanded in 1918, but their artistic success inspired several members to form the Theatre Guild, which became the most prestigious theatre group in America.

The goal of the Theatre Guild, a fully professional company, was to present quality plays not likely to interest commercial producers. By 1920 it had become America's most respected theatre group, presenting a number of plays each year to a largely subscription audience. Lee Simonson was the Guild's major designer; their most typical style was a modified realism.

Figure 14-3 A tenement house on fire in *One Third of a Nation*, a "living newspaper" production by the Federal Theatre Project, 1938.

the Federal Theatre Project put thousands of unemployed theatre people to work. It gave continuous employment to Black actors and encouraged new production techniques using original plays by new authors. It mounted about 1200 productions during the four years of its existence and played to more than 30 million people in almost all states of the union. Sixty-five percent of its performances were free.

In spite of its diversity, the Federal Theatre Project is now remembered largely for developing the "living newspaper"—a documentary-type drama that integrated factual data with cinematic form and short dramatic scenes. Each script centered around an immediate social problem. For example, *Triple A Plowed Under* (1936) dealt with the plight of the farmer; *Power* (1937) with rural electrification; and *One Third of a Nation* (1938)—the most famous—with slum housing. In most of the plays the central character was an ordinary citizen who raises questions about a current problem and is then given background information and possible solutions. The living newspaper took its dialogue from speeches, newspaper stories, and other documents. Epic theatre inspired many of its techniques, such as the use of slide projections, treadmills, sound amplifiers, and presentational acting styles with narrators. The political tone of many works eventually alienated Congress. In 1937 Marc Blitzstein's *The Cradle Will Rock* was prohibited from opening because federal bureaucrats considered it subversive and dangerous. Its producers, John Houseman and Orson Welles, resigned from the Federal Theatre in protest and opened the play themselves as the first production of the Mercury Theatre. Other attackers claimed that the Federal Theatre was both immoral and communistic. Although the theatrical profession rallied to defend it for having rescued thousands of artists from poverty and for contributing to the cultural life of the nation, Congress cut off the project's appropriations on June 30, 1939, because of the political tone of many plays. Finally, newsreels shown in movie houses supplanted the idea of the living newspaper.

The Mercury Theatre Orson Welles (b. 1915) and John Houseman (b. 1902) formed the Mercury Theatre in 1937, first presenting *The Cradle Will Rock* after its difficulties under the Federal Theatre. Welles had already established a reputation as an actor with his portrayal of Marlowe's Doctor Faustus and as an imaginative producer with his production of *Macbeth* set in Haiti with an all-Black cast.

Between 1937 and 1939 the Mercury Theatre presented works by Buchner, Shaw, and Shakespeare. While its greatest success was *Julius Caesar*, played in German storm-trooper uniforms as a comment on fascism, its most "infamous" success was the Welles's radio broadcast for CBS of the *War of the Worlds* (1938), which chronicled a Martian invasion of earth. Many listeners thought the invasion was real, and panic ensued.

The Lafayette Street Theatre Before 1915 a few musicals had been written for Black casts, making Black performers like Bert Williams (1876–1922) and Eubie Blake (1883–1983) Broadway musical-comedy stars.

Dialogue from
One Third of a Nation

Mr. Borah Is the Senator going to discuss the question of the causes of slums? Why do we have those awful degraded conditions?

Loudspeaker Senator Robert F. Wagner, of New York.

Mr. Wagner I think it is a very simple matter. It is because of low incomes received by the individuals who live in the slums. That is the fundamental difficulty. If overnight we could increase their incomes by a more fair distribution of the wealth of the country, we would not have any slums.

Loudspeaker Senator C. O. Andrews, of Florida.

Mr. Andrews Mr. President, I should like to ask the Senator from New York where the people who live in slums come from?

Mr. Wagner A great many of them have been here a long time. What does the Senator mean by, "Where do they come from"? Whether they come from some other country?

Mr. Andrews I think we ought not to offer any inducement to people to come in from our country or foreign countries or anywhere else and take advantage of our government in supplying them with houses. For instance, if we examine the birth records in New York, we will find that most of the people there in the slums were not born in New York, but the bright lights have attracted them from everywhere and that is one reason why there are so many millions in New York without homes.

Hallie Flanagan, *Arena: The History of the Federal Theatre* (1940)[1]

In 1915 Anita Bush organized the All-Colored Dramatic Stock Company in New York. After one season its direction passed to Robert Levy at the Lafayette Theatre. Most of the company's repertory was taken from Broadway, but it gave Black actors their longest continuous employment in regular drama up to that time. Playwrights also began to write serious plays for Blacks that ignored the "step-and-fetch-it" stereotype. It was a time when color prejudices were breaking down, at least on the stage, and many Blacks were winning admiration and applause as writers and actors.

Eugene O'Neill wrote *The Emperor Jones*, in which a Black actor played the leading role in a serious American play on Broadway for the first time; DuBose and Dorothy Heyward wrote *Porgy*, later to become the opera *Porgy and Bess*; Marc Connelly, *The Green Pastures*; Paul Green, *In Abraham's Bosom*; and Black playwright Langston Hughes, *Mulatto*. Such Black actors as Richard Harrison, Frank Wilson, Rose McClendon, and Abbie Mitchell found vehicles for their considerable talents. Paul Robeson (1898–1976), who became the greatest Black actor of his time, appeared in O'Neill's original production of *All God's Chillun Got Wings* in 1924. His great talent as a singer was soon recognized on the concert stage and his stature as an actor was later confirmed, especially by his performance of *Othello* (Figure 14-4).

While Black theatre had made its presence felt, the end of the Federal Theatre Project in 1939 was soon followed by the demise of the Lafayette Theatre. An audience for serious Black plays had not been developed sufficiently to support the theatre, and Black playwrights were not yet seen as "commercial" by New York producers.

THE DIRECTORS

The modern American theatre has often been spoken of as a director's theatre. The importance of the director had been established in the first quarter of the twentieth century by such *régisseurs* as Augustin Daly and David Belasco.

Between 1940 and 1960 a new group of master artists emerged who were able to perceive all the potentials of drama and embody them in vividly exciting productions. The most influential figures among them were Elia Kazan, Harold Clurman, José Quintero, and Tyrone Guthrie.

Elia Kazan (b. 1909) and designer Jo Mielziner, collaborating on such plays as Tennessee Williams' *A Streetcar Named Desire* and Arthur Miller's *Death of a Salesman*, established a production style that dominated the commercial theatre until about 1960. Kazan's combination of realistic "method" acting with theatricalist staging has practically become an American idiom. He made his reputation as a director on Broadway in 1942 with Thornton Wilder's *The Skin of Our Teeth*, and his subsequent career has been filled with stage and film successes.

Kazan's staging has been admired for its power and simplicity. His working methods are meticulous. After careful study of the play, he decides where the emphasis should be and discusses his concepts in great detail with his cast. It has been said that actors revere his judgment and trust his sense of the theatrical, which is always tempered with good taste.[2]

Harold Clurman (1901–1980) remained throughout his long career an articulate spokesman for the director in the commercial theatre. Firmly established as a Broadway director in the 1940s, by 1959 he had more than 50 productions to his credit, including such popular successes as *The Member of the Wedding* (1950), *Bus Stop* (1955), and *A Touch of the Poet* (1958). As a director Clurman was intensely emotional, even volatile. His purpose was "to make the play as written, clear, interesting, enjoyable, by means of living actors, sounds, colors, movements."[3] Today the newly renovated civic theatre complex on 42nd Street in New York contains the Harold Clurman Theater.

With the growth of the television industry in the 1950s and rising production costs on Broadway, producers looked for "safe" vehicles with broad appeal to attract audiences. The number of productions mounted on Broadway steadily declined as ticket prices rose. In

Figure 14-4 Paul Robeson as Othello learns the truth about Desdemona's innocence from Margaret Webster as Emilia in the 1944 Theatre Guild production in New York.

the season of 1949–1950, only 59 new productions were mounted. There had to be an alternative. One solution was to diversify the theatre by moving Off Broadway. The new theatres that opened away from Broadway were able to cut production costs, bring in new materials, and encourage new playwrights.

The Circle in the Square was the first of the new Off-Broadway stages to gain prestige. José Quintero (b. 1924) and Theodore Mann (b. 1924) opened their theatre in 1951 in a former nightclub. Gone was the proscenium stage; in

its place was a rectangular acting area with audiences seated around three sides. Quintero directed Tennessee Williams' *Summer and Smoke*, a failure on Broadway, to high critical praise. He triumphed again with a revival of Eugene O'Neill's *The Iceman Cometh* in 1956 and that same year directed the Broadway production of *Long Day's Journey Into Night*.

While Quintero was directing presumably noncommercial American classics 50-odd blocks from Broadway, other directors, such as Margo Jones in Dallas, Zelda Fichandler in

Figure 14-5 O'Neill's *A Moon for the Misbegotten*, directed by José Quintero on Broadway in 1973. Left to right: Ed Flanders, Colleen Dewhurst, and Jason Robards, Jr.

Washington, D.C., Jules Irving and Herbert Blau in San Francisco, and Tyrone Guthrie in Minneapolis, further decentralized American theatre, creating a full-blown regional theatre movement by 1970.

An established British director, Tyrone Guthrie (1900–1971) inaugurated a Shakespeare Festival Theatre in 1953 in Stratford, Ontario. Ten years later he came west and founded the Tyrone Guthrie Theatre in Minneapolis—a

unique seven-sided thrust stage encircled by 1441 seats—one of the most prestigious regional theatres in the United States. Guthrie instituted a classical repertory and the Guthrie became known for its spectacular revivals of Greek and Shakespearean plays. Guthrie's concept of resident theatres presenting revivals in repertory was dominant until about the mid-1970s when, among other events, new plays came onto the regional scene.

THE PLAYWRIGHTS

Following World War II American playwrights came into their own. Earlier they had served stars, managers, groups, and their work had been preempted by classical European plays—largely British imports. Three names stand out as the shapers of midcentury American playwriting: Eugene O'Neill, Tennessee Williams, and Arthur Miller.

O'Neill got his start in George Pierce Baker's playwriting class around 1912 and with the Provincetown Players in the 1920s. His 25 full-length plays represent experiments with novel theatrical devices and dramatic techniques, including the use of masks and working dynamos.

Tennessee Williams, our most celebrated playwright since O'Neill, began to learn his craft at the University of Iowa's Writers' Workshop in 1938. Between 1945 and 1960 numerous productions of *The Glass Menagerie, A Streetcar Named Desire*, and *Summer and Smoke* made his name synonymous with serious commercial theatre.

Williams has been rivaled only by his contemporary Arthur Miller, who began his playwriting career as a student at the University of Michigan at Ann Arbor. Miller's first success, *All My Sons* in 1947, established his reputation as a socially committed dramatist.

Between 1945 and 1960 the American playwright was largely subject to the Broadway hit-or-miss syndrome. The Off-Broadway movement and its offspring Off-Off Broadway, with Joseph Papp at the Public Theatre and Ellen Steward at La Mama ETC, helped to alter this situation.

THE COLLECTIVES

The hallmark of the American avant-garde in the 1960s was the collective creation of texts. Among the many groups at work, the most notable were the Living Theatre, the Open Theatre, and the Bread and Puppet Theatre in New York. Each was organized around a central figure who functioned as leader, guru, parent, mentor, director, writer, actor, and teacher. They were Judith Malina and Julian Beck ("the Becks") of the Living Theatre, Joseph Chaikin of the Open Theatre, and Peter Schumann of the Bread and Puppet Theatre.

The Living Theatre The Becks and the Living Theatre were the foremost gurus of the sixties' Off-Off Broadway groups. Their zeal and talents were directed to a peace-loving, nonviolent revolution to overhaul society and to the creation of a performance style to confront that society. Their theatre reached its fullest expression in *Paradise Now* (1968)—a marathon work whose performance lasted as long as the audience endured. The performance was like a freely structured religious service in which the audience was both encouraged to take part and assaulted for its middle-class values. It was made up of a series of rites: shouted epithets, prayer, yoga, "universal intercourse" practiced for the achievement of sexual freedom, and so on. The work revealed the core of a Living Theatre performance: an anarchist spirit, nonviolent stances, onstage nudity, pacifist beliefs, and a search for solutions outside the political system (Figure 14-6). Money was the prime evil and its destruction the prime goal.

The Living Theatre began in 1948 in a New York cellar on Wooster Street. In 1959, in a converted space on 14th street, the Becks produced Jack Gelber's *The Connection*, a disturbing play about heroin addicts. The addicts' environment, of which the audience was a part, was naturalistically reproduced, as was their life style. This well-received production was followed by Kenneth Brown's *The Brig* (1963),

---

> **Collective** an association of people who share a common vision and who work together to develop a common style of performing.

Figure 14-6 *Paradise Now: The Revolution of Cultures,* as performed by the Living Theatre. in 1968. Actors form a living totem pole in one of many theatrical rites.

which recreated the repetitive and senseless routine of a day in a Marine prison camp. The critical success of this production was undermined by the Living Theatre's encounter with the U.S. Internal Revenue Service (Figure 14-7). The government closed the theatre for nonpayment of taxes and the Becks went to jail for a short time. When they came out they took their group (some 40 men, women, and children) into self-imposed exile in Europe where they have remained off and on.

As social and political conditions changed in the 1970s, the Living Theatre's influence waned. However, unlike the disbanded Open Theatre, the Living Theatre is still a viable producing group, although, for economic reasons as much as for philosophical ones, they have split into three groups or "cells." Their goal of "theatre as politics" remains the same as they tour Europe, performing street theatre and playing in traditional theatres. Their collective creation *Prometheus,* showing the struggle between the liberator of humankind and Zeus, the subjugator and destroyer, has been performed by the group recently in Poland, France, and Italy.

Much of our current theatre is indebted to the liberating influence of innovative groups like the Living Theatre.

Figure 14-7 The Living Theatre production of Kenneth Brown's *The Brig*, New York, 1963, about life in a Marine prison camp. Internal Revenue Service agents locked up the theatre on 14th Street during the run of this production.

The Open Theatre Joseph Chaikin (b. 1935) and Peter Feldman founded the Open Theatre in New York in 1963. This experimental company put aside nonessentials like costume, makeup, scenery, and properties, emphasizing the actor and texts that examined contemporary political and social problems.

Under Chaikin's leadership the Open Theatre involved actors, directors, playwrights, and sometimes audiences in developing theatre pieces, using physicalization to convey situation, relationships, character, sound, and action. The group's backgrounds, interests, training, and life styles were put to use in workshop performances. Writers participated in the workshops before writing anything down, relating their scripts to the group's improvisations from which they selected the most effective work within a given social and political context. The scripts were usually performed by the same actors who had been in the workshops. In this way Megan Terry (b. 1932) wrote *Viet Rock; a Folk War Movie* and *Mutation Show*, and Jean-Claude van Itallie (b. 1936) scripted *America Hurrah!* and

The Serpent. These two playwrights worked consistently with the Open Theatre in the sixties.

Chaikin developed two performance techniques that later came to be known as "Open Theatre techniques": sound and movement, in which the actor developed physical movements and sounds to communicate emotions, and character transformation, in which the actor switched from one identity to another without establishing motivation or realistic transitions. The results of these techniques were "image plays," which presented an image or series of images coordinated by a central theme or idea. Communication with the audience depended upon the effectiveness of the actor's sound-and-movement patterns and the transformational roles.

In van Itallie's *Interview*, one of his three short plays produced as *America Hurrah!* in 1966, Chaikin's group recreated the mechanical behavior, isolation, and depersonalization of urban America. *Interview* begins and ends with automatic questions: What's your name? What job do you want? What experience have you had?

Paradise Now: The Revolution of Cultures
(Performed by the Living Theatre, 1968)
Rite I: The Rite of Guerilla Theatre

When the audience has almost completely assembled, the actors enter the theatre, mingling with the spectators in the aisles and on the stage and in the lobby. Each actor approaches a spectator and, addressing him individually, speaks the first of five phrases directly to him. At first he speaks in a very quiet, urgent, but personal voice.

Phrase 1

I AM NOT ALLOWED TO TRAVEL WITHOUT A PASSPORT.

He goes from spectator to spectator and repeats this phrase. With each repetition, his voice and body express greater urgency and frustration. He speaks only this phrase. If the spectator addresses him, he listens to the spectator but repeats only this phrase. The spectator may mock him, encourage him, question him. The spectator may be passive, sympathetic, superficial, witty, profound, cynical, hostile. The actor uses this response to increase his expression of the frustration at the taboos and inhibitions imposed on him by the structure of the world around him. He is obsessed with the meaning of the prohibition and by the ramifications of the prohibition. He cannot travel freely, he cannot move about at will, he is separated from his fellow man, his boundaries are official: the Gates of Paradise are closed to him.

He hears his fellow actors flipping out and is affected by the community of protest. He experiences the spectators' growing frustration at the sense of a lack of communication. By the end of two minutes, all of the actors have reached a point close to hysteria. They are shouting the words with anguish and frustration. They are flipping out. The Cherub with the Flaming Sword is standing at the frontiers and at the customs stations. At the end of two minutes the actors go beyond words into a collective scream. This scream is the pre-revolutionary outcry. (Flashout.)*

At this point the actors return to the artist's quiet center. They stand still and breathe.

Pause and begin again.

Phrase 2

I DON'T KNOW HOW TO STOP THE WARS.

Again each actor begins by addressing the spectators quietly and personally. He expresses his own passionate frustration at his inability to abolish even the most obvious evil: War. His guilt, his responsibility, his need. He cries out against the system and the culture which block his peacemaking efforts. The spectators' response, whether negative, positive, or

---

*Whenever this happens in the play, the actor by the force of his art approaches a transcendent moment in which he is released from all the hangups of the present situation.

passive, increases his horror at his inability to stop the killing. Passion and frustration mount in crescendo until they reach the point of the collective scream. (The Flipout and Flashout.)
Pause and begin again.

Phrase 3

YOU CAN'T LIVE IF YOU DON'T HAVE MONEY.

Beginning quietly and personally the actors repeat this phrase. Two minute crescendo. There is no way to sustain yourself on this planet without involvement in the monetary system. The actors see in the spectators' responses the floundering economics of the structure. It makes them crazy. It makes them crazy to realize that many spectators do not know that they are talking about death by starvation. Et cetera. (Flipout. Scream. Flashout.)
Pause and begin again.

Phrase 4

I'M NOT ALLOWED TO SMOKE MARIJUANA.

Two minute crescendo. From the horror of death by starvation to the horror at the prohibition of pleasures. (The same legislators sign the bills that permit napalm and prohibit pornography.) The sense of living in an insane world mounts. The Culture of Laws and Prohibitions is making us crazy. (Flipout. Scream. Flashout.)

Pause and begin again.

Phrase 5

I'M NOT ALLOWED TO TAKE MY CLOTHES OFF.

Two minute crescendo. Even the nearest, the most natural, is prohibited. The body itself of which we are made is taboo. We are ashamed of what is most beautiful; we are afraid of what is most beautiful. The corruption of the fig leaf is complete corruption. We may not arouse each other; we may not act naturally toward one another. The Culture represses Love. (Flipout.)

Having come to the final human absurdity that the body is somehow bad, the actors do not scream about it, but act it out by removing as much of their clothing as the law allows. As they reach the climax of their flipout they begin to tear their clothes off in a frenzy while shouting out *I'M NOT ALLOWED TO TAKE MY CLOTHES OFF.* They are left standing in the aisles and on the stage, the forbidden areas of their bodies covered, the rest exposed. It is an active demonstration of the Prohibition. When the action has reached this legal limit, the actors say once more *I'M NOT ALLOWED TO TAKE MY CLOTHES OFF* and flash out. They are standing outside the Gates of Paradise. First Assault on the Culture. (Flashout.)[4]

How many years' experience? Age? Dependents? Social security number? and so on. In the middle are short scenes revealing the sounds and rhythms of people's lives—those of a telephone switchboard operator, a cocktail party loner, an analyst's patient (Figure 14-8).

After 10 years of intensive work, the Open Theatre disbanded, according to Chaikin, largely to avoid becoming an institution. Chaikin has since worked at the Public Theatre and at La Mama ETC. Megan Terry founded her own company, the Omaha Magic Theatre. Other members of Chaikin's group started the Medicine Show Theatre Ensemble.

Interview

In *Interview*, playwright Jean-Claude van Itallie writes into the stage directions the various characters that the actors become (Third Interviewer, Telephone Operator, and so on). He also describes the sounds and movements that the actors must improvise to resemble telephone circuits and their sounds.

[*The Third Interviewer slips out of the subway as though it were her stop and sits on a box, stage right, as a Telephone Operator. The other actors form a telephone circuit by holding hands in two concentric circles around the boxes, stage left; they change the hissing sound of the subway into the whistling of telephone circuits.*]

Telephone Operator Just one moment I will connect you with Information.

[*The Telephone Operator alternates her official voice with her ordinary voice; she uses the latter when she talks to her friend Roberta, another operator whom she reaches by flipping a switch. When she is talking to Roberta, the whistling of the telephone circuits changes into a different rhythm and the arms of the actors, which are forming the circuit, move into a different position.*]

Telephone Operator Just one moment and I will connect you with Information. Ow! Listen, Roberta, I said, I've got this terrible cramp. Hang up and dial again, please; we find nothing wrong with that number at all. You know what I ate, I said to her, you were there. Baked macaroni, Wednesday special, maple-nut fudge, I said. I'm sorry but the number you have reached is not—I can feel it gnawing at me at the bottom of my belly, I told her. Do you think it's serious, Roberta? Appendicitis? I asked. Thank you for giving us the area code but the number you have reached is not in this area. Roberta, I asked her, do you think I have cancer? One moment, please, I'm sorry the number you have reached—ow! Well, if it's lunch, Roberta, I said to her, you know what they can do with it tomorrow. Ow! One moment, please, I said. Ow, I said, Roberta, I said, it really hurts.

[*The Telephone Operator falls off her seat in pain. The whistling of the telephone circuit becomes a siren. Three actors carry the Telephone Operator over to the boxes, stage left, which now serve as an operating table. Three actors imitate the Telephone Operator's breathing pattern while four actors behind her make stylized sounds and movements as surgeons and nurses in the midst of an operation. The Telephone Operator's breathing accelerates, then stops. After a moment the actors begin spreading over the stage and making the muted sounds of a cocktail party: music, laughter, talk. The actors find a position and remain there, playing various aspects of a party in slow motion and muted tones. They completely ignore the First Interviewer who, as a Girl At The Party, goes from person to person as if she were in a garden of living statues.*][5]

Figure 14-8 *Interview* was produced by the Open Theatre as part of *America Hurrah!* in New York in 1966 on a bare stage with gray lighting. Wearing nondescript clothing, the actors worked in a depersonalized space with modules (a set of boxes) as furniture and props. The sparseness and colorlessness of the stage reinforced the playwright's statement about the quality of urban American life.

The Bread and Puppet Theatre Peter Schumann founded the Bread and Puppet Theatre in New York in 1961. Unlike many radical theatres growing out of the social and political unrest of the 1960s, the Bread and Puppet Theatre flourishes today, relocated to Plainfield, Vermont. Its plays—performed in streets, gyms, churches, and sometimes in theatres—reflect Shumann's mysticism. Developed from biblical and legendary sources and using both live actors and larger-than-life-sized puppets, the plays advocate the Christian virtues of love, charity, and humility. By 1983 the group had performed more than 70 works thoughout the United States and Europe.

According to Schumann, "bread and theatre belong together." Audiences at a Bread and Puppet performance are handed a loaf of bread. Each person, in turn, breaks off a piece and hands the rest to the next person, who does the same and passes the loaf along. When everyone has tasted bread, the performance begins. Thus audiences have participated in an instantly recognizable religious ritual—sharing the staff of life, symbol of one of humankind's basic needs.

Schumann's idea was to bring theatre to the

> **"** *The power of bread is obvious. People are hungry. The job of bread-baking involves baking the loaves well for chewing and digestion and making them available to everybody.*
>
> *Puppeteers and artists never know for sure what they are good for and what their job does for other people. We want to join the bread-bakers, make good bread and give it out for free.*
>
> *The world in which we live seems to consist mainly of politics or the organizations of man. War and hunger have to be abolished; water, air and soil have to be brought back to life. . . .*
>
> *War is made up by the mind, and poverty and hunger exist through our inefficiencies. Our mind is hungry, and Jesus says: man does not live from bread alone. . . . What is the purpose of a puppet show? To make the world plain, I guess, to speak simple language that everybody can understand. To seize the listener, to persuade him to the new world. To spark the movement of the listeners.* **"**
>
> Peter Schumann, "The World Has to Be Demonstrated Anew" (1970)[6]

people by going out into the streets with processions made up of tin-horn bands, gigantic puppets (manipulated by actors, as are the Bunraku puppets of the Oriental theatre), masked actors, and short plays on contemporary themes. The street performances are always free; for indoor performances the theatre charges one dollar. Schumann likes to avoid a traditional theatre space ("It's too comfortable, too well known . . . It conditions [the audience's] reactions.")[7] But they play wherever the puppets can fit into the space.

One of Schumann's most lasting and famous puppets has been the "Gray Lady"—a Vietnamese peasant woman, who is often carrying her dead baby. She is a recurring symbol of the poor, hungry, meek, and victimized. Sometimes there are several Gray Ladies. Ten to 15 feet tall, they represent the archetypal mother figure and the suffering women of Vietnam. Entirely gray, their Oriental faces are fixed in pain; their huge gray hands move slowly but powerfully; their gray, angular heads, necks, and torsos are draped with gray cloth so that they appear to float through space; and long gray cloth covers their bodies.[8] The Gray Ladies have been central characters in *A Man Says Goodbye to His Mother* and *The Gray Lady Cantata*. Other celebrated **Bread and Puppet Theatre** pieces are *Fire* and *The Cry of the People for Meat* (Figure 14-9).

A Bread and Puppet street performance begins with actors in grubby white pants and shirts, colored bandanas around their foreheads, and wearing an assortment of headgear (including giant masks) proceeding through the streets beating drums, rattling tambourines, and blowing trumpets. An actor in a pig's head rolls over and over on the pavement and cavorts with the people on the sidewalks. Audiences join the procession if they feel like it and chat with the actors. The gaiety of the company is infectious. At a certain spot the company will stop to perform their short play; the audience watches in rapt attention, absorbing its message.

If the procession then goes indoors, Schumann announces the program for that evening. He dominates the action as he works with the lights and conducts the actors when they sing or chant. Crouched on the floor he speaks through a hand mike, relating the simple story of the play as it unfolds. When necessary he takes part in the action, accompanies on the violin, helps the actors with their masks and costumes. He stage-manages the show before our eyes. There is no attempt to conceal the mechanics of performing. When not in a scene the actors sit on the floor watching or stand by to make noises and effects. Their gentleness, humor, caring, and concern

(text continues on p. 418)

a

Figure 14-9 (a) Peter Shumann's *Gray Lady's Sonata,* as performed in 1971 by the Bread and Puppet Theatre. The Gray Lady puppets were Schumann's homage to the suffering women of Vietnam during the war. (b) *Stations of the Cross*, performed in 1972 by the Bread and Puppet Theatre, directed by Peter Schumann. The giant puppet mask, manipulated by actors, is typical of Bread and Puppet Theatre productions.

b

Oklahoma (1943) with book and music by Richard Rodgers and Oscar Hammerstein with choreography by Agnes De Mille.

It is frequently said that musical comedy is the only truly *original* form of American theatre. American musical comedies are imitated today from London to Tokyo, and companies of *Chorus Line, Evita,* and *Annie* tour throughout the world.

Musical comedy began as a popular entertainment whose main ingredients were beautiful chorus girls, popular music and dance numbers, and stand-up comedians. Between 1907 and 1931 Florenz Ziegfeld presented a new edition of the *Ziegfeld Follies* each year. In 1928 a new theatrical form was born when Jerome Kern and Oscar Hammerstein II came along with *Showboat,* giving birth to musicals with coherent story lines. Musical comedy has never been the same since. The new musical reached its apogee in Richard Rodgers' and Oscar Hammerstein's *Oklahoma* (1943) with choreography by Agnes De Mille, in which music, story, setting, and dance were fully integrated. Rodgers, Hammerstein, and De Mille repeated their formula for the integrated musical in *Carousel* (1945).

Major changes in musical comedy have been few since the 1940s. Some writers adapted literary works and straight plays for the musical stage. Shakespeare was responsible for *Kiss Me, Kate* and *West Side Story*; James Michener, *South Pacific*; Thornton Wilder, *Hello, Dolly!*; Cervantes, *Man of La Mancha*; George Bernard Shaw, *My Fair Lady*; Voltaire, *Candide*; and Sholem Aleichem, *Fiddler on the Roof.*

A natural consequence of integrating story, music, lyrics, and dance was the need for strong directors and choreographers. One result has been the emergence of the director-choreographer entrusted with staging the entire production. The prestige and influence of the director-choreographer contributed to the so-called *concept musical,* in which a staging device or personal imprint takes precedence over the narrative. It is hard to imagine *West Side Story* and *Fiddler on the Roof* without Jerome Robbins; *Hello, Dolly!* and *42nd Street* without Gower Champion; *Pippin* and *Chicago* without Bob Fosse; *A Chorus Line* and *Dreamgirls* without Michael Bennett; *Sweeney Todd* and *Evita* without Harold Prince. In addition, the teams of Richard Rodgers and Oscar Hammerstein, Alan Jay Lerner and Frederick Loewe, Stephen Sondheim and Harold Prince are synonymous with the integrated musical.

The American musical theatre has evolved as a distinctive Broadway product. Its creators shoot for Broadway, make their mark there, and send out national touring companies of hits like *Annie, Ain't Misbehavin'*, and *The Best Little Whorehouse in Texas*. Unlike many successful serious Broadway plays, the winning American musical is a prized gift that Broadway frequently shares with the nation and the world.

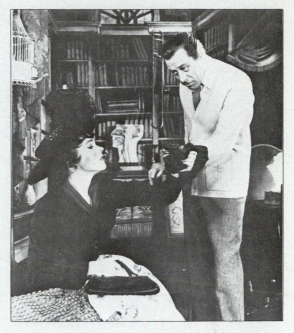

The musical *My Fair Lady* (1956), adapted by Alan Jay Lerner and Frederick Loewe from *Pygmalion* by George Bernard Shaw. Rex Harrison is seen as Professor Henry Higgins and Julie Andrews as Eliza Doolittle.

Hello, Dolly! a Broadway musical starring Carol Channing (center), 1964. The book is based on Thornton Wilder's play, *The Matchmaker*. Music by Jerry Herman.

42nd Street, 1980 Broadway musical, directed and choreographed by Gower Champion.

Nine, 1982 Broadway musical with book by Arthur Kopit and directed by Tommy Tune.

Left: *The Wiz*, 1975 Broadway musical, directed by Geoffrey Holder.

Below: *A Chorus Line*, conceived, directed, and choreographed by Michael Bennett, opened on April 15, 1975.

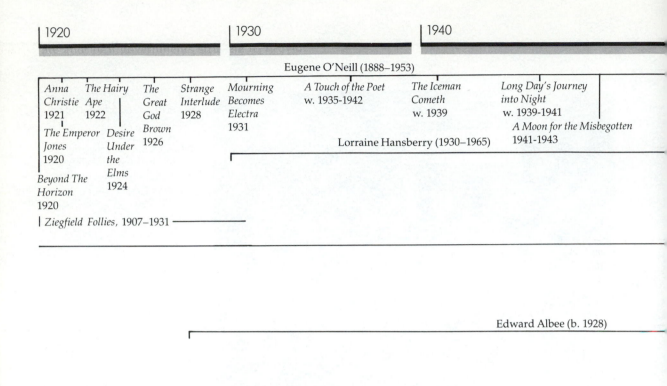

| 1920 | 1930 | 1940 |

Eugene O'Neill (1888–1953)

Anna	*The Hairy*	*The*	*Strange*	*Mourning*	*A Touch of the Poet*	*The Iceman*	*Long Day's Journey*
Christie	*Ape*	*Great*	*Interlude*	*Becomes*	w. 1935-1942	*Cometh*	*into Night*
1921	1922	*God*	1928	*Electra*		w. 1939	w. 1939-1941
The Emperor	*Desire*	*Brown*		1931			*A Moon for the Misbegotten*
Jones	*Under*	1926					1941-1943
1920	*the*				Lorraine Hansberry (1930–1965)		
Beyond The	*Elms*						
Horizon	1924						
1920							

| *Ziegfield Follies, 1907–1931* ——————————————

Edward Albee (b. 1928)

Clifford Odets (1906–1963)

Waiting for	*Golden*
Lefty, 1935	*Boy*
	1937
Awake and	
Sing, 1935	
Paradise	
Lost, 1935	

are part of the total action. As the piece ends, the actors again share bread with the audience just as they have shared their art, their vision of the world's evils, and their compassion. What Schumann is trying to communicate, according to James Roose-Evans, is his essential vision of man and God.[9]

A 1981 production of Georg Buchner's *Woyzeck* at New York's Theatre for the New City marked a new departure for the Bread and Puppet Theatre. Not only was it the first time they used a human actor as the lead performer (George Bartenieff played Woyzeck; all other characters were puppets), but it was also the first

time one of their performances had been based on a text not originally conceived by Schumann and the group.

DRAMATIC CONVENTIONS

O'NEILL'S ECLECTICISM

Eugene O'Neill was the first large talent to emerge among American playwrights in the second quarter of the twentieth century. His

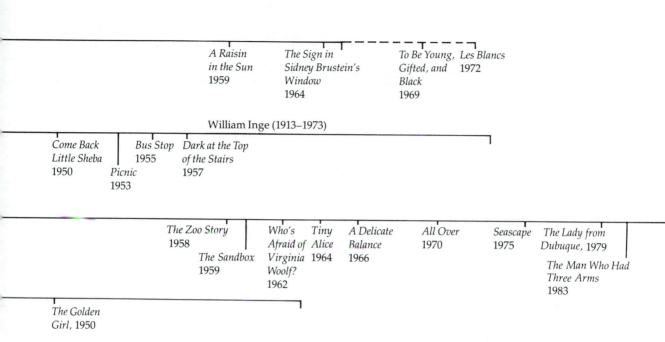

1950   **1960**   **1970**

A Raisin in the Sun 1959   *The Sign in Sidney Brustein's Window* 1964   *To Be Young, Gifted, and Black* 1969   *Les Blancs* 1972

William Inge (1913–1973)

Come Back Little Sheba 1950   *Bus Stop* 1955   *Dark at the Top of the Stairs* 1957   *Picnic* 1953

The Zoo Story 1958   *Who's Afraid of Virginia Woolf?* 1962   *Tiny Alice* 1964   *A Delicate Balance* 1966   *All Over* 1970   *Seascape* 1975   *The Lady from Dubuque,* 1979   *The Man Who Had Three Arms* 1983

The Sandbox 1959

The Golden Girl, 1950

---

powerful eclecticism—his freewheeling range of subjects, forms and styles—touched upon all the major movements of modern European writing and stagecraft: naturalism, expressionism, symbolism, and realism, as well as Greek mythic trilogies and six-hour productions.

Desire Under the Elms, produced by the Provincetown Players and designed by Robert Edmond Jones in 1924, is considered the first great American tragedy. O'Neill placed his characters on a small New England farm and developed a story of intimate relationships among an elderly husband, his young wife, and his son by a previous marriage. Bound to each other by social

convention, the characters finally release their caged emotions in an explosion of spiritual violence. This becomes the pattern of O'Neill's finest plays, including *Mourning Becomes Electra, The Iceman Cometh,* and *Long Day's Journey into Night.*

O'Neill brought to American drama a powerful insight into passion and suffering. Families (usually his own) became microcosms for broad conflicts and tragic emotions. He also had a large, frequently undisciplined, talent for theatrical expression. Plays like *Desire Under the Elms, The Emperor Jones* and *The Hairy Ape* demand multilevel scenery, jungle drums, masks, dyna-

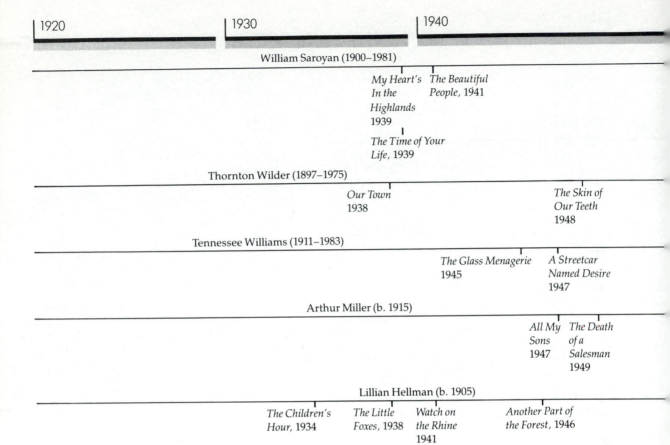

1920	1930	1940

William Saroyan (1900–1981)

My Heart's In the Highlands 1939   *The Beautiful People*, 1941

The Time of Your Life, 1939

Thornton Wilder (1897–1975)

Our Town 1938   *The Skin of Our Teeth* 1948

Tennessee Williams (1911–1983)

The Glass Menagerie 1945   *A Streetcar Named Desire* 1947

Arthur Miller (b. 1915)

All My Sons 1947   *The Death of a Salesman* 1949

Lillian Hellman (b. 1905)

The Children's Hour, 1934   *The Little Foxes*, 1938   *Watch on the Rhine* 1941   *Another Part of the Forest*, 1946

❝ *The playwright of today must dig at the roots of the sickness of today as he feels it—the death of the old God and the failure of science and materialism to give any satisfactory new one for the surviving primitive religious instinct to find a meaning for life in, and to comfort its fears of death with. It seems to me that anyone trying to do big work nowadays must have this big subject behind all the little subjects of his plays or novels, or he is scribbling around the surface of things.* ❞

Eugene O'Neill, letter to George Jean Nathan[10]

mos, fiery stokeholds of oceanliners, and scenery suggesting the fantasies of the protagonist's brain.

In his last and greatest plays, O'Neill produced volumes of dialogue (even monologues) for his characters and torrents of emotional despair. *The Iceman Cometh* takes place in a Soho bar where O'Neill's down-and-out characters are verbally bombarded into pain and confusion by Hickey, O'Neill's salesman of hopelessness. Equally lacerating is *Long Day's Journey into Night*. Among the whiskey bottles, drugs, tattered furniture, and games of four-handed solitaire, the Tyrone family (read O'Neill's parents) assault each other with old grievances, guilt, and anguish. The family lives in a hell of their own

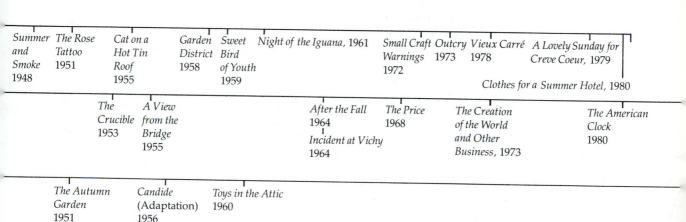

1950   1960   1970

Summer and Smoke 1948   *The Rose Tattoo* 1951   *Cat on a Hot Tin Roof* 1955   *Garden District* 1958   *Sweet Bird of Youth* 1959   *Night of the Iguana,* 1961   *Small Craft Warnings* 1972   *Outcry* 1973   *Vieux Carré* 1978   *A Lovely Sunday for Creve Coeur,* 1979

Clothes for a Summer Hotel, 1980

The Crucible 1953   *A View from the Bridge* 1955   *After the Fall* 1964   *Incident at Vichy* 1964   *The Price* 1968   *The Creation of the World and Other Business,* 1973   *The American Clock* 1980

The Autumn Garden 1951   *Candide* (Adaptation) 1956   *Toys in the Attic* 1960

making. They place themselves, as one critic has said, "on an operating table that allows for no anesthetic. When the light fails, they are still— but not saved."[11]

O'Neill is the American playwright who has most consistently embraced the task of writing tragedy. However, unlike classical tragedy of fulfillment despite pain and death, O'Neill's American version is a *tragedy of frustration*, whose subjects range from unrequited love to lost dreams.

HELLMAN'S MELODRAMA

From the productions of the touring Hallams to the wildly successful *Uncle Tom's Cabin, melo-*

drama was a major style of nineteenth-century American theatre. The term became widely used to describe a play having a serious action ordinarily caused by the villainy of an unsympathetic character. Melodrama's characters are clearly divided—either sympathetic or unsympathetic. Usually the main character is seen in circumstances that threaten death or ruin from which he or she is rescued at the last possible moment. The villain's destruction brings about the happy resolution. Today we apply the term *melodrama* to such diverse theatre pieces (and also to movies and television plays) as Lillian Hellman's *The Little Foxes* (1939), Lorraine Hansberry's *A Raisin in the Sun* (1959), and Joseph Walker's *The River Niger* (1972).

EUGENE O'NEILL

Eugene O'Neill (1888–1953) was born in New York City to the famous actor James O'Neill and Ella Quinlan O'Neill. He became one of America's greatest playwrights.

As an infant he toured with his mother and his actor father. But during his school years he lived at home in Manhattan with his mother, who had now become a drug addict. He was to record this traumatic experience from his childhood in one of his most famous plays, *Long Day's Journey into Night.*

O'Neill entered Princeton University in 1906 but dropped out to dissipate in New York with his older brother Jamie. Married in 1909 to Kathleen Jenkins, he soon left his wife and a young son to begin a series of sailing adventures that took him to England and South America. Between voyages he drank excessively and generally lived the life of a derelict. After his return to New York and his subsequent divorce, he toured as an actor with his father and brother in *The Count of Monte Cristo.* He continued to drink and once attempted suicide. In 1912, resolving to become a playwright, he took a job on the *New London Telegraph* but, discovering that he had a case of mild tuberculosis, entered a Connecticut sanatorium. Here he read the plays of August Strindberg, which were to be a major influence on his work.

In 1914 O'Neill joined George Pierce Baker's 47 workshop at Harvard. Although greatly encouraged by Baker, he was unable to return for a second seminar because his father failed to advance the money. About this time he joined the Provincetown Players, who produced his *Bound East for Cardiff,* written in 1913–1914. The theatre moved to New York as the Playwright's Theatre and O'Neill went with them. *Beyond the Horizon,* written in 1917 and produced in 1920, was O'Neill's first Broadway play. *Anna Christie, The Emperor Jones,* and *The Hairy Ape* opened in 1921–1922. Meanwhile O'Neill had married short story writer Agnes Boulton. Daughter Oona O'Neill (to marry Charlie Chaplin) was born in 1925. The family had moved to Bermuda in 1924 where he wrote *Marco Millions* and *The Great God Brown. Lazarus Laughed* and *Strange Interlude* also date from this period. In 1929 he divorced again and married actress Carlotta Monterey; they settled in Tours, France, where he began his trilogy, *Mourning Becomes Electra,* in 1931.

The O'Neills returned to the United States for the Broadway production of *Mourning Becomes Electra.* For the next 22 years, O'Neill worked on a series of plays that showed American family life corrupted by possessiveness and materialism. The cycle of nine plays that he envisioned in 1936 was never completed—only *A Touch of the Poet* written in 1935–1942 and *More Stately Mansions,* written in 1936, were finished.

In 1936 O'Neill was awarded the Nobel Prize for literature, but poor health prevented him from going to Sweden to accept it. His remaining years were productive despite illness and physical disability. He wrote *The Iceman Cometh* (1939), *Long Day's Journey into Night* (1941), *Hughie* (1941), and *A Moon for the Misbegotten* (1943). He died in Boston on November 27, 1953.

LILLIAN HELLMAN

Lillian Hellman (b. 1905), born in New Orleans and educated in New York, began her writing career as a book reviewer for the *New York Herald Tribune* and as a play reader for New York producers.

In 1925 she married Arthur Kober, author and playwright, and in 1930 they went to Hollywood as script readers for Metro-Goldwyn-Mayer. Divorced in 1932, Hellman returned to New York; two years later her first play, *The Children's Hour*, was produced successfully on Broadway.

Continuing to write plays, she toured Europe, observed the Spanish Civil War along with Ernest Hemingway and other Americans, and became an outspoken antifascist. In 1939 *The Little Foxes*, starring Tallulah Bankhead, was produced. It is her best and remains her most popular play. During the war years she wrote *Watch on the Rhine* (1941) and *Another Part of the Forest* (1946).

Hellman continued to speak out against the evils of fascism and all injustice. Her activities on behalf of novelist Dashiell Hammett, whose books were banned from overseas government li-braries by the House of Representatives Un-American Activities Committee (HUAC) brought her before the committee in 1952. Like many others, she refused to reveal names of associates and friends in the theatre who might have had Communist connections. Her famous statement that she read before the committee ended with the words: "I cannot and will not cut my conscience to fit this year's fashions . . ."[12] The committee subsequently dropped charges against her.

After the war Hellman wrote *The Autumn Garden* (1951) and adapted *The Lark* (1955) and *Candide* (1956). *Toys in the Attic* (1960) was her last unqualified success. After the failure of *My Mother, My Father, and Me* (1963), she abandoned drama for autobiography: *An Unfinished Woman* (1969), *Pentimento* (1973), *Scoundrel Time* (1976), and *Maybe* (1980).

Although her plays now seem old-fashioned, oversimplified, and contrived, she brought to Broadway, movies, and television memorable characters caught up in suspenseful situations that often examined sensitive social and political issues of the time.

Lillian Hellman wrote melodramas for Broadway for almost three decades. *The Little Foxes*, her most successful star vehicle (the part of Regina Giddens has been played by Tallulah Bankhead, Anne Bancroft, and, most recently, Elizabeth Taylor), tells the story of rapacious greed among a family of rising industrialists of the new South around 1900. Her antifascist plays, *Watch on the Rhine* and *Another Part of the Forest*, and *The Autumn Garden* and *Toys in the Attic*, her last Broadway success, assured her a reputation as a major playwright.

Hellman's tightly constructed melodramas skillfully depict human perversity and evil. The destructive power of evil—its ability to corrode family relationships—is a common theme.

Figure 14-10 A scene from *Waiting for Lefty* by Clifford Odets, 1935. This Group Theatre production at the Civic Repertory Theatre, New York, was directed by Odets and Sanford Meisner.

CLIFFORD ODETS

Clifford Odets (1906–1963), born in Philadelphia to Lithuanian Jewish immigrants, rose from an obscure actor in summer stock to the Group Theatre's leading playwright. Four of Odets' plays were staged by the Group in one year: *Till the Day I Die* (1935), *Waiting for Lefty* (1935), *Awake and Sing* (1935), and *Paradise Lost* (1936).

The 1930s were Odets' most celebrated years. He began his career as primarily a polemical dramatist with *Waiting for Lefty*. His struggle to find a form that would express his and the Group's ideas brought forth *Paradise Lost* (1936), *Golden Boy* (1937)—his greatest hit, *Rocket to the Moon* (1938), and *Night Music* (1940).

To aid the financially failing Group, Odets began working in 1936 as a Hollywood screenwriter and producer. Of his later plays, including *The Big Knife* (1949), and *The Flowering Peach* (1954), only *The Country Girl* (1950) was a Broadway success.

Odets' playwriting fortunes delined with the economic upswing of the war years. The Depression world, which had shaped Odets, had ended. His loyalty (and Communist party membership) was challenged in the 1950s by the House Committee on Un-American Activities, and his career was essentially over. At the time of his death in 1963, he was writing for NBC television but the country's most promising playwright of the 1930s had passed into obscurity.

In 1981 Margaret Brennan-Gibson published the first of a two-volume biography called *Clifford Odets: American Playwright The Years from 1906 to 1940.*

ARTHUR MILLER

Arthur Miller (b. 1915), a native New Yorker, enrolled in the University of Michigan, Ann Arbor, in 1934, twice winning the Avery Hopwood Award for playwriting. After receiving his degree in 1938, he returned to New York, joined the Federal Theatre Project, and began writing for radio, films, and the theatre. His first play on Broadway, *The Man Who Had All the Luck* (1944), ran for only four performances. But *All My Sons*, produced in 1947, won the New York Drama Critics Circle Award; *Death of a Salesman* (1949) received the same award together with the Pulitzer Prize.

Because Miller, like Odets and Hellman, espoused left-wing political causes, he also came under the scrutiny of the congressional committee investigating alleged Communist influence in the arts. After *The Crucible* opened in 1953, he was refused a passport to attend the play's Brussels premiere, presumably because *The Crucible* invited comparisons between the Salem witch trials and the contemporary American hysteria over Communism. Rumors spread that Miller was a Communist sympathizer, even a Communist. In 1956 he was called (along with Hellman and others) before HUAC, where he denied that he was a Communist but declined to name others who might have been. He was cited for contempt of Congress, but the ruling was reversed by the courts in 1958.

Miller's much-publicized marriage to film star Marilyn Monroe in 1956 ended in divorce four years later. In 1964, after a nine-year absence, he returned to the New York stage with *After the Fall*, a strongly autobiographical drama based on his marriage to the actress. While he has written four full-length plays since then, none has received the critical attention awarded to *All My Sons* and *Death of a Salesman*, now considered American classics. His most recent Broadway plays are *A View from the Bridge* (expanded to a full-length play in 1965), *The Price* (1968), *The Creation of the World and Other Business* (1972), and *The American Clock* (1980).

ODETS' AND MILLER'S SOCIAL REALISM

Midcentury American playwriting continued a strong current of realism and social protest in the plays of Clifford Odets and Arthur Miller. Both playwrights responded to the apparent breakdown of the capitalist economy with its business failures, unemployment, bread lines, poverty, and broken dreams.

As playwright-in-residence of the Group Theatre, Odets wrote four plays for production: *Till The Day I Die, Waiting for Lefty* (Figure 14-10), *Awake and Sing,* and *Paradise Lost.* His later plays, more troubled and somber, included *The Big Knife* and *The Country Girl.*

Odets' characters are New Yorkers—half-educated Jews, Italians, and Irish, who speak the ungrammatical jargon of the streets, drugstores, subways, bars, sports arenas, and union halls.

His dialogue, crackling with realistic speech, is often succinct and memorable. One of Odets' characters says, "I'm so nervous, look, I weighed myself twice in the subway." Leo Gordon in *Paradise Lost* ruminates: "We cancel our experience. This is an American habit."[13]

Arthur Miller's plays have strong social and psychological themes. *All My Sons* takes up the issue of war profiteering; *Death of a Salesman,* the worship of success and the perversion of the American dream; *The Crucible,* the tendency for the narrowly moral to persecute the liberal and the outspoken.

Miller's basic premise is that American society is a purveyor of myths and prejudices that provide the false values and dreams to which we subscribe. He implies that the individual has little choice. Joe Keller in *All My Sons* and Willie

---

Waiting for Lefty

In Clifford Odets' one-act drama, the theatre becomes a meeting hall of the taxi drivers' union, which is about to take a strike vote. Union officers are onstage; members are dispersed among the audience.

Lefty, the members' militant representative, has not yet arrived at the meeting. Fatt, the union secretary, and others belittle the strike talk. They are jeered. Fatt tells the union members that Lefty has run out on them. Several members come forward to justify Lefty. One man speaks of his financial difficulties, which he fears the strike will only make worse. A war-profiteering industrialist also speaks. A young taxi driver and his girl bitterly agree that they cannot afford to marry on his wages. Finally, the members are brought to action by the discovery of a management spy in the hall and by the news that Lefty has been killed by an unknown assailant. They then vote to strike and the play ends with shouts of "Strike! Strike! Strike!"

Agate [*to audience*] What's the answer, boys? The answer is, if we're reds because we wanna strike, then we take over their salute too! Know how they do it? [*Makes Communist salute.*] What is it? An uppercut! The good old uppercut to the chin! Hell, some of us boys ain't even got a shirt to our backs. What's the boss class tryin' to do—

make a nudist colony outa us? [*The audience laughs and suddenly* Agate *comes to the middle of the stage so that the other cabmen back him up in a strong clump.*]

Agate Don't laugh! Nothing's funny! This is your life and mine! It's skull and bones every incha the road! Christ, we're dyin' by inches! For what? For the debutant-ees to have their sweet comin' out parties in the Ritz! Poppa's got a daughter she's gotta get her picture in the papers. Christ, they make 'em with our blood. Joe said it. Slow death or fight. It's war! [*Throughout this whole speech* Agate *is backed up by the other six workers, so that from their activity it is plain that the whole group of them are saying these things. Several of them may take alternate lines out of this long last speech.*]

You Edna, God love your mouth! Sid and Florrie, the other boys, old Doc Barnes —fight with us for right! It's war! Working class, unite and fight! Tear down the slaughter house of our old lives! Let freedom really ring.

These slick slobs stand here telling us about bogeymen. That's a new one for the kids—the reds is bogeymen! But the man who got me food in 1932, he called me Comrade! The one who picked me up where I bled—he called me Comrade too! What are we waiting

Loman in *Death of a Salesman* conform and are destroyed. John Proctor in *The Crucible* and Eddie Carbone in *A View from the Bridge* refuse to conform and also are destroyed. Nevertheless, Miller's plays are not wholly pessimistic. He has a kind of faith in humanity, a suspicion that the individual may be able, in the end, to retain his integrity. As Willie Loman's wife, Linda, says of her husband:

> for. . . . Don't wait for Lefty! He might never come. Every minute—[*This is broken into by a man who has dashed up the center aisle from the back of the house. He runs up on stage, says*]:
>
> *Man* Boys, they just found Lefty!
>
> *Others* What? What? What?
>
> *Some* Shhh. . . . Shhh. . . .
>
> *Man* They found Lefty. . . .
>
> *Agate* Where?
>
> *Man* Behind the car barns with a bullet in his head!
>
> *Agate* [*crying*] Hear it, boys, hear it? Hell, listen to me! Coast to coast! HELLO AMERICA! HELLO. WE'RE STORMBIRDS OF THE WORK-ING-CLASS. WORKERS OF THE WORLD. . . . OUR BONES AND BLOOD! And when we die they'll know what we did to make a new world! Christ, cut us up to little pieces. We'll die for what is right! put fruit trees where our ashes are!
> [*To audience*]: Well, what's the answer?
>
> *All* STRIKE!
>
> *Agate* LOUDER!
>
> *All* STRIKE!
>
> *Agate and Others on Stage* AGAIN!
>
> *All* STRIKE, STRIKE, STRIKE!!!
>
> [*Curtain*][14]

I don't say he's a great man. Willy Loman never made a lot of money. His name was never in the paper. He's not the finest character that ever lived. But he's a human being, and a terrible thing is happening to him. So attention must be paid. He's not to be allowed to fall into his grave like an old dog. Attention, attention must be finally paid to such a person.[15]

Miller's plays written after a long absence from the stage (beginning in 1964 with *After the Fall* and *Incident at Vichy*) have largely sacrificed dramatic action for doctrinal exposition. Always a socially committed and even didactic writer, Miller has moved increasingly away from creating characters whose confrontations arise out of their inner motivations to those who speak to each other in abstractions about life.

The Price, Miller's most recent critical success, is perhaps the least didactic of these plays. Gregory Soloman, the elderly furniture dealer in *The Price*, says, "Let me give you a piece of advice. It's not that you can't believe nothing, that's not so hard—it's that you still got to believe it. *That's* hard."[16] The play brings two brothers—one a policeman, the other a successful surgeon—to the top floor of the brownstone that was their family home before 1929. They have not seen or talked with one another for 16 years, and now, surrounded by the furniture of the past, they try to justify their past choices through mutual recriminations. They play out their charges and countercharges in the presence of the retired appraiser, who finds in the furniture an opportunity to begin again. He embodies Miller's idea that "life is the product of belief beyond disbelief."[17]

Odets and Miller represent a central trend in American drama—protest against social injustice, persecution, and psychological mistreatment—a trend that took on renewed momentum during the Vietnam war years in plays by David Rabe, Megan Terry, and Joseph Walker.

LORRAINE HANSBERRY

Lorraine Hansberry (1930–1965) was born in Chicago to a prosperous Black family. The youngest of four children, she spent two years at the University of Wisconsin at Madison, then went to New York where she studied African history under W.E.B. DuBois and worked on a monthly journal, *Freedom*, published by Paul Robeson.

In 1959 *A Raisin in the Sun* was produced on Broadway, and Hansberry attained immediate fame as the youngest American and the only Black dramatist to win the Best Play of the Year award. She continued to write and work until her untimely death from cancer a few months before her thirty-fifth birthday. *The Sign in Sidney Brustein's Window* (1964) was running on Broadway at the time of her death.

In addition to her plays, essays, and journals, Hansberry contributed significantly to the Black movement by writing the text for a photographic journal, *The Movement: A Documentary of a Struggle for Equality* (1964). Her 90-minute television drama, *The Drinking Gourd* (1960), com-missioned by NBC for the Civil War centennial, was shelved as "too controversial," although many of its scenes were forerunners of later television plays like Alex Haley's *Roots*.

After her death her husband, Robert Nemiroff, edited *To Be Young, Gifted, and Black* (1969), and *Les Blancs: The Collected Last Plays of Lorraine Hansberry* (1972). The musical *Raisin* was produced in 1978.

A landmark in the American theatre, *A Raisin in the Sun* ran for 530 performances. Its title and theme are based on a poem by Langston Hughes that asks, "What happens to a dream deferred?" The play derives its power from the conflicts among the members of the Younger family, each of whom has a different dream, a separate plan, for escaping the dreary life of their Chicago ghetto. Hansberry neither asserts that it will be any easier for the Youngers to live in their new "integrated" neighborhood nor states that all whites are villains. In all of her work Hansberry remains objective about "good" and "bad" people regardless of race.

LORRAINE HANSBERRY'S MULTICULTURAL REALISM

Lorraine Hansberry represents the development of significant work by Black American playwrights from the forties well into the sixties. The earliest extant play by a Black American playwright is William Wells Brown's *The Escape, or the Leap from Freedom*, written in 1858 but never produced. In the years that followed, Blacks wrote music, skits, and jokes for minstrel shows and later for vaudeville and musical revues. However, most regular plays *about* Blacks were almost all written by white playwrights, among them Eugene O'Neill. The first Black-authored plays appeared on Broadway in the 1920s. Langston Hughes's *Mulatto*, dealing with the bitterness and suffering that can result from illicit relationships between the races, appeared in 1934. Richard Wright adapted his powerful novel *Native Son* (1941) for the stage with the help of Paul Green.

The civil rights movement of the 1950s became a major stimulus to Black playwriting and especially to such women writers as Alice Childress, Adrienne Kennedy, and Lorraine Hansberry. In 1959 Hansberry wrote *A Raisin in the Sun*, a poignant drama about Black family life that won the New York Drama Critics Circle Award for the best American play of the year. During her brief career she wrote plays that are distinct for their multicultural richness. Although her dramatic situations are centered around Black urban family life in the fifties and sixties, she touched upon the changing relationships in our society between Black and White,

rich and poor, male and female in a way that virtually no American playwright had ever done before.

During the 1960s the nation became acutely conscious of the need for racial justice and equality. Black writers began to express themselves with vehemence and passion, not only on the subject of racial injustice, but on the more enduring subject of their unique history, culture, and way of life. The result was the emergence of many vigorous and talented Black playwrights—both men and women. Among them were LeRoi Jones (Imamu Amiri Baraka, b. 1934), with *Dutchman* (1964) and *Slave Ship*

A Raisin in the Sun

In the final scene of *A Raisin in the Sun*, the son, Walter Younger, asserts his authority as head of the household and his human rights. Speaking to Lindner, the white neighborhood's representative who is offering cash to the Younger family not to move, Walter says:

. . . Well—we are very plain people . . .

Lindner Yes—

Walter I mean—I have worked as a chauffeur most of my life—and my wife here, she does domestic work in people's kitchens. So does my mother. I mean—we are plain people . . .

Lindner Yes, Mr. Younger—

Walter [*Really like a small boy, looking down at his shoes and then up at the man*] And—uh—well, my father, well, he was a laborer most of his life.

Lindner [*absolutely confused*] Uh, yes—

Walter [*looking down at his toes once again*] My father almost beat a man to death once because this man called him a bad name or something, you know what I mean?

Lindner No, I'm afraid I don't.

Walter [*finally straightening up*] Well, what I mean is that we come from people who had a lot of pride. I mean—we are very proud people. And that's my sister over there and she's going to be a doctor—and we are very proud—

Lindner Well—I am sure that is very nice, but—

Walter [*starting to cry and facing the man eye to eye*] What I am telling you is that we called you over here to tell you that we are very proud and that this is—this is my son, who makes the sixth generation of our family in this country, and that we have all thought about your offer and we have decided to move into our house because my father—my father—he earned it. . . . We don't want to make no trouble for nobody or fight no causes—but we will try to be good neighbors. That's all we got to say. [*He looks the man absolutely in the eyes.*] We don't want your money. . . .[18]

(1969); Ed Bullins (b. 1935) with *The Electronic Nigger* (1968) and *The Taking of Miss Janie* (1975); Lonne Elder, III (b. 1933) with his award-winning *Ceremonies in Dark Old Men* (1969); Douglas Turner Ward with *Day of Absence* (1967) and *The Reckoning* (1969); and Adrienne Kennedy (b. 1931) with *Funnyhouse of a Negro* (1964) and *Cities of Bezique* (1969). The creativity of these Black playwrights has enriched the modern American theatre over a period of 20 years.

WILLIAMS' AND ALBEE'S "NEW" REALISM

With *The Glass Menagerie* Tennessee Williams continued a trend in American drama that focused on the family as a crucible of tragic action. Here the family unit consisted of a dominating mother, an absent husband, a handicapped daughter, and an alienated son. In 1945, with the opening of this play, Williams was recognized as a major new talent. His writing showed a deep compassion for human suffering and a genuine lyricism of style. Abandoning the straightforward cause-and-effect plot, he wrote a play of short scenes, intermingling past and present time. He controlled the action through the memories of the son, who finally, like his father before him, walked out on a demanding Amanda, a routine job, and a stifling existence. The play is composed of the son's memories of events leading up to that passage into life.

Williams' career was part and parcel of the Broadway hit-or-miss syndrome. His plays were either colossal successes or abysmal failures. *Summer and Smoke* (1948), a Broadway flop, later achieved success Off-Broadway. In contrast, *Cat on a Hot Tin Roof* was successful on Broadway, on the road, and on film. The cat on the hot tin roof is the sensual Maggie whose husband, running away from his homosexuality, is driven to drink. The play deals with his and his father's struggle to accept two truths: the son's sexual preference and the father's incurable cancer. Williams' characters protest against the "mendacity" of the system they live in.

Until the 1960s Williams averaged better than a new play every two years. Again and again he told the story of the outsider who, by virtue of his or her differentness—physical defect, sexual preference, alcoholism, or artistic inclin-

TENNESSEE WILLIAMS

Tennessee Williams (1911–1983) was born Thomas Lanier Williams in Columbus, Mississippi, son of a traveling salesman and Episcopalian minister's daughter. The family moved to St. Louis in 1918. He was educated at Missouri University, Washington University in St. Louis, and later the University of Iowa, where he received his B.A. degree.

In 1939 *Story* magazine published his short story, "A Field of Blue Chicken," the first work to appear under his nickname "Tennessee," which was given to him because of his Southern accent. That same year he compiled four one-act plays under the title *American Blues,* and won a prize in the Group Theatre's American play contest. This aroused the interest of New York agent Audrey Wood, who asked to represent him.

In 1945 *The Glass Menagerie* marked Williams's first major success and established him as an important American playwright. It was followed by his major plays: *A Streetcar Named Desire* (1947), *The Rose Tattoo* (1951), *Cat on a Hot Tin Roof* (1955), *Sweet Bird of Youth* (1959), and *The Night of the Iguana* (1961). Although his recent plays failed to please critics, he continued to write and be produced in New York and London until his death.

ations—is victimized by an uncongenial society. But Williams was not a social protest writer. He looked deep within his characters and found the enemy: the character's own psyche, the ravages of time or a Godless, indifferent universe. Whatever the case, there is no escape. Williams delivered his audience into an interior world of eroticism, memories, and dreams. Taken out of conventional box settings, the characters' lies and truths, emotions and memories, come across with great theatricality and inner truth.

Edward Albee, best known for *Who's Afraid of Virginia Woolf?*, also writes family dramas of bruised psyches engaged in battles to the death. Albee started out in the 1960s in the company of absurdists Samuel Beckett and Eugene Ionesco with *The Zoo Story* and *The American Dream*. His one unqualified critical success has been *Who's Afraid of Virginia Woolf?*, a realistic portrait of two mutually destructive couples. His other plays, including *A Delicate Balance, All Over,* and *Seascape*, have collected mixed reviews. Albee is recognized as a serious but uneven playwright.

In Albee's plays life is measured in terms of loss, love by its failure, contact by its absence. Whether his plays take place on a Central Park bench, in a university professor's house, or in an upper–middle-class apartment, the situation is

Figure 14-11 The original 1962 New York production of *Who's Afraid of Virginia Woolf?*, directed by Alan Schneider, with Arthur Hill as George, Uta Hagen as Martha, and George Grizzard as Nick. Martha dances with Nick, and their flirtation excludes her husband, who contemplates the couple.

EDWARD ALBEE

Edward Albee (b. 1928), American playwright and director, was born in Washington, D.C., and adopted by Mr. and Mrs. Reed A. Albee of the Keith–Albee theatre chain. He attended Hartford's Trinity College but left after a year and a half to work at odd jobs: radio copywriter, waiter, telegram messenger.

In 1958 he wrote *The Zoo Story*, a one-act play, and in 1959 *The Death of Bessie Smith*; both were produced abroad and acclaimed by critics before they premiered in New York. In 1962 Albee made a successful Broadway debut with *Who's Afraid of Virginia Woolf?* This full-length play established him as a major playwright. Since then Albee has written *Tiny Alice* (1964), *A Delicate Balance* (1966), *All Over* (1971), *Seascape* (1974), *The Lady from Dubuque* (1980), *Lolita* (1980), and *The Man Who Had Three Arms* (1983), and directed the 1976 New York revival of *Who's Afraid of Virginia Woolf?*

Jerry's story about his landlady's vicious dog is an effective account of human efforts to make contact (to win affection or to annihilate). In the end Jerry and the dog reach perhaps a more painful accommodation—they ignore one another. The sense of loss is acutely felt.

Jerry ALL RIGHT. [*as if reading from a huge billboard*] THE STORY OF JERRY AND THE DOG! [*natural again*] What I am going to tell you has something to do with how sometimes it's necessary to go a long distance out of the way in order to come back a short distance correctly; or, maybe I only think that it has something to do with that. But, it's why I went to the zoo today, and why I walked north . . . northerly, rather . . . until I came here. All right. The dog, I think I told you, is a black monster of a beast: an oversized head, tiny, tiny ears, and eyes . . . bloodshot, infected, maybe; and a body you can see the ribs through the skin. The dog is black, all black; . . . I worried about that animal the very first minute I met him. Now, animals don't take to me like Saint Francis had birds hanging off him all the time. What I mean is: animals are indifferent to me . . . like people [*he smiles slightly*] . . . most of the time. But this dog wasn't indifferent. From the very beginning he'd snarl and then go for me, to get one of my legs. Not like he was rabid, you know; he was sort of a stumbly dog, but he wasn't half-assed, either. It was a good, stumbly run; but I always got away. He got a piece of my trouser leg, look, you can see right here, where it's mended; he got that the second day I lived there; but, I

kicked free and got upstairs fast, so that was that . . . Anyway, this went on for over a week, whenever I came in; but never when I went out. That's funny. Or, it *was* funny. I could pack up and live in the street for all the dog cared. Well, I thought about it up in my room one day, one of the times after I'd bolted upstairs, and I made up my mind. I decided: First, I'll kill the dog with kindness, and if that doesn't work . . . I'll just kill him. [*Peter winces*] Don't react, Peter; just listen. So, the next day I went out and bought a bag of hamburgers, medium rare, no catsup, no onion; and on the way home I threw away all the rolls and kept just the meat.

[*Action for the following, perhaps*]

When I got back to the rooming house, the dog was waiting for me. I half opened the door that led into the entrance hall, and there he was; waiting for me. It figured. I went in, very cautiously, and I had the hamburgers, you remember; I opened the bag, and I set the meat down about twelve feet from where the dog was snarling at me. Like so! He snarled; stopped snarling; sniffed; moved slowly; then faster; then faster toward the meat. Well, when he got to it he stopped, and he looked at me. I smiled; but tentatively, you understand. He turned his face back to the hamburgers, smelled, sniffed some more, and then . . . RRRAAAAGGGGGHHHH, like that . . . he tore into them. It was as if he had never eaten anything in his life before, except like garbage. Which might very well have been the truth. I don't think the landlady ever eats anything but garbage. But. He ate all the hamburgers, almost all at once, making sounds in his throat like a woman. *Then*, when he'd finished the meat, the hamburger, and tried to eat the paper, too, he sat down and smiled. I think he smiled; I know cats do. It was a very gratifying few moments. Then, BAM, he snarled and made for me again. He didn't get me this time, either. So, I got upstairs, and I lay down on my bed and started to think about the dog again. To be truthful, I was offended, and I was damn mad, too. It was six perfectly good hamburgers with not enough pork in them to make it disgusting. I was offended. But, after a while, I decided to try it for a few more days.

. . .

Now, here is what I had wanted to happen: I loved the dog now, and I wanted him to love me. I had tried to love, and I had tried to kill, and both had been unsuccessful by themselves. I hoped . . . and I don't really know why I expected the dog to understand anything, much less my motivations . . . I hoped that the dog would understand.

[*Peter seems to be hypnotized*]

It's just . . . it's just that . . . [*Jerry is abnormally tense, now*] . . . it's just that if you can't deal with people, you have to make a start somewhere. WITH ANIMALS! [*much faster now, and like a conspirator*] Don't you see? A person has to have some way of dealing with SOMETHING. If not with people . . . if not with people . . . SOMETHING. . . .

Where better to make a beginning . . . to understand and just possibly be understood . . . a beginning of an understanding, than with . . .

[*HERE Jerry seems to fall into almost grotesque fatigue*]

. . . than with A DOG. Just that; a dog.

[*Here there is a silence that might be prolonged for a moment or so; then Jerry wearily finishes his story*]

A dog. It seemed like a perfectly sensible idea. Man is a dog's best friend, remember. So: the dog and I looked at each other. I longer than the dog. And what I saw then has been the same ever since. Whenever the dog and I see each other we both stop where we are. We regard each other with a mixture of sadness and suspicion, and then we feign indifference. We walk past each other safely; we have an understanding. It's very sad, but you'll have to admit that it is an understanding. We had made many attempts at contact, and we had failed. The dog has returned to garbage, and I to solitary but free passage. I have not returned. I mean to say, I have *gained* solitary free passage, if that much further loss can be said to be gain. I have learned that neither kindness nor cruelty by themselves, independent of each other, creates any effect beyond themselves; and I have learned that the two combined, together, at the same time, are the teaching emotion. And what is gained is loss. And what has been the result: the dog and I have attained a compromise; more of a bargain, really. We neither love nor hurt because we do not try to reach each other. . . .[19]

essentially the same. Albee's people exist apart—in separate rooms, cages, and skins. How, then, do they try to engage one another? Violence is one way. Jerry dies in *The Zoo Story*; Martha and George battle in *Virginia Woolf*. Love is another form of connection, but Albee's characters either withdraw from sex (as does Tobias in *A Delicate Balance*) or fail in their efforts at consummation (as Nick in *Virginia Woolf*).

Absence of contact is Albee's main preoccupation, but his concerns include the collapse of American values. In his preface to *The American Dream* he says that the play is "an attack on the substitution of artificial for real values in our society."[20] While Albee has disavowed solutions, his plays show the inescapable anxieties that are generated in a materialistic society. He has written: "I've always thought . . . that it was one of the responsibilities of playwrights to show people how they are and what their time is like in the hopes that perhaps they'll change it."[21]

REPRESENTATIVE PLAY

A Streetcar Named Desire
Written by Tennessee Williams; produced by Irene M. Selznick at the Ethel Barrymore Theatre on December 3, 1947; directed by Elia Kazan with Marlon Brando, Kim Hunter, Karl Malden, and Jessica Tandy

BACKGROUND

A Streetcar Named Desire (originally called *The Poker Night*) was presented two years after Tennessee Williams' first success, *The Glass Menagerie*. From director Elia Kazan's notebook, Williams' writings, and the first-night reviews, we learn about the evolution of the production from script to Pulitzer Prize-winning play.

Kazan approached the play as a "poetic tragedy"—as Blanche DuBois' tragedy and as "the last gasp" of a dying civilization. The director saw the play as the final dissolution of a person who once had great potential and who, even in her demoralization, is worth more than the "healthy, coarse-grained figures who kill her."[22] In these roles Kazan cast little-known actors: Marlon Brando as Stanley Kowalski, the vulgar brother-in-law; Kim Hunter as Blanche's self-effacing sister; Karl Malden as the gentle suitor; and Jessica Tandy as the rueful Blanche. All were to become stage and film actors of considerable reputation.

Three days before the play's opening, Wil-

A Streetcar Named Desire

In *A Streetcar Named Desire*, Blanche DuBois, her family's Mississippi estate sold, arrives at the New Orleans tenement home of Stella and Stanley Kowalski, her pregnant sister and brother-in-law. Blanche's faded gentility clashes with Stanley's male ego. As she seeks protection from the world, she competes with Stanley for Stella's affections but finds herself no match for his sexual hold over her sister. She tries to charm Mitch, Stanley's poker-playing friend, into marrying her. However, Stanley destroys Blanche's hopes for marriage by telling Mitch about her past drunkenness and promiscuity. As Stella reproaches Stanley for his cruelty, her labor pains begin and Stanley rushes her to the hospital.

Blanche is visited by a drunken Mitch, who accuses her of lying to him and makes an effort to seduce her. Stanley returns to find Blanche dressed for a party, fantasizing about an invitation to go on a cruise with a wealthy friend. Angered by her pretensions, Stanley starts a fight with her that ends in rape. In a final scene some weeks later, Blanche, her mind gone, is taken from the Kowalski home to a mental hospital.

liams published an article in the *New York Times* called "On a Streetcar Named Success," in which he reflected upon the hit–flop syndrome of the Broadway theatre. At that moment he was riding high on success at age 36. He described the precarious life of the successful playwright—the suites in first-class hotels, elaborate room service, patient hotel managers, late-night parties, storms of royalty checks, fawning friends and acquaintances—which could change overnight. Nevertheless, Williams stated, he wrote plays because

> it is only in his work that an artist can find reality and satisfaction, for the actual world is less intense than the world of his invention and consequently his life, without recourse to violent disorder, does not seem very substantial. The right condition for him is that in which his work is not only convenient but unavoidable.[23]

The opening-night reviewers for the *New York Times*, *Daily News*, *Post*, and *Herald Tribune* were ecstatic, calling the play "brilliant," "powerful," "a masterpiece," and "a smash hit." They compared Williams to Clifford Odets, William Saroyan, and Eugene O'Neill. Brooks Atkinson, the *New York Times* reviewer, best put the new play in perspective. He wrote that *Streetcar* gained its stature and excitement from the world *within* the theatre. It was not a social

---

Stage Directions for
A Streetcar Named Desire

SCENE ONE

The exterior of a two-story corner building on a street in New Orleans which is named Elysian Fields and runs between the L & N tracks and the river. The section is poor but, unlike corresponding sections in other American cities, it has a raffish charm. The houses are mostly white frame, weathered grey, with rickety outside stairs and galleries and quaintly ornamented gables. This building contains two flats, upstairs and down. Faded white stairs ascend to the entrances of both.

It is first dark of an evening early in May. The sky that shows around the dim white building is a peculiarly tender blue, almost a turquoise, which invests the scene with a kind of lyricism and gracefully attenuates the atmosphere of decay. You can almost feel the warm breath of the brown river beyond the river warehouses with their faint redolences of bananas and coffee. A corresponding air is evoked by the music of Negro entertainers at a barroom around the corner. In this part of New Orleans you are practically always just around the corner, or a few doors down the street, from a tinny piano being played with the infatuated fluency of brown fingers. This "Blue Piano" expresses the spirit of the life which goes on here.

Two women, one white and one colored, are taking the air on the steps of the building. The white woman is Eunice, who occupies the upstairs flat; the colored woman a neighbor, for New Orleans is a cosmopolitan city where there is a relatively warm and easy intermingling of races in the old part of town.

Above the music of the "Blue Piano" the voices of people on the street can be heard overlapping.

[*Two men come around the corner, Stanley Kowalski and Mitch. They are about twenty-eight or thirty years old, roughly dressed in blue denim work clothes. Stanley carries his bowling jacket and a red-stained package from a butcher's. They stop at the foot of the steps.*][24]

play absorbed in the great issues of the times; it solved no problems and arrived at no general moral conclusions. Nor did it deal with representative men and women. But, as Atkinson wrote, it was a work of art where audiences sat in the theatre in the "presence of truth."

> Out of nothing more esoteric than interest in human beings, Mr. Williams has looked steadily and wholly into the private agony of one lost person. He supplies dramatic conflict by introducing Blanche to an alien environment that brutally wears on her nerves. But he takes no sides in the conflict. He knows how right all the characters are—how right she is in trying to protect herself against the disaster that is overtaking her, and how right the other characters are in protecting their independence, for her terrible needs cannot be fulfilled. There is no solution except the painful one Mr. Williams provides in his last scene.[25]

THE SCENE

Williams' opening stage direction is a page in length. In this description he evokes atmosphere and graphic details of place, time, light, and sound: New Orleans, Elysian Fields Avenue, a May twilight, blue sky, barroom piano music. Working from the script, designer Mielziner visualized a single setting with several levels that showed all rooms of the apartment simultaneously. The two dreary rooms are flanked on one side by the bathroom, in which Blanche takes incessant warm tub baths, and on the other by iron stairs leading up to the other apartment. The walls of the set are transparent, showing the French Quarter beyond. The furniture and details (the naked lightbulb, for example) are clues to the Kowalski life style that will destroy Blanche's fragile truce with reality. She has nowhere to go—this "scene" is her last refuge—and when this environment becomes threatening she retreats into a fantasy world devoid of cruelty, aging, and death (Figure 14-12).

THE TRAGIC ACTION

Streetcar's tragic action encompasses an individual and the passing of a way of life. In novelist Margaret Mitchell's phrase, Blanche DuBois' genteel South has "gone with the wind." In one of the play's famous speeches, Blanche accuses her ancestors of "epic fornications," which destroyed the family fortune and genteel life style. One measure of Blanche's tragic fall is her own immediate past in Laurel, Mississippi, where according to Stanley's sources, she also engaged in epic fornications at the Flamingo Hotel with soldiers from the local army base, with traveling salesmen, and with a high school student, the last causing her to lose her teaching job.

Despite all of the many writings on *Streetcar* as a modern tragedy, director Kazan's interpretation remains one of the best. He saw Williams' tragedy embodied in Blanche, as "a twisted, pathetic, confused bit of light and culture . . . snuffed out by the crude forces of violence, insensibility and vulgarity which exist in our South—and this cry is the play."[26]

From Kazan's viewpoint, the tragic action is the final dissolution of a person of worth—who once had great potential—and who as she goes down escapes the forces of insensitivity and violence. Blanche's psychotic breakdown is precipitated by Stanley's public revelations about her sexual activities and by her loss of Mitch, security, and love. Poised against Stanley's basic animal cynicism, Blanche is defeated. Her final refuge is a mental institution and the "kindness" of strangers.

Central to the tragic action is Belle Reve, "beautiful dream," of the plantation lost by Blanche and Stella's prodigal family. Around it Blanche has created her own beautiful dream to make the world around her more gentle, hospitable, and safe. In her fantasy world she is beautiful; dressed in elaborate silks, furs, and jewels; and pursued by wealthy, well-mannered suitors. But like a paper moon (an image from a popular song that Blanche sings repetitively), the illusion tears, revealing a harsh reality.

As part of her fantasy life, Blanche puts on

Figure 14-12 Stanley Kowalski's friends play poker while Blanche Du-Bois is taken away to an asylum. The foreground of the photo shows the realistic details of Jo Mielziner's setting: bed, tables, and chairs. Stanley comforts Stella on a stairway while Blanche is led away by a doctor and nurse in an upstage area that seems far removed from the poker game.

superior airs that alienate Stanley and Stella who fail to understand her desperation. Stanley, not fully aware of her helplessness, becomes her enemy. Just as he tears the paper lantern off the lightbulb, revealing the drabness of the room and Blanche's aging features, so he also smashes her illusions forever. Just as her ancestors destroyed Belle Reve and a way of life, so, too, Stanley destroys her sustaining make-believe world.

Blanche DuBois is one in a long line of tragic heroines in Western drama. She is as alone in her dilemma and in as much mental anguish as Sophocles' Antigone or Ibsen's Hedda Gabler. One facet of Blanche's tragedy is that she is unable to reconcile her dual nature and her two worlds (the past and the present). Her sexuality, which she calls "brutal desire," is at odds with her self-image as a cultured, refined woman. To

escape this conflict, she carries about with her the Old South's romantic notion of women; innocent, untouched, marrying husbands who protect, defend, and maintain their honor.

In contrast, Stella, Stanley, and Mitch are not tragic figures. Closing her mind to the past, Stella lives in the present. Stanley's sexuality, her pregnancy, are the important facts in her life. Stella, refusing to acknowledge her dependency, lives through her husband. Stanley is king in his castle and Blanche enters as a dangerous foe. Blanche tries to make Stella face up to the facts of her sister's existence, but fails. Blanche's famous speech to Stella that ends with the warning *"Don't—don't hang back with the brutes!"* is a measure of her sensibilities and why she is doomed in the Kowalski world.

Mitch, on the other hand, is a mama's boy wanting to escape while at the same time seeking his mother's perfection in other women. At the end he gives up Blanche and returns to his mother's "absolute sovereignity." He would also be a tragic figure if he were aware of his dilemma (Figure 1-3, p. 10).

> *Blanche* He acts like an animal, has an animal's habits! Eats like one, moves like one, talks like one! There's even something—sub-human—something not quite to the stage of humanity yet! Yes, something—ape-like about him, like one of those pictures I've seen in—anthropological studies! Thousands and thousands of years have passed him right by, and there he is—Stanley Kowalski—survivor of the stone age! Bearing the raw meat home from the kill in the jungle! And you —*you* here—*waiting* for him! Maybe he'll strike you or maybe grunt and kiss you! That is, if kisses have been discovered yet! Night falls and the other apes gather! There in the front of the cave, all grunting like him, and swilling and gnawing and hulking! His poker night!—you call it—this party of apes! Somebody growls—some creature snatches at something—the fight is on! *God!* Maybe we are a long way from being made in God's image, but Stella—my sister—there has been *some* progress since then! Such things as art—as poetry and music—such kinds of new light have come into the world since then! In some kinds of people some tenderer feelings have had some little beginning! That we have got to make *grow!* And *cling* to, and hold as our flag! In this dark march toward whatever it is we're approaching. . . . *Don't—don't hang back with the brutes!*[27]
>
> (sc. 4)

CHARACTER

Williams' characters, with the exception of Blanche, are in their late twenties and early thirties. They wear the clothes of working-class people; their activities are eating, drinking, bowling, playing poker, and making love. Blanche is about five years older than her sister. She enters the Kowalski world dressed as for a garden party in white suit, hat, and gloves. Williams describes her appearance:

> Her delicate beauty must avoid a strong light. There is something about her uncertain manner, as well as her white clothes, that suggest a moth.[28]

In Williams' world moths do not long survive contact with the light (Figure 14-13).

The relationship among Blanche, Stanley, Stella, and Mitch are based on the law of the jungle: The weaker, in this case Blanche and Mitch, are physically and psychologically violated by Stanley, the stronger. Stanley's need to dominate and control his world destroys Mitch's happiness and Blanche's ability to cope with reality. Stella long ago has given up the vestiges of gentility for the sexual satisfactions of her life with Stanley.

Williams' characters fall into two categories: survivors and nonsurvivors. In a clash the sensitive and the fragile fall before the coarse and the brutal in Williams' violent world of the new South.

LANGUAGE

Since *The Glass Menagerie* Williams has been acknowledged as a poet of the theatre. His ear for rhythmic dialogue—the soft cadences of Southern speech with its characteristic poeticisms—is matched only by his theatrical images and symbolic sounds woven into the play's texture and meaning: the evening sky that "invests the scene with a kind of lyricism"; the "Blue Piano" of the New Orleans' barroom that expresses the spirit of loss and despair hovering in the air that Blanche DuBois breathes.

Figure 14-13 *A Streetcar Named Desire*, 1948. Uta Hagen succeeded Jessica Tandy as Blanche Du-Bois.

On the verbal level Williams' language universalizes a specific experience. For instance, Blanche stands bewildered before the tenement building unable to believe that her sister lives in this place. Eunice, a neighbor, says:

What's the matter, honey? Are you lost?

Blanche [*with faintly hysterical humor*] They told me to take a street-car named Desire, and then transfer to one called Cemeteries and ride six blocks and get off at—Elysian Fields![29]

In three lines of dialogue Williams has described the history of Blanche's ancestors and her own sexual desires, which have resulted in death and dying.

The play's visual language is a matter of contrasts. The red-stained package of meat that Stanley throws to his wife contrasts with Blanche's mothlike quality and her white garden party clothes. Blanche's drinking contrasts with her self-image as a genteel, untouched virgin. The barroom music of the present contrasts with the polka music of Blanche's memories. She is haunted by a scene that took place years earlier at the Moon Lake Casino where she danced a polka with her young husband (Allan Grey) who, unable to face his homosexuality, walked out of the casino and shot himself. The memory recurs with greater frequency as she retreats from the present into a past of her own creation. As she gains Mitch's love, the polka tune fades out, but as she loses Mitch, it returns drowning out the sounds of Stanley's voice and the poker games.

STREETCAR'S MODERNISM

A Streetcar Named Desire, now almost 40 years old, continues to appeal to present-day audiences. Williams' characters and themes touch the core of contemporary experience. The play brings to mind our culture of narcissism with its ethic of self-preservation and psychic survival. Blanche DuBois and Stanley Kowalski are both narcissistic individuals. One loses and the other wins out. Blanche is also an *outsider* alienated from the self and society, a fashionable character in current literature. Blanche's aloneness and sexual reaching out are familiar themes in contemporary novels, films, and plays. More traditionally, Williams also presents Blanche as a fragile individual struggling to survive in an indifferent and brutal environment. Blanche's fears of aging, loneliness, and homelessness are popular materials for today's mass media. Nor are the scenes of blatant sensuality and sexual violence outdated either in our society or in our theatre.

According to Williams, we all ride that "Desire" streetcar—desiring love, connection, and protection. We want to be taken in, to belong; yet at the same time we want to be left alone with our illusions and paper lanterns because they make the world a little easier to bear. The character of Blanche DuBois, created in 1947, epitomizes this, and the action of Williams' play shows us these truths about ourselves.

ESSAY: From Stage to Film

Almost from the beginnings of sound motion pictures, Hollywood has looked to novels and plays as material for films. Successful Broadway plays, particularly, have been prime Hollywood targets. This connection between the modern American theatre and its technological cousin, film, is worth examining. The film industry provides jobs for actors, writers, directors, and designers. Moreover, film can make a play like *A Streetcar Named Desire* accessible to millions far away from Broadway. The Hollywood connection is a vital part of the American theatre world.

The 1951 movie version of Tennessee Williams' *A Streetcar Named Desire* is an American film classic. It represents a mix of theatrical and film talent. Warner Brothers retained Elia Kazan as director and commissioned him to produce a script. Of the original Broadway cast, Marlon Brando, Kim Hunter, and Karl Malden were signed on. However, the producers felt that Jessica Tandy was not sufficiently well known to "sell" the film to the American public. They turned to Vivien Leigh (1913–1967), the British stage and film actress who had captured America's imagination as Scarlett O'Hara in *Gone with the Wind* in 1939. Leigh was cast in the role of Blanche DuBois, and her performance (with Brando) electrified film audiences (Figure 14-14).

> ❝ Carson McCullers concludes one of her lyric poems with the line: 'Time, the endless idiot, runs screaming ''round the world.'' ' It is this continual rush of time, so violent that it appears to be screaming, that deprives our actual lives of so much dignity and meaning, and it is, perhaps more than anything else, the arrest of time which has taken place in a completed work of art that gives to certain plays their feeling of depth and significance. ❞
>
> Tennessee Williams,
> "The Timeless World of a Play" (1950)[30]

Figure 14-14 The film version of *A Streetcar Named Desire,* 1951. Vivien Leigh as Blanche and Marlon Brando as Stanley confront each other in one of the film's climactic moments. Elia Kazan directed.

SUMMARY

American commercial theatre put down indigenous roots in less than 150 years. From English touring companies and home-grown amateur productions, the American theatre developed theatre centers and buildings; playwrights, actors, directors, designers, and producers; training programs; professional theatres on and beyond Broadway; and a continuing tradition of the avant-garde.

New York City has been the locus of American professional theatre since about 1890, and Blacks, Hispanics, American Indians, and women have contributed to its multicultural richness. The full significance of these and other groups is only beginning to be assessed by historians and critics.

Reflecting the diversity of the country and its

people, American theatre has been characterized chiefly by a healthy eclecticism. In the 1860s towns far and wide had resident companies supporting a "star." These were displaced by touring companies bringing new plays, stars, and scenery to the provinces. New York was the center for packaging these tours; by the turn of the century it also was the locus of the commercial theatre run by such renowned artist-managers as Steele MacKaye, Augustin Daly, and David Belasco. In 1896 businessmen-managers set out to monopolize the touring business. The Syndicate, organized by Charles Frohman, became a powerful enterprise, rewarding compliant stars and managers and breaking those who opposed it. However, the Syndicate itself was soon broken by the determined efforts of actors, managers, and producers led by David Belasco and the Shubert Brothers.

Since the first quarter of the twentieth century, star-centered performances have alternated with ensemble acting inspired by Stanislavsky and the tours of the Moscow Art Theatre to New York in the 1920s. Unions developed to protect the professional artist. University departments evolved to teach theatre to amateurs and aspiring young professionals. In scenic design the new European stagecraft of Appia and Craig inspired American designers like Robert Edmond Jones, Kenneth Magowan, and Lee Simonson, who, in turn, influenced an entire second generation. Europe's theatres and writers also influenced American production techniques and aspiring American playwrights.

Independent theatres like the Provincetown Players and the Washington Square Players in the 1920s encouraged new playwrights by giving them a home away from the commercial pressures of Broadway. Eugene O'Neill emerged from the Provincetown Players; Clifford Odets, Paul Green, and William Saroyan from the Group Theatre. The same was true for actors, directors, and designers. Moreover, the Federal Theatre Project during its brief history (1935–1939) gave employment to theatre artists of all races throughout the country.

The star system and the Broadway production have been the backbone of American commercial theatre. But group work has been the hallmark of the theatrical avant-garde. From the experiments of the Group Theatre with Stanislavsky's methods in the 1930s to the Living Theatre's confrontations with audiences in the 1960s, the artistic vision and energies of small groups of like-minded theatre people led American theatre in new directions. In the mid-twentieth century American theatre was notable for the work of groups devoted to particular attitudes and methods—political, artistic, and ethnic. The Mercury Theatre, the Lafayette Street Theatre, the Actors Studio, the Living Theatre, the Open Theatre, and the Bread and Puppet Theatre have all made unique contributions to American culture and society.

American theatre has a special identity as a director's theatre. In the late 1940s and 1950s, Elia Kazan, Harold Clurman, and José Quintero created a style of "modified" or "selected" realism for the staging of plays by O'Neill, Miller, and Williams, in particular. Modified realism as a production style continues to dominate this theatre. It represents less dependence on illusionism and a greater emphasis on theatricality. Stage settings rely on suggestion instead of detailed representation of period and place. As staging became more theatrical, plays became freer in structure and less concerned with external details than with inner psychological truths. O'Neill, Miller, Williams, Hellman, and Albee have written plays of harrowing psychological insight.

Stage realism has also been an appropriate setting for the social protest plays written since the 1930s and the Depression years. Odets, Miller, and Hansberry have written plays that treat of political and social injustices against identifiable groups. In the 1960s a new wave of Black writers emerged who not only protested racial injustice but also took up the more enduring subjects of Black history and culture. At the end of the sixties the American theatre had gathered its forces for a great theatrical renascence whose emphasis was to be on the new playwright, the far-flung resident theatres, and independent groups whose social and political consciousness would determine their artistic direction.

A Streetcar Named Desire by Tennessee Williams, our representative play, was produced on Broadway in 1947. One of the greatest American plays, it is a poetic tragedy about an individual and a dying way of life. The 1947 production brought together many elements discussed in this chapter through the modified realism of Williams' writing, Jo Mielziner's design, and Elia Kazan's staging; the method of the Group Theatre and the Actor's Studio in Kazan's directing and Strasberg's training of the play's actors Marlon Brando, Karl Malden, and Kim Hunter.

Hollywood has always looked to novels and plays as material for films. The film industry provides jobs for actors, writers, directors, and designers and makes plays accessible to millions far away from Broadway. The filming of *A Streetcar Named Desire* is an integral part of artistic practice in the United States.

PLAYS TO READ

Desire Under the Elms by Eugene O'Neill

The Little Foxes by Lillian Hellman

A Streetcar Named Desire by Tennessee Williams

Death of a Salesman by Arthur Miller

A Raisin in the Sun by Lorraine Hansberry

SOURCES

Hansberry, Lorraine. *A Raisin in the Sun*. New York: New American Library, 1961. Paperback. In addition to the cast listing for the 1959 New York premiere of Hansberry's play at the Ethel Barrymore Theatre, this edition includes a number of photographs from the motion picture starring many of the original Broadway cast, including Sidney Poitier, Claudia MacNeil, and Ruby Dee. Also in *A Raisin in the Sun*. New York: New American Library, 1966. Paperback. This edition includes *The Sign in Sidney Brustein's Window*.

Hellman, Lillian. *The Little Foxes*. In *Six Plays*. New York: Random, 1979. Paperback. It also contains *The Children's Hour, Days To Come, Watch on the Rhine, Another Part of the Forest*, and *The Autumn Garden*.

Miller, Arthur. *Death of a Salesman*. New York: Penguin Books, 1976. Paperback. Also *Death of a Salesman: Text and Criticism*. Edited by Gerald Weales. New York: Viking Penguin, 1977. Paperback. This is a popular edition with students and instructors since it not only contains the play but also includes major criticism on Miller's most respected work.

O'Neill, Eugene. *Desire Under the Elms*. In *Three Plays*. New York: Random, 1959. Paperback. This volume also contains *Strange Interlude* and *Mourning Becomes Electra*. Also in *Three Plays*. New York: Random House, 1973. Paperback. This edition includes *Anna Christie, The Emperor Jones*, and *The Hairy Ape*.

Williams, Tennessee. *A Streetcar Named Desire*. New York: New American Library, 1973. Paperback. A reprint of Williams' 1947 *New York Times* article entitled "On a Streetcar Named Success" is included as a preface. Also published by New Directions (New York, 1980). Paperback.

NOTES

1. Hallie Flanagan, *Arena: The History of the Federal Theatre* (New York: Quell, Sloan & Pearce, 1940), p. 219.

2. Garff B. Wilson, *Three Hundred Years of American Drama and Theatre: From Ye Bare and Ye Cubb to Chorus Line* (Englewood Cliffs, N.J.: Prentice-Hall, 1982), p. 299.

3. Toby Cole and Helen K. Chinoy, eds., *Directors on Directing: A Source Book of the Modern Theatre* (Indianapolis Bobbs-Merrill, 1976), p. 38.

Reprinted by permission of Bobbs-Merrill Educational Publishing.

4. Judith Malina and Julian Beck, *Paradise Now: Collective Creation of The Living Theatre* (New York: Random House, 1971), pp. 18–19. Copyright © 1971 by Judith Malina and Julian Beck. Reprinted by permission of Random House, Inc.

5. Jean-Claude van Itallie, *America Hurrah!* (New York: Coward-McCann, 1966), pp. 43–45. Reprinted by permission of Coward-McCann, Inc.

6. Peter Schumann, "The World Has to Be Demonstrated Anew," *Poland* (March 1970), 4. Reprinted by permission of *Poland*.

7. James Roose-Evans, *Experimental Theatre: From Stanislavsky to Today* (New York: Universe Books, 1970), p. 138. Reprinted by permission of Universe Books.

8. Margaret Croyden, *Lunatics, Lovers and Poets: The Contemporary Experimental Theatre* (New York: Dell, 1974), p. 221.

9. Roose-Evans, *Experimental Theatre*, p.140.

10. Joseph Wood Krutch, *The American Drama Since 1918* (New York: Random House, 1939), pp. 92–93.

11. Walter Kerr, *New York Herald Tribune* (November 8, 1956). Reprinted by permission of Walter Kerr.

12. Lillian Hellman, *Scoundrel Time* (Boston: Little, Brown, 1976), p. 98.

13. Clifford Odets, *Six Plays of Clifford Odets*, intro. Harold Clurman (New York: Grove, 1979), p. 191. Reprinted by permission of Grove Press, Inc.

14. Odets, *Waiting for Lefty* in *Six Plays of Clifford Odets*, pp. 30–31. Reprinted by permission of Grove Press, Inc.

15. Arthur Miller, *Death of a Salesman* in *Collected Plays* (New York: Viking, 1957), p. 162. Copyright 1949 by Arthur Miller. Copyright renewed 1977 by Arthur Miller. Reprinted by permission of Viking Penguin, Inc.

16. Arthur Miller, *The Price* (New York: Viking, 1968), p. 37. Copyright © 1968 by Arthur Miller and Ingeborg M. Miller, Trustee. Reprinted by permission of Viking Penguin, Inc.

17. Gerald Weales, *The Jumping-Off Place: American Drama in the 1960s* (New York: Macmillan, 1969), p. 23. Reprinted by permission of Gerald Weales.

18. Lorraine Hansberry, *A Raisin in the Sun* (New York: Random House, 1959), pp. 137–138. Copyright © 1958, 1959 by Robert Nemiroff as Executor of the Estate of Lorraine Hansberry. Reprinted by permission of Random House, Inc.

19. Edward Albee, *The Zoo Story* (New York: Coward-McCann, 1959), pp. 30–36. Copyright © 1960 by Edward Albee. Reprinted by permission of Coward-McCann, Inc.

20. Edward Albee, *The American Dream* (New York: Coward-McCann, 1963), pp. 53–54. Reprinted by permission of Coward-McCann, Inc.

21. Weales, *The Jumping-Off Place*, p. 35. Reprinted by permission.

22. Elia Kazan, "Notebook for *A Streetcar Named Desire*" in *Directors on Directing*, p. 364.

23. Tennessee Williams, "On a Streetcar Named Success," *New York Times*, November 30, 1947, pt. 2, p. 3. © 1947 by The New York Times Company. Reprinted by permission.

24. Tennessee Williams, *A Streetcar Named Desire*, pp. 9–10. From *Theatre of Tennessee Williams*, Volume I. Copyright 1947 by Tennessee Williams. Reprinted by permission of New Directions Publishing Corporation.

25. Brooks Atkinson, " 'Streetcar' Tragedy, Mr. Williams' Report on Life in New Orleans," *New York Times*, December 14, 1947, pt. 2, p. 1. © 1947 by The New York Times Company. Reprinted by permission.

26. Cole and Chinoy, *Directors on Directing*, p. 364. Reprinted by permission.

27. Williams, *Streetcar Named Desire*, pp. 80–81. Reprinted by permission.

28. Williams, *Streetcar Named Desire*, p. 11. Reprinted by permission.

29. Williams, *Streetcar Named Desire*, p. 15. Reprinted by permission.

30. Williams, "The Timeless World of a Play," *The Rose Tattoo* (New York: New Directions, 1950), p. vi. Tennessee Williams, *Theatre of Tennessee Williams, Volume II.* Copyright © 1958 by Tennessee Williams. Reprinted by permission of New Directions Publishing Corporation.

FIFTEEN

AMERICAN THEATRE: THE PRESENT

A MODERN PERSPECTIVE

While Broadway remains the mecca for American commercial theatre, both commercial and nonprofit theatres have proliferated beyond Broadway and throughout the United States.

Commercial interests have encroached upon New York's Off-Broadway theatres, but New York's Public Theatre and La Mama Experimental Theatre Club, for example, have continued to provide alternative performance spaces for nonprofit artists and groups. Moreover, the resident theatre movement has established a network of professional theatres (called LORT theatres for League of Resident Theatres) across the country. It is difficult today to find a major city that does not have one or more professional resident theatres. Finally, small groups of like-minded theatre people have banded together to make theatre out of their ethnic, political, and social concerns, providing alternatives to our more established theatrical institutions.

Whereas experimental theatre in the sixties was defined by groups working in collaboration to create the text, the current experimental theatre, due as much to economics as to artistic vision, is different. Today artists are engaged in the use of autobiography ("the self as text") and in working out new strategies for dealing with the content of self-exploration. The most successful avant-gardists staging their personal mythologies are Richard Foreman, Robert Wilson, Spalding Gray, Meredith Monk, and Lee Breuer. At present the Mabou Mines, with whom Lee Breuer has been associated from its beginnings, is the leading avant-garde company of the 1980s.

Above all, since the mid-seventies American theatre has seen the emergence of the new playwright. Among them Sam Shepard, who was championed in his development by the Performance Group, the Public Theatre, La Mama ETC, and others, stands tall. Shepard's career is a weathervane of the direction of American playwriting today.

REPRESENTATIVE THEATRE:
The Public Theatre

As you walk up the littered subway stairs at New York's Astor Place, you surface in an area of wide streets surrounded by large red brick warehouses. You are between the West Village and the East Village where the Public Theatre is located on Lafayette Street. Washington Square and New York University lie to the West, and to the South sits the Bowery.

The New York Shakespeare Festival theatres, under the leadership of Joseph Papp, operate year-round in two locations: the open air Delacorte Theatre in Central Park and the Public Theatre.

The Festival began in 1956 as a free summer theatre in Central Park producing Shakespeare. The outdoor Delacorte Theatre, seating 2236, was built there in 1962 as a permanent location. Soon Papp looked for a year-round home and an outlet for the production of new American plays. He obtained funds to convert the Astor Library, a New York City landmark, into the Public Theatre, which opened with the original production of *Hair* in 1967.

More than 100 plays were produced in the first decade at the Public. Among its award-winning productions were *No Place to Be Somebody, Sticks and Bones, That Championship Season, Short Eyes, Streamers, For Colored Girls . . . , Runaways, A Chorus Line,* and revivals of *The Threepenny Opera, The Cherry Orchard,* and *The Pirates of Penzance.*

The Public has several characteristics of theatres operating today. It is a multistoried building with a number of spaces offering a variety of performance activities. On any one week at the Public, two or more plays can be seen in the newly renovated theatres, along with films, poetry readings, and jazz concerts. Ticket prices are low, making the theatres accessible to all types of theatregoers, especially to students.

Productions at the Public are eclectic in style and in content. Shakespeare and other classics are produced in old and new dress. Shakespeare's *Two Gentlemen of Verona* was adapted as a musical, and Gilbert and Sullivan's *The Pirates of Penzance* also appeared, with new musical sounds. Moreover, the theatre is devoted to the production of new plays by new playwrights, and new directors and actors have gotten their start at the Public, returning there for premiere productions. Its spaces are also used to showcase the work of avant-garde companies like the Mabou Mines and for solo performances by individual artists.

Figure 15-1 (a) The Public Theatre, headquarters of the New York Shakespeare Festival Theatre at 425 Lafayette Street, New York. The building was formerly the Astor Library. (b) The Delacorte Theatre in Central Park.

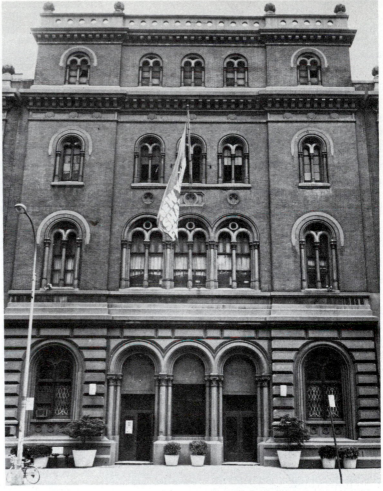

a

b

A small enterprise in the fifties eking out its existence, today the Public is "big time." Joe Papp's entrepreneurial skills are fulfilling his dreams on Lafayette Street. With the proceeds from *A Chorus Line* and *The Pirates of Penzance*, he has established an endowment for the Public Theatre. There are six theatre spaces, and Papp is committed to shows for cable television. Moreover, the Public now has an arrangement with the Royal Court (London) to showcase new British plays and to transport new American plays to London.

Joseph Papp is a controversial figure. Legendary stories evolve around him and artists develop love-hate relationships with him. But the Public Theatre under his auspices consistently provided a model for nonprofit theatre in the seventies and continues to do so today.

CONDITIONS OF PERFORMANCE

BACKGROUND

Beginning with the 1950s the United States became an *affluent society* as most Americans benefited from an expanding economy and expanding government services. By 1970 the population had increased to 203,000,000 and had shifted from metro centers to the suburbs. The "Sun Belt," or southern half of the country from the Carolinas to California, experienced the greatest population growth of the decade.

But the affluent society had its less idyllic side. The inner cities, emptied of its White, middle-class population, began to decay. The Vietnam war divided Americans, talented young people dropped out of a society they no longer believed in, political leaders were assassinated, the Watergate break-in followed by President Richard M. Nixon's resignation created a cli-

---

JOSEPH PAPP

Joseph Papp (b. 1921) is producer of the New York Shakespeare Festival Theatres in New York City.

Papp, born in Brooklyn, began his theatre career as a Broadway stage manager. He founded the Shakespeare Theatre Workshop in 1953, which became the base for the New York Shakespeare Festival. Here actors in street clothes, with no scenery or props, performed Shakespeare before small invited audiences. Between 1953 and 1962 the Workshop gave performances at the Emmanuel Presbyterian Church and then moved into Central Park as a Shakespeare Festival in 1956 and as an official branch of the city's arts activities. In 1962 the permanent Delacorte Theatre was built in Central Park for the Festival, where on an average of two Shakespeare plays are produced each year. In 1967 Papp founded the Public Theatre.

Papp relocated the New York Shakespeare Festival at Lincoln Center in 1973 but returned in 1977 to the Public Theatre, which became his base of operations. Papp has received wide recognition for his contributions to the theatre, including the Antoinette Perry (Tony) Award for Distinguished Service to the Theatre (1957–1958), the ANTA annual Award for Outstanding Contribution to the Art of Living Theatre (1965), and several Pulitzer Prizes.

---

mate of skepticism about the nation's moral leadership.

In the 1980s the nation's crime rate has soared. The nation's illiteracy rate also is rising as the public school system fails to keep its promises for quality education for all Americans. Inflation, crime, and unemployment are considered by most Americans the most serious national problems. While inner cities deteriorate and local governments struggle to provide day-to-day services, the political leadership in Washington, D.C., strives to balance the nation's finances and to keep a strong military posture. While spending on military hardware has increased, poverty programs, health-care services, and other programs are being cut back.

In 1980 Broadway theatre attendance peaked and the resident theatre movement burgeoned across the country, but times are already changing on the American art scene. The National Endowment for the Arts (created by President John F. Kennedy in 1965) is threatened with a significant reduction of federal funding. Although faltering, the American theatrical renascence has not yet failed.

In the regional theatres new plays are being performed, some finding their way to Broadway and onto college campuses. Although the artistic directors of these far-flung theatres (from Los Angeles to Boston) admit it is a temptation *not* to think of Broadway as they read new scripts, they remain true to their newfound concern: to develop the American theatre through the American playwright. This endorsement is one of the most notable features of the American theatre of the 1980s.

THE TROIKA: BROADWAY, OFF BROADWAY, AND OFF-OFF BROADWAY

Broadway Critic Martin Gottfried describes the American theatre since the Second World War as split by two natural forces—one tugging toward change, the other pulling toward tradition. Broadway represents the tradition of the success-oriented, expensive, star-studded, professional theatre of big musicals, melodramas like *Deathtrap*, and the occasional tour de force like *The Gin Game* or *Nicholas Nickleby*. Sometimes Shakespeare, with superstars like James Earl Jones and Christopher Plummer in *Othello*, makes it to Broadway.

Broadway is replicated in touring com-

1970

——————— Vietnam War 1957–1975 ———————

| Richard M. Nixon President, 1969–1974 | Nixon resigns the presidency 1974 |

Nixon's visits to China end two decades of isolation, 1971

Gerald R. Ford, President 1974–1976

Watergate break-in at Democratic National Committee Headquarters 1972

War between Israel and Egypt 1973

> **"**The natural place to begin is with [Broadway's] commercial nature. On the one hand, the profit motive provides the strictest test for the ability of a dramatic work to reach an audience. On the other, it identifies Broadway theatre as an investment enterprise. Backers are convinced that a play (which in marketplace terminology is called a 'property') is so good that it will receive marvelous reviews, run three years, tour for three more with three companies, be produced abroad and finally, heaven allowing, be sold to Hollywood. Like the tax-advantage purchase of paintings, it is a business proposition with warming cultural overtones as well as show business glamour.**"**
>
> Martin Gottfried, *A Theatre Divided* (1967)[1]

American pull-out
in Vietnam, 1975

Jimmy Carter
President, 1977–1980

Americans taken
hostage in Iran, 1980

North Vietnam
overruns South
Vietnam, 1975

Israel/Egypt
Treaty signed
at Camp David
1979

Ronald Reagan,
President, 1981–1984

Anwar Sadat of Egypt
assassinated, 1981

Jerry Falwell
and the "Moral
Majority," 1979

Russians invade
Afghanistan,
1980

Sandra Day O'Connor
first woman appointed
to the U.S. Supreme
Court, 1981

Poland's trade union
"Solidarity" declared,
1981; martial law in
Poland, Dec. 1981

Guatemala, San Salvador,
and Nicaragua erupt
into bitter fighting
between leftist and rightist
groups, 1980s

panies, summer stock, musical tents, cultural centers, institutional theatres, and even our large repertory theatres. This is the "legitimate" theatre in the very best sense, including, as it does, almost everybody in the theatre who has training, experience, technique, and craft.

Off Broadway Off Broadway is an area many blocks from Broadway that is home to a number of smaller theatres. It is associated with the adventuresome spirit of producers and artists who, in the 1960s, looked for solutions to high production costs and excessive union demands. For a few years the Off-Broadway theatres (seating about 200) were an alternative to Broadway's supercommercialism. Offbeat plays could be produced cheaply and new talent (writers, actors, and directors) could be tried out without the penalty of high overhead. The Circle-in-the-Square, one of the leaders in the sixties, revived "noncommercial" plays by Eugene O'Neill and Tennessee Williams and produced such new plays as *Hot L Baltimore* (1973) by Lanford Wilson.

Off-Off Broadway With encroaching union demands on the Off-Broadway theatres (and the lethal hit-or-miss success syndrome they encouraged), other solutions were sought. Also, theatre groups that took for their themes the Vietnam war and generally left-wing political positions were driven even further from Broad-

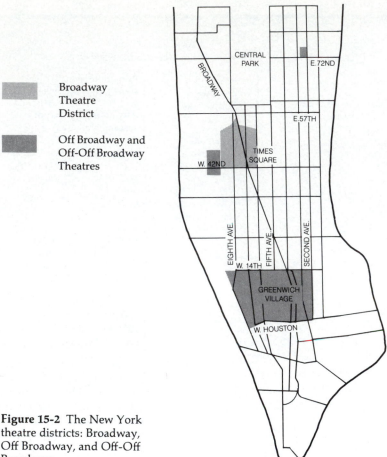

Figure 15-2 The New York theatre districts: Broadway, Off Broadway, and Off-Off Broadway.

way (and into smaller spaces). As early as 1959 Café Cino had been started by Joseph Cino; it was quickly followed by Al Carmines' Judson Poets' Theatre and Ellen Stewart's Café La Mama (now called La Mama ETC). These were nonprofit, independent organizations serving the needs of new playwrights and new audiences. They established permanent quarters for the production of new and frequently unpopular plays. The collectives—the Living Theatre, the Open Theatre, the Bread and Puppet Theatre—opened up in warehouses, lofts, and garages deep within the East and West Villages. Others

pushed for noncommercial productions of forgotten classics by Garcia Lorca, Georg Buchner, and Gertrude Stein. New playwrights emerged from the Off-Off-Broadway experiments, including Edward Albee, Jack Gelber, Julie Bovasso, Rochelle Owens, Paul Foster, Megan Terry, Tom Eyen, Leonard Melfi, Jean-Claude van Itallie, María Irene Fornés, Ed Bullins, David Rabe, Lanford Wilson, and Sam Shepard.

Off-Off-Broadway theatre in general has been labeled amateurish because of erratic production techniques and enthusiasms for the radical. For a while the *Village Voice* became the journalistic spokesperson for the Off-Broadway movements, while *Variety* and *Backstage* continued to speak for the commercial theatre in terms of grosses, road potential, stock possibilities, and movie sales.

There is an ebb and flow among this troika. The Public Theatre is the best example of an Off-Off-Broadway institution sustaining avant-garde companies and new playwrights while feeding Broadway with its broad-based successes like *A Chorus Line* and *The Pirates of Penzance*. Off Broadway also nourishes performers who move between the two entities; Off-Broadway writers like Edward Albee, Lanford Wilson, and Mary Beth Henley have also become commercial successes.

RESIDENT THEATRES

The terms *resident* and *regional* have been used interchangeably to describe professional theatres located outside New York. Established in the fifties and sixties, *resident* theatres from Seattle to Boston have been heralded as alternatives to the commercialism of Broadway and to the theatre's centralization in New York.

Today there are about 60 theatres in 51 cities with budgets ranging from $200,000 to more than $5 million. They produce over 600 productions yearly to audiences of more than 12,000,000. Many have touring programs. Most perform seasons of from 5 to 10 months, generally to subscription audiences.

In a society as diverse as that of the United States, these resident theatres make up a matrix that some call the country's *national* theatre. What are these theatres like? Why do they have permanent artistic staffs but, unlike their European counterparts, no permanent companies?

American resident theatres usually have a continuity of artistic leadership. They have main stages with second and even third stages for new and experimental works. Many still cling to the more obvious classics and standard modern works (Shakespeare, O'Neill, Miller, and Williams). Others produce lesser-known plays from the European repertoire and new plays by American playwrights. Actors Theatre in Louisville has a new American play festival; the Yale Repertory Theatre has its Winterfest series; the Mark Taper Forum in Los Angeles has a New Theatre for Now festival.

One of the most remarkable effects of the resident theatre movement has been the development of more sophisticated and adventurous audiences. They are making possible the greater diversity of plays produced and the second and even third stages. However, although there is usually continuity of artistic leadership, there has been no continuous support system. The resident theatres depend upon a precarious balance of federal dollars (now dwindling), private foundation money, and subscribers' dollars. This financial balancing act hurts the artist the most. Although most theatres hire permanent administrative staff and artistic leadership (like the artistic director), they have not yet been able to fund a resident company for the entire season. The artists themselves often support the theatre by accepting minimal salaries until they grow tired and move on into film, television, and the commercial theatre. They are then replaced by new actors and the cycle begins again. This talent drain is wearing at best, discouraging at worst. But the resident theatre movement is strong, although still looking for permanent funding and resident companies.

It would be inaccurate to picture the resident theatres as having no connections with the commercial theatre. In the last decade Broadway has been enlivened by the products of these theatres: *A Chorus Line, Runaways,* and *The Pirates of Penzance* from the Public Theatre; *The Gin Game* from Actors Theatre in Louisville; *Children of a Lesser God* from the Mark Taper Forum in Los Angeles; and *American Buffalo* from the Long Wharf Theatre in New Haven. The dangers inherent in the Broadway connection are that distinctions will blur between commercial and nonprofit theatre and that the regional theatres will settle for a goal of finding commercial property that will make it to Broadway and return big money to the theatre back home.

Some of the 70+ LORT Theatres

Theatre	City	Artistic Director
Actors Theatre of Louisville	Louisville	John Jory
American Conservatory Theatre (ACT)	San Francisco	William Ball
American Repertory Theatre (ART)	Boston	Robert Brustein
Arena Stage	Washington, D.C.	Zelda Fichandler
Circle in the Square	New York City	Theodore Mann
Circle Repertory Company	New York City	Marshall W. Mason
Dallas Theatre Center	Dallas	Adrian Hall
Denver Center Theatre	Denver	Donovan Marley
El Teatro Campesino	San Juan Bautista	Luis Valdez
Goodman Theatre	Chicago	Gregory Mosher
Guthrie Theatre	Minneapolis	Liviu Ciulei
Hartford Stage Company	Hartford	Mark Lamos
Indiana Repertory Theatre	Indianapolis	Tom Haas
Long Wharf Theatre	New Haven	Arvin Brown
Manhattan Theatre Club	New York City	Lynne Meadow
Mark Taper Forum	Los Angeles	Gordon Davidson
McCarter Theatre Company	Princeton	Nagle Jackson
Milwaukee Repertory Theatre	Milwaukee	John Dillon
Missouri Repertory Theatre	Kansas City	Patricia McIlrath
Negro Ensemble Company (NEC)	New York City	Douglas Turner Ward
New Federal Theatre	New York City	Woodie King, Jr.
New York Shakespeare Festival	New York City	Joseph Papp
Oregon Shakespearean Festival	Ashland	Jerry Turner
Organic Theatre Company	Chicago	Stuart Gordon
Playmakers Repertory Company	Chapel Hill	Gregory Boyd
Repertory Theatre of St. Louis	St. Louis	Steven Woolf
Seattle Repertory Theatre	Seattle	Daniel Sullivan
Trinity Square Repertory Company	Providence	Adrian Hall
Virginia Museum Theatre	Richmond	Tom Markus
Williamstown Theatre Festival	Williamstown	Nikos Psacharopoulos
Yale Repertory Theatre	New Haven	Lloyd Richards

SUBSIDIZING THE ARTS

The idea of subsidy to theatres is a relatively new concept in the United States. In 1962 the Ford Foundation gave grants totaling $6.1 million to nine resident theatres. The Rockefeller Foundation soon followed. Then the federal government jumped into the funding business, subsidizing theatres on a large scale. In 1964 the National Council on the Arts was formed, and in 1965 Congress established the National Endowment for the Arts, with Roger L. Stevens as its head. Joining the foundations and federal government in giving financial support were cultural centers, state governments, corporations, and private citizens. All were a direct stimulus for the boom in resident theatres in the 1960s.

However, unlike European nations, the United States has never had a national arts policy underpinned by a philosophy of subsidy. Many theatres profited and used their monies wisely. Others did not and fell by the wayside. Now, with an inflated economy and federal deficits, both public and private subsidies are falling off. In response to the economic trends of the times, many theatres are faced with shortened seasons and reduced companies.

ALTERNATIVE THEATRES

Black Theatre The Negro Ensemble Company (NEC), one of the oldest and best-known Black theatre groups in New York City, was founded in 1967 by Robert Hooks, Douglas Turner Ward, and Gerald Krone. Their aim was to provide a forum for the presentation of theatrical materials relevant to the Black experience. The focus was to be upon the new Black playwright.

Since 1967 NEC has produced 80 plays, including new plays by Imamu Amiri Baraka (formerly known as LeRoi Jones), who wrote Dutchman and Slave Ship: A Historical Pageant, and by Ed Bullins, author of The Electronic Nigger and Clara's Ole Man. The most influential Black playwrights of the 1960s, they wrote agitprop dramas to spur the development of Black consciousness. Since then the mission of such Black

playwrights as Lonne Elder III (Ceremonies in Dark Old Men), Ntozake Shange (For Colored Girls Who Have Considered Suicide When the Rainbow Is Enuf), Samm Art-Williams (Home), and Charles Fuller (A Soldier's Play) has subtly changed as they have moved beyond writing about confrontations with White people and stereotyped behavior (Figure 15-3).

Charles Fuller, for example, explores the internal psychological effects of racism on Black people and Shange, the experiences of modern Black women. Recently, Douglas Turner Ward, NEC artistic director, said in an interview: "We are not presenting plays whose themes are exclusively intended for Blacks. The plays of Sean O'Casey are set in Ireland, but has anyone ever suggested those plays are intended for the enjoyment of only the Irish? Of course not. Why shouldn't the same be true of the Black play?"[2]

Using a resident company of actors, directors, and designers, NEC has produced new plays almost exclusively. Its productions have provided a major share of the body of contemporary Black dramatic literature.

Chicano Theatre El Teatro Campesino was started by Luis Valdez in 1965 as part of the organizing effort for Cesar Chavez's United Farmworkers (UFW) union in California. El Teatro's original purpose was to dramatize the issues of the Delano grape strike and to urge farmworkers to join the union, as well as to promote Chicano pride and erase the lingering stereotypes of Chicanos. By 1967 El Teatro Campesino had moved from Delano and had left the UFW to focus on broader issues of Chicano culture and consciousness.

Since the theatre grew out of specific economic action, agitprop skits called actos were the basis of performances. Farmworkers playing farmworkers (Valdez, a former member of the San Francisco Mime Troupe, was the exception) effectively dramatized conditions of Chicanos in the fields. Comedy—satire, slapstick, and clowning—was the main element of their work, developed after picketing hours and performed on

Figure 15-3 The Negro Ensemble Company (NEC) produced Charles Fuller's *A Soldier's Play* in New York in 1982. Left to right: Denzil Washington and Charles Brown.

picket lines, in marketplaces, and on farms. Based on Valdez's manifesto

Inspire the audience to social action;
Illuminate specific points about social problems;
Satirize the opposition;
Show or hint at a solution;
Express what people are feeling;

the *actos* became political acts themselves. They made theatre of the exploitation of farmworkers, of racial prejudices, of the need for solidarity between Chicano peasants and Vietnamese peasants, and of the Chicano struggle against stereotyping (Figure 15-4).

During the late sixties the California grape strike and the Vietnam war furnished vital issues on which to focus. In the 1970s El Teatro Campesino became less political and more mystical. The group moved to San Juan Bautista, California, in 1971. The progression from politics toward myth (*mitos*) was closely tied to the Chicano search for identity—to become "de-Anglicized." While other Chicano companies, such as Tenaz (El Teatro National De Aztlan), became more radical, Valdez said of El Teatro's break with radical politics: "Now our acts are the acts of human beings living and working on this earth. . . . We are still very much the political theatre, but our politics are the politics of the spirit—not of the flesh, but of the heart."[3]

Figure 15-4 Luis Valdez (standing), artistic director and resident playwright of El Teatro Campesino, plays the *Esquirol* or Scab in one of his early actos. Other actors with masks and signs depict satirical stereotypes in *La Conciencia del Esquirol* or *The Conscience of the Scab.* Actos were presented at many of the nightly rallies of the Farmworkers Union.

Valdez's experiment mirrored the two faces of popular theatre in the United States in the *actos*—a theatre that grew out of the experiences it sought to portray—and the religious *mitos*—a theatre of spiritual retreat from social action.

Since 1975 El Teatro has concentrated on representing Chicano consciousness realistically rather than through the *mitos*.

Feminist Theatre There are more than 100 feminist theatres listed in *Women in American Theatre* (1981), located in San Francisco, Minneapolis, New York, Boston, Pittsburgh, Washington, D.C., and elsewhere. "Feminist theatre" or "women's theatre" was born in the early seventies. The movement has survived for more than a decade but not without change. It now has a history (many theatres have come and gone) and a body of writing, together with a documented political and artistic impact on American culture and our way of thinking about women's concerns.

In its beginnings feminist theatre portrayed women almost solely as victims; today it shows how women have gained control of their lives. From both viewpoints feminist theatre has dealt largely with perceptions of how society fosters specific gender roles, male as well as female. Central to feminist performance has been the valuing of women's experiences, such as role stereotyping, sexual initiation, mother-daughter

At the Foot of the Mountain

At the Foot of the Mountain is a women's theatre collective located in Minneapolis. It was founded in 1974 in a spirit of "protest, celebration, and hope." The theatre's mission is to "create and produce plays, community events and rituals which spring from the lives of women." Its methods are largely improvisational and often draw on the life experiences of the women in the company.

In its beginnings the collective depended more on energy, inspiration, and consensus than on any formal administrative structure. However, Martha Boesing, the theatre's playwright and de facto artistic director, has been instrumental in changing this with the appointment of Phyllis Jane Rose as managing director.

The theatre group, which got its name by casting the *I Ching* until it came up with "the spring at the foot of the mountain," is dedicated to creating an ensemble of women performers who share similar artistic and political values. At its founding the theatre included 3 women, 3 men, 3 children, plus 43 plants, 1 cat, 4 cars, and a 24-foot U-Haul truck. The first season consisted of two plays by Martha Boesing: *Pimp* and *Gelding*.

By 1976 the group had become entirely a women's collective. In that first all-woman season, *Raped*, a powerful company-created piece, set the theatre's performance style as well as its type of subject: prostitution, addiction, marriage. Boesing believes that theatre ought to be one of the "healing arts," and talks easily about matriarchal cultures in which theatre appears to have been associated with medicine and healing.

Boesing's plays, such as *Junkie; The Web; Ashes, Ashes, We All Fall Down*, achieve their combined artistic and political goals not by narrative means but by emotional effects. Her plays have been described as "collages" of scenes. *Ashes* (1982) is a "ritual drama about nuclear madness and the denial of death." The play focuses on a family's denial of its mother's fatal disease interwoven with society's toying with nuclear war as we careen toward the end of the world.

While Boesing remains the theatre's resident playwright, the work of other women is now produced and the company is expanding its season and touring program.

---

bonding, rape, and childbirth. The aim has been to communicate women's experiences by placing women's mental and physical needs at the center of the plays.

By extension, a feminist theatre avoids gender roles even in its organization. Most also avoid leadership roles. Some theatres employ only women and perform only for women. Some women-only companies perform for audiences of men and women. In other companies both men and women perform for mixed audiences. Some consider artistic aims more important than political goals or social ends; some declare the opposite.

Of the notable theatres that have survived into the eighties, we find companies as diverse in size and goals as in their geographies: The Omaha Magic Theatre (Nebraska), At the Foot of the Mountain (Minneapolis), the Caravan Theatre (Lexington, Massachusetts), Los Angeles Feminist Theatre, Spider Woman Theatre Workshop (Brooklyn), Rhode Island Feminist Theatre, and Women's Experimental Theatre (New York City).

A further outgrowth of this movement has been the attention given in recent years by the publishing industry to plays written by feminists. Among the best are Martha Boesing's *The Story of A Mother* (1977), Roberta Sklar's, Sondra Segal's, and Clare Coss's *The Daughters Cycle Trilogy: Daughters, Sister/Sister, Electra Speaks* (1976), María Irene Fornés' *Fefu and Her Friends* (1977), and Adele Shank's *Stuck* (1981).

CURRENT PLAYWRITING

American theatre mythology says that the successful playwright is the playwright produced on Broadway. However, this mythology has been challenged increasingly in the past 20 years. The O'Neill Center, Off-Off-Broadway theatres, and resident and institutional theatres have discovered the "new" play as a commercially viable entity; they are reading new scripts, producing new plays, and scheduling new play festivals. Some playwrights are closely associated with resident theatres: Marsha Norman and Mary Beth Henley with Actors Theatre of Louisville; Samm Art-Williams and Charles Fuller with the Negro Ensemble Company; Tom Eyen and Rochelle Owens with La Mama ETC; David Rabe and Elizabeth Swados with the New York Shakespeare Festival Theatre. The O'Neill Center in Waterford, Connecticut, holds an annual playwright's institute for selected new playwrights to work on their scripts with the aid of professional actors, directors, and critics. All of this indicates a level of playwriting activity perhaps never seen before in the United States.

THE CHANGING AVANT-GARDE

Avant-garde (a French military term meaning "vanguard," or "being in the forefront") has been applied since the nineteenth century to advanced and experimental movements in the arts. The word implies change in art forms as well as an effort on the artist's part to become free from established tastes. In general, the *avant-garde* is associated with a wide segment of Western culture, including fauvism, cubism,

ELLEN STEWART

Ellen Stewart is the phenomenon known as La Mama. Founder of Café La Mama theatre in 1963, she has been its producer, manager, fund raiser, and guardian. Café La Mama began in a basement on 9th Street in New York City, making several moves (always just one step ahead of city housing authorities) to other locations before finding a permanent home on 4th Street in 1969.

From the beginning Ellen Stewart understood the importance of playwrights. She rang a cowbell before each performance, greeting audiences with "Welcome to La Mama; dedicated to the playwrights and all aspects of the theatre."

Stewart's hospitality attracted playwrights, actors, and directors to La Mama as a place to work and experiment. Tom Eyen, Paul Foster, Rochelle Owens, Julie Bovasso, and María Irene Fornés were some of the many writers. Of this aspect of her producing, Stewart said in an interview: "People sometimes wonder at my choice of plays. I've been criticized for choosing amateurish writing. . . . I happen to think I am right. If a script 'beeps' to me, I do it. Audiences may hate these plays but I believe in them. The only way I can explain my 'beeps' is that I'm no intellectual but my instincts tell me automatically when a playwright has something."[4]

After La Mama's first European tour in 1965, during which the group received rave notices as the "New American Theatre," New York critics took notice and foundations provided funding. On April 2, 1969, Café La Mama became La Mama ETC (Experimental Theatre Club). Since then La Mama has become a worldwide organization with branches in Bogotá, Amsterdam, Tokyo, and elsewhere, and Ellen Stewart and her theatre have become an American institution.

Right: Lighting designer Jennifer Tipton's 1981 designs for *The Catherine Wheel,* choreographed by Twyla Tharp and produced at the Winter Garden Theatre, Broadway. *The Catherine Wheel* demonstrates the lighting designer's collaboration with scenic and costume designer, choreographer, and dancers.

Opposite: Designer Ming Cho Lee's spectacular setting for the play *K2* by Patrick Meyers: a sheer ice wall representing K2, the world's second highest mountain. In the play two climbers are trapped on the icy ledge just below the summit. *K2* opened in 1982 at Arena Stage, Washington, D.C., before going to Broadway.

Right: John Conklin designed sets and costumes, including masks and puppets, for the Hartford Stage Company's 1979 production of Brecht's *Galileo.* Conklin aims for control over the theatrical space and color, and he prefers to design both scenery and costumes as crucial elements in the designer's arsenal of weapons in capturing the esssence of a theatrical piece. In *Galileo,* Conklin's giant puppets filled the theatrical space, commenting visually on the play's action and meaning.

JOANNE AKALAITIS

JoAnne Akalaitis (b. 1937) was educated at the University of Chicago where she received a B.A. in philosophy in 1960. She trained for the stage at the Actor's Workshop in San Francisco. Here in 1964 Lee Breuer, Ruth Maleczech, Philip Glass, David Warrilow, and JoAnne Akalaitis began working together within a loose coalition of artists. They continued this association in Europe from 1966 to 1969, when they formed the Mabou Mines, named for a small town in Nova Scotia. From 1970 to 1973 Mabou Mines was a resident company of La Mama ETC; since 1975 they have performed at the New York Shakespeare Festival's Public Theatre.

Akalaitis has worked as actress, designer, and director with the group and performed in all of Breuer's *Animations.* Among the productions she has directed and designed are *Cascando* (1976), an adaptation of a Beckett radio play; *Dressed Like an Egg* (1978), adapted from the writings of Colette; *Southern Exposure* (1979) and *Dead End Kids: A History of Nuclear Power* (1980), revived in 1982 to coincide with the special United Nations session on nuclear disarmament. Outside of Mabou Mines, Akalaitis has directed *Request Concert* (1981) at the Interart Theatre and *Red and Blue* (1982) at the New York Shakespeare Festival. She is at work on the film script for *Dead End Kids.*

She has won five Obie Awards for work Off Broadway, and received a Guggenheim fellowship to continue her work in experimental theatre.

dadaism, surrealism, abstract expressionism, pop art, theatre collectives, and atonal music.

The "new" theatre combines the sense of collective creation that distinguished experimental theatre from the 1950s to the mid-1970s with the personal creation of the solo performer of the 1980s. The political, social, aesthetic, and environmental struggles that forged theatrical groups with activist purposes in the sixties have largely disappeared along with many of those groups, now defunct, bankrupt, or living in exile. Others, such as the Wooster Group, Re. Cher. Chez, and Spiderwoman Theatre Workshop, have sprung up in the eighties.

What is the new direction of theatrical experiments? Who are the new faces of the 1980s? Some have conjectured that the new wave is led by the *performer* (rather than the *actor* who pretends to be someone else) whose method is the monologue. In an inflated economy, money has been a large factor in the attraction of solo performances. One-person shows naturally cost less.

A former member of Houston's Alley Theatre and New York's Performance Group, Spalding Gray's solo work dates from 1979. He composes his own pieces out of personal experiences, memories, tapes of interviews, old clothes from thrift shops, and old family photograph albums. Sitting at a table he quietly improvises in front of a small audience until his improvisations cohere into set routines. *Rumstick Road, Nayatt School,* and *Seven Scenes from a Family Album* are "rememberings"—a means of putting together in performance what the experience of living has fragmented.

There is a strong relationship between Spalding Gray's work and Lee Breuer's with the Mabou Mines. Even though the Mines is a company (Re. Cher. Chez is their new experimental studio), they also tend to personal expression in subject matter and performance style. Breuer constructs a highly personal version of his own inner world. But he uses autobiography to project the self into a *social context* for which he needs a company. Plays like *The*

Shaggy Dog Animation relate his inner and outer worlds to each other.

More recently, director JoAnne Akalaitis, one of the original founders of the Mabou Mines, has taken up social issues with *Dead End Kids: A History of Nuclear Power* (1980), a history of nuclear power from the alchemists to the cold war. By dramatizing historical and scientific facts with grotesque humor, eye-searing images and corrosive aural sounds, she has found a way to make audiences think about the unthinkable all over again.

DRAMATIC CONVENTIONS

THE COMIC REALISM OF NEIL SIMON

Neil Simon, according to *Variety*, is the most financially successful playwright in the history of the American theatre. He is also the only playwright in history to have had four plays running on Broadway at one time. He is equally successful writing film scripts, dividing his time between California and New York—Hollywood and Broadway.

Simon's early comedies deal with lovable eccentrics who are masters of the one-liner and the easy gag. Simon's main setting has remained family realism—recognizable New York apartments and hotel rooms. His plays affirm the enduring qualities of people plagued by inconsequential misunderstandings and events. The personal relationship is the source of the comic confusion: the slob living with Mr. Neat Guy; the reluctant bride who locks herself in the hotel bathroom to the distress of her parents; the middle-aged husband trying to carry on an affair.

Simon's recent plays have more serious overtones. His themes have darkened; they are now sexual infidelity, divorce, alcoholism, death. Almost mechanically, Simon sets up the decline, fall, and escape of his characters whose wisecracks cloak their anguish and hide their

NEIL SIMON

Neil Simon (b. 1927) is a playwright and producer. He began his writing career by supplying sketches for television shows: The "Phil Silvers Arrow Show," the "Garry Moore Show," the "Phil Silvers Show," and the "Sid Caesar Show." His first full-length Broadway play was *Come Blow Your Horn* in 1961. Since then he has written some 14 Broadway successes along with books for such musicals as *Sweet Charity* and *They're Playing Our Song*. His screenplays include *The Out-of-Towners*, *The Heartbreak Kid*, *Murder by Death*, *The Goodbye Girl*, and *The Cheap Detective*.

fears. In *The Sunshine Boys*, two elderly vaudeville partners who are unremittingly hostile to each other explain why they spent 43 years together. One says of the other: "As an actor, no one could touch him. As a human being, no one wanted to touch him."[5]

Simon's humor depends on our recognition of the objects of his barbed wit. His paranoid or aggressive one-liners puncture American urban society where contemporary neurosis runs rampant. In *The Prisoner of Second Avenue* (1972), the prisoner's wife, Edna, describes their expensive cell: "You live like some kind of a caged animal in a Second Avenue [New York City] zoo that's too hot in one room, too cold in another, over-charged for a growth on the side of the buildings they call a terrace that can't support a cactus plant, let alone two human beings."[6] Simon's middle-class urban audience chuckles in recognition. Still, Simon's plays have endured, not because of his clever gags, but because they end by promising their neurotic victims rosier

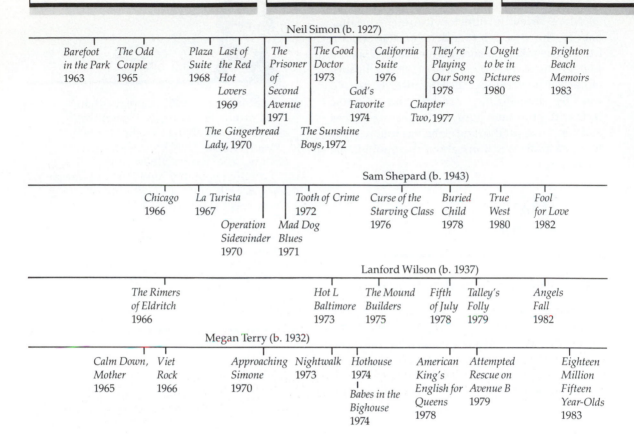

1960				1970						1980

Neil Simon (b. 1927)

| Barefoot in the Park 1963 | The Odd Couple 1965 | Plaza Suite 1968 | Last of the Red Hot Lovers 1969 | The Prisoner of Second Avenue 1971 | The Good Doctor 1973 | California Suite 1976 | They're Playing Our Song 1978 | I Ought to be in Pictures 1980 | Brighton Beach Memoirs 1983 |

God's Favorite 1974   Chapter Two, 1977

The Gingerbread Lady, 1970   The Sunshine Boys, 1972

Sam Shepard (b. 1943)

| Chicago 1966 | La Turista 1967 | Tooth of Crime 1972 | Curse of the Starving Class 1976 | Buried Child 1978 | True West 1980 | Fool for Love 1982 |

Operation Sidewinder 1970   Mad Dog Blues 1971

Lanford Wilson (b. 1937)

| The Rimers of Eldritch 1966 | Hot L Baltimore 1973 | The Mound Builders 1975 | Fifth of July 1978 | Talley's Folly 1979 | Angels Fall 1982 |

Megan Terry (b. 1932)

| Calm Down, Mother 1965 | Viet Rock 1966 | Approaching Simone 1970 | Nightwalk 1973 | Hothouse 1974 | American King's English for Queens 1978 | Attempted Rescue on Avenue B 1979 | Eighteen Million Fifteen Year-Olds 1983 |

Babes in the Bighouse 1974

futures and possible escapes. Simon's most popular comedies are *Barefoot in the Park, The Odd Couple, Plaza Suite,* and *The Sunshine Boys.*

THE BIZARRE REALISM OF SHEPARD AND MAMET

Sam Shepard and David Mamet are playwrights in their thirties. While their backgrounds are diverse, the common denominator in their work is a bizarre realism that leaves the audience uncomfortable, if not stunned, by the events they see and hear: rampant snakelike computers (Shepard's *Operation Sidewinder*), petty criminals plotting in junkshops (Mamet's *American Buffalo*), and rock musicians battling for the ratings

(Shepard's *Tooth of Crime*). In Shepard's *Buried Child,* vegetables are sliced up with malicious energy and a baby's skeleton is cradled on stage; in *American Buffalo* petty criminals plot revenge over losing five cents.

These playwrights, leaders of a third postwar generation of writers that includes Arthur Kopit, Lanford Wilson, David Rabe, John Guare, Ronald Ribman, Megan Terry, and Jean-Claude van Itallie, test the American character, family, and dreams and find them wanting. Shepard and Mamet have a distinct sensitivity to the American scene (fast-food joints), the American idiom (jive talk), and the mindless violence that has become an accepted American way of life (theft, murder, and rape). Their staged events

María Irene Fornés (b. 1930)

Tango Palace 1961	The Successful Life of 3 1965	Dr. Kheal 1968	The Curse of the Langston House 1972	Aurora 1973	Fefu and Her Friends 1977	Eyes on the Harem 1979
	Promenade 1965	Molly's Dream 1968				

Arthur Kopit (b. 1937)

Indians 1968	Wings 1978	Nine (book) 1982	End of The World 1983

Jean-Claude van Itallie (b. 1936)

America Hurrah 1966	The Serpent 1968	Nightwalk 1973	Bag Lady 1979

David Rabe (b. 1940)

The Basic Training of Pavlo Hummel 1971	In the Boom Boom Room 1973	Streamers 1976	Goose And Tom Tom 1982
Sticks and Bones 1971			

David Mamet (b. 1947)

Duck Variations 1971	Sexual Perversity in Chicago 1974	A Life in the Theatre 1977	Lakeboat 1980	Glengarry Glen Ross 1983
	American Buffalo 1975	The Water Engine 1977	Lone Canoe, 1978	
		Reunion, 1977		
		The Woods, 1977		

Ntozake Shange (b. 1948)

For Colored Girls Who Have Considered Suicide/When the Rainbow Is Enuf, 1976	Spell #7 1979	Boogie-Woogie Landscapes 1980

and use of sexually explicit language result in a bizarre realism—recognizable places and events twisted and warped by violence. Brutal or ugly images strike the ear and eye, such as Shepard's rock musicians attempting to annihilate each other with sound and Mamet's environments cluttered with the detritus of the affluent society.

THE INTERIOR MONOLOGUE

The traditions of social and psychological realism continue to dominate American drama. While dialogue has become more sexually explicit and writers deal with Black, Puerto Rican, Chicano, and feminist consciousness, dramatic conventions remain largely those of the well-made play: small casts, intensive play structure, conversational dialogue, and end-of-act crises. However, Samuel Beckett, along with stream-of-consciousness novelists, has been influential in injecting a new convention in playwriting and performance—*the interior monologue.*

Beckett's monologues and narrative voices in his novels and plays, together with his minimal staging (an old man, a table, and a tape recorder; a woman buried in a mound of sand; two lips speaking), have influenced the work of Sam Shepard, Arthur Kopit, Lee Breuer, Spalding Gray, and others. The aim of the convention is the same as in the stream-of-consciousness novel: to present the conscious and unconscious thought processes of the narrator. To take us into the character's or speaker's consciousness in the theatre, playwrights have introduced electronic amplification, sound tracks, and voice-overs. In Lee Breuer's *Shaggy Dog Animation* (1978), nine performers, sometimes with microphones, speak for Rose, the heroine. In Spalding Gray's works, film projections supplement the speaker's verbal images with visual ones. In Arthur Kopit's *Wings* (1978), as a stroke victim struggles to readapt to her broken world of hospitals, doctors, and therapists, random noises from her immediate environment are amplified through a sound system along with her disconnected thoughts and unintelligible words.

All this material, along with stage directions for achieving the aural effects, is provided by the playwright as part of the play's dramatic conventions. The text becomes as much a performance score as a piece of literature.

SAM SHEPARD

Sam Shepard (b. 1943) began his theatrical career as a bit actor. Since 1964 he has dominated avant-garde theatre in New York and London. Among his best-known plays are *Cowboys* (1964); *Chicago* (1965); *Red-Cross* and *La Turista* (1967); *Operation Sidewinder* and *The Unseen Hand* (1970); *Mad Dog Blues* (1971); *The Tooth of Crime* (1972); *Angel City* and *Curse of the Starving Class* (1976); *Buried Child* (1978); *True West* (1980); and *Fool for Love* (1982). He has also acted in such films as *Days of Heaven, Resurrection,* and *The Right Stuff.* He wrote the screenplay *Zabriskie Point* with Michelangelo Antonioni and others. Shepard has received the Obie Award eight times for distinguished playwriting and the 1979 Pulitzer Prize for *Buried Child.* He currently works with the Magic Theatre in San Francisco.

DAVID MAMET

David Mamet, born in 1947 in Chicago, worked during high school as a busboy at Second City, Chicago's famous improvisational cabaret. After several years at Goddard College in Vermont and at the Neighborhood Playhouse in New York, he returned to Chicago. *Sexual Perversity in Chicago* (1974) was produced while Mamet was teaching writing and theatre at the University of Chicago. He became the founding artistic director of Chicago's St. Nicholas Theatre Company where he worked between 1973 and 1976. His first full-length play, *American Buffalo,* was produced in Chicago in 1975 and debuted on Broadway with Robert Duvall in 1977. It was named Best Play of 1977 by the New York Drama Critics' Circle. Recent plays include *A Life in the Theatre, The Water-Engine, The Woods,* and *Lakeboat.* Since 1978 Mamet has been associate artistic director and playwright-in-residence at the Goodman Theatre in Chicago.

The moment of a stroke, even a relatively minor one, and its immediate aftermath, are an experience in chaos. Nothing at all makes sense. Nothing except perhaps this overwhelming disorientation will be remembered by the victim. The stroke usually happens suddenly. It is a catastrophe.

It is my intention that the audience recognize that some real event is occurring; that real information is being received by the victim, but that it is coming in too scrambled and too fast to be properly decoded. Systems overload.

And so this section must not seem like utter "noise," though certainly it must be more noisy than intelligible. I do not believe there is any way to be true to this material if it is not finally "composed" in rehearsal, on stage, by "feel." Theoretically, any sound or image herein described can occur anywhere in this section. The victim cannot process. Her familiar world has been rearranged. The puzzle is in pieces. All at once, and with no time to prepare, she has been picked up and dropped into another realm.

In order that this section may be put together in rehearsal (there being no one true "final order" to the images and sounds she perceives), I have divided this section into three discrete parts with the understanding that in performance these parts will blend together to form one cohesive whole.

The first group consists of the visual images Mrs. Stilson perceives.

The second group consists of those sounds emanating outside herself. Since these sounds are all filtered by her mind, and since her mind has been drastically altered, the question of whether we in the audience are hearing what is actually occurring or only hearing what she believes is occurring is unanswerable.

The third group contains Mrs. Stilson's words: the words she thinks and the words she speaks. Since we are perceiving the world through Mrs. Stilson's senses, there is no sure way for us to know whether she is actually saying any of these words aloud.

Since the experience we are exploring is not one of logic but its opposite, there is no logical reason for these groupings to occur in the order in which I have presented them. These are but components, building blocks, and can therefore be repeated, spliced, reversed, filtered, speeded up or slowed down. What should determine their final sequence and juxtaposition, tempi, intensity, is the "musical" sense of this section as a whole; it must pulse and build. An explosion quite literally is occurring in her brain, or rather, a series of explosions: the victim's mind, her sense of time and place, her sense of self, all are being shattered if not annihilated. Fortunately, finally, she will pass out. Were her head a pinball game it would register TILT—game over—stop. Silence. And resume again. Only now the victim is in yet another realm. The Catastrophe section is the journey or the fall into this strange and dreadful realm.

In the world into which Mrs. Stilson has been so violently and suddenly transposed, time and place are without definition. The distance from her old familiar world is immense. For all she knows, she could as well be on another planet.

In this new world, she moves from one space or thought or concept to another without willing or sometimes even knowing it. Indeed, when she moves in this maze-like place, it is as if the world around her and not she were doing all the moving. To her, there is nothing any more that is commonplace or predictable. Nothing is as it was. Everything comes as a surprise. Something has relieved her of command. Something beyond her comprehension has her in its grip.

Arthur Kopit, *Wings* (1978)[7]

FEMINIST PLAYS: MARÍA IRENE FORNÉS

Of the many women writing feminist plays to-day, María Irene Fornés stands out as one of the most enduring. As playwright, director, and de-signer, her plays show meticulous attention to visual and verbal detail. Slight on the surface and seemingly nonrealistic, they, nevertheless, offer a criticism of reality.

Tango Palace (1963), developed for the Actor's Workshop of San Francisco, displays her con-cern with acting rather than with plot or char-acter development. *The Successful Life of Three* (1965), created with The Open Theatre, an ex-tended pun on the eternal love triangle, deals with the sexual affinities of our culture.

Although highly praised for *Promenade, Dr. Kheal,* and *Molly's Dream, Fefu and Her Friends* placed Fornés in the mainstream of feminist writing in the seventies. First produced by the New York Theatre Strategy in 1977, and di-rected by Fornés, the play literally carries the audience along with the actresses through its several environments. Part One takes place at noon in the living room of a New England country house with the audience watching from the auditorium. Part Two occurs in the after-noon in four different environments: the lawn, the study, the bedroom, and the kitchen. The audience is divided into four groups and each group is guided into each of the four spaces. The scenes are performed simultane-ously. When one scene is completed, that part of the audience moves into the next space and the scene is performed again for the next group. Each scene is repeated four times until each group has seen all four scenes. Part Three takes place in the evening in the living room with the entire audience again watching from the auditorium.

Although this use of audience participation is a holdover from the environmental practices of the sixties, the play's concerns, centering upon the women's relationships and the envi-

MARÍA IRENE FORNÉS

María Irene Fornés (b. 1930) was born in Havana, Cuba. A member of New York's Theatre Strategy since 1972 (and its presi-dent since 1973), she has been a promi-nent figure in the Off-Broadway theatre since the mid-sixties and has worked with some of the foremost experimental theatres in the country, including the Fire-house Theatre, Washington Square Church, Theatre Genesis, Judson Church, the Open Theatre, and La Mama ETC. Of some 15 plays, the best known are *The Successful Life of Three* (1965), *Promenade* (1965), *Dr. Kheal* (1968), and *Fefu and Her Friends* (1977). She has directed many of the original productions herself and de-signed the environments for them. Fornés has received numerous grants from the John Jay Whitney Foundation, Yale Uni-versity, the Rockefeller Foundation, and the Guggenheim Foundation. She has been the recipient of Obie awards for *The Suc-cessful Life of Three, Promenade,* and *Eyes on the Harem.* Her early plays are collected in a volume entitled *Promenade and Other Plays* (1971).

ronments where they live out their lives, are current.

The actual event of the play is the gathering of seven women in Fefu's house. Aside from the hostess, Fefu (married to Philip who never ap-pears), there is Julia in her wheelchair, the pair Christina and Cindy, histrionic Emma, ex-lovers Paula and Cecilia, and Sue, who is the least in-dividualized of the women. Fefu has been toying with a shotgun before the guests arrive. The

Figure 15-5 María Irene Fornés' *Fefu and Her Friends*, at the American Place Theatre, New York, 1978.

" The play is about women. It's a play that deals with each one of these women with enormous tenderness and affection. I have not deliberately attempted to see these women 'as women have rarely been seen before.' I show the women as I see them and if it is different from the way they've been seen before, it's because that's how I see them .The play is not fighting anything, not negating anything. My intention has not been to confront anything. I felt as I wrote the play that I was surrounded by friends. I felt very happy to have such good and interesting friends. "

María Irene Fornés,
Women in American Theatre (1981)[8]

women appear. They have come together to organize a meeting to raise funds for supporting art as a learning tool. After the meeting, where they have rehearsed what they are going to say and wear, a few women go into the kitchen ostensibly to make coffee. There, like children, they engage in a water fight. At one point the handicapped Julia suddenly "walks" into the living room to get coffee. Soon Fefu taunts Julia with her psychosomatic illness. Interrupted in her tirade by one of the women, Fefu takes the gun outside. A shot is heard and Julia bleeds from the forehead. Fefu comes in with a dead rabbit, stands behind the bleeding Julia, and speaks the play's closing lines: "I killed it . . . I just shot . . . and killed it . . . Julia."[9]

Julia, wounded in body and spirit, represents

In the bedroom Julia lies on a mattress on the floor. There is a sink on the wall. There are dry leaves on the floor although it is not the fall season of the year. The sheets are linen and Julia wears a white hospital gown. Julia hallucinates in a still and luminous sort of way. This speech is the play's centerpiece, pointing out that women's minds, like their bodies, are made to suffer until they become cripples.

Julia The human being is of the masculine gender. The human being is a boy as a child and grown up he is a man. Everything on earth is for the human being, which is man. To nourish him.—There are evil things on earth for man also. For him to fight with, and conquer and turn its evil into good. So that it too can nourish him. There are Evil Plants, Evil Animals, Evil Minerals, and Women are Evil.—Woman is not a human being. She is: 1-A mystery. 2-Another species. 3-As yet undefined. 4-Unpredictable; therefore wicked and gentle and evil and good which is evil. If a man commits an evil act, he must be pitied. The evil comes from outside him, through him and into the act. Woman generates the evil herself. God gave man no other mate but woman. The oxen is good but it is not a mate for man. The sheep is good but it is not a mate for man. The mate for man is woman and that is the cross man must bear. Man is not spiritually sexual, he therefore can enjoy sexuality. His sexuality is physical which means his spirit is pure. Women's spirit is sexual. That is why after coitus they dwell in nefarious feelings. Because that is their natural habitat. That is why it is difficult for them to return to the human world. Their sexual feelings remain with them till they die. And they take those feelings with them to the afterlife where they corrupt the heavens, and they are sent to hell where through suffering they may shed those feelings and return to earth as man.[10]

everything that Fefu and the other women have had to fight against to maintain their equilibrium in a male-dominated society. Julia's wheelchair is the chief symbol of society's maiming of its women. Her symbolic death underscores Fefu's strength and tenacity. Fefu's ability to kill "it" also points up Fornés' consistent theme throughout her plays: the triumph of the irrational in the lives of women. We see their helplessness, their childishness, their sexual feelings, their displaced anger; we hear of their violations and their feelings of purposelessness.

Feminist writers of the seventies, like Martha Boesing, Adrienne Kennedy, Ntozake Shange, Adele Shank, Marsha Norman, and Wendy Wasserstein, take up the problems of women who have learned to see themselves as commodities and as vessels of male pleasure and caprice. Some of the plays are aggressively strident, others compassionate. All are concerned with exploring basic feminist issues, usually with universal female characters, and with raising audience consciousness.

Fornés writes: "And if they [women] shall recognize each other, the world will be blown apart."[11]

REPRESENTATIVE PLAY

Buried Child
First presented at the Magic Theatre, San Francisco, in 1978 and Off Broadway at the Theatre de Lys in the 1978–1979 season; directed by Robert Woodruff

BACKGROUND

Sam Shepard first attracted critical attention in 1963 with Off-Broadway productions at Theatre Genesis of *Cowboys* and *Rock Garden*. His first full-length play, *La Turista* (1967), presented at the American Place Theatre, won an Obie Award. Since then his plays have been produced at Lincoln Center, Princeton and Yale universities, the Performing Garage, La Mama ETC, the Magic Theatre, the Open Theatre, the American Place Theatre, the Public Theatre, and the Royal Court (London).

Several things distinguish Shepard as a playwright. While he is a well-known and respected name in theatre circles, he has never been produced on Broadway. A prolific writer, he is a persistent social critic of the American scene. His major plays—*The Tooth of Crime, Operation Sidewinder, Buried Child,* and *The Curse of the Starving Class*—expose the dry rot that has undermined the faith and commitment of Americans to the triple pillars of society—God, family, and country. Shepard's style is eclectic, varying from surrealistic to naturalistic and containing a mixture of wild humor, explosive violence, and harrowing revelation. His stage images are unsettling.

Shepard's background is important in understanding his two major themes: "identity" and "roots." Born in the Midwest, he grew up in California where rootlessness is a way of life. At the same time California in its Los Angeles aspect is the place that most visibly embodies the values of the American dream: overnight success, stardom, fame, personality cults, and a prefabricated culture. The term for Hollywood, "tinsel town," accurately conveys the culture's glitter and emptiness, its lack of roots and lasting values.

THE SCENE

Written in three acts, *Buried Child* takes place in the midwestern living room of Dodge and Halie's home. Shepard's stage directions describe a room with tattered sofa, faded shade on a single floor lamp, night table littered with pill bottles, and an old-fashioned television set flickering blue light but with no image or sound. A wooden staircase covered with frayed carpet leads off stage left. Upstage is a large screened-in porch beyond which are dark elm trees.

This is a scene of illness, incest, adultery, personal violation, and spiritual emptiness. The American values of family, religion, and brotherhood have decayed along with Dodge and Halie's relationship with each other and with their children, Tilden and Bradley, and their grandson, Vincent. The grown children of this marriage are maimed: Bradley is an amputee; Tilden is a functional illiterate. Vincent, Tilden's son, is a displaced person wandering throughout the West with his girlfriend, Shelly.

Although when she first enters the house, Shelly describes the scene as something like "a Norman Rockwell cover," she has got it wrong. Rockwell's *Saturday Evening Post* covers pictured bright-cheeked, chubby children with their warm and loving gray-haired grandparents—all smiling in well-fed, well-clothed benevolence. In contrast Shepard's scene is more like something out of painter Edward Hopper's portfolio of America as an empty, sterile wasteland of decayed houses, red and white gasoline stations and yellowing motel rooms with garish neon signs.

The modern palliatives, religion and drugs, are not efficacious here. Only whiskey, sex, and routine chores seem to make Shepard's characters feel the emptiness less.

Figure 15-6 This midwestern farm house is reminiscent of the house in
Buried Child. (*Farm Boy,* Archie Lieberman, 1974.)

THE ACTION

Vincent's *quest* for his roots (and identity) is the play's central action. In *Buried Child* Shepard is writing within the mainstream of Western drama from *Oedipus the King* to *Who's Afraid of Virginia Woolf?* The grandson returns to his family and finds out who he is in the play's harrowing climax.

Shelly, the Californian, is also without roots. Asked where she comes from she replies, "Originally?" She is "originally" from Los Angeles. She makes fun of the traditional-looking house and shouts with laughter when Vince calls softly for his "grandma." When Dodge fails to recognize his grandson, Shelly asks if Vince has got the wrong address. Vince answers, "It's not the wrong address! I recognize the yard."

The action of *Buried Child* reveals the rottenness at the heart of the American family. Dodge, the father, is dying, hastening the process with whiskey and cigarettes. The former all-American fullback, Tilden, is a jailbird. Another son, Ansel, has been slain sometime ago in a Mafia-style killing. The mother, Halie, carries on an adulterous affair with the local Protestant minister, Father Dewis, and flaunts their relationship in front of husband and sons. Into this scene arrives the grandson in search of his roots. What he discovers about his origins are bigotry (Ansel would "still be alive today if he hadn't married into the Catholics"), hypocrisy (the clergy as seducer), adultery (Halie's affair), absence of a work ethic (Dodge's farm hasn't been worked in years), incest and child murder (a baby's corpse is secretly buried in the backyard).

As the family's terrible secret is revealed, we are symbolically shown the decayed fiber of the American family. Tilden's remarkable ceremony of laying corn shucks on his father's sleeping body is a gentle gesture, offset by Bradley's malicious shaving of Dodge's head while his father is sleeping. Both the gentle and violent gestures point up the play's moral ambivalence. The family has been engaged for years in covering up the murder of a baby born to Halie and Tilden and later drowned by Dodge and buried in the back yard. The revelation of

Figure 15-7 *Buried Child,* Theatre de Lys, New York, 1978. (a) Bradley (Jay Sanders, stage left) is threatened with his own artificial leg by Christopher McCann. Shelly (Mary McDonnell) looks on. (b) Dodge (Richard Hamilton) collapses among the carrot tops as Tilden (Tom Noonan) and Shelly (Mary McDonnell) watch.

the secret crime cleanses, like the spring rain. At this moment Dodge dies and Vince settles down on the sofa to assume his inheritance.

With Dodge's confession and death, the family's guilt is exorcised. Halie can now "see" what was not visible to her before—the corn, carrots, potatoes, and peas growing in the mysterious field behind the house. Tilden, who has seen it much earlier because he knows the truth, unearths the child's corpse and carries it upstairs to Halie's bedroom—where it was conceived. This fantastic field, according to critic Richard Gilman, is a metaphor for fecundity and at the same time a hope for the future against bitter hidden truths.[12]

CHARACTER

Shepard's characters are all searching out their personal histories, which might explain who they are and how they came to be that way. In *Buried Child* it is Vince's search.

The lives of Shepard's characters are filled with incidents of murder, adultery, incest, mutilation. The past, once so promising, is filled with horror: one son killed in a gangland murder; the baby drowned; another son maimed in a chain-saw accident. Without the normal touchstones of love, family, and friendship, Shepard's characters live in a world that is indifferent to their betrayal, guilt, and violence.

Nevertheless, there is always a seeker among Shepard's marginal characters; here it is Vince. Vince discovers that his family does not know him. They are locked together in mutual dependence, caring for the sick and looking after the physically and psychologically lame. But these are surface gestures; beyond this they do not care. Angry and ineffectual, they assert themselves in the present, for the past has too many hidden meanings and there is no future. Looking at a photo from his youth, Dodge insists: "That isn't me! That never was me! This is me. This is it. The whole shootin' match."[13]

LANGUAGE

In *Buried Child* figures of everyday speech—the bromides, exclamations, and metaphors of middle-class American life—are arranged in such a way that they take on a fresh, almost frantic, meaning. Characters reach moments of bafflement and mutual understanding without ever abandoning the flat tones of ordinary conversation.

The play opens with a monologue (a solo speech) spoken offstage by Halie. She talks on and on about the weather and the state of Dodge's health while we look at Dodge lying on the living room sofa coughing away his life. Their relationship is as empty as the stark room and the imageless and soundless television screen. But the solo speech is significant in the development of Shepard's work. The three solo speeches in *Buried Child* (the remaining two belong to Dodge and to Vince) signal a shift in emphasis away from characters who are obsessive and self-absorbed to characters who are reaching out, however tentatively, to establish relationships.

Like many contemporary playwrights, Shep-

ard is master of the unexpected stage metaphor: an enormous number of vegetables dumped in the middle of the stage, a freestanding artificial leg, and a baby's mud-covered skeleton carried onstage. Tilden enters with an armful of unshucked corn. After he shucks it he gently spreads the husks across the sleeping body of his father. He repeats this ceremony until the floor is clean of corn husks and Dodge is completely covered by them. The symbolism is vivid. Dodge is a husk of his former self emptied by age, sickness, and guilt of his potency and usefulness. He no longer farms the land, but rather remains indoors isolated from the soil that holds his crime. Another symbol of impotence is Bradley's artificial leg, which he takes off while he sleeps and stands in one corner of the room.

SHEPARD'S POSTMODERNISM

Shepard's vision of America's myths and rituals, of dreams of power and of family love, of modern drift and disconnection, is sharply projected in *Buried Child*. Although personal, his vision is, nevertheless, accessible to anyone familiar with Western drama's tradition of a hero's quest to discover identity and meaning.

Shepard's scene in *Buried Child* is the American Midwest, but these midwesterners of the 1970s are out of touch with the soil, once the quintessential sign of America's work ethic and its psychic vitality. The American dreams of familial love, personal integrity, and success achieved by hard work have been replaced by the reality of disease, betrayal, and death. Nevertheless, Shepard admits of the possibility of reviving those dreams and values in a postmodern world. As Dodge goes gently into death after the harrowing revelation of his murder of the unwanted child, the back yard springs into growth with a life-sustaining abundance, establishing the old agrarian rhythm of birth, death, and rebirth. The American soil may be a sterile wasteland because of the degeneration of American character and values, but both are capable of renewal.

Postmodernism is a word frequently heard in discussions of new architecture, art, dance, design, music, and theatre. The word implies that modernism no longer exists and that a long history of artistic achievement has come to a halt. The thrust of postmodernism has been to add to art forms what has formerly been kept out: story telling, deliberate incongruity, and aesthetic bad manners. It has thrived on ground that modernism once ruled off limits—insult, images steeped in kitsch, triviality—but is also marked by energy, independence, and freedom from intimidation. The artist Paul Klee once said, "the artist should make art as if no one had ever made it before." Add to this rambunctiousness and irreverence and you have a good sense of the postmodern. Many of Sam Shepard's plays and the work of the Mabou Mines fall into the postmodern category.

ESSAY

The American theatre has found a new home in the resident, not-for-profit theatres across the country, which have encouraged new playwrights and produced their plays. Among resident theatres that have been particularly hospitable to the avant-garde is Joseph Papp's Public Theatre, which has reserved space on its second stage for the work of groups like the Mabou Mines. *The Shaggy Dog Animation* at the Public is representative of many of the new theatrical techniques and conventions: the staging of personal histories, social fables, stream-of-consciousness techniques, and satirical portraits of American pop culture.

The Mabou Mines in Performance
Lee Breuer's *Shaggy Dog Animation* at the Public Theatre (1978)

Lee Breuer wrote three animations (*The Red Horse, The B. Beaver,* and *The Shaggy Dog*) in the period 1968–1978 when he was artistic director of the Mabou Mines. The first two animations were originally performed at La Mama Experimental Theatre Club and *Shaggy Dog* at the Public.

Animations, as we know from early Walt Disney, are filmed cartoons in which animals talk and take on human personalities. Breuer adapted the idea to the theatre. Animals, instead of people, are the principal characters. Drawing on a rich and popular tradition of beast fables ranging from the medieval *Reynard the Fox* to Disney's lovable *Bambi*, Breuer creates his own fables of contemporary life and manners, showing us how people function as social "animals."

Breuer chooses his animals with care. The natural activities of each animal's life, whether horse, beaver, or dog, coincide with human modes of feeling and perception. For example, the horse evokes feelings of untamed power, the beaver builds defenses, and the dog exists in a master-slave relationship. All are metaphors for certain human intellectual and emotional positions.[14]

However, as with many of the new experimentalists, the source of Breuer's material is himself. The animals are Breuer's "mask"—a way of distancing himself from his material. Like storytellers of old, the animals tell their personal histories. They delight in word play—verbal and visual puns—but they do not engage in traditional stage dialogue.

Breuer disregards the conventional uses of plot, dialogue, setting, time, and character in favor of an open-ended form. The texts are even printed in capital letters. The idea of life passages which Gail Sheehy and other writers have made fashionable is substituted for plot; monologue for dialogue; personal space for setting.

LEE BREUER

Lee Breuer (b. 1937) was one of the founders of the Mabou Mines Ensemble. Breuer got his start in theatre with the San Francisco Actor's Workshop and in 1963 began his own experimental company. He spent five years in Europe (1965–1970), studying the work of the Berliner Ensemble in East Germany and Jerzy Grotowski in Poland. He directed *Mother Courage and Her Children* in Paris; Brecht's *Messingkauf Dialogues* at the Edinburgh Festival; and Beckett's *Play* in Paris. In 1970 he brought the company of *Play* to New York as the Mabou Mines and worked as their artistic director until the group adopted a collaborative directorship in 1976.

In addition to writing the company's three animations, Breuer has directed other Mines productions and worked with other companies: *Mabou Mines Performs Samuel Beckett* (1975), which included his own adaptation of *The Lost Ones*; *A Prelude to Death in Venice* (1980) and *The Saint and the Football Players*, which he also choreographed, for the American Dance Festival; Genet's *The Screens* (1980) and Shakespeare's *The Tempest* (1981) for the New York Shakespeare Festival. He has taught at New York University, the Yale Drama School, and the University of California. At present he is artistic director of Re. Cher. Chez, the Mabou Mines' studio for the experimental performing arts.

Memory controls dramatic time, and a chorus of nine actors takes the place of individual characters in conflict. However, Breuer's chorus, unlike the Greek chorus that gives information and emotional responses to events taking place before it, serves as an individual voice.

As in the Oriental theatre, the voice is sep-arated from the character. Actors take turns enacting events from the animal's life rather than imitating them, helped by electronic music, films, photographs, puppets, sculpted space, and kinetic movement. What is remarkable is Breuer's ability to accommodate the most experimental styles of art with theatre history and literary tradition in a form derived from Walt Disney cartoons.[15]

In *The Shaggy Dog Animation* the narrative voice belongs to a dog named Rose, visualized as a human puppet. The cast of characters also includes another dog (Broadway), a rabbit (Bunny), and two humans (John and Leslie). They appear in what are essentially a series of soap opera adventures that take place in California, Las Vegas, and New York.

Shaggy Dog is a love story of Rose and John, dog and master, woman and man. The animation follows an almost classical narrative line: Our heroine comes to know the truth about herself by going through a series of meaningful experiences. Rose the dog (read also person), chained in an emotional relationship with her master, finds a new freedom. She develops a feminist consciousness. As the story progresses it makes fun of the traditions of Western love; it mocks love's illusions, pain, sentimentality, and silliness. But it also acknowledges its ecstasy.

Shaggy Dog is slick, stylish, and controlled by sound and light technicians. The glossy setting (illuminated sound track dial as background, shaggy white carpeting, and chrome-plated dollhouse furniture) is decorated with the gadgetry of a technological society. Rose refers to her "Hobart 700 Speed Queen Dishwasher with pot-scrubbing action." This love story for the electronic age is based on the clichés of romance filtered through the language and sounds of the mass media—disc jockeys, movies, sound tracks, popular songs, and other elements of our pop culture.

Rose (played by Linda Wolfe's handsomely sculpted puppet) is a puppet, dog, woman, and artist. Hers is the narrative voice speaking to John, the dog's owner and the woman's lover;

Figure 15-8 *Shaggy Dog Animation*, 1978. JoAnne Akalaitis and Linda Hartinian sing Rose the Puppet's thoughts as she reads in her high-tech john.

she reflects on their relationship which ended three years ago (21 years in a dog's life). The Prologue is a kind of radio play—a shaggy dog story—performed before an illuminated radio dial. In Part I ("the mechanism of attachment"), Rose recalls the high points of her love affair. In Part II ("the wages of attachment"), Rose and John break up. The voice sings: "GOODBYE. DEAR. I SAID. AND SANK INTO THE NIGHT LIKE A PIECE OF BACON IN A BOWL OF SPLIT PEA SOUP. . . ."[16] Sick with grief, Rose overeats, throws temper tantrums when John is with his new girlfriend, takes a new lover. She does everything humans do to compensate for a broken heart.

By the end of Part II Rose no longer needs John (she has worked through her grief); she leaves him on a New York street at four o'clock in the morning when they are out for a "walk." Rose is now liberated and it is John's turn to suffer.

Part III (a "Dear John" letter) takes place three years later. John is now a puppet himself, both literally and figuratively. He simultaneously dials "John's Anonymous" and a girlfriend. Their positions are reversed and John is into "self-pity," the modern panacea for all ills. The play ends with a voice on the sound track singing Rose's thoughts, conveying one final time the clichés of a love relationship.

Figure 15-9 *Shaggy Dog Animation,* 1978. Bill Raymond with John the Puppet as he telephones "John's Anonymous" and a girlfriend.

I HEAR YOU KNOCKING. BUT YOU CAN'T COME IN. SING ME A CHORUS OF CHERRY PIE. WRONG LIFE BABY. NEXT TIME. MAYBE. I TELL YOU THE TRUTH. ONLY SLEEPING DOGS LIE.[17]

As a writer Breuer is a social critic. He recycles the clichés (the junk) of our popular culture and makes us see and hear it for what it is: a parody of ourselves. But, like Sam Shepard, Lee Breuer is also an optimist. He believes that, like Rose, we can liberate ourselves from false value systems and relationships and become authentic individuals.

SUMMARY

The current American theatre is an amalgam of professional, not-for-profit, alternative, and amateur theatre. New York City (Broadway in particular) remains the nexus of professional, commercial activity. However, in the past two decades the resident theatre movement has created a network of professional, nonprofit theatres within our major cities. Moreover, "people's" theatres dedicated to the social and political concerns of ethnic groups have absorbed the artistic energies of many of our younger theatre artists.

In New York Off-Broadway and Off-Off-Broadway theatres sprang up in the sixties as alternatives to the high cost of producing on Broadway and to the limited types of shows produced there. Joseph Papp's New York Shakespeare Festival theatres—the Delacorte and the Public—are among the most successful. Ethnic theatres have also emerged as part of the alternative theatre movement. Black, Chicano, and Puerto Rican groups have as their artistic and political goals the raising of our consciousness about minority issues. In the early seventies feminist theatres devoted to women's concerns joined other alternative groups in producing plays dealing with specific artistic and social issues.

The growth of the resident and experimental theatre movement was made possible in the sixties by grants from foundations and from the National Endowment for the Arts, established by Congress in 1965. However, almost 20 years later, the United States, unlike European nations, has still not developed a coherent national arts policy underpinned by a philosophy of subsidy.

Since the mid-seventies the direction of the theatrical avant-garde has shifted from the collectives to the solo performer creating a text out of his or her life experiences. The solo work of Spalding Gray is an example of this trend. The Mabou Mines company also adheres to highly personal expression in their subject matter and performance style.

While Neil Simon's plays, large-scale musicals, British imports, and tried-and-true revivals sustain the Broadway theatre, in the last decade there has been a resurgence of playwriting among all groups. Part of the reason lies in the devotion of such entrepreneurs as Joseph Papp, Ellen Stewart, and Douglas Turner Ward to new scripts and writers. One interesting outcome of the resident theatre movement has been the discovery that there is a large audience across the United States for new plays and that many of these have commercial potential. Never before in the history of the American theatre have so many new plays been produced by so many producing groups. The names of some of the new American playwrights are Megan Terry, Lanford Wilson, Arthur Kopit, Jean-Claude van Itallie, Sam Shepard, David Rabe, David Mamet, Ntozake Shange, María Irene Fornés, Mary Beth Henley, and Christopher Durang.

For the past 25 years the New York Shakespeare Festival theatres under the aegis of producer Joseph Papp have been instrumental in shaping contemporary American theatre. The Public Theatre, the Off-Off Broadway wing of the Festival, is our representative theatre in this chapter because it has served so long as a model for other nonprofit groups. Papp's successes with new plays, some of them commercial hits, and experimental artists and groups make the Public Theatre unique in our time.

Sam Shepard's Pulitzer Prize-winning play *Buried Child* and *The Shaggy Dog Animation* by the Mabou Mines company at the Public Theatre let us survey trends in playwriting and performance techniques in the nonprofit theatres. Shepard and the Mabou Mines share a unique vision of American society and they express this vision with diverse theatrical means.

The American theatre, like the country, is complex, diverse, and multicultural. While we can only conjecture about the theatrical scene of the late 1980s, the patterns we see today probably will continue to be influential: financial retrenchment, the conservatism of Broadway producers, artists at work in different media, experimentation of small groups and solo performers, and the nurturing of new playwrights.

PLAYS TO READ

American Buffalo by David Mamet
Buried Child by Sam Shepard

Wings by Arthur Kopit

Fefu and Her Friends by María Irene Fornés

SOURCES

Fornés, María Irene. *Fefu and Her Friends*. New York: Performing Arts Journal Publications, 1980. Paperback. *Fefu and Her Friends* is reprinted in *Word Plays: An Anthology of New American Drama*. New York: Performing Arts Journal Publications, 1980. Paperback. The anthology also contains *Domino Courts* by William Hauptman, *The Vienna Notes* by Richard Nelson, *Boy on the Straight-Back Chair* by Ronald Tavel, *Naropa* by Jean-Claude van Itallie, and *Starluster* by John Wellman.

Kopit, Arthur. *Wings*. New York: Hill and Wang, 1978. Paperback. *Wings* has a preface by the playwright describing the genesis of the play. Shortly after his commission in 1976 to write a radio play for the drama project of National Public Radio, Kopit's father suffered a major stroke, which rendered him incapable of speech. This experience became the material for the radio play and the stage version of *Wings*.

Mamet, David. *American Buffalo*. New York: Grove, 1977. Paperback.

Shepard, Sam. *Buried Child*. New York: Urizen, 1979. Paperback. This edition contains an introduction by playwright Jack Richardson and two other plays by Shepard: *Seduced* and *Suicide in B♭*. Also in *Sam Shepard: Seven Plays*. New York: Bantam Books, 1981. Paperback. This edition has an introduction by critic Richard Gilman and includes the plays *True West, Curse of the Starving Class, The Tooth of Crime, La Turista, Tongues*, and *Savage/Love*.

NOTES

1. Martin Gottfried, *A Theatre Divided: The Postwar American Stage* (Boston: Little, Brown, 1967), pp. 27–28.

2. George Goodman, "Black Theater: Must It Appeal to Whites?" *New York Times*, January 10, 1982, pt. 2, p. 1. Copyright © 1982 The New York Times Company. Reprinted by permission.

3. John Harrop, "The Agitprop Pilgrimage of Luis Valdez and El Teatro Campesino," *Theatre Quarterly*, 5, No. 17 (1975), 32–35. Reprinted by permission of *Theatre Quarterly*.

4. "Mother Is at Home at La Mama," *New York Times*, March 30, 1969, pt. 2, p. 5. Copyright © 1969 The New York Times Company. Reprinted by permission.

5. Neil Simon, *The Sunshine Boys* (New York: Random House, 1973), p. 23. Reprinted by permission of Random House.

6. Neil Simon, *The Prisoner of Second Avenue* (New York: Random House, 1972), p. 15. Reprinted by permission of Random House.

7. Arthur Kopit, *Wings* (New York: Hill and Wang, 1978), pp. 9–10. Reprinted by permission of Hill and Wang, a division of Farrar, Straus and Giroux, Inc. Excerpt from *Wings* by Arthur Kopit, copyright © 1978 by Arthur Kopit.

8. Beverley B. Pevitts, "Fefu and Her Friends," in *Women in American Theatre: Careers, Images, Movements: An Illustrated Anthology and Sourcebook*, eds. Helen K. Chinoy and Linda W. Jenkins (New York: Crown, 1981), pp. 319–320. Copyright © 1981 by Helen Krich Chinoy and Linda Walsh Jenkins. Reprinted by permission of Crown Publishers. Inc.

9. María Irene Fornés, *Fefu and Her Friends* in *Word Plays: New American Drama* (New York: Performing Arts Journal Publications, 1980), p. 41. Reprinted by permission of Performing Arts Journal Publications.

10. Fornés, *Fefu and Her Friends* in *Word Plays*, p. 25. Reprinted by permission.

11. Pevitts, "Fefu and Her Friends," in *Women in American Theatre*, p. 316. Reprinted by permission.

12. Richard Gilman, "Introduction," in *Sam Shepard: Seven Plays* (New York: Bantam, 1981), pp. xxiv–xxv.

13. Sam Shepard, *Buried Child* (New York: Urizen, 1979), p. 54.

14. For a discussion of Breuer's three animations, along with the texts, see Bonnie Marranca and Gautam Dasgupta, eds., *Animations: A Trilogy for Mabou Mines*, intro. Bonnie Marranca (New York: Performing Arts Journal Publications, 1979).

15. Marranca, *Animations*, p. 13.

16. Lee Breuer, *The Shaggy Dog Animation* in *Animations* (New York: Performing Arts Journal Publications, 1979), p. 130. Reprinted by permission of Performing Arts Journal Publications.

17. Breuer, *The Shaggy Dog Animation* in *Animations*, p. 154. Reprinted by permission.

SUGGESTED READINGS

CHAPTER 1

Brockett, Oscar G. "The Humanities: Theatre History." *Southern Speech Communication Journal* 41 (Winter 1976), 142–150.

Brook, Peter. *The Empty Space.* New York: Avon, 1969.

Cole, David. *The Theatrical Event: A Mythos, A Vocabulary, A Perspective.* Middletown, Conn.: Wesleyan University Press, 1975.

Esslin, Martin. *The Anatomy of Drama.* New York: Hill and Wang, 1977.

Goffman, Erving. *The Presentation of Self in Everyday Life.* Garden City, N.Y.: Doubleday, 1959.

Huizinga, Johan. *Homo Ludens: A Study of the Play Element in Culture.* Boston: Beacon, 1955.

Hunningher, Benjamin. *The Origin of the Theater.* New York: Hill and Wang, 1961.

Innes, Christopher. *Holy Theatre, Ritual and the Avantgarde.* London: Cambridge University Press, 1982.

Kirby, E.T. *Ur-Drama: The Origins of Theatre.* New York: New York University Press, 1975.

Piaget, Jean. *Play, Dreams, and Imitation in Childhood.* Translated by C. Gattegno and F.M. Hodgson. New York: Norton, 1962.

Southern, Richard. *The Seven Ages of the Theatre.* New York: Hill and Wang, 1961.

Turner, Victor. *From Ritual to Theatre: The Human Seriousness of Play.* New York: Performing Arts Journal Publications, 1982.

CHAPTER 2

Beckerman, Bernard. *Dynamics of Drama: Theory and Method of Analysis.* New York: Alfred A. Knopf, 1970.

Bentley, Eric. *The Life of the Drama.* New York: Atheneum, 1964.

Goldman, Michael. *The Actor's Freedom: Toward a Theory of Drama.* New York: Viking, 1975.

Langer, Susanne K. *Feeling and Form: A Theory of Art.* New York: Scribner's, 1953.

Marranca, Bonnie, ed. *Theatre of Images.* New York: Drama Book Specialists, 1977.

Nichol, Allardyce. *The Theory of Drama.* New York: Crowell, 1931.

Schechner, Richard. *Public Domain: Essays on the Theatre.* Chicago: Bobbs-Merrill, 1969.

Styan, J.L. *Drama, Stage, and Audience.* London: Cambridge University Press, 1975.

————. *The Elements of Drama.* London: Cambridge University Press, 1960.

CHAPTER 3

Historian Arthur W. Pickard-Cambridge is considered the principal authority on the fifth-century Greek theatre. His monumental works on the period are as follows: *Dithyramb, Tragedy, and Comedy* (1962), 2nd ed., rev. T.B.L. Webster; *The Dramatic Festivals of Athens* (1968), 2nd ed., rev. John Gould and D.M. Lewis; and *The Theatre of Dionysus in Athens* (1946), all published by Oxford University Press in London.

Arnott, Peter D. *The Ancient Greek and Roman Theatre.* New York: Random House, 1971.

Bieber, Margarete. *The History of the Greek and Roman Theatre.* 2nd ed. Princeton, N.J.: Princeton University Press, 1961.

Butler, James H. *The Theatre and Drama of Greece and Rome.* San Francisco: Chandler, 1972.

Duckworth, George E. *The Nature of Roman Comedy.* Princeton, N.J.: Princeton University Press, 1952.

Else, Gerald F. *The Origin and Early Form of Greek Tragedy.* Cambridge, Mass.: Harvard University Press, 1965.

Kitto, H.D.F. *Greek Tragedy: A Literary Study.* London: Oxford University Press, 1950.

Kott, Jan. *The Eating of the Gods: An Interpretation of Greek Tragedy.* Translated by Boleslaw Taborski and Edwa Czerwinski. New York: Random House, 1973.

Webster, T.B.L. *Greek Theatre Production.* 2nd ed. London: Methuen, 1970.

CHAPTER 4

The standard source on medieval theatre is Edmund K. Chambers, *The Medieval Stage* (1903), 2 vols., published by the Clarendon Press in Oxford.

Brooke, Iris. *Medieval Theatre Costume.* New York: Theatre Arts, 1968.

Craig, Hardin. *English Religious Drama of the Middle Ages.* New York: Oxford University Press, 1955.

Huizinga, Johan. *The Waning of the Middle Ages: A Study of the Forms of Life, Thought and Art in France and the Netherlands in the Dawn of the Renaissance.* New York: St. Martin's, 1949.

Nelson, Alan H. *The Medieval English Stage: Corpus Christi, Pageants and Plays.* Chicago: University of Chicago Press, 1974.

Potter, Robert. *The English Morality Play: Origins, History and Influence of a Dramatic Tradition.* London: Routledge & Kegan Paul, 1975.

Southern, Richard. *The Medieval Theatre in the Round.* London: Faber & Faber, 1957.

Tuchmann, Barbara W. *A Distant Mirror: The Calamitous Fourteenth Century.* New York: Alfred A. Knopf, 1978.

Wickham, Glynne. *Early English Stages, 1300–1660.* 2 vols. New York: Columbia University Press, 1959–72.

————. *The Medieval Theatre.* New York: St. Martin's, 1974.

Woolf, Rosemary. *The English Mystery Play.* Berkeley: University of California Press, 1972.

CHAPTER 5

There are two standard sources tracing the history of the English stage for this period. They are Edmund K. Chambers, *The Elizabethan Stage* (1923), 4 vols., and Gerald E. Bentley, *The Jacobean and Caroline Stage* (1941–1968), 7 vols., both published by Oxford University Press in London.

Beckerman, Bernard. *Shakespeare at the Globe 1599–1609.* New York: Macmillan, 1962.

Berry, Ralph. *On Directing Shakespeare: Interviews with Contemporary Directors.* New York: Barnes & Noble, 1977.

Campbell, Lily Bess. *Scenes and Machines on the English Stage During the Renaissance.* London: Cambridge University Press, 1923. Reprinted, New York: Barnes & Noble, 1960.

Harbage, Alfred. *Shakespeare's Audience.* New York: Columbia University Press, 1941.

Hodges, C. Walter. *The Globe Restored.* Rev. ed. New York: Oxford University Press, 1968.

Kott, Jan. *Shakespeare Our Contemporary.* Translated by Boleslaw Taborski. New York: Doubleday, 1964.

Shakespeare Survey: An Annual Review of Shakespearean Study and Production. New York: Macmillan, 1948–present.

CHAPTER 6

The best source book on *commedia dell'arte* is by Pierre Louis Duchartre, *The Italian Comedy: The*

Improvisation Scenarios Loves Attributes Portraits and Masks of the Illustrious Characters of the Commedia dell'Arte, translated by Randolph T. Weaver (New York: Dover, 1966).

Herrick, Marvin I. *Italian Comedy in the Renaissance.* Urbana, Ill.: University of Illinois Press, 1960.

Kahan, Gerald. *Jacques Callot: Artist of the Theatre.* Athens, Ga.: University of Georgia Press, 1976.

Lea, Kathleen M. *Italian Popular Comedy,* 2 vols. New York: Russell and Russell, 1962.

Nagler, Alois M. *Theatre Festivals of the Medici, 1539–1637.* New Haven, Conn.: Yale University Press, 1968.

Nicoll, Allardyce, *The World of Harlequin.* London: Cambridge University Press, 1963.

———. *Masks Mimes and Miracles: Studies in the Popular Theatre.* New York: Cooper Square Publishers, 1963.

Strong, Roy. *Splendor at Court: Renaissance Spectacle and the Theater of Power.* Boston: Houghton Mifflin, 1973.

CHAPTER 7

The standard authority on dramatic and theatrical history of the period is H.C. Lancaster, *A History of French Dramatic Literature in the Seventeenth Century* (1929–1942), 5 vols., published in Baltimore by the Johns Hopkins Press.

Barthes, Roland. *On Racine.* Translated by Richard Howard. New York: Hill and Wang, 1964.

Bjurstrom, Per. *Giacomo Torelli and Baroque Stage Design.* Stockholm: Almqvist and Wiksell, 1961.

Blitzer, Charles. *Age of Kings.* The Great Ages of Man Series. New York: Time–Life Books, 1967.

Lough, John. *Paris Theatre Audiences in the Seventeenth and Eighteenth Centuries.* London: Oxford University Press, 1957.

Turnell, Martin. *The Classical Moment: Studies in*

Cornielle, Molière and Racine. New York: New Directions, 1948.

Wiley, W.L. *The Early Public Theatre in France.* Cambridge, Mass.: Harvard University Press, 1960.

CHAPTER 8

For years the standard authorities on the Restoration theatre were Leslie Hotson, *The Commonwealth and Restoration Stage* (Cambridge, Mass., 1928); and Montague Summers, *The Restoration Theatre* (London, 1934) and *The Playhouse of Pepys* (London, 1935). More recent scholarship both in England and America has produced extensive histories of the day-to-day activities of the London stage, its managers, actors, playwrights, and other personnel between 1660 and 1800.

Fraser, Antonia. *Royal Charles: Charles II and the Restoration.* New York: Alfred A. Knopf, 1979.

Highfill, Philip H., Jr., et al. *A Biographical Dictionary of Actors, Actresses, Musicians, Dancers, Managers, and Other Stage Personnel in London, 1660–1800,* 6 vols. Carbondale, Ill.: Southern Illinois University Press, 1973–1978.

Holland, Peter. *The Ornament of Action: Text and Performance in Restoration Comedy.* London: Cambridge University Press, 1979.

Leacroft, Richard. *The Development of the English Playhouse.* London: Methuen, 1973.

Loftis, John, Richard Southern, Marion Jones, and A.H. Scouten. *The Revels History of Drama in English, 1660–1700,* vol. 5. London: Methuen, 1976.

The London Stage, 1660–1800, 11 vols. Edited by Emmett L. Avery, Arthur H. Scouten, Charles B. Hogan, and George W. Stone, Jr. Carbondale, Ill.: Southern Illinois University Press, 1960–1968.

Lynch, James J. *Box, Pit and Gallery: Stage and Society in Johnson's London.* Berkeley: University of California Press, 1953.

Nicoll, Allardyce. *The Garrick Stage: Theaters and Audiences in the Eighteenth Century.* Edited by

Sybil Rosenfeld. Manchester: Manchester University Press, 1980.

————. *History of the English Drama, 1660–1900*, 6 vols. 4th ed. London: University of Cambridge Press, 1955–1959.

Southern, Richard. *Changeable Scenery: Its Origin and Development in the British Theatre*. London: Clarendon Press, 1952.

CHAPTER 9

Agne Beijer's decorative book, *Court Theatres of Drottningholm and Gipsholm* (1933) contains photographs of existing eighteenth-century Scandinavian theatres. These illustrations of the period's theatre architecture, interiors, stages, machines, and movable scenery give us an excellent idea of what these theatres looked like and how they were used. Today these theatres are more than museum pieces; they are used for performances in period costumes with the original stage scenery and machines.

Albright, H.D., ed. *André Antoine's Memories of the Théâtre Libre*. Translated by Marvin Carlson. Coral Gables, Fla: University of Miami Press, 1964.

Barzun, Jacques. *Darwin, Marx, Wagner: Critique of a Heritage*. 2nd ed. Chicago: University of Chicago Press, 1981.

Bentley, Eric, ed. *The Theory of the Modern Stage: An Introduction to Modern Theatre and Drama*. Baltimore, Md.: Penguin, 1968.

Bruford, Walter H. *Theatre, Drama and Audience in Goethe's Germany*. London: Routledge & Kegan Paul, 1950.

Carlson, Marvin. *The French Stage in the Nineteenth Century*. Metuchen, N.J.: Scarecrow Press, 1972.

————. *The German Stage in the Nineteenth Century*. Metuchen, N.J.: Scarecrow Press, 1972.

DeHart, Steven. *The Meininger Theater: 1776–1926*. Ann Arbor: UMI Research Press, 1983.

Grube, Max. *The Story of the Meiningen*. Coral Gables, Fla.: University of Miami Press, 1963.

Marker, Frederick, and Lise-Lone Marker. *The Scandinavian Theatre: A Short History*. Totowa, N.J.: Rowman and Littlefield, 1975.

Steiner, George. *The Death of Tragedy*. New York: Hill and Wang, 1968.

Waxman, Samuel M. *Antoine and The Théâtre-Libre*. Cambridge, Mass.: Harvard University Press, 1926. Reprint. New York: Benjamin Blom, 1964.

CHAPTER 10

Constantin Stanislavsky's system has been disseminated throughout the world in his writings and by his colleagues and students. The following books describe the evolution of his system for helping the actor do the job he or she sets out to do: *My Life in Art* (1952), *An Actor Prepares* (1948), and *Building a Character* (1977). Translated by Elizabeth R. Hapgood and published in new editions by Theatre Arts, New York.

Braun, Edward. *The Theatre of Meyerhold: Revolution on the Modern Stage*. New York: Drama Books, 1979.

Chinoy, Helen K., ed. "Reunion: A Self-Portrait of the Group Theatre." *Educational Theatre Journal* 28, No. 4 (December 1976), 445–552.

Clurman, Harold. *The Fervent Years*. New York: Alfred A. Knopf, 1945.

Cole, Toby, and Helen K. Chinoy. *Actors on Acting*. Rev. ed. New York: Crown, 1970.

Crawford, Cheryl. *One Naked Individual*. Indianapolis: Bobbs-Merrill, 1977.

Garfield, David. *A Player's Place: The Story of The Actors Studio*. New York: Macmillan, 1980.

Gorchakov, Nikolai M. *Stanislavsky Directs*. Translated by Miriam Goldina. New York: Funk & Wagnalls, 1954.

Hethmon, Robert H., ed. *Strasberg at the Actors Studio*. New York: Viking, 1965.

Houghton, Norris. *Moscow Rehearsals: An Account of Methods of Production in the Soviet Theatre*.

New York: Octagon, 1936. Reprinted, New York: Harcourt Brace Jovanovich, 1975.

Lewis, Robert. *Advice to the Players.* New York: Harper & Row, 1981.

———. *Method—or Madness?* New York: Samuel French, 1958.

Munk, Erika, ed. *Stanislavski and America: An Anthology from the Tulane Drama Review.* New York: Hill and Wang, 1966.

Sayler, Oliver M. *Inside the Moscow Art Theatre.* New York: Brentano's, 1925.

Schmidt, Paul, ed. *Meyerhold at Work.* Austin: University of Texas Press, 1980.

Stanislavsky, Constantin. *Stanislavski Produces Othello.* Translated by Helen Nowak. New York: Theatre Arts Books, 1948.

———. *The Sea Gull Produced by Stanislavski.* Edited by S.D. Balukhaty. Translated by Davis Magarshack. New York: Theatre Arts Books, 1952.

———. *Stanislavsky on the Art of the Stage.* Translated by David Magarshack. New York: Hill and Wang, 1961.

———. *An Actor's Handbook.* Edited and translated by Elizabeth Reynolds Hapgood. New York: Theatre Arts Books, 1963.

———. *Stanislavski's Legacy.* Edited and translated by Elizabeth Reynolds Hapgood. Rev. ed. New York: Theatre Arts Books, 1968.

Strasberg, Lee. Introduction to *Acting, a Handbook of the Stanislavski Method.* Compiled by Toby Cole. Rev. ed. New York: Crown, 1955.

Styan, J.L. *Chekhov in Performance: A Commentary on the Major Plays.* London: Cambridge University Press, 1971.

Toporkov, Vasily Osipovich. *Stanislavsky in Rehearsal: The Final Years.* Translated by Christine Edwards. New York: Theatre Arts Books, 1979.

CHAPTER 11

While not issued consecutively (volumes 3, 4, and 8 are still missing from the series), the six

volumes of *Bertolt Brecht: Collected Plays,* edited by Ralph Manheim and John Willett (New York: Random House, 1971–1977), contain new translations of Brecht's major plays: *A Threepenny Opera, The Good Person of Szechwan, Life of Galileo, Mother Courage and Her Children, The Caucasian Chalk Circle,* and *Coriolanus.* The editors have also included such relevant materials as Brecht's production notes, letters, conversations, and textual variations.

Bentley, Eric. *The Brecht Commentaries—1943–1980.* New York: Grove, 1981.

Esslin, Martin. *Brecht: The Man and His Work.* Rev. ed. New York: Norton, 1971.

Gorelik, Mordecai. *New Theatres for Old.* New York: Samuel French, 1940.

Patterson, Michael. *Peter Stein: Germany's Leading Theatre Director.* New York: Cambridge University Press, 1981.

Piscator, Erwin. *The Political Theatre: A History, 1914–1929.* New York: Avon Books, 1978.

Special Brecht Issues: *Tulane Drama Review* 6, No. 1 (1961). *The Drama Review* 12, No. 1 (Fall 1967).

Theaterarbeit. Dresden: Dresdner Verlag, 1952.

Willett, John. *The Theatre of Bertolt Brecht: A Study of Eight Aspects.* New York: New Directions, 1959.

Willett, John, ed. and trans. *Brecht on Theatre: The Development of an Aesthetic.* New York: New Directions, 1964.

Witt, Hubert, ed. *Brecht As They Knew Him.* Translated by John Peet. New York: International, 1974.

CHAPTER 12

Of the few general studies of the post-war European theatre, perhaps the most valuable are John Gassner's *Theatre in Our Times* (New York: Crown, 1954); Lander MacClintock's *The Age of Pirandello* (Bloomington, Ind.: Indiana University Press, 1951); Jacques Guicharnaud's *Modern French Theatre* (New Haven, Conn.: Yale University Press, 1975); and Martin Esslin's *The Theatre of the Absurd* (3rd ed. New York: Penguin, 1980).

Artaud, Antonin. *The Theatre and Its Double.* Translated by Mary C. Richards. New York: Grove, 1958.

Barrault, Jean-Louis. *Reflections on the Theatre.* Translated by Barbara Wall. 1951. Reprinted, Westport, Conn.: Hyperion, 1979.

Chiari, Joseph. *The Contemporary French Theatre: The Flight from Naturalism.* London: Oxford University Press, 1958.

Croyden, Margaret. *Lunatics, Lovers, and Poets: The Contemporary Experimental Theatre.* New York: Dell, 1974.

Fowlie, Wallace. *Dionysus in Paris: A Guide to Contemporary French Theatre.* New York: Peter Smith, 1960.

Knapp, Bettina L. *Off-Stage Voices: Interviews with Modern French Dramatists.* Ed. Alba Amoia. Troy, N.Y.: Whitson, 1975.

O'Connor, Garry. *French Theatre Today.* London: Pitman, 1975.

Pirandello, Luigi. *Naked Masks: Five Plays by Luigi Pirandello.* Edited by Eric Bentley. New York: Dutton, 1958.

Sayler, Oliver M. *Max Reinhardt and His Theatre.* 1924. Reprint. New York: Arno, 1968.

Styan, J.L. *Max Reinhardt.* London: Oxford University Press, 1982.

Wave: British Drama for the Seventies* (New York: Hill and Wang, 1971).

Addenbrooke, David. *The Royal Shakespeare Company: The Peter Hall Years.* London: William Kimber, 1974.

Ansorge, Peter. *Disrupting the Spectacle: Five Years of Experimental and Fringe Theatre in Britain.* London: Pitman, 1975.

Beauman, Sally. *The Royal Shakespeare Company: A History of Ten Decades.* New York: Oxford University Press, 1982.

Browne, Terry. *Playwright's Theatre: The English Stage Company at The Royal Court.* London: Pitman, 1975.

Cook, Judith. *Directors' Theatre.* London: Harrap, 1974.

Findlater, Richard, ed. *At the Royal Court: Twenty-Five Years of the English Stage Company.* New York: Grove, 1981.

Hayman, Ronald. *The Set-Up: An Anatomy of the English Theatre Today.* London: Methuen, 1973.

Hinchliffe, Arnold P. *British Theatre, 1950–1970.* London: Oxford University Press, 1974.

Marowitz, Charles, and Simon Trussler, eds. *Theatre At Work: Playwrights and Productions in the Modern British Theatre: A Collection of Interviews and Essays.* New York: Hill and Wang, 1968.

Worth, Katharine J. *Revolutions in Modern English Drama.* London: Bell, 1973.

CHAPTER 13

John Russell Taylor has been a consistent chronicler of the British theatre scene for the last three decades. His emphasis has been upon the emerging new playwright, or the "angry young" writer, introduced to the English stage in the person of John Osborne in 1956. Taylor's writings are found in *Anger and After; A Guide to the New British Drama* (London: Methuen, 1977); *The Angry Theatre: New British Drama,* rev. ed. (New York: Hill and Wang, 1969); and *The Second*

CHAPTER 14

John Gassner's *Theatre at the Crossroads: Plays and Playwrights of the Mid-Century American Stage* (New York: Holt, Rinehart and Winston, 1960) and *The Theatre in Our Times* (New York: Crown, 1954) and Joseph Wood Krutch's *The American Drama Since 1918* (New York: Braziller, 1957) afford us the best understanding of trends in American playwriting from 1918 to about 1970. The writings of designers Kenneth Macgowan and Robert Edmond Jones in *Continental*

Stagecraft (New York: Harcourt, Brace, 1922, reprinted by Benjamin Blom, 1964) and Lee Simonson in *The Stage Is Set* (New York: Harcourt, Brace, 1932) provide the best perspective on the new stagecraft of the New York theatre from the 1920s to the late 1940s.

Abramson, Doris E. *Negro Playwrights in the American Theatre.* New York: Columbia University Press, 1969.

Biner, Pierre. *The Living Theatre.* 2nd ed. New York: Horizon, 1972.

Bordman, Gerald. *American Musical Comedy: From Adonis to Dreamgirls.* New York: Oxford University Press, 1982.

Buttitta, Tony, and Barry B. Witham. *Uncle Sam Presents: A Memoir of the Federal Theatre, 1935–1939.* Philadelphia: University of Pennsylvania Press, 1982.

Clark, Brian. *Group Theatre.* New York: Theatre Arts Books, 1971.

Engel, Lehman. *American Musical Theatre.* Rev. ed. New York: Macmillan, 1975.

Hewitt, Barnard. *Theatre USA 1668–1957.* New York: McGraw-Hill, 1959.

Neff, Renfreu. *The Living Theatre USA.* Indianapolis: Bobbs-Merrill, 1970.

Pasolli, Robert. *A Book on the Open Theatre.* Indianapolis: Bobbs-Merrill, 1970.

Price, Julia. *The Off-Broadway Theatre.* Metuchen, N.J.: Scarecrow, 1962. Reprinted, Brooklyn: Greenwood, 1974.

Smith, Cecil. *Musical Comedy in America.* New York: Theatre Arts Books, 1950.

Weales, Gerald. *American Drama Since World War II.* New York: Harcourt Brace Jovanovich, 1962.

———. *The Jumping Off Place: American Drama in the 1960s.* New York: Macmillan, 1969.

Wilson, Garff B. *Three Hundred Years of American Drama and Theatre: From Ye Bare and Ye Cubb to Chorus Line.* 2nd ed. Englewood Cliffs, N.J.: Prentice-Hall, 1982.

CHAPTER 15

Although many books have been published over the last decade on new trends in the American theatre, the best sources for day-to-day accounts of what's happening in today's theatre are major newspapers and magazines. The *New York Times,* the *Washington Post,* the *Los Angeles Times,* the *Chicago Tribune, Variety, Backstage,* and the *Village Voice* record daily and weekly activities. Such magazines as *Time, Newsweek, U.S. News and World Report,* the *Nation,* and the *New Yorker* review performances on a weekly basis. Then there are the quarterly "little" magazines—*The Drama Review, The Performing Arts Journal, Theatre Crafts, Theater*—that deal with experimental theatre, publish scripts, and analyze noncommercial trends in the contemporary theatre, both American and European.

Brown, Janet. *Feminist Drama: Definition and Critical Analysis.* Metuchen, N.J.: Scarecrow Press, 1979.

Brustein, Robert. *Critical Moments: Reflections on Theatre and Society, 1973–79.* New York: Random House, 1980.

———. *Revolution as Theatre: Notes on the New Radical Style.* New York: Liveright, 1971.

Chinoy, Helen K., and Linda Walsh Jenkins, eds. *Women in American Theatre: Careers, Images, Movements. An Illustrated Anthology and Sourcebook.* New York: Crown, 1981.

Croyden, Margaret. *Lunatics, Lovers, and Poets: The Contemporary Experimental Theatre.* New York: McGraw-Hill, 1974.

Cohn, Ruby. *New American Dramatists: 1960–1980.* New York: Grove, 1982.

Gottfried, Martin. *A Theatre Divided: The Postwar American Stage.* Boston: Little, Brown, 1967.

Greenberger, Howard. *The Off-Broadway Experience.* Englewood Cliffs, N.J.: Prentice-Hall, 1971.

Lahr, John. *Astonish Me: Adventures in Contemporary Theatre.* New York: Viking, 1973.

Marranca, Bonnie and Gautam Dasgupta. *American Playwrights: A Critical Survey,* 2 vols. New York: Drama Books, 1980–1982.

Poland, Albert, and Bruce Mailman, eds. *The Off Off Broadway Book: The Plays, People, Theatre.* Indianapolis: Bobbs-Merrill, 1972.

Price, Julia. *The Off-Broadway Theatre.* Metuchen, N.J.: Scarecrow Press, 1962. Reprinted. Brooklyn: Greenwood, 1974.

Sainer, Arthur. *The Radical Theatre Notebook.* New York: Avon, 1975.

Schevill, James. *Breakout! In Search of New Theatrical Environments.* Chicago: University of Chicago Press, 1972.

Schechner, Richard. *Environmental Theatre.* New York: Hawthorn, 1973.

————. *The End of Humanism: Writings on Performance.* New York: Performing Arts Journal Publications, 1982.

Shank, Theodore. *American Alternative Theater.* New York: Grove, 1982.

Theatre Profiles 6: A Resource Book of Nonprofit Professional Theatres in the United States. New York: Theatre Communications Group, 1983.

Ziegler, Joseph. *Regional Theatre: The Revolutionary Stage.* New York: Da Capo, 1973.

ILLUSTRATION CREDITS

CHAPTER 1

page 6: Top: Courtesy The National
  Theatre of Great Britain
  Bottom: Courtesy The Guthrie
  Theatre/Photo: Robert Ashley Wilson
page 7: Top: Courtesy Arena Stage,
  Washington, D.C.
  Bottom: Courtesy The Oregon
  Shakespeare Festival/Photo:
  Hank Kranzler
page 9: Museum of Modern Art Film Stills
  Archives
page 10: The New York Public Library at
  Lincoln Center, Vandamm Collection
page 14: © George E. Joseph
page 15: The New York Public Library at
  Lincoln Center, Courtesy of
  Alan Schneider
page 18: © Max Waldman
page 20: © Martha Swope

CHAPTER 2

page 27: © Martha Swope
page 29: © Bert Andrews
page 30: © Martha Swope
page 31: Courtesy Playmakers Repertory
  Company
page 34: Courtesy Stratford Festival
  Theatre Ontario, Canada/Photo:
  Robert C. Ragsdale
page 36: Courtesy The Berliner Ensemble
page 38: © Johan Elbers
page 44: Courtesy Royal Shakespeare
  Company/Photo: Donald Cooper
page 45: Courtesy Royal Shakespeare
  Company/Photo: Donald Cooper
page 47: Top: The New York Public Library
  at Lincoln Center, The Billy Rose
  Theatre Collection
  Bottom: Culver Pictures, Inc.

CHAPTER 3

page 53: The Bettmann Archive, Inc.
page 59: Top: © George E. Joseph
  Bottom: © Joseph Abeles
page 61: Top: The Metropolitan Museum
  of Art, Rogers Fund, 1908
  Bottom left: The Metropolitan
  Museum of Art, Fletcher Fund, 1924
  Bottom right: The Metropolitan
  Museum of Art, Rogers Fund, 1906

page 64: Courtesy Greek National Tourist
  Organization
page 65: Courtesy Greek National Tourist
  Organization
page 66: Top: Anderson/Art Resource
  Bottom: Alinari/Art Resource
page 67: Anderson/Art Resource
page 73: The Metropolitan Museum of Art,
  Rogers Fund, 1906
page 77: Courtesy Royal Shakespeare
  Company/Photo: Donald Cooper
page 81: © Kenn Duncan

CHAPTER 4

page 91: Victoria and Albert Museum
page 92: Bibliothèque Nationale, Paris
page 93: The Bettmann Archive, Inc.
page 95: The Bettmann Archive, Inc.
page 97: Courtesy The Historic New
  Orleans Collection/Photo:
  Charles Genella
page 102: Musée Condé; Photographie
  Giraudon/Art Resource
page 104: Courtesy City of York, England
page 105: Courtesy City of York, England
page 107: © Douglas H. Jeffery

CHAPTER 5

page 114: The Bettmann Archive, Inc.
page 117: By permission of the Folger
  Shakespeare Library
page 125: The Duke of Devonshire/
  Chatsworth Collection/Courtauld
  Institute of Art
page 127: Top: Reprinted by permission of
  Oxford University Press
  Bottom: The Oregon Shakespeare
  Festival/Photo: Hank Kranzler
page 130: © George E. Joseph
page 134: © George E. Joseph
page 139: Courtesy Royal Shakespeare
  Company

CHAPTER 6

page 143: Courtesy Musée Baron-Gérard,
  Ville De Bayeux, France
page 147: Harvard Theatre Collection
page 157: Harvard Theatre Collection
page 158: Top: The Art Institute of Chicago
  Bottom: Courtesy Randolph Umberger
page 159: Top: Harvard Theatre Collection

page 165: Courtesy the San Francisco
  Mime Troupe/Photo:
  Gerhard E. Gscheidle
page 166: Courtesy the San Francisco
  Mime Troupe/Photo:
  Gerhard E. Gscheidle

CHAPTER 7

page 169: The Bettmann Archive, Inc.
page 174: Harvard Theatre Collection
page 176: Harvard Theatre Collection
page 177: The Bettmann Archive, Inc.
page 181: The Bettmann Archive, Inc.
page 182: Courtesy KaiDib Films
  International, Glendale, California
page 183: Courtesy KaiDib Films
  International, Glendale, California
page 188: Left: The Bettmann Archive, Inc.
  Right: Historical Pictures Service,
  Chicago

CHAPTER 8

page 195: Courtesy Yale University Library;
  William Lawrence *Elizabethan Playhouse*
page 199: The New York Public Library
  Prints Division, Astor, Lenox and
  Tilden Foundations
page 202: Harvard Theatre Collection
page 203: Harvard Theatre Collection
page 205: Harvard Theatre Collection
page 207: Harvard Theatre Collection
page 209: Harvard Theatre Collection
page 210: Harvard Theatre Collection
page 211: Wide World Photos
page 222: © Douglas H. Jeffery

CHAPTER 9

page 227: The New York Public Library at
  Lincoln Center, Billy Rose Theatre
  Collection
page 228: The New York Public Library at
  Lincoln Center, Billy Rose Theatre
  Collection
page 232: The Bettmann Archive, Inc.
page 239: Courtesy of Drottningholms
  Theatermuseum, Stockholm
page 240: Courtesy Drottningholms
  Theatermuseum, Stockholm
page 247: Top: Historical Pictures Service,
  Chicago
  Bottom: Culver Pictures, Inc.

page 248: Top: The New York Public Library at Lincoln Center, Billy Rose Theatre Collection
Bottom: © Beata Bergström
page 249: Top: Teatermuseet, Copenhagen
Bottom: © Zoë Dominic
page 259: Courtesy J. F. Kennedy Center, Washington, D.C./Photo: Jack Buxbaum

CHAPTER 10

page 264: Top: TASS from SOVFOTO
Bottom: NOVOSTI from SOVFOTO
page 273: NOVOSTI from SOVFOTO
page 275: The New York Public Library at Lincoln Center, Billy Rose Theatre Collection
page 276: Top: Alexander Bakshy, *The Path of the Modern Russian Stage and Other Essays*
Bottom: TASS from SOVFOTO
page 277: Top: TASS from SOVFOTO
Bottom: The New York Public Library at Lincoln Center, Billy Rose Theatre Collection
page 285: Alexander Bakshy, *The Path of the Modern Russian Stage and Other Essays*
page 288: © Martha Holmes

CHAPTER 11

page 293: Courtesy The Berliner Ensemble
page 296: The New York Public Library at Lincoln Center, Billy Rose Theatre Collection
page 304: Courtesy KaiDib Films International, Glendale, California
page 305: Culver Pictures, Inc.
page 308: Courtesy Guthrie Theatre
page 310: Courtesy Guthrie Theatre

CHAPTER 12

page 320: Museo Del Prado, Madrid/VAGA, New York
page 322: Max Reinhardt Archive, Special Collections, Glenn G. Bartle Library, State University of New York at Binghamton
page 323: Max Reinhardt Archive, Special Collections, Glenn G. Bartle Library, State University of New York at Binghamton

page 327: Wide World Photos
page 331: Courtesy Cultural Services of the French Embassy, New York
page 336: Courtesy KaiDib Films International, Glendale, California
page 337: Top: Courtesy KaiDib Films International, Glendale, California
Bottom: Courtesy Nikolai Dance Theatre/Photo: Milton Oleaga
page 342: © George E. Joseph
page 345: Wide World Photos
page 347: Courtesy French Cultural Services of the French Embassy, New York

CHAPTER 13

page 356: © Catherine Ashmore
page 360: Top: Wide World Photos
Bottom: Courtesy Royal Shakespeare Company/Photo: Clive Totman
page 361: Reproduced by permission of the Governors of the Royal Shakespeare Theatre, Stratford-upon-Avon, England
page 363: © Douglas H. Jeffery
page 364: © Douglas H. Jeffery
page 366: Top: Courtesy The Shakespeare Birthplace Trust, The Shakespeare Centre, Stratford-upon-Avon
Bottom: © Douglas H. Jeffery
page 367: © Douglas H. Jeffery
page 372: © Zoë Dominic
page 373: © Douglas H. Jeffery
page 376: © Martha Swope
page 377: © Zoë Dominic
page 379: Wide World Photos
page 382: © Martha Swope
page 383: © Martha Swope
page 384: © Martha Swope

CHAPTER 14

page 395: Culver Pictures, Inc.
page 396: Harvard Theatre Collection
page 400: Culver Pictures, Inc.
page 403: The New York Public Library at Lincoln Center, Vandamm Collection
page 404: Wide World Photos
page 406: Courtesy Dr. Mark Hall Amitin & The Living Theatre/Photo: Gianfranco Mantegna
page 407: Wide World Photos

page 411: Courtesy International Creative Management, New York
page 413: Courtesy Dr. Mark Hall Amitin & The Bread & Puppet Theatre/Photo: Theo Ehrhardt
page 414: The New York Public Library at Lincoln Center, Billy Rose Theatre Collection
page 415: Wide World Photos
page 416: Top: © Martha Swope
Bottom: © Kenn Duncan
page 417: Top: © Kenn Duncan
Bottom: © Martha Swope
page 424: The New York Public Library at Lincoln Center, Billy Rose Theatre Collection
page 431: © Joseph Abeles
page 437: The New York Public Library at Lincoln Center, Vandamm Collection
page 439: The New York Public Library at Lincoln Center, Vandamm Collection
page 441: Museum of Modern Art Film Stills Archive

CHAPTER 15

page 448: Courtesy New York Shakespeare Festival
page 456: © Bert Andrews
page 457: Courtesy El Teatro Campesino/Photo: George Ballis
page 460: Top: Courtesy Arena Stage, Washington, D.C./Photo: George de Vincent
Bottom: Courtesy Twyla Tharp Dance Foundation Inc./Photo: Martha Swope
page 461: Courtesy Hartford Stage Company, Connecticut
page 469: © Martha Holmes
page 472: © Archie Lieberman
page 473: Top: © Gerry Goodstein
page 477: Courtesy Mabou Mines/Photo: Johan Elbers
page 478: Courtesy Mabou Mines/Photo: Carol Rosegg

Color insert: © Max Waldman Archives, 1984

INDEX

Abraham and Isaac, 108
Abstract expressionism, 459
Absurdists, 136, 286, 328–330, 340–343
  definition of, 329, 340
  plays of, 33, 42, 48, 345–351
  theatre of, 25, 317, 326, 329–330, 334, 340–343, 374
Acharnians (Aristophanes), 58, 68
Ackermann, Konrad, 231
Acting, 12, 23, 119, 173–175, 267, 362, 396–397, 402
  method acting, 275, 278, 289, 397, 402
  Stanislavsky system, 267–268, 278
Actor-manager, 172, 173, 241, 245, 267
Actors Equity Association (AEA), 397
Actors Studio (New York), 275, 278, 288, 397, 442, 443
Actors Studio Theatre (New York), 287–288
Actors Theatre of Louisville (Kentucky), 453, 459
Actors' Workshop of San Francisco, 17, 426, 462, 468
Actos, 455, 457
Adamov, Arthur, 191, 330, 331, 340
Adams, Maude, 395
Adaptations, 28–32, 48, 205, 381, 384
Adler, Luther, 287
Adler, Stella, 399
Adrian, Max, 359
A-effect, 298
Aeschylus, 42, 57, 59, 60, 68
After the Fall (Miller), 427
Afterpiece, 72, 201, 213
Agamemnon (Aeschylus), 42, 58, 59, 69, 82
  plot of, 59
Age of Gold (Mnouchkine), 32
Agent (theatrical), 395, 430
Agitprop, 295, 382, 455
Agon, 70, 73
Ain't Misbehavin' (musical), 414
Akalaitis, Joanne, 462, 463
  biography of, 462
Akins, Zoe, 399
Albee, Edward, 287, 431–434, 452
  biography of, 431
  quotation from, 434
Alcestis (Euripides), 68, 76
Alchemist, The (Jonson), 118, 129, 204
Aldwych Theatre (London), 359, 374, 381

Aleichem, Sholem, 414
Aleotti, Giovan Battista, 155
Alexander (Euripides), 75
Alexandrine, 184
Alexandrinsky Theatre (St. Petersburg), 269, 271
Alfred Jarry Theatre (Paris), 327
Alienation effect, 298, 313
All Against All (Adamov), 330
All-Colored Dramatic Stock Company (New York), 402
All for Love (Dryden), 212
All God's Chillun Got Wings (O'Neill), 402
All My Sons (Miller), 405, 425, 426
All Over (Albee), 431
Allegory, 312
Allen, Woody, 189
Alley Theatre (Houston), 41, 462
Alleyn, Edward, 113, 117, 123
Allio, René, 189, 221, 223
Alternative theatre, 164, 455–459
Amadeus (Shaffer), 359, 371, 376, 377, 386
America Hurrah! (van Itallie), 407, 411, 444, 465
American Blues (Williams), 430
American Buffalo (Mamet), 288, 453, 464, 465, 466, 479, 480
American Clock, The (Miller), 425
American Dream, The (Albee), 431, 434
American Kings English for Queens (Terry), 464
American Laboratory Theatre (New York), 278
American Place Theatre (New York), 471
American Theatre, 388–481
American Theatre Association (Washington, D.C.), 398
Aminta (Tasso), 161
Amphitryon (Plautus), 69, 74
Amphitryon 38 (Giraudoux), 326, 338
An Actor Prepares (Stanislavsky), 265
And They Handcuffed The Flowers (Arrabal), 330, 339
Andorra (Frisch), 312
Andreini, Francisco, 143, 144, 147
Andreini, Isabella, 144, 147
Andria (Terence), 69
Andromache (Euripides), 82
Andromaque (Racine), 178, 184
Andronicus, Livius, 62
Angel City (Shepard), 466
Angels Fall (Wilson), 464

Animations, 462, 475, 476, 481
  definition of, 475
Anna Christie (O'Neill), 258, 422, 443
Annie (musical), 414
Another Part of the Forest (Hellman), 423, 443
Anouilh, Jean, 325, 326, 338, 351
Antigone (Sophocles), 68, 70, 82, 338, 437
Antonioni, Michelangelo, 466
Antoine, André, 227–229, 231, 244–245, 254, 262, 268, 317, 321
  biography of, 229
  as director, 244–245
  on directing, 244
  quotation from, 228
Antony and Cleopatra (Shakespeare), 138
Apollinaire, Guillaume, 334
Appen, Karl von, 299, 302, 307
Appia, Adolphe, 241, 259, 332, 398, 442
Approaching Simone (Terry), 464
Architect and Emperor of Assyria, The (Arrabal), 330, 339
Architettura (Serlio), 154, 155, 160
Archon, 56, 62
Arden, John, 221, 361
Arena stage, 5
Arena Stage (Washington, D.C.), 7
Ariane (Corneille), 195
Ariosto, Ludovico, 146, 160
Aristophanes, 57, 58, 72–73
  biography of, 58
Aristotle, 23, 24, 25, 55, 58, 70, 72, 76
  definition of tragedy, 70
Armin, Robert, 119
Arrabal, Fernando, 330, 339
Arsenic and Old Lace (Kesselring), 19
The Art of the Theatre (Craig), 277
Art-Work of the Future, The (Wagner), 246
Artaud, Antonin, 326, 327, 330, 332, 334, 351, 353
  biography of, 327
  theories of, 327
Artistic director, 355, 435, 450, 458, 466, 476
  list of American, 454
As You Desire me (Pirandello), 338
As You Like It (Shakespeare), 80
Ashcroft, Peggy, 354, 362
Ashes, Ashes, We All Fall Down (Boesing), 458

Ashley, Elizabeth, 9
Asides, 132
Assumption of Hannele, The (Hauptmann), 274
At the Foot of the Mountain (Minneapolis), 458
Atellan farces, 146, 153
Athalie (Racine), 179
Atkinson, Brooks, 10, 21, 287, 291, 391, 435, 436, 444
  quote from, 436
Attempted Rescue on Avenue B (Terry), 464
Auclair, Michael, 191
Audiberto, Jacques, 330
Audiences, 2, 4–5, 17–19, 164, 269–270, 385, 405
  Elizabethan, 122–123
  Greek, 62
  medieval, 98
  modern, 269–270
  nineteenth-century European, 245
  Renaissance Italy, 153
  Restoration, 209
  seventeenth-century French, 180
Aurora (Fornés), 465
Automobile Graveyard, The (Arrabal), 330, 339
Autos, 94
  sacramentales, 94, 108
Autumn Garden, The (Hellman), 423, 443
Avant-garde, 330–331, 334, 350, 447, 475
  definition of, 459
Avignon Festival (France), 168, 327
Awake and Sing (Odets), 424, 425
Ayckbourn, Alan, 28

Baal (Brecht), 297, 306
Babes in the Bighouse (Terry), 464
Baby Want a Kiss (musical), 287
Bacchae, The (Euripides), 76
Backstage (newspaper), 453
Bag Lady (Van Itallie), 465
Bajazet (Racine), 179
Baker, George Pierce, 398, 405, 422
Balcony, The (Genet), 339, 344
Bald Soprano, The (Ionesco), 33, 317, 329, 339, 340, 341, 344–350, 352
  Representative Play, 344–350
Ballad opera, 205, 214–215
Ballet, 153, 175, 177, 238,
Ballets d'entrees, 177, 192

Bambi (film), 475
Bancroft, Anne, 423
Bankhead, Tallulah, 423
Baraka, Imamu Amiri (LeRoi Jones), 429, 455
Barbican Centre (London), 359, 360
Barefoot in the Park (Simon), 464
Barrault, Jean-Louis, 29, 48, 316, 327, 331, 351
  as director, 327–328
Barry, Elizabeth, 202, 204, 223
Barry, Philip, 398
Barrymore, Ethel, 391, 395
  biography of, 391
Barrymore, John, 391
Barrymore, Lionel, 391
Barton, John, 44, 49, 52, 368
Basic Training of Pavlo Hummel, The (Rabe), 465
Bataille, Nicholas, 317, 331, 344, 346
Bates, Alan, 354, 361, 373, 377, 379, 386
Bathhouse, The (Mayakovsky), 281
Baty, Gaston, 325
Bauer, Wolfgang, 312
Baxley, Barbara, 287
Bay, Howard, 298, 305, 398
Baylis, Lilian, 362
Bayreuth Theatre (Bavaria), 231, 245–247, 260, 337
B. Beaver Animation, The, 475
Bear, The (Chekhov), 279, 289
Beast fables, 475
Beaumont, Francis, 113, 119, 123, 129, 204
Beaux' Stratagem, The, 212, 213, 215–220, 220–223, 224
  dialogue from, 216, 219, 220
  Essay, 220–223
  Representative Play, 215–220
Beck, Julian, 405, 444
Beckerman, Bernard, 49, 141
Beckett, Samuel, 3, 13, 14–15, 17, 26, 142, 164, 257, 317, 328–331, 334, 339, 340–343, 352, 431, 466
  biography of, 343
  quotation from, 343
Becque, Henri, 253
Bedbug, The (Mayakovsky), 281
Before Sunrise (Hauptmann), 251
Beggar, The (Sorge), 294
Beggar's Opera, The (Gay), 213, 214, 215, 219, 301
  quotation from, 215
Behan, Brendan, 363

Behn, Aphra, 206, 212
Behrman, S. N., 398
Bèjart, Madeleine, 180, 186
Bel Geddes, Norma, 398
Belasco, David, 394, 395, 396, 402, 442
Belasco Theatre (New York), 391
Belgrade Theatre (England), 138
Bellerose (Pierre le Messier), 174, 192
Ben Hur (Wallace), 274
"Benefit," 200, 201–202, 206
Bennett, Michael, 414
Bentley, Eric, 28, 48, 261, 314
Berain, Jean, 192
Bérénice (Racine), 178, 179
Bergman, Ingmar, 248, 249, 258
Berlau, Ruth, 302, 313
Berliner Ensemble, The (East Berlin), 220, 293, 297–298, 300, 301–303
Berne, Eric, 23
Bernhard, Thomas, 312
Bernhardt, Sarah, 17, 394
Best Little Whorehouse in Texas, The (musical), 414
Betrayal (Pinter), 371, 374
A Better Class of Person: An Autobiography 1929-1956 (Osborne), 378
Betterton, Thomas, 201, 203, 204, 206, 207
Beyond the Horizon (O'Neill), 422
Biedermann and the Firebugs (Frisch), 312
Big Knife, The (Odets), 424, 425
Bingo (Bond), 369–370
Biomechanics, 271
Birds, The (Aristophanes), 58, 68
Birmingham Repertory Theatre (England), 362
Birthday Party, The (Pinter), 371, 373, 374
Björnson, Bjorn, 235
Black Theatre, 442, 455, 465, 479
Blackfriars Theatre (London), 112, 113, 115, 119, 123–124
Blacks, The (Genet), 339, 343, 344
Blakely, Colin, 361, 386
Blank verse, 131, 135, 140, 232
Blau, Herbert, 17, 404
Blin, Roger, 316–317, 331
Blitzstein, Marc, 401
Boesing, Martha, 458, 459, 470
Bolcom, William, 287
Boleslavsky, Richard, 263, 278, 289
Bond, Edward, 221, 312, 361, 368–369, 370
  biography of, 369
  quotation from, 368, 369

Boogie-Woogie Landscapes (Shange), 465
Booth, Edwin, 394
Booth stage, 102, 103, 146, 167
Booth Theatre (New York), 391
Borders, 157
Bosse, Harriet, 237
Boucicault, Dion, 28
Bound East for Cardiff (O'Neill), 422
Bourgeois Gentleman, The (Molière), 184
Bovasso, Julie, 452, 459
Box set, 239, 241, 258, 316, 431
Boy on the Straight-Back Chair (Tavel), 480
Bracegirdle, Anne, 202, 203, 204, 207, 208, 213, 223
biography of, 203
Braggart Warrior, The (Plautus), 69, 74
Brahm, Otto, 231, 234, 254, 259, 262, 321
Brand (Ibsen), 235
Brandes, George, 229
Brando, Marlon, 9, 287, 392, 397, 434, 440–441
Braque, Georges, 334
Bread and Puppet Theatre (Vermont), 164, 405, 411–413, 442, 452
Breasts of Tiresias, The (Apollinaire), 334
Breath (Beckett), 343
Brecht, Bertolt, 24–25, 33, 36, 215, 292, 294, 295, 297–303, 306–307, 311
as director, 302–303
biography of, 297
quotation from, 299
Brenton, Howard, 316, 368
Breton, André, 334, 353
Breuer, Lee, 38, 447, 462, 466, 475, 476, 478, 481
biography of, 476
Brig, The (Brown), 405, 406
Brighella, 173
Brighton Beach Memoirs (Simon), 464
Britannicus (Racine), 179
Broadway, 287, 381, 391, 394, 402–403, 414, 446, 450–453
Brockett, Oscar G., 57, 90, 108
Broken Jug, The (Kleist), 242
Brook, Peter, 3, 12, 19, 21, 137, 311
as director, 364–365
quotation from, 3, 364
Brooks, Mel, 189
Brothers, The (Terence), 69, 74
Brown, Kenneth, 405
Brown, William Wells, 428
Bryden, Bill, 106
Buchner, Georg, 232, 234, 250, 251, 257, 260, 401, 418, 452
Buffequin, George, 175
Building a Character (Stanislavsky), 265
Bullins, Ed, 430, 452, 455
Buontalenti, Bernardo, 156, 159, 167

Buratini, 153
Burattino, 153
Burbage, Cuthbert, 115
Burbage, James, 111, 113, 115, 123
Burbage, Richard, 113, 115, 117, 119, 123
Buried Child (Shepard), 464, 466, 479, 480, 481
Representative Play, 471–474
Burlesque, 205, 213, 394
Burned House, The (Strindberg), 237
Burrell, John, 358, 362, 385
Bus Stop (Inge), 402
Busch, Ernst, 36, 302, 303, 307
Butley (Gray), 374
Byrd Hoffman School of Byrds (New York), 38, 40

Cabaret Voltaire (Zurich), 333
Café Cino (New York), 452
Café La Mama (New York), 452, 459
Cagney, James, 321
Caird, John, 381
Calderón de la Barca, Pedro, 94
Caldwell, Zoe, 308, 310
"Calendar," 192
California Suite (Simon), 464
Caligula (Camus), 328, 338, 351
Call, Edward Payson, 310
Callot, Jacques, 148, 160, 163, 167
biography of, 150
Calm Down, Mother (Terry), 464
Camus, Albert, 328, 338, 339, 341, 351, 352
quotation of, 328
Candide (Bernstein and Hellman), 414, 423
Canterbury Festival (England), 368
Canterbury Tales, The (Chaucer), 87, 99
Captives, The (Plautus), 74
Caravan Theatre (Lexington, Mass.), 458
Careless Husband, The (Cibber), 213, 215
Caretaker, The (Pinter), 362, 371, 372, 373, 386
Carmines, Al, 452
Carnival of Thieves (Anouilh), 338
Carnovsky, Morris, 399
Carousel (Rodgers and Hammerstein), 414
Carros, 94, 108
Cartel des Quatre, 325
Cascando (Beckett), 462
Casket, The (Plautus), 69, 160
Castro, Guillén de, 178
Cat on a Hot Tin Roof (Williams), 430
Catharsis, 298
Catiline (Ibsen), 235
Cats (musical), 136, 138
Caucasian Chalk Circle, The, (Brecht),

33, 36–37, 106, 297, 302, 303, 307, 314, 315
diagram of, 36–37
quotation from, 306, 310
Representative Play, 307–311
Cavander, Kenneth, 44, 49
Central School of Speech and Drama (London), 362, 374
Ceremonies in Dark Old Men (Elder), 430, 455
Ceremony, 330, 343
Cervantes, Miguel de, 414
Chaikin, Joseph, 41, 405, 407, 410
Chairs, The (Ionesco), 339, 340, 352
Chamber plays (Strindberg), 237, 274
Champion, Gower, 414
Champmeslé, Marie Desmares, 175, 192
biography of, 175
Changeling, The (Middleton and Rowley), 129
Changing Room, The (Storey), 369, 370, 371
Chaplin, Charlie, 28, 142, 164, 422
Chapter Two (Simon), 464
Character, 24, 78, 135, 188, 256–257, 286, 306, 346–347, 380, 438, 473–474
Chariot and pole system, 155, 156, 238
Charles II, King of England, 196–199, 206, 207
biography of, 197
Charley's Aunt (Thomas), 19
Chaucer, Geoffrey, 87, 99
Cheap Detective, The (film), 463
Chekhov, Anton, 263, 265, 266–267, 269, 270, 276, 279–282, 286
biography of, 279
dramaturgy of, 279–282, 286
modernism of, 286
quotation from, 280, 281, 286
realism of, 279
Cheney, Sheldon, 398
Chereau, Patrice, 191
Cherry Orchard, The (Chekhov), 80, 276, 279, 280, 284, 289, 290, 364, 447
Chester cycle (England), 90, 91, 103, 108
Chicago (Shepard), 414, 464, 466
Chicano Theatre, 455–457, 465, 479
Chichester Festival Theatre (England), 365, 368
Chicken Soup with Barley (Wesker), 370
Children of a Lesser God (Medford), 453
Children of the Chapel Royal, 123
Children's Hour, The (Hellman), 423, 443
Childress, Alice, 429
Chinese Wall, The (Frisch), 312
Chiton, 60, 62
Chlamys, 60

Choreographer, 414
Chorus (Greek), 57, 70, 476
Chorus Line, A (musical), 382, 414, 447, 449, 453
Christmas Carol, A (Dickens), 28, 31, 384
Chronegk, Ludwig, 244, 259
  biography of, 244
Chronicles (Holinshed), 128, 133
Chronicles of Hell (Ghelderode), 325, 338
Chrystie Street Settlement (New York), 278
Cibber, Colley, 204, 205, 206, 213, 215, 223
Cid, The (Corneille), 180, 184, 192
Cinna (Corneille), 178
Cino, Joseph, 452
Cinthio, Giraldi, 160
Circle in the Square (New York), 30, 403, 404, 451
Cities of Bezique (Kennedy), 430
City Dionysia (Athens), 52, 54, 55, 56, 59, 75
Clara's Ole Man (Bullins), 455
Classicism, 232, 252
Claudel, Paul, 326
Climactic action, 132
Climactic structure, 33, 34–35, 48
  diagram of, 34–35
Climax, 33, 131
Clouds, The (Aristophanes), 58, 68
Clurman, Harold, 274, 397, 398, 399, 402, 442, 444
  as director, 402
Cocoanut Grove Playhouse (Miami), 15
Collaborative art, 11
Collective, 40, 312, 397, 405–413, 458
  definition of, 405
Colosseum (Rome), 66
Combined Company, 394
Come and Go (Beckett), 329, 343
Come Blow Your Horn (Simon), 463
Comédie Française (Paris), 171, 175, 183, 245, 327, 331
Comedy, 25–26, 63, 181, 205, 230, 334–335, 346, 376, 455–456, 463
  genteel, 213, 215
  Greek comedy, 72–73
  Roman comedy, 73–74
  sentimental, 205, 215
Comedy of manners, 194, 204–205, 213–214, 215, 220, 362
Comic action, 186–187
Comic actor (Greek), 57
Comic actor (Roman), 63
Commedia dell'arte, 74, 142–167, 168, 179
  characters:
    Arlecchino, 143, 152, 153, 160, 164

Brighella, 143, 149, 151, 152, 153, 160, 164
    Capitano, 144, 151, 152, 153, 160
    Dottore, 152, 160
    inamorata, 147, 158, 160, 161
    inamorato, 160
    Pantalone, 143, 144, 152, 160, 164, 165
    Pedrolino, 152, 160
    Pulcinello, 152, 160
  companies, 161, 170
Communist Manifesto, The (Marx), 231
Community theatre, 398
Complication, 41, 42, 48
Comte, Auguste, 252
Concept musical, 414
Condemned of Altona, The (Sartre), 327
Conditions of Performance
  American theatre (contemporary), 449–463
  American theatre (modern), 392–418
  British theatre (modern), 357–368
  commedia dell'arte, 144–153
  Elizabethan theatre, 111–127
  epic theatre, 294–303
  European theatre (19th century), 229–247
  European theatre (postwar), 317–334
  French theatre (17th century), 171–181
  Greek theatre (classical), 54–62
  Italian Renaissance court theatres, 153–157
  medieval theatre, 86–98
  Roman theatre (classical), 62–63
  Russian theatre (19th century), 265–274
Conference of Birds (Brook), 364
Confidant, 74, 179, 185
Confidenti Company, 147, 148, 167
Confidential Clerk, The (Eliot), 370
Conflict, 32, 68, 130
Confrérie de la Passion (Paris), 101, 170, 175, 192
Congreve, William, 203, 204, 214, 215
  biography of, 214
Connection, The (Gelber), 405
Connelly, Marc, 402
Conquest of Granada (Dryden), 212
Conscious Lovers, The (Steele), 213, 215
Constant Couple, The (Farquhar), 217
Constructivism, 332, 333, 351
Continental Seating, 246, 293
Contractor, The (Storey), 369, 370, 371, 386
Copeau, Jacques, 325, 351, 356
  as director, 325
Coral (Kaiser), 306
Coriolanus (Shakespeare), 111, 138, 307

Corn Is Green, The (Williams), 391
Corneille, Pierre, 168, 173, 178, 180, 184, 192
  biography of, 178
Cornell, Katherine, 399
Cornish Round (England), 96
Corpus Christi, 85, 86, 89, 90, 94, 103, 108
  definition of, 89
Corrales, 94, 95
Corrigan, Robert W., 48, 333, 353
Coss, Clare, 459
Costigan, James, 287
Costumes, 60, 63, 93, 121, 150–153, 176–177, 239–241, 268–269, 301
Cothurnus, 60, 62
Cottesloe Theatre (London), 6, 106, 107, 358
Count of Monte Cristo, The (Dumas père), 422
Country Girl, The (Odets), 424, 425
Country Wife, The, 195, 196, 212, 224
  quotation from, 196
Couplet, 130, 147
Court theatre, 143, 153–157, 192, 226, 227, 229, 238, 250, 258
Covent Garden Theatre (London), 196, 197, 199, 200, 201, 204, 223
Coventry productions (England), 85, 91, 103, 108
Cowboys (Shepard), 466, 471
Cradle Will Rock, The (Blitzstein), 401
Craig, Edward Gordon, 277, 281, 332, 398, 442
Crawford, Cheryl, 275, 397, 398, 399
Creating a Role (Stanislavsky), 265
Creation and the Fall of Lucifer, 85
  quotation from, 86
Creation of the World and Other Business, The (Miller), 425
Creditors (Strindberg), 237
Crime and Punishment (Dostoevsky), 133
Crisis, 41, 42, 48
Critique of Pure Reason (Kant), 231
Cromwell, Oliver, 113, 194, 198, 370, 371
Cross-Purposes (Camus), 327, 338
Crucible, The (Miller), 425, 426, 427
Crucifixion Play (Wakefield), 108
  Representative Play, 103
Cry of the People for Meat, The (Bread and Puppet Theatre), 412
Cubism, 333, 459
Curse of the Langston House, The (Fornés), 465
Curse of the Starving Class (Shepard), 464, 466, 471, 480
Curtain Theatre (London), 111, 112
Cycles (Medieval), 89, 94, 98, 99–101, 103, 106
Cyclops (Euripides), 72, 76

Cymbeline (Shakespeare), 124
Cyrano de Bergerac (Rostand), 160

Dadaism, 333, 351, 459
Daly, Augustin, 394, 395, 402, 442
Dance, 60, 94, 122, 153, 177, 208, 231, 294
Danish Royal Theatre (Stockholm), 249
Danton's Death (Buchner), 234, 251, 260
Darwin, Charles, 229, 231, 252, 253
Daughters Cycle Trilogy, The (Sklar), 459
Davenant, William, 196, 199, 201, 206, 207, 212, 223
David Copperfield (Dickens), 28–29, 384
  plot of, 31
Davis, Ronnie G., 164, 167
Day of Absence (Ward), 430
Daykarhanova, Tamara, 287
Days of Heaven (film), 466
Days To Come (Hellman), 443
De Architectura (Vitruvius), 154
De Loutherbourg, Philip James, 206, 208, 224
De Mille, Agnes, 414
Dead End Kids: A History of Nuclear Power (Akalaitis), 462, 463
Dean, James, 278, 397
Death of a Salesman (Miller), 46–47, 402, 425, 426, 427, 443, 444
  quotation from, 427
Death of Bessie Smith, The (Albee), 431
Death of Ivan the Terrible, The (Tolstoy), 263
Death of Pompey, The (Corneille), 178–179
Deathtrap (Levine), 450
Deathwatch (Genet), 339, 343, 344, 352
Debary, Jacques, 191
Decroux, Etienne, 164, 326
Dee, Ruby, 443
Dekker, Thomas, 113
Delacorte Theatre (New York), 14, 447, 449, 479
Delaney, Shelagh, 363, 386
Delicate Balance, A (Albee), 431, 434
Dench, Judi, 138
Desire Under the Elms (O'Neill), 419, 443
Dessau, Paul, 300, 301, 302, 309, 313
Deus ex Machina, 60, 62, 166, 185, 187, 219
Deutsches Theater (East Berlin), 301, 302, 321
Devil and the Good Lord, The (Sartre), 339
Devine, George, 221, 355, 356, 381, 385, 386
  quotation from, 355, 357
Dexter, John, 292, 362, 364–365, 368, 376, 386

Dialectic, 306–307, 311
Dialogue, 22
Dickens, Charles, 28, 31, 381, 382, 383, 384, 385, 386
Dionysus, 52, 54, 56, 60, 62, 82
  definition of, 56
Diorama, 274
Directing, 241–245, 325, 327–328, 330, 362–368, 402–404, 414
Director, 12, 270
  as creative artist, 12, 270
  as interpretive artist, 12, 270
Dirty Hands (Sartre), 338, 339
Discovery space, 116
Disney, Walt, 475, 476
Dithyramb, 55, 62
Divine Comedy, The (Dante), 87, 98, 103
Dr. Faustus (Marlowe), 103, 118, 122, 128, 401
Doctor in Love, The (Molière), 173
Dr. Kheal (Fornés), 465, 468
Doctrine and Discipline of Divorce (Milton), 216
Doggerel, 99, 101, 230
Doll's House, A (Ibsen), 235, 236, 249, 254, 257, 258, 261, 280, 391
Domino Courts (Hauptman), 480
Don Carlos (Schiller), 232, 251
Don Juan (Molière), 32
Dorset Garden Theatre (London), 196, 200, 207, 223
Double Dealer, The (Congreve), 214, 220
Drama, 22, 43, 205, 226
Drama Centre, The (London), 362
Dramaten (Stockholm), 240
Dramatic action, 24, 32
Dramatic Conventions, 41–43, 63–75, 98–103, 128–132, 157–161, 181–186, 212–215, 250–254, 278–282, 303–307, 334–344, 368–377, 463–470, 418–434
  American, 418–434, 463–470
  commedia dell' arte, 157–161
  contemporary British, 368–377
  Elizabethan, 128–132
  epic, 303–307
  European (postwar), 334–344
  French (17th century), 181–186
  Greek, 63–73
  medieval, 98–103
  nineteenth-century European, 250–254
  Restoration, 212–215
  Roman, 73–75
  Russian (19th century), 278–282
Dramatic forms, 22–32, 48
Dramatic structure, 32
Dramatists Guild, The (New York), 397
Dran, 22, 43
Dreamgirls (musical), 414

Dream Play, A (Strindberg), 106, 240, 248, 260, 261, 280
  preface to, 238, 261
Dresden Opera House (Germany), 246
Dressed Like an Egg (Colette), 462
Drew, John, 391
Drew, Louisa Lane, 391, 394
Drinking Gourd, The (Hansberry), 428
Drottningholm Court Theatre (Sweden), 229
Drummond, Alexander M., 398
Drums in the Night (Brecht), 306
Drury Lane Theatre (London), 195–196, 199, 200, 201, 204, 215, 241
  Photo Essay, 210–211
Dryden, John, 201, 204–205, 206, 209, 212
DuBois, W.E.B., 428
Duchess of Malfi, The (Webster), 118, 129, 315
Duck Variations (Mamet), 465
DuCroisy, 186
Duerrenmatt, Friedrich, 311, 312
Dulcitius (Hrotsvitha), 101
Dullin, Charles, 325, 327, 331
Dumbshow, 122, 138
Dumbwaiter, The (Pinter), 374
DuParc, Mlle., 175, 192
Durang, Christopher, 479
Duras, Marguerite, 29
Dutchman (Baraka), 429, 455
Duvall, Robert, 466
Dynamite Tonight (musical), 287

Each in His Own Way (Pirandello), 326, 338
Earl of Leicester's Men, 113
Early Days (Storey), 371
Early Morning (Bond), 369, 370
Earth Spirit (Wedekind), 251
Easter (Strindberg), 261
Eastwood, Clint, 252
Ecclesiazusae, The (Aristophanes), 58
Edgar, David, 381, 383
Edinburgh Festival (Scotland), 368, 476
Edward II (Marlowe), 118, 129, 191
Egmont (Goethe), 250
Einstein on the Beach (Wilson), 40
Eisler, Hanns, 301, 302, 313
Ekkyklema, 58, 62
El Teatro Campesino (California), 164, 455–457, 480
Elder, Lonne, III, 430, 455
Elder Statesman, The (Eliot), 370
Electra (Euripides), 68, 76, 79, 80
Electronic Nigger, The (Bullins), 430, 455
Elements of drama, 23–25
  diagram of, 24

Eliade, Mircea, 8, 21
Eliot, T.S., 370
Elizabethan theatre, 110–141
Elliott, Patricia, 30
Emblem, 93, 121, 263
Emilia Galotti (Lessing), 232, 250
Emperor Jones, The (O'Neill), 419, 422, 443
Empress of Morocco, The (Settle), 207
Endgame (Beckett), 339, 341, 343
Enemies (Gorky), 280, 290
Enemy of the People, An (Ibsen), 235, 236, 261, 263
Engel, Erich, 302, 304
English Stage Company (London), 220, 221, 354, 355–356, 361, 377
Ensemble, 234, 289, 292, 312, 397, 398, 442
Entertainer, The (Osborne), 368, 370, 378
Entertainment, 10–11
Epic theatre, 25, 292–314, 400
    acting style, 297–298, 313
    definition of, 297
    designers, 298–299, 302
    diagram of, 299
    dramaturgy, 303–307
    half-curtain, 299, 300
    narrator in, 303
    theory and practice, 295–297
    visual elements, 298–301
Epidaurus Festival Theatre (Greece), 65
Epilogue, 201, 206, 213
Episode, 69, 70, 99, 232, 297, 313
Episodic plot and structure, 33, 36–37, 48, 128–129, 140, 303
    diagram of, 36–37
Equus (Shaffer), 359, 362, 365, 371, 376, 387
    quotation from, 365
Escape, or the Leap from Freedom, The (Brown), 428
Escurial (Ghelderode), 326, 338
Essays:
    Chekhov in Modern Performance, 286–288
    Commedia in Modern Performance, 164–167
    Eighteenth-Century Comedy in Modern Performance, 220–223
    Epic Theatre in Contemporary Performance, 311–313
    From Stage to Film, 440–441
    Ghosts in Modern Performance, 257–260
    Greek Tragedy in Modern Performance, 79–81
    Life and Adventures of Nicholas Nickleby in Modern Performance, 381–385

Mabou Mines in Performance, 475–478
Medieval Theatre in Modern Performance, 106–108
Molière in Modern Performance, 189–192
Shakespeare in Modern Performance, 136–146
Theatricalism and the Absurd in Modern Performance, 350–351
Esslin, Martin, 21, 321, 328, 330, 344, 350, 352, 353
Esther (Racine), 179
Ethel Barrymore Theatre, The (New York), 391–392, 434, 443
Ethelwold, Bishop of Winchester, 88
Etherege, Sir George, 194, 205, 212, 213, 216, 220, 224
Eumenides, The (Euripides), 59, 82
Eunuch (Terence), 69, 74
Euripides, 44, 54, 69, 72, 74, 75–79, 81, 185
    biography of, 76
    and the chorus, 57
    modernism of, 78
European theatre (19th century), 226–261
Evans, Edith, 362
Evans, Maurice, 362
Everyman, 87, 103, 108, 323, 325, 351
    description of, 325
Every Man in His Humour (Jonson), 118, 129
Evita (musical), 414
Evreinov, Nikolai, 272
Ewell, Tom, 15
Existentialism, 286, 319, 328, 339–340, 342, 343
Exit the King (Ionesco), 329, 341
Exodus, 57
Exorcist (Sachs), 102
Exposition, 41–42, 48, 129–130
Expressionism, 234–235, 294–295, 296, 332, 333, 419
    definition of, 294
Eyen, Tom, 452, 459
Eyes on the Harem (Fornés), 465, 468

Fabula Atellana, 74
Faithful Shepherd, The (Guarini), 161
Fando and Lis (Arrabal), 330, 339
Fantesca, 160
Farce, 28, 30, 73, 112, 146, 173, 213, 230, 294, 341
    definition of, 28
    French (17th century), 169–170, 173, 174, 178, 179
    medieval, 99, 101–102
Farm, The (Storey), 370, 371
Farquhar, George, 205, 212, 213–220, 221

biography of, 217
modernism of, 220
Father, The (Strindberg), 237, 261, 280
Faust (Goethe), 242, 251, 260
Fauvism, 333, 459
Federal Theatre Project, 305, 394, 399–401, 402, 425, 442
Fefu and her Friends (Fornés), 459, 465, 468, 480
    text of, 470
Feiffer, Jules, 189
Feldman, Peter, 407
Feminist theatre, 457–459, 465, 468–470, 479
Fergusson, Francis, 24, 28
Fescennine verses, 146
Festival of Two Worlds (Spoleto, Italy), 39
Festivals, 386
Feydeau, Georges, 30
Fichandler, Zelda, 403
Fiddler on the Roof (musical), 414
Fields, W.C., 28
Fifth of July (Wilson), 464
Figaro, Le (newspaper), 228, 332
Film, 8–9, 19, 440–441, 443
Finlay, Frank, 359
Finney, Albert, 354, 361, 378, 386
Fire (Bread and Puppet Theatre), 412
Firehouse Theatre (Chicago), 468
Fiske, Minnie Maddern, 395
First Studio (MAT) (Russia), 267, 280
Five Finger Exercise (Shaffer), 371, 376
Flanagan, Hallie, 399, 401
Fletcher, John, 113, 119, 123, 128, 204
Flies, The (Sartre), 328, 339, 340, 352
    plot of, 340
Flowering Peach, The (Odets), 424
Fonda, Jane, 252
Fool, The (Bond), 369
Fool for Love (Shepard), 464, 466
Footlights, 156, 176, 208, 241, 270, 271
For Colored Girls Who Have Considered Suicide When the Rainbow is Enuf (Shange), 447, 455, 465
Ford, John, 119, 129
Foreman, Richard, 38, 40, 48, 441
    biography of, 40
Fornés, María Irene, 48, 452, 459, 465, 468–470, 479, 480
    biography of, 468
    quotation from, 469, 470
    text of, 470
Forrest, Edwin, 394
Fortune Theatre, The (London), 111, 113, 117, 124, 127
42nd Street (musical), 414
47 Workshop (Harvard University), 422
Fosse, Bob, 414
Foster, Paul, 452, 459

Fouquet, Jean, 102
Fourth wall, 245
Fragments of a Trilogy (Serban), 79, 81, 82
Frazer, Sir James, 4
Freeway (Shank), 459
Freie Bühne (Berlin), 231, 234
French Academy (Paris), 178, 181, 184
French Lieutenant's Woman, The (film), 371
French theatre, 168–193
Freud, Sigmund, 111, 136, 137, 229, 260, 272, 334, 363
Friends, The (Wesker), 370
Fringe companies (England), 368, 385, 386
Frisch, Max, 311, 312
Frogs, The (Aristophanes), 58, 60, 68
Frohman, Charles, 395, 442
Frohman, Daniel, 395
From Morn to Midnight (Kaiser), 296, 306
From Moses to Mao (Savary), 350
Frost, Robert, 106
Fruits of Enlightenment, The (Tolstoy), 280
Fuller, Charles, 455, 459
Funeral Ceremonies (Genet), 344
Funnyhouse of a Negro (Kennedy), 430
Futurism, 332, 334, 351
    definition of, 332–333

Galileo (Brecht), 297, 307, 314
Gammer Gurton's Needle (Mr. S.), 112
Garfield, David, 291
Garrick, David, 202, 204, 210, 362,
    biography of, 204
Gas I, II (Kaiser), 306
Gaskill, William, 220–221, 368, 369
    biography of, 221
Gassner, John, 109
Gaultier-Garguille (Huges Guéru), 173, 174
Gay, John, 213, 214, 215, 219, 301
Gelber, Jack, 452
Gelosi Company (Italy), 143–144, 147, 148, 149, 161, 168
Genêt, Jean, 317, 329–330, 331, 334, 343–344, 345, 476
    biography of, 344
Gesamtkunstwerk (Master Art Work), 246
Gest, 306
Gesture, 24
Ghelderode, Michel de, 325, 338, 351
Gherardi, 148
Ghosts (Ibsen), 24, 42, 228, 235, 253, 321, 322
    diagram of, 34–35
    Essay, 257–259
    plot of, 255
    quotation from, 256

Representative Play, 254–257
    showing climactic play structure, 33, 34–35
    stage directions from, 236
Ghost Sonata, The (Strindberg), 237, 238, 261, 280
Giacometti, Alberto, 331
Giehse, Therese, 302
Gielgud, John, 354, 358, 362, 385
Gill, Peter, 368
Gilman, Richard, 480
Gin Game, The (Coburn), 450, 453
Gin Lane (Hogarth), 198, 199
Gingerbread Lady, The (Simon), 464
Giraudoux, Jean, 180, 325, 326, 338, 381
Glass Menagerie, The (Williams), 392, 405, 430, 434, 438
Glass, Philip, 462
Globe Theatre, The (London), 110, 111, 115–116, 118, 119, 121
    burning of, 122, 123
    in Photo Essay, 126–127
Glyndebourne Festival (England), 368
God's Favorite (Simon), 464
Godfather II, The (film), 278
Goethe, Johann Wolfgang von, 226, 232–233, 234, 241–243, 250–251
    as director, 241–243
    biography of, 242
    on acting, 241–242, 260
    staging of *Wallenstein's Camp*, 243
Goffman, Erving, 16
Gogol, Nikolai, 266, 271, 289, 290
Going in Style (film), 278
Golden Bough, The (Frazer), 4
Golden Boy (Odets), 424
Goldoni, Carlo, 164, 165, 167
Goldsmith, Oliver, 194, 205, 213, 224, 386
Gone With The Wind (novel), 440
Good Doctor, The (Simon), 464
Good Soldier Schweik, The (Hacek), 295
    description of, 298
Good Woman of Setzuan, The (Brecht), 80, 297, 307
Goodbye Girl, The (Simon), 464
Goodman, Edward, 399
Goodman Theatre (Chicago), 466
Goodman's Fields Theatre (London), 204
Goon Show (radio), 374
Goose and Tom Tom (Rabe), 465
Gorboduc (Sackville and Norton), 112
Gorelik, Mordecai, 298, 315
Gorky, Maxim, 254, 266, 267, 268, 270, 280, 289, 290
Gottfried, Martin, 450, 480
    quotation from, 450
Gottshed, Johann Christoph, 231, 232
Götz von Berlichingen (Goethe), 232, 238, 239, 242, 250

Government Inspector, The (Gogol), 290
Governor's Lady, The, 396
Grabow, Carl, 240
Graham-Jones, Sebastian, 106
Grand Magic Circus, The (France), 350–351, 352
Gray, Simon, 374
Gray, Spalding, 40, 41, 447, 462, 466, 479
    biography of, 41
Gray Lady Cantata, The (Bread and Puppet), 412
Great Expectations (Dickens), 384
Great God Brown, The (O'Neill), 422
Greek chorus, 5, 309, 476
Greek National Theatre, The (Athens), 52
The Greeks (Barton and Cavander), 44, 49
Greek theatre, 52–83, 267
Green, Paul, 275, 399, 402, 428, 442
Green Pastures, The (Connelly), 402
Grein, J.T., 254
Grillparzer, Franz, 232
Grimes, Tammy, 27
Grizzard, George, 431
Gros-Guillaume, 173–174
Grosses Schauspielhaus (Berlin), 323, 351
Grosz, George, 296, 298, 304
    drawing by, 296
Grotowski, Jerzy, 476
Grouch, The (Menander), 73
Groundlings, 123
Group Theatre, The, 275, 398–399, 424
Grünewald, Matthias, 230
Guare, John, 464
Guarini, Giambattista, 146, 161
Guerilla theatre, 164, 408
Guernica (Picasso), 320
Guicharnaud, Jacques, 181, 192, 193
Guildhall School, The (London), 362
Guinness, Alec, 362
Guthrie, Sir Tyrone, 110, 137, 358, 362, 385, 402, 404
Guthrie Theatre, The (Minneapolis), 6, 17, 290, 308, 310
Gwyn, Nell, 197, 206, 208, 223

Hagen, Uta, 431, 434
Haigh, Kenneth, 377, 379
Hair (musical), 447
Hairy Ape, The (O'Neill), 419, 422, 443
Haley, Alex, 428
Hall, Peter, 138, 292, 356, 358, 359, 362, 365, 374, 377, 385
    as director, 365
    quotation from, 365
Hallam, William, 197, 381

Hamburg Dramaturgy, The (Lessing), 231, 250
Hamburg Theatre (Germany), 231
Hamlet (Shakespeare), 3, 13, 24, 33, 43, 111, 120, 130, 131, 132, 202, 277, 363, 374–375
  plot of, 13
  quotations from, 3, 120, 130
Hammerstein II, Oscar, 414
Hampton, Christopher, 361
Handel, George Frederick, 214, 231
Handke, Peter, 312
Hands, Terry, 368
Hansberry, Lorraine, 28, 421, 428–429, 442, 443, 444
  biography of, 428
Hanswurst, 160, 231, 232
Happenings, 24
Happy Days (Beckett), 339, 341, 343
Harbage, Alfred, 141
Hardy, Alexandre, 178
Hare, David, 361, 368
Harlequin, 148, 160
Harold Clurman Theatre (New York), 402
Harris, Julie, 278, 397
Harrison, Richard, 402
Harvey, William, 171
Hasenclever, Walter, 294
Haunted House, The (Plautus), 69
Hauptman, William, 480
Hauptmann, Elisabeth, 302, 313
Hauptmann, Gerhart, 232, 234, 251, 253, 267, 274, 289
Havoc, June, 287
Haymarket Theatre (London), 196, 197, 200, 201, 215, 223
Haynes, Joe, 368
Heartbreak Kid, The (Simon), 463
"Heavens," 127
Hebbel, Friedrich, 232, 234, 251
Hecuba (Euripides), 82
Hedda Gabler (Ibsen), 235, 236, 249, 261, 263, 274, 280, 437
Hellman, Lillian, 28, 421–423, 425, 442, 443, 444
  biography of, 423
Hello, Dolly! (musical), 414
Hell's Mouth (Medieval), 86, 92, 93, 101, 106, 108
Henley, Beth, 453, 459, 479
Hennings, Betty, 249
Henry IV (Shakespeare), 129
Henry V (Shakespeare), 129, 137
Henry VI (Shakespeare), 128
Henry VIII, King of England, 122, 123
Henry Street Settlement (New York), 399
Henslowe, Philip, 111, 113, 115–117, 140
  Diary, 113, 116
Hermitage Theatre (Moscow), 263

Herne, James A., 395
Herod and Miriamne (Hebbel), 251
Heroic drama, 204, 205
Herr Puntila (Brecht), 307
Herrmann, Karl Ernst, 312, 313
Hessian Courier, The (Buchner), 260
Heyward, Dorothy, 402
Heyward, DuBose, 402
Heywood, Thomas, 119
Hill, George, 431
Himation, 60
Hippolytus (Euripides), 68, 76, 185
Histriones, 146
Hochhuth, Rolf, 312
Hodges, C. Walter, 126, 127
Hoffman, Dustin, 278, 397
Hofmannsthal, Hugo von, 322
Hogarth, William, 198, 199, 209
Holberg, Ludwig, 235
Holden, Joan, 164, 165
Hollander, Anne, 177, 193
Home (Storey), 370, 371, 455
Homecoming, The (Pinter), 362, 371–374, 386, 387
  plot of, 374
  quotation from, 373, 375
Homer, 54
Hooks, Robert, 455
Hope Theatre, The (London), 113
Horace (Corneille), 178
Hostage, The (Behan), 363
Hôtel de Bourgogne (Paris), 168, 169–170, 174, 175, 180
Hothouse (Pinter), 464
Hot L Baltimore (Wilson), 451, 464
Houghton, Norris, 268, 290
Houseman, John, 401
House of Representatives Un-American Activities Committee (HUAC), 423, 424, 425
Howard, Alan, 18, 138
Howard, Sidney, 398
Hrotsvitha, 86, 101
  biography of, 101
Hubris, 79
Hughes, Helena, 379
Hughes, Langston, 402, 428
Hughie (O'Neill), 422
Huizinga, Johan, 93, 109
Hull House Players (Chicago), 398
Humanism, 111, 145
Humorists, The (Shadwell), 212
Hunter, Kim, 392, 434, 440, 443
Hurrah, We Live! (Toller), 307
Hurwicz, Angelika, 307
Hypokrites, 56

I Balli de Sfessania (Callot), 150
I Remember Mama (musical), 258
Ibsen, Henrik, 227, 228, 235, 236, 241, 248, 249, 254–258, 280

biography of, 235
modernism of, 257
Iceman Cometh, The (O'Neill), 403, 419, 420, 422
Ik, The (Brook), 364
Iliad (Homer), 54
Ill Seen, Ill Said (Beckett), 343, 353
Illustre Théâtre (France), 172, 174, 180
I'm Talking About Jerusalem (Wesker), 370
Image plays, 407
Imaginary Invalid, The (Molière), 179, 180, 182, 184
Imitation, 22, 23
Imperial Opera (Moscow), 271
Importance of Being Earnest (Wilde), 187
Imposter, The (Molière), 186, 188
Improvisation, 142, 146, 147–148, 164, 231, 267, 350, 363, 364, 382, 458, 462, 466
In Abraham's Bosom (Green), 402
In Celebration (Storey), 369, 370, 371
In the Boom Boom Boom (Rabe), 465
In the Jungle of the Cities (Brecht), 306
Inadmissible Evidence (Osborne), 370, 378
Incident at Vichy (Miller), 427
Independence Theatre (London), 254
Indian Queen, The (Dryden), 203, 210
Indians (Kopit), 465
Inns of Court (London), 112
Insect Comedy, The (Capek), 336
Inspector General, The (Gogol), 266, 271, 272, 273, 289, 290
  plot of, 272
Interart Theatre (New York), 462
Interlude, 94, 108, 112
Intermezzi, 150, 153
International Centre for Theatre Research in Paris (Brook), 364
Interview (van Itallie), 407, 410, 411
  text of, 410
Intimate Theatre (Stockholm), 237
Intrigue and Love (Schiller), 250
Intrigues, 205
Invasion, The (Adamov), 330
Investigation, The (Weiss), 43, 312
Ion (Euripides), 82
Ionesco, Eugene, 28, 33, 317, 329, 339, 340–341, 344–350
  biography of, 341
  interview with, 341
  modernism of, 350
  Representative Play, 344–350
Iphigénie auf Tauris (Goethe), 242
Iphigénie (Racine), 179
Irving, Jules, 17, 404
Ivanov (Chekhov), 279, 290

Jack, or the Submission (Ionesco), 352
Jackson, Glenda, 354

Jackson, Sir Barry, 362
Jacques Damour (Zola), 227
Jarry, Alfred, 326, 351
   biography of, 326
Jefferson, Joseph, 394, 395
Jellicoe, Ann, 220, 221, 361
Jessner, Leopold, 294
Jeu de paume, 170
Jeux de théâtre, 270
Jodelle, Etienne, 170
John F. Kennedy Center for the Per-
   forming Arts, The (Washington,
   D.C.), 40, 258, 259, 260
John Gabriel Borkman (Ibsen), 261
Johnson, Samuel, 204, 212
Jones, Ernest, 363
Jones, Inigo, 124, 125, 140, 156, 157
   biography of, 125
Jones, James Earl, 450
Jones, LeRoi (Imamu Amiri Baraka),
   429, 455
Jones, Margo, 403
Jones, Robert Edmond, 398, 399, 419,
   442
Jongleurs, 87, 101
Jonson, Ben, 118, 125, 128–129
Josephson, Ludvig, 235
Jourdan, Louis, 30
Jouvet, Louis, 325, 326
Joyce, James, 235
Jubilee (Chekhov), 289
Judith (Giraudoux), 338
Judson Church (New York), 468
Judson Poets' Theatre (New York), 452
Julius Caesar (Shakespeare), 40, 137,
   138, 244
Jumpers (Stoppard), 371, 375
Junkie (Boesing), 458
Just Assassins, The (Camus), 328, 339,
   352

Kabuki Theatre (Japan), 267
Kachalov, Vassily, 263, 289
Kafka, Franz, 43
Kaiser, Georg, 294, 296, 306
Kammerspiele Theater (Berlin), 312,
   321
Kane, John, 18
Kant, Immanuel, 229, 231
Kaprow, Allan, 24
Kathen von Heilbron (Kleist), 251
Kazan, Elia, 12, 402, 434, 440, 441,
   442, 443, 444
   quotation from, 434, 436
Kean, Charles, 244
Keaton, Buster, 142
Keene, Laura, 394
Kemble, John Philip, 204
Kempe, Will, 123
Kennedy, Adrienne, 11, 48, 429, 430,
   470

Kern, Jerome, 414
Kernodle, George R., 121, 141
Kerr, Walter, 444
Kierkegaard, Sören, 229
Killer, The (Ionesco), 329, 339
Killigrew, Thomas, 196, 201, 206, 212,
   223
King and No King, A (Fletcher and
   Beaumont), 129
King Lear (Shakespeare), 119, 129, 133,
   204
King of Sodom (Arrabal), 330
King's Men, The (company), 113, 116,
   133, 140
Kingsley, Sidney, 399
Kiss Me Kate (musical), 414
Kitchen, The (Wesker), 32, 370
Klee, Paul, 475
Kleist, Heinrich von, 232, 233, 234,
   242, 250, 251, 312
Knight, Shirley, 287
Knights, The (Aristophanes), 58
Knipper, Olga, 263, 269, 283, 289
Knowles, Christopher, 39
Koch, Frederick, 398
Kokoschka, Oscar, 294
Komos, 73
Konig, Michael, 312
Kopit, Arthur, 464, 465, 466, 467, 479,
   480
Kordax, 60
Kott, Jan, 136, 141
Kotzebue, August Friedrich von, 233,
   234, 251, 260
Kouril, Miroslav, 332
Krapp's Last Tape (Beckett), 339, 343
Krone, Gerald, 455
Kronenberger, Louis, 198, 200, 222
Krutch, Joseph Wood, 213, 214, 225,
   255, 261, 444
Kyd, Thomas, 111, 115, 119, 128, 140

La Mama Experimental Theatre Club
   (New York), 446, 447, 452, 459,
   462, 468, 471, 475, 480
La Mocedades del Cid (Castro), 178
La Thebaide (Racine), 184
La Turista (Shepard), 464, 466, 471,
   480
Lady from Dubuque, The (Albee), 431
Lady from the Sea, The (Ibsen), 261
Lafayette Street Theatre (New York),
   401–402, 442
Lagerkvist, Pär, 235
Lahr, Bert, 15
Lahr, John, 21
Lakeboat (Mamet), 465, 466
L'Amant Militaire (San Francisco
   Mime Troupe), 164, 165, 167
   quotation from, 165
Langham, Michael, 290

Language, 23, 78, 132–133, 135,
   188–189, 257, 286, 347, 380, 438,
   474
Lark, The (Anouilh), 339, 423
Lasch, Christopher, 316
*Last Days of Solitude of Robinson Crusoe,
   The* (Savary), 350
Last of the Red Hot Lovers (Simon), 464
Laughing Audience, The (Hogarth), 209
Laughton, Charles, 315
Lazarus Laughed (O'Neill), 422
Lazzi, 148, 151, 157, 160, 161, 166
Le Ballet de la Nuit, 177
Lear (Bond), 370
League of Resident Theatres (LORT),
   454
   list of, 454
LeCompte, Elizabeth, 40, 41
Lecomte, Valleran, 172, 173
Le Gallienne, Eva, 257
Leigh, Vivien, 9, 440, 441
*Le Mémoire de Mahelot, Laurent et
   d'autres décorateurs de l'Hôtel de
   Bourgogne* (Mahelot), 175
LeNoir, Charles, 172, 176
Lenz (Buchner), 260
Leonce and Lena (Buchner), 251, 260
Lerner, Alan Jay, 414
Les Blancs (Hansberry), 428
Les Comédiens du Roi (France), 173
Lessing, Gotthold Ephraim, 231, 232,
   250
Lesson, The (Ionesco), 339, 340, 352
Let's Get a Divorce and Other Plays, 48
Letter for Queen Victoria, A (Wilson),
   38–39, 40
Levy, Robert, 402
Lewenstein, Oscar, 355
Lewis, Robert, 275, 397
Lewisohn, Alice, 399
Lewisohn, Irene, 399
Libation Bearers, The (Aeschylus), 59,
   82
Licensing Act of 1737, 201
   description of, 201
*Life and Adventures of Nicholas Nickleby,
   The* (Dickens, RSC), 381–385,
   386, 387
Life and Times of Joseph Stalin, The
   (Wilson), 40
Life Class (Storey), 370, 371
Life in the Theatre, A (Mamet), 465, 466
Life-scripts, 23
Life with Father (Lindsay & Crouse),
   138
Lighting, 121, 156, 176, 183, 208, 241,
   301, 316, 325, 328
Lillo, George, 213
Lincoln's Inn Fields Theatre (London),
   196, 200
Little Foxes, The (Hellman), 28, 421,
   422, 443

Littlewood, Joan, 363, 365, 386, 387
  as director, 363
Living Newspaper, The (Federal Theatre Project), 305, 400
Living Theatre, The (Europe), 164, 397, 405–406, 442, 444, 452
Loca, 96, 102
Loewe, Frederick, 414
Lolita (Albee), 431
London Academy of Music and Dramatic Art (LAMDA), 362
London Merchant, The (Lillo), 213
London Theatres, 116
  list of, 116
Long Day's Journey into Night (O'Neill), 403, 419, 420, 422
Long Wharf Theatre (New Haven), 453
Look Back in Anger (Osborne), 354, 357, 361, 362, 368, 370, 385, 386, 387
  quotation from, 379, 380
  Representative Play, 377–381
Lorca, Garcia, 452
Lord Admiral's Men (company), 113, 116, 117, 140
Lord Chamberlain's Men (company), 113, 116, 119, 133, 140
Los Angeles Feminist Theatre, 458
Lost Ones, The (Beckett), 476
Louis XIV, King of France, 171, 172, 177, 184, 186, 192
Louvre, The (Paris), 173, 182
Love and a Bottle (Farquhar), 217
Love and Honour, 207
Love Canoe (Mamet), 465, 466
Love for Love (Dryden), 212, 214, 224
Love Letters on Blue Paper (Wesker), 370
Lower Depths, The (Gorky), 254, 268, 270, 280, 289, 290
Lucky Chance, The (Behn), 206
Ludi (Roman festivals), 62, 82
Lugné-Pöe, Aurelién-Marie, 326
Lulu Plays (Wedekind), 234
Luther (Osborne), 370, 378
Lysistrata (Aristophanes), 58, 68, 72, 73
Lyttelton Theatre (London), 6, 358

Mabou Mines (New York), 38, 447, 462, 475, 476, 479, 481
Macbeth (Shakespeare), 119, 121, 122, 129–140, 401
  quotations from, 131, 132, 135, 136
  Representative Play, 133
Macbett (Ionesco), 339, 341
Macgowan, Kenneth, 397, 398, 442
Machiavelli, Niccolò, 145, 146, 160
MacKaye, Percy, 395, 442
MacKaye, Steele, 394
Macklin, Charles, 204, 223, 224
MacNeil, Claudia, 443

Mad Dog Blues (Shepard), 464, 466
Madden, John, 258
Madeleine Renaud–Jean-Louis Barrault Company (Paris), 327, 345, 357
Maeterlinck, Maurice, 274, 289, 290
  quotation from, 274
Magic Flute, The (Mozart), 243
Magic Theatre (San Francisco), 466, 471
Mahelot, Laurent, 175, 176, 177
Maid of Orleans, The (Schiller), 251
Maids, The (Genet), 338, 343, 344, 352
Maid's Tragedy, The (Fletcher and Beaumont), 129
Malden, Karl, 10, 278, 392, 397, 434, 440, 443
Maleczech, Ruth, 462
Malina, Judith, 405, 444
Malvern Festival (England), 362, 368
Mamet, David, 464–465, 466, 479, 480
Man and the Masses (Toller), 306
Man Is Man (Brecht), 302, 307, 314
Man in the Glass Booth, The (Shaw), 374
Man of La Mancha (musical), 414
Man of Mode, The (Etherege), 205, 212, 224
Man Says Goodbye to His Mother, A (Bread & Puppet), 412
Man Who Had All the Luck, The (Miller), 425
Man Who Had Three Arms, The (Albee), 431
Man with Bags, The (Ionesco), 339, 341
Management (theatre), 56, 62, 89, 116, 146, 172, 199, 203–232, 266, 320–325, 358–361, 394
Mandrake, The (Machiavelli), 160
Mann, Theodore, 403
Mansions (Medieval), 86, 91, 92, 102, 108, 116, 150, 170, 175
Manual for Constructing Theatrical Scenes and Machines (Sabbattini), 157
Marathon 33 (Havoc), 287
Marat/Sade (The Persecution and Assassination of Jean-Paul Marat As Performed By the Inmates of the Asylum of Charenton Under the Direction of the Marquis de Sade) (Weiss), 43, 166, 311, 312, 359, 363, 364
Marceau, Marcel, 142, 164
Marco Millions (O'Neill), 422
Mardi Gras, 97
Maria Magdalena (Hebbel), 234, 251
Marinetti, Filippo Tommaso, 332
Marinsky Theatre (Moscow), 271
Marionettes, 153, 192
Mark Taper Forum (Los Angeles), 453
Marlowe, Christopher, 99, 103, 115, 118, 128–129, 140, 191, 251
  biography of, 118
Marowitz, Charles, 364

Marranca, Bonnie, 38, 481
Marriage à la Mode (Dryden), 212
Marriage Proposal, The (Chekhov), 279, 289
Marston, John, 113, 119
Marx Brothers, The, 28, 142, 164
Marx, Karl, 229, 231
Mary Stuart, Queen of Scots, 112–113, 115
Mary Stuart (Schiller), 232, 242, 243, 244, 245, 251
Masks, 335, 343, 365, 376, 412, 419, 475
  Greek and Roman, 56, 57, 60, 63, 75
  commedia dell'arte, 143–148, 150–153, 160, 161, 164
Masques, 95, 124, 133, 140, 156
Masque of Blackness, The (Jonson), 125
Masque of Oberon, The, 124
Massinger, Philio, 119
Master Builder, The (Ibsen), 261
Mastersinger of Nuremberg, The (Wagner), 230
Matisse, Henri, 334
Mayakovsky, Vladimir, 281
Maybe (Hellman), 423
Mazarin, Cardinal, 171
McCarthy, Kevin, 287
McClendon, Rose, 402
McCullers, Carson, 440
McCullough, John, 394
McKellen, Ian, 138, 139, 354
McLuhan, Marshal, 334
McManus, Mark, 107
McWhinnie, Donald, 373
Measure for Measure (Shakespeare), 111, 137
Mechane, 58
Medea (Euripides), 40, 68, 69, 76, 78, 79, 80, 81
Medicine Show Theatre Ensemble (New York), 410
Medici, Lorenzo de, 144
Medieval drama, 192
Medieval theatre, 84–109
Meiningen Company, 226, 231, 242, 243–244, 258, 266, 280, 323
  ensemble style, 244
Meiningen Court Theatre, 243–244
Meisner, Sanford, 399
Melfi, Leonard, 452
Mélite (Corneille), 178
Melodrama, 26–28, 29, 233, 251–252, 365, 385, 421, 423, 450
  definition of, 421
Melos, 26
Member of the Wedding, The, 402
Mémoire de Mahelot, Laurent, et d'Autres Décorateurs, Le, 176, 177
Memorial Theatre (Stratford, England), 359
Menander, 55, 73

Merchant, The (Plautus), 370
Merchant, Vivian, 354
Merchant of Venice, The (Shakespeare), 204, 323
Mercury Theatre, The (New York), 137, 401, 442
Messenger's report, 185
Messingkauf Dialogues (Brecht), 476
Metatheatre, 334, 335, 338
Metropolitan Opera Company (New York), 292, 364
Meyerhold Theatre (Moscow), 271
Meyerhold, Vsevolod, 270–272, 274, 280, 283, 289
  acting style of, 271
  as director, 270–272
  biography of, 271
  drawing by, 273
  quotation from, 270–271
Michener, James, 414
Middleton, Thomas, 119, 129
Midsummer Night's Dream, A (Shakespeare), 18, 19, 137, 140, 141, 180, 321, 381
Mielziner, Jo, 46–47, 392, 398, 436, 437, 443
  designs of, 437
Miles Gloriosus, 160
Miller, Arthur, 46, 48, 405, 425, 426–427, 442, 443, 444, 453
  biography of, 425
Miller, Jonathan, 368
Milton, John, 196, 216
Mime, 74–75, 146, 164, 231, 260, 343, 382
Mimes, 87, 101
Mimesis, 23
Minna von Barnhelm (Lessing), 250
Minotis, Alexis, 52
Minstrel, 394
Minstrel shows, 428
Miracle of the Rose, The (Genêt), 344
Miracle plays, 101, 108
Misanthrope, The (Molière), 179, 180, 184
Mise en scène, 268, 270, 298
Miser, The (Molière), 180, 184
Miss Julie (Strindberg), 236, 237, 253, 260, 261, 280
  preface to, 236, 261
Miss Sara Sampson (Lessing), 250
Misunderstanding, The (Camus), 352
Mitchell, Abbie, 402
Mitchell, Margaret, 436
Mithridate (Racine), 179
Mitos, 456, 457
Mnouchkine, Ariane, 31, 32
  biography of, 32
Modern theatre (19th century), 262–291
Modern Theatre Is the Epic Theatre, The (Brecht), 299

Modernism, 106, 135–136, 189, 257, 286, 350, 381, 475
  cycle plays, 106
  Molière, 189
  Shakespeare, 135–136
Molière (Jean-Baptiste Poquelin), 26, 168, 172–175, 179, 181, 182, 185, 186, 188, 270
  biography of, 180
  modernism of, 189
  Representative Play, 186–189
Molière Cycle (Vitez), 169
Molly's Dream (Fornés), 465, 468
Monk, Meredith, 447
Monologue, 378, 442, 462, 474, 475–476
  interior, 465–467
Monroe, Marilyn, 425
Mons (France), 192
Montdory (Guillaume des Gilleberts), 172, 173, 178, 192
Monteverde, Claudio, 153
Montfleury (Zacharie Jacob), 174, 192
Month in the Country, A (Turgenev), 266
Monty Python, 28
Mood, 244, 281, 286, 301
Moon for the Misbegotten, A (O'Neill), 422
Morality plays, 94, 95, 99, 102–103, 108, 323
More Pricks Than Kicks (Beckett), 343
More Stately Mansions (O'Neill), 422
Morosco Theatre (New York), 287
Moscow Art Theatre (Russia), 263–265, 268–270, 280–281
Moscow Philharmonic Society (Russia), 263
Moskvin, Ivan, 263, 289
Mother Courage and Her Children (Brecht), 41, 297, 298, 300, 306, 307, 309, 476
  plot of, 300
  Model Book of, 315
Mother-in-Law (Terence), 69, 74
Mourning Becomes Electra (O'Neill), 419, 422, 443
Movement: A Documentary of a Struggle for Equality, The (Hansberry), 428
Mozart, Wolfgang Amadeus, 230, 242, 245
Mulatto (Hughes), 402, 428
Multicultural, 342, 441
Mummings, 95, 98
Munch, Edvard, 321, 322
Murder By Death (film), 463
Music, 60–62, 93, 122, 153, 177, 208, 231, 297, 301, 313, 315, 439
Music and the Art of the Theatre (Appia), 241
Musical, 294, 396, 414–417, 428, 450, 451, 479

Music-drama (Wagner), 226, 235, 245, 246
Mutation Show (Terry), 407
My Fair Lady (musical), 414
My Life in Art (Stanislavsky), 244, 265, 268, 269, 281, 290
  quotation from, 268, 269
My Mother, My Father, and Me (Hellman), 423
Mystery-Bouffe, (Mayakovsky), 281
Myth, 68, 339, 364, 456
Myth of Sisyphus, The (Camus), 351, 352, 377
  quotation from, 328

Napier, John, 44, 137, 381
Naropa (van Itallie), 480
Narr, 230
Narrative, 297
Narrow Road to the Deep North (Bond), 369, 370
Nathan the Wise (Lessing), 250
National Alliance of Theatrical Stage Employees, 397
National Council of the Arts, 455
National Endowment for the Arts, The (N.E.A.), 450, 455, 479
National Theatre (Bergen, Norway), 235, 258
National Theatre (London), 6, 358–359, 362, 365, 370, 374, 376, 378, 385, 386
National Theatre (Oslo, Norway), 229
National Theatre (Prague), 332, 336
Native Son (Wright), 428
Naturalism, 227–229, 237, 238, 253–254, 382, 395, 405, 419, 471
Naturalism in the Theatre (Zola), 253
  quotation from, 253
Naumachia, 156
Nayatt School (Gray), 41, 462
Nazimova, All, 263, 289
Negro Ensemble Company (NEC) (New York), 29, 455, 456, 459
Neher, Caspar, 298, 299, 302, 304, 313
Neighborhood Playhouse (New York), 398, 399, 466
Nelson, Richard, 480
Nemiroff, Robert, 428
Nemirovich-Danchenko, Vladimir, 263, 265, 266, 270, 283, 289
Neoclassicism, 178, 205, 235
  decorum, 178, 181, 184
  genre, 181
  poetic justice, 181, 185
  rules of, 178–186
  unities of time, place, action, 178, 179, 181, 184, 185, 186
  verisimilitude, 181, 184
  verse, 179, 181, 184
Neuber, Caroline, 232

Neville, John, 258
New Comedy, 55, 63, 73
New stagecraft, 398, 442
New Tenant, The (Ionesco), 339
New York Shakespeare Festival, 14, 59, 447, 449, 459, 462, 476, 479
Nicomède (Corneille), 173
Night and Day (Stoppard), 371
Night Music (Odets), 424
Night of the Iguana, The (Williams), 430
Nightingale, Benedict, 387
Nightwalk (Terry), 464, 465
Nikolais, Alwin, 337
No Exit (Sartre), 328, 338, 339, 351
No Man's Land (Pinter), 371, 374
No Place to Be Somebody (Gordone), 447
Noh Theatre (Japan), 267, 295, 303
Norman, Marsha, 459, 470, 479
Norton, Thomas, 112
Not I (Beckett), 329, 343
Notes and Counter Notes: Writings on the Theatre (Ionesco), 28, 340, 353
Nunn, Trevor, 136–138, 140, 381, 382, 384, 385, 386
    biography of, 138
    quotation from, 384, 385
Nurseries, 201, 267

Oberammergau (Bavaria), 84–85
O'Casey, Sean, 455
Octoroon, The (Boucicault), 28
Odd Couple, The (Simon), 464
Odéon Théâtre (Paris), 228
Odes, 54, 57, 60, 69, 70, 72
Odets, Clifford, 275, 399, 424–426, 427, 435, 442, 444
    biography of, 424
Odyssey (Homer), 54
Oedipus at Colonus (Sophocles), 68
Oedipus the King (Sophocles), 24, 25, 69–72
    plot of, 70
    quotation from, 71
Oenslager, Donald, 399
Off Broadway, 403, 405, 446, 450–453, 468, 471
Off-Off-Broadway, 317, 368, 405, 450, 451–453, 459
Oh, What a Lovely War! (Littlewood), 363
O'Horgan, Tom, 320
Okhlopkov, Nikolai, 272
Oklahoma (musical), 414
Old Bachelor, The (Congreve), 214
Old Comedy, 58, 60, 72
Old Times (Pinter), 371, 374
Old Vic Company (London), 137, 320, 354, 358, 359, 362, 385
Oldfield, Anne, 215
Oliver Twist (Dickens), 384
Olivier, Sir Laurence, 23, 137, 354,

356, 358, 359, 362, 363, 365, 378, 385
Olivier Theatre, The (London), 6, 358
Omaha Magic Theatre (Nebraska), 410, 458
Ondine (Giraudoux), 326, 338
On Humor (Pirandello), 338
On the Razzle (Stoppard), 371
One Third of a Nation (Federal Theatre Project), 305, 400, 401
    quotation from, 401
1001 Nights (Savary), 350
O'Neill, Eugene, 394, 404, 405, 418–421, 428, 442, 443, 451, 453
    biography of, 422
    quotation from, 420
O'Neill, James, 395, 422
O'Neill Center, The (Connecticut), 459
Ontological-Hysteric Theater (New York), 38, 40
Open Theatre (New York), 164, 407, 410, 411, 452, 468, 471
Opera, 153, 156–157, 175, 177, 238, 245, 250, 295, 382
Opera and Drama (Wagner), 246
Operation Sidewinder (Shepard), 464, 466, 471
Orateur de troupe, 172
Orbecche (Cinthio), 160
Orchestra, 54, 62, 154
Oregon Shakespearean Festival Theatre, The (Ashland), 7, 127
Oresteia (Aeschylus), 59, 68, 82, 322, 327
Orfeo (Monteverde), 153
Origin of Species, The (Darwin), 231, 253
Orphan, The (Otway), 212
Orton, Joe, 361
Osborne, John, 354, 356, 370, 385, 386, 387
    biography of, 378
    modernism of, 381
    Representative Play, 377–381
Ostrovsky, Alexander, 266, 289
Othello (Shakespeare), 14, 24, 42, 130, 131, 279, 402, 403, 450
Other Place, The (Stratford-upon-Avon, England), 136
Otherwise Engaged (Gray), 374
O'Toole, Peter, 361
Otto, Teo, 298, 299, 301, 302
Otway, Thomas, 212, 224
Our Lady of the Flowers (Genêt), 344
Ouspenskaya, Maria, 278
Out-of-Towners, The (film), 463
Owens, Rochelle, 452, 459

Pacino, Al, 278, 288, 397
Page, Geraldine, 278, 287, 397

Pageant, 85, 90, 95, 98, 102, 121
Pageant master, 90, 102
Pageant wagon, 85, 91, 96, 103, 106, 108
Pagliaccio. 160
Palais Royal (Paris), 171, 173, 182, 187, 192, 226
Palamedes (Euripides), 75
Palladio, Andrea, 143, 149, 158, 161
Pandering to the Masses (Foreman), 40
Pandora's Box (Wedekind), 251
Pantagleize (Ghelderode), 326, 338
Pantomime, 74–75, 142, 213
Paolo Paoli (Adamov), 330
Papp, Joseph, 342, 405, 447, 449, 475, 479
    biography of, 449
Parabasis, 73
Parable, 308, 311, 314
Parade float (Mardi Gras), 97
Paradise Lost (Milton), 196, 424, 425, 426
    quotation from, 426
Paradise Now: Collective Creation of the Living Theatre, 405, 406, 408–409, 444
    text of, 408–409
Parados, 57, 62, 65, 77
Parigi, Giulo, 156, 167
Parterre, 169, 177
Passion play, 85, 99
    Lucerne, 85
    Mons, 85
    Valenciennes, 85
Passion, The (York cycle), 106
Pastoral, 172, 178
Patriot For Me, A (Osborne), 370, 378
Pavilion, 116
Peace (Aristophanes), 58
Peachum Print, The, 122
Peer Gynt (Ibsen), 106, 235, 311, 312–313, 315
    quotation from, 313
Pelican, The (Strindberg), 237
Pelléas and Mélisande (Maeterlinck), 274
Penchenat, Jean-Claude, 31
Penguin Touquet (Foreman), 40
Pennell, Nicholas, 35
Penthesilea (Kleist), 233, 251
Pentimento (Hellman), 423
Pepys, Samuel, 198, 206, 208, 209
    biography of, 198
    Diary of, 198, 208
Performance Group (New York), 40, 41, 447, 462
Performance style, 384–385
Performing Garage (New York), 471
Periaktoi, 58, 62, 157
Peripety, 72
Persians, The (Aeschylus), 57, 68
Persona, 258
Personal History of the American Theatre, The (Gray), 41

Perspective, 167, 192
Petit Bourbon (Paris), 173, 175, 182, 192
Phaedra (Racine), 175, 179, 184, 185, 192, 193
  plot of, 185
Phaedra (Seneca), 69
Philaster (Beaumont and Fletcher), 129
Philoctetes (Sophocles), 68
Phormio (Terence), 69, 74
Photo Essays:
  American Design and Stage Technology, 460–461
  Drury Lane Theatre Past and Present, 210–211
  Comédie Française, 182–183
  Elizabethan Theatre Past and Present, 176–177
  Epic Theatre in Performance, 304–305
  Greek Theatre Past and Present, 64–65
  Ibsen and Strindberg in Performance, 248–249
  Medieval Fixed and Processional Stages, 96–97
  Moscow Art Theatre in Performance, 276–277
  "New" Stage Realism, 366–367
  Roman Theatre Past and Present, 66–67
  Styles of Developing Scripts into Performance, 44–47
  Theatres of Renaissance Italy, 158–159
  "Theatrical" Styles in Scenery, Costumes, and Lighting, 336–337
  Types of Contemporary Theatres, 6–7
Physicists, The (Duerrenmatt), 312
Piaget, Jean, 23
Picasso, Pablo, 320, 334
Pickup, Ronald, 223
Pickwick Papers (Dickens), 28
Pierre Pathelin (farce), 87, 101, 108
Pierrot, 160, 363
Pillars of Society (Ibsen), 236, 260
Pimp (Boesing), 458
Pinakes, 58
Pinter, Harold, 365, 368, 370–374, 375, 386, 387
  biography of, 374
  quotation from, 375
Pippin (musical), 414
Pirandello, Luigi, 326, 334–335, 338–339, 343, 351, 352
  quotation from, 334, 335, 338
Pirates of Penzance, The (Gilbert and Sullivan), 447, 449, 453
Pirsig, Robert M., 252, 261
  quotation from, 252

Piscator, Erwin, 294–298, 304, 307, 313
Piscator Theater (Berlin), 304, 307
Pitoëff, Georges, 325
Plain Dealer, The (Wycherley), 205, 212
Planchon, Roger, 168, 189, 191, 192, 193, 292
  biography of, 191
Platea, 92
Plautus, 62, 63, 69, 73, 74, 82, 146
Play, 22, 23
Play (Beckett), 476
Play of Adam, 86
Play structure, 33, 37, 48, 69–70, 466
  classical, 69–70
  climactic, 33, 34–35
  episodic, 33, 36–37
  intensive, 466
  situational, 33, 37, 48
Plays to Read, 82, 108, 140, 167, 192, 224, 260, 289, 314, 352, 443, 479–480
Play-within-the-play, 41, 42, 43, 180, 309, 326, 334, 375, 377
Playwriting, 11, 98–99, 118–119, 178–179, 232–238, 325–326, 328–330, 351, 362, 368–377, 459
Plaza Suite (Simon), 464
Plot, 23, 24, 251, 334, 341
  commedia, 146, 147, 157, 160, 161
  double, 36, 41, 43, 74, 130
  Greek, 68–70, 72–73
  medieval, 101, 102
  Roman, 74
  simultaneous, 42–43
  structure, 32–33, 68–70, 297, 303
Plowright, Joan, 359, 361, 386
Plummer, Christopher, 450
Plutus (Aristophanes), 58, 68
Poetics (Aristotle), 23, 55, 70, 83
Point Judith (Gray), 41
Point of attack, 41, 42
Poitier, Sidney, 443
Polly (Gay), 214
Popular entertainments, 153, 333
Porgy (Heyward), 402
Porgy and Bess (Heyward), 402
Portable stage, 148, 164
Postmodernism, 474, 475
  definition of, 475
Postwar Theatre (European), 316–353
Pot of Gold (Plautus), 74
Power (Federal Theatre Project), 400
Power of Darkness, The (Tolstoy), 280
Prague Institute of Scenography, 332
Prelude to Death in Venice, A (Breuer), 476
Pretenders, The (Ibsen), 235
Price, Jonathan, 21
Price, The (Miller), 425, 427, 444
  quotation from, 427

Prince, Harold, 414
Prince, The (Machiavelli), 145
Prince of Homburg, The (Kleist), 233, 251, 312
Princesse qui a perdu L'Esprit, La (Gelosi Co.), 147
Prisoner of Second Avenue, The (Simon), 463, 464, 480
Private Life of the Master Race, The (Brecht), 307
Processional staging (Spain), 94–95
Producer, 113, 115, 275, 395, 396, 397, 451, 459, 479
Prologue, 56, 73, 149, 170, 172, 201, 206, 208, 213, 308, 477
Promenade (Fornés), 465, 468
Prometheus (Living Theatre), 406
Prometheus Bound (Aeschylus), 68
Promptbook, 270
Properties, 176, 207–208, 239–241, 298, 300, 313, 316, 325, 385
  commedia dell'arte, 146, 148, 150, 162
  Elizabethan, 116, 121
  medieval, 93, 94
  modern realism, 268–269, 270, 271
Proscenium arch, 159, 161, 170, 182, 183, 192, 270, 284
Proscenium stage, 5, 6
Provincetown Players (New York), 398, 399, 405, 411, 422, 442
Prozess, The (Weiss), 43
Pryor, Richard, 28
Psychomachia, 103
Public playhouse, 111, 115–116
Public Theatre, The (New York), 80, 140, 342, 446, 447, 453, 471, 475, 479
  Representative Theatre, 447–449
Punch, 152, 160
Punch and Judy, 160
Puppets, 411, 412
Pygmalion (Shaw), 27

Quare Fellow, The (Behan), 363
Queen Anne, of England, 197, 198
Queen Elizabeth I, of England, 111, 112, 115, 124, 133
  biography of, 115
Queen Mary I, of England, 112, 115
Quem Quaeritis trope, 13–14, 88, 98, 108
  quotation from, 88
Querelle de Brest (Genêt), 344
Quintero, José, 402, 403, 404, 442
  as director, 403

Rabe, David, 427, 452, 459, 464, 465, 479
Racine, Jean, 179, 184, 186, 233, 250
  biography of, 179

Radok, Alfred, 332
Raisin (musical), 428
Raisin in the Sun, A (Hansberry), 28, 421, 428, 429, 443, 444
   text of, 429
Raissoneur, 335
Ralph Roister Doister (Udall), 112
Raped (At the Foot of the Mountain), 458
Rape of Lucrece, The (Shakespeare), 119
Realism, 227, 234, 252–253, 286, 316, 366–367, 395, 428, 430–434, 463, 464–465
   definition of, 278
   modified, 399, 442, 443
   "new," on the British stage, 354–385
   Pinter's, 370–374
   psychological, 262, 270, 288, 289, 340, 354, 465
   selected, 398, 442
   simplified, 398
   social, 262, 289, 321, 465
   working class, 368–369
Re. Cher. Chez. (New York), 462, 476
Reckoning, The (Ward), 430
Recruiting Officer, The (Farquhar), 212, 216, 220
Red and Blue (Akalaitis), 462
Red Cross (Shepard), 466
Redemption (Tolstoy), 281
Redford, Robert, 252
Redgrave, Michael, 359, 362
Red Horse Animation, The (Breuer), 475
Red Room, The (Strindberg), 237
Rees, Roger, 385
Regiebuch, 268, 325
Regional theatre (America), 164, 274, 289, 362, 381, 390, 404, 450, 453
Régisseur, 243, 259, 323, 402
Regularis Concordia, 88
Rehearsal at Versailles, The (Molière), 180, 181
   quotation from, 180
Reid, Sheila, 223
Reinhardt, Max, 294, 306, 316, 320, 321–325, 351, 352, 398
   as actor, 321
   as director, 321–325
   biography of, 321
   quotation from, 321
Relapse, The (Vanbrugh), 205, 213
Renaissance (German), 230
Renaissance (Italy), 142, 153–157
Renaud, Madeleine, 327, 345
Repertory system, 116, 172–173, 200, 206
Representative Plays:
   Bald Soprano, The (Ionesco), 344–350
   Beaux' Strategem, The (Farquhar), 215–220
   Buried Child (Shepard), 471–474

Caucasian Chalk Circle, The (Brecht), 307–311
Crucifixion Play, The (Wakefield Cycle), 103–106
Ghosts (Ibsen), 254–258
Look Back in Anger (Osborne), 377–381
Macbeth (Shakespeare), 132–136
Streetcar Named Desire, A (Williams), 434–441
Tartuffe (Molière), 186–189
Three Cuckolds, The (*commedia* scenario), 160–164
Three Sisters, The (Chekhov), 283–286
Trojan Women, The (Euripides), 75–79
Representative Theatres:
   Drury Lane Theatre (London), 195–196
   Ethel Barrymore Theatre, The (New York), 391–392
   Gelosi Company (Italy), 143–144
   Globe, The (London), 111
   Hôtel de Bourgogne (Paris), 169–170
   Moscow Art Theatre (Russia), 263–265
   Public Theatre, The (New York), 447–449
   Royal Court Theatre (London), 355–357
   Theater am Schiffbauerdamm (East Berlin), 293–294
   Theatre at York (England), 85–86
   Théâtre des Noctambules (Paris), 317
   Théâtre Libre (Paris), 227–229
   Theatre of Dionysus (Athens), 53–54
Request Concert (Kroetz), 462
Resident theatre, 394, 404, 446, 453–455, 475, 478, 479
Resident theatre movement, 227, 243, 362
Resistible Rise of Arturo Ui, The (Brecht), 307
Resolution, 41, 42, 48
Resounding Tinkle, A (Simpson), 221
Restoration and 18th Century Theatre, 194–225
Restoration of Arnold Middleton, The (Storey), 317, 370
Resurrection (film), 466
Resurrection of Our Lord Jesus Christ, The, 96
Reunion (Mamet), 465
Revenger's Tragedy, The (Tourneur), 138
Revue (musical), 428
Reynard the Fox (Anonymous), 475
Reynolds, George F., 141

Rhapsodes, 82
Rhinoceros (Ionesco), 329, 339, 340, 341
Rhoda in Potatoland (Foreman), 40
Rhode Island Feminist Theatre, 458
Ribman, Ronald, 464
Rice, Elmer, 394
Rich, John, 197, 224
Richardson, Ian, 354–355, 358
Richardson, Jack, 480
Richardson, Sir Ralph, 354, 362, 385
Richardson, Tony, 138, 377
Richelieu, Cardinal, 171, 181, 182
Ride Across Lake Constance, The (Handke), 312
Rienzi (Wagner), 246
Right You Are, If You Think You Are (Pirandello), 326, 335, 338, 353
   quotation from, 335
Rimers of Eldritch, The (Wilson), 464
Ring of the Niebelungs, The (Wagner), 246
Rise and Fall of the City of Mahagonny, The (Brecht), 292, 314
Ritual, 4, 52, 140, 316, 330, 343, 352, 364, 365, 456
Rivals, The (Sheridan), 205, 213
River Niger, The (Walker), 28, 29, 421
Robbers, The (Schiller), 250
Robbins, Jerome, 414
Robeson, Paul, 402, 403, 428
Robson, Flora, 362
Rocket to the Moon (Odets), 424
Rock Garden (Shepard), 471
Rodgers, Richard, 414
Roman drama, 73–75
Roman *habit,* 207
Roman theatre, 62–63
Romanticism, 226, 233, 235, 250–251, 252, 260, 294
   tenets of, 233
Romeo and Juliet (Shakespeare), 126, 129, 382
Room, The (Pinter), 371, 374
Rooney, Mickey, 321
Roose-Evans, James, 418, 444
Roots (Wesker), 370, 428
Rose, Phyllis, 458
Rose Bruford College, The (London), 362
Rosencrantz and Guildenstern Are Dead (Stoppard), 362, 371, 374, 375, 376
Rose Tattoo, The (Williams), 430, 445
Rose Theatre, The (London), 111, 113, 117
Rosmersholm (Ibsen), 235, 280
Rousseau, Jean Jacques, 27
Route 1 & 9 (Gray), 41
Rover, The (Behn), 212
Royal Academy of Dramatic Art (RADA) (London), 362, 374
Royal Court Theatre (London), 355–357, 385, 386, 449, 471

Royal Court Theatre (*continued*)
  directors of, 355
  Representative Theatre, 355–357
Royal Dramatic Theatre (Stockholm), 229, 237, 249
Royal Hunt of the Sun, The (Shaffer), 365, 371, 376
Royal Opera Company (London), 365
Royal Shakespeare Company (RSC) (England), 12, 28, 136–138, 358, 359–361, 362, 374, 381, 385, 386
Rueda, Lope de, 99
Rules for Actors (Goethe), 241, 243, 261
  quotation from, 243
Rumstick Road (Gray), 41, 462
Runaways (musical), 447, 453
Ryall, David, 221

Sabbattini, Nicola, 157
Sachs, Hans, 101–102, 230
Sackville, Thomas, 112
Saint and the Football Players, The (dance), 476
Saint-Denis, Michel, 358
Saint Genêt: Actor and Martyr (Sartre), 343
St. Nicholas Theatre Company (Chicago), 466
Sakonnet Point (Gray), 41
Salzburg Festival (Austria), 324, 325, 351
San Francisco Mime Troupe, 142, 164–167, 455
Saroyan, William, 275, 399, 435, 442
Sartre, Jean-Paul, 328, 338, 339–340, 343, 351, 352
Satin Slipper, The (Claudel), 327
Satire, 205, 312, 313, 346, 363, 455
Satyr play, 54–57, 60, 62, 63, 72, 75, 76
Savage/Love (Shepard), 480
Savary, Jerome, 350–351, 352
Saved (Bond), 312, 368, 369, 370, 372, 386
  plot of, 369
Saxe-Meiningen, Duke of, 234, 243–244, 259, 260
  as director, 243–244
Scaena frons, 63
Scala, Flaminio, 147, 148, 157, 161
  biography of, 148
Scamozzi, Vincenzo, 149, 158
Scapin, 148, 151, 160
Scaramouche, 160
Scenario, 144, 146, 147, 148, 150, 157, 160, 161, 167
Scenery, 126–127, 147–148, 206–207, 238–239, 267–268, 298–300, 304–305, 328, 332–333, 366–367, 398, 460–461
  Elizabethan, 116, 121, 126–127
  Greek, 58, 63

medieval, 91–92, 94–95
movable, 94, 108, 155, 156, 175, 192
perspective, 154–156
Scenographer, 12
Schaubühne am Halleschen Ufer (West Berlin), 292, 311, 312, 314
Schechner, Richard, 40, 41
Schédadé, Georges, 330
Schiller, Friedrich, 226, 232, 233, 234, 242, 243, 250–251
Schiller Theatre (West Berlin), 43
Schlegel, August Wilhelm, 233
Schneider, Alan, 15, 302, 315, 431
  quotation from, 302
School for Husbands, The (Molière), 179
School for Scandal, The (Sheridan), 205, 208, 213, 224, 391
School for Wives, The (Molière), 179
Schroeder, Friedrich, 238, 239
Schumann, Peter, 405, 411, 412, 413, 418, 444
  quotation from, 412
Schweyk in the Second World War (Brecht), 315
Sciopticon, 238
Scoundrel Time (Hellman), 423, 444
Screens, The (Genêt), 327, 339, 343, 344, 345, 476
Scribe, Eugène, 279
Sea, The (Bond), 369, 370
Seagull, The (Chekhov), 269–270
  opening night of, 269–270
  plot of, 282
  quotation from, 281, 282
Seascape (Albee), 431
Second Shepherds Play, The, 101, 108
Secrets, 92
Seduced (Shepard), 480
Segal, Sondra, 459
Self-as-text, 447
Self-Service (Kaprow), 24
Self-Tormentor (Terence), 69, 74
Sellers, Peter, 28
Selznick, Irene M., 434
Seneca, Lucius Annaeus, 62, 69, 74, 130
Sense of Detachment, A (Osborne), 370
Sententiae, 74
Serban, Andrei, 52, 79, 80, 81, 82, 320, 342
Serlio, Sebastiano, 154, 155, 160, 167
Sermon joyeux, 102
Serpent, The (van Itallie), 407, 465
Serreau, Jean-Marie, 331
Servant of Two Masters, The (Goldoni), 167
Seven Against Thebes (Aeschylus), 68
Seven Scenes from a Family Album (Gray), 462
1789 (Mnouchkine), 32
1793 (Mnouchkine), 32
Sex and Death to the Age 14 (Gray), 41

Sexual Perversity in Chicago (Mamet), 465, 466
Shadwell, Thomas, 205, 212
Shaffer, Peter, 355, 365, 368, 371, 374, 376–377, 386, 387
Shaggy Dog Animation, The (Breuer), 463, 466, 475, 477, 478, 481
  quotation from, 477, 478
Shakespeare, William, 13, 14, 18, 33, 43, 111, 118, 119, 127–133, 136, 137, 250, 359, 362
  biography of, 119
  modernism of, 135–136
Shakespeare Festival Theatre (England), 358, 359, 362, 385
Shakespeare Festival Theatre (Ontario), 35, 404
Shakespeare Theatre Workshop (New York), 449
Shaman, 4
Shange, Ntozake, 455, 465, 470, 479
Shank, Adele, 459, 470
Shaw, George Bernard, 215, 401, 414
Shaw, Irwin, 399
Shaw, Robert, 374
Sheehy, Gail, 475
Shepard, Sam, 447, 452, 464–465, 466, 471–475, 478, 479, 480, 481
  biography of, 466
  modernism of, 475
Sheridan, Richard Brinsley, 194, 205, 206, 213, 224, 386, 391
She Stoops to Conquer (Goldsmith), 205, 213
She Would If She Could (Etherege), 212, 213
Short Eyes (Pinero), 447
Short Organon for the Theatre, The (Brecht), 25
Showboat (musical), 414
Shubert Brothers (Sam, Lee, Jacob J.), 395, 396, 442
Shubert Organization (New York), 396
Shubert Theatre, The (New York), 17, 391
Siddons, Sarah, 204
Sides, 120
Sign in Sidney Brustein's Window, The (Hansberry), 428, 443
Sikinnis, 60
Similitude, 215, 220
Simon, Neil, 463–464, 479, 480
  biography of, 464
Simonson, Lee, 398, 399, 442
Simpson, N.F., 221, 361
Sintesi, 333
Sisyphus (Euripides), 54, 75
Six Characters in Search of an Author (Pirandello), 326, 335, 338, 353
Skene, 58, 62
Skin of Our Teeth, The (Wilder), 402

Skinner, Otis, 395
Sklar, Roberta, 459
Slave Ship (Baraka), 429, 455
Slice-of-life, 228, 253
Smith, Maggie, 223, 249, 359
Smith, Priscilla, 59
Soccus, 63
Socialist realism, 267, 271, 332
Sociétaire, 173, 326
Society of Art and Literature, 263
Society for Stage Directors and
    Choreographers, 397
Sogetto, 157
Soldier's Play, A (Fuller), 455
Soliloquy, 74, 131, 132, 134, 135, 140,
    185
Solo performance, 447, 462, 479
Sondheim, Stephen, 414
Song of the Lusitanian Bogey, The (Weiss),
    43
Sophocles, 3, 8, 14, 24, 48, 57, 58, 68,
    69, 72, 79, 82, 279, 437
Sorge, Reinhard, 294
Sorrows of Young Werther, The
    (Goethe), 242
Sotties, 102
Sound-and-movement, 407
Sound effects, 269, 313, 385
Sound poems, 333
Southern Exposure (Akalaitis), 462
Southern, Richard, 206, 225
South Pacific (musical), 414
Spanish Tragedy, The (Kyd), 128
Special effects, 92, 177
Spell #7 (Shange), 465
Spider Woman Theatre Workshop
    (New York), 458, 462
Spring's Awakening (Wedekind), 234,
    251
Stafford-Clark, Max, 368
Stage business, 146, 147, 150, 157,
    162, 164, 244, 286, 289
Stage realism, 262, 263, 268, 269, 272,
    279, 289, 294, 343, 351, 354
Staging, 5, 92, 94, 99, 108
Staging of Wagner's Music Dramas, The
    (Appia), 241
Stanislavsky, Constantin, 263,
    265–269, 276, 280–281, 397
    as director, 265, 270
    biography of, 265
    method of acting, 265, 267–268,
    271, 288
    quotation from, 268, 269
Stanislavsky System, 265, 278
Stanley, Kim, 287, 288
Stapleton, Maureen, 278, 397
Starluster (Wellman), 480
Star system, 266–267, 362, 394, 397,
    442
State of Siege (Camus), 328, 338, 352
Steele, Richard, 212, 215

Stein, Gertrude, 452
Stein, Peter, 52, 311, 312, 313, 314
    biography of, 312
    epic techniques of, 313
Steiner, George, 23, 251, 252, 261
    quotations from, 252, 339
Stephens, Robert, 223, 359
Stevens, Roger L., 455
Stevens, Thomas Wood, 398
Stewart, Ellen, 80, 350, 405, 452, 479
    biography of, 459
    quotation from, 459
Stichomythia, 70
Sticks and Bones (Rabe), 447, 465
Stock characters, 147
Stoppard, Tom, 355, 362, 368, 371,
    374–376, 386
Storey, David, 361, 368, 369–370, 371,
    386
    biography of, 370
Storm and Stress group, 250
Storm Weather (Strindberg), 237
Story of A Mother, The (Boesing), 459
Stowe, Harriet Beecher, 28, 394
Strange Interlude (O'Neill), 287, 422,
    443
Stranitzky, Joseph Anton, 231
Strasberg, Lee, 262, 275, 287, 288, 289,
    397, 398, 399, 443
    biography of, 278
Strasberg, Susan, 278, 287
Strasberg at the Actors Studio, 278
Streamers (Rabe), 447, 465
Stream-of-consciousness, 466, 475
Streetcar Named Desire, A (Williams), 9,
    10, 391–392, 430, 440, 441, 443,
    444, 445
    plot of, 434, 437
    quotation from, 437, 438, 439
    Representative Play, 434–441
    stage directions from, 435
*Streetscene: A Basic Model for an Epic
    Theatre* (Brecht), 299
Strehler, Giorgio, 292, 314
Strindberg, August, 227, 236, 240,
    248, 280, 422
    biography of, 237
Stroll in the Air, A (Ionesco), 329, 339
Stronger, The (Strindberg), 261
Subplot, 33, 43, 184, 250
Successful Life of 3, The (Fornés), 465,
    468
Suicide in B♭ (Shepard), 480
Sullen Lovers, The (Shadwell), 212
Summer (Bond), 370
Summer and Smoke (Williams), 403,
    405, 430
Summer Folk (Gorky), 280
Sunken Bell, The (Hauptmann), 251
Sunshine Boys, The (Simon), 463, 464,
    480
Suppliants, The (Aeschylus), 68

Surrealism, 326, 332, 333, 334,
    350–353, 459, 471
    definition of, 334–335
Svoboda, Josef, 332, 336
    biography of, 332
Swados, Elizabeth, 79, 459
Swan Theatre, The (London), 111,
    119, 126
Sweeney Todd (musical), 274, 414
Sweet Bird of Youth (Williams), 430
Sweet Charity (Simon), 463
Symbol, 24, 274, 281, 333, 412
Symbolism, 257, 272–274, 289, 294,
    332, 419, 474
Syndicate, The, 395, 396, 442

Tairov, Alexander, 272
Taking of Miss Janie, The (Bullins), 430
Tale of Two Cities, A (Dickens), 28, 384
Talking pieces, 40–41, 48
Talley's Folly (Wilson), 464
Tamburlaine (Marlowe), 118, 128
Tamiroff, Akim, 263
Tandy, Jessica, 9, 10, 392, 434, 440
Tango Palace (Fornés), 465, 468
Tardieu, Jean, 330
Tartuffe (Molière), 26, 27, 168, 179,
    180, 184, 185, 187–193
    quotation from, 187, 189, 190
    Representative Play, 186–189
Taste of Honey, A (Delaney), 363, 386
Tavel, Ronald, 488
Taylor, Elizabeth, 423
Taylor, John Russell, 378, 387
Taylor, Laurette, 9
Teatro Farnese (Italy), 113, 159, 161
Teatro Olimpico (Italy), 112, 145, 149,
    158
Teatro Piccoló (Milan), 292, 314
Tempest, The (Shakespeare), 119, 122,
    124, 129, 476
Tenaz (El Teatro National De Aztlan),
    456
Terence (Publius Terentius Afer), 62,
    63, 69, 73, 74, 82, 101, 131, 146
Terry, Ellen, 277
Terry, Megan, 48, 407, 410, 427, 452, 464,
    479
That Championship Season (Miller), 447
Theater am Schiffbauerdamm (East
    Berlin), 293–294, 304, 307, 315
Theatre and Its Double, The (Artaud),
    327, 331, 353
    quotation from, 331
Theatre Arts Magazine, 398
Theatre at Delphi (Greece), 64
Théâtre de Babylone (Paris), 15
Théâtre de Campagnol (Paris), 31
Théâtre de France (Paris), 331, 345
Théâtre de la Cité (France), 168, 189,
    191, 292

Théâtre de L'Athénée (Paris), 325
Théâtre de L'Oeuvre, (Paris), 326
Theatre de Lys (New York), 471
Théâtre des Noctambules (Paris),
    317, 331, 340, 344, 347
    Representative Theatre, 317
Théâtre du Babylone (Paris), 331
Théâtre du Marais (Paris), 170, 171,
    173, 175
Théâtre du Soleil (Paris), 31
Théâtre du Vieux Colombier, 320, 325,
    356
Theatre event, 2, 8, 11, 327
Theatre for Fifty Days, The (commedia
    scenarios), 148
Theatre games, 270
Theatre Genesis (New York), 468, 471
Théâtre Guénégaud (Paris), 175
Theatre Guild (New York), 278, 399,
    403
Theatre in everyday life, 16–17
Theatre-in-the-round, 313
Théâtre Libre (Paris), 234, 237, 244,
    254, 317
    Representative Theatre, 227–229
Théâtre Montparnasse (Paris), 228
Théâtre National Populaire (TNP)
    (France), 191
Theatre of Cruelty, 327, 330, 364
Theatre of Dionysus (Athens), 56, 62,
    63, 75
    Representative Theatre, 53
Theatre of images, 38–40, 48
Theatre of Marcellus (Rome), 66
Theatre of the Absurd, 37, 317,
    329–330, 350
Theatre of the Absurd, The (Esslin), 352,
    353
Théâtre panique (panic theatre), 330
Theatre Royal (London), 210, 223, 363
Theatre space, 4
Theatre Strategy (New York), 468
Théâtre supérieure, 170
Theatricalism, 270, 289, 316, 317,
    320–325, 326, 332, 351, 352, 402
    definition of, 320
Theatricality, 311, 326, 343, 344,
    350–351, 352, 368, 374–377, 386,
    442
Theatron, 4, 62
Thérèse Raquin (Zola), 253
Thesis drama, 339
Thesmophoriazusae (Aristophanes), 58
Thespis, 5, 56
    biography of, 56
The Theatre (London), 112, 113, 117,
    140, 161, 168
They're Playing Our Song (Simon), 463,
    464
Thief's Journal, A (Genet), 344
13 Rue de L'Amour (Feydeau), 30
This Sporting Life (Storey), 370

Thorndike, Sybil, 362
Three Cuckolds, The, 160, 167
    Representative Play, 161–163
Three Musketeers, The (Dumas père),
    191
Threepenny Opera, The (Brecht), 297,
    301, 304, 306, 307, 314, 356, 447
Three Places in Rhode Island (Gray), 40
Three Sisters, The (Chekhov), 263, 279,
    280, 283–286, 287–288, 289, 290
    plot of, 283
    Representative Play, 283–286
Thrust stage, 5, 6, 404
Thunderstorm, The (Ostrovsky), 266
Thyestes (Seneca), 69, 74
Thymele, 62
Tieck, Ludwig, 233
Till the Day I Die (Odets), 424, 425
Time, 23, 24, 475, 476
    actual, 24
    event, 24
Tiny Alice (Albee), 431
Tiring house, 96, 111, 116, 120, 126,
    127, 269
'Tis Pity She's A Whore (Ford), 129
Titus Andronicus (Shakespeare), 138
To Be Young, Gifted, and Black
    (Hansberry), 428
To Damascus I (Strindberg), 236
Toller, Ernst, 294, 306
Tolstoy, Alexei, 263
Tolstoy, Leo, 228, 234, 266, 267, 278,
    280–281, 289
Tom Jones (film), 378
Tongues (Shepard), 480
Tonight We Improvise (Pirandello), 326,
    338
Tooth of Crime, The (Shepard), 41, 464,
    466, 471, 480
Torelli, Giacomo, 155, 167, 175
Torquato Tasso (Goethe), 242
Total work of art, 259–260
Touch of the Poet, A (O'Neill), 402,
    422
Touring company, 394, 442, 450
Tournament, 95
Tourneur, Cyril, 119, 138
Toys in the Attic (Hellman), 423
Trackers, The (Sophocles), 72
Trade guild, 85, 86, 89, 90, 94, 99, 100,
    108
Tragedy, 25, 112, 130–132, 179, 181,
    232, 256, 419, 421, 434, 436, 443
    Greek and Roman, 55, 68–72, 74
Tragic action, 75, 133–134, 255, 436
Tragical in Daily Life, The (Maeter-
    linck), 274, 290
    quotation from, 274
Tragicomedy, 22, 25, 26, 48, 172, 181,
    284
    modern, 26
Tragic vision, 25

Training programs (educational),
    397–398
Trapdoor, 92, 116, 127, 135
Traveller Without Baggage (Anouilh), 338
Travesties (Stoppard), 371, 375
Trial, The (Kafka), 43
Trial of Lucullus, The (Brecht), 314
Trilogy, 53, 54, 59, 62, 326, 422
Triple A Plowed Under (Federal Theatre
    Project), 400
Triumph of Isabella, The, 91
Troilus and Cressida (Shakespeare), 137
Trojan War Shall Not Take Place, The
    (Giraudoux), 325, 338
Trojan Women, The (Euripides), 44, 53,
    57, 58, 68, 69, 75–82
    quotation from, 44, 53, 76, 78
    Representative Play, 75–79
Trope, 88
Troupe de Monsieur, 173
True Chronicle History of King Leir, 128
True West (Shepard), 464, 466, 480
Tsar Fyodor Ivanovich (Tolstoy), 263,
    268, 269
Tuchman, Barbara W., 108
Turgenev, Ivan, 266, 278, 289
Turlupin, 173, 174
Twelfth Night (Shakespeare), 129
Twin Menaechmi, The (Plautus), 69, 73,
    74, 82
Two Gentlemen of Verona (Shake-
    speare), 447
Tynan, Kenneth, 356
    quotation from, 356–357
Tyrone Guthrie Theatre (Minneapo-
    lis), 6, 404
Tyzack, Margaret, 35, 258
Tzara, Tristan, 333

Ubu enchaîné (Ubu Bound) (Jarry), 326
Ubu Roi (King Ubu) (Jarry), 326
Uffizi Teatro (Italy), 159
Uhl, Frida, 237
Ullmann, Liv, 258, 259, 260, 261
Uncle Tom's Cabin (Stowe), 28, 394,
    395, 421
Uncle Vanya (Chekhov), 263, 279, 280,
    289, 290
Unconscious, 238, 257, 260, 272–274, 334
    definition of, 272–274
Unfinished Woman, An (Hellman), 423
Unions, 397, 442, 451
United Company, 203
United Scenic Artists, 397
Uniti Company, 147, 167
Unseen Hand, The (Shepard), 466
Ure, Mary, 377, 379

Vakhtangov, Yevgeny, 272
Valdez, Luis, 455, 456, 457, 480
    quotation from, 456–457

Valenciennes Passion Play (France), 92, 98, 99
Vanbrugh, Sir John, 205, 213, 224
Van Itallie, Jean-Claude, 48, 407, 410, 444, 452, 464, 465, 479, 480
Variety (newspaper), 453, 463
Vaudeville, 394, 428, 463
Vega Carpio, Lope Félix de, 99
Venice Preserved (Otway), 212
Venus and Adonis (Shakespeare), 119
Versailles (France), 172, 182, 186, 192
Verse, 99, 235, 257, 354, 362
Vice figure, 103, 108
Vienna Notes, The (Nelson), 480
Vietnam Discourse (Weiss), 312
Viet Rock: A Folk War Movie (Terry), 407, 464
View from the Bridge, A (Miller), 425, 427
Vigarani, Carlo, 182
Vikings of Helgeland, The (Ibsen), 235
Vilar, Jean, 316, 328, 329, 351, 352, 359
  as director, 328, 329
  quotation from, 329
Village Voice, The (newspaper), 452
Virtuoso, The (Shadwell), 205
Visions of Simone Machard, The (Brecht), 315
Visit, The (Duerrenmatt), 312
Visual elements, 58–62, 91–93, 121–122, 147–153, 153–157, 175–177, 238–241, 267–269, 298–301, 332–334, 398
  commedia dell' arte, 147–153
  Elizabethan theatre, 121–122
  epic theatre, 298–301
  European theatre (19th century), 238–241
  French theatre (17th century), 175–177
  Greek theatre, 58–62
  Italian court theatre, 153–157
  medieval theatre, 91–93
  Moscow Art Theatre, 267–269
  post-war European theatre, 332–334
Vitez, Antoine, 29, 30, 168
Vitrac, Roger, 334
Vitruvius, 58, 154, 155, 167
Vivian Beaumont Theatre (New York), 59
Volpone (Jonson), 118, 129
Von Essen, Siri, 237
Vultures, The (Becque), 253

Wagner, Richard, 226, 230, 231, 245–246, 251, 259, 260
  as director, 245–246
Wagner, Wieland, 337
Waiting for Godot (Beckett), 13–15, 17,

19, 26, 329, 331, 343
  plot of, 15
  quotation from, 14
Waiting for Lefty (Odets), 424, 425, 426–427, 444
  text of, 426–427
Wakefield Cycle, The (England), 85, 101, 103, 108
Walker, Joseph, 28, 29, 421, 427
Wallace, Lew, 274
Wallenstein's Camp (Schiller), 243, 251
Walpole, Robert, 197, 201, 214
Waltz of the Toreadors (Anouilh), 339
Wandering Scholar, The (Sachs), 102
War of the Roses, The (Shakespeare, Hall), 359
War of the Worlds (radio), 401
Ward, Douglas Turner, 29, 430, 455, 479
  quotation from, 455
Wardle, Irving, 223, 225
Warrilow, David, 462
Washington Square Church (New York), 468
Washington Square Players (New York), 398, 399, 442
Wasps (Aristophanes), 58, 68
Wasserstein, Wendy, 470
Watch It Come Down (Osborne), 370, 378
Watch on the Rhine (Hellman), 423, 443
Water Engine, The (Mamet), 465, 466
Waterston, Sam, 14
Way of the World, The (Congreve), 203, 212, 213, 214, 215
  quotation from, 215
Weavers, The (Hauptmann), 234, 251, 253
Web, The (Boesing), 458
Weber, Carl, 302, 315
  quotation from, 302
Webster, John, 118, 129, 140
Webster, Margaret, 403
Wedding Feast, The (Wesker), 370
Wedekind, Frank, 232, 234, 251, 260
Weigel, Helene, 302, 304, 307
  biography of, 302
  quotation about, 302
Weill, Kurt, 215, 292, 297, 301
Weimar classicism, 241
Weimar Court Theatre (Germany), 226, 231, 234, 241, 258
Weinstein, Arnold, 287
Weiss, Peter, 43, 166, 311, 312, 359, 364
  biography of, 43
Welles, Orson, 40, 137
Well-made play, 278, 294, 328, 378, 466
  definition of, 278
Wellman, John, 480
Wesker, Arnold, 32, 221, 361, 370

West of Suez (Osborne), 370, 378
West Side Story (musical), 414
When We Dead Awaken (Ibsen), 235, 236, 258, 260, 274
White Devil, The (Webster), 118, 129
Who's Afraid of Virginia Woolf? (Albee), 287, 431, 434, 472
Wickham, Glynne, 91, 96, 98, 108, 109
Wild Duck, The (Ibsen), 235, 236, 261, 263, 274, 280
Wilde, Oscar, 187, 215
Wilder, Thornton, 402, 414
Wilks, Robert, 215, 217
Williams, Clifford, 368
Williams, Emlyn, 391
Williams, Heathcote, 361
Williams, Samm Art-, 455, 459
Williams, Tennessee, 3, 9, 12, 17, 237, 391, 392, 394, 402, 403, 405, 430–431, 434–440
  biography of, 430
  modernism of, 440
  quotation from, 435, 440
Williamson, Nicol, 378
William Tell (Schiller), 251
Wilson, Angus, 356
Wilson, Frank, 402
Wilson, Lanford, 451, 452, 453, 464
Wilson, Robert, 38, 39, 40, 48, 447
  biography of, 40
Wilson, Snoo, 368
Wings (Kopit), 465, 466, 480
  text of, 467
Wings and borders, 156
Wings and shutters, 206
Wings-in-grooves, 125, 155
Winter's Tale, The (Shakespeare), 124, 138
Wit, language of, 215
Wolfe, Linda, 476
Woman, The (Bond), 369, 370
Woman of Andros, The (Terence), 74
Women's Experimental Theatre (New York), 458
Wood, Audrey, 430
Wood, John, 27
Woodruff, Robert, 471
Woods, The (Mamet), 465, 466
Wooster Group, The (New York), 41, 462
Works Progress Administration (WPA), 399
Worth, Irene, 258, 342
Woyzeck (Buchner), 232, 234, 251, 418
Wren, Christopher, 195, 210
Wright, Richard, 428
Wycherley, William, 194, 195, 196, 205, 212, 213, 216, 219, 220

Yale Repertory Theatre (Connecticut), 453

York cycle (England), 85–86, 99, 100, 103, 104, 105, 106, 107
  list of playlets, 100
Young Barbarians Today (Arrabal), 330, 339
Young, Roland, 399

Zabriskie Point (film), 466
Zanni, 143, 146, 149, 152, 160, 161, 230
Zartan (Savary), 350, 351
Ziegfeld, Florenz, 414
Ziegfeld Follies, 414
Zirkus Schumann (Vienna), 322, 351

Zola, Emile, 227, 228, 234, 237, 253, 260
  quotation from, 253
Zoo Story, The (Albee), 431–434
  text of, 432–433
Zykovs, The (Gorky), 290